Continental Corporate Power

Wallace Clement

CONTINENTAL CORPORATE POWER

Economic Elite Linkages between
Canada and the United States

McClelland and Stewart

To John and Marion Porter
for their contribution to
Canadian social science
and their kindness.

The Canadian Publishers
McClelland and Stewart Limited
25 Hollinger Road, Toronto M4B 3G2

Canadian Cataloguing in Publication Data

Clement, Wallace.
Continental corporate power

Bibliography: p.
Includes index.
ISBN 0-7710-2150-X bd.   ISBN 0-7710-2151-8 pa.

1. Corporations – Canada.   2. Corporations –
United States.   3. Elite (Social sciences) –
Canada.   4. Elite (Social sciences) – United States.
5. Canada – Economic conditions – 1965-   *
6. United States – Economic conditions – 1971-
I. Title.

HD2809.C54   338.7′4′0971   C77-001457-7

Contents

Preface   1

Chapter One
A Continental Economy and Corporate Power   6
I.   The Canadian Quandary   7
II.   The Power of Corporations   9

Chapter Two
A Framework for Analysis of the Continental System   14
I.   Changes in International Capitalism: From Mercantile to
        Industrial Capital   15
II.   Relations between Nations: The World System   20
III.   The Continental System: Capitalist Class Fractions   23

Chapter Three
Setting the Stage for a Continental Economy   33
I.   Common British Origins and Colonial Rule (to 1776)   34
II.   Mercantilism and the Impact of the American
        Revolution (1770 to 1830)   35
III.   Prelude to an Industrial System and the Civil War (1830
        to 1860)   41
IV.   The Railway Era (1860 to 1900)   44
V.   Consolidation of Corporate Capitalism (1900 to 1913)   54
VI.   The First World War: U.S. Expansion and Canadian
        Growth (1913 to 1929)   65
VII.   The Depression Years (1929 to 1939)   73

Chapter Four
Consolidating the Continental Economy   80
I.   The Wartime Economy   81
II. U.S. Investment in Canadian Resources and
     Manufacturing and Its Results   82
III. U.S. Ownership and "Canadian" Capital   88
IV. Changes in the Profile of U.S. Investment in Canada   90

Chapter Five
**Multinational Corporations Operating
from the United States and Canada**   97

I.   Multinational Corporations and Class Fractions   97
II. A Profile of U.S. Expansion   103
III. Asymmetry in U.S.-Latin American Relations   109
IV. Foreign Investment in the United States   110
V.   Canadian Foreign Investment – Is It Merely
     Go-Between?   113
VI. A Comparative View of the Countries of the Western
     Hemisphere   124

Chapter Six
Continental Corporate Structures and Interlocking   132
I.   Conglomerates, Corporate Continuity, and
     Concentration   132
II. Dominant U.S. Corporations and Their Canadian
     Relations   141
III. Interlocking among Dominant U.S. and Canadian
     Corporations   162
IV. Continental Connections: Interlocking between
     Dominant U.S. and Canadian Corporations   172

Chapter Seven
**The Economic Elite in Canada and the United States:
I. Careers, Class and Kinship**   183
I.   Career Patterns of the Economic Elite   184
II. Class Origins of the Economic Elite   206
III. Inheritance and Current Kinship Ties in the Economic
     Elite   211

Chapter Eight
The Economic Elite in Canada and the United States:
II. Corporate, Ascriptive, and Social Characteristics   215
I.   Corporate Characteristics of the Elite   215
II.   Ascriptive Characteristics of the Elite   223
III.   The Elite As a Social Group   235
IV.   Relations between Elites   245

Chapter Nine
Relations between the U.S. and Canadian Elites and Managers 251
I.   Multinational Activities of the U.S. Economic Elite and
        Foreign-Born in the Elite   251
II.   Managerial Migration between Canada and the United
        States   257
III.   Multinational and Continental Activities of the
        Canadian Elite   278

Chapter Ten
Implications of the Continental Economy for Canadian Society 289
I.   The Nature of the Canadian Elite: The Question of
        Domination   290
II.   Effects of the Continental Economy on Canadian
        Society   295
III.   The Canadian State in the Continental Economy   298

Appendices
I.   Foreign Ownership of Industrial Groups in Canada,
        1972   305
II.   Control of Industrial Groups in Canada, 1972, by
        Assets, Sales, and Profits   306
III*a*. Value of Insurance in Force of the Thirteen Dominant
        Canadian Life Insurance Companies in Canada, the
        United States, and the United Kingdom, 1970   308
III*b*. Assets of Dominant Canadian Life Insurance
        Companies Held outside Canada, 1970   309
III*c*. Value of Insurance in Force of Dominant Canadian Life
        Insurance Companies in Countries Other Than Canada,
        the United States, and the United Kingdom, 1970   310

IV*a*.   Branches of Canadian Chartered Banks outside Canada,
1972   312
IV*b*.   Foreign Holdings of Canadian Banks, 1971   313
V.   Determining Dominance in U.S. Corporations   315
VI.   Dominant U.S. Corporations (All Sectors)   316
VII.   Average Sizes of Dominant U.S. Corporations by Sector   327
VIII.   Trends in Corporate Interlocking in the United States,
1899 to 1970   328
IX.   Interlocking among 194 Dominant U.S. Corporations   330
X.   Interlocking among Dominant U.S. and Canadian
Corporations   332
XI.   Studies of the U.S. Economic Elite and Executives   332
XII.   Methodological Note on Biographical Data for the Elite   339
XIII.   The "Ownership/Control" Debate in the United States:
The Power of Property   340
XIV.   Immigration Data and Migration Theories   348
XV.   Procedures Used in a Survey of Canadian-Born,
U.S.-Resident Managers   352
XVI.   Two Methods of Determining Class Origins of Managers   356

Notes   358

References   374

Index   385

Preface

In an earlier study entitled *The Canadian Corporate Elite* I attempted to portray some aspects of change in Canada's socio-economic history, specifically changes in economic power that have taken place since John Porter's study of this subject in 1951, reported in *The Vertical Mosaic*. Although some have interpreted it otherwise, my first study raised at least as many issues as it resolved. Broadly, these may be divided into three problem areas: boundaries (Canada in a continental context), relations between systems of power (Canada's corporate and state systems), and class (Canada's class structure as affecting and affected by these other problem areas). As before, the last two areas, while deserving of more thorough attention, will be discussed but not attacked directly in favour of a detailed analysis of Canada's place specifically within the system of continental capitalism and generally within the world order.

While the essence of my earlier work was the emergence and current structure of economic power in Canada, this study has as its focal point developments in the U.S. economic structure, especially as they have affected Canada's economy and social structure. It searches for external effects upon internal developments and the extensions of each national economy into a continental system.

In addition to having direct relevance for the understanding of relations between Canada and the United States, this study can be regarded as part of a growing literature on international capitalism and its implications for modern national societies generally. A great deal of work has been done to explain relationships between the United States and "Third World" nations but very little on the U.S. relationships with "go-between" nations like Canada. Given the worldwide tendency of international capitalism, the understanding of such relationships must be expanded. It is most important to assess the impact of these international relations on the internal power structures of the nations involved. By going beyond the traditionally accepted political boundaries to study the broader economic system of which these states are a part, it is possible to assess the extent to which internal developments are influenced by external forces.

The idea of looking for external centres of power with an importance in Canada is not a new one. In presenting his analysis of the economic elite in Canada for 1951, John Porter stated that "rather than a Canadian elite we should perhaps be searching for a foreign or international

1

elite...[it is] in some respects unrealistic to accept national boundaries as the boundaries of any economic system," adding that it was necessary for the purpose of analysis to delineate some boundaries.[1] Porter's studies have now led him in other directions. In this work, I am attempting to expand, in some senses, the limits he adopted for his earlier study. That being said, however, even though it extends the analysis into the continental system and to a limited extent beyond, this study does not completely resolve these earlier bounds. While the heart of Canada's international economic relations is with the United States, there remains an even broader world system of capitalism to be taken into account. The spiral is a never ending one.

The existence of an international economy is certainly not of recent origin. The Mesopotamians had international trading companies, and the East India Company, founded in 1600, was a major international force following the first Elizabeth's reign. For centuries both Canada and the United States were on the receiving end of Pax Britannica, and many European rivalries have been played out in North America. Trade has long been central to the international system. But international capitalism has undergone important transformations with the burgeoning of the modern multinational corporation. Although important trade links still exist, the exchange of commodities between two independent units (whether companies or nations) characteristic of earlier eras differs radically from the intra-organizational transfers of products and profits within one multinational spanning several nations, so dominant in today's trade.

Many aspects of international capitalism must be explored. There are ownership links of both a direct controlling nature and a portfolio or investment nature; there are international interlocking of directorships and migrations of businessmen, common social circles in the club rooms of the advanced nations, and common associations such as the Canadian-American Committee. There are also agreements between governments such as the Canada–United States Auto Pact. All are in some sense related.

There is no attempt here to claim that interlocking directorships, social connections, or common class origins explain all or even most capitalist relationships either within the United States or between the United States and Canada. What is claimed, however, is that they do serve as strong social indicators of broader capitalist relations, expressed on a human level. The broad trends evident in capital formations, accumulation and concentration, foreign investment, and other economic indicators are expressed in the way people relate to one another and provide the context for these relationships. In other words, sociology complements political economy.

A historical review of economic relations between Canada and the United States is necessary for even the most limited understanding of the forces and developments that become manifest in the type of people who have built the continental economy. In the context of the theoretical issues outlined in Chapter 2, historical background will explain why large-scale Canadian capitalists have been unable to visualize their markets (whether commodity, capital, resource, or even labour) in Canada or elsewhere without taking the United States into account. It will also illustrate why only capitalists in the financial, communications, transportation, utilities, and media sectors in Canada have been able, by means of legislation and their own indigenous power bases, to protect themselves from direct U.S. domination and why the rest of the economy – resources and manufacturing in particular – is dominated to a high degree by U.S. capital. Since much of the activity in the Canadian-controlled sectors is predicated on the others, Canadian capitalists are forced into an unusual relationship with U.S. capitalists. To begin to delineate some of the features of this association will be a major purpose.

Having set out this background, I will explore some of the consequences of this relationship. The usual list of "defensive expansionism" (which hastened Canada's move to the West to protect its boundaries from U.S. encroachment), accelerated industrialization (industrialization from without), branch plants (owned and controlled outside the country to meet external needs), capital drains (caused when branch plants send more money to their parents than comes into the country as new capital), or resource depletion (caused by exporting unprocessed raw materials to meet foreign demand), only scratches the surface.

To understand the structure of the economic relationship between Canada and the United States, it is necessary to examine the main organizations involved. These are the largest corporations within each country, called here dominant corporations because they control most of the economic activities in each country. This includes an analysis of the relative degrees of concentration within various economic activities, but it also involves determining which U.S. corporations penetrate Canada and contrasting this foreign control with their multinational (or worldwide) activities. This perspective allows for an understanding of Canada's special place in the U.S. sphere of influence. After the dominant corporations in each country are identified, the relationships between these corporations are also examined, particularly in terms of the patterns of interlocking directorships which indicate the nature of the relationships between corporations engaged in different domestic economic activities. An analysis of the continental interlocks between dominant Canadian and U.S. corporations follows, to observe the continental exchanges of their respective economic elites.

After setting the stage by examining the structural relations, it is necessary to clarify some of the social dimensions of the relationship between Canada and the United States, particularly regarding the types of people controlling the dominant corporations in each country and the kinds of bonds they have established.

A further section of this study is an examination of the Canadian economy within the North American context to determine the mobility and opportunity it affords Canadians. It cannot be designed as a comparative study in the usual sense of two separate systems in convergence with or divergence from one another but is instead an analysis of North America with special reference to Canada. This part of the study deals with international managerial migration and elite mobility, a hitherto unexplored aspect of stratification, making use of immigration data, a survey of persons who were born in Canada but have moved into management positions in the United States, and an examination of the U.S. activities of members of the Canadian economic elite.

The core of this study is an analysis of corporate concentration and the economic elites in both Canada and the United States and of corporate and elite linkages between the two nations. It has involved gathering data on the top corporations of each country (194 in the United States and 113 in Canada) and biographical information on nearly three thousand members of the economic elite (2,007 in the United States and 798 in Canada). To supplement this information, I gathered original survey data on a sample of business executives who are Canadian born but now U.S. residents (302 answered questionnaires). Data on the flow of managers between the two countries were obtained from immigration statistics. To this original research I have added a great deal of supplementary material drawn from contemporary and historical studies of each country and its respective economic elite, from government statistics on capital flows and investments between the two countries, and from various studies of multinational corporations.

It is no longer possible to provide an adequate understanding of the power structure of Canadian corporations without expanding the horizons of the study outside into the United States and, to a limited extent, beyond. I am satisfied that this work is complete, at least in its broad outlines, and now needs to be developed through more detailed case studies of particular companies, industries, and decisions. Such work will require development of alternative methodologies and approaches to the problem. Limits to the "power" perspective are inherent in elite studies, for they focus on only one dimension of inequality. If the implications of the particular kind of corporate power structure characteristic of Canadian society are to be fully explored, it is necessary to turn directly to those affected. To do this will require making a class analysis of Canadian society that takes into account the concentrated and exclusive structure of power this study has found. It will also have to recognize the realities of extensive foreign control in Canada's productive sectors, for both have shaped the contemporary labour force.

I would like to acknowledge the assistance of many people in preparing this study. I thank Carl Cuneo of the Department of Sociology, McMaster University, for his critical thinking; Daniel Drache, Department of Political Science, Atkinson College, York University, for his knowledge of Canadian political economy; from Carleton University, Dennis Olsen for his understanding of Canadian society, Dennis Forcese for his encouragement and persistence, Leo Panitch for his insights and many abilities, and finally, John Porter for his stimulating comments and tolerance in encouraging me to carry on productive debate with him. More than any others, these six people have personally helped me come to my present level of understanding of corporate power and Canadian society through written comments and many hours of discussion. They share in this work in many ways, although they do not all agree with what is now written. For this I assume responsibility.

I would also like to thank my critics (of whom there are many) who have forced me to sharpen my analysis and my thinking. Most have given careful consideration to what I have written, and I hope for further exchanges to advance my own understanding. I would also like to thank many businessmen (who shall remain unnamed) for spending time with me in interviews and discussions on the nature of corporate power and the continental economy. I would also like to thank those who kindly answered the questionnaire sent to them.

On the financial side, Muni Frumhartz, then Chairperson of the Department of Sociology and Anthropology at Carleton, made funds available to further my research; Peta Sheriff, Chairperson of the Department of Sociology, McMaster University, also made university funds available. The Canada Council helped fund my studies. On the technical side, Lillian Giavedoni arranged my keypunching and helped make the computer count for me; Lesley Clement was a most able and thorough research assistant for one summer, spending many hot hours in the National Library. At McClelland and Stewart, I wish to thank Peter Saunders, Peter Milroy, Anna Porter, and James Marsh for their continuing encouragement and assistance. Janet Craig has acted as my editor and has helped with the presentation of a very complex subject.

Finally, and most important, Elsie Clement has typed several drafts of this study and has been as tolerant as anyone has the right to ask. Chris and Jeff Clement have also put up with me, and I owe them all a great deal for the time this study has stolen from them.

Although a reader should always be wary of oversimplification, the task of analysis is to abstract patterns and give meaning to complex phenomena. The line is a fine one and not always easy to follow. This analysis attempts to identify major trends and forces in Canadian–U.S. economic relations, and of necessity it must simplify. But it is hoped that the essence of the relationship is not missed in the process. To say the relationship is complex is to state the obvious; to abstract the crux of the relationship is the task.

Wallace Clement

CHAPTER ONE

A Continental Economy and Corporate Power

Canada is an independent nation-state enveloped by spill-over from the most powerful capitalist society in the world, which includes some of the costs and benefits of that society's wealth. While Canada's economy is largely controlled and shaped by U.S. capitalists, these capitalists do not operate in a complete power vacuum in Canada. What has been forged over the past century is an alliance between the *leading* elements of Canadian and U.S. capital that reinforces mutually the power and advantage of each. The particular type of economic development Canada has experienced has occurred in the context of two overriding factors: the dominant place of financial capitalists in Canada and the presence of the world's largest industrial giant immediately adjacent. Together these features have determined the nature of the continental economy.

Leading forces of capitalism in both Canada and the United States benefit from this alliance. Canada provides important natural resources and market outlets for U.S. industrialists, while the economic activity arising from U.S. resource extraction, transportation, and production is the bread and butter of Canada's leading capitalists. This is an unequal alliance, however: U.S. capitalists control the major areas associated with production, the cornerstone of an industrial society; Canadian capitalists have their strength in areas of circulation and service to production. Production is made up of the key economic activities of manufacturing and resource extraction, while circulation and service consist of financial activities, transportation, and utilities. Thus the alliance, while unequal, represents a merging of efforts and interests, giving Canadian and U.S. capitalists an affinity.

The earlier break of the southern colonies from Great Britain permitted the emergent United States an autonomous pattern of industrialization in contrast to Canada's continuance as a mediator between the imperial centre and its own resources. The United States has since become an expanding empire and centre for most of the world's largest multinational corporations. In contrast, Canada's capitalists have been engaged in consolidating and protecting their limited areas of economic power, in large part in reaction to the outward thrust of the United States. The major thesis of this study is that this broad pattern of the United States as an expanding empire and Canada as a country confined by U.S. expansion has had tremendous ramifications for the patterns of ownership within the Canadian economy, for the relationships between

6

corporations, and for the nature of the economic elites of each country.

Not all Canadian capitalists are pleased with this arrangement, but most do not see beyond the immediate economic gains arising from this method of nation building and surplus extraction. Nevertheless, the central tendency is clear. For those commanding the uppermost positions in Canada's economy, as the United States goes, so goes Canada. The two economies have become intertwined in a multitude of ways. But their interpenetration does not mean that they have become the same. Indeed, it is precisely because of the way they have come together that they are so distinctive; that is, because they have come together in an unequal alliance, Canada's economy has been shaped to conform to the dominance of the United States.

An analysis of the Canadian economy and of those who control it must then be one that includes an examination of the United States and of those who control its economy. This being so, Canada cannot be characterized as an advanced independent capitalist society, nor can it be grouped with the various peripheral nations often called "the Third World," although it shares some traits with each type. Herein lies the Canadian quandary.

I. The Canadian Quandary

Canada is a bundle of paradoxes. Its economic development has been uneven because of external and internal factors. It is both underdeveloped and overdeveloped, a resource hinterland and an advanced manufacturer, capital rich and capital poor. This quandary was manifested in a speech made by the late prime minister Lester B. Pearson: "Our desire to share in the material benefits of continental growth and development and also to maintain an independent political and social and cultural identity, seems at times to result in a split personality, a kind of national schizophrenia."[1]

But Canada's peculiar pattern of development cannot be reduced to the problem of identity. The roots go much deeper and evolve out of Canada's political economy. "Political economy" means the connection between a country's economy and social relations viewed with a historical perspective; in the Canadian case, its relationships with foreign economies have moulded the nature of the Canadian economy and the capitalists who control it, while they in turn shape social relations within Canada.

Canada is a secondary power in the world economic order and has a distorted economic system because of its colonial origins and because its industrialization proceeded in the shadow of an industrial giant – "shirttail" development. Throughout its history Canada has conformed to the pressures of external demands and internal opportunism. Instead of employing the techniques of autonomous development, Canadian capitalists and members of the state elite have adapted Canada's economy as part of a much broader economic system – the capitalist world economic order – and particularly today as an integral part of a continental economic system.

The division of activity between the economic elites of Canada and the United States follows from radically different formative forces in each country and the different types of capitalists each has produced and sustained. The American Revolution of the 1770s, the Civil War of the 1860s, and the imperialism of the mid-twentieth century are the three major landmarks often cited to distinguish U.S. from Canadian history. But these landmarks are the outcomes of broader internal differences. Canada never went to war to break with Britain, it never successfully resolved its major internal conflict (between French and English) by civil war, and it has never had the power to take the rest of the capitalist world as its domain. Moreover, Canada's late attempt at nation building occurred within the orbit of the largest and most aggressive industrial nation in history, the United States.

Within the Canadian economy, this division of activity has meant that Canadian capitalists have retained control of activities associated with finance, transportation, utilities, and the mass media, while foreign, predominantly U.S., capitalists have held the strongest position in resource extraction and manufacturing. The reasons for this division will be explored theoretically in the following chapter and empirically throughout the remainder of this study. It is also the purpose of this study to provide an analysis of the causes, consequences, and costs of this division of activity. Frank Underhill stated the proposition in 1929: "The real problem on this continent is not the political relationship between two supposedly mutually exclusive and independent entities called Canada and the United States, but the economic relationship between the classes who make up the North American community."[2] Since this was written, the problem has grown dramatically with the creation of multinational corporations and the flows of capital, control, and personnel that have followed.

Amazingly little new research is available on this question. Although there has been a great deal of study of foreign investment in Canada, few writers have looked outside Canada to analyse the external forces that have become reflected in Canada's economy. Few have examined the U.S. power structure to see how it relates to Canada. The intersection of the economic power structures (including corporations and people) of Canada and the United States will provide the focus for the analysis undertaken here. I propose to explain the continental interpenetration by examining both the "push" and the "pull" factors on each side within a set of assumptions based on corporate capitalism. In *The Canadian Corporate Elite: An Analysis of Economic Power*, I explored some of the pull factors in Canada – the dominance of a financial economic elite and the underdevelopment of an indigenous group of industrial and resource entrepreneurs. In this study I intend to contrast them with patterns of U.S. economic development. But this analysis claims to be more than a comparison of U.S. and Canadian economic elites and corporations, although this is an important component. Instead, the focus is on the relationship between them as well as the patterns within each.

II. The Power of Corporations

To understand the effects of continental corporate power it is necessary to understand corporate power. Why can it be said that dominant corporations – or to be more precise, the members of the economic elite (who hold the top decision-making posts in these corporations) – are powerful, and just what is the nature and extent of their power? "Power" is the ability of some people to mobilize resources for particular ends. "Resources" is simply a general concept for anything that is valued, such as capital, raw materials, labour power, or products. Power is always a *relational* concept, meaning that someone has more resources than someone else and thus has the ability to make more of an impact in terms of that resource. The following is a rather simple outline of some of the types of resources, and hence corporate power, located in corporations. It is not meant to be an exhaustive list but rather an illustration of some aspects of corporate power to be analysed.

The most obvious areas where economic power resides are costs and prices paid for goods, services, or credit. Obviously broad constraints exist here, at the bottom the cost of production and at the top the limits of the "market." But these are much broader than might be supposed. Production costs are made up of a great number of components, many of which include factors resulting from other costs charged at a rate the market will bear. For example, an important cost of production is labour, but the price of labour – which has remained at a fairly steady proportion of the total cost of production – includes the socially necessary costs of survival and reproduction. Today these essentials include transportation, shelter, and food. If these essentials are being purchased by labour at the price the market will bear, then this obviously affects the cost of labour, and hence the cost of production. The upper limit is imposed by the illusive market. Of course, the market is no more than the sum of all those offering goods, services, or credit and all those wanting these things. The first group is highly variable in terms of the number of alternative sources, and the second also varies in response to created wants (such as those instilled by advertising). Where there are few outlets for particular goods, services, or credit, a monopoly market tends to exist. The more demand the controllers of these valued commodities can create through such things as planned obsolescence, advertising, and narrowing alternatives (such as the alternative of economical and efficient public transit to the automobile), the greater the price they can command. Thus the upper limit is made flexible by control over the marketplace. To reiterate, the economic elite has quite extensive power over costs and prices.

Corporate power also has a dominant position in capital accumulation. While it cannot be said that the elite can absolutely determine profits, it would be equally misleading to suggest that they are without a strong hand in keeping profits high. Again, their impact will vary with the relative command over the market. The elite is able to determine, however, what proportion of profits will be paid out in dividends and what proportion will be held as retained earnings. The single most important source of funds for capital accumulation is built into the corporation. The second important source is financial intermediaries, especially the giant banks and life insurance companies, and to the extent that the largest corporations and the largest sources of financial capital are tied into one another, monopoly over the capital necessary for new or renewed development exists. To whom are the economic elite responsible in these decisions? Only to the stockholders – in other words, mainly to themselves and thousands of small investors whose only option is to sell their shares if they do not like the policy. Since their power is *private* there is no public accountability for their decisions.

Besides its influence on prices and capital accumulation, the power of corporations and their elite extends to wages and salaries. In spite of unions, wages are still set by capitalists. Wages are determined at the upper level by productivity, again the responsibility of the elite, and below it by collective bargaining – at least for the third of the labour force that is unionized. Included in the corporations' bag of tools for collective bargaining are the capacity to withstand prolonged strikes by shifting operations elsewhere (including the ultimate threat of closing down an operation), the long-term strategy of avoiding strike-bound areas, the ability to call on a reserve army of unemployed, and the use of back-to-work orders issued by the state. In the setting of wages there is also considerable leverage. Regarding salaries, and more specifically executive compensation, the elite has the special privilege of being able to determine its own rewards and schemes for payment. These typically consist of a combination of salary, bonus, and stock options – all determined by themselves, for themselves. These types of rewards are also used as an important enticement for lower-level management aspiring to the elite and are an effective social control on them for performance and reliability. In large part corporate salaries set the pace for settlements in smaller industries and the state sector, thus having an impact beyond their immediate scope.

By being able to determine the nature of production – whether it will be capital or labour intensive, clean or dirty, safe or hazardous, secure or intermittent – the elite have great control over the quality of life. By turning off and on the fiscal taps for research and development, they affect greatly the kind of technology developed and, once developed, how and whether it will be used. They exert great influence on the nature of the labour force. By deciding which skills will be rewarded highly and what proportion of the labour force, the economic elite can affect the overall number of jobs – how many will be clerical, how many managerial, and how many blue collar. This control in turn provides feedback to the educational system regarding how many people may become engineers, scientists, lawyers, or M.B.A.s (Masters of Business Administration) because corporations are the largest source of jobs for these occupations.

To argue that corporations do not have a great impact on the nature of the labour force would be to assume that the way their elites choose to perform their activities is the only way – that there are not many different ways to organize production and administration, that human ingenuity for social organization has been exhausted and we are thus limited to production lines and giant bureaucracies. Any experimentation that has been carried out by corporations has been evaluated in their terms – profitability – not in human terms based on the ensuing quality of life and experience for those actually doing the work. Efficiency for corporations has to be governed by their own terms of reference, and these terms insist that the capital invested must return a "reasonable rate of profit," not that the people doing the work put out a socially useful product or service and do so under the best possible working conditions.

As the power contained in the corporation over the nature of the labour force goes right to the heart of what is important in a society, so does its impact on the values of the people in that society. It has already been suggested that by setting the reward structure corporations are able to entice individuals to different careers. Then within these careers they dictate standards of performance, particularly by promoting those deemed to meet these standards. In so doing, corporations tend to mould certain types of individuals. Corporations also mould individuals in other ways and otherwise affect social values. The most obvious expression of this power is in advertising and the promotion of mindless consumption. To argue that advertising does not direct people and serve to stabilize the monopoly position of corporations over particular goods and services is to suggest that advertising does not work and is wasted. But the effects of consumerism are of greater importance: it serves to squander the resources of a society, both human and natural. Corporations command great armies of people and convert large quantities of natural resources to consumer products, but where are the criteria governing the use of these resources? The criteria are in the heads of the elite; their values determine the use of these resources. But in a capitalist society they are not accountable for these values.

Finally, although it does not complete the list of areas where this elite wields power, there is the power to determine the basic investment patterns of a nation. Investment patterns are decisions regarding the location of various facilities – plants and offices – and the kinds of activities that will be pursued, such as mining, petroleum extraction, nuclear energy, and so forth. Corporate expansion patterns have an effect on which regions will be developed, whether raw materials will be processed or shipped elsewhere, where bureaucratic facilities will be established – the very shape of the country. This kind of economic power is very far-reaching and bears on the entire phenomenon of economic planning with all its ramifications. Certainly the state can have an impact here, but that impact is muted. To entice a corporation to perform certain operations in a specific location, the state must offer sufficient inducements of capital or concessions (such as forgivable loans or tax holidays). In other words, it must lure the corporation on the corporation's own terms – and those terms are the private accumulation of profit.

When this concentration of power transcends national boundaries on the scale that has occurred between Canada and the United States, the issue of corporate power becomes of even greater significance. In the words of Herbert Marshall and his colleagues in the classic, *Canadian-American Industry*, "businessmen and capitalists in either country have always been attracted by economic opportunities in the other, and found few obstacles to investing in and developing them" and "this has been a movement in both directions," although the relative impact on each nation has certainly not been equal.[3]

The power and importance of corporations and the elites that run them in both national and international operations will vary with time and place. Capitalism has many phases and faces. In its formative stages it is progressive and productive, creating goods and services, giving rise to a free labour market, and mobilizing large pools of capital. It also has enormous costs that are not shared equally by all the nations or people involved. It alienates the labour of many and concentrates capital among the few. It is often wasteful of resources, both natural and human. There are also many kinds of capitalists, ranging from the small owner to the conglomerate financier, operating in anything from the capitalism of small-scale economies to the enormous enterprises of the current U.S. system.

In the world of international corporate power it is only the largest corporations and the individuals who run them that are of major consequence. The scope of their power is reflected in their ability to determine the direction of economic activity and development at home and abroad. They also have enormous international influence because they can affect the political and military power of both their home and other nations. Compared to political or, more especially, military power, economic power keeps a low profile, but it is nevertheless effective. Companies both national and multinational can hide behind a variety of name brands and subsidiaries in an attempt to blend with the locals. Thus international corporate power can often be exercised with very little public knowledge or scrutiny, not to mention accountability. Moreover, because certain members of the U.S. economic elite have such concentrated and significant power in some economic activities in Canada (for example, the automobile or oil industries), they have much broader influence and create a particular environment within which the state and economic elites of Canada must exercise their own power. These Canadian power holders have to decide whether to co-operate or to enter into conflict with the U.S. economic power holders. Most often they have co-operated because they have seen co-operation as conducive to their own well-being.

The economic elite are not the only individuals with weight in directing the economy, but in Canada and the United States they are by far the *most* important, the *most* powerful.

CHAPTER TWO

A Framework for Analysis
of the Continental System

Economic patterns in Canada have been shaped by foreign capital, but this country has not languished completely underdeveloped. Indeed, some parts have been overdeveloped to the relative neglect of other parts, resulting in the pattern called uneven development. While Canada is not a "Third World" country, it has in common with such countries an extremely high foreign control of basic resources, an indigenously controlled manufacturing sector that is relatively underdeveloped (much of major secondary manufacturing being under external control), and an overdeveloped commercial sector. On the other hand, it exhibits some of the characteristics of an advanced capitalist nation, having fairly extensive foreign investments of its own, a highly developed commercial and service sector, and an elaborate state system built on the model of Western liberal democracies.

Before a concrete analysis of the continental economy is launched, it is necessary to establish a framework that will aid in making sense of this material. To do this requires setting out some concepts and theories concerning the nature of capitalism, the nature of the world economy, and the effects of both on various fractions of the capitalist class. This chapter foreshadows later chapters and provides the broad outlines of some later findings.

Uneven development is characteristic of all liberal democracies, but some are able to shift the greatest part of this burden to other countries. Even the most powerful of all, the United States, has not been completely successful in this, however – witness the position of Blacks and Mexican Americans and native peoples. But generally, other nations have borne the brunt of this unevenness. In Canada the phenomenon of internal exploitation as exhibited in the position of native peoples and French Canadians and in regional inequalities has also been great, but Canada too has been able to shift some of the burden abroad, although not nearly as extensively as the United States.

Why is it that the United States has been able to shed its past position of being the recipient of the uneven development of others while many nations have not been as successful? The literature on development provides a key theory: development possibilities that exist at one period may no longer prevail at a later time precisely because a new context of powerful industrial centres comes into existence that can deter development of alternative centres.* Thus, in many underdeveloped countries the impact of foreign ownership of industries and resources has reinforced the position of commercial capitalism (in the business of the circulation of commodities and money) at the expense of industrial capitalism (in the business of production). Moreover, the consequence of foreign control has been to siphon off capital from underdeveloped areas rather than to channel capital to them. Herein the theory parallels Canada's pattern of development.

I. Changes in International Capitalism: From Mercantile to Industrial Capital

There was a world economic order based on mercantile capitalism well before the emergence of industrial production. With industrialization this international system took on new meaning and greater scope, revolving around the search for natural resources to feed the factories and workers of metropolitan nations and later for product markets. During the era of merchant dominance, capitalists were interested primarily in the staples of the colonies, such as fish, fur, and timber. In the era of colonial control, commercial capitalists began to export portfolio capital in the form of loans, usually guaranteed by the colonial governments, to companies constructing canals and railways and setting up financial lending institutions, all of which facilitated extraction of staples. As capitalism in centre nations transformed itself from the entrepreneurial to the corporate stage by the merging of industrial and commercial capital, and as many former colonies became nation-states, the nature of foreign investment began to shift from portfolio to direct control. Capitalists established production and extraction industries in the new nations but retained control from the metropolitan nation, and the nature of dominance was transformed from primarily political to primarily economic. At the same time, multinational corporations began to emerge.

A crucial shift in the world economy from the dominance of trade to the dominance of capital flows occurred about 1850 during the consolidation of the industrial revolution in Britain and marked the transformation from mercantile to industrial capitalism. Such transformations occurred in central nations with much greater ease than in peripheral nations. As Paul Baran has pointed out, metropolitan (or central) control tended to inhibit the transformation from mercantile to industrial

---

* Paul Baran, in *The Political Economy of Growth*, has concluded that "in most underdeveloped countries capitalism had a peculiarly twisted career." He states that "the new firms, rapidly attaining exclusive control over their markets and fencing them in by protective tariffs and/or government concessions of all kinds, blocked further industrial growth while their monopolistic price and output policies minimized the expansion of their own enterprises.... Monopolistic industry...extends the merchant phase of capitalism by obstructing the transition of capital and men from the sphere of circulation to the sphere of industrial production" (pp. 176-77).

capitalism in the periphery. In the presence of foreign investments "there could be no spread of small industrial shops" because foreign capitalists "erected single large-scale modern plants which were sufficient to meet the existing demand."

Although the total amount of capital needed for such a venture was frequently large, the part of it spent in the underdeveloped country was small, with the bulk of the outlays involved taking place abroad on the acquisition of foreign-made machinery, of foreign patents, and the like. The stimulating effect on the economy as a whole resulting from such investments was accordingly slight. What is more [this]...reduced greatly or eliminated entirely the chances of another enterprise being launched in the same field.[1]

Foreign control of this type forced local interests to remain in traditional merchant pursuits and was important in preventing them from moving into industrial areas.

As in many peripheral nations, the transition between mercantile and industrial capital in Canada was not smooth. Merchant capitalists remained locked into the sphere of circulation because of both external pressure and the safe and lucrative nature of that territory.* Indigenous industrial capitalists in Canada who followed the path from local manufactories to national corporations in the sphere of production were often stymied because they lacked the necessary financing and transportation to markets, both activities controlled by dominant Canadian capitalists in circulation. Canadian industrialists also ran into the stone wall of foreign industrialists who entered the country directly or exported their products to Canada to supplement their industrial operations at home. These foreign capitalists could overpower most Canadian industrialists because of the greater resources their home markets gave them. They had not only a greater capacity to develop technology but also easier access to capital, which was often used to buy up Canadian industries when they were large enough to enter the national market. The Canadian commercial capitalists, whose "commodity" was money, only increased the burden of small industrialists by treating their firms in the same way – "products" to be bought and sold, not to be nurtured and valued for their intrinsic productive value.

In the early stages of international capitalism Canadian merchants and their counterparts in the United Kingdom engaged in buying and selling commodities. Canadian merchants acted as intermediaries between Canadian resources (staples) and foreign markets. Supply was often easier to control than demand, particularly when foreign "de-

---

* In *Development and Underdevelopment: A Marxist Analysis*, Geoffrey Kay makes a distinction between *productive* and *circulation* capital that corresponds to the different economic activities: "the production of commodities in the one case; the buying and selling of them in the other" (p. 86). Industrial capitalists operate in the sphere of production and commercial capitalists in the sphere of circulation. Merchants were prominent among commercial capitalists during the early stages of capitalism, financiers during the later stages.

mand" was determined by other merchant capitalists abroad or by industrial capitalists who processed the resources. Because the exchange of commodities was predicated on the transportation of goods, it was easy for Canadian capitalists to make a transition into transportation, the basis of their commerce.* Thus they backed development first of canal systems and later of railways and found British capitalists willing to support their ventures.

The transition from mercantile to financial capitalism was also a logical one. As Geoffrey Kay has pointed out, "the circulation of commodities requires complex financial arrangements, such as the provision of funds to productive capital at the start of the circuit, and the supply of consumer credit at its close. These are undertaken by specialist firms such as banks, merchant banks and building societies, who all have one thing in common; the only commodity they handle is money."[2] Thus when mercantilism declined, merchant capitalists in Canada, as elsewhere, began to move into financial institutions such as banks and the trust, insurance, and mortgage companies, all of which specialize in the "sale" of money and are in the sphere of circulation. Given the easy movement into financial activities and the barriers to movement into areas of production, Canada's top capitalists committed themselves, and Canada with them, to a vulnerable position in the world system. They sought out and found foreign capitalists willing and able to enter the sphere of production in Canada.

The consequences were far-reaching. Because Canadian capitalists had specialized in circulation, they soon became dependent upon foreign capitalists in control of Canadian production. In a metropolitan nation the consequences would not have been so important, for, as Kay says, "in capitalist society no fundamental contradiction exists between the sphere of circulation and the sphere of production because both are under the control of the same class."[3] While the spheres were indeed under the control of the same class in Canada, they were not controlled by the same class fractions.† There was, however, a non-antagonistic

---

* Transportation, like financial capital, is in the sphere of circulation, but it resembles production in that it tends to be a long-term activity that ties up capital. In Canada railway and canal construction were made low-risk by government guarantees and concessions. Historically, transportation in Canada is clearly aligned with financial capital because most railways were commercially oriented to opening trade in a resource-based economy. In the United States the railways had a more industrial orientation and were used to open markets for products, particularly in the northeastern and north-central regions. In the South, however, they remained oriented much longer toward staple production (cotton), and this type of staple lent itself to industrial production (textiles) in a way Canada's key staples of fish, fur, and wheat did not. The purpose of railways was clearly quite different for the various types of North American capitalists and economic activities.

† Class fractions are divisions *within* as opposed to *between* classes. The capitalist class as a whole is distinguished from other classes because it owns and controls the means of production, thus employing the labour power of others. Within the capitalist class, however, divisions occur that may or may not be antagonistic, such as those between the spheres of production and circulation, between foreign and indigenous capitalists, and between large- and medium-sized capital. These fractions will be returned to later in this chapter.

relationship between the two fractions in Canada – the indigenous fraction in circulation and the foreign-controlled fraction in production. The division of activity actually reinforced the continental economy and the relationship between these two fractions in Canada.

In metropolitan nations, merchant capitalists succumbed to industrial capitalists. Kay notes that mercantile capitalism "created the preconditions for a thorough-going revolution in the means of production, but its fractional interests, its desire to protect narrow monopolistic privileges, blocked their realisation. As a result the first struggle of industrial capitalism was against its own progenitor: the industrial revolution was a historic defeat for merchant capital."[4] In Canada, however, no groundwork was laid for the defeat of merchant capitalists by industrial capitalists. As a colony, Canada's industrial needs were often met by foreign industrialists. Thus Canada differed from metropolitan nations in that it was not a Canadian industrial revolution that defeated its merchant capitalists but rather the industrial revolution in the United Kingdom and eventually the United States. Stymied by the repeal of the Corn Laws and the end of mercantilism, Canada's merchant capitalists were left out in the cold, floundering for a new imperial centre to tie to. The United States and its industrial economy provided the desired mooring place, and Canadian capitalists clung to the initiative of foreign industrial capitalists as a surrogate for indigenous development.

With Canada's economy shaped to conform to the resource demands of industrial societies, particularly the United States but to some extent the United Kingdom and Europe, the internal power of capitalists in circulation in Canada was reinforced although they were relegated to a subordinate international position. The Second World War proved to be the crucial watershed for Canadian industrialization. At the very outset of the war, the Canadian state took charge, pumping millions of dollars directly and millions more in tax exemptions and depreciation allowances into production facilities (both private and public), playing an important role in industrializing the country. After the war it dismantled that part of the industrial economy it had directly established, putting these means of production on the auction block. Most of the buyers were industrial capitalists from the United States seeking to ensure the same dominant position in Canada that they had already established at home. Canada had clearly emerged from the underdeveloped world. U.S. industrialists now perceived it as a place for direct investment and accumulation in the sphere of production, particularly in manufacturing, in contrast to the earlier emphasis on resources. This shift was facilitated by the proximity of Canada and by its relatively wealthy market, which could have its tastes trained to match those of the U.S. market.

Canada was also politically stable compared to the underdeveloped world, and there was no fear for direct investment in production facilities. Unlike merchant capitalists, industrial capitalists* require long-

---

* For a review of the development of Canada's labour force, see H.C. Pentland, "The Development of a Capitalistic Labour Market in Canada," *CJEPS* 25 (1959).

term capital and therefore much greater security, as well as a trained and available labour force. In short, after the industrial revolution produced its changes in the United Kingdom and United States, Canada's dominant capitalists were left controlling the means of circulation rather than the means of production. As a result, Canadian capitalists dominated the internal economy but were dependent in the international system. When the ties shifted to the United States, Canada's capitalists turned to servicing U.S. capital, again remaining primarily in circulation and service but under the general hegemony of U.S. corporate capitalism.

While these transformations in international capital were occurring, there was also a shift in the locus of international power from Britain to the United States. At the same time there was a dramatic switch from mercantilism to corporate capitalism, and the first stages of the modern multinational corporation took place.[5] As will be illustrated later, U.S. industrial capitalists have historically been much more powerful at home and abroad than have their counterparts in Britain and Canada. This circumstance will explain many of the differences in the patterns of U.S.- and U.K.-led relations in Canada.

The United States was the first "new" nation to develop a powerful, internally generated industrial base, and when other countries started on the road to industrialization, United States companies already had the technological and financial base from which to expand into these developing areas. The worldwide system of branch plants integrated with and controlled by U.S.-based patents created major linkages between parent and subsidiary as well as within the investing nation. In Canada these developments caused a disarticulation between finance and industry. A new form of dependency, international in structure and different from earlier types, had been created. The result of these broad developments has been to create an international structure of dependency.

Theotonio Dos Santos has identified three historical periods of dependency for Latin America of which the first was "colonial dependence," predominant during the seventeenth century, when commercial and financial capitalists, along with metropolitan governments, dominated colonial empires through trade policies. The second, beginning near the end of the nineteenth century, was "financial-industrial dependence," wherein capital was consolidated in the centre nations from which external expansion emanated, especially in a search for raw materials, and caused a pattern of "foreign-oriented development." Finally, after the Second World War there was a change to "technological-industrial dependence," which was "based on multinational corporations which began to invest in industries geared to the internal market of underdeveloped countries."[6]

In the Canadian experience the "technological-industrial" phase of dependence occurred much earlier than Dos Santos's date in many areas of manufacturing, simultaneously with early ventures in pursuit of resources, although it was not firmly consolidated and expanded until the period after the Second World War. In fact, Canada was largely regarded as simply a part of the home market by many U.S. capitalists and, as a result, was integrated into the consolidation process occurring within the United States at the turn of the century. Canadian manufacturing corporations are weak today because of their weak foundations and this tradition of dependence. As V.O. Marquez, then chairman of Northern Electric (now called Northern Telecom), told a Canadian Manufacturers' Association meeting, "Canada's problem is that technology and innovation from parent corporations and other easily accessible sources have been so readily available and so economically attractive in the short term, that the growth of systematic, broad-based, indigenous innovative and technological capability has been severely inhibited."[7] To understand why this has happened requires a detailed analysis of the continental economy and those who control it.

This brief summary of the changes in international capitalism provides a set of concepts and relationships useful for understanding the historical emergence of Canada and the United States within the context of European dominance. It also serves as a theoretical introduction to the differences and similarities between Canada and "Third World" nations in their relations with metropolitan nations. Left to explore are some further aspects of the place of Canada and the United States within the world capitalist order, particularly with regard to the types of fractions that have emerged within the capitalist classes of these nations, and the relationship between elites and classes, focusing on how classes reproduce themselves across generations.

II. Relations between Nations: The World System

Capitalism is a worldwide system of organizing production. Canada, as a liberal democracy, is a capitalist nation; its means of production are predominantly under private control. Capitalists are able to operate inside and outside their country, unhampered by national boundaries within this larger system. In fact, the capital they command, the resources they exploit, and the products they produce are the essential elements, transferred between the various units, making up the entire complex of economic relations between nations. But superimposed on this primary economic system are sets of political units, nation-states, that redirect, influence, and stimulate patterns of capital flows, resource extraction, and production.

As suggested earlier, it is imperative to identify which classes are involved in these relations between nations and how they fit into the overall system. For example, the argument that "Canadians" are losing control of "their" economy to the United States is based on a false premise, that "Canadians" own "their" economy. In liberal democracies the predominant kind of ownership is private, not public. Canadians collectively have never owned or controlled the Canadian economy. Rather, it has been owned and controlled by private individuals and organized into corporate entities. Such individuals and their corporate entities are the main actors in the international capitalist system. For purposes of abstraction and conceptualization we will start by referring to these relations simply as relations between nations. As refinements are developed the class structures can be taken into account.

The literature on relations between nations is rich in examples and explanatory theories of the variety of associations that can and have been established. For the purpose of analysing the continental economy, however, it is important to narrow the field to those theories that are of direct, immediate relevance. This can be done by identifying relations of a similar type through application of two key analytical concepts in the study of international relations. These are (1) the degree of intensity of these relations and (2) the degree of symmetry or asymmetry between nations.[8] Canada's relationship with the United States is highly intensive since such a great amount of raw material, products, and capital crosses their border. In fact, they are probably the two most intensely related nations, based on capitalism, that could be found. Further, the relationship between them is highly asymmetrical because they are grossly unequal in power and population, the United States being some eleven times larger in population and many times wealthier than Canada. Thus the search for models of international relations that will have some relevance for Canadian–U.S. relations can be narrowed to those with highly intensive relations and an asymmetrical relationship. It leads directly to the wealth of literature that has recently appeared to analyse relations between Latin American countries and advanced capitalist nations. While a great deal can be learned from these "Third World" analyses, it would be misleading to use them to characterize relations between Canada and the United States without first subjecting them to a critical appraisal. The models (that is, components and relationships deemed important) are certainly useful, but the theories that account for the relationships must be reappraised in light of the Canadian experience.*

Dependency models developed primarily for Latin America's relations with advanced capitalist nations are useful for our purposes because they integrate both national and international class relations. They analyse indigenous class structures in light of their relations with foreign centres. A central feature of them all is the unequal relationship

---

* The following section draws on various writings that have attempted to theorize about the nature of Latin American dependency. For a more thorough review, see my "A Political Economy of Regionalism in Canada" in *Conflict and Consensus: Multiple Loyalties in the Canadian State*, ed. D. Glenday, A. Turowetz, and H. Guindon. The major writers and works covered there include Andre Gunder Frank, *Latin America: Development or Revolution*; Johan Galtung, "Structural Theory of Imperialism," *Journal of Peace Research* 2, 1971; Osvaldo Sunkel, "Transnational Capitalism and National Disintegration in Latin America," *Social and Economic Studies* 22 (1973); and Norman Girvan, "The Development of Dependency Economics in the Caribbean and Latin America: Review and Comparison," *Social and Economic Studies* 22 (1973).

between interdependent classes, which form asymmetrical associations either within nations or between nations. In other words, it is argued that there is a chain of exploitive relations linking various classes and regions from the local to the regional to the national and international levels, all serving to drain power and resources from the lower levels and accumulate them at the higher levels. In terms of the continental economy between Canada and the United States, this chain imagery is important for understanding how relations between these two nations can affect regional disparities within Canada, particularly the presence of most of the U.S. branch manufacturing plants in Southern Ontario and the consequent aggravation of regional disparities within Canada. The inequality among nations stressed in dependency models also enforces inequalities within nations.

The dependency models not only stress the general inequality among nations but also show how asymmetrical relationships tend to create alliances between the dominant classes of the metropolitan and peripheral nations, reinforcing the power of each while fragmenting the subordinate classes of the two nations. Thus it is insufficient to focus only on the dominance of one nation over another because there are classes in both nations that benefit from the structure of dominance. It is therefore important to analyse the nature of the relationship between the dominant class in the peripheral nation and that in the metropolitan nation. Applied to relations between Canada and the United States, this analysis focuses on the parts of Canada's capitalist class that become aligned with the capitalist class of the United States and are thus active participants in the general pattern of dominance.

There is also a suggestion in the literature on dependency, most evident in the work of Osvaldo Sunkel, that at least part of the dominant class in peripheral nations becomes "internationalized" with the development of multinational corporations. Sunkel maintains that in the peripheral nation "international mobility will correspond to the internal mobility, particularly between the internationalized sectors of developed and underdeveloped countries."[9] The implication is that members of the dominant class from peripheral nations will encounter few barriers in moving from local branches of multinationals to headquarters in metropolitan nations. Data in later chapters will test how this proposition stands up when officials from branches of U.S. plants in Canada move to the parent companies; these data will also test whether members of the dominant classes of "Third World" nations have been recruited to top positions in U.S. multinationals. Although neither of these patterns is very pronounced, the data will show that an important core of leading Canadian capitalists have retained their indigenous operations within Canada and have also been recruited to the board rooms of some of the dominant U.S. corporations. The evidence suggests that although there has been some "continentalization" of members of the Canadian economic elite, there has been little "internationalization" of citizens of "Third World" nations to top positions in U.S. multinationals. The dependency models can certainly suggest features to focus on in understanding relations between Canada and the United States, but it is clear that the continental relationship is not the same as that between metropolitan and peripheral nations.*

III. The Continental System: Capitalist Class Fractions

Few would not agree that the United States is a metropolitan, developed, centre or core nation, depending upon the particular perspective used, but Canada cannot be so easily placed. The paradoxes of Canada's economic structure have already been stressed several times, but there is yet another complexity. Johan Galtung has suggested that some nations may be called "go-between" in that they mediate between central and peripheral nations.[10] These go-between nations are not clearly in either camp and may be expected to exhibit some of the characteristics of both central and peripheral nations. This is an important clue to an understanding of Canada's place in the continental system and its role in the world system because a great deal of "Canadian" foreign investment in the "Third World" and elsewhere is of this go-between type; that is, much of this investment flows from firms in Canada which in turn are subsidiaries of other companies controlled outside Canada (see Chapter 5). The go-between nation theory identifies both Canada's specific location within the continental economy and its general world position.

Galtung did not elaborate on the meaning of "go-between nation" except to suggest that it acts as a mediator between central and peripheral nations, that it would be ahead of the periphery but behind the centre in technological development, and that it would deal in semi processed materials rather than the finished products of the centre or the raw materials of the periphery. While each of the features would generally apply to Canada, important questions remain unanswered. For instance, what effect would this go-between position have on the class formation of such a nation? If some fractions act as intermediaries or agents for foreign interests, are all therefore subordinate to outside interests?

---

* Immanuel Wallerstein's work is the most ambitious attempt to come to grips with the issue of international capitalism, although it is by no means complete at this point. In *The Modern World System: Capitalist Agriculture and the Origins of the European World Economy in the Sixteenth Century*, he sets the valuable but enormous task of providing a "world-system perspective." At the moment, Wallerstein's main divisions between "core," "peripheral," and "semi-peripheral" states are problematic in terms of Canada, missing necessary refinements for placing it within the world system. The work by Malcolm Alexander, a student of Wallerstein's, may overcome this difficulty by using the term "semi-industrial" to characterize countries such as Canada, Australia, and Argentina that have industrial social structures but peripheral trade patterns ("The Political Economy of Semi-Industrial Capitalism"), but this remains work in progress.

Certain members of the Canadian economic elite (the fraction of the capitalist class controlling the largest corporations in Canada) are integrated into the world order in two distinct ways: as go-betweens of foreign, predominantly United States, interests and through their own indigenously controlled corporations. Canada has a rather unique role as mediator of foreign-controlled capital, as holder of its own foreign investments, and as host to extensive foreign investment. Thus a framework differing somewhat from the one emerging from the dependency literature is needed for placing Canada in the world system.

This initial complexity is simplified because, as was suggested earlier, the various types of investments are located in rather clearly defined economic activities. Foreign investment in Canada tends to be centred in the manufacturing and resource sectors (the sphere of production), while the finance, transportation, and utilities sectors (the spheres of circulation and service) tend to be indigenously controlled. Canadian-based foreign investments follow the same pattern; in the sphere of production they are go-between, and in the spheres of circulation and service they are directly Canadian. There are, of course, exceptions, but they are typically exceptions that sustain the general pattern.*

What must be identified now are the components of various fractions of the capitalist class in Canada and their relationship to foreign ownership. Starting with the divisions within the Canadian capitalist class already discussed, several class fractions can be distinguished, making use of the criteria of locus of control and size and sector of economic activity. Thus it is important to distinguish between indigenous fractions (those with a Canadian-owned and controlled base of power) and comprador fractions (those whose main allegiance is to a foreign-controlled base of power in Canada), both of which can be further subdivided into national and international components depending on their scope of control. Compradors are the senior executives and directors of branch plants who follow the directives and policies of their foreign headquarters.† Secondly, a distinction is required between the most powerful or dominant capitalists and middle-range capitalists based on the amount of economic control they command. Dominant corporations are companies that control the greatest amount of economic activity in the most important areas of the economy, and dominant capitalists are persons who control these corporations.° The third distinction is identification of the major economic sector, production or circulation and service, to which the fraction belongs.

---

* It will be demonstrated in Chapter 5 that many of the Canadian-based and controlled foreign investments in the sphere of production are actually controlled by financial capitalists through two major holding companies, Argus Corporation and Power Corporation.

†For an elaboration of the term *comprador* and its origin, see Clement, *The Canadian Corporate Elite*, p. 119ff.

° The concept "dominant corporations" will be explained in Chapter 6 for both Canada and the United States. There are 113 dominant corporations in Canada and 194 in the United States, when all subsidiaries are taken as part of their parent company.

In Canada these characteristics tend to cluster, so that three major fractions of the capitalist class can be distinguished (the few who fall outside these types do not represent large analytical categories). The first of these is a *dominant indigenous* fraction, very active in finance, transportation, and utilities, to a lesser extent in trade, and much less in manufacturing and resources (and then primarily in food and beverages, steel, and pulp and paper).* This fraction is both national and international in scope. In this study it will be referred to as the indigenous Canadian economic elite – that set of people who hold the uppermost positions in Canadian-controlled dominant corporations. The second is a *middle-range indigenous* fraction, active mainly in relatively small-scale manufacturing and not international in scope. Many members of this fraction act in a service capacity to dominant foreign corporations in the sphere of production, while others serve regional markets inside Canada. Because they are often dependent on the dominant indigenous fraction for sources of capital and access to markets, they are vulnerable to the power of the two dominant fractions of the capitalist class. The third is a *dominant comprador* fraction. It is active in manufacturing and resources, is both national and international, and is located in branch plants of foreign-controlled multinationals. The comprador fraction can be further subdivided by source of control (whether the United States, United Kingdom, or elsewhere), where the U.S. component is clearly the most important in Canada. This fraction will be represented in this study by the comprador Canadian economic elite, those holding the uppermost positions of foreign-controlled dominant corporations in Canada. The fact that this fraction is also international reflects its go-between role. Although dependent itself on foreign capitalists in the parent companies of foreign-based multinationals, it also acts as an intermediary for a significant amount of foreign direct investment flowing out of Canada.†

Fractions of the U.S. capitalist class are not as difficult to classify using these three distinctions as their counterparts in Canada, a reflection of the fragmentation of the Canadian capitalist class because of foreign dominance and the unity of its U.S. counterpart. The basic differences, of course, are that foreign-controlled capital plays an insignificant role in the United States and no fraction is go-between. Still, there are the distinctions based on size and degree of international investment. The U.S. economic elite – those who control the uppermost positions (senior executives and directors) of dominant corporations in

---

*The historical reasons for the participation of indigenous Canadian capitalists in the areas of food and beverages, steel, and pulp and paper will be explored in Chapter 3.
†The following is an example of the comprador elite's foreign investment: Ford Motor Co. of the United States holds 85 per cent of the stock in Ford Motor Co. of Canada, thus making the Canadian operation a branch plant. This Canadian-based company in turn holds 100 per cent of Ford Motor Co. of Australia, New Zealand, South Africa, and Singapore and operates plants in Malaysia. The history of Canada's go-between role will be explored in Chapter 3 and the contemporary pattern will be developed in Chapter 5.

the United States – is both national and international.* There is also a middle-range fraction of the capitalist class, which is national and occasionally multinational and continental. There is no need to make a distinction based on economic sectors because U.S. control dominates in them all, but a difference exists in the degree of international and continental investment depending on sector as well as in the sectors' relationships with each other.

Finally, a component of both the U.S. and Canadian elites forms a continental elite through a series of interlocking directorships and social ties in both countries. This continental elite is based not only on Canada–United States and United States–Canada interlocks between parent and subsidiary companies but also on important exchanges between dominant Canadian-controlled and U.S.-controlled companies outside the parent-subsidiary relationship. From the perspective of a continental economy, it is important to identify the fractions of the capitalist classes of both countries involved in this continental elite and to assess the importance of the tie.

A Note on Class and Elites

Before proceeding with the empirical analysis that is at the core of this study, it is important to clarify the meaning given to two terms: the economic elite and the capitalist class. An *elite* is a set of uppermost positions in any area of life that is hierarchically organized. The *economic elite* is that set of people holding senior executive and directorship positions (the uppermost positions) within dominant corporations (the largest companies). The *capitalist class*, on the other hand, includes all those in a particular relationship to capital, that is, those who own, control, and/or manage (at a senior level) all corporations employing the labour power of others, including their families.† In a sociological analysis, it is more convenient, in making an empirical examination of the people involved, to focus on the economic elite than on the capitalist class as a whole; moreover, the economic elite is the leading force of the capitalist class and controls most of the privately owned resources. Focusing on the elite of a class rather than the class as a whole makes possible a more detailed analysis of the social characteristics of that elite. Identifying an elite is simply a methodological technique for objectively singling out the people occupying the most powerful positions

* Included in international operations are the distinctions between those who are multi-national and those who are continental; that is, those who control operations in the United States and throughout the world and those who control operations in the United States and Canada only. Since virtually all dominant U.S. corporations are both continental and multinational (with some exceptions to be explored later), there is little point in making this analytical distinction for elites, although it is important for corporate activity.

† For a more detailed discussion of social class and elites, see Clement, *The Canadian Corporate Elite*, pp. 5-11.

in any activity. It is not a substitute for a class analysis; it is simply a mechanism for making an analysis of characteristics for a particular fraction of a given class.

A further point requiring clarification is how members of the capitalist class and particularly the economic elite reproduce themselves, that is, the question of continuity within the elite and how people are recruited to elite positions. Ralph Turner has drawn a distinction between two basic types of mobility: contest and sponsored. Contest mobility is characterized by an open system where an individual gains some desired end by competing with others on their own merits in a "contest" governed by "fair play"; in other words, it characterizes the type of mobility portrayed in the dominant ideologies of liberal democracies in which there is fluid movement of individuals with equal opportunity for all. Sponsored mobility, on the other hand, means that established powers select recruits based on criteria set by themselves. There is a "controlled selection process. In this process the elite or their agents, who [they feel] are best qualified to judge merit, *call* those individuals to elite status who have the appropriate qualities."[11] As an example of sponsored mobility, Turner provides the telling illustration of private clubs "where each candidate must be 'sponsored' by one or more of the members." This type of mobility is in opposition to the dominant ideology of open and free competition, where the criteria of access are those established by the broad community as opposed to closed selection by those already in power. Under the sponsorship system, the values and qualities deemed important are exemplified by a few who are able to set the "standards" of admission. For a sponsorship system to exist it is necessary, first, to have a hierarchically organized activity and, second, to have top positions filled by appointment rather than broadly based election. This relatively simple distinction is important for understanding the process of elite selection and recruitment. The theoretical complexities of the distinction actually have much older intellectual roots, and more recent analysts have refined and developed the core idea contained in the dichotomy.

The notion of social "closure," the basis of a sponsorship system, was first introduced by Max Weber, who specified some of the criteria and processes involved in creating "communities" of interest:

> When the number of competitors increases in relation to the profit span, the participants become interested in curbing competition. Usually one group of competitors takes some externally identifiable characteristic of another group of (actual or potential) competitors – race, language, religion, local or social origin, descent, residence, etc. – as a pretext for attempting their exclusion.... The jointly acting competitors now form an "interest group" towards outsiders.... Such closure, as we want to call it, is an ever-recurring process; it is the source of all guild and other group monopolies.[12]

Recently Weber's theory of social closure has been revived and applied empirically. For example, Gertrud Neuwirth uses it with reference to race relations and communities. She says, "Communities are defined in terms of the solidarity shared by their members, which forms the basis of their mutual orientation to social action." The formation of communities leads to a situation where "community members will tend to monopolize economic, political, and/or social advantages. The process aimed at such monopolization is called 'community closure.' Such closure may, of course, be achieved to varying degrees ranging from the total exclusion of outsiders to the admittance of certain new members who fulfill specified conditions."[13]

Although Neuwirth does mention the implications of closure for economic power, her main application leads in a different direction from that to be pursued here. The major theoretical application of these concepts to social classes has been the work of Frank Parkin, continuing from Weber's concepts.

Parkin's article on social closure in formation of classes provides some important analytical suggestions for developing the relationship between social classes and the economic elite. Specifically, it helps to develop the relationship between the concepts of power, class, and elites. Following Weber, Parkin says that social closure "means the process by which social collectivities seek to maximize rewards by restricting access to a circle of eligibles." He identifies in social closure "two general strategies for staking claims on resources: those based upon the power of *exclusion* and those based upon the power of *solidarism*."[14] Exclusion, he argues, is the key mode of closure in systems of stratification, while solidarism is more the reaction of those excluded. Those in power attempt to remain in power by controlling the means of access and using their position to enhance their own continuity and that of others they deem acceptable. As Parkin says, "The rise and consolidation of ruling groups has been affected by the restrictions of access to valued resources, such as land, esoteric knowledge, or arms, to a limited circle of eligibles."[15] Aristocracies used "family" as a means of closure, but for capitalists property and position have taken the place of descent. This does not mean, however, that inherited private property has lost its centrality to capitalism.*

The purpose here is to develop an understanding of elite recruitment in dominant corporations, and because these corporations are characterized by stability and a sponsorship type of access the following discussion will be confined to practices of closure adopted by members of the economic elite. The two broad types of criteria used for exclusion are *ascribed* and *acquired* characteristics. Although there is some overlap between the two, the essence of their difference can be maintained. Ascribed attributes are characteristics over which an individual has no

---

* The continuing central role of private property is examined in Appendix XIII, and the theoretical foundations and their application to Canada are examined in the section on "Owners, Directors, Managers and Technocrats: The Ownership and Control Debate" in my *The Canadian Corporate Elite*, pp. 11-23.

control such as sex, class of birth, region of birth, race, or ethnicity, while acquired characteristics are at least partly the result of the activities or careers of the persons themselves. At least some acquired characteristics will be affected by origins, such as traits acquired from education at a particular university because of parental responsibility for choice of institution and cost of tuition, while others are not likely to be, such as the "loyalty" and "endurance" of those making the "long crawl" through the corporation. Under a sponsorship system either ascribed or acquired characteristics can be used as means of exclusion. For example, a person may have a position of power because his parents selected him to inherit a corporate post or transferred property to him. On the other hand, an individual may have been selected by those already in power because he has what are considered desirable attributes (desirable, that is, to those already in power). By examining both kinds of attributes in the economic elite it is possible to determine what types of characteristics have eliminated others and evaluate to what degree the elite is open or closed to the population.

There are other power centres besides the corporate sector in liberal democracies, notably the state, and it is possible that persons may gain privileges in them that can be translated into advantages for their offspring. A concept broader than the capitalist class is therefore needed to encompass these other holders of power. This broader set of people, which includes the entire capitalist class and its families and the state elite and its families, will be called the upper class. All members of the economic and state elites are therefore regarded as members of the upper class because of their current positions, but they may have been drawn from other classes. If their class of origin differs from their current class position, they have experienced upward mobility. This key characteristic of the elite is one of the traits that will be examined.

To summarize, the strength or effectiveness of closure among the economic elite will be variable, and, similarly, the particular attributes selected as a means of exclusion will vary, as will be evident when the attributes of the Canadian and U.S. economic elites are empirically analysed in the following chapters. It will be possible to determine the extent to which the upper class is able to transfer the privileges and prerogatives of power to its offspring through marriage, inheritance, and advantages such as private schools. It will also be possible to see what other characteristics (whether ascribed or acquired) of people with middle- and working-class backgrounds are used for exclusion or selection. These include educational training in science, law, or commerce; experience and knowledge through experience, such as that gained from political or military careers or intracorporate experience; and honorific or token appointments that may be made for women or Blacks. It will be argued that the upper class has been successful in continuing to transfer its privileges among the economic elite through generations. That is, the upper class sets the pace and determines the criteria of admission or exclusion for elite positions by socializing those sponsored in the corporations and in the club room circuit. Persons born into the upper class tend to hold their elite positions longer than those born outside it, and the latter tend to be more transitory or reach the elite only after long crawls.

The assertion that the economic elite is able to absorb the leading elements outside the upper class into its ranks on terms set by itself makes an important qualification to the mobility of some persons into the upper realms of decision making. It is saying that private property – the primary transmitting mechanism of the upper class – can be complemented by key outsiders – politicians, lawyers, technicians, and the like – who are well rewarded for their ability to make capital grow. In fact, these outsiders can become part of the upper class and transmit their privilege to their offspring because they earn at such high rates and are rewarded with stock options. This approach attempts to conceptualize the self-perpetuating nature of the elite and show how it uses its power to provide continuity between generations while at the same time absorbing "desirable" outsiders. The extent to which this occurs and the characteristics selected will be important for understanding the nature of the economic elite; moreover, formulated this way, access to the elite is an empirical proposition which can be examined in light of the data.

What are the implications of these practices for the relationship between social mobility and social classes? Theoretically, social mobility and social classes exist as independent aspects of stratification; that is, recruitment is independent of the class structure. In practice they turn out to be interdependent dimensions of inequality with class of origin determining, in large part, class of destination. The degree to which classes are open or closed, whether in terms of intergenerational or intragenerational mobility, will affect the way class cultures are established and the way class will be experienced. While the extent of mobility will affect the way class boundaries are experienced or formed, closure allows both change and continuity by drawing in outsiders but admitting them only if properly socialized and acceptable, thus preserving the essential nature of the upper class and its institutions.

What then is the relationship between the economic elite and the upper class? They are both part of what C.Wright Mills called "the higher circles," that is, "a set of groups whose members know one another socially and at business, and so, in making decisions, take one another into account. The elite, according to this conception, feel themselves to be, and are felt by others to be, the inner circle of the 'upper social classes.'"[16] More recently, G.William Domhoff has stressed the linkage between the concepts *class* and *elite*, defining the power elite "as active, working members of the upper class and high-level employees in institutions controlled by members of the upper class. The power elite has its roots in and serves the interests of the social upper class."[17] While the strength and importance of Domhoff's work is empirical rather than theoretical, it does point clearly to the class-elite linkage by analysing the "cohesiveness," "consciousness," and "consensus" among members of the upper class and elite in the United States. Domhoff considers both in-group interaction and differential life-styles to be the basis of class consciousness. He uses intermarriage, private schools, clubs, summer and winter resorts, and acquaintance patterns to illustrate "social cliques."[18] His purpose in using these indicators is to show that the power elites in the United States are rooted in and act on behalf of the upper class, thus forming a class unity which transcends particular corporations, positions, or individuals.

E.Digby Baltzell, working from a different ideological perspective from Domhoff's, has also advanced the relationship between the concepts *class* and *elite*. He has recognized that the concept *elite* tends to have a rather temporary perspective and is limited to individuals rather than facilitating a historical focus. He argues that

in any comparatively stable social structure, over the years, certain elite members and their families will tend to associate with one another in various primary group situations and gradually develop a consciousness of kind and a distinctive style of life. The *upper class* concept, then, refers to a group of *families*, descendents of successful individuals (elite members) one, two, three, or more generations ago, who are at the top of the social (subjective) class hierarchy.[19]

The extent to which an elite will be able to reproduce itself intergenerationally will determine the strength and viability of an upper class in terms of its ability to acquire most of the advantages a society has to offer. The existence of a traditional upper class means that elites are able to transfer their advantages to their offspring; it also means that the upper class enjoys the benefits of most of the resources an elite is able to extract from the rest of the population. In other words, elites who transform their power into upper-class privileges are a major means of reproducing inequality. Essential to the relationship between the elite and the upper class are sets of families and institutions such as private schools and clubs that provide stability and direction for the elite. The upper class serves as the reservoir for elite members and enjoys the majority of the benefits. It is primarily a class of inheritance, but it is also a class of nomination in that people of middle-class origin, and occasionally people of working-class origin, are drawn into it if they adhere to the values and "rules" of the upper class and are of value to it.

The upper class is a property class, a set of families who own large amounts of surplus capital. While the middle and upper reaches of the working class have personal property – homes, automobiles, pension plans, and even small portfolios for savings – they do not own sufficient capital to invest for control. Some elements of the upper class are *rentiers* who have sufficient capital to live off its interest; they manage their portfolios but do not mobilize their capital for control. Other elements of the upper class use their wealth for accumulation and hence exercise their ownership rights for control, to command corporations and ensure their interests are taken into account. These are the active members of the upper class – the economic elite. It is also possible to become a member of the economic elite without first being a member of the upper class, but these members tend to accumulate large amounts of property on the road to the elite.

Finally, the capitalist class exists as a class because of its relationship to property, a relationship that also produces a working class, which sells its labour power to capitalists in return for wages. In this study the focus is on developments in the capitalist class and particularly its most powerful arm, the economic elite. Because of the narrowness of this focus it excludes, except in a peripheral way, an analysis of classes outside the capitalist class that develop alongside and in response to this dominant class. Nevertheless, it is crucial to keep in mind that this capitalist class is directly related to the working class through its control over property and the power this brings. To provide a well-rounded approach to all classes requires a methodology broader than the one adopted here, and only when this is done can the full implications of concentrated power in a few dominant corporations controlled by the economic elite be specified.*

---

* An important example of such a methodology is that of Harry Braverman's *Labor and Monopoly Capital: The Degradation of Work in the Twentieth Century.* I am planning to develop a class analysis of Canadian society that will have a broader frame of reference than the power focus of the present study but will take into account the power structure and patterns of economic development uncovered here.

CHAPTER THREE

Setting the Stage for a Continental Economy

Consolidation and concentration – the transformation from entrepreneurial to corporate capitalism – were processes that went on throughout the nineteenth and early twentieth centuries in North America, but their time sequences and results differed in the Canadian and U.S. economics. Because of dissimilar types of relationships between industrial and financial capital and different external relations (particularly the continued external ties of British North America long after the breakaway of the thirteen colonies), industrial development proceeded at a different rate in present-day Canada, leaving it behind the United States and vulnerable to U.S. corporate penetration. The closeness of the two economies and the differences in their rhythms of development account for the current continental configurations.*

In what is now the United States, abrupt breaks with the past occurred twice. The first was the split from Britain following the Declaration of Independence in 1776 and the second was the result of the Civil War in the 1860s, with the defeat of a commercial South by an industrial North. Developments in Canada have been more gradual; parallel events were much less dramatic and much less productive of change. Not until the First World War did the British connection finally disintegrate, and the central role of Canada's commercial interests was never really ended. U.S. financial capitalists differed from their Canadian counterparts in that they were independent of external ties – in Canada's case, with Britain – and the emerging industrial interests were able to gain a much stronger hold in the formative stages of U.S. development.

---

*Since I have not done original historical research, I cannot claim originality in this historical chapter, aside from attempting to synthesize the work of others and to lend to that work some interpretation of how developments within the United States can be used to explain its impact on Canada. Although literally hundreds of sources have been surveyed for the material in this chapter, a few works stand out as most important: H.G.J. Aitken, *American Capital and Canadian Resources* (1961); J.B. Brebner, *North Atlantic Triangle* (1945); Cleona Lewis, *America's Stake in International Investments* (1938); Herbert Marshall, Frank Southard, and Kenneth Taylor, *Canadian-American Industry* (1936); O.J. McDiarmid, *Commercial Policy in the Canadian Economy* (1946), Tom Naylor, *The History of Canadian Business, 1876-1914*, 2 vols. (1975); and Mira Wilkins, *The Emergence of Multinational Enterprise* and *The Maturing of Multinational Enterprise* (1970, 1974). To avoid repetition, material contained in chapters 2 and 3 of my *The Canadian Corporate Elite* has simply been summarized. The focus of this chapter is not on internal Canadian development but on developments in the United States and their impact on Canada, set in the context of indigenous Canadian patterns.

A basic contradiction in Canadian society is that although it is an advanced industrial society, its own capitalists are mainly commercial and not industrial; that is, the industrial initiative has been sustained by external forces emanating primarily from the United States while the indigenous industrial forces have often been suppressed by domestic commercial interests. Analysis of these phenomena will make it possible to contrast uneven development within Canada with the indigenous industrialization of the United States.

I. Common British Origins and Colonial Rule (to 1776)

The first ties of both Canada and the United States were transatlantic and were cemented for both by charter companies. Each was subject to a grand mercantilist design.[1] The economies of the colonies reflected demand in the British ruling class for certain staples and, in part, the British social structure, as members of the aristocracy were sent to manage the affairs of the colonies. The result was the establishment of landed estates in what is now the United States, mainly for the production of tobacco, cotton, and grain, and, throughout the colonies, charter companies for the accumulation and transportation of commercial commodities. A class of small merchants and traders arose at a time when, as Myers says,

> the great chartered companies monopolized the profitable resources. The land magnates exacted tribute for the slightest privilege granted. Drastic laws forbade competition with the companies, and the power of law and the severities of class government were severely felt by the merchants. The chartered corporations and the land dignitaries were often one group with an identity of men and interests.[2]

The colonial merchants were under two kinds of constraints: they could distribute only goods imported by the charter companies and they were prevented from manufacturing their own goods, so that they could not diversify. When they did attempt to compete, export duties were imposed, and ultimately the British Parliament prohibited export from the colonies of a number of simple manufactured products. As would be expected, "smuggling became general."[3] Navigation acts formalized the trade restrictions and protected the colonies for British manufactures, to be carried in British ships. Some merchants then expanded into land speculation and some became agents for British commercial houses. But in the rural areas of the colonies, craft shops and small manufactories began to emerge in the form of small grain and paper mills and iron works to serve local needs. Many of these early manufactories proved successful; for example, by 1775 the production of pig and bar iron in the colonies had become greater than the English and Welsh combined[4] and was placed under restrictions by the British government.[5]

In the mid-eighteenth century, New France too was feeling the wrath of the British, ending with the Conquest in 1760. British North America was also subjected to charter companies from Britain in pursuit of fish and fur. But the northern colonies were less favoured than the southern for development of a market to support local manufactories, and much of the hinterland lay under the quasi-military rule of the Hudson's Bay Company.[6]

Marked differences in geography and demography distinguished the two groups of colonies, differences that were to be more telling as time passed. In the words of Donald Creighton, "Two colonial societies, rooted in two different American landscapes, had come into existence on the continent; and while one was scattered sparingly along the giant system of the St. Lawrence and the lakes, the other, more compact and populous, had grown up on the Atlantic seaboard."[7] British North America was basically a source of raw materials; the thirteen colonies were oriented to settlement. But the main difference was to be expressed in the reaction of the more populous colonies of the eastern seaboard to the constraints of colonial rule.

II. Mercantilism and the Impact of the American Revolution (1770 to 1830)

The economies of the thirteen colonies differed noticeably from one another, with the most radical contrast between the commercial Northeast and the plantation South. The consequent difference in their relations with Britain is best illustrated by the post-revolutionary debts claimed by British merchants. Of the three million pounds in claims, 84 per cent was against southern plantations and only 16 per cent against commercial interests in the Northeast. This situation can be attributed to the peculiarities of British mercantilism:

> In broad outline this was a system of commercial restriction by which the colonies became a captive market for the manufactures of the mother country and an exclusive source of supply for certain exotic commodities...the colonies which produced exportable staples that complemented the products of the mother country were more highly regarded than those which produced competitive commodities.... In contrast with the semi-open and commercially active economy of the northern provinces, the economy of the plantation provinces was integrated with that of the mother country in what was essentially a closed and metropolitan oriented system of trade, shipping and finance.[8]

The southern plantation system, exporting staples and importing manufactured products, complemented British mercantilism. There also emerged in the South a merchant-factor class that mediated between the two economies and often extended short-term credit.

Thus the southern slave society was tightly bound to the British sys-

tem. As Brebner put it, using a distinction made earlier between circulation and production, "The south was willing enough to accept both
goods and workers from British suppliers. The north wanted to make its
own goods or buy them in the cheapest market and it contained few
slaves...."[9] These contradictory forces were bound to manifest themselves in the pressures brought to bear on the British government (and
ultimately within the United States itself). Merchant-factors were also
prominent in the North, but of a different kind: "while the merchants
and factors in the southern colonies were mostly Englishmen and
Scotsmen who became Loyalists during the Revolution, those to the
north were generally native Americans, who, with few exceptions, supported or at least acquiesced in the colonial cause."[10]

This is an important distinction between kinds of merchants because,
as Harold Innis pointed out, the fur trade, primary staple of British.
North America at this time, had a capital structure very similar to that
of the plantations:

> The effectiveness of short-term credit in commercialism based on
> the fishing industry was in striking contrast to the limitations of long-
> term credit in the fur trade and in the plantation colonies. Staples
> demanding long-term credit were dependent on capital control in re-
> lation to the metropolitan development of Great Britain. Under these
> conditions the effectiveness of staple interests was evident in political
> influence and legislation. With dependence on commercialism as in
> New England the essentially close relationship between the economic
> and political institutions of the British Empire disappeared.[11]

Innis's statement explains the difference between the northeastern
colonies and the British North American colonies regarding the revolutionary impetus and draws an important distinction between the types
of commercialism in these two areas. The commercialism of a staple
economy permeates all the institutions of that economy, including the
political hold of the imperial centre, and its products are designed primarily for the imperial centre's requirements. But the commercial merchants of the Northeast traded with Britain as well as on their own; that
is, they were not so completely committed to the mercantile system as
the commercial interests of a staple economy had to be and indeed were
obstructed by the mercantile policy when laws were passed to inhibit
their trade patterns.

In the thirteen colonies, in the decades prior to the Revolution, a
mercantile class based on commerce and landholdings became established.[12] Even in this period "the upper classes and the older colonial
families maintained, at least regionally, strong standards of social and
religious decorum and they had fallen into deeply engrained habits of
living."[13] The same pattern prevailed later in British North America
with the Family Compact of Upper Canada, the Chateau Clique of
Lower Canada, and the Maritime Oligarchy of the East Coast.[14] It is
important to stress the regional character of these classes. Just as there

were cleavages in British North America between York (Toronto), Montreal, and Halifax, so there were cleavages in the thirteen colonies between North and South. There was also a fundamental difference in the nature of these cleavages. The thirteen colonies differed over two modes of production – the plantation economy based on slavery and the nascent industrial economy based on free wage labour. In British North America the regional differences took place within one mode of production – a mercantile economy with limited labour requirements where all three regions, acting as mediators between Canada's resources and the British Empire's demand, were drawn into rather than away from the empire.*

But the luxury of an empire was not without its costs. Britain was feeling the high administrative costs of managing its colonies, and added to its burden was the debt accumulated from the Seven Years' War. Opinion in Parliament was strongly in favour of forcing the colonies to pay for themselves. There was also pressure from British commercial interests feeling competition from the northeastern colonies. These interests led Parliament to impose revenue-producing and restrictive measures; these acts, in turn, provided the catalyst for the revolutionary impetus in the northeastern colonies. The most unpopular were the Proclamation Line of 1763, the Stamp Act of 1765, the Townshend Duties of 1767, and the Tea Act of 1773. All had their greatest effect in the northeastern colonies. The final repressive measure, interestingly enough, was the Quebec Act of 1774, imposed to appease interests in British North America. Its purpose was to keep the West available as a hinterland to insure the supply of fur and timber staples. The "recipients of the royal bounty, in the shape of great tracts of land, were to be British (English and Scottish) merchants, army officers, and rich landlords, and not the colonials."[15] In Van Alstyne's terms, "the Quebec Act threw the weight of the Imperial Government behind the commercial empire of the St. Lawrence...."[16] The colonials of the Northeast were convinced that their interests were betrayed. In contrast, on the horizon

> The Constitution held out to merchants and manufacturers the advantages of a large free-trade area, a single national currency, the protection of commercial credits in all the states, and a stimulus to business that would come with the issuing of sound public securities. Merchants and shipowners also stood to profit from federal laws giving preference to American-owned ships and from the backing in foreign trade of a strong government endowed with effective bargain-

* In Creighton's words, "The British-Canadian merchants were soon to become distinguished for their obstinate loyalty to the empire and for their old-fashioned devotion to the mercantile system." Moreover, as Canadian merchants of the time argued in London, British North America "was a valuable colony. It conformed perfectly to the requirements of mercantilism. It supplied the staples, furs, fish and oil; it consumed and did not compete with British manufactures; and it provided an outlet for British shipping" (*Empire of the St. Lawrence*, pp. 30-31, 44).

ing power. Manufacturers and artisans could now link to the Union for additional benefits in the shape of bounties and tariffs.[17]

The immediate impact of the American Revolution on the economy of the newly formed United States was not as impressive as the promises of the Constitution had suggested, although the long-term implications were to be enormous. The American Revolution did not upset the economic interests that had been solidifying for some time in the Northeast; in fact, it reinforced their position. It did temporarily hinder the South's commerce, but after the smoke had cleared, the British once again sought out the commodities of the South. Indeed, Barrington Moore, Jr., observed that "since it did not result in any fundamental changes in the structure of society, there are grounds for asking whether it deserves to be called a revolution at all. At bottom it was a fight between commercial interests in England and America, though certainly more elevated issues played a part as well."[18] Whether a revolution or not, it propelled the United States along a path not to be followed by Canada until a century later, and it broke the distorting ties with an external economy.

Following the colonial break, land remained an important source of wealth, but the landowning class was soon surpassed in power by the trading classes. It was the merchant class that "provided the early American banks with stockholders who were partly men of inherited wealth, accumulated in the colonial era, and partly *nouveaux riches* ...and the fact that the early American banks had been dominated by socially prominent cliques exerted in time a considerable influence."[19] These merchants were not averse to tapping the British capital markets for their ventures, as the British connections of George Peabody, who was instrumental in forming J.S. Morgan and Company, demonstrated.[20] A class of manufacturers who "came from the old class of mechanics and craftsmen" and were often backed "with the financial aid of merchants who had capital to invest" began to appear.[21] But their production was typically on a small scale and adapted to the local markets. Nathan Appleton was an example of those who left "mercantile pursuits" to invest in large-scale textile manufacturing.[22] Merchant interests were thus important to the nascent industrial interests in the United States. With colonial barriers to trade on the world market gone, a "boom in overseas trade beginning in 1793 created surplus capital which could be fed into industry as the profits from trade declined" during the Napoleonic Wars.[23]

The fact that most of the manufacturing enterprises in the United States as the nineteenth century opened were relatively small is underscored by the low number incorporated at that time.* In 1800, there

---

* These early manufactories were small but rapidly becoming organized. For example, "New York's Central Committee of Mechanics was founded in 1785 and soon thereafter became the Manufacturing Society of New York. An Association of Tradesmen and Manufacturers in Boston was matched by the Pennsylvania Society for the Encouragement of Manufactures and Useful Arts" (W.A. Williams, *The Contours of American History*, pp. 142-43).

were 255 corporations in transportation and public service, 67 in banking, and only 6 in manufacturing. But the period of small firms with low capital requirements, high competition, and local markets was not to last long. Soon the commercial interests, with their large pools of capital, would turn their attention to the home market. "One after another, between 1812 and 1830, the bigger houses abandoned world trading and shifted their capital to internal ventures such as banking, transportation, acquiring of western land, and manufacturing."[24] The economy of the United States was changing, and manufactories were assuming a more important part. Williams sees the "rise of manufactures to a position of parity" symbolized by the creation of the congressional Committee on Commerce and Manufactures in 1819[25] and this transformation was also reflected in changes in the labour force. For instance, half the immigrants arriving between 1783 and 1812 went into non-agrarian jobs. And other activities were expanding; banks increased from 29 in 1800 to 246 in 1816, and U.S. ships were carrying over 90 per cent of the country's trade by 1816."[26]

Not all of the country's capitalization was supplied internally. The Bank of the United States was 56 per cent foreign owned when it folded in 1841. British investors held the greater part of the $7-million bond issue of the Erie Canal, the first successful venture of its sort in the United States, completed in 1825, and many early railway bonds.[27] The British capital market was as available to the United States as to British North America, even after the break with the mother country.

Nor had the success of the Revolution quelled U.S. aspirations to take control of the entire continent, including the territory that is now Canada. The War of 1812 was only the most dramatic expression of these aspirations. Thomas Jefferson, among others, thought it "a mere matter of marching" into the British provinces to proclaim their "liberation" because "on the eve of the War of 1812 eight out of every twelve persons in Upper Canada were of American origin, and two thirds of the elected members of the provincial legislature had been born in the United States."[28] While the U.S. forces drastically underestimated the British resistance and were successfully repelled, the British ended the war by signing a commercial convention in 1815 and in 1818 a boundary convention extending the boundary westward along the 49th parallel.

The more important immediate effect of U.S. independence on British North America came via Britain. With the thirteen colonies lost as an important source of staples, Britain turned to Canada for other requirements besides furs.* Canada was to be a "granary and commercial

---

* Donald Creighton notes that "the emergence of the United States as an independent nation produced an immense dislocation in British imperial trade in the North American world. The trade relations between Great Britain and her Atlantic possessions on the one hand and the United States on the other were too vital to be severed....Canada's position was slightly dubious. Canada wanted a little something from both parties. It wanted free trade in the interior of North America; but it also wanted mercantilism on the Atlantic Ocean..." (*Empire of the St. Lawrence*, p. 103).

complement to the West Indies...and as the United States forced her way back into imperial commerce, Canada grew in value as a supplier, a market, and an *entrepot.*"[29] During the Napoleonic Wars, competition from U.S. merchants was so diminished by the Embargo Act of 1807 and the Non-Intercourse Act of 1809 that Canadian commercial capitalists were presented with a golden opportunity. The result was "the abrupt elevation of British North America from obscurity and poverty to prominence and prosperity. Britain discovered that she needed not only all the timber, lumber, and wheat which they could produce, but all that they could attract to their ports from the United States."[30] Montreal and Quebec City boomed as timber ports and shipbuilding centres.

When the wars ended, however, the British trade with the West Indies was successfully challenged by the United States, and by 1822 the hope that this U.S. trade would be diverted through the Maritimes was dashed. More important now was the St. Lawrence, as the entry point for Montreal merchants' trade to the interior and a trade avenue for the American West to the world outside.[31]

In the end, the British North American colonies were destined to occupy a subordinate economic position. Brebner summarized their vulnerable location in the North Atlantic triangle: "Against British and American strengths, the British North American colonies had little to offer. In every field of production and sale, except the fur trade, they were seriously inferior to the Americans, largely for want of equal resources and capital of their own, but partly because of their subordination to British imperial policies."[32] The weakness of the colonies in the four decades after the Revolutionary War had several sources. The small, primarily self-sufficient rural population provided little demand for manufactured goods. In addition, the United States was a lure to new arrivals, so that the population in the Canadas remained low. Spelt estimates that about 60 per cent of the immigrants arriving in Montreal between 1827 and 1837 crossed over to the United States.[33] Furthermore, the capital structure of the period aggravated the situation as H.C. Pentland has noted:

> So long as economic life in Canada consisted in the looting of surface resources (furs, seals, timber) capital requirements were limited to the provision of short-term mercantile capital, circulating capital.... Long-term commitments [in fixed capital], horror of the mercantile system, could be avoided...the weight of Empire was all against manufacturers. [34]

The United States was drawing off immigrants to serve as a skilled labour force and a market for manufactured products, but more important, it no longer bore the constraints upon manufacturers imposed by empire. It was free to march on its path to indigenous industrialization. While merchants of British North America still looked overseas to the imperial centre, capitalists in the United States were turning inward toward industry.

III. Prelude to an Industrial System and the Civil War (1830 to 1860)

The foundation for an industrial system was being firmly built in the United States prior to the Civil War. Although predominantly small and oriented to food production, cotton milling, and other commodities, the manufactories of the period had an independence not possible under colonial rule. By 1860, 1,385,000 workers, or about a sixth of the labour force, found employment in these manufactories. Taking into account persons engaged in supplying raw materials and circulation of manufactured goods, the census reported that a third of the U.S. population was supported (directly or indirectly) by manufacturing.[35] Although most of this manufacturing activity was centred in New England and the Middle Atlantic regions, centres in the eastern North Central area were also becoming important for manufacturing and merchandising, especially in clothing and agricultural machinery.

Meanwhile, the South remained a plantation economy. "In 1850 the annual value of manufactures produced in the free states was more than four times the output of manufactures in the slave states.... In 1857, the free states had 17,800 miles of railway lines; the slave states only 6,800 miles."[36] While the economic bonds between the Northeast and Old Northwest were cemented by rails, shipping, and a flow of goods, the South was still operating within a completely different economic system. Instead of the integrated transportation network of rails, canals, and ports taking shape in the North, in the South "roads tended to radiate outward from the cotton country, and were mainly engaged in getting southern staples to seaports."[37] The southern staple economy was reflected in a social structure with a small but powerful ruling class of plantation owners, a class of independent farmers with few or no slaves, and the slaves themselves.* But it was in the North that the great fortunes of the era were being accumulated, in trade, promotion, railway and canal construction, private banking, and, to a lesser extent, manufacturing.[38]

As the U.S. economy developed, the corporate form of organization became more evident, stimulated by the advantages of limited liability in the competitive and risk-ridden manufacturing sector and the need to raise large amounts of capital for turnpikes, canals, and railways in the transportation sector. And government aid, especially in the trans-

---

* According to Hacker, 15 per cent of the slaveholding families had three quarters of all the slaves, and only one quarter of the white families in the South held any slaves in 1860 (*The Course of American Economic Growth and Development*, p. 169, Table 28). Slavery did not become widespread in British North America because of "the unsuitability of slavery as a solution to Canada's labour problems.... Only in a plantation agriculture, with a need for continuous, large inputs of low-grade routinized labour, could slavery pay" (H.C. Pentland, "The Development of a Capitalist Labour Market in Canada," *CJEPS* 25 (1959): 452; see also S.B. Ryerson, *The Founding of Canada*, pp. 233-41).

portation sector, became commonplace "as a supplement and stimulus to private enterprise, not a substitute for it," supplying between 25 and 30 per cent of the capital requirements.[39] The other major source of capital was the British bond market, which at its peak provided $30 to $40 million annually and "for more than three-quarters of a century furnished American railways the principal market for their securities."[40] Like British North America, the United States enjoyed easy access to British loan capital but, unlike British North America, without the constraints of empire to mould it to an external economy.

Prior to about 1850, the U.S. commercial banks were engaged largely in financing the transportation of goods, but after that time they funnelled substantial amounts of capital into industry. The autonomous unit banking system, in which each bank pursued its own local policies, facilitated this kind of financing; the number of banks increased from 5 in 1791 to 338 in 1818, 834 in 1850, and 1,562 in 1860. In contrast, there were only twenty-one Candian banks by 1868, each controlling policies in its own branches spread throughout the country. A cost of the unit banking system in the United States was frequent failures, but it had enormous advantages for local manufacturers because of each bank's autonomy.

Aside from the private U.S. banks, for example the House of Morgan in Britain and Lazard Frères in Europe (whose purpose was to channel funds to the home market), there was little foreign investment during this period. Mira Wilkins's survey of the period concludes: "Although American traders, individual citizens, and some corporations had made foreign direct investments before the Civil War, two prerequisites for international business were absent: the first was speedy transportation and communication to distant places; the second was the transformation of the American corporation into a national enterprise."[41] In other words, it was not until U.S. corporations became national rather than regional that the necessary conditions for foreign expansion would be met.

For British North America, a new stage in international capitalism was marked by the abolition of the Corn Laws in 1846 and the commitment of Britain to free trade. The Union of the Canadas in 1841 had eased the capital position by allowing standardization of tariff policy and promoting the stability needed to encourage loans from the British capital market. Now the repeal of the Corn Laws undermined the position of many merchants, especially in Montreal, some of whom put forward the Annexation Manifesto of 1849 in response to loss of preferential treatment within the empire.* At the same time, various indigenous

---

* In the words of Donald Creighton, "The movement for annexation to the United States was the appropriate conclusion of all the distress, disappointments and resentments of these years. It was the last gesture of revulsion from a system which had been broken in pieces and a plan which had failed. Up to the very end the conservative merchants of Canada had accepted the economic limitations of the empire" (*Empire of the St. Lawrence*, p. 370).

British North American interests were already pressing for tariff protection. While farmers (whose products were, of course, traded by commercial capitalists) attained some satisfaction with a tariff for their products in 1843, it was not until 1858 that nascent manufacturers received a measure of protection. Indeed, "the second British Empire appeared indifferent to the development of manufacturing in the colonies, and industrially Canada had not advanced far by 1846."[42] The Reciprocity Treaty of 1854 between British North America and the United States did not even include manufactured goods.[43] The treaty provided for free trade in staples, agricultural and forestry products, fish, and minerals, and the main impact was on lumber and grain production in Canada.

Already behind the United States in output, even in this early period, most of the manufacturing that did exist was very local and employed only a few hands.* Dominant control in Canada was still with commercial interests and these major interests were turned to the St. Lawrence corridor and railway expansion to the West to develop a more sophisticated though traditional staple economy.†

The weakness of the manufacturing community in Canada, reflected in some state policies, can be understood best in connection with the banking structure, which differed greatly from that of the United States. Tom Naylor states:

> The country banks [in the United States], and to some extent the American state and local banks, were excellent vehicles for industrialization as long as fixed capital requirements were low. But as the capital intensity of industry grew...[investment banks in the U.S.] involved a close link between industry and finance like the country banks, though of course the scale was vastly different.
>
> The financial structures that evolved in the Province of Canada lacked any tradition of either investment banking or institutions analogous to country banks. As a colony...Canada was a staple-extracting hinterland servicing British markets, and its banking system took a form appropriate to facilitating the movement of staples from Canada to external markets rather than promoting secondary processing industries.[44]

During the formative stage of industrialization, both financial institutions and the state failed manufacturers in British North America. Transportation and sale of staples, such as lumber and agricultural products in later years, continued to be the mainstay of the dominant com-

---

*Spelt reports that according to the *Canadian Economist* of August 8, 1846, Upper Canada "had not yet produced any manufactured goods, except potash, which were of such a quality that they could compete in foreign markets. In general, manufacturing, in the modern meaning of the word, was almost non-existent" (*Urban Development*, p. 74).

†G. Tulchinsky's study "The Montreal Business Community, 1837-1853" illustrates the dominant place commercial capitalists occupied in Canada's ruling class, focusing on shipbuilding, import/export trade, merchandising, and railways.

mercial class, and as long as this structure persisted, only limited capital would flow into manufacturing from Canadian sources.

In the United States, tensions were building between the staple-producing South and the commercial-industrial North. The bloody settling of this conflict was to favour northern interests and resolve the contradiction of two opposing modes of production operating under one state. Barrington Moore, Jr., went so far as to write about the Civil War as "The Last Capitalist Revolution." He attributed much of the importance of the war to the throwing off of the last vestiges of colonial structures. Because the South was still a staple economy, it remained tied to foreign markets and had a social structure unconducive to industrialization. For example, "by 1849, sixty-four percent of the cotton crop went abroad, mainly to England. From 1840 to the time of the Civil War, Great Britain drew from the Southern states four-fifths of all her cotton imports."[45] Moreover, like the earlier capitalist revolution in England and Europe, in which the capitalist class overthrew the aristocratic order, the Civil War, as Moore sees it, was important to the United States as a means to assert the power of town over country, free wage labour over slavery, and free markets over inherited privilege. In practical immediate terms, Northern capitalists were after "a moderate amount of government assistance in the process of accumulating capital and operating a market economy: more specifically, some tariff protection, aid in setting up a transportation network...sound money, and a central banking system."[46] In one sense the quarrel was over state power and an open national market system unencumbered by regional divisions. This is not to say that moral abhorrence of slavery was not a factor, only that this sentiment was also rooted in the political economy of the day.

Like all wars, the Civil War had the effect of stimulating economic activity (in British North America as well as the North), and with this shot in the arm, U.S. cottage industries that composed the bulk of U.S. manufacturing were to enter the post-war period ripe with a more potent national industrial system that the world (especially Canadians) would soon see first hand.

IV. The Railway Era (1860 to 1900)

Internal rivals defeated, unburdened by the baggage of an aristocracy or colonial ties, disregarding any native peoples in the way, the rejuvenated industrial capitalists of the North set out westward to forge a new frontier and carve out a national market for their products. For three decades after the Civil War, the West was the frontier and the railroads were actively recruiting immigrants to fill the territories. Although rising industrialists were to some extent protected by tariffs, their main boost was to come from the building of the railways, of which the main spin-offs were the capital and product markets. The shift from a predominantly commercial and agrarian society to one based on industry and finance was remarkably swift.

Between 1860 and 1900, 163,000 miles of track were added to the 30,000 that had existed in 1860, and with this construction boom came the first important indigenous demand for primary metal products and, of course, a locomotive industry. These outlets could now support a modern factory system, and the corporations controlling the railways themselves were the most important capital consumers of the period. Their stocks provided an important source of gain for speculators. According to Hacker's estimates, railway construction itself (not counting the suppliers) accounted for a fifth of the entire capital formation of the country in the 1870s, declining to 15 per cent in the 1880s and 7.5 per cent by the 1890s.[47]

Financial institutions flourished under these conditions by tapping indigenous sources of capital and by acting as intermediaries for foreign, particularly British, banking houses. After the Civil War, the unit banking system had become rationalized with the formation of the National Banking System, providing for the first time some uniformity and security to the collage of banks spread throughout the country. But, in spite of the multitude of banks, only a handful of investment banking houses were large enough to underwrite "the financial needs of American big business. As might be expected, in a situation where there were many companies seeking money and only a few powerful wholesalers of securities, the investment houses set the rules of the trade."[48] The leading investment banking houses were J.S. Morgan and Company; Kuhn, Loeb; Kidder, Peabody; First National Bank; and National City Bank. There was a tightly knit financial community; the leading investment and commercial banks, as well as the four top life insurance companies, all had their headquarters in New York. In addition to these national institutions that formed the capital pools for large corporate ventures, there were also many state banks, rising from 247 in 1868 to 9,322 by 1900, and these were important for local business interests. As Douglas points out, even by "1912 there were only thirteen banks in the country whose capital and surplus were large enough to lend $1 million to a single customer."[49] Thus, there were both concentration and diversification within the banking structure; it was a structure that helped support both big and small companies, unlike the British North American charter banks that were biased toward the former.

The giant bankers with their great capital pools were frequently responsible for the initial movement from industrial to finance capitalism (or, as it is also called, corporate capitalism). In this, J. Pierpont Morgan was the master craftsman, creating in his time such durable companies as General Electric, United States Steel, and International Harvester. Concentrated financial institutions produced concentrated industrial corporations in their own image by consolidating related firms into giant complexes. Even at this early period (around the 1880s) a tradition that has endured up to today was practised: "Since bankers usually acquired vital interests in the companies they financed, it became a common practice to put bank presidents and directors on the boards of trustees in charge of railway and manufacturing companies. By way of reciprocity, heads of industrial corporations were also installed among the directors of banks."[50] At the top the distinction between leading corporations in finance and industry became blurred very early. This business was not as risk-ridden as it may have appeared on the surface, and certainly not as risky as for the entrepreneurs who established the initial firms. The strategy to minimize risk was simple. Take all the small competitive firms and amalgamate them into one giant corporation and price any that failed to co-operate out of the market.

Railways were among the first to feel the rationalization of corporate consolidation: the New York Central, the Baltimore and Ohio, and the Union Pacific were all products of consolidation. But they were not alone. Also products of the first merger movement initiated by both financiers and industrialists were American Can, American Telephone and Telegraph, American Tobacco, E.I. du Pont de Nemours, Eastman Kodak, National Lead, Pittsburgh Plate Glass, Standard Oil of New Jersey, United Shoe Machinery, and United States Rubber. In a few short years, the centre of corporate capitalism in the United States was pieced together. There were 2,722 manufacturing and mining consolidations between 1897 and 1902 alone.

But where had all of these companies come from? The "average tariff rate on durable commodities increased to 47 per cent in 1864 from about 20 per cent in the pre-Civil War period,"[51] but tariffs alone cannot explain the rapid expansion; they can only explain why the expansion occurred in U.S. manufacturing rather than in imported products. Much of the reason for expansion was the railways, both because they were themselves important consumers of industrial products and because they allowed companies to tap a national market that was rapidly expanding with immigration. The emergence of a steel industry, especially between 1870 and 1875, is an important case in point.[52] In 1870, only 30,500 tons of Bessemer steel rails were produced; production rose by 1880 to 850,000 tons and by 1890 to nearly two million.[53] And, in addition to the rails themselves, steel bridges were coming into use, as were structural steel in buildings and plate in shipbuilding.

These new conditions caused the number of manufacturing establishments to expand rapidly from 140,000 in 1859 to 250,000 only ten years later,* with the most rapid growth occurring in the eastern North Central region. No sooner had expansion occurred than the forces of

---

* In contrast, there were only 39,000 manufacturing establishments in Canada in 1870, reflecting both a smaller population and a lower level of industrialization.

consolidation began to take over. The electrical industry was among the fastest to concentrate and illustrates how most concentration came about, either instigated by financial capitalists or initiated by industrialists themselves. A case in point was Thomas A. Edison, the inventor and industrialist, for whom needed capital was provided by J.P. Morgan and other financiers to form Edison Electric Light in 1878. When competing firms emerged, they were consolidated with Edison Electric in General Electric in 1892, with financial capitalists in control. Other consolidations arose mainly out of industrial interests themselves, of which George Westinghouse's Westinghouse Electric was an example in 1886. In 1905, T.W. Lawson, stressing that Westinghouse "owed nothing to extraneous influences," wrote of how he assisted Westinghouse in repelling the attack by General Electric and its backer, J.P. Morgan, so that the company was able to expand and remain free of the dominant financial interests in control of its rival.[54] Reflecting the pattern of consolidation paralleling concentration, the two electrical companies soon entered into "working agreements as to the joint use of patents and divided between them the major portion of the manufacturing business."[55]

Similar developments occurred in the meat-packing industry between 1865 and 1873, with Armour, Morris, and Swift emerging at the top.[56] A major force stimulating consolidation was the depression of the 1890s. Out of a list of 318 combinations, 303 were formed between 1888 and 1903.[57] Corporate lawyers, of whom W.H. Moore was an example, were instrumental in reorganizations such as those of the Diamond Match Company and the National Biscuit Company in 1890.

To protect themselves against the ravages of competition, many industrial combines began to form trusts. Oil refining, led by John D. Rockefeller's Standard Oil Company of Ohio, was the classic example. In the space of ten years after its formation, Standard took control of over 90 per cent of U.S. refining. In 1882, Rockefeller used a holding company to form a trust with the name of the Standard Oil Company of New Jersey.

As an industry-by-industry consolidation was taking place, the common interests of this new class had to be managed, and in 1895 the National Association of Manufacturers was formed. In the words of its president, NAM "would speak with one voice on every occasion of common defense and on all occasions pertaining to [manufacturers'] general welfare."[58]

While railways enabled manufacturers to expand their markets, they also facilitated combination and vertical integration. The pre–Civil War industries, geared to local markets, had given way by 1880 to a system in which "80 per cent of the three million workers in mechanized industry labored in factories."[59]

Corporate capitalism in this era began to implement stock issues as a source of capital. Before 1880 these were characteristic mainly of the railways, but soon all large companies began to take on the corporate form of organization. This was encouraged by the "Supreme Court decision of 1886 which declared that the Fourteenth Amendment protected the corporation."[60] In his important survey of these transformations, Alfred D. Chandler, Jr., says, "By the end of the century...many American industries had become dominated by a few great enterprises that, besides manufacturing goods, sold them directly to retailers or even to the ultimate consumer, and purchased or even produced their own essential materials and other supplies."[61] In other words, they had also become integrated operations.

Changes in the size and control of industry also resulted in changes in patterns of administration, a turning from the entrepreneur to the executive. In terms of control, the corporate form of organization created a definite hierarchy of power. "Within the ranks of management there developed a clear-cut separation between the top executives – the financiers who directed the competitive strategy and who made other strictly entrepreneurial decisions – and the supervisors who oversaw operating divisions, traffic departments, and the like."[62]

What was the role of the state in this formative period in U.S. capitalism? As in British North America, the state had been active in creating the transportation infrastructure. By 1861, $188 million was invested in canals, $137 million coming from state and municipal governments, and similar assistance was provided for railways. But unlike British North America, where the state was ultimately forced to take over many of the canals and railways in order to rationalize these crucial transportation services, in the United States, "with the sale of the great majority of publicly constructed canals and railroads to corporations the precedent became firmly established that henceforth the ownership and operation of these transportation facilities would be the province of private enterprise."[63]

In reaction to pressure from the Progressives and to the concentrated power of the trusts, the federal government passed regulating legislation; moreover, as Gabriel Kolko has pointed out, "business had no vested interest in pure, irrational market conditions, and grew to hate the dangerous consequences inherent in such situations.... The first federal regulatory effort, the Interstate Commerce Commission, had been cooperative and fruitful; indeed, the railroads themselves had been the leading advocates of extended federal regulation after 1887."[64] Trust busting and the Sherman Act of 1890 were to have some effect in the following period, but "court decisions were handed down which seemed to limit the scope of the Sherman Act.... Several of the earlier trusts besides Standard Oil had survived the panic [of the nineties] and had been reorganized to conform to the law, notably, the American Sugar Refining Company and the American Tobacco Company."[65] Business was too important and powerful to be confined by the state; in fact, it was the chosen instrument of development and nation building. Moreover, market expansion itself helped dilute concentration. At times business had to be subsidized and at others to be protected from its own ravages, but it was too productive a force to be hemmed in.

The post-Civil War boom created great pools of capital, held not only in corporations but also by individuals and families. The captains of finance and industry amassed great fortunes. It has been said that "before the war the number of millionaires ranged in the low hundreds, [but] by 1892 the number was somewhere between 3,045 and 4,047."[66] In aggregate terms, 12 per cent of the population had 88 per cent of the national income, and unequal distribution of income increased between 1870 and 1900.[67] The enormous expansion in national wealth was not equally shared by all; the most powerful benefited the most, both absolutely and relatively.

Among the capitalist class it was the railway owners and financiers that gained the most in terms of wealth, while the small manufacturers were also slowly beginning to amass wealth. The growth of large bureaucratic organizations was producing both a new middle class and, for the first time, a national upper class. E. Digby Baltzell's analysis of the making of a national upper class demonstrates that "a national, inter-city, metropolitan upper class was becoming a reality in America: for the first time, in the last part of the nineteenth and early twentieth centuries, the New England boarding schools and the fashionable eastern universities provided the sons of the new and old rich from many cities with a common experience and set of subcultural standards."[68] Using a series of indicators such as the founding of key private schools and clubs and the issuing of social registers, he was able to conclude that "a centralized elite and upper class quite naturally follows from a centralized economy."[69] It is interesting to note that some of the key U.S. private schools for boys – Taft, Hotchkiss, Groton, and Choate – date from between 1884 and 1896, while many of their Canadian counterparts were established much earlier; for instance, Upper Canada College was founded in 1829. The Toronto Club (Canada's most prestigious) was formed in 1835. This reflects two important differences between Canada and the United States. First, Canada's economy was much more concentrated than that of the United States, in spite of its being much smaller. Secondly, the Canadian upper class differed from that of the United States, being based in commerce and tied to British tradition.

Canada moved gradually to Confederation in 1867 for a very different reason from the one that led to the war for independence initiated by the northeastern colonies almost a century earlier. Kenneth Buckley has summarized the forces at work:

> Whereas the New England colonies had revolted against the restrictions of a mercantile empire, the Canadian colonies threatened to revolt when the restrictions were removed. Confederation in 1867

was part of the reaction to free trade. It reflected an evolution of political institutions within the British North American colonies as means to support economic development in the interests of commercial capitalism on the St. Lawrence.[70]

While U.S. capitalists were directing their energies inward to establish a national market and an industrial system, leading Canadian capitalists were still acting as mediators between the country's resources and outside economies. Canada's two nodal points, Montreal and Toronto, continued to be the seats of commercial power as they pressed hard for railways to the West to protect their resource hinterland; it was a policy of "defensive expansionism" to protect the West from U.S. encroachment by building railways and stimulating immigration.[71] Like earlier canal construction, railway building in Canada was a step behind that in the United States. For a variety of reasons, railways in Canada were both costly and without the same immediate spin-offs, with the notable exception of the steel industry, which was taken over by the same clique that controlled railway construction. [72]

As has been argued, Canada's financial institutions evolved so as to complement the staple economy based on the mediation of resources rather than an industrial structure. Before 1900, they financed commercial interests that not only acted as mediators between Canadian staples and the British market but also carried on trade of a go-between nature, sending products originating in the United States to Great Britain.* Only later would grain exports from the Canadian West account for the larger share of the commodity trade. The long persistence of trade in agricultural staples is noteworthy. Brebner said of the comparative position: "The pattern of the future for the whole continent was indicated, when, some time about 1890, manufacturing became a more valuable economic activity than agriculture in the United States. The same thing happened in Canada about 1920."[73]†

This was not because Canadian capitalists lacked access to large capital pools. Quite the contrary; as the railways demonstrated, large amounts of capital were available. It was rather the way this capital was put to use that made the difference. It was not simply the amount of

---

*Tom Naylor points out that "a financial structure geared to aiding and abetting the long distance movement of raw materials grew up to complement the commercial system. And the great works of commercial infrastructure, notably the railways, which absorbed an enormous share of public capital account expenditures, evolved in such a way as to open the agricultural, lumber, and mining frontiers to produce raw materials for export" ("Canada's International Commercial Expansion to 1914," *Our Generation* 10 (1975):6). Naylor also states that "in 1878, some $10 million of Canada's total of $46 million of exports to the U.K. were re-exports. Of this entrepot trade, 95% was in agricultural products, accounting for nearly half of the Dominion's total agricultural exports to Britain" (*History of Canadian Business, 1867-1914*, vol. II, 238).

†O.J. Firestone says that only 19 per cent of the gross national product and 13 per cent of the employment in 1870 were in manufacturing while agriculture accounted for 34 and 50 per cent, respectively (*Canada's Economic Development, 1867-1953*, p. 204).

capital available, it was also that the source of the capital determined the use to which it was to be put. Neither British financial houses nor Canadian banks favoured risky manufacturing when secure outlets were available.

Besides staples and rails, another important "acceptable" capital outlet was utilities. As with the railways, investments in electric and gas utilities were often guaranteed by the state, and if that was not enough, the monopoly position of utilities provided a secure investment. Thus Canada's commercial capitalists expanded into the field of utilities. H.V. Nelles provides a valuable analysis of the workings of this system with the example of the Electrical Development Company. The securities and interlocking directorships of this company follow a line running directly to the bankers, insurance directors, railway men, and leading political figures (all difficult to distinguish from one another) in both Toronto and Montreal.[74] Canada's dominant capitalists were willing to diversify their activities, but only under certain conditions.

Was the problem simply that Canadian politicians lacked foresight, that they were oblivious to the interests of manufacturers or did not wish to promote an industrial society? Did Canadian financial capitalists simply have a blind spot for the profits that could be turned in manufacturing? The answer cannot be that simple. It must be sought in the political economy of Canadian capitalism.

No one could help but observe what was happening in Canada, least of all Sir John A. Macdonald, who masterminded the famous National Policy of 1879. Macdonald's argument in favour of this policy that was to cure every woe Canada ever experienced claimed that

the welfare of Canada requires the adoption of a National Policy, which, by a judicious readjustment of the Tariff, will benefit and foster the agricultural, the mining, the manufacturing and other interests of the Dominion; that such a policy will retain in Canada thousands of our fellow countrymen now obliged to expatriate themselves in search of employment denied them at home, will restore prosperity to our struggling industries, will prevent Canada from being made a sacrifice market, will encourage and develop an active interprovincial trade, and moving (as it ought to) in the direction of a reciprocity of Tariffs with our neighbours.[75]

No doubt Macdonald believed the policy of railway building, tariffs, and immigration would serve Canada's interests best, at least those dominant interests that ruled the state. But there was little reason to believe that tariffs alone were the answer to building an indigenous manufacturing class. Indeed, there is evidence that tariffs had little or only an intermittent effect on how this class would eventually develop. McDiarmid found that among "industries awarded special tariff protection...domestic producers were supplying more than 90 per cent of the goods consumed in their respective fields.... On the other hand, sugar refining had received generous protection during the late fifties and early sixties, yet less than 60 per cent of the sugar consumed came from Canadian refineries." Not tariffs but capital sources explain the situation: "Canadian manufactures were indeed placed at some disadvantage because of credit conditions. While investment capital was scarce in Canada and credits expensive for Canadian manufacturers, long-term British credits were available to Canadian dealers in British goods."[76] The National Policy did *stimulate* manufacturing, but it did nothing to *sustain* it. Again the reason was that Canada's financial structure was geared to two functions – an intermediary role with external economies and secure long-term guaranteed investment. What incentive was there to invest in the precarious manufactories of central Canada or the Maritimes when these other avenues were open? It was not until two conditions were met that Canada's dominant capitalists would enter the field of manufacturing. The first was profitability and the second security. When this is understood, little mystery remains in their behaviour.

Naylor has identified two avenues to industrialization. In the first, "industry can grow up 'naturally' by a process of capital accumulating in a small-scale unit of production, perhaps even artisanal in character, the profits of which are reinvested in the enterprise to finance its growth from within." With this method, capital is generated from within and the producer remains in control. "A second path implies direct development into large-scale enterprise...and with capital from outside the enterprise."[77] The second method promotes outside control. Both processes were under way in Canada before the turn of the century, but few of the first type were able to make it successfully past the initial stages. Two factors insured that the second type of development would become dominant in Canada. First, the indigenous financiers would consolidate smaller manufactories into corporate complexes through promotion, takeover, and merger, and second, the foreign-controlled branch plants of U.S. industry would either establish new operations in Canada or take over existing ones.

For example, small manufactories developed in the Maritime provinces and were even stimulated by the National Policy, yet at the turn of the century they fell under the control of financiers from central Canada.[78] In central Canada itself, manufacturing in the steel industry, cotton mills, and sugar refineries was subject to the same kind of financial forces.* Consolidation was also occurring rapidly in Canada; between 1891 and 1900 alone there was a reduction from 130 plants to 66 in Ontario and from 69 to 41 in Quebec.[79]

---

* A thorough account of the "decentralized and insecurely rooted" manufacturing enterprises in Canada can be found in O.J. McDiarmid, *Commercial Policy in the Canadian Economy*, pp. 88-89, 147-99. They were usually low-capital firms with few employees and oriented to the local market. A possible exception was the agricultural machinery industry, led by Massey-Harris, that was prospering with the expanding market.

It is important, however, to turn attention to the other force that was only beginning to build in Canada, early U.S. capital. Accounts of investments prior to the turn of the century vary, but the general consensus is that they were neither large in number nor vital to the U.S. operations. From 1860 to 1879 there were only a few instances of U.S. plants in Canada, and after that time only a slow, though steady, growth of branches occurred.[80]

The case of Canadian General Electric illustrates what was occurring. The firm was organized when Senator Frederick Nicholls merged three Canadian subsidiaries of U.S. electrical companies and one Canadian company. By 1895, Senator Nicholls owned most of the shares of the company, which operated through manufacturing agreements with General Electric of the United States. A decade later the company was "entirely Canadian" with "exclusive rights in Canada." This relationship continued until 1923 and Senator Nicholls's death, when "the American company purchased the majority of the common stock of Canadian General Electric."[81] This history has three features common among manufacturing industries at the turn of the century: consolidation by a financier (Nicholls), technological dependence on a U.S. company, and eventual takeover by the U.S. parent to integrate the branch into its worldwide operations.

The specific pattern in the resource industry was only slightly different. Petroleum was found in 1857 in southwestern Ontario (two years before the Drake well in Pennsylvania), and in 1880 Imperial Oil was formed. At its inception it was Canadian controlled, but by 1898 John D. Rockefeller's Standard Oil held the majority interest. "American enterprise occupied an important though hardly a dominating position in the Canadian industry from 1850 to 1890."[82] In other resources, however, "in 1891 the Royal Commission on the Mineral Resources of Ontario proudly reported that Americans owned one-half of the mines in the province."[83]

Between 1890 and 1914, thirty-six of the U.S. manufacturing companies studied by Mira Wilkins established foreign manufacturing operations. Of these, thirty-four either established or obtained through a predecessor company plants in Canada.[84] The depression from 1893 to 1897 restricted demand in the United States, and many companies sought external markets to dump surplus products. Soon exports became significant, and to sustain this business, sales branches were established leading to further investments and eventually to branch plants. In addition, the consolidation movement in the United States created giant firms that began to move out of the country in search of expanded markets and raw materials.[85] In Cleona Lewis's words, "Until the closing decade of the nineteenth century, the outward flow of capital thus set in motion was of negligible proportions. With the passing of the American frontier, however, the pressure for markets encouraged an expansion of America's foreign investments."[86] These forces are reflected in U.S. investment patterns in Canada. In 1867 U.S. direct investment amounted to only $15 million, but by 1900 it had risen to $175 million direct, besides $30 million in portfolio loans. The basic difference between U.S. and U.K. investment in Canada is revealed by the fact that in 1900 there was only $65 million in direct U.K. investment but $1,000 million in portfolio investment.[87]

After 1850 there was some significant Canadian involvement in U.S. activities. James J. Hill,* the U.S. railway promoter who was born near Guelph, Ontario, in 1838 and migrated to St. Paul, Minnesota, in 1856, made several deals with the leading Canadian financiers George Stephen of the Bank of Montreal and Donald Alexander Smith of the Hudson's Bay Company.[88] In fact, the Bank of Montreal was Hill's financial support in many of his railway enterprises.[89] Most Canadian banks

> found it necessary almost from the beginning to maintain agents or branches in New York. Particular banks, depending on their field of service and type of customers, had branches in other American cities; for example, the Bank of Nova Scotia in Minneapolis (1855 to 1892), in Chicago (from 1892 on), and in Boston (since 1899)...they played an important part in the New York market, especially in the early days.[90]

Generally, it may be argued that there was tremendous expansion in the United States before the turn of the century; there was a dynamic element that did not prevail in Canada† – it lacked colonial ties, a state-directed opening of the West, and a dominant financial ruling class with dependent external ties. But though this expansion provided conditions for the development of a free-wheeling industrial system, it also allowed the Robber Barons of laissez-faire capitalism to fight their battles for profit at the expense of the people. The gestation costs of the most powerful industrial system in the world were high, yet, in another way, so were those of Canada's financially dominated economy.

V. Consolidation of Corporate Capitalism (1900 to 1913)

As the United States entered the twentieth century, industrial expansion proceeded apace. Although there was a tremendous merger move-

---

* Hill is reported to have said, "Canada is merely a portion of our western country, cut off from us by accident" (quoted in Stephen Scheinberg, "Invitation to Empire: Tariffs and American Economic Expansion in Canada," *BHR* 47 (1973):220).

† Aitken states that in spite of the construction of the Canadian Pacific, the last decades of the century in Canada were "a phase of slow growth" (*American Capital and Canadian Resources*, p. 30). Canada did not experience the industrial "take-off" that took place in the United States. See G.W. Bertram, "Economic Growth in Canadian Industry, 1870-1915," *CJEPS* 39 (1963).

ment, the economy was growing and new areas were opening so rapidly that, in spite of consolidation, competition remained. Kolko found that between 1899 and 1909, the number of manufacturing companies grew by 29 per cent and "new mergers...were unable to stem the tide of competitive growth."[91] The apparent paradox of increase in both consolidation and competition can only be explained by the number of new openings for investment. The reason was swift technological innovation, and the creation of new industries, that were taking place more rapidly than consolidation in the manufacturing sector. Only under rapid economic expansion could the two processes co-exist.

The census of 1900 "reported seventy-three industrial combinations capitalized at more than $10,000,000, most of them dominating more than one-half of production in their fields."[92] Moreover, between 1895 and 1904, 3,012 firms were absorbed.* Yet the appearance of new industries, such as those active in metal, machinery, rubber, petroleum, and chemicals, must also be stressed. The automobile industry is an important example. Between 1906 and 1920, 126 firms were founded, although only 84 remained in operation by 1920 (by 1926 the number had dropped to 44; by the early 1960s, three accounted for 90 per cent of the production).[93]

While expansion characterized the manufacturing industries, the market was closing in land transportation, and consolidation bred concentration: "By 1900 most of American land transportation was handled by about twenty five great systems informally allied in six groupings."[94] The finance sector followed much the same course as manufacturing, as the Pujo Committee of the House of Representatives found in 1913.[95] Between six hundred and eight hundred mergers of banks had occurred between 1900 and 1909, but the actual number of banks continued to rise until 1920.[96]

The rise of corporate capitalism was well under way; the corporate form of organization by 1900 accounted for two thirds of the manufacturing output where only a few years earlier small manufactories had been most prominent. Corporate capitalism gave new order and stability to the system. As Williams has argued, "The political economy had to be extensively planned, controlled, and co-ordinated through the institution of the large corporation if it was to function in any regular, routine, and profitable fashion."[97] The basic elements of this capitalism, as summarized by Dusky Lee Smith, are "private ownership of the means of production, increased participation of the state in the political economy, centralization of the major institutions, imperialism, efficiency, and functionalism." Part of the justification for the transi-

---

* In his authoritative study of mergers between 1895 and 1920, R.L. Nelson states, "The eight leading merger industries were primary metals, food products, petroleum products, chemicals, transportation equipment, fabricated metal products, machinery, and bituminous coal. Together, they accounted for 77 per cent of merger capitalizations and 68 per cent of net firm disappearances by merger" (*Merger Movement in American Industry*, pp. 52-53).

tion was provided by intellectuals. Smith's analysis of the period concludes, "In varying degrees, the founding fathers of American sociology were ideological protagonists for corporate capitalism."[98]

Two forces important in the previous period were again at work in creating the new corporate order. The first was the role of promoters and financial capitalists in combining various manufacturing firms into corporate complexes (particularly notable during the great merger movement from 1899 to 1904); the other was the growth of corporations out of the retained earnings of manufacturing companies themselves.* Kolko says that from 1900 to 1910, "70.4 per cent of the new funds in manufacturing came from internal sources, and this led to a general independence from outside financial power."[99] Chandler found that manufacturing companies were beginning to diversify and integrate several of the economic functions related to their production; "by the early twentieth century nearly all the companies making semifinished product goods controlled the mining of their own raw materials."[100] Whether by financial or industrial initiative, leading corporations were increasingly taking on the form of organization they currently have, and the corporations themselves were important engines for the production of surplus capital that could be reinvested. The corporate form of organization and associated stability also facilitated their becoming important outlets for the capital of financial capitalists.

Corporate capitalism in the United States meant more than an organizational change and more than the merging of industrial and financial interests; it also meant the meshing of economic and political policy. Gabriel Kolko's *The Triumph of Conservatism* on the Progressive era in the United States illustrates the role big business had in the formulation of government policy and how this resulted in the stabilization of business in the United States at the turn of the century through state regulation. His view is that

> Progressivism was initially a movement for the political rationalization of business and industrial conditions, a movement that operated on the assumption that the general welfare of the community could be best served by satisfying the concrete needs of business. But the regulation itself was invariably controlled by leaders of the regulated industry, and directed towards ends they deemed acceptable or desirable.[101]

For example, because of pressure from several quarters, the Federal Reserve Bank Act was passed in 1913. Although most demand for the act came from the Progressives, Kolko has argued that the "major function, inspiration, and direction of the measure was to serve the

---

* Chandler noted that "consolidation and departmentalization meant that the leading industrial corporations became operating rather than holding companies...of the 50 companies with the largest assets in 1909, only United States Steel, Amalgamated Copper, and one or two other copper companies remained purely holding companies" ("The Structure of American Industry in the Twentieth Century," *BHR* 43 (1965):88).

banking community in general, and large bankers specifically."[102]*

In response to the irrationality of the marketplace, it was important to create political, social, and economic conditions conducive to the long-term profitability of corporations. Regulation could create these conditions. But, as Kolko maintains, this was particularly true when corporations became national in scope; *federal* regulation helped national corporations cope with state boundaries. Arguing against the position that increased state regulation is necessarily "progressive," he said that "if the criterion is not the presence or absence of government intervention but the degree to which motives and actions were designed to maintain or preserve a particular distribution or locus of power, the history of the United States from Theodore Roosevelt through Woodrow Wilson is consistently conservative."[103] Thus, following the turn of the century, a system of state and corporate cooperation was established in response to transformations that had been occurring within the economy. The economy was national in scope, characterized by a corporate form of organization, and there was a meshing of industrial and financial interests into corporate complexes.

The emergence of corporate capitalism also meant that the exercise of corporate power was systematized. Central figures and families, still in command, began to surround themselves with technical, administrative, and legal experts to carry out many of the operations of the companies where they held controlling interests. John Pierpont Morgan, like his father before him, created and controlled a far-reaching financial and industrial empire.[104] Other important empire builders were Frederick Weyerhaeuser, Andrew Carnegie, and members of the Guggenheim, Mellon, Rockefeller, du Pont, and Gould families.

Corporate capitalism also had its effects in the international capital market. Lewis has contended that in the era of entrepreneurial capitalism, foreign investment in U.S. manufacturing was discouraged, but the "advent of the industrial corporation marked the beginning of large-scale industry and eventually was instrumental in drawing foreign capital into outstanding American undertakings."[105] Foreign portfolio capital had earlier been prominent in railways and utilities, the first sectors to adopt the corporate form of organization. When the corporate form was adopted by industrials, they too became attractive as investments. Before the First World War, important British portfolio investment was made in several industrials, including Eastman Kodak, United Fruit, and General Electric, over $1 million in each case, but the most important outlet was United States Steel, with $34.6 million in U.K. loans. Nevertheless, industrials then accounted for only 13 per cent of British holdings in the United States against 87 per cent in rail-

---

* The system's overseeing body was the Federal Reserve Board, composed of five presidential appointees, the Comptroller of the Currency, and the Secretary of the Treasury. It oversaw the Federal Reserve banks in twelve districts, each with a board of nine members, six representing stockholding banks (three bankers and three others) and three others appointed by the board (T.C. Cochran, *The American Business System*, pp. 87-88).

ways and utilities.[106] It is important to note that portfolio investment is not controlling ownership; it provides capital pools from which the corporate owners can draw for expansion. The corporate form thus attracted British capital for U.S. industrial expansion before the First World War. These funds helped project the United States into world leadership in such industries as steel, where it accounted for 40 per cent of the world output in 1913.

In this era the United States was beginning to expand beyond its borders with a few colonial adventures into the Caribbean and Philippines, but these were as much military and political as economic. Before the war, most of the attention remained on shoring up its home markets, although a few external excursions were to provide a toehold for later multinational expansion. For example, First National City Bank (now Citicorp) had branches in London and five Asian countries in 1902, adding seven Latin American branches by 1914.[107] Many of the early foreign branches of industrials continued previous export patterns and were fostered by the desire to maintain export markets.[108] Production plants were also drawn to foreign locations by the prospect of lower labour costs outside the United States. A further stimulus was provided by capital surpluses that had been built up in corporations. Cochran and Miller suggest that by 1913, "savings were mounting faster than new investments in productive enterprises";[109] Wilkins adds that "well before the First World War, American direct foreign investment was not merely in extractive industries and utilities; indeed, by 1914 a surprising number of 'genuine' U.S.-headquartered multinational manufacturing companies had already come into existence."[110] The most important location for these foreign firms was to be Canada.

Generally, the period from 1900 to 1913 in Canada was much like the railway era in the United States, one of rapid growth, but with some important differences. The major railways were complete or nearing completion, and substantial parts of an industrial system were beginning to take their places. It was a period that "saw the agricultural settlement of the western prairies, the opening up of a mining frontier on the Canadian Shield, the development of the newsprint industry, and the beginnings of large-scale hydroelectric development."[111]

Much of Canada's prosperity during the period was the result of world conditions, especially the stimulation given by wheat exports to Europe. Wheat was of such consequence to Canada not because it produced more than the United States (it did not) but because it consumed less. With one-twelfth the population of the United States, Canada achieved a much greater surplus from a somewhat smaller total yield. The increased European demand for foodstuffs and the rising prices benefited the traditional commercial interests as well as the farmers because of the increased use of their mediating services, such as transportation and short-term financing.

But the upsurge of agriculture with wheat as a new staple was not without its consequences. Between 1896 and 1913 the population of the West (mainly agricultural) increased by a million, growing from 7 per cent to 20 per cent of Canada's total population.* Canada remained a rural society for much longer than the United States. For example, the source of capital for agricultural investment was not from traditional financial sources: "Prairie farm investment was financed almost entirely from the real savings of settlers and immigrants."[112] These conditions meant that manufactories remained small and oriented toward local rural markets. Moreover, by the time Canada was beginning to develop a national manufacturing market, U.S. manufacturers were ready to define their market as continental. Thus much of the consolidation that occurred in Canada was from the beginning on a continental rather than a national basis. The transition from commerce and agriculture to an industrial society did not take place as smoothly in Canada as it had in the United States because dominant Canadian interests remained oriented toward supplying the international economy rather than toward developing an internal market. In addition, much of the necessary capital was monopolized by the dominant financial interests.

Under circumstances in which dominant industrial firms in the United States were expanding faster than their market and shifting into Canada, and while consolidation was being undertaken by Canadian financial capitalists, the Canadian movement into corporate capitalism was bound to differ from that in the United States. The Canadian sectors that moved into corporate capitalism through indigenous forces, engineered either by Canadian financiers or by independent manufacturing consolidations, and in primary manufacturing, were reasonably able to compete in their traditional sectors: steel, pulp and paper, and food and beverages. Other sectors with new technology in secondary manufacturing and without an earlier base were most susceptible to control by U.S. companies already settled in such industries. These formative stages were of central importance because once the patterns became established, many companies rode the wave of industrial development and became the dominant companies of today.

External consolidation was sometimes a force for movement into corporate capitalism, as was the case in the automobile industry.† U.S.

* The filling of Canada's West was assisted by the fact that "the best lands of the United States plains had been settled, but excellent free land was still available in Canada" (A.E. Safarian, *The Canadian Economy in the Great Depression*, p. 19).

† Important to these early automobile developments were patent rights. In her analysis of Ford Motor Co. and General Motors, Lewis notes that "patent rights represented the larger part of a company's contribution toward the establishment of foreign subsidiary or affiliate" (*America's Stake in International Investments*, pp. 300-2). Reliance on imported technology was characteristic of many manufacturing companies in Canada, especially in the electrical and chemical-based industrials. Glen Williams states that "Canadian manufacturers made heavy use of U.S. patents in their production, so much so that the proportion of Canadian patents issued to Canadians fell from 100 per cent in 1869, to 33 per cent in 1884, to only 16 per cent in 1908" ("Canadian Industrialization: We Ain't Growin' Nowhere," *This Magazine* 9 (1975):8; see also Wilkins, *Emergence of Multinational Enterprise*, pp. 142-44).

automobile companies made their first expansions into Canada but not without some compliance from Canadian manufacturers, as Wilkins's account makes clear:

> In 1904 Gordon M. McGregor, a Canadian maker of carriages, visited Henry Ford and suggested to him that Ford cars be manufactured in the Dominion. Ford agreed. McGregor raised the capital in Canada and in the United States to finance this venture. Henry Ford and the Detroit stockholders in the Ford Motor Company got controlling interest (51 per cent) in the new Canadian Ford unit in exchange for patents, drawings, and Henry Ford's services. The Dominion enterprise was to handle Ford business in the entire British Empire, excluding England and Ireland; it started at once to manufacture Ford cars in Canada – behind the Dominion tariff wall.[113]

The Ford arrangement is important because the factors in the decision included not only the Canadian market, protected by a 35 per cent tariff, but also the export market in all British colonies and ex-colonies, a marketing pattern later to be reinforced by Imperial Preference. (This pattern of moving into Canada for access to the Commonwealth was also followed by other firms including Heinz and Quaker Oats.)

General Motors moved into Canada under slightly different conditions. Robert McLaughlin had been a carriage manufacturer since 1868 and with his sons, R.S. and G.W. McLaughlin, founded the McLaughlin Motor Car Company in 1907 by acquiring the Canadian rights for the Buick car. In 1914, General Motors and the McLaughlin Carriage Company were sharing ownership in the subsidiary company (with the McLaughlins having a slightly larger share). By 1918, General Motors of Canada, a wholly owned subsidiary of the U.S. parent, owned both companies. Robert McLaughlin's sons became president and vice-president of General Motors of Canada.[114]

Other methods for external consolidation of Canadian companies were also evident. Some of these instances have been summarized by Naylor:

> Sherwin-Williams Paints was a merger of three firms, one Canadian, one British, and one American, which remained under the American parent's control via licensing. Two large licensed joint ventures in mining equipment and machinery, the Canada Rand Drill Co. (1899) and the Ingersoll Rock Drill Co. (1882), were combined in 1912 as the Canadian-Ingersoll-Rand Co. parallelling the parent's [sic] merger. In 1906 Bell Canada, one-quarter owned by ATT, bought control of Northern Electric and Manufacturing, in which Western Electric held part interest. Imperial Wire & Cable was also jointly owned and in 1914 the two were merged into Northern Electric of which 44% of the stock was held in the U.S.[115]

Unlike instances in the automobile industry, where much of the initiative for U.S. takeover came from small Canadian manufacturers, these cases illustrate direct U.S. initiatives that served to realign Canadian-based companies.

A further example illustrates another kind of pattern, one used by the Aluminum Company of America (Alcoa). This company had had a plant in Canada at Shawinigan Falls since 1899, but its rapid growth did not occur until somewhat later under the stimulus of the U.S. Sherman Antitrust Act. Alcoa's president, A.V. Davis, had "decided to enter into accords with European industrialists," but this would have been disallowed under the U.S. law. A new subsidiary was therefore formed in Canada to organize the Canadian operation and also the U.S. export business. This was done "with the full knowledge of the U.S. Justice Department" and "the Canadian subsidiary of Alcoa made a new pact with the foreign producers, regulating the aluminum trade *outside* the United States."[116]

Thus, for reasons different from those that had motivated Ford and later Imperial Preference branch plants, Alcoa also became a participant in Canada's early go-between role in the international economy. Sherwin-Williams was another early example; it "allocated [to] its Canadian affiliate control of the English subsidiary, which in turn controlled those in India, South Africa, Shanghai and even France."[117] Jersey Standard transferred its holdings in Peru to Canadian affiliates in 1913-14 for the same purpose, and in 1913 Western Electric transferred its foreign stocks to its Canadian affiliate. Wilkins notes, "Thus, Canadian enterprises of pre-World War I years, as later, often served more than their ostensible purpose."[118]

Bonuses offered by Canadian municipalities to entice manufacturers to build within their limits were added incentives to U.S. companies. They included free land, tax exemptions, and sometimes even free utilities. Ninety-five municipalities in Ontario were engaging in these practices by 1900.[119] Wilkins has pointed out, however, that "legislation involving patents, tariffs, industry incentives, and 'made in Canada' rulings – would not have been enough to 'force' investments by American manufacturing firms in Canada...unless American companies desired to sell in Canada and unless the market was there (or could be created), Americans would not have invested."[120] The inducement was clearly there.

But a further point must be added to Wilkins's observation. If there had not been a vacuum in the Canadian market, that is, if Canadian firms had supplied the whole market, the inducement to invest in Canada would also have been lowered. The evidence is that the U.S. firms did in fact meet much of the demand, for, "almost three-fifths of the new plant machinery installed in Canadian factories between 1900 and 1914, the period of greatest industrial expansion from 1879 to 1914, was foreign in origin. Over 90 per cent of this machinery came from the United States. Much of the remaining two-fifths of plant machinery which was Canadian in origin, was actually manufactured by U.S. branch plants or licensed ventures in Canada."[121] The question was not one of demand but which capitalists would be supported to fill the demand.

Meanwhile, the consolidation process was guided toward central Canada and rapid expansion was occurring. Between 1900 and 1910, the value of manufacturing output increased from $215 million to $564 million, led by the expansion of the iron and steel industry during the railway boom and the tenfold increase in pig iron consumption between 1896 and 1913.[122] Other important Canadian activities at the time included textiles, sawmilling, and food processing, but concentration of industry in central Canada accompanied expansion in the areas of textiles, boot and shoe production, furniture making, and tobacco. By 1910, Ontario and Quebec accounted for four-fifths of all manufacturing in Canada.

In the United States, the merger movement was accompanied by an absolute increase in the number of firms. In Canada the pattern differed. Between 1904 and 1911, 196 companies disappeared into forty-one industrial combines; the number of firms actually fell between 1900 and 1910.[123] Furthermore, the style of mergers changed over the course of the decade. Naylor observes that financing for early mergers was "largely industrial in origin.... But after 1907 mergers showed distinctly new characteristics...new mergers involved outside promoters, generally Montreal, but to a lesser degree Toronto and Halifax financiers as well...[and] did not involve any sort of industrial risk capital."[124] Thus, fewer Canadian manufacturers and other industrialists were able to secure the degree of autonomy from financial interests achieved by their opposite numbers in the United States in the transition to corporate capitalism. These mergers were often financed by portfolio investment from Britain through the mediation of Canadian financiers. The most prominent figure in this financially controlled merger movement was Max Aitken (Lord Beaverbrook), followed by Louis Forget and E.R. Wood.*

What types of relationships existed between manufacturing and finance, aside from promotions? According to Naylor's calculations, little support was provided for small manufacturers by the large capital pools, and this is reflected in the causes of business failure.† But where financial interests moved into corporate capitalism, the situation was reversed. Naylor notes:

---

* Tracing Max Aitken's career, Naylor found that he had been involved in the promotion of "Canada Power, Calgary Power, Western Canada Power, Cape Breton Trust, Union Bank of Halifax, Demerara Electric Co., Camaguey Electric and Traction, Puerto Rico Co., Robb Engineering, Standard Ideal Co., Canada Car & Foundry Co., Canada Cement, and the Steel Company of Canada" (*Canadian Business*, II: 188). This is an impressive list by any standards.

† During the period 1890 to 1913, "the rate of all business failure due to 'lack of capital,' including manufacturing failures, ranged between 65 and 75% growing steadily, while during the same period the American rate was less than half of this.... The American failure rate due to lack of capital fell over the period, while the Canadian rate rose" (Naylor, *Canadian Business*, I: 84-85).

The Montreal commercial community, branching out into cotton manufacturing, sugar refining, iron and steel, and the like, secured bank accommodations through their holding directorships on the banks. This accommodation for the old commercial elite reflected again the bias of the pattern of Canadian industrial development in favour of established wealth and away from the new entrepreneurial class which was promoting industrialization throughout southern Ontario.... Indirectly, the banks assisted the concentration of industry in some areas by discriminating by size among industrial borrowers. In 1913, small firms paid up to ten per cent for the same accommodation granted large ones for five or six per cent.... In mining, the banks would not advance money for development work – this remained the stockholders' responsibility. After the mine actually began shipping ore to the smelter and getting a return on it, the bank might lend on security of the ore.[125]

The situation was also complicated by the presence in Canada of U.S. industrialists preparing international moves in search of expanded markets and sources for raw materials. Clearly, Canadian manufacturers in the process of forging an industrial system faced less encouraging conditions than those existing in the United States.

During the period under consideration, a further transition from the old commercial staples (fur, fish, timber, and wheat) to the new industrial staples (minerals, newsprint, and fuel) was occurring. The shift occurred both in markets and in the technological requirements for extraction and use of materials. The market shifted from Europe to the United States. The old staples had required little technology for extraction or use, but the new ones, the raw materials of industry, needed a more highly developed capital base for the new technology.[126] It has been said that the "new axis of continental integration, symbolized by the ownership, technique and market orientation of the new staple industries, cut across the east-west lines of national consolidation laid down by the wheat economy."[127]

Ironically, many of the new staples that fostered this continental integration were uncovered during the construction of railways, intended to be the great device for national integration. Asbestos was found in 1876 near Thetford, Quebec, during railway construction; nickel was discovered by the Canadian Pacific Railway near Sudbury, Ontario, in 1883; silver, gold, and copper were uncovered near Cobalt when the Timiskaming and Northern Ontario Railway was under construction in 1903.[128]

The most impressive development from these discoveries took place in the nickel industry. Between 1902 and 1913, Canadian production rose from 45 per cent of the world's requirement of ore and matte to 70 per cent, including all of the U.S. market.[129] Initially, several firms working in close relationship with one another were involved, but in 1902 they were consolidated in the International Nickel Company with capitalization of $25 million. "Ultimate control rested in the hands of the financial group behind the United States Steel Corporation, under the leadership of J.P. Morgan."[130] This powerful complex successfully resisted government attempts to force refining of the nickel in Canada until the threat to expropriate, reinforced by the war, was made.[131]

With nickel and the other minerals, as with all the new staples, Canada was continuing its historical pattern of supplying resources to the world. And in this activity, as in the manufacturing sector, Canada was increasingly being drawn into the continental economy. By 1912, there were "some 200 American 'branch' manufactories" and by 1914, "Canada clearly had more U.S.-controlled manufacturing plants than any other foreign nation."[132]

While Canadian manufacturers were at a disadvantage in the capital markets, U.S. multinational branches in Canada could receive capital injections from several sources – from the parent companies' retained earnings, from U.S. financial capitalists through the parents, or from Canadian financial capitalists, who invested in the branches directly or through the multinational headquarters because of their stable position. It thus became something of a self-fulfilling prophecy that Canadian industrial capitalists who were not allied with Canadian financial capitalists would be weak and unprotected from the onslaught of U.S. branch plants.

As in the earlier period, some Canadian investment was being made in the United States, but the impact of these investments relative to U.S. investment in Canada was insignificant because of the scale of the two countries. As Brebner suggests, "relative to wealth and population, Canada's industrial investment in the United States was larger than its American counterpart in Canada, indeed American branches of Canadian business concerns had a way of becoming larger than their parents; but when set against the American total they were about as completely lost to general view as the corresponding human migrants."[133] Just after the turn of the century, Canadian banks held assets of over $100 million in foreign countries; this figure rose to $229 million by 1913. At the same time, their assets were generally double their liabilities in foreign countries.[134] Canadian railways had a prominent role in northern sections of the United States. By 1914, the Canadian Grand Trunk, the Canadian Northern, and the Canadian Pacific together had $55.2 million of their stock invested in the United States; they had 7,197 miles of line in the United States by 1912.[135] There were also instances of manufacturing companies with branches in the United States. Moore Corporation, organized by S.J. Moore, had U.S. interests from 1893 onward, including the American Sales Book Company with capital stock of $4 million in 1911. Moore's business-form and paper-box operations continued to grow until by 1934 the Moore companies had eleven plants in the United States but only four in Canada. Another important early entrant to the U.S. market was Massey-Harris Harvester. Registered in the United States in 1910, it was soon acquiring and consolidating several U.S. companies.[136] Both Moore and Massey remain important Canadian multinationals today.

In general, Canadian society before the First World War remained different from that of the United States. This is reflected in occupational terms by the fact that in 1911 only 14 per cent of the labour force in Canada was in manufacturing occupations relative to 21 per cent in the United States. Even more telling is the strong emergence in the United States, around the turn of the century, of a new middle class that was adapting to many of the organizational and technical aspects of the new corporate form. This class did not develop as early in Canada. The United States, the technological leader, was producing large numbers of highly skilled people in professions like engineering. There was pressure for expansion of post-secondary education. In Canada there was a willingness to import both technology and highly qualified personnel, with corresponding down-playing of education. Training continued to be oriented towards the older professions of medicine or law rather than the technical fields. As time went by, the gaps tended to widen rather than narrow.

VI. The First World War: U.S. Expansion and Canadian Growth (1913 to 1929)

The First World War marks dramatically a shift in the world economy; it signalizes the end of British prominence, particularly in manufacturing but also in capital markets. The war itself did not increase manufacturing output in the United States as greatly as it did in Canada, particularly since the United States entered the war later. But following the war, the United States emerged unscathed as the leading force in the international economy. Also, the effect of gearing the U.S. economy to wartime had brought political and economic leaders into close alliance. One result was to reorganize and consolidate the railways into a few large companies under private ownership.

The experience of the war clearly demonstrated to businessmen that the state need not be a threat to their private interests; indeed, the state could be used to further their interests. During the war, a number of control agencies were established to co-ordinate the U.S. war effort. The men who ran them were the same ones that ran the private corporations. The key agencies and their heads were

> Food Administration, presided over by Herbert Hoover, a mining industrialist; Fuel Administration, presided over by Harry A. Garfield, former President of the Cleveland Chamber of Commerce and Director of the Cleveland Trust Co.; War Industries Board, directed by Bernard Baruch, a Wall Street financier and stockmarket operator; War Trade Board, directed by Vance McCormick, of the family associated with the International Harvester Co.... Businessmen pre-

dominated, made the decisions, gave the orders, set the prices, determined legitimate costs, and set allowable profit margins.[137]

More important than the internal experience and alliances that had been forged was the unity of interest created concerning external relations.[138] President Wilson is reported to have said, "There is nothing in which I am more interested than the fullest development of the trade of this country and its righteous conquest of foreign markets." To this end, business and government created a series of associations and forums directed at promoting U.S. direct investments abroad. B.I. Kaufman says of these developments:

> Secretary of Commerce William C. Redfield and Commissioner Edward Hurley of the Federal Trade Commission worked closely with such groups as the AMEA and the Pan American Society in organizing a major new national business association, the National Foreign Trade Council (NFTC). Headed by James Farrell, President of United States Steel Corporation, the NFTC was composed of fifty of the nation's leading industrialists, bankers, merchants, and transportation executives. The first truly national association devoted exclusively to promoting foreign trade and representing all economic sectors, it quickly became the most important organization of its kind.[139]

The point is not that the United States was uninvolved in the international economy earlier than this but that for the first time a conscious, co-ordinated movement involving both the state and private interests was taking place for the purpose of expanding the United States internationally.

Another development, not unrelated to the links between business and government, concerned the relationship between finance and industry. After the war, industrialists were able to establish several sources of capital in addition to the bankers. Williams has noted that the industrialists' "own operations produced much of the capital they needed, and once the government was brought into the new system as a purchaser of goods and services on a large and routine scale, they could and did deal directly with this new source of capital."[140] Moreover, following the war, another group became important both as a source of capital and for public relations – the small stockholders. For example, American Telephone and Telegraph had an increase in the number of shareholders owning five or fewer shares from some 50,000 in 1920 to 210,000 in 1930.[141] Industrialists could thus use the security market as leverage in their dealings with the banks. This is not to say that the banks did not remain important capital sources and holders of stock, only that industrialists in the United States, as opposed to Canada, had a degree of freedom from the dominance of financial capitalists that allowed them to deal with financial institutions as equals rather than as dependants.

Important developments were occurring within the banks them-

selves. While there were bank mergers before the war, the total number of banks continued to rise until just after the war. At the turn of the
century, there were 12,400 commercial banks in the United States, rising to 31,000 by 1920. Then the decline began, with a fall to 25,000 in
1929. The Great Depression then took its toll of the remaining banks;
8,800 suspended operations between 1930 and 1933, leaving about
15,000.[142] The fact that the number of banks was halved in thirteen
years may seem dramatic but not in comparison with the fate of Canadian banks. In 1874 there had been fifty-one banks in Canada, but by
1925 only eleven remained.

There was also a second merger movement in the mining and manufacturing industries, beginning about 1925 and peaking in 1929. This
merger movement differed from the earlier one primarily because a few
leading companies were already established in most of the key areas.
The result was that "horizontal mergers did not often involve the largest firms in the industry but, instead, those in the tier just below them:
the third and fourth largest."[143] This is illustrated by the automobile
industry, where in 1912 seven companies produced half the cars but by
1923 ten were producing 90 per cent. In 1925 "a group of production
men and New York financiers organized a rival to Ford and General
Motors," the Chrysler Corporation, which itself acquired the Dodge
Company in 1928. From this point on, the Big Three continued to sell
over 80 per cent of the passenger vehicles in the United States.[144]
Another type of merger was vertical, usually carried out by larger firms
for the purpose of acquiring companies related to their primary operations. Mergers were complemented by a program of diversification that
was being carried out by the largest companies, especially in high-
technology industries.[145] In the dairy industry there was a radical re-
organization with National Dairy Products acquiring 331 dairy companies between 1923 and 1932 and Borden Company buying up 207
between 1928 and 1932.[146] Broadly, the level of concentration that was
achieved by the end of this period was to remain fairly constant until
the 1960s.

The period 1914 to 1929 is a crucial one in U.S. external economic
relations because in it the nation was transformed from a net debtor to
a net creditor. In other words, in 1914 there was more foreign investment in the United States ($7,200 million) than U.S. investment
abroad ($3,514 million), but by 1929, while the amount of foreign in-
vestment remained fairly steady ($8,931 million), U.S. investment
abroad increased almost fivefold (to $17,009 million).[147]* In compara-
tive terms, by 1925 there was about the same amount of U.S. direct
investment within Canada alone as the total amount of all foreign direct

* The one exception to the general pattern, which remains an anomaly in the United
States today, was the European-controlled Royal Dutch Shell group. This group entered the United States in 1902 and, by buying up various companies and properties,
grew along with the other U.S.-controlled oil companies during the rapid expansion of
1906 to 1932 (see Lewis, *America's Stake in International Investments*, pp. 94-95).

investment in the United States, in spite of the fact that the United States was twelve times the size of Canada.*

U.S. foreign expansion was evident elsewhere, but Canada remained the single most important target of U.S. direct investment – both as a market and as a source of raw materials. From a U.S. perspective, direct investment fell into three main types: first, "direct subsidiaries and other affiliates of American corporations whose chief field of operations is the United States," such as the automobile companies or International Business Machines (IBM); second, "American corporations organized for the specific purpose of operating abroad," such as mining companies, utilities, and railways, the outstanding examples being International Telephone and Telegraph (ITT) and Anaconda Copper; finally, "direct ownership by American individuals of stock of foreign corporations," for example, Dome Mines or International Nickel.[148] Establishment of branches or affiliates obviated the need for exports and avoided tariffs. Some companies expanded abroad to reach sources of raw materials and cheaper labour or because greater profits were to be made from foreign operations. The result was the appearance after the First World War of a large number of multinational companies with worldwide operations, including U.S. banks. In 1920, twelve U.S. banks had 181 foreign offices, mainly started in the two years after the war, though none were in Canada.[149] Following the war, the three top U.S. automobile manufacturers were all multinational.

Why was it that Canada received so much of this U.S. investment? Obviously proximity was important, and so was encouragement by Canadian politicians and businessmen; but this is not the whole explanation. It is necessary to look at the overall strategy of U.S. investments abroad. Summarizing the basic motives behind two distinct thrusts of U.S. direct investment, Wilkins says: "Whereas market-oriented interests of manufacturers, oil, and mining enterprises tended to be largest in industrial nations, investments based on supply strategies, as in times past, predominated in the western hemisphere (Latin America and Canada), and then in less developed nations around the world."[150] *Canada is the only country that is attractive to both supply- and market-oriented motives.*† This quality, combined with the availability and com-

---

* Indeed, in terms of the U.S. capital relationship with Canada, the period after the war up to 1926 reflects a pattern different from any that existed earlier or later. During this time there was actually more U.S. portfolio investment in Canada than direct, while at the same time the amount of U.S. direct investment in Canada increased from $520 million in 1913 to $1,403 million in 1926. Thus the United States during this period was not only adding to its direct investments in the form of branch plants but was also supplying most of Canada's foreign portfolio capital. Overall, the effect was to raise the U.S. proportion of all foreign capital sources in Canada from 22 per cent to 54 per cent (see Kari Levitt, *Silent Surrender*, p. 66, Table 3).

† Wilkins lists fifty U.S.-owned multinationals in 1929 with both market- and supply-oriented investments. Of these, thirty-one had market-oriented investments in Canada while thirteen had supply-oriented ones. Only four of the companies operating in Canada had *only* supply-oriented investments without also having market-oriented ones (*The Maturing of Multinational Enterprise*, pp. 143-45, Table VII, 2).

patibility of Canada, explains the dramatic influx of investment.

In Canada, the immediate impact of the war on the economy was much more significant than it was in the United States. Canada had entered the war at the beginning and experienced it for four years; the United States was involved only towards the end. The direct effect was apparent in the munitions requirements, which spurred manufacturing, and in pulp and paper, metals, and motor vehicles because of demand and world prices, as well as government subsidies.[151] The general effect was promotion of rapid expansion, even greater than in the United States; "between 1923 and 1929 the index of manufacturing production rose by 37 per cent, and that of mining production by 60 per cent."[152] The peak reached by 1929 in manufacturing was not achieved again until the Second World War. What these figures do not indicate, however, is whether this expansion was carried out by Canadian firms or by U.S. firms within Canada.

While the United States was emerging from the war as a net creditor nation, Canada remained a net debtor. Between 1914 and 1919 a 32 per cent increase in U.S. direct investment in Canada took place. The total increased from $618 million to $814 million, but this $196 million increase was unevenly spread across various sectors, with manufacturing alone increasing by $179 million (to $400 million) and mining by $41 million (to $200 million). Merchandising rose by only $3 million (to $30 million), petroleum by $5 million (to $30 million), utilities by $7 million (to $15 million), and railways by $7 million (to $76 million). Agriculture *fell* by $51 million (to $50 million). In other words, almost all of the total increase in U.S. direct investment went into manufacturing, with mining the only other sector with a significant increase.[153*] During the war years the amount of direct investment added by U.S.-controlled manufacturing almost doubled what it had been at the outset of the war. Aggregate figures mask the heavy concentration of investment in manufacturing during this period, especially in light of the halving of the amount invested in agriculture. By 1924, over 70 per cent of U.S. direct investment in Canada was located in "industrial raw materials and secondary manufacturing" compared to half in 1914.[154]

In the meantime, after the war commercial banks in Canada (of which there were only ten by 1928) continued to hold "bonds, and, to a very minor extent, equities, but their chief activity was the financing of inventories and receivables.... The sociological basis of an adequate market for new equity issues did not appear. Internal financing and direct use of personal savings remained the characteristic mode of applying venture capital."[155] The financial structure thus continued to reinforce and support existing corporations or those that could enter from outside, but a developed security market, as in the United States,

---

* There were an additional $8 million in miscellaneous investments in 1914 and $13 million in 1919.

that could be used to provide initial capitalization for new indigenous entrants failed to emerge.*

Another effect of the war was to redirect almost all of Canada's search for external capital from London to New York: "In 1913 Canada had raised 74.2 per cent of its foreign capital requirements in London and only 13.5 per cent in New York. Within two years those proportions were almost exactly reversed."[156] The shift was important in a number of respects, not the least of which was the ending of the traditional capital source for Canadian promoters.

Several U.S. companies entered Canada during the war explicitly to participate in the business boom – Aetna Explosives, Procter and Gamble, Chrysler – but most of the growth occurred in existing U.S.-controlled companies – du Pont, Ford, Imperial Oil, and others. Some companies that were Canadian controlled, like Canadian General Electric, reverted to a subsidiary status. Other moves into the Canadian market were made by suppliers of major firms that had been established earlier in Canada. This was particularly obvious in the automobile industry; "whereas in 1919 U.S. capital was estimated to control about 61 per cent of the Canadian motor car industry, by the end of the 1920s U.S.-controlled corporations produced over 83 per cent of the Dominion's cars, trucks, and parts."[157] Firestone Tire and Rubber, B.F. Goodrich and Company, Goodyear Tire and Rubber, Seiberling, and U.S. Rubber all followed the big three automakers into Canada.

One further fact made Canada more susceptible to U.S. investment than other countries: U.S. businessmen regarded Canada as part of the domestic market.† Therefore, even companies that were not multinational were continental, as the aircraft industry illustrates. "The nascent U.S. aircraft industry was little interested in foreign investments; those investments made were in Canada and were part of the industry's U.S. domestic expansion."[158] All the U.S. companies acted in unison.

---

* Mergers accelerated toward the end of the period. Of the 374 consolidations that took place from 1900 to 1933, 231 occurred between 1925 and 1930 (L.G. Reynolds, *The Control of Competition in Canada*, p. 6n). Many mergers in the food industry resulted when U.S. parents such as General Foods, Standard Brands, and National Biscuit joined several U.S. companies together, simultaneously merging their Canadian subsidiaries (Wilkins, *Maturing of Multinational Enterprise*, pp. 63n-64n). J.C. Weldon has shown that the twenties constituted the period of greatest consolidation until after World War II. In this decade, 327 consolidations absorbed 654 enterprises ("Consolidations in Canadian Industry, 1900-1948," in *Restrictive Trade Practices in Canada*, ed. L.A. Skeoch, p. 238).

† The go-between role of Canada reinforces the view that it was seen as part of the U.S. domestic market. "By 1929, among the U.S. corporations using Canadian holding companies for certain overseas business were Union Carbide (for Norway), Kelvinator Company (for England), Ford Motor Company (for the British empire outside of Britain and Ireland), Standard Oil of New Jersey (for Peru and Colombia), and Aluminum Company of America (for the world outside of the United States). In each of these cases, the parent U.S. enterprise operated in the Dominion along with using a Canadian unit for the added foreign business relations; these were not simply devices for getting out from under U.S. law" (Wilkins, *Maturing of Multinational Enterprise*, p. 139).

Between 1926 and 1929 the five top companies in the U.S. aircraft industry established branches in Canada.

Appropriately, given Canada's roots in a staple economy, the greatest boom after the war was in pulp and paper, an industry that combined new technology with an old natural resource. The expansion was dramatic and based on increased demand in the United States, where the level of newsprint production remained the same from 1913 to 1929 while consumption skyrocketed. Imports had to fill the gap, rising from 220,000 tons in 1913 to 2,421,000 in 1929. Canadian producers responded, and "in 1929 Canada accounted for about 65 per cent of world exports of newsprint. Of the 1929 output 90 per cent was exported, and 90 per cent of this was exported to the United States."[159] Mergers in the 1920s changed a small competitive industry into a concentrated industry with three companies controlling half the production and another handful the remainder.[160]

The state did not simply sit by while these developments transpired; it intervened *on behalf of the industry*. As Nelles has noted:

> Certainly the state had intervened with unprecedented force and directness into the affairs of the pulp and paper industry; but it must be noted that it did so on terms dictated by the leaders of the industry itself. Government was not regulating business in the public interest, but rather it was acting as the political extension of an industrial cartel. It merely assumed that the objectives of the Newsprint Association of Canada were identical with the public interest.[161]

Who controlled the pulp and paper industry? A good deal was U.S. controlled with some important Canadian participation. In 1914, of the $221 million in U.S. direct investment in Canadian manufacturing, $74 million was in pulp and paper. Between 1914 and 1916, "four new, giant American paper and pulp mills were constructed across the northern border" because the product was much cheaper to make in Canada ($30.52 a ton in the United States and $26.38 in Canada), and there were no duties on exports.[162] By 1929 the three largest Canadian pulp and paper companies were International Paper and Power, Abitibi Power and Paper, and Canada Power and Paper. U.S. capital participated in all three, but only International Paper and Power was U.S. controlled.[163] Abitibi was Canadian owned and was among the largest companies. From the beginning there was substantial direct U.S. participation in the pulp and paper industry as there had not been in the earlier staple exports to Europe. No longer were staples to be the exclusive domain of indigenous interests.

Between 1919 and 1929, U.S. direct investment in Canada increased from $814 million to $1,657 million. Of this $814 million increase, $420 million was in manufacturing and $118 million in mining, while merchandising increased by $8 million, petroleum by $25 million, and railways dropped by $3 million. Agriculture fell further by $20 million but utilities rose by $230 million (to $245 million).[164]*

In the mining industry, control varied depending upon the metal. In gold extraction Canadians owned 70 per cent and the United States 27 per cent in 1921; ownership in nickel was 48 per cent U.S., 43 per cent British, and only a fraction Canadian.[165]† In oil production U.S. companies dominated, led by Imperial Oil (73 per cent owned by Standard Oil of New Jersey in 1927) while other companies sold imported oil in Canada.

Only in production of hydro-electric power did the state resist U.S. ownership. The resource industries, particularly pulp and paper, mining, and aluminum, were the most active protagonists of cheap, efficient power. Beginning with Ontario and over the years in most other areas, the provinces took the lead in providing hydro-electric power. Why did the state take this action? The most thorough analysis of this question has been provided by H.V. Nelles, and his answer is clear: "Power was far too precious as an agent of industrial expansion to be left under the control of monopoly capital, Canadian or American."[166] As it had been with canals and railways, the state would be the initiator of the necessary infrastructure of economic activity; it would provide the necessary conditions for private capital accumulation.°

At the continental level the most powerful corporations and capitalists operated freely on both sides of the border. The fact that U.S. industrial and resource capitalists were strong in Canada reflects their power base at home. Nor were Canadian capitalists barred from operating in the United States. In fact, the banks and railways already had extensive operations there, and industrial and resource interests followed; a powerful firm, the Steel Company of Canada, had both coal and ore properties in the United States. "In 1917 it acquired an interest in two ore properties, and in 1924 and 1926 in two additional ore properties, all in the Lake Superior region. In 1918 it purchased 1,617 acres of coking coal in Pennsylvania for $1,090,000, but in 1919 these were consolidated with other holdings so that it has [in 1936] a one third interest in 4,438 acres."[167]

The difference was the shortage of indigenous Canadian industrial

---

* Miscellaneous investment of an additional $65 million was made between 1919 and 1929.

† According to Wilkins, "In Canada, in 1929 the U.S.-controlled International Nickel Company sold more than 90 per cent of the world's nickel.... By 1929, Americans owned not only most of Canadian nickel mining, but also the bulk of the Dominion's copper, gold, and asbestos output" (*Maturing of Multinational Enterprise*, pp. 106-7).

° Nelles also raised and answered another question: "Did an interventionist public philosophy significantly alter the pattern of resource development in the province [Ontario] from the continental norm? After surveying the record the answer must be a qualified no, the qualification being the important exception of Hydro. If anything, the proprietary relationship made it easier for business to establish a firm grip upon the instruments of the state. In this, Hydro was not an exception, for it was run by businessmen, for businessmen, in what was always referred to as a 'businesslike' manner" (*Politics of Development*, pp. 489-90).

corporations. Much of the reason for this continued to lie in the shortage of venture capital. Canadian capitalists cared little whether their money came from Canadian or U.S. sources, just so long as it came, and the most secure investments were in the United States. The *Monetary Times* in 1918 remarked on the extent of private Canadian holdings of U.S. securities:

> There is still a considerable amount of high-grade United States investment stocks held in the Dominion. Before the war the business in Wall Street stocks transacted by Montreal and Toronto brokers probably exceeded the business done in Canadian stocks. Many Canadian capitalists and financiers were accustomed to carry considerable lines in the United States stocks; also the wealthy American residents in Canada and the highly paid executive officials of large United States branch industrials located in this country, naturally leaned towards United States securities.[168]

Lines of interest ran with lines of capital, not with lines drawn by politicians on maps.

VII. The Depression Years (1929 to 1939)

War brought the state and the economy together; depression had a similar effect. When business faltered during the Great Depression, it clamoured more than ever for the state to "set things right again." Big Business had to fend off the interests of farmers, unions, and small businessmen to keep hold of the reins of state power – and the depression was costing Big Business a great deal of credibility. The full decade of the 1930s and the Second World War would have to pass before the earlier pattern of aggressive foreign expansion could be pursued again.

Manufacturing output in the United States declined 48 per cent from 1929 to 1932; Canada dropped 40 per cent, France 26 per cent, and the United Kingdom 18 per cent.[169] The Hawley-Smoot tariff (almost doubling the average duties to 40 per cent) became law in 1930, but it turned out to be "an aggravation of the crisis" as "America naively construed foreign commerce as the right to sell, with little or no obligation to buy in exchange."[170] The international reaction was to declare economic war and to erect counter-tariffs and quotas, resulting in cutting U.S. exports in half. Ironically, a further outreaching of U.S. branches resulted, especially in Canada; "to escape this threat of boycott, American manufacturers during the first two years of the Hawley-Smoot Act set up two hundred and fifty-eight separate factories in foreign countries, including seventy-one across the Canadian line."[171] Branch plants seemed to come to Canada whether it was Canada or the United States that imposed the tariff.

Within the United States, the effect of the depression was to reinforce concentration by eliminating many smaller competitors. Hearings investigating the concentration of economic power toward the end of the period found that three automobile companies had 86 per cent of the output, two beef products companies had 47 per cent, three can companies had 90 per cent, five cement companies had 40 per cent, three cigarette companies had 78 per cent, two plate-glass companies had 95 per cent, four iron ore companies had 64 per cent, and three steel companies had 61 per cent.[172] Although domestic cartels were illegal, international ones could not be controlled. Such companies as Anaconda Copper, Bendix Aviation, Diamond Match, du Pont, General Electric, Standard Oil of New Jersey, United States Steel, and Westinghouse "entered into agreements...with foreign producers often to restrict production in order to raise prices and increase profits, and still more commonly to divide world markets and exchange patents."[173]

In spite of this enormous concentration of power, or possibly because of it, many firms began to fail and there was a general retrenchment in the world economy. By 1935 the value of U.S. foreign investment had declined from its peak in 1929. "In 1931 and 1932 some American companies with plans for foreign plants cancelled such projects. Some U.S.-owned foreign facilities stopped operations. Certain U.S. subsidiaries and affiliates abroad changed nationality, that is, the American parent sold them to Australians, Englishmen, or Canadians."[174] Many U.S. companies were driven to establish branches in Canada and elsewhere because of the U.S. tariffs; but the conditions were poor, and many of these failed.

Economic relations between Canada and the United States in the 1930s can be divided into two periods: retaliation and reconciliation. Retaliation to the Hawley-Smoot tariff of 1930 brought the Bennett tariff of 1930-31 and the Ottawa Agreements (or Imperial Preference) of 1932. Reconciliation brought the Reciprocal Trade Agreements of 1935. The effect of the preferential trade agreements was to open Commonwealth markets to goods manufactured in Canada. As a result, more U.S. companies moved into Canada; of the 1,350 U.S. companies in Canada in 1934, 26 per cent were established between 1930 and 1934.[175] This movement did not last long, however, and "in 1935 Canada and the United States succeeded in negotiating their first comprehensive trade agreement since 1854-1866. Under this agreement Canada extended most-favoured-nation treatment to the United States and obtained significant tariff reductions on exports of important primary products to the United States. This new departure was to have a substantial effect on the direction of Canadian trade."[176] The number of new branch plants established in Canada after 1935 dropped substantially because of these liberalized trade agreements. At the same time the size of investments began to rise, returning to the pre-depression peak by 1939-40. The agreements, because they opened the door to raw materials, helped to maintain Canada's focus on resource extraction and export.

From 1929 to 1940, U.S. direct investment in Canada rose by only

$446 million, a great drop from the increase between 1919 and 1929. Manufacturing attracted $123 million (a lower rate of increase than earlier) while merchandising rose considerably by $74 million (to $112 million) and petroleum by $65 million (to $120 million). Mining, however, *fell* by $131 million (to $187 million) and agriculture continued its fall as an outlet for direct investment by $20 million to a low of $10 million. Utilities, including railways, continued the earlier increase, rising by $89 million (to $407 million).[177]*

Virtually all major U.S. manufacturers had plants in Canada by 1930 and, of the total manufacturing done in Canada, one-third came from these plants. U.S. interests controlled about the same proportion of mining, smelting, and petroleum production and 30 per cent of the utilities. At that time there were just over a thousand U.S.-controlled firms operating in Canada; about half of them were in manufacturing and about 10 per cent in each of merchandising, pulp and paper, and mining and smelting. Two years later there were more than two hundred U.S.-controlled companies in Canada with a capitalization of over $1 million, of which 110 were in manufacturing, 23 in mining, 44 in utilities, and 47 in merchandising.[178] U.S.-controlled companies in Canada also exhibited a remarkable degree of concentration. Only thirty-five firms administered over 60 per cent of the U.S.-controlled capital.[179] The U.S. presence was firmly entrenched.

Even at this period, U.S. investment in Canada tended to be concentrated in certain activities while avoiding others. It controlled a large share of the production of rubber goods (64 per cent), machinery (42 per cent), automobiles (82 per cent), electrical apparatus (68 per cent), non-ferrous metals (50 per cent), non-metallic minerals (44 per cent), and chemicals (41 per cent). In the agricultural implement business,† the U.S.-controlled International Harvester Company had about 40 per cent of Canadian sales. The Canadian-controlled Massey-Harris Company's sales in Canada were only half as large as International's, but its total sales were 50 per cent greater. Three other U.S. implement com-

---

* Miscellaneous investment of an additional $246 million was made between 1929 and 1940.

† John Warnock has traced the "relative destruction of the farm machinery industry in Canada" resulting from free trade. Although U.S. branches were established as early as 1847, they were primarily sales agencies. After its formation in 1902, International Harvester dominated the U.S. market, controlling 75 per cent of the retail market although escaping anti-trust action. "International Harvester tried to purchase the Massey-Harris firm. This failed. As an alternative, they established a branch-plant in Canada in 1903.... During the 19th century, Massey-Harris was the dominant firm in the farm machinery field with over 50% of total Canadian sales. During the 1920's and 1930's, this dropped to around 20%, but with International the two firms controlled around 60% of the Canadian market." After the tariff was removed in 1944, production in Canada experienced a major setback. "In 1941 imports were around 50% of the total sales in Canada. By 1947 this had risen to 72%; by the 1960's, imports accounted for over 80%.... In 1942, exports were 7% of total production. This rose to 51% by 1952. However, exports were only around one-half of the value of imports" ("Free Trade Fantasies: The Case of the Farm Implements Industry," *This Magazine* 9 (1975):36-38).

panies had between 11 and 19 per cent of Canadian sales.[180] It was not that the Canadian company was small but simply that two-thirds of its market was outside Canada, leaving most of the Canadian market open to U.S. companies. Because of U.S. dominance in automobiles, the proportion of U.S. control of iron products in Canada was about 39 per cent, but only 12 per cent of basic steel was actually U.S. controlled. The three dominant primary steel producers were the Steel Company of Canada, Dominion Steel and Coal, and Algoma Steel. The dominant company in the United States, United States Steel, sold its Canadian properties to Dominion Steel and Coal in 1937. Pulp and paper were the outlet for over a quarter of U.S. direct investment in manufacturing, but U.S. sources controlled "only" 34 per cent of production. In textiles, telephones and telegraphs, and finance, with the exception of some areas of insurance, little U.S. investment was evident.

U.S. plants were also highly concentrated geographically in Canada. In 1934, two-thirds of all U.S. plants were located in Toronto (32 per cent), Montreal (13 per cent), Hamilton (5 per cent), the Niagara Frontier (7 per cent), or nearby border cities (9 per cent). Of all the manufacturing establishments in Canada in 1931, 42 per cent were in Ontario and 31 per cent in Quebec, but of the U.S.-controlled plants, 66 per cent were in Ontario and 16 per cent in Quebec.[181] In this way the Ontario-centred branches of U.S. manufacturing firms tended to aggravate the problem of regionalism in Canada.

Important sectors of the resource industries continued to be dominated by U.S. interests. International Nickel was not a U.S. subsidiary, but 43 per cent of its stock was owned by Americans, compared to 34 per cent held by British and 22 per cent by Canadian owners, and its board was composed of thirteen American, seven Canadian, and five British members.[182] Petroleum was still dominated by Imperial Oil, a subsidiary of Standard Oil of New Jersey, but 95 per cent of the crude was imported.

Six U.S. retailing chains were important in Canada by the 1930s, Great Atlantic and Pacific Tea, H.L. Green, S.S. Kresge, Liggett, Mercantile Stores, and F.W. Woolworth companies. They were simply Canadian divisions of U.S. retailing systems. Dominion Stores was different; it was not a subsidiary but had 71 per cent of its shares held in the United States.[183] American Telephone and Telegraph Company had a 24 per cent interest in Bell Telephone of Canada in 1934 in addition to various patent and research agreements.

U.S. banks continued to expand abroad, rising from a low of only 26 foreign branches in 1913 to 156 by 1919 and a high of 181 in 1920. But after that time there was a decline to 120 by 1924, remaining at 118 in 1935, when "of the total number established abroad, about 37 per cent were in Central and South America, 27 per cent in the West Indies, 19 per cent in Asia, 15 per cent in Europe, three branches or 1½ per cent in Mexico, and one branch in South America."[184]

Canada is conspicuous by its absence. The reason may well be the

lack of openings in Canada, with only ten banks in 1930, the four largest accounting for 80 per cent of the business. On the other hand, five
Canadian banks at this time had thirteen branches in the United States.
In addition, "the larger Canadian investment bankers, especially A.E.
Ames and Company, Ltd., Wood Gundy and Company, and Dominion
Securities, have New York offices. And 92 Canadian investment trusts
hold American securities."[185] Twenty U.S. life insurance companies
were operating in Canada in 1932, accounting for about 32 per cent of
the insurance in force. There was also a reciprocal process. In 1932
fourteen Canadian life insurance companies did business in the United
States accounting for 22 per cent of their total sales although it was only
8 per cent of the total of all life insurance in force in the United States
(in contrast, the U.S. companies' operations in Canada equalled only 2
per cent of the insurance in force at home).[186] It was not that the Canadian life insurance companies were any less active continentally than
their U.S. counterparts, it was simply that the U.S. market was so much
larger that it could absorb any foreign presence much more readily than
the smaller Canadian market.

Aside from financial institutions, Marshall and his colleagues were
able to locate some seventy-six Canadian companies operating in the
United States in the early 1930s with 138 branches and subsidiaries. For
example, there were three paper mills, of which Fraser Companies was
most important (they had a ten-year contract with Sears, Roebuck and
Company for their catalogues), and another eight companies in paper
products. Together they operated seventeen factories and six sales outlets. After prohibition ended there were twelve breweries and distilleries, including Hiram Walker-Gooderham and Worts and Distillers Corporation-Seagrams. Canada Packers also operated several meat-packing
plants and George Weston Company had bakeries. In 1932, Loblaw
Groceterias operated 132 stores in the United States. Algoma Steel and
Stelco had coal properties. All together, nine iron, steel, and mineral
product companies had seventeen factories in the United States.[187]

Canadian operations in the United States were distinguished from
their counterparts mainly by size, both of the companies themselves
and of their respective markets. In the aggregate, Canadian companies
had an insignificant impact on the U.S. economy, while about a quarter
of Canada's total economy was U.S. owned and the proportion was
much higher in key sectors. Moreover, U.S. penetration of Canada was
much more systematic than Canadian penetration of the United States.
Canadian companies in the United States were generally there in search
of specific resources, as in the case of the steel companies, or to complete a Canadian transportation network, as in the railways. A few companies, such as Massey-Harris and Moore Corporation, could claim an
important international presence.

This chapter has explored the historical developments and processes leading to patterns of continental capitalism prior to the Second World War. The American Revolution marked a radical break for the thirteen colonies from the hegemony of Britain. The industrial North defeated the commercial South in the Civil War. In the United States, industrial capitalists were thus encouraged to engage in an independent indigenous development process, whereas in Canada commercial classes continued to dominate, and these U.S. industrialists transformed themselves into corporate capitalists. The result has been that different fractions of the capitalist class have become dominant in the two countries. In the United States there was a clear progression from the small entrepreneur to the national corporation to the multinational corporation, and this final phase of U.S. development, in turn, had its impact in Canada. Along with the retardation of industrialization imposed by Canadian financial interests, imported industrialization from the United States severely limited indigenous development in Canada.

It may well be that if the Canadian economy had been allowed to evolve free from foreign influence after the break with the British, the manufacturing and later the resource sectors would finally have emerged and consolidated smoothly with financial capital into a system of corporate capitalism in a "balanced" development of industry and finance. But, of course, this was not the environment in which manufacturing and resource development occurred. To the south, engaged in a process of consolidation, was the most powerful industrial economy of the world. Facilitated by Canadian commercial capitalists and the state, both anxious for resource extraction and industrial capacity in Canada, the U.S. industrial giants brought much of Canada's nascent industry into their fold and bought up most of the resources, in large part because they were needed in the United States where these same U.S. interests controlled the market. Canadian capitalists and the state were not completely duped in the transaction. The state has often pressed, although not always hard, to have part of the processing and production of these resources and products done in Canada, but seldom has it pressed to have this activity controlled by Canadians. Canadian capitalists have participated in the U.S. penetration in a multitude of ways, and at least the most powerful ones have gained considerably.

Many of the seeds for the current high levels of U.S. direct investment in Canada were planted in the 1920s, supplemented by others immediately after the Second World War, and nourished on the rapid post-war resource and industrial boom. This investment was meant to care for two mutually reinforcing U.S. needs – sources for raw materials (both resource and industrial) and outlets for markets (both industrial and retail). In the process many potential openings in the Canadian economy closed, filled by U.S. corporations. Aside from the early indigenous industrial pursuits, steel, beverages, food, and pulp and paper, most vacuums were quickly filled. New resources activities – especially petroleum – were brought into the circle of world resource monopolies led by the United States. Many U.S. companies in the manufacturing and resource sectors were at the stage of consolidation when Canadian firms in these areas were only beginning to become stabilized. The periods of merger and consolidation *within* the United States generally coincide with the periods of buying and establishing U.S. branches in Canada. Just as many of the branches of U.S. firms established in Canada were not perceived as "foreign" by U.S. investors, their naïve reception by the Canadian state was as companies that would become "Canadianized."

The dominance of the financial sector in Canada has also had its effects. In the formative stages, industrialists often provided the entrepreneurial skills, found market outlets, and took the major risks, while financial capitalists acted as catalysts by providing the much-needed capital for expansion. They were catalysts in the sense that they favoured particular industrialists and particular industrial activities over others, thus stimulating growth of a select range from the multitude of possibilities. Even in the later stages when the internal requirements of giant corporations are largely self-financing, external capital access is essential for large-scale expansion into new areas and for acquisition of other companies. Financial capitalists still have a guiding role even in the era of advanced corporate capitalism. Ordinarily, financial capitalists during the formative stages have a range of options only among the industrialists of their own nation. In Canada the situation was far from typical because industrialists from the United States were willing and able to move in. Moreover, they came with a more highly developed technological base than their Canadian counterparts had and with secure home markets. Rather than run the risks of supporting indigenous Canadian industrialists, given the inviting option of U.S. companies, financial capitalists frequently chose to support the more stable and secure companies from the United States. Thus, by feeding some and starving others, Canadian financial capitalists had a large part in preparing the current place of Canada in the world system.

Alone, national financial capital is inherently weak. It requires secure long-term capital outlets. Thus it is typically found closely integrated with national industrial capital during the era of corporate capitalism. But this is not the only outlet; only to mention giant transportation and utility projects or, in Canada's case, externally controlled industrial capital, and even the state and its sponsored activities illustrates the variety of alliances possible for financial capital. Given the powerful place of financial capitalists in Canada, it is understandable that they have used all these outlets – giant transportation and utilities projects, often sponsored by the state, financing foreign manufacturers both within Canada and directly in their parent companies, and specific Canadian companies complementing their interests. What is important is the direction and relative proportion of each activity and alliance. It will be the task of remaining chapters to specify the contemporary nature of these relationships.

CHAPTER FOUR

Consolidating the Continental Economy

From 1940 to 1957, the ruling class of this country was radically reshaped. In 1939, the United Kingdom still seemed a powerful force, and the men who ruled Canada were a part of the old Atlantic triangle. They turned almost as much to Great Britain as to the United States, economically, culturally, and politically. After 1940, the ruling class found its centre of gravity in the United States.

George Grant[1]

Crucial to an understanding of the dominant place held by U.S. capitalists in Canada's sphere of production are the events of the period immediately following the Second World War. The following figures illustrate the rapidity of the change: in 1946, 35 per cent of Canada's manufacturing was foreign controlled; by 1953, foreign control had risen to 50 per cent, and by 1957 to 56 per cent; in mining and smelting the corresponding increases were from 38 per cent to 57 per cent to 70 per cent.[2]* In the course of a decade after the Second World War, both the manufacturing and the mining and smelting sectors of the Canadian economy, the productive cornerstones, ceased to be predominantly Canadian owned and became predominantly foreign owned. Why?

We have already seen the background for the processes and forces that proceeded headlong in this post-war period. In the United States the forces of production were strong and outward looking; in Canada they were left underdeveloped partially because of the action of Canadian capitalists in control of the sphere of circulation and partially because of the early entry of U.S. industrialists. The uneven development of Canada's economy reached a stage in this vital period in which the vacuum in Canadian production would be filled by outsiders. To understand both the outward thrust of the U.S. economy and the receptivity of the Canadian, it is necessary to begin with the war years themselves and their effects on the two economies.

---

*When speaking generally of foreign direct investment in Canada, we are really referring to U.S. investment because about 80 per cent of all foreign direct investment in Canada after the 1930s has been controlled from the United States.

I. The Wartime Economy

In the wake of the Great Depression came the Second World War – a mechanized war, an industrial war – which boosted the U.S. economy out of its slump. Recovery enabled U.S. corporate capitalism to move once more into a commanding position in the world system. C. Wright Mills has observed:

> In capitalistic economies, wars have led to many opportunities for the private appropriation of fortune and power. But the complex facts of World War II make previous appropriations seem puny indeed. Between 1940 and 1944, some $175 billion worth of prime supply contracts – the key to control of the nation's means of production – were given to private corporations. A full two-thirds of this went to the top one hundred corporations – in fact, almost one-third went to ten private corporations.[3]

"Of plants built directly by the government, about half, over seven billion dollars' worth, were constructed and operated under contracts with only thirty-one corporations."[4] As indirect incentives, companies were also able to amortize over five rather than twenty or thirty years and to purchase government-run operations after the war at low rates.

It is tempting to say that the war rebuilt the United States economy, but this would not be correct; it simply served to enlarge existing corporations.* It did, in a sense, rebuild the society. In 1940, there had been seven million unemployed in the United States, but by 1944 there was only 1 per cent unemployment. Unlike the First World War, which increased output by a mere 7 per cent, this was a total war for the United States, and output more than doubled in six years. By 1945 the war was using 57 per cent of the national income.[5] In addition to consuming such a large share of the national income, the war caused shortages of many raw materials – copper, tin, zinc, and especially iron ore – and provoked a worldwide search for sources of these materials, particularly in Canada, the backdoor storehouse.

As in the First World War, "dollar-a-year" businessmen were brought in to run the Office of Production Management, Office of Price Administration and Civilian Supply, the War Resources Board, and other government war agencies established for the U.S. effort in World War II: such men as William S. Knudsen and Charles E. Wilson of General Motors, Edward R. Stettinius of U.S. Steel, John D. Biggers of Libbey-Owens-Ford, Charles Wilson of General Electric, Ralph Budd of Great Northern Electric, Donald Nelson of Sears, Roebuck, or Wil-

---

* A.D.H. Kaplan says, "The Federal Trade Commission reported that, during the period 1940-46, the process of war mobilization and demobilization saw the merging of not less than 1,658 companies: nearly one-third of these were absorbed by corporations having assets of $50 million or more. These developments in turn implied that the disparity between big business and the rest of the economic structure had been accentuated by the wartime experience" (*Big Enterprise in a Competitive Society*, p. 33).

liam Jeffers of Union Pacific Corporation. Business again took over the state apparatus. What is more, the Second World War did not end war for the United States. By 1950, the U.S. government was again putting over $18 billion into the treasuries of one hundred corporations – including $2.4 billion to General Motors and $1.2 billion to United Aircraft[6] – for war materials for the United Nations action in Korea.

In terms of increasing production, the second war had a similar effect in Canada. By 1943, 60 per cent of employees in manufacturing were working on war materials.[7] David Wolfe says that "the key factor in accelerating [Canada] out of the slump of the 1930's was the impetus provided by the Second World War. The primary result of the war was the relative growth of secondary industry" fostered by curtailing imports and accelerating demand.[8] Under the direction of C.D. Howe, the Department of Munitions and Supply spent $900 million on crown corporations and $15 billion on war supplies. The change was rapid; production rose from $1.2 billion in 1939 to $2.9 billion in 1945, resulting in an average annual growth rate of 23 per cent during the war.

As in the United States, accelerated amortization helped private corporations. For example, the Aluminum Company of Canada (Alcan) saved $164 million in this way on its Shipshaw power project alone. "Altogether the accelerated depreciation rates were applied to capital investments worth $1.4 billion undertaken by 4,212 companies during the five year period. This constituted four fifths of all manufacturing investment at the time."[9] Modern industrialization came to Canada courtesy of the war and the Canadian state.

The presence of U.S. ownership in manufacturing was of little consequence; like the domestic companies, U.S.-controlled firms converted for wartime. The Foreign Exchange Control Board, designed to control Canadian resources for the war, was established in 1939 and issued licences to foreign subsidiaries in Canada, not wishing "to upset any existing arrangements which the Canadian companies have with their parent companies by way of inter-company accounts."[10] War would not stand in the way of the continental economy – it would consolidate it.

II. U.S. Investment in Canadian Resources and Manufacturing and Its Results

"Personally, I am afraid of foreign investments. The record does not show that our foreign investments to date have been very profitable, except for those in Canada, which I do not regard as a foreign country" (the treasurer of a large U.S. company in 1946).[11]

U.S. direct investment abroad had experienced severe setbacks during the depression beginning in 1930. As Table 1 indicates, the total value of that investment actually fell in real terms between 1929 and 1946. Cutbacks had been greatest in Latin America and Europe, each of which lost some $400 million from 1929 to 1946; U.S. investment in

TABLE 1

Total Book Value of U.S. Foreign Direct Investment, 1929 to 1970 – Selected Years ($ billions)

	1929	1946	1950	1957	1963	1970
Canada	2.0	2.5	3.6	8.6	13.0	22.8
Latin America	3.5	3.1	4.6	8.1	9.9	14.7
Europe	1.4	1.0	1.7	4.1	10.3	24.5
Other	0.6	0.6	1.9	4.4	7.5	16.1
TOTAL	7.5	7.2	11.8	25.2	40.7	78.1

(SOURCE: R. Vernon, *Manager in the International Economy*, 2nd ed., p. 205, Table X.1.)

Canada actually increased by $500 million over the period, but then again Canada was not regarded "as a foreign country."[*]

Table 1 also illustrates that in the immediate post-war expansion of $4.6 billion over the course of only four years, U.S. direct investment took certain directions. While increased investments in Canada and Latin America came quickly, the increase in Europe was somewhat delayed. Canada and Latin America were both sources of raw materials much sought by the United States following the war. The dismantling of the Canadian war economy was lucrative for those buying up businesses.[†] Canada was also a market outlet, as was Europe; but the European market had not yet stabilized following the massive destruction of the war, and there were few businesses to buy at that point.

Nowhere and at no time (except by military conquest) has the increase in control from outside been so rapid as it was in Canada following the war. The figures on p. 80 show the swiftness of this takeover. Although there had been signs of the trend – the early branch plants founded to bypass the National Policy tariff of 1879 and subsequent tariffs and the expansion of U.S. companies in the 1920s – it took the war-induced industrialization in the mid-1940s to consolidate the continental economy. Trade patterns after the decline of British dominance led the way, but the difference between trade and foreign ownership is

---

[*] The U.S. businessman's habit of not regarding Canada "as a foreign country" also shows up in some U.S. studies of multinational corporations. F.T. Knickerbocker says in *Oligopolistic Reaction and Multinational Enterprise*, "Canada was excluded because a number of U.S. firms considered their Canadian operations an integral part of their domestic operations; their reasons, therefore, for establishing a Canadian subsidiary are not very likely to be the same as their reasons for establishing subsidiaries in other countries" (pp. 33-34). Yet, the practice of excluding Canada from such studies eliminates these issues from the realm of investigation.

[†] Government war plants (worth $200 million) were sold off by the Crown Assets Allocation Committee, directed by C.D. Howe. "By 1947, $107 million worth of these plants had been sold or leased to private industry, generally at one third the price of their original construction cost" (D.A. Wolfe, "Political Culture, Economic Policy, and the Growth of Foreign Investment in Canada," p. 88).

the difference between independence and dependence.

Induced in large part by the depletion, actual or foreseeable, of materials within U.S. boundaries following the war, many U.S. companies in both the manufacturing and the resource sectors received added incentive to tap supplies in Canada. They were welcomed by Canadian politicians and businessmen, and a receptive environment for continental integration was formed. The pattern of U.S. investment in resources was noted by Aitken in 1959: "Capital inflows from the United States since World War II have been heavily concentrated in areas of the economy that contribute directly to exports to the United States. Approximately 70 per cent of the total inflow of direct capital investment from the United States in the period 1946-1955 went into the petroleum, mining, and pulp and paper industries." [12]

After the Leduc find in 1947, oil was a major contributor to the postwar boom in resources. But Canada's oil came into production when the major oil companies had already carved out their markets. By 1952 "it was apparent that the further development of the Canadian oil industry depended less upon the discovery of additional reserves than upon access to markets."[13] The local prairie market being small, the markets of central Canada and the United States would have to be tapped. Pipelines were required, and the necessary technology was mainly U.S. controlled. When Interprovincial Pipe Line was formed in 1950, it was to transmit the oil from Alberta to Imperial Oil's Sarnia refinery and the major markets; today, Imperial Oil continues to hold a one-third interest in Interprovincial. Half of the U.S. capital that entered Canada between 1946 and 1953 went into petroleum. By 1954, Canadian oil was supplying the entire market between Vancouver and Toronto; by 1957, 70 per cent of the petroleum and natural gas industries in Canada were U.S. controlled.

Development of Canadian iron ore resources was a method adopted by U.S. steel companies after the war to guarantee their supply sources. In 1949, five U.S. steel companies (Armco Steel, National Steel, Republic Steel, Youngstown Sheet and Tube, and Wheeling Steel), along with Hollinger Mines (a Canadian company) and Hanna Ore Mining (a U.S. company), formed the Iron Ore Company of Canada to develop iron ore in Quebec. Shortly thereafter other U.S. companies, notably Kennecott Copper and U.S. Steel, also began active mineral exploration.[14]

This tremendous push into Canadian resources by U.S. firms (from both the resource and the manufacturing sectors) must be seen as part of a conscious effort. After the Second World War, and further reinforced by the Korean War, the U.S. government was moved to investigate its resource requirements for the future. The result was the Paley Report, appropriately entitled *Resources for Freedom*. It identified twenty-nine key commodities, and Canada was specified as a likely major source for twelve of them. Because Canada was considered secure (politically and militarily), it was the logical target of attention rather than Latin America.

In 1950, U.S. direct investment in mining in Latin America had been about double that in Canada. In recorded history, U.S. direct investment in mining in Latin America had always been higher than in Canada. By 1960, however, U.S. stakes in mining in Canada surpassed those in the whole of Latin America. This was not because of the exhaustion of Latin American mineral resources. Rather the reason lay in the conditions of doing business in Latin America that compared unfavorably with the more suitable investment climate in Canada.[15]

Furthermore, the conscious effort by U.S. capitalists and their government was met by a like-minded Canadian state. As Wolfe has observed, during the 1950s, "in the case of the GATT tariff reductions, Canadian negotiations concentrated on gaining easier access for Canadian raw materials to foreign markets. [C.D.] Howe and the Government tended to view the resource industries as the lead sector of the Canadian economy that would provide the stimulus for the expansion of industry in the manufacturing and service sectors."[16] C.D. Howe, the great "salesman," said in a speech in Boston in 1954, "Canada has welcomed the participation of American and other foreign capital in its industrial expansion. In Canada, foreign investors are treated the same as domestic investors."[17] Prime Minister Louis St-Laurent also supported Howe's position, arguing that foreign capital somehow became "nationalized" once it had entered Canada.[18] It is not entirely clear that St-Laurent's belief was right. What is clear is the success of this government policy, a policy that promoted the old pattern of export of Canadian resources and foreign ownership of manufacturing within Canada.

Even in terms of manufactured goods, a resource-based product, pulp and paper, remained the prime Canadian export to the United States, accounting for about half of all exports at the end of the 1950s. Aitken surveyed pulpwood, nickel, petroleum, and natural gas and concluded that these natural resources "were initially developed by United States capital and entrepreneurship, with the aid of United States technology to serve the United States market."[19] At the end of the fifties, three-fifths of all Canadian exports were destined for the U.S. market and over 70 per cent of these exports were raw materials for U.S. industries.[20]

As a result of its particular form of development, Canada has become very much an extension of the U.S. economy. In 1974, exports accounted for 23 per cent of Canada's Gross National Product (GNP).[21] By contrast, in 1968, when exports made up only 4 per cent of the GNP of the United States, they comprised 24 per cent of the Canadian GNP.[22] Much of the advantage of the United States over Canada in trading terms results from sheer size. While in world terms Canada's GNP is of moderate size (certainly not small), compared to the GNP of the United States it is puny. For instance, in 1970, the United States had trade worth $8,810 million with Canada while Canada's trade to the United States was worth $10,920 million – not a very dramatic difference. Yet these figures accounted for only 20.7 per cent of the total U.S. trade but 65.4 per cent of Canada's total.[23] Nevertheless, the differences between Canada and the United States include more than size; they also reflect the types of goods exported to and imported from the United States and radically different trade levels per capita. A *Toronto Star* article reported in the summer of 1976: "We import more manufactured goods per person than any other major nation: twice the European average and four times the American. Last year, Canada imported $10 billion more manufactured end-products than it exported."[24]

While this trade pattern has long been characteristic of Canada, its intensity has been increasing rapidly since World War II. Writing at the beginning of the sixties, Aitken noted: "Since Canada became a nation in 1867, the value of Canadian-American trade has increased some eighty-fold; during the same period, total world trade has increased only about twenty times."[25] Over the course of Canada's first century, the proportion of imports originating in the United States has increased from about one-third to over two-thirds of the whole and the proportion of Canadian exports going to the United States has increased from about one-half to two-thirds. Recently, the increasing density of Canada's trade relationship with the United States has continued to grow, as Table 2 shows. But to assume that little has changed in Canada's economic relations with the United States because the high degree of trading in the post-war era is similar to that in the era from the turn of the century to the Second World War is to overlook the important way in which this "trading" has changed. In the earlier period, it was correct to suggest a market relationship in which capitalists in Canada bought from and sold to capitalists in the United States. Now 75 per cent of all "trading" by foreign-controlled companies in Canada represents intracompany transfers within one corporation that straddles the

TABLE 2

Canadian Trade Patterns, 1961, 1971, and 1974
(in percentages)

	U.S.	U.K.	Other Commonwealth	Other	Total
EXPORTS					
1961	54.0	15.8	5.7	24.5	100
1971	67.2	7.9	3.9	21.0	100
1974	65.9	6.0	3.5	24.6	100
IMPORTS					
1961	67.0	10.7	5.1	17.2	100
1971	70.1	5.4	4.0	20.5	100
1974	67.3	3.6	4.0	25.1	100

(SOURCE: Calculated from *Canada Year Book, 1975*, p. 728, Table 18.29.)

boundary between Canada and the United States. Although the proportion of total Canadian trade accounted for by branch plants is not known, the fact that most of the key exporting activities are foreign controlled suggests that the proportion is high.

A statement by Mitchell Sharp, then Secretary of State for External Affairs, describes the situation graphically:

> The Canada-U.S. relationship, as it has evolved since the end of the Second World War, is in many respects a unique phenomenon. It is by far our most important external relationship, but it is more than an external relationship. It impinges on virtually every aspect of the Canadian national interest, and thus of Canadian domestic concerns.... The North-South pull has, of course, been a factor throughout Canadian history. At the time of Confederation and until the 1920s, however, there were strong countervailing forces promoting an East-West bias in Canada's economic development.... Over time, however, the exploitation of our mineral and forestry resources assumed more importance and these found a large and expanding market in a rapidly industrializing United States. The economic axis was gradually turning in a North-South direction.[26]

As Canada has shifted from the east-west to the north-south axis, the nature of the resources has also changed from the old staples of fish, fur, timber, and wheat to the new staples of petroleum, minerals, and pulp and paper. This has led Daniel Drache, following a long tradition of political economists in Canada who have focused on staples, to conclude that "what we have in Canada is a hybrid or 'incomplete' form of capitalism, which might be called *advanced resource capitalism*, where capitalist relations are based on a very highly developed resource exploitation."[27] Canada occupies this position because it is both an important market for manufacturers *and* a source of resources for U.S. capitalists. The result is that the current level of U.S. control amounts to 58 per cent of manufacturing and 74 per cent of mining in Canada. At the same time Canada has been supplying a large portion of U.S. import requirements, in 1973 42 per cent of the aluminum, bauxite, copper, lead, nickel, tin, and zinc, which together were worth $1 billion, while oil and gas exports added a further $2 billion and pulp and paper another $2.5 billion.[28]

Insights into the implications of these developments for Canadians are provided by Pierre Bourgault:

> When we examine the nature of our imports and exports, we find that we export mainly raw materials and resource-based products, while importing mostly manufactured goods, particularly those which have a high knowledge content [i.e. technology and skilled labour]. Our pride in being a trading nation must be tempered by the realization that we excel in the sale of those products that most developed countries want, on which they impose no tariffs, and which they

use to make products for sales abroad, thus creating jobs for their citizens. [29]

Bourgault also points out that Canada imports some of the same raw materials that it exports but in "more science-intensive forms"; these are resources such as nickel, aluminum, pulp and paper, platinum, natural gas, petroleum, and asbestos. He is led to question the value for Canada of such trading patterns but leaves little doubt why foreign capitalists have found Canada such an attractive place to invest. In fact, Canada is so attractive that it has been the recipient of almost 40 per cent of all investments made abroad by multinational corporations.[30]

One consequence of this pattern, as expressed in the study *Foreign Direct Investment in Canada*, is that "some 90 per cent of patents issued in Canada are registered to foreign owners, of which two-thirds are owned by United States residents."[31] Not only did its technological lead give the United States an important wedge for entering Canada, but the effect of its branch plants has also been to appropriate the means of innovation and further reinforce its strength within the sphere of production.

III. U.S. Ownership and "Canadian" Capital

While U.S. control was being extended over more and more Canadian resources and manufacturing industries, the proportion of U.S. capital actually imported to support these investments was falling. The Gordon Commission reported in 1957 that "the net use of foreign resources was about one-quarter in 1926-30, compared to 6% in 1946-54; direct foreign financing fell from about one-half to one-quarter between the two periods."[32] Where was the financing coming from? Aitken shows that for 1959, of the total sources of funds for U.S. direct investment in Canada, 26 per cent came from the United States, 7 per cent from Canadian sources outside the company, 32 per cent from depreciation and depletion allowances, and 31 per cent from net income.[33] Even this early, some seven-tenths of the sources for expansion of U.S. direct investment were coming from within Canada or were financed from Canadian operations.

To what extent were new arrivals from the United States "pioneers" and to what extent were they simply taking over existing Canadian operations? A United Nations report in 1974 analysed the patterns of 187 U.S. multinationals. It found that before 1946, 29 per cent of the U.S. firms entering Canada came by acquisition of existing Canadian companies. Between 1946 and 1957 this method of entry increased to 45 per cent, and between 1958 and 1967 it rose to 58 per cent. This, it should be noted, is much higher than in all other countries entered by U.S. firms, where the proportions were 24, 28, and 41 per cent, respectively, for each period.[34] In other words, relative to other places where U.S.

multinationals operate, in Canada the tendency was to take over existing companies rather than open new ones.

The method of financing and the method of entry together show that increasingly in the post-war period U.S. firms were expanding their Canadian operations with capital obtained in Canada. Both processes contributed to the rapid increase in the U.S. share of control in both resources and manufacturing.

Kari Levitt has argued that dependence is characteristic of Canada's relationship with the United States, showing that "in the period 1960-67, remitted profits by American subsidiaries in Canada ($5.9 billion) exceeded new capital inflows ($4.1 billion) by $1.8 billion."[35] Clearly, the effect of foreign direct investment, such as that characteristic of multinational corporations, is to increase dependence over time and lead to underdevelopment of the economy of the host country in the sense of draining off more capital than is initially invested.

The paradoxical position of Canada is that while the amount of U.S. investment in Canada continues to grow, financed out of retained earnings, Canadian financial capital, and profits remitted to U.S. parents, this country is now a net exporter of capital to the United States. There are additional remittances of various kinds; for example, between 1946 and 1968, interest payments on foreign capital amounted to $5.085 billion, and of this, 88 per cent went to the United States. This amount has been increasing rapidly, with $500 million going to the United States in 1968 alone. In that year 82 per cent of all dividend payments went to the United States. Dividend payments to the United States amounted to $10.3 billion between 1926 and 1968, of which $7.5 billion was paid between 1950 and 1968.[36] Further forms of remittance to the United States are professional fees, royalties, management fees, rent, research, franchise, advertising, and insurance, which amounted to $1.715 billion in 1969 alone.[37] Unlike earlier periods when many of the patents held by U.S. companies were used in Canada by Canadian companies, the current situation finds patent use almost exclusively a branch-plant phenomenon. A special Statistics Canada survey found that "out of more than $250 million paid to non-residents in respect of royalties, patents, copyrights and trademarks, management and administrative services, and franchises and similar rights, some $240 million emanated from direct investment enterprises."[38] In other words, about 96 per cent of all these payments were from branch plants.

By 1970, dividend payments to foreign parents were up to $806 million, or two-fifths of the branch plants' total earnings, and the excess of payments over receipts of direct investment was $473 million, reflecting both a high increase in foreign control and high foreign payments. *Foreign investments in Canada are now so lucrative that they can both expand within Canada and export capital to their parents.* "In the periods 1956 to 1958 and 1959 to 1961, when intense capital formation occurred, Canada's net use of foreign resources amounted to between one third and two fifths of net capital formation. In the next six years, however, the relative use of foreign resources was almost halved to one fifth...the relative use of foreign resources fell to 12% in the period 1968 to 1970."[39]

Thus the issue for Canadians to consider is no longer new inflows of U.S. direct investment, for they have virtually ceased; the issue is now the expansion of foreign control almost entirely through retained earnings from Canadian operations and Canadian financial capital. More than ever, the argument that Canada is capital poor and needs foreign investment appears absurd. On the contrary, Canada *is becoming* capital poor because it has so much foreign investment and that investment is generating dividends that drain funds back to the foreign parent.

As was suggested earlier, the nature of direct investment is such that when it matures it begins internal generation of sufficient funds for growth and requires less new direct inflow to continue to expand. In Canada, this point was reached between 1962 and 1963 when undistributed earnings began to be greater than new capital inflows. In the seventeen years from 1946 to 1962, net capital inflow contributed $6.4 billion to the expansion of foreign direct investment in Canada compared to $4.4 billion through net increases of undistributed earnings (59.5 per cent capital inflow, 40.5 per cent undistributed earnings). In the next eight years, from 1963 to 1970, these two sources combined yielded an almost identical amount of capital ($10.8 billion from 1946 to 1962 and $10.6 billion from 1963 to 1970), but the relative contribution of the two factors was reversed. In the more recent period, net capital inflows contribute 44.4 per cent while undistributed earnings account for 55.6 per cent.[40]

These calculations do not include earnings that flow back to parent companies, which follow a similar trend, or borrowings within Canada that add to foreign-controlled direct investment. Of the total U.S.-controlled investment of $27.7 billion in 1970, Canadians owned $3.46 billion in the form of debt and $2.37 billion through equity, other non-residents owned $0.467 billion, and the remaining $19.28 billion belonged to U.S.-controlled Canadian corporations. Canadian investors through debt or equity had thus committed some $5.8 billion to U.S.-controlled companies. This is Canadian capital's share (about 21 per cent) in U.S. direct investment.[41] It suggests that there is a form of alliance or partnership between the dominant fractions of Canadian and U.S. capitalists in their management of the continental economy.

IV. Changes in the Profile of U.S. Investment in Canada

The profile of U.S. direct investment in Canada by sector between 1926 and 1970 shows a steady proportion directed to finance (hovering between 6 and 8 per cent) and a similar steady pattern in merchandising (about 6 per cent). A sharp decline occurred in investment in utilities, particularly during the fifties, after peaking at over 20 per cent of the total before the Second World War and subsequently declining to about 2 per cent by 1960. There was a steady slight upward trend from 10 to 13 per cent in the amount going to mining and smelting. But the major change was in the petroleum and natural gas sector, where investment rose from between 6 and 7 per cent before World War II to 25 per cent, where it has remained in the post-war period. The war is also the watershed in overall manufacturing, dividing investment of almost 60 per cent from a steady post-war 43 per cent. Within manufacturing, there has been a steady decline in wood and paper from a high of 13 per cent in 1926 to a low of 8 per cent in 1970.[42] This *relative* decline in the proportion of U.S. direct investment going to manufacturing is a result of the increasing importance of petroleum and natural gas in the later period. In other areas of the world, the proportion of U.S. direct investment going to manufacturing has been increasing (from 33 per cent to 40 per cent since World War II), but Canada remains behind Europe in this respect, Canada having 43 per cent compared to Europe's 55 per cent but being well ahead of Latin America (24 per cent), Africa (14 per cent), and Asia (18 per cent). In the world view of U.S. multinationals, Canada is both a market and a source of raw materials while other areas tend to be specialized as one or the other, thus confirming the argument made earlier that Canada has a dual role within the U.S. sphere of influence.

Table 3 provides a retrospective view of U.S. control in non-financial industries in Canada. The steady pattern of an increasing share of control in manufacturing and in mining and smelting is readily apparent, while fluctuations in petroleum and natural gas mainly reflect other foreign interests (Britain and the Netherlands). Much lower levels of control in transportation and utilities are also evident.

TABLE 3

U.S. Control of Canadian Non-Financial Industries, 1926 to 1970 – Selected Years *(in percentages)*

SECTOR	1926	1930	1939	1948	1954a*	1954b*	1960	1965	1970
Manufacturing	30	31	32	39	45	41	44	46	47
Petroleum & gas	–	–	–	–	–	67	64	58	61
Mining & smelting	32	42	38	37	54	49	53	52	59
Railways	3	3	3	3	2	2	2	2	2
Other utilities	20	29	26	24	11	7	4	4	4

*Petroleum and natural gas included in manufacturing and mining and smelting before 1954.
(SOURCE: Calculated from Canada, *Canada's International Investment Position, 1968 to 1970*, pp. 144-45, Table 28.)

Placing this pattern of U.S. control within the context of all non-financial industries in Canada, as in Table 4, highlights predominant

U.S. control in manufacturing and resources and the lesser place of private Canadian interests and other foreign interests in these sectors.* What this table does not suggest, but Appendix I illustrates clearly, is that the proportion of foreign control expressed in terms of assets is considerably lower than the proportion of profits. In other words, foreign investment in the mining and manufacturing sectors is much more profitable than Canadian ownership in these same areas. While foreign interests controlled 65 per cent of the mining assets in 1972, these assets generated 69 per cent of the sales and 73 per cent of the profits. In manufacturing as a whole, foreign interests had 56 per cent of the assets and sales but 65 per cent of the profits in 1972. Appendix I also illustrates the low levels of foreign ownership in the utilities, wholesale and retail trade, and finance sectors not shown in Table 4. These facts confirm the historical division of activity, with Canadian capitalists dominant in circulation and service and foreign interests dominant in production, discussed in earlier chapters.

TABLE 4

Control of Non-Financial Industries in Canada, 1970
(in percentages)

SECTOR	CANADA Gov't.	Private	U.S.	OTHER FOREIGN	Total
Manufacturing	2	37	47	14	100
Petroleum & gas	2	22	61	15	100
Mining & smelting	1	29	59	11	100
Railways	73	25	2	—	100
Other utilities	69	24	4	3	100
Merchandising & construction	1	87	8	4	100
Total	22	42	28	8	100

(SOURCE: Calculated from Canada, *Canada's International Investment Position, 1968 to 1970*, pp. 146-47, Table 29.)

Table 5 provides a broad perspective of the difference between capital controlled and owned in Canada and in the United States. It reveals that the capitalists of the two countries controlling this capital engage in different activities. Canadian interests own more than they control in manufacturing, mining, and smelting and especially in petroleum and natural gas, where they own 43 per cent of the whole but control only

* A detailed classification of proportion of ownership and control of assets, sales, and profits is provided in Appendices I and II. There are major differences depending on the indicator used. For example, U.S. manufacturers in Canada employ 30 per cent of the people but represent 60 per cent of control in assets (Canada, *Canadian Statistical Review, Historical Summary 1970*, p. 214). This illustrates that U.S. manufacturing is highly capital intensive and tends to create fewer jobs in Canada than Canadian manufacturing.

TABLE 5

Relative Distribution of Ownership and Control of
Capital Employed in Canadian Non-Financial Industries,
1972

| | Total Capital Employed* ($ billions) | PER CENT OF CAPITAL | | | | | |
| SECTOR | | Owned | | | Controlled | | |
		Can.	U.S.	Other	Can.	U.S.	Other
Manufacturing	28.4	47	44	9	42	43	15
Petroleum & gas	15.0	43	46	11	25	58	17
Mining & smelting	7.8	44	46	10	42	47	11
Railways	6.0	85	7	8	98	2	—
Other utilities	25.9	81	16	3	92	5	3
Total non-financial	105.0	66	27	7	65	26	9

*Based on book value of long-term debt and equity (including retained earnings) employed in enterprises in Canada.
(SOURCE: Canada, *Canada's International Investment Position, 1968 to 1970*, p. 65, Statement 23.)

25 per cent. On the other hand, they have control over more than they own in railways and other utilities. This situation arises because, as discussed earlier, there are different control rights associated with different types of capital. In the productive sectors U.S. capital tends to be direct investment and Canadian capital is portfolio investment.

These figures also contain clues to tendencies, particularly regarding the types of capital Canadian and U.S. capitalists use in the various sectors and the relative strength each type of capital gives these capitalists in terms of their ability to control. Not only the availability of capital but also the use to which it is put is of importance. For example, in rubber manufacturing, Canadians supplied 31 per cent but controlled only 1 per cent of total capital employed. In the aluminum industry, Canadians invested 24 per cent, but control was 100 per cent foreign. In chemicals, Canadians invested 34 per cent but controlled only 19 per cent; the figures in petroleum were 39 per cent of the capital and 24 per cent of the control, in mining, 41 per cent of the capital and 30 per cent of the control, in smelting and refining, 53 per cent of the capital and 33 per cent of the control.[43] In capital terms, the difference lies in the tendency of Canadian capitalists to portfolio investment and of U.S. capitalists to direct investment. In organizational terms, the U.S. capitalists build branch plants and the Canadians supply the capital to do the building. In terms of favoured sectors, U.S. capitalists invest in manufacturing and resources, Canadian capitalists invest in finance, transportation, and utilities and lend capital to U.S. firms in the productive sectors.

The most recent data available on foreign direct investment in Canada only reaffirm the patterns outlined here.* At the end of 1973, the total of foreign direct investment climbed to $32.8 billion, an increase of 11 per cent over the previous year compared to increases of 6 per cent in each of the two previous years. This increase represented an expansion in one year of $3.3 billion, but only $725 million, or 22 per cent of it, came from direct investment inflows; the rest was accounted for by retained earnings and capital borrowed in Canada. And the pattern of the past persisted: the United States accounted for 79 per cent of all foreign direct investment in Canada at the end of 1973.[44]

It is important to recognize that while parts of an economic system may be dependent on external capitalists, not all parts are necessarily externally dependent. Nor must all the various parts be in conflict; some parts may be in conflict while others are in alliance. The relations of the three fractions of the capitalist class outlined earlier (p. 25) with one another can be understood in terms of their place in the continental system. The dominant indigenous elite has entered into an alliance with the dominant comprador elite (and thereby with the foreign elite that controls the parent companies) because each group operates in relatively distinct though complementary economic activities, the former in finance, transportation, and utilities and the latter in manufacturing and resources. Even when the dominant indigenous elite has entered the manufacturing and resource sectors, it has gone into the components of these sectors that are long established in Canada and, again, relatively distinct from foreign-controlled activities. The food and beverages, steel, and pulp and paper industries provide the most significant examples of this trend. The third fraction, the middle-range indigenous capitalists mainly in manufacturing, is much weaker in access to both markets and capital than either of the other two fractions and often in direct conflict with them. It is this fraction that is frequently forced to sell out and join the ranks of the comprador elite or *rentier* capitalists. As has been shown, the weak position of the middle-range national capitalist class throughout history cannot be totally divorced from the dominant position of the indigenous elite in finance, transportation, and utilities.

Once again, it is crucial to place these patterns of investment in their economic sectors. If the sectors are taken individually, it is evident that the middle-range fraction of the indigenous capitalist class centred in manufacturing is most directly affected.† In 1967, U.S. direct invest-

---

* Government statistics on corporations and foreign investment in Canada are generally three to five years out of date by the time they are released. The Canadian government is not renowned for either gathering statistics of this kind or making what it gathers widely available.

† In the resource sector, foreign investment creates little conflict with middle-range indigenous capitalists because that class was never able to develop significantly in this sector. For example, 99.5 per cent of the assets and 98.9 per cent of the sales in petroleum and coal products are foreign controlled. The participation of Canada's dominant class has been primarily in promotion and speculation of stocks rather than in resource production.

ment in Canada was concentrated in manufacturing (44 per cent) and resources (39 per cent) and very little flowed into other sectors (finance, 8 per cent; trade, 5 per cent; utilities, 2 per cent).[45] These figures (and those presented above) illustrate the relative direction of U.S. direct investment and multinational activity in Canada by sector, but they do not compare the relative volume with Canadian-controlled investment. A comparison can be made by studying the net change in the book value of investments in Canada over the thirteen years ending in 1967 (the most recent period for which these data are available). In manufacturing, U.S.-controlled branches have added $5.9 billion compared to the $4.7 billion added by Canadian-controlled companies; in resources, the comparative additions are $6.2 billion to $2.6 billion. On the other hand, there was no U.S. investment in railways, but Canadians added $1.4 billion; in the other sectors, the comparative figures were in utilities, $0.3 billion and $10.6 billion; in merchandising and construction, $0.6 billion and $7.2 billion.[46] These figures show that the pattern of underdevelopment characteristic of Canada in the post-war period as a result of U.S. branch plants has persisted in specific sectors, notably manufacturing and resource, but has had limited direct influence elsewhere.

A Note on Canada's Industrial Coming-of-Age

It is difficult to identify precisely the date when Canada came of age industrially. Some may even argue that because of the extensive amount of foreign control in its industries, Canada has still not reached that point. But examined in terms of social structure, standard of living, and output, Canada is an industrial society even if it has a strong bias towards resource and commercial activity. Illustrating the confusion over the beginning of the period of industrialization, O.J. Firestone says, "If the criterion of industrialization is the proportion of national income derived from manufacturing then Canada became more industrial than agricultural during World War I. If the definition is extended to cover employment, then Canada's industrial coming-of-age is very recent dating back only to the early years of World War II."[47] It may be argued that the basis for an industrial society was established prior to the beginning of the Second World War, but the major transformations projecting Canada's social structure into its present form did not take place until the war.

When we use the proportion of the labour force in agriculture as an indicator, the recent shift is readily apparent. This proportion fell from 26 per cent in 1941 to 16 per cent by 1951, to 10 per cent by 1961, and to 6 per cent by 1971. On the other hand, the evidence shows that the decline in agricultural labour did *not* produce a corresponding rise in the proportion of the labour force employed in secondary production. For the crucial period 1946 to 1963, the proportion employed in production of primary goods fell from 29 per cent to 13 per cent, as would be expected with the decline in agriculture. Nevertheless, the proportion engaged in secondary production increased only slightly, from 31 to 32 per cent, in the same period. A very large portion of the shift went to the service sector, rising from 40 to 55 per cent, with the lion's share going to trade, finance, insurance, real estate, and "other" services. What has also been clear in this shift is an increase in the proportion of the labour force employed as paid workers as opposed to self-employed. In 1956, 79 per cent of the workers in Canada were paid workers, but by 1972, 88 per cent were in this category. There was a corresponding decline from 12 to 6 per cent of those working for themselves and a decline from 6 to 4 per cent of those who were employers.[48]

Canada is obviously no longer an agrarian society, but neither is it particularly oriented to secondary production. Rather, as Canada became industrialized it tended to expand in the service sectors of the economy. At the same time, there has been a "rationalization" of labour with the decline of numbers of self-employed workers and even of those who are employers. This pattern in the occupational structure of Canadian society reflects Canada's economic development. No clear progression from primary to secondary to tertiary activities took place in Canada as it had in the United States. In Canada the economy changed from primary to tertiary without developing the area of secondary production. Here again can be seen the uneven nature of Canada's development and the effects of external control.

CHAPTER FIVE

Multinational Corporations Operating from the United States and Canada

Placing the connection between Canada and the United States in the broader context of the relations of each with other parts of the world system makes possible a better understanding of their differences and similarities as recipients and sources of foreign direct investment. It also permits an analysis of the ambiguous role Canada plays in the international economy, both as a go-between and as a direct participant. These views help us to place U.S. investment in Canada within a larger perspective and in particular to see how Canada differs from other countries that are also on the receiving end of extensive foreign direct investment. A thorough analysis of these relations is beyond the scope of this study, but even this limited excursus provides some insights into these complex issues and sheds light on the peculiarities of Canada's relationship with the United States. We will see that U.S. investment affects not only the internal relations of Canada but also its relations with other nations. The repercussions of the U.S. economy on Canada are indeed far reaching.

I. Multinational Corporations and Class Fractions

Since about two hundred of the estimated three hundred world corporations usually classified as multinational are U.S. based, it is appropriate to think of them as "*national* enterprises with multinational operations."[1] Although various definitions are available, the one adopted in *Foreign Direct Investment in Canada* is as comprehensive as any: a multinational corporation is "the embodiment of foreign direct investment by a single business enterprise which straddles several economies (a minimum of four or five) and divides its global activities between different countries with a view to realizing overall corporate objectives."[2] As implied in the definition, multinationals have a worldwide division of activities that gives them flexibility, and in general their enormous size gives them sufficient economic power to rationalize production and resource extraction throughout the world to the advantage of their national base. This structure requires centralized

97

control over the activities of subsidiaries and decision making based on assessments of worldwide maximization of profit.*

Corporate strategy in multinationals is established by members of "centre" elites at headquarters and carried out by the "periphery" elites that manage the affairs of branch plants within the designated limits. Profitability is gauged within the broad time and space limits set by the parent and not with respect to particular local interests. Vertically linked subsidiaries are valued for their contribution to the whole production process by supplying raw materials, while horizontally linked subsidiaries are important to the extent that they add to the overall profit of the parent through production and sales. In organizational terms, vertically linked operations must meet the production quotas established by the parent and closely co-ordinate their activities, while horizontally linked subsidiaries may achieve greater flexibility as long as profits increase satisfactorily. In either case, it is the parent that specifies the policy under which they must operate. Integration can take many forms, but, as J.N. Behrman points out, centralization is made to work by the "establishment of a hierarchy of abilities to commit the company to capital expenditures" in which expenditures over a specified size or contrary to established policy must be approved at the level of the parent's board of directors.[3]

The amount of discretion available to the management of Canadian branch plants was discussed in the Watkins Report. It stated that

in 20 per cent of the subsidiaries there was very substantial decentralization of decision-making with respect to both operations and policies, with the parent's direct influence largely felt through its representation on the Canadian board. In another 20 per cent, policy determination was highly centralized with varying degrees of operational freedom. The remaining 60 per cent represented cases where there was a high degree of operational decentralization, and with the officers of the subsidiary playing a role in policy determination, particularly in initiating changes, *though final authority lay elsewhere.* Where major policy changes were involved, however, the officers of the parent company had to be consulted [emphasis added].[4]

The authors of this report said further that in very nearly all cases where important policies are to be altered, where major expenditures are involved, or where senior appointments are to be made in the subsidiaries, the officers of the parent company take part. In the areas of

* *Foreign Direct Investment in Canada* goes on to say, "Size and consequent financial strength, together with flexibility, confer great economic power on the MNE [multinational enterprise]. It can often negotiate more favourable terms of entry to a country than any other investor. It can switch production from an affiliate in one country to an affiliate in another. It can more readily circumvent local monetary and fiscal policy. It may be able to mobilize home government support if threatened. It is this power which makes the MNE a challenge for governments, not only of small countries but of larger ones as well" (p. 56). This commentary is unsatisfactory because it reifies multinationals and does not go behind organizations to the classes and people who control them.

production, marketing, labour, and the like, however, there was apt to be more decentralization.

A recent legal case, reported by Larry Pratt, illustrates in some detail the degree of autonomy "enjoyed" by Imperial Oil, the Canadian subsidiary of Exxon Corporation. This case is particularly interesting because it provides an unusual opportunity to examine the inside of a key multinational and because of the importance of oil companies in the world system. Only some of the most telling evidence can be included here. Involved is a suit by Nova Scotia Power Corporation (NSPC) against Imperial concerning an agreement to supply oil:

> While the case centred primarily on the issue of whether Imperial was entitled to pass on to its customer, the power board [NSPC], the burden of tax increases imposed in Venezuela, the evidence revealed much about the way Exxon directly involves itself in Imperial's pricing and crude purchasing policies. "The judges found," Oilweek reported, "that Imperial does not have independence of action in deciding where its crude supplies come from or an ability to bargain directly with the supplier. This function is carried out by the planning and analysis group of Exxon International in New York." Imperial has no representation among this small group, thus the company cannot control its own source of crude supply. "The ultimate decisions rested with Exxon Corporation," concluded Justice L.S. Hart.[5]

After examining further evidence, Pratt concludes that it "effectively lays to rest the lingering myth of Imperial's autonomy; neither it, nor any other foreign-controlled oil company operating in Canada, enjoys independence of action, particularly in areas such as the tar sands where billions of dollars are at stake."[6] Major decisions, decisions that have society-wide effects, are made by the headquarters of the multinationals, not by those hired to run their affairs in branch plants.

Technological advances in communications and transportation in the fifties and sixties made possible the kind of control adopted by the multinationals. Lines of control were strengthened, increasing the ability of the centre elite to command branches around the world. Management techniques, combined with new technologies and the demands of worldwide operations, permitted new organizational systems to develop.*

Alcan Aluminium, a Montreal-based multinational, can serve as an example of multinational organization and planning. Alcan has 42 per cent of its assets outside Canada and operates subsidiaries in thirty-

---

* Technology and rapid communications mean that fewer decisions need to be made on the spot, so that local people, who will have no part in policy making, can be recruited to carry out orders and fewer employees have to be sent from the parent. Robert Perry points out in Galt, USA: "There are, in fact, very few Americans in Galt; fewer who bear high titles in the American-owned companies. Canadians hold most of the senior jobs. Rather, the American presence takes the form of sheafs of policy and operating instructions, report forms, engineering manuals, patent-use contracts and technical-aid agreements" (p. 27).

three countries. A five-man "Group Executive Committee" controls operations of the company and organizes its management of half the "free world's" aluminum production and sales. It co-ordinates mining of bauxite in the Caribbean, ore smelting in Canada and Norway where hydro electricity is cheaply available, fabrication of products, and, finally, sales throughout the world. All operations are overseen by the finance department; according to the annual report for 1974, "Alcan's operations are interlinked on an international basis because of the geographical dispersion of raw materials, economic energy sources and ultimate markets for fabricated and primary aluminum. Strategic, logistical and financial planning are, therefore, centralized at corporate headquarters in Montreal but direction of current operations, market development and preliminary planning are largely decentralized."[7] These three activities are supervised by executive vice-presidents who, in turn, account to the president. Various national subsidiaries account to general managers who report to Montreal.

Some Alcan plants are organized to serve local markets; others serve regions, for example the German branch serves continental Europe. In 1974, only 15 per cent of Alcan's sales were in Canada; 27 per cent were in the United States, 17 per cent in the United Kingdom, 13 per cent in other European Economic Community countries, and 28 per cent elsewhere. Distribution of sales is wide and raw materials also come from a variety of sources. In 1974, 38 per cent of the alumina used came from Canada, smelted from bauxite mined in Guinea and Guyana, 36 per cent from Alcan Jamaica, 15 per cent from Australia, and 11 per cent was purchased. Alcan's organization is based on ability to control operations and supply markets, not on political divisions.

Although area managers meet regularly in Montreal to offer suggestions and make reports, final decisions are based on overall corporate performance and are made by the five executive members. "At Alcan all major projects, whether entirely new, such as the British smelter, or already allowed for in the forward plans, have to receive an individual appropriation from Montreal." Prices are all established by Montreal, as is the rate of return expected from subsidiaries. "Within the parameters established by head office Alcan's managers have considerable freedom of action to run their own affairs," but with the tight financial controls, price setting, and control over investment, little autonomy remains.[8]* Multinationals are capable of a decentralization of operations necessary to meet local conditions, but they necessarily maintain centralized control of policy making and centralized profit taking, with profits from all operations flowing back to the parent for allocation at its board's discretion.

This kind of organizational structure affords multinationals many ad-

* The multinational ownership structure of Alcan and International Nickel Company of Canada will be examined in detail in Chapter 6.

vantages, particularly over national corporations and governments.* In addition to control and development of advanced technology protected by licences and royalties, they have access to large sources of expansion capital, either internally generated or from various pools both at home and in their countries of operation where their stability is an asset often unavailable to local companies. They also have great market power, operating in non-competitive situations and buying and selling in a variety of markets. With great capital reserves, they can shift investments and operations to "take advantage of new technology, marginal changes in transportation costs, wages, taxes or population movements, with no consideration of the human havoc that such moves create."[9] Conducting operations in several areas allows multinationals to integrate markets and produce "distinctive" products or to exploit natural resources on a large scale so that they can control both markets and sources of raw material.

Flexibility and resources also allow multinationals to plan on a larger scale and for greater time periods than national corporations can do. For example, Exxon is currently projecting operations into the 1990s, and a group of a hundred corporations has commissioned the Hudson Institute to study the "future corporate environment" from 1975 to 1985.[10] In contrast, politicians must envisage the future in the much shorter perspective of a term of office in the liberal democracies. Multinationals may also avoid taxes or other government measures by shifting operations to other countries or by threatening to do so. International capitalism is the multinational's greatest defence against adverse local conditions, and it can use this weight to counter regulatory powers of governments, whether at home or abroad.

Although at the subsidiary level there is frequently a hybrid management composed of both nationals and representatives from the parent (with both groups selected at the discretion of the parent board), there is seldom much foreign content within the parent, as later chapters will show. There are two unequal sets of management, one operating from the parent company and the other national, representing local executives and other outsiders deemed important. As has been suggested earlier, multinational corporations do not internationalize their own managements but they do *de*nationalize a part of the national elite. The drawing of the local elite into the international system, however, "helps to bolster the strength of certain local elite groups and is usually

---

* In his study of Falconbridge Nickel Mines, a Canadian-based multinational, John Deverell illustrates the variety of political systems this company has done business with: "Falconbridge and subsidiaries have co-existed with a wide range of political philosophy in government, from Canada's liberal democracy to the Dominican Republic's militarized pseudo-democracy, Amin's military dictatorship in Uganda, and the apartheid regimes of Rhodesia, South Africa and Namibia.... What all these societies including Canada have in common is considerable freedom for private capital, and this is a political principle about which the corporate managers and owners care a great deal" (*Falconbridge*, pp. 177-78). See also p. 120n.

seen as a threat to the strength of others."[11] To the extent that the presence of foreign multinational branch plants displaces them, members of the local elite often aspire, according to Raymond Vernon, "to control the government apparatus rather than to be modern businessmen, technicians, and managers."[12]

Outside control, as expressed in multinational branch plants, has several effects on the activities of the local elite. Some of the members will be drawn directly into the international system by working for these branches; another group will be drawn into an alliance with international business because of their association with international capital, although not working directly for that business; and another segment will be either displaced from existing local operations or prevented from developing these activities because the "space" is foreign controlled.

Among the persons who run multinationals there is a sense of unity, of common purpose, that binds them together against their critics. The following account is simply one instance of this:

> *David Rockefeller* called on the business community in Britain and elsewhere yesterday for a united effort in refuting what he termed "the proliferating critics" of multinational corporations.
>
> The chairman of the Chase Manhattan Corporation said in an address at the stock exchange in Manchester, England, that "We should be doing all in our power to lift the siege that is taking shape around the beleaguered multinational companies."
>
> He terms the multinationals "the most important instruments in the unprecedented expansion that has taken place in world trade."[13]

And it is not simply on the ideological level that multinationals are bound together. The Orion Bank, formed in 1970, is the most impressive example of multinationals themselves entering into joint ventures. It operates in more than a hundred countries and its six members are at the top of the international financial community: Chase Manhattan (third largest bank in the United States), Royal Bank of Canada (Canada's largest), National Westminster Bank (Britain's second largest), Westdeutsche Landesbank (Germany's second largest), Credito Italiano (Italy's fourth largest), and Mitsubishi Bank (Japan's fourth largest). With this aggregation of financial resources, the Orion is able to support other multinationals. For example, in 1971, Canadian-controlled "Massey-Ferguson wanted to raise $25 million in Euro-currencies at a time of general credit squeeze and slow trading in the agricultural industry. Rather than go around the market for a million here and a million there, Orion decided to handle the entire deal itself. Old correspondent ties between Chase and Royal and between Royal and National Westminster led to the formation of Orion."[14]

Although international capitalism may be as old as capitalism itself, it has taken on a new quality in the multinational corporation. Portfolio investment was characteristic of formal colonies in which there was trade of the products of the imperial centre. Usually guaranteed by the

colonial government, portfolio investment was used to create the economic infrastructure of the area – particularly canals, roads, railways,
utilities, and similar services. Direct investment, the capital expression
of multinationals, is more typical of informal empires where the government of the country in which investment is made does not usually
mediate directly in the financing and where tariff walls have been
erected either for revenue or to encourage on-site plants or the direct
extraction of resources. Markets are ensured by entering them directly,
that is, in economic rather than political terms.

While direct investment and multinationals are now characteristic of
all capitalist societies, the relative power is not evenly distributed.
Based on data for 1971, *Multinational Corporations in World Development*
shows that the United States held 52 per cent of the worldwide stock of
foreign direct investment, followed by the United Kingdom with 14.5
per cent, France with 5.8 per cent, Germany with 4.4 per cent, Switzerland with 4.1 per cent, and Canada with 3.6 per cent.* Below Canada in
the list are Japan (2.7 per cent), the Netherlands (2.2 per cent),
Sweden (2.1 per cent), Italy (2.0 per cent), and Belgium (2.0 per cent);
all other countries together account for well under five per cent.[15] Similar distribution is found when the 650 largest industrials are examined
by country, except that Japan moves from seventh to second place. The
United States alone owns 358 of these, accounting for 55 per cent. Canada owns seventeen (2.6 per cent) and is sixth on the list.[16]

In the countries listed, the source of foreign direct investment is
concentrated in a few of the largest firms. The focus of this study will
now be turned to an analysis of the foreign investments held by dominant U.S. companies, keeping in mind that this one country alone is the
home base for over half the world's largest multinationals.

II. A Profile of U.S. Expansion

When examining U.S. corporate interests outside the country it is not
necessary to study the entire U.S. social structure or even the entire
economy because only a select group of corporations and individuals
control U.S. foreign direct investment. Multinational corporations, particularly U.S. multinationals, are predominantly derived from the largest domestic corporations, a small number of which account for most of
the capital abroad. As D. Johnson points out, "Only forty-five U.S.
corporations each with investments in excess of one hundred million
dollars account for 57 per cent of all American foreign investment. One
hundred and sixty-three firms account for 80 per cent of all foreign
investment."[17]

To put U.S. foreign investment in some perspective, it should be
recognized that foreign investment flowing from the United States is

---

* Part of the Canadian direct investment is go-between and part of the investment of
others may be also, so that the U.S. share of control may be even larger.

directly related to the growth of the U.S. economy (see Chapter 3). As the U.S. economy grew, so did its foreign investments. Mira Wilkins* points out that U.S. direct investment abroad in proportion to total GNP at home in 1966 was the same as it had been in 1914 – 7 per cent (although the proportion had dropped between 1929 and 1946). Both the GNP and the amount of foreign direct investment, however, had increased twenty times over that period.[18] It is primarily the size of the U.S. economy and its continuous growth that account for increases in U.S. direct investment. The most recent period, however, has seen an increase in foreign direct investment in proportion to GNP; it was at 8 per cent by 1970 and rising faster than the domestic U.S. economy between 1955 and 1970.[19]

The best source of data on U.S. multinationals is the impressive Harvard Multinational Enterprise Project which was begun in 1966 and has been the basis for several books and theses.[20] The project focuses exclusively on industrial corporations and multinationals, however, and ignores the non-industrial economic sectors and non-multinationals. There are, obviously, great differences in the extent to which specific U.S. corporations are multinational. Size has already been discussed as a decisive criterion. Economic sector is another, as Table 6 shows. Over two-thirds of the 194 dominant corporations are multinational,† but most of the multinationals are concentrated in manufacturing (85 per cent of dominants), resources (100 per cent), and banks (85 per cent). Half the dominant trade companies are multinational, as are a third of the life insurance and other finance companies, but only 13 per cent of utilities and 6 per cent of the transportation companies.

Of the twenty dominant commercial banks, seventeen are multinational, and the three non-multinationals are the smallest of the twenty. An enormous expansion of multinational banks took place mainly in the decade of the sixties. In 1960 there were only 124 branches of U.S. banks outside the country (only nineteen of them in Europe); by 1969 there were 460 foreign branches and the main expansion was in Europe (where there were now 103).[21] While from 1953 to 1962, between $1.3 and $2.0 billion in assets of the U.S. banks were outside the United States, in 1965 this increased to $7.2 billion and by 1968 had reached $16 billion.[22] Even though there has been an increase in the number of bank branches in Europe, in 1961 over three-quarters of the foreign branches were still located in non-industrial societies outside Europe. Canada is one of the few countries where foreign banks are restricted, and it has only one U.S. bank, the Mercantile Bank. Latin America accounted for about half of the U.S. foreign branches in every year

---

* The most detailed and informed analysis of U.S. multinationals is the two-volume work of Mira Wilkins: *The Emergence of Multinational Enterprise* (1970) and *The Maturing of Multinational Enterprise* (1974).

† In the next chapter the continental operations of dominant U.S. corporations will be contrasted with the multinational operations presented here.

TABLE 6

Proportion of 194 U.S. Dominant Corporations That Are Multinational, by Economic Sector, 1975

Sector	Total Dominant*	Number Multinational†	Per Cent Multinational
TOTAL FINANCE	35	22	63
Banks	20	17	85
Life insurance	9	3	33
Other	6	2	33
TOTAL TRADE	10	5	50
TOTAL TRANSPORTATION	17	1	6
Railways	8	0	0
Airlines	7	0	0
Other	2	1	50
TOTAL UTILITIES	16	2	13
TOTAL RESOURCES	13	13	100
Metal mining	2	2	100
Oil & gas extraction	11	11	100
TOTAL MANUFACTURING	103	88	85
Food	9	9	100
Beverages	2	2	100
Tobacco	3	2	66
Textiles	1	1	100
Apparel	1	1	100
Paper & wood	7	4	57
Chemicals	9	9	100
Petroleum refining	9	9	100
Rubber	5	5	100
Pharmaceuticals	4	4	100
Soap & cosmetics	2	2	100
Glass, cement & concrete	2	2	100
Metal manufacturing	14	7	50
Metal products	3	3	100
Appliances	5	5	100
Measuring, scientific	2	2	100
Motor vehicles & parts	5	5	100
Aircraft & parts	7	4	57
Farm & industrial machinery	4	4	100
Office machinery	5	5	100
Other machinery	4	3	75
TOTAL OF ALL SECTORS	194	131	68

*The basis for selecting these 194 dominant corporations will be discussed in Chapter 6. See also Appendix V.

†"Multinational" is defined as operating in five or more countries and/or having over one-fifth of deposits in foreign countries.

(SOURCE: Various *Moody's Manuals*, company reports, and *Fortune* magazine.)

from 1918 to 1969. Among the banks, First National City Bank (Citicorp) stands out as the most powerful multinational. In 1974, it had 252 overseas branches in forty-four countries. Citicorp alone has 40 per cent of all the U.S. banks' foreign installations. It makes 45 per cent of its loans abroad and makes 62 per cent of its profits outside the country.[23] In contrast to the banks, only three of nine dominant U.S. life insurance companies and two of six other dominant finance companies can be considered multinational.

Trade is the other sector in which multinational importance is increasing. In fact, during the 1960s, trade accounted for almost the same proportion of new foreign investment as the mining sector, although both were well behind manufacturing and petroleum. While F.W. Woolworth Company has long been multinational, Sears, Roebuck and Company, the largest U.S. retailer, did not become multinational until the 1960s, and Safeway Stores expanded at the same time. Half of the largest retailers are not yet multinational.[24] Both the transportation and the utilities sectors remain essentially national corporations. The only multinational transportation company is Greyhound, and the only two multinationals in utilities are Tenneco Incorporated and El Paso Natural Gas. All of the other thirty dominant companies in transportation and utilities are national corporations.

The fact that all the dominant companies in the resource sector are multinational should come as no surprise.* In fact, many corporations that are manufacturing companies in the United States are resource companies in their multinational operations, changing sectors as they move abroad in search of natural resources to feed their manufacturing needs. For the most part, the search for raw materials by U.S. multinationals has taken place in Canada, Latin America, and, to a lesser extent, Africa and Asia. In 1964, for example, mining and smelting operations in Canada accounted for $1.7 billion, in Latin America, $1.1 billion, and in Africa, $0.4 billion of a total of $3.6 billion in U.S. direct investment in this sector, or over 90 per cent.[25]

The outstanding aspect of the manufacturing sector in terms of multinational operations is that only 15 of 103 dominants are *not* multinational. Of these, three are in the aircraft and parts sector, reflecting the national character of airlines; seven are in metal manufacturing, representing the steel industry, another sector of national character (although all but one of these fourteen metal manufacturing companies have Canadian operations, mainly in the resource sector); and three are in the pulp and wood sector (again, all having Canadian operations).

Generally, a multinational outlook pervades U.S. dominant companies, but there are marked differences by sector. For most of the multinationals the United States is the main base of operation, but for eight-

* Resource companies were the first U.S. companies to become multinational. At the turn of the century, about 60 per cent of U.S. direct investment abroad was in resources, and only 15 per cent was in manufacturing. By the 1970s, 42 per cent was in manufacturing and 36 per cent in resources (see Government of Canada, *Foreign Direct Investment in Canada*, p. 52).

een dominant companies, foreign operations accounted, in 1973, for half or more of their income.[26] The two main traditional incentives for U.S. industries to make direct investments abroad have been, first, the search for resources required for production and consumption at home, and second, market expansion to be linked to outlets for their production. Only recently have "service" types of foreign activities become prominent, often to complement U.S. business abroad, to search out profitable capital outlets, or, in the case of trade, to serve expanded retail markets.

The post-war expansion of U.S. direct investment has indeed been great, rising from $7.2 billion in 1949 to over $25 billion by 1957 and $60 billion by 1967. It has seen an increasing proportion of the whole committed to industrial sectors of the economy while high levels in resources were maintained. A much greater proportion of U.S. direct investment in the manufacturing sector has gone to industrialized nations than to underdeveloped areas, reflecting attempts by U.S. multinationals to tap these markets. Corresponding to the move of direct investment to manufacturing has been its *relative* shift away from Latin America and toward Europe, with Canada's proportion remaining fairly stable. The proportion of all U.S. direct investment in Latin America dropped steadily from 43 per cent in 1949 to 17 per cent in 1967. Europe picked up the difference, increasing from only 14 per cent in 1949 to 30 per cent by 1967; Canada ranged between 31 and 35 per cent during the period. Europe's share of manufacturing investment increased from 24 per cent in 1950 to 40 per cent by 1966. Canada, however, remains the single most important country as an outlet for U.S. direct investment and receives the lion's share in virtually all sectors, as Table 7 illustrates. Once again, there is a pattern in which Canada is a

TABLE 7

U.S. Foreign Direct Investments by Area and Sector, 1969

Area	Percentage of Investment* in				Total investment by area	
	Manufacturing	Petroleum	Mining	Other	%	($ billions)
Canada	32	24	49	32	31	$21.1
Latin America	15	20	34	27	20	13.8
E.E.C.	22	12	—	11	15	10.2
U.K.	16	9	—	7	11	7.2
Other Europe	5	6	1	13	6	4.2
Southern Dominions†	7	5	9	4	6	3.9
Asia and other Africa	5	25	7	7	11	7.4
Total in $ billions	$29.5	$18.3	$5.6	$14.3		$67.7

*Foreign direct investments are defined here as 25 per cent or more equity.
†Southern Dominions are Australia, New Zealand, and South Africa.
(SOURCE: Calculated from *Survey of Current Business*, October 1970:28.)

prime recipient in all sectors while advanced nations are high in manu-facturing and low in resources and underdeveloped areas are low in manufacturing and high in resources.

The parent corporation tends *not* to provide the funds used for U.S. direct investment, and, as U.S. multinational operations mature, it will continue to decline as a source for expansion. A U.S. Department of Commerce survey reports that between 1957 and 1959, only 25 per cent of the funds for foreign operations came from the U.S. parents, and by the more recent period 1966 to 1970, the amount was only 15 per cent. About half the funds came from internal earnings and over a quarter were borrowed outside the United States.[27]

On the other hand, foreign investment is increasingly important for the earnings of U.S. corporations, as indicated in Table 8. Domestic earnings actually dropped between 1950 and 1960, but the difference was made up by foreign earnings. Although between 1950 and 1964 domestic profits of U.S. companies increased by 66 per cent, for the same period profits from foreign operations increased by 271 per cent (and more than half of these profits came from operations in under-developed countries). The profitability of foreign enterprise is of parti-cular importance to dominant economic interests in the United States because the eight largest companies alone accounted for 25 per cent of the profits in this period, and each of them is a multinational.[28]

TABLE 8

U.S. Earnings (in $ billions), Foreign and Domestic, 1950 to 1965

	Foreign		Domestic	
	Earnings	Per cent	Earnings	Per cent
1950	$2.1	9	$21.7	91
1955	3.3	13	22.2	87
1960	4.7	19	20.6	81
1965	7.8	18	36.1	82

(SOURCE: Calculated from Magdoff, *The Age of Imperialism*, p. 183.)

Although in recent years there has been a relative shift in U.S. in-vestment away from Latin America as a greater proportion is allocated to other areas of the world, Latin America has actually experienced an increase. For example, by 1965 the United States had increased its rela-tive hold on "Third World" countries to 60 per cent of all foreign investment.[29]

III. Asymmetry in U.S.–Latin American Relations

Because such a large part of U.S. direct investment is in Latin America (next in importance only to Canada), it is valuable to examine briefly some of the implications of the presence of U.S. multinationals in that region. In this way a rough comparison with Canada can be made at the end of this chapter.

Between 1960, when the United States had a $653-million balance of trade advantage, and 1965, when the advantage had doubled to $1.3 billion, a total balance of trade of $6.4 billion favoured the United States to the deficit of Latin America.[30] Much of the deficit is attributable to the repatriation of capital by U.S. multinationals, which, for example, drew out about 98 per cent of their profits made in Latin America in 1967.[31] U.S. investment in Latin America drains capital from that region instead of providing the capital for its development. Between 1950 and 1965, when there was an outflow of direct investment to Latin America of $3.8 billion, income of $11.3 billion from this investment returned to the United States. In addition to this net deficit of $7.5 billion for Latin America, U.S. investments financed out of retained earnings and capital sources within the region increased from $4.5 billion to $10.3 billion.[32] In the five years from 1960 to 1965, income on all U.S. investment in Latin America totalled $6.4 billion, 73 per cent of it from direct investment. In 1960 the total income from all U.S. investment was $858 million; by 1965 it had increased 45 per cent to $1.25 billion.[33]

Relative to return on investment from all "Third World" countries in 1964, the average return on U.S. investment in Latin America amounted to 17.6 per cent, without adding "invisible" payments.[34] Invisible payments cover the costs of debt service, royalties, and other financial services. Payments for Latin America's invisible financial services from 1961 to 1963 amounted to 40 per cent of its foreign exchange earnings, and payments for foreign transportation and other services were another 21.5 per cent, together totalling 61.5 per cent of Latin America's foreign exchange earnings without receipt of any goods in return.[35]

U.S. aid to Latin America constitutes a method of promoting U.S. corporate capitalism there and subsidizes U.S. multinationals. U.S. foreign aid typically takes the form of tied loans, not grants, and is designed to subsidize U.S. agriculture and industry. For example, between 1948 and 1958 more than half the goods shipped under the foreign aid program went in ships registered in the United States, and 68 per cent of the aid money had to be spent in the United States.[36] Built into the U.S. Foreign Assistance Act is a provision that the President is to cut off aid in the event of actions by recipients against U.S. corporations.[37] The act also forces the recipients to buy in the U.S. market, so that 95 per cent of the payments for machinery and vehicles in the mid-sixties were made to U.S. companies while 90 per cent of all AID (Act for International Development) payments were to U.S. corporations.[38] The result has been that 11 per cent of all U.S. exports come directly from foreign aid.[39] Foreign aid, therefore, keeps markets abroad open for U.S. products while tying recipients further into the U.S. economy with increased debt. Foreign aid is the "price" the United States pays for maintaining its economic empire, although direct interventions do occasionally have to be called upon to supplement control by co-optation.

U.S.-owned manufacturing plants in Latin America are primarily oriented toward capturing local markets and bypassing tariffs. For example, the sales of U.S.-owned manufactured goods in Latin America for 1965 amounted to $5,073 million (92.5 per cent) locally, $101 million (1.8 per cent) in exports to the United States, and $310 million in other exports (5.7 per cent).[40] Ironically, as Wilkins reports,

> by 1970 the book value of U.S. direct investments in manufacturing in Latin America *as a whole* remained less than such stakes in either Canada or the United Kingdom. The reason lay in currency depreciations, smaller markets (because of low per capita income), and political uncertainty. But even if the rise in U.S. direct investments in manufacturing in Latin America was not as dramatic as that in Europe, the additions to U.S. stakes in Latin American manufacturing in response to host government pressures were unquestionably important. Indeed, the very import-substitution by direct foreign investors that took place *because* of governments' nationalistic measures came to be regarded by Latin American nationalists as a new cause for alarm over foreign domination.[41]

The tariff walls that were created within Latin America after the Second World War had an effect comparable to that of Canada's National Policy tariffs. But while there are parallels between Latin America and Canada in relation to the United States, there are also marked differences that need to be taken into account. Much of the dissimilarity results from Canada's own foreign investments.

IV. Foreign Investment in the United States

Before turning to Canadian foreign investments, the phenomenon of foreign investment in the United States should be examined, but briefly, because it has had little impact. Overall, at the year end of 1969, foreigners had claims of $91 billion on the United States while the United States had $141 billion in claims on other countries. But even this difference is deceptive because over half the U.S. claims abroad were in the form of subsidiaries and branches whereas only 16 per cent of foreign claims on the United States were in this form. In fact, over a third of the foreigners' claims on the United States were in the form of bank claims, compared to less than a tenth in the opposite direction.[42] The country with the greatest amount of foreign investment in the United States in 1969 was Britain with $3.5 billion (almost 30 per cent of the total), followed by Canada with $2.4 billion (or about one-quarter of the total), the Netherlands (17 per cent), Switzerland (12 per cent), Germany (5 per cent), France (3 per cent), and Japan (2 per cent).[43]

By the end of 1974, all foreign direct investment in the United States totalled $26.5 billion. Again Britain led, but now with only 21 per cent of the total, followed by Canada with 20 per cent ($5.3 billion) and the Netherlands with 18 per cent.[44] While undeniably large in value, these investments have virtually no impact on control of the U.S. economy.

Only seventeen of the *Fortune* 500* for 1975 are controlled outside the United States, and only two of these are in the Top 200 (Shell Oil, no. 14, with 42 per cent held in the Netherlands and 28 per cent in Britain, and Standard Oil Company (Ohio), no. 87, with 25 per cent held by British Petroleum). Three "Canadian" companies appear on the 500 list: Joseph E. Seagram & Sons (no. 257), 100 per cent Canadian-owned; Texasgulf Incorporated (no. 304), of which 30 per cent is held by the Canada Development Corporation; and ESB Incorporated (no. 380), 100 per cent controlled by International Nickel of Canada. The Netherlands and Britain control three joint ventures and three companies each in the Top 500; Belgium, Switzerland, Japan, and France have one each, and there is an additional British-French joint venture. Therefore, British direct investment is involved in seven of the seventeen companies, Dutch in six, and Canadian in three, and these are the only other multiple representations in the list.[45]

Other Canadian companies have U.S. operations, but they are smaller than the *Fortune* 500. The following companies expanded their U.S. operations in 1974: Bell Canada (over $1 million in construction, investment, and acquisition of AVM Corporation), Moore Corporation ($7 million in expansion and construction), Massey-Ferguson (over $1 million in construction and joint ventures), Noranda Mines ($70 million in expansion), and MacMillan Bloedel ($8 million in acquisition and construction).[46]

The average annual rate of growth of Canadian direct investment in the United States between 1962 and 1971 was 5.8 per cent, compared to an average rate of 7.9 per cent for the same period by U.S. direct investment in Canada. Similarly, in 1962 Canadian investment in the United States was 17.0 per cent of U.S. investment in Canada, but by 1971 this ratio had fallen to 13.9 per cent. U.S. investment was penetrating the Canadian economy faster and to a much greater extent in the decade of the sixties than Canadian direct investment capital vis-à-vis the United States.[47]

* The *Fortune* 500 is an annual listing of the five hundred largest industrial corporations in the United States, ranked by sales.

Foreign investment in the United States is restricted "in defense or other industries vital to the national interest such as nuclear energy, transportation and communication," but other areas are open. In 1973, however, there was an increase of $3.5 billion in foreign direct investment in the United States, raising the total to $20 billion (compared to $120 billion in U.S. direct investment abroad). These developments created some concern, particularly regarding the bid to take over Lockheed Aircraft (subsequently blocked) and reports of Iran's interest in Pan American World Airways.[48]

Early in 1975, the Zarb Report issued by the U.S. Federal Energy Administration (FEA) focused on the matter of foreign investments in the United States, particularly in the energy field. It found $4.4 billion in foreign direct investment in this sector (compared to U.S. foreign oil interests of $30 billion), or under 12 per cent of the total investment in U.S. energy. "Four European-based companies – the United Kingdom's Burmah and British Petroleum, Belgium's Petrofina and the Netherlands' Shell – 'account for more than 90 per cent of the foreign ownership control' the FEA report said."[49] Foreign investment in U.S. oil reflects the worldwide concentration in this resource; oil is the only area with any significant foreign ownership within the United States.

The United States appears to have little reason to fear the oil countries' investments. Rose reports that OPEC (Organization of Petroleum Exporting Countries) had under $100 million in direct investments in the United States in 1974, and these were mainly in real estate and some small banks. He says that "the OPEC countries have put nearly all their money into portfolio investments – i.e., bank deposits, bonds, and noncontrolling stock purchases. Robert Gerard is a high Treasury official who makes it his business to keep track of OPEC investments in the U.S. Says he, 'From everything we have been able to learn, the OPEC investor is behaving like a nervous grandma who turns her money over to Morgan Guaranty and says: "Here, invest it as conservatively as possible."'"[50]

Indeed, although the U.S. government has been quick to respond, there is little basis for this concern over any foreign investment in the United States, certainly not compared to that expressed elsewhere over U.S. investments in the rest of the world. Total foreign direct investments in the United States amount to less than 18 per cent of the same type of U.S. investment abroad. Foreign direct investment is essentially a one-way street: from the United States to Canada, to Latin America, and to Europe, with little traffic in the opposite direction. On a world scale, oil is the only exception to this general pattern; on the continental level, the exceptions are in those areas where Canadian capitalists have their strength.

V. Canadian Foreign Investment – Is It Merely Go-Between?

The relationship between the United States and Latin America is, theoretically at least, quite simple: the United States is the centre economy and Latin America is its periphery. The United States operates directly in Latin America through multinational corporations, whose primary purpose is to extract resources for use in the United States and to provide an expanded market for manufactured products. Canada's economic relationships with other countries are not so easily summarized because Canada is simultaneously an importer and an exporter of foreign direct investment and a substantial part of the exported direct investment goes through foreign-controlled branch plants in Canada.

Speaking of Canada's international investment position up to 1914, Tom Naylor says:

> Capital exports went almost exclusively to two areas – to the United States and to the Caribbean and South America. Since the one was a major metropolis and the others economic hinterlands, the role performed by the Canadian ventures in the two areas was very different. The American investments represented substantial outflows of capital from Canada: the others did not, for the South American and Caribbean investments were devices for draining funds from these areas.[51]

Even at this early period, Canada was playing two roles as investor, a subordinate one in the United States and a dominant one in conjunction with the United States and Britain in Latin America (including the Caribbean). To Latin America, Canada was a metropolitan nation with aggressive investment policies, but at the same time Canada was subject to similar kinds of forces from the United States. Only an unevenly developed economy in Canada could have produced these different projections abroad and, as was demonstrated earlier, this uneven development has characterized and continues to characterize Canada.

Naylor places Canadian foreign investments prior to 1914 in seven categories, depending on the nature of the activity and whether it was dominant or subordinate:

> (1) Bank establishments in the United States to facilitate capital movements and commodity exchange between the U.S. and Canada....
> (2) Insurance companies established branches in the U.S. which, unlike the banks, actively solicited business there. However, the insurance companies were substantial net exporters of capital from Canada [holding large U.S. portfolios]....
> (3) Railway extensions and operations in the U.S. were considerable [but essentially extensions of Canadian operations]....
> (4) A sizeable amount of individual, as well as institutional, portfolio investments existed in the U.S.

(5) The smallest group of Canadian investments in the U.S. were direct investments in industry, horizontally or vertical extensions of Canadian oligopolies....

(6) A network of banks was established across the Caribbean...active in developing and dominating local banking business. Insurance companies, too, established a dominant position in local business. Both extracted funds for export back to Canada, and their holdings of local securities were virtually non-existent.

(7) Railways and utilities operations in Latin America...were designed to develop local traffic and resources. The utilities were generally wholly owned direct investments.[52]

Many of these early ventures into Latin America were within the context of the British Empire, in which commercial capitalists took the dominant part. These Canadian capitalists acted as intermediaries in the world capitalist system, especially in Latin America. According to Naylor, "Canadian banks and insurance companies abroad played an indispensible [sic] role in the promotion of these enterprises.... The Commerce, for example, serviced the Rio and Sao Paulo utilities, the Bank of Montreal served as banker for some of the principal Mexican operations, while Herbert Holt's Royal Bank backed Van Horne's Caribbean escapades."[53] Developments in Latin America paralleled those in Canada, even down to including the same men; "utility and railway promotions in Latin America...were undertaken by the same groups of Montreal and Toronto financiers in the same alliances."[54] A prominent example of such ventures at the turn of the century was Brazilian Traction, Light, Heat and Power Corporation (now Brascan), a holding company created by Canada's foremost financiers – among them Edward Rogers Wood and the Hon. Senator George Albertus Cox – who were intimately associated with Dominion Securities and many other financial activities.[55] Some of the men involved with Brascan were also behind the push of Canadian banks and insurance companies abroad. But with the withdrawal of the British Empire following World War I, much of the financial, political, and military support necessary to sustain these developments by Canadian capitalists also receded. Although some of these early companies continue today, a new twist has been added to many recent "Canadian" ventures in Latin America.

The pattern of "Canada's foreign investment" outside of North America must be seen in the context of the degree of U.S. control of Canada's resources and manufacturing. Most of Canada's foreign direct investment now is in the United States, but to say this does not correctly reflect Canada's total position. For example, in 1968, 55 per cent of Canada's direct investment was located in the United States but produced only 41 per cent of its income receipts from all foreign sources. Britain returned only 8 per cent of the receipts from 12 per cent invested. But a different situation existed relative to other countries; although they received only 33 per cent of Canadian direct investment, areas outside the United States and Britain returned 52 per cent of the income.[56]

Recently, an increasing share of Canadian direct investment has veered away from the United States. Although Canadian direct investment in the United States was increasing in dollar value from \$2.041 billion to \$3.251 billion from 1965 to 1970, it was falling from 59 to 53 per cent of the total.[57] The pattern with respect to portfolio investment, however, is different; it remains the pattern Naylor observed for the turn of the century. Canada's portfolio investment abroad in 1970 was \$2.7 billion, and 85 per cent of it was mainly in stocks of corporations.[58] Since 85 per cent of Canadian portfolio investment is located in the United States, there is no need to examine movements of Canada's portfolio capital to the rest of the world. Nevertheless, about half of the Canadian direct investment abroad is located outside the United States and this fact requires a more detailed analysis. But first, Canada's overall place in the capital market must be indicated.

By 1973, Canada had assets abroad of about \$30 billion and external liabilities totalling about \$63 billion.[59] In other words, about twice as much foreign capital was invested in Canada as Canada had invested in other countries. The two facts are not unrelated, and the nature of their relationship requires that an important distinction be drawn in all statistics measuring Canada's role in Latin America. This is the distinction between Canadian-controlled investment abroad and investment originating with foreign-controlled companies operating out of Canada. The first is *indigenous* Canadian foreign investment, the second *go-between* investment. One reflects the relatively autonomous power position of Canada, the other Canada's dependent position within the context of U.S. capital.*

Table 9 shows where the two types of "Canadian" foreign direct investment go by sector. It should be kept in mind that all these statistics exclude banks and insurance companies (because they report to other agencies), which will be dealt with in detail shortly. The difference between indigenous and go-between foreign direct investment is mainly in the areas of utilities and railways, where Canadian-controlled companies dominate, and in manufacturing, petroleum, and mining, where foreign-controlled companies are pre-eminent.

Between 1969 and 1970, an important shift occurred in the distribution of indigenous and go-between foreign direct investment by country of destination. This resulted mainly from a "new" investment

---

* Changes in classification now make them difficult to use for aggregate analysis of change. The *Fortune* list of Top 300 industrials outside the United States now lists U.S. subsidiaries as Canadian companies (with the result that five "Canadian" companies have been added to the list: Ford, Imperial Oil, Gulf Oil, Texaco, and General Electric) but excludes subsidiaries of comparable size (General Motors, Chrysler, and IBM). Shell Canada is also excluded because it is consolidated with the U.K./Netherlands' parent, Royal Dutch/Shell Group. Also included among the twenty "Canadian" companies are Alcan and INCO, both with substantial foreign holdings but neither a branch plant (see *Financial Post* 27 Sept. 1975:C-4).

TABLE 9

Types of Canadian Direct Investment Abroad
by Industry, 1970

Industry	Per Cent Indigenous	Per Cent Go-between
Manufacturing	49.2	56.8
Merchandising	2.0	9.3
Petroleum	6.2	11.2
Mining	3.8	10.4
Railways	7.7	0.8
Other utilities	21.1	2.1
Financial*	7.3	6.0
Other	2.8	3.4
	100	100

*Banks and life insurance, Canada's two key areas of foreign investment, are not included here, thus making the comparison somewhat deceptive.
(SOURCE: Canada, *Canada's International Investment Position, 1968 to 1970*, p. 29, Statement 10.)

classification of almost $600 million by a utilities company in South and Central America.[60] As a result of this government reclassification, the pattern of investment in developing and developed countries has changed for the indigenous and go-between types of investment. In 1969, only 12 per cent of indigenous direct investment went to developing countries (a rise of only one percentage point since 1965), but it jumped to 26 per cent in 1970. Conversely, go-between investment in developing countries appears to decline from 24 per cent to 22 per cent in 1970. In spite of these changes through reclassification, there were still important differences with respect to the location of the two types of direct investment, as Table 10 shows. Again (keeping in mind that banks and insurance companies are excluded), these figures show that indigenous investment has pulled well ahead of go-between investment in South and Central America, rising from only $67 million to $656 million between 1969 and 1970, although the increase is mainly a reflection of the reclassification noted earlier.* On the other hand, go-between direct foreign investment exceeds indigenous investment in Europe outside the E.E.C. and in Africa, Asia (by about four times), and Australasia (by about three times).

A few very large firms are the source of most Canadian direct investment abroad (again aside from banks and life insurance companies). The concentration is even higher than that among companies in the

*This shift in indigenous foreign investment in South and Central America "was principally a result of the reclassification to direct from portfolio investment of the overseas investments of a major enterprise. This enterprise, previously accorded the special tax status of a foreign business corporation, began to establish sizeable diversified investments in Canada" (Canada, *Canada's International Investment Position, 1968 to 1970*, p. 23). The company is probably Brascan, although it is not certain.

United States. Statistics Canada concludes from the data in Table 11: "While about 800 Canadian enterprises had direct investments abroad in 1970 with a value of $6.2 billion, 11 enterprises alone accounted for

TABLE 10

Canadian Direct Investment Abroad by Location and Type of Control, 1970

Location	Canadian Enterprises Controlled from			
	Canadian (Indigenous)	U.S./Other (Go-between)	Canadian (Indigenous)	U.S./Other (Go-between)
	($millions)		(percentages)	
United States	2,339	912	58.0	42.4
Other North America	282	226	7.0	10.5
South & Central America	656	164	16.3	7.6
United Kingdom	328	258	8.1	12.0
E.E.C.	203	101	5.0	4.7
Other Europe	77	108	1.9	5.0
Africa	61	73	1.5	3.4
Asia	27	107	0.7	5.0
Australasia	63	203	1.6	9.4
Total	4,036	2,152	100	100
Developed	2,998	1,677	74.3	77.9
Developing	1,038	475	25.7	22.1

(SOURCE: Calculated from Canada, *Canada's International Investment Position, 1968 to 1970*, p. 92, Table 4.)

TABLE 11

Canadian Direct Investment Abroad, by Type of Control and Size of Investment, 1970

	Number	$ Millions	% Total	Average Size ($ millions)
INDIGENOUS Investment of				
over $100 m.	8	2,861	70.9	357.6
$25-100 m.	13	561	13.9	43.2
ALL	539	4,036	100	7.5
GO-BETWEEN Investment of				
over $100 m.	3	1,183	55.0	394.3
$25-100 m.	10	533	24.8	53.3
ALL	257	2,152	100	8.4

(SOURCE: Calculated from Canada, *Canada's International Investment Position, 1968 to 1970*, p. 94, Table 6.)

two thirds of the total."[61] Although go-between investments averaged somewhat larger than indigenous investments, there were twenty-one indigenous investments of over $25 million but only thirteen go-between. Alone, these twenty-one indigenous investments accounted for 85 per cent of all investments of this type while the thirteen go-between investments accounted for 80 per cent in that category. Although the number of companies is small, the average size of the largest investments is very substantial.

A specific examination must now be made of the central source of indigenous Canadian foreign investments, the banks and life insurance companies. There are thirteen dominant Canadian life insurance companies, accounting for 93 per cent of the assets of all such companies in Canada and 89 per cent of the gross income and 95 per cent of the net income of all life insurance companies in Canada. Over 25 per cent of the insurance in force of ten companies out of the thirteen is outside Canada.* None of the next seven largest companies has as much as 25 per cent of insurance in force outside Canada. In other words, the ten multinational life insurance companies are all dominant in Canada. Measured in terms of assets outside Canada, all of the multinationals have at least 10 per cent of their assets located outside Canada, ranging as high as 55 per cent (Manufacturers Life, with Sun Life close behind at 53 per cent). The three dominant insurance companies that are not multinational have a maximum of 0.3 per cent of their assets outside Canada. Of the multinational dominants, two have over 50 per cent of their assets outside Canada, six have between 25 per cent and 50 per cent, and the remaining two have 22 per cent and 11 per cent, for an average of 43 per cent. Great West Life is a dominant company with 44 per cent of its insurance in force outside of Canada, but this amount is completely concentrated in the United States. In fact, most of the foreign insurance in force of the multinationals is located in the United States or the United Kingdom; nevertheless, a substantial amount resides in other nations, such as the $1,215 million in South Africa, the $734 million in Jamaica, and the $270 million in Trinidad and Tobago. Particular companies tend to concentrate their business in specific nations.

In banking, the other part of the cornerstone of indigenous Canadian capitalism, the same multinational pattern among dominant companies emerges. There are five dominant banks in Canada, accounting for 90 per cent of the assets, 91 per cent of the income, and 91 per cent of the net income of all banks in Canada. All five dominants have multinational operations, but some are more heavily involved than others. Two criteria have been used to determine which chartered banks are multinational: the number of branches outside Canada and the foreign hold-

* Parts *a*, *b*, and *c* of Appendix III provide detailed information on the foreign operations of Canada's dominant life insurance companies, including insurance in force and assets held outside Canada.

ings of the chartered banks.* The first criterion has to do with ways in which deposits are received and other traditional banking activities, while the other measures the degree of each bank's corporate control through ownership. Respecting bank branches outside Canada in 1972, the Bank of Montreal had ten, five of which were located in the United States (it also had holdings in ten countries); the Bank of Nova Scotia had sixty-nine, forty-one of them located in the West Indies; the Canadian Imperial Bank of Commerce had fifty-seven, twenty-three in the United States and thirty-two in the West Indies; the Toronto-Dominion Bank had only four, the fewest of all the five dominant banks (although it did have holdings in six countries);† and finally, the Royal Bank had eighty-five, the most of all, with fifty-eight located in the West Indies. All the dominant banks have extensive direct holdings outside Canada. The Royal Bank, for example, holds 100 per cent of seven international companies, including the Royal Bank Trust Company (West Indies) Limited, which has subsidiaries in Jamaica, Barbados, Trinidad, Guyana, and the Cayman Islands.

Although banks and insurance companies as a group have the most extensive multinational operations of all the companies controlled by the indigenous Canadian capitalist class, some other prominent indigenous companies are also active in this respect. For example, Massey-Ferguson has 90 per cent of its sales, 62 per cent of production, and 84 per cent of its assets outside Canada and operates subsidiaries in twenty-two foreign countries.° George Weston Limited, another dominant Canadian company, has extensive multinational operations.[62] Others in this category (or their subsidiaries) include Brascan, Canron, Cominco, Consolidated-Bathurst, Distillers Corporation–Seagrams, Hiram Walker Gooderham and Worts, Hollinger Mines, Laurentide Financial, Montreal Trust, Moore Corporation, Noranda Mines, Northern Telecom, Royal Trust, and the Steel Company of Canada. There are also companies in Canada that are themselves substantially foreign controlled and have extensive foreign holdings: Anglo-Canadian Telephone, Canadian International Power, Dominion Bridge, Falconbridge

---

* Parts *a* and *b* of Appendix IV provide detailed information on the foreign operations of Canada's dominant banks, including branches outside Canada and foreign holdings.
† For the year end October 1976, the Toronto-Dominion Bank, the least multinational of the five dominant banks, had made $23.2 million of its after-tax balance of revenue from foreign operations. This amounted to one-quarter of its total after-tax revenue of $92.1 million. Moreover, 37 per cent of its total assets in 1976 were in the form of foreign currency assets. It may be safely concluded that the Toronto-Dominion is a multinational bank (*Globe and Mail* 9 Dec. 1976: B16).
° "70%-75% of the net sales for Massey in 1975 [were] outside North America, while 75%-80% of the U.S. firms' [International Harvester and John Deere] sales were *in* North America. Massey has been world-oriented for 25 years" (*Financial Post* 13 March 1976:21). For a detailed study of this company, see E.P. Neufeld's *A Global Corporation: A History of the International Development of Massey Ferguson Limited.*

Nickel Mines,* Ford Motor Company of Canada, McIntyre Mines, Pacific Petroleums, Patino Mines, Rio Algom Mines, Sherritt Gordon Mines, and Westcoast Petroleum. Two other Canadian-based multinationals, Alcan Aluminium and International Nickel Company, have substantial holdings from outside Canada.†

Along with the banks and life insurance companies, two holding companies are giants among the multinationals. One is Power Corporation, which controls at least five major Canadian multinationals: Laurentide Financial Corporation, Montreal Trust, Great West Life, Imperial Life, and Consolidated-Bathurst. The other is Argus Corporation, important because of its 16 per cent controlling interest in Massey-Ferguson and its 20.3 per cent interest in Hollinger Mines, which in turn holds 10 per cent of Noranda Mines, which has 26 per cent of Placer Development; all four companies are multinationals. Between them these two dominant holding companies have substantial ownership in at least five major Canadian multinationals in the production sector. Companies in the transportation/utilities service sector are also active through production-based multinationals such as Cominco, a subsidiary of Canadian Pacific, or Northern Telecom, a subsidiary of Bell Canada.

If it can be demonstrated that part of the indigenous Canadian capitalist class is able to operate internationally – that is, if it is not merely go-between – the case for its internal strength in Canada is reinforced. It would be difficult to argue that the Canadian capitalists who control these powerful corporations are merely go-between. It is correct, however, to say that a substantial part of so-called Canadian foreign investment is merely go-between. While not all members of the indigenous elite in Canada engage in multinational operations, it is apparent that many do. Canadian capitalists who do operate multinationally tend to be at the commanding heights of the Canadian economy.

The pattern of foreign direct investment sent out from Canada is a reflection of the internal pattern seen earlier. The Canadian-controlled component tends to be centred in finance and transportation/utilities, and many of the Canadian manufacturing and resource companies represented abroad are tied to the Canadian holding companies, Power Corporation and Argus Corporation. The foreign-controlled or go-between component is almost exclusively in manufacturing and resources.

One of the few detailed studies of Canada's investment abroad is

---

* John Deverell's *Falconbridge: Portrait of a Canadian Multinational* is an important case study of a company controlled in the United States (by Superior Oil and the Howard B. Keck family) but operating from a Canadian base.

† For a more detailed examination of these two companies, see Chapter 6. Pierre Bourgault says that Alcan "does have a large part of its product development in the U.K." while INCO "does most of its product development in the U.S." This suggests that the fact that they are Canadian based has little impact on Canada's technological development (*Innovation and the Structure of Canadian Industry*, p. 126).

Canada-West Indies Economic Relations, by Kari Levitt and Alister McIntyre. They found that "in the fields of banking, insurance, and bauxite-alumina production Canadian investment not only is significant, but is the main portion of investment in each of those particular industries." [63] The financial operations were Canadian controlled and based in Canada. Half of Canadian investment in the West Indies was located in Jamaica, with further concentration in Guyana and the remainder of the eastern Caribbean. About three-fifths of the Canadian investment in the area was in bauxite-alumina and a little under one-fifth in finance, with lesser amounts in utilities, agriculture, manufacturing and other areas. Outside the sectors of banking and insurance, Canadian capital lagged "far behind the United States and Britain," particularly in "the new manufacturing sectors...it is estimated that American companies account for nearly 80% of the direct investment that has taken place since the 1950's." Banking in Jamaica is dominated by the Bank of Nova Scotia, which has been there since 1889, and in the rest of the Caribbean the Royal Bank, along with the British-controlled Barclay's Bank, dominates. In the insurance business, Canadian companies are dominant in the entire Caribbean, controlling 70 per cent of the business. [64] In Jamaica they account for 21 per cent of the insurance in force with North American Life the dominant company; Confederation Life and Crown Life dominate in Trinidad and Tobago, Crown Life and Imperial Life in the Bahamas. In Guyana it is North American Life and in the Dominican Republic Confederation Life. Although these operations in underdeveloped areas may not be crucial to the companies themselves, they do dominate *some* sectors of these small societies and withdraw capital from these areas. In one area of manufacturing, distilling in Jamaica, it is a Canadian-controlled firm, Distillers Corporation–Seagrams, that dominates.

The same general pattern appears in Central and South America, with over three-quarters of Canadian investment located in only seven countries: Argentina, Brazil, the Dominican Republic, Mexico, the Netherlands Antilles, Peru, and Venezuela. [65] Brazil is another area where a review of Canadian investment has been done. Here Canada accounted for only 7 per cent of all foreign investment in 1974 and was in fifth position behind the United States, West Germany, Japan, and Switzerland. Nevertheless, Brazilian operations are important for specific Canadian-controlled companies. In 1974, Brascan sent half of its $108-million profit from Brazilian business back to Canada, and Massey-Ferguson sent back a third of its $10-million profit. [66] Massey-Ferguson controls 50 per cent of the tractor market in Brazil. Brascan is well known for its utility operations in Brazil, begun in 1901, but recently, in conjunction with MacMillan Bloedel, the company has been moving into development of a forest products industry and is involved in another venture with Swift-Armour. Besides being Brazil's largest private utility company, Brascan now has over thirty other operations "including a pineapple plantation, breweries, hotels, cable television and financial services.''[67]* More than thirty major Canadian companies are active in Brazil. These companies clearly profit from their Brazilian activities, but they are not in a position to dominate the Brazilian economy, except in such specific areas as utilities and tractors. Otherwise the dominant external force in the area is the United States. While Canadian multinationals cannot be said to have dominated any of these areas in the way U.S. multinationals have, they were helped into the region first as protégés of the British Empire (particularly in the Caribbean) and now in the wake of the United States. They depend to a large extent on the climate created and maintained by the United States in its sphere of influence (reinforced by political and military control) for their continued operation. Thus some Canadian capitalists have enjoyed great privileges within that sphere of influence.

The Statistics Canada publication *Canada's International Investment Position* offers the following explanation of "Canadian" direct investment abroad:

A significant amount represents the direct extension of corresponding activities of the owners in Canada or developments ancillary to their Canadian operations. Broadly representing the extension of Canadian enterprises are investments abroad in beverages, agricultural implements, mining and smelting, pulp and paper, automobiles, business forms, merchandising and petroleum. A further part of Canadian direct investment abroad is related to the provision of raw materials, such as bauxite, for Canadian enterprises, and yet another is the direct extension of transportation facilities such as Canadian owned railway and pipeline facilities in the United States.[68]

Other factors mentioned are markets, socio-political ties, "country of control of the investing enterprise," and historical factors (Commonwealth ties and tariff preferences). In mining, for example, Canadian-controlled companies have made only 4 per cent of their direct investment, but foreign-controlled companies have put in over 10 per cent. This suggests that Canadian direct investment in mining primarily reflects a worldwide operation rather than a particularly Canadian extension into the world economy. On the other hand, finance and utilities are held under strong Canadian control, and their extensive operations emanate from powerful indigenous sectors and are thus Canadian initiated.

As the number and size of Canadian multinationals have grown, so have political and business support agencies to reinforce the extension of these multinationals into the world. It should be made clear, however, that politically and militarily, Canada has not attempted to protect these multinational operations directly, nor would it be likely to suc-

---

* J.H. Moore, president of Brascan, recently argued in favour of "bigness" so that his company can "compete efficiently in world markets." Of Brascan's $2.25 billion in investments, "only" $293 million are in Canada (mainly in John Labatt Ltd.); most of the rest are in Brazil, with some mining interests in the United States and Australia (*Globe and Mail* 7 May 1976: B1; 3 June 1976: B5).

ceed in such an attempt. This does not say that the Canadian state has not provided other types of support, only that it does not have the international power to provide the type of political/military umbrella the United States can provide. But to some extent, the U.S. umbrella also protects Canadian operations within the U.S. sphere of influence.

The Canadian state provides a number of services to multinationals including the Trade Commissioner Service, which has seventy-nine trade offices in fifty-six countries. "Its primary role is to promote Canada's export trade and generally to protect its commercial interests abroad," and it provides marketing consultants, searches out foreign buyers, recommends "modes of distribution and suitable agents," and furnishes tariff, exchange control, and other information. "At no time, however, does a commissioner handle any money since he is not an agent but rather provides personalized assistance to the Canadian exporter in his territory."[69]

Another government agency assisting multinationals is the Export Development Corporation (EDC); "it is the purpose of the EDC to facilitate the development of Canada's export trade by providing insurance, guarantees, loans and other financial facilities that enable Canadian firms to meet international credit competition." A twelve-man board (a chairman and six directors from the civil service and five from "private business") administers its affairs. Two of the private businessmen in 1971 were Paul Leman, president of Alcan (which has received $14.7 million in credits from the agency) and the late A.F. Mayne, at that time president of Kennecott Canada and director of six other "Canadian" multinationals. In 1971, 85 per cent of the EDC insurance coverage was in Africa, Asia, Latin America, and the Caribbean. One EDC loan of note (over $26 million) was made to Brazil and in 1971 was guaranteed by the Brazilian government. It stipulated that $23 million of the $26.5 million must be used to buy equipment from seven "Canadian" companies, all foreign-owned (six in the United States and one in Britain).[70]

Private associations have also emerged to support multinational activity. One such agency is the Pacific Basin Economic Council (PBEC), which, according to its sixteen-page advertisement in *Fortune* (September 1972), "is a unique organization operating in the interests of private enterprise under a covenant pledging its membership to strengthen business and economic relationships among its member countries and to generate greater economic and social progress among the developing countries of the Pacific region." The explicit political nature of this organization was indicated by K.H.J. Clark, president of PBEC and also of the International Nickel Company of Canada, when he said, "Many of the action proposals our committees are studying have to be implemented by or with governmental co-operation so PBEC is keeping in touch with the national governments of the five member states and with the developing nations of the Pacific region."

Canadian involvement in PBEC can be seen on two levels, one the fact that "150 Canadian corporations have taken an active interest in

PBEC" and the other, the high degree of Canadian participation in the executive. In addition to Clark as president, other Canadians are W.D.H. Frechette, director-general (also an executive vice-president of the Canadian Manufacturers' Association), W.D.H. Gardiner, a committee chairman (also vice-president of the Royal Bank), J.H. Stevens, deputy chairman of economic development (also president of Canada Wire and Cable), and A.H. Hart, Q.C., chairman of the transportation committee (also a senior vice-president of Canadian National Railways). Through organizations like PBEC, Canadian multinationals are attempting to open the way for future foreign investments and extend their corporate interests to underdeveloped areas of the world, in this instance co-operating with the United States, Australia, New Zealand, and Japan.

Canadian businessmen are also active in the Inter-American Development Bank[71] and other associations, one of the most important being the Canadian Association for Latin America. It was formed in 1969, "largely on the initiative of Grant Glassco and Robert Winters of Brascan" and now has 140 members. "Half the association's annual budget of $180,000 comes from its members. The other half comes about equally from a grant from the Department of External Affairs and a contract with the Canadian International Development Agency." Its current president is Thomas Bata of Bata Shoes, which has eighty-seven shoe manufacturing plants in various parts of the world. [72]

Outside of banking and insurance and a few specific areas, Canadian indigenous capitalism is not strong internationally, although it does have an international presence. But within banking it is important. As W. Earle McLaughlin, chief executive of the Royal Bank, told the Vancouver Board of Trade, "In international trade and finance, we *are* big.... Certainly as far as international trade is concerned, it has been an advantage to be big. We have been able to operate successfully in the international sphere because we are big and people have confidence in us."[73]

VI. A Comparative View of the Countries of the Western Hemisphere

From a comparative perspective, the economic relations of the United States with Canada have been less "troublesome" than those with Latin America, for a variety of reasons – proximity, language, similar form of government. But two further reasons, perhaps less obvious, have also been important. First, because the United States entered Canada industrially on the ground floor, its industrial dominance grew as the industrial and resource sectors grew. As U.S. industrials moved in, they usually did not have to oust *powerful* capitalists already in these sectors. Second, U.S. branch plants provided just what the powerful commercial capitalists wanted in their search for secure outlets and production for their capital to serve. The U.S. companies were a safe surrogate for the rough-and-ready competition of indigenous industrialists.

It was not until after the Second World War that the United States became a global power of the first order, but much earlier it had become a continental power. While it has expanded in both respects in the last thirty years, the United States has continued to show great interest in the continental economy because that was its first and easiest place of expansion. It has even been argued that "success" in Canadian operations stimulated U.S. multinationals to move further abroad. I.A. Litvak and C.J. Maule suggest that "one might even argue that Canada has inadvertently been a catalyst to this growth. The success of U.S. subsidiaries in Canada has motivated many a 'parent firm' to extend its international operations – an intermediary step in evolving into a multinational corporation."[74] Canada's go-between role has had many dimensions.

Two factors distinguish Canadian multinational activity from that of the United States. Size is the first and most obvious. With only one-eleventh the population of the United States, even if Canada operated abroad to the same degree, its impact would still be overwhelmed by the U.S. presence. The second and not so obvious factor is the go-between nature that we have observed, indicative of the high degree of foreign control within the resource and manufacturing sectors of the Canadian economy. Although in areas of indigenous strength, particularly finance and utilities, there is a long-standing thrust of investment from Canada to Latin America, the overall standing of Canada within the hemisphere is still a paradoxical one displaying simultaneous dependence and dominance.

The comparative places of Canada and the United States are evident in Table 12, which summarizes over a three-year period the flow of direct investment and income from investment both into and out of these countries. The figures show that (on an annual average) U.S. corporations have made more direct investment by $2,894 million in the rest of the world than the rest of the world has made in the United

TABLE 12

Annual Flows of Direct Investment and Investment Income, United States and Canada, Average for 1968 to 1970 *($ millions)*

| | DIRECT INVESTMENT | | | INCOME FROM DIRECT INVESTMENT | | |
	Inward	Outward	Net	Inward	Outward	Net
United States	727	-3,621	-2,894	8,107	-866	7,241
Canada	651	-274	378	171	-579	-408

(SOURCE: United Nations, *Multinational Corporations in World Development*, p. 169, Table 20.)

States, and the United States receives $7,241 million more in income from direct investment than is paid out. Canada's position is just the reverse. More direct investment flows in than flows out, and more income from direct investment flows out than flows in. While the United States receives annually $4,347 million more in income from direct investment than flows out in direct investment, in Canada $30 million more flows out in income payments than flows in through foreign direct investment. Thus the United States tends to be overdeveloped by its relationship with the rest of the world; Canada's relations in the aggregate lead to its underdevelopment.

In this era of international capitalism, it is whether a nation or region integrates its economic activities on a worldwide scale or whether it is a satellite to the integrated activities of other nations that determines its status as developed or underdeveloped. A relationship between equals can be considered to be symbiotic, but relationships between powerful and weak nations are parasitic. The contemporary relationships between Canada and Britain or Europe may be rough examples of symbiosis; the relationships between the United States and Canada or Latin America, and to a lesser extent between Canada and Latin America, may be considered parasitic. It has become apparent that the kind of relationship one nation establishes with another and the degree of autonomous development it enjoys are linked to the power of that nation vis-à-vis other nations as capitalism became increasingly international in orientation.

An *underdeveloped* society is no longer an *un*developed society but one whose development is controlled from outside. It is now impossible to speak of "underdeveloped" societies without in turn examining "overdeveloped" societies, that is, societies developed beyond their internal potentials and therefore relying in part on the outside world for affluence. Overdevelopment is the concomitant of the underdevelopment discussed by A.G. Frank, who contends that "underdevelopment, far from being due to any supposed 'isolation' of the majority of the world's people from the modern capitalist expansion, or even to any continued feudal relations and ways, is the result of the integral incorporation of these people into the fully integrated but contradictory capitalist system which has long since embraced them all."[75]

When there is large-scale withdrawal of capital through profits, dividend payments, interest payments, and a variety of other "services" performed by the foreign parent corporation, there will be development *in* the country but not development *of* the country, so that indigenous capital required to achieve autonomy is withdrawn. When this system of developing underdevelopment exists, there are no economic solutions to break the cycle because the necessary capital is not available indigenously; the only way to put an end to the process is political or military.

The dependence produced by multinational corporations is not simply characteristic of relations between advanced and underdeveloped nations but is also a relationship built into the structure of multinationals. One of the ironies of foreign direct investment is that once it is set in motion, its own logic turns it into a Catch-22 situation. A subsidiary that is encouraged not to expand will continue to return a substantial rate of surplus to its parent because its retained earnings will not be reinvested but returned to the parent. On the other hand, a company that is encouraged to reinvest its "made abroad" surplus abroad will continue to grow, generating a greater surplus and returning a lower proportion but an absolutely greater amount to the parent, while expanding the parent's control abroad. In either case, capital will be withdrawn from the subsidiary.

Dependency relations are established because it is in the interest of powerful nations to maintain that kind of relationship and as a consequence to contribute to the underdevelopment of the less powerful nation. The relationship is valuable to a powerful nation not only because of the capital it produces but also because it ensures raw materials, a labour supply, and markets. It is in the interest of powerful nations to maintain a state of "artificial backwardness," to use T. Balogh's phrase, and it is also in the interest of the elite of the less powerful areas to maintain this relationship because it reinforces their position vis-à-vis the rest of the population and, as a consequence, binds their privileged position to the maintenance of the existing structure of inequality.[76]

Obviously, there are degrees of development, overdevelopment, and underdevelopment – varying positions on the chain – evident in the economic relationship of the United States, Canada, and Latin America. From the preceding, it becomes apparent that because of uneven development, even within a particular country such as Canada, the various sectors of the economy can experience differing degrees of dependence and underdevelopment. In Canada, manufacturing and resource exploitation have been externally induced and have become dependent upon U.S. capital, markets, and development while the circulation and service sectors have been controlled by a highly developed sector of the indigenous capitalist class that has chosen to extend itself into other underdeveloped areas of the world rather than compete with foreign interests in its own country. Latin America, in turn, bears the brunt of both systems: U.S. multinationals in pursuit of resources, markets, and extension of their internal manufacturing and Canadian extensions of the financial and utilities sectors. This relationship holds whether one is considering direct U.S. involvement or indirect (go-between) involvement through U.S.-controlled subsidiaries operating from a Canadian base. The U.S. capitalist class benefits from both relationships because its manufacturing and resource activities give it extensive control in Canada and also in Latin America where it also benefits from financial activities.

A country's development is affected also by the stage of capitalism in which it finds itself when outside intervention occurs. For example, the indigenous control in Canada of the finance, transportation, and utilities sectors is largely attributable to the historical environment in which they were developed. It was an era when Canada was receiving British portfolio investment, which allowed capitalists in these sectors to pay off their debts and gain autonomy. The resource and manufacturing sectors, on the other hand, have been developed by U.S. multinationals with direct investment and have remained under outside control instead of achieving autonomy.

Many Latin American countries experienced a similar development in the transportation sector, especially railways, which were typically state-built, but they did not gain the same autonomy in finance. In the Caribbean it has been in large part the highly developed banking and insurance companies from Canada, which began operations in the area as early as 1889, that limited the indigenous potential in this sector. Mining and petroleum enterprises were in many cases initiated by indigenous Latin American capitalists, but very early in their development U.S. direct investment appeared equipped with large capital reserves, technology, and markets, so that these sectors were soon taken over. Manufacturing has principally been originated by U.S. multinationals extending their operations to avoid tariffs and using local resources and labour.

This suggests that the degree of development a country can reach is also influenced by the manner in which the outside intervention makes its contact and the stage of internal development of the country at the time. When there is external intervention, an entrepreneurial class does not arise from the society but is typically created out of an extension of the landed aristocracy or substituted for by foreign corporations. Secondly, when profits are generated, they are reinvested by the controllers of the external investment. Eventually, more capital is sent out than is sent in, leaving the country capital-poor rather than generating more capital for indigenously controlled reinvestment. The national government is also usually left capital-poor because it has contracted heavy loans to set up basic services, such as railways and utilities, and must begin the long process of servicing the debt by taxing the indigenous population. Doing so is particularly difficult when tax incentives have been used to induce outside development. And because foreign development creates powerful positions within the country and recruits influential nationals, increasing dependence follows.

Uneven levels of development in an underdeveloped country are reinforced as some areas become industrialized and rely on maintaining internal colonies for their own positions of power. This is particularly the case where influential citizens from the indigenous landed aristocracy are recruited to powerful positions within branch plants because this status reinforces their power position within the country. They are able to maintain traditional social structures without competition because emerging industrial interests that might see it as advantageous to destroy the old power structure are limited in their growth.

There is a partial instance of this pattern in the early construction of Canadian canals and railways, which involved heavy government subsidies besides "reliance upon government as the pipeline to foreign capital. It also gave a particular cast to the power structure of the Canadian economy. Relative backwardness, as in other cases, encouraged centralization of power and an intimate alliance of political and economic leadership."[77] Here an alliance between powerful financial interests and politicians was reinforced and encouraged by the way foreign capital was channelled into Canada. The utilities network was initially constructed with foreign portfolio capital that had to be serviced through public funds. The same pattern occurs in many Latin American countries where local power structures are reinforced through outside funding designed to provide services essential to corporate development.

Within Canada the externally induced activities dominant during the initial staple phase and later during the advanced staple phase, in pursuit of more technologically oriented resources such as pulp and paper, oil and gas, and minerals, served to reinforce leading Canadian capitalists while at the same time shaping the Canadian economy in the interests of external markets and needs. The result was a concentration on extractive industries and a lack of industrial development.

The experiences of Canada and Latin America, when compared, are similar in the underdevelopment of industrial sectors, although Canada's level of industrialization is much higher. In each case, local capitalists gained their positions of power by acting as mediators between indigenous natural resources and external markets. All the governments were concerned with raising revenues through taxes, royalties, and duties to service loans they had made to finance the transportation and utilities sectors. Both areas have been caught in the web of mutual dependence between external and internal elite groups that reduces the likelihood that an indigenous elite from the industrial sector may rise to dispute successfully the power of the internationally dependent elite. This has been a similar experience for both Latin America and Canada.

In the triangle of relationships among the United States, Canada, and Latin America, some members of each elite are commonly allied in a mutually rewarding association. It should be noted, however, that the alliance is imposed by the nation that commands the greatest resources. The go-between nation that is forced to rely on the powerful member does not have this ability, but the benefits accruing from this intermediary role can be said to make Canada an "affluent annex" in the sense of being a subsidiary or supplementary structure of the United States. This comfortable position does not prevent some of the more powerful members of the Canadian capitalist class from engaging in independent multinational ventures. Where it applies to Latin America it does not prevent aspiring elites from attempting to gain independence from the United States, particularly through political means. This argument is only asserting that, within the international system of capitalism organized through multinational corporations, the structural relationship among the three areas is such that the United States is dominant and Canada enjoys the advantages of being intermediary and the disadvantages of being dependent while Latin America remains primarily dependent, as long as its external ties are unbroken.

In terms of international stratification the United States has a hegemonic place in the group of three, but the power of national elites within their particular nations should not be underestimated. In Canada and Latin America important areas of decision making and national sectors remain under indigenous control. Only in the sectors where a strong native elite long ago established roots and has been able to protect a sphere of influence with legislation does national control remain predominant.

Two levels of inequality have been focused on here, inequality between nations and inequality within nations, each of which is related to and reinforced by the other. The distributive mechanism that dominates economic relations between the United States, Canada, and Latin America is the multinational corporation, which serves as a means of withdrawing resources, capital, and decision-making power from underdeveloped areas. The result of this withdrawal is that under the existing economic structure the lesser partners will not generate internal capital needed to break out of the cycle. Rather, they will continue to be dominated; this is the character of foreign direct investment and its instrument, the multinational corporation.

The political consequences of dominance are important in two respects. First, sectors that are dominated by multinationals are being developed for the requirements of the multinationals, not for the establishment of an integrated national economy. Secondly, the degree of freedom for decision making by the political elites of these nations has been eroded. It does not appear that the capitalist framework can provide economic solutions to dependence on powerful corporations. Political solutions may break the chain, although many contingencies can prevent them from being applied or succeeding. Besides being strong on their own, multinationals are able to call on their parent governments for political or military intervention. They also have their alliances with powerful political and economic elite groups in the nations in which they operate.

Since Canada's economy is at once developed and underdeveloped, its economic elite is both powerful and dependent. To reduce the question to whether Canada is "exploited or exploiter" in the world system misses the fact that its elites exhibit both qualities.

Taking a broad view of the world order, it is clear that Canada sits firmly among the advantaged. It is futile to argue that this is not so because there are so many poor and deprived persons in Canada; even in the United States, with over half the world's wealth, a quarter of the population lives in poverty.[78] Rank in the world order is based on the distribution of resources among the nations, not the inequalities of distribution within them.

Proximity to the United States cannot be the entire explanation for Canada's intimate relationship with that country, but proximity has facilitated the bringing together of the two economies. Geographical determinism aside, Canada's shared border with the United States is a significant factor because it facilitates transport of raw materials from Canada to the United States, it makes possible a continental rather than a national commodity market, and, in the political-military sense, it prevents, within certain bounds, an autonomous Canadian world stance.

As suggested earlier, there is a tendency to conceptualize international relations exclusively in terms of nations. For a more detailed analysis of the continental system, however, it is necessary to examine the relations of specific corporations and specific class fractions. Some elements of the Canadian capitalist class have become internationalized and are international powers in their own right; others are internationalized through their relations with foreign-controlled corporations. Still other elements are relatively autonomous in relation to the internationalized sectors but are not unaffected by them. Overall, however, it would not be correct to view Canadian capitalists as imperialist in their own right. To the extent that they have participated in foreign investment, it has been largely in the remnants of the old British Empire and in the backwash of the United States. In some areas, particularly banking and life insurance, they have become important international actors but not on a scale, or with political-military support from the Canadian state, that could be considered independently imperialist. Were the U.S. umbrella to collapse, as the British Empire did earlier, they would be caught in the downpour.

The separation of power between the Canadian economic elite and the U.S. economic elite operating in Canada is not one that creates a "countervailing" situation. Instead, the elites tend to reinforce one another within one continental economic system in which the U.S. economic elite dominates.

CHAPTER SIX

Continental Corporate Structures and Interlocking

Investigations of economic concentration, ownership ties, and corporate interlocking are three approaches to establishing trends and patterns in the economic power relations between and within Canada and the United States. This chapter will follow each of these approaches by comparisons of contemporary developments within the two countries and by analysis of their interpenetration in both corporate and elite terms.

I. Conglomerates, Corporate Continuity, and Concentration

At the current stage of economic development in Canada and the United States, and indeed in most liberal democracies, a pattern is visible in which a few corporations control the lion's share of the assets, revenue, and profits of each key economic sector while below them are many smaller companies. Outside these key sectors there are typically many firms, small in comparison to the giants, that are highly competitive with each other. Capitalism, however, has a built-in tendency to concentrate capital into fewer and fewer larger units.

Two concepts relating to these economic facts require clarification. The first is *concentration*, which refers to the result of two processes, consolidation and growth. When concentration takes place, the scale of economic control is increased because the resources are gathered within a few companies and the number of companies is reduced. It can be the result of a few firms outstripping the others or of the horizontal merging of several firms in the same business to form one large company. The second is *centralization*, in which either one firm vertically integrates a group of companies in related economic spheres (such as raw materials, transportation, production, or distribution) or several firms form a consortium (joint action) to undertake specific activities in which they all share. Both processes have the effect of lodging economic power within a few dominant corporations.

As the forces of concentration and centralization work themselves out, the areas controlled by dominant corporations expand, impinging on the ability of the competitive sectors and corporations to survive. Following from these processes, three economic sectors can be delineated in liberal democracies: the *competitive sector*, characterized by high

132

labour intensity, low capital and productivity, instability, and low unionization and wages (for example, the service industries); the *monopoly sector*, which is characterized by high capital and high output per worker, large-scale production and markets, high wages and unionization, stability, and long-range planning (for example, the automobile industry); and finally, the *state sector*, which includes both direct state economic activities (crown corporations, for example) and others contracted for (such as road construction).[1] These three types can be reduced to two systems, in J.K. Galbraith's terms, the "market system" and the "planning system."[2] Within the planning or monopoly sector there are both private and public corporations, although the latter are of more importance in Canada than in the United States where the private economy is usually primed by means of contracts and subsidies.

In spite of concentration of capital in dominant activities, a class of small businessmen persists – particularly in the retail trades but also in such activities as insurance agencies – which helps to give an impression of competition to an otherwise concentrated system. But even among the traditional activities of small businessmen there is a growing absorption into the realm of big business. Franchises, agencies, and chains all provide an element of openness, competition, and entrepreneurship but not power. As far as the overall command of the economy is concerned, it is the giants on the peaks, the dominant corporations, that set the tone and direction by owning and/or controlling the majority of the capital, sales, profits, and labour force. What was once a local merchant's shop is now often a store belonging to a larger chain, owned by a corporate complex but administered by a local manager who is, in turn, accountable to corporate executives. The store managers may earn as much as or even more than the local merchant, but they do not have the same control over the enterprise – the hours, the merchandise, the prices, or even the location. Backed by the corporate complex, the manager has access to greater corporate reserves or borrowing power from the bank. But in the end, local managers do not have the same accumulated assets to sell off for retirement or to pass on to their children. These privileges now return to the owners of the complexes themselves, to the economic elite that gives direction to and derives the greatest benefits from corporate capitalism.

Conglomerates, Mergers, and Acquisitions

The historical transformation of corporate capitalism was examined earlier, as were some major merger movements at the turn of the century, in the 1920s, and immediately after the Second World War. The mid-sixties witnessed another period of mergers, this time serving both to centralize control and to increase concentration as the number of mergers exceeded economic expansion. According to W.F. Mueller, "Practically all of the increase between 1947 and 1968 in the top 200's share of industrial assets is directly attributable to mergers."[3] The importance of mergers to the growth of dominant corporations is evident in Ralph Nelson's finding that of the top hundred manufacturing companies, "more than three-fifths had at least one important merger at some time in the company's history."[4] Table 13 provides detailed information on recent mergers and acquisitions* valued at over $10 million among U.S. companies.

TABLE 13

U.S. Mergers and Acquisitions in Manufacturing and
Mining, 1963 to 1971

Year	Total Mergers	Acquisitions worth over $10 million		
		Number	Horizontal & Vertical	Conglomerate
1963	861	82	25	57
1964	854	91	32	59
1965	1,008	91	27	64
1966	995	101	22	79
1967	1,496	168	27	141
1968	2,407	207	32	175
1969	2,307	155	29	126
1970	1,351	98	12	86
1971	1,011	66	8	58

(SOURCE: United States, *Statistical Abstract of the United States, 1974*:491, Table 809.)

The late 1960s experienced simultaneously an increasing number of mergers, an increase in the number of acquisitions valued at over $10 million, and a dramatic increase in the proportion of these large mergers that were conglomerate in nature rather than of the more traditional horizontal and vertical types. Among the largest U.S. mergers and acquisitions† have been the takeover of Consolidated Coal by Continental Oil, Douglas Aircraft's merger with McDonnell Aviation, Atlantic Refining's merger with Richfield Oil and then with Sinclair Oil, the combination of Getty Oil with S. Kelly Oil and Tidewater Oil, Montgomery Ward's takeover of Container Corporation of America, Chase National Bank's takeover of the Bank of Manhattan to form Chase Manhattan, Manufacturers Trust's merger with Hanover Bank

---

* A *merger* is the combination of two or more companies into one "new" company; an *acquisition* is the buying of one company by another. A *conglomerate*, on the other hand, is a heterogeneous company, the product of either mergers or acquisitions, engaged in a variety of unrelated activities. Mergers or acquisitions by companies in the same activity are horizontal and those in complementary activities are vertical.

†The largest mergers and acquisitions are not the only ones of importance. For example, Beatrice Foods (a dominant U.S. company) has acquired over four hundred relatively small companies during the past twenty-five years on its road to the top (see *Fortune* 93 (April 1976):2).

to form Manufacturers Hanover, Guaranty Trust's merger with J.P. Morgan to form Morgan Guaranty, and takeovers by Chemical Corn Exchange of New York Trust to form Chemical New York, of Armour by Greyhound, of Jones and Laughlin by LTV Corporation, and of Continental Baking by International Telephone and Telegraph.

Regarding U.S. business, the *Economic Report on Corporate Mergers* says, "The Federal Trade Commission has calculated that expenditure on acquisitions has risen from less than 5 per cent of new corporate investment in the early 1950s to over 50 per cent by 1968."[5] The principal means of growth has now changed from creating new economic activities to buying up the companies of others. And as Table 13 illustrates, the conglomerate merger has become the major means of doing so.

Jon Didrichsen finds the beginning of the movement to conglomerate diversification in the period after World War II, suggesting as reasons for this development surplus capital and the pressure from anti-trust legislation.[6] Because anti-trust legislation steers corporations away from buying companies in their own sector, conglomerate acquisitions are an alternative capital outlet. There are two conglomerate strategies; in one type a company finds that its primary product line is either stagnating or in decline and relies on diversification to supplement the original line. The other type, more aggressive and entrepreneurial, is one in which a major holding company makes diverse acquisitions as a means of rapid growth. Examples of the first type would be Beatrice Foods, PepsiCo, Incorporated, and Philip Morris, each of which has diversified from its primary activity, while the "true" conglomerate is typified by Gulf and Western Industries, ITT, Textron Incorporated, and Transamerica Corporation, whose activities are extremely varied within each company. Between 1966 and 1970 alone, seventy-two industrials from the *Fortune* 500 disappeared because of these developments.[7]

In Canada also there has been a definite movement toward conglomerates; holding companies, exemplified by Argus Corporation and Power Corporation, are prominent, but such traditional companies as Canadian Pacific can also be included.* Among Power Corporation's holdings are Canada Steamship Lines, Consolidated-Bathurst, Great-West Life Assurance, Investors Group, Imperial Life Assurance, Laurentide Financial Corporation, and Montreal Trust. In the Argus Corporation group are British Columbia Forest Products, Dominion Stores, Hollinger Mines, Massey-Ferguson, and Standard Broadcasting. A few of Canadian Pacific's holdings are Canadian Pacific Investments,

---

*There are also examples of diversified operations by industrial corporations. For example, in 1974 John Labatt Ltd. received 52 per cent of its gross sales from brewing, 26 per cent from consumer products (Catelli, Laura Secord), and 22 per cent from industrial products; Molson Companies received 48 per cent from brewing, 20 per cent from consumer products and services, 29 per cent from retail merchandising (Safeway, Beaver, and Aikenhead), and 2.5 per cent from petroleum marketing equipment (*Financial Post* 29 Nov. 1975:17).

Canadian Pacific Steamships, Canadian Pacific Transport, Cominco, Great Lakes Paper, Marathon Realty, and Pan Canadian Petroleum. In Canada, unlike the United States, there is very little pressure from anti-trust laws to encourage growth of conglomerates. Instead, they seem to be fostered by the financial gains to be made from buying and selling companies, the security of diverse holdings, and the power that can be wielded through pyramiding.*

The conglomerate movement has important implications for the operation of the continental economy. Vertical and horizontal mergers and expansion, as we have seen, made specific Canadian markets and resources vulnerable to U.S. control, but conglomerate expansion makes virtually all Canadian economic enterprises (aside from those protected by legislation – banks, insurance companies, and mass media) susceptible to takeover.

The master craftsman of Canadian conglomerate formation has been Paul Desmarais of Power Corporation, who, "with his seventy companies and nearly $7 billion in assets, has yet to establish a single new enterprise."[8] Conglomerate organization requires a combination of decentralized management and centralized control. For example, Power Corporation exercises fiscal and appointment control over its many companies, such as Canada Steamship Lines (CSL). While it is unlikely that Paul Desmarais takes part in the scheduling of CSL's ships, it is evident that he is able to regulate the number of ships, the level of service, and other activities by controlling the purse-strings and the hiring of managers capable of running the organization effectively (or replacing them if they fail to do so). Even the *process* of attempting to add to a conglomerate's holdings can be a lucrative business. For example, in November 1974, Abitibi Paper, after a battle with Power Corporation, gained control of Price Company, making Abitibi the world leader in newsprint manufacturing. But in the process, Power still gained. Consolidated-Bathurst, "the corporation that Abitibi finally outbid to gain control of Price, made a profit of perhaps $10-million in the course of losing the battle by selling Thursday afternoon a bloc of Price stock it had acquired only Tuesday night as part of its own takeover bid."[9] And Consolidated-Bathurst is controlled by Power Corporation.

One aspect of consolidation must be stressed because it has a bearing on later parts of this study: mergers, acquisitions, and especially conglomerate takeovers do not *necessarily* displace the owners and senior managers of the smaller companies swallowed up. These people are often absorbed into the new, larger organization, and, as often occurs in

---

* Pyramiding is the practice by which one company uses various tiers of companies to control others worth many times the original investment. For example, if one company owns 51 per cent of another company which in turn owns 51 per cent of a third company, the first company has a controlling interest in the third at only a fraction of the investment required to own it directly. The rest of the company's financing comes from minority owners.

these transactions, the owners of smaller concerns may become substantial shareholders in the new corporation as the result of an exchange of shares. The same thing can happen when foreign companies buy out Canadian operations, further integrating Canadian capitalists into an international system rather than displacing them altogether.

Continuity among Top Corporations

The U.S. financial corporations of consequence today were established earlier than the industrials – for instance, the ancestors of three dominant banks, Chemical New York, Chase Manhattan, and the First National City Bank, were all established just following the American Revolution – but at the beginning of the twentieth century, U.S. industrials proceeded to catch up rapidly. This was the era of the movement from entrepreneurial to corporate capitalism. At present, the same proportion of both large industrial and non-industrial U.S. corporations dates from the first decade of this century or earlier – about four-fifths of each. The pattern of continuity in Canada is similar with respect to non-industrials, but industrials did not catch up with them, a phenomenon already dealt with extensively. It has been found in a study of concentration and continuity in Canadian top corporations that least 41 of the 183 companies dominant in 1951 had been reduced to 17 in 1972 through acquisition and merger.[10]

In the United States several writers have attempted to determine the "survivorship" of top industrial corporations over an extended period of time.[11] They have listed the largest one hundred industrials for various years to see how many continue on the list over a considerable period. Generally, the survival rates have been quite high. On the 1960 list there were about a third of the top one hundred from 1909, half from 1919, three-fifths from 1929, and three-quarters from 1948. I have reconstructed this study using a somewhat different approach and found, using the top one hundred from 1974, that twenty-eight had been on the top one hundred list in 1909, forty-two in 1919 or earlier, fifty-three in 1929 or earlier, sixty five in 1948 or earlier, and seventy-seven in 1960 or earlier. Some of the ancestors of the twenty-three "new" entrants may have appeared in the top one hundred before, but it was not possible to trace them. Both studies show that there has been a fairly high degree of continuity among the one hundred largest U.S. industrial corporations, with over half the current hundred having been among the top hundred before 1930.

Of the twenty-two current industrials on the *Fortune* 500 list that did not exist in 1954, none are in the top hundred; six are in the second hundred, five in the third, three in the fourth, and eight in the rank of the smallest hundred.[12] Figure 1 illustrates the degree of continuity among the largest five hundred of 1954 and of 1974. In percentages, 57 per cent of the industrials appear on both lists, and 32 per cent of the 1954 top five hundred merged with companies on the 1974 list, ac-

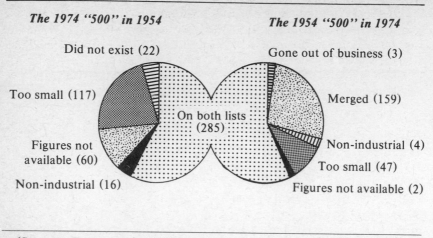

Fig. 1.   Survivorship among companies on the *Fortune* 500 industrial list between 1954 and 1974.

counting for about 90 per cent of all the earlier top five hundred. Of the remaining, 0.6 per cent had gone out of business, 9.4 per cent were too small to be listed, 0.8 per cent were no longer industrials, and figures were not available for 0.4 per cent. These figures also demonstrate the high degree of continuity among the largest U.S. industrials when 90 per cent of the current largest five hundred have sprung from the largest five hundred of twenty years ago.

Corporate Concentration in the United States and Canada

Paralleling other developments, concentration within the five hundred largest industrial corporations has also been occurring apace, since these five hundred now account for a greater share of the total market. "Their share of total industrial sales rose from around half in 1954 to around two-thirds" by 1974, and their portion of earnings rose "from two-thirds to three-quarters over the two decades."[13] For a similar period, 1955 to 1970, the proportion of workers in manufacturing and mining in the United States employed by the top five hundred rose from 44.5 per cent to 72 per cent.[14] While mergers do not account for all of this increased concentration, their impact is nevertheless crucial. Commenting on these activities in 1968, J.R. Felton noted that "the mining and manufacturing assets acquired by merger were equal to approximately 45 per cent of the new investment...the role of mergers in exacerbating the problem of over-all concentration of economic power is clear and unmistakable."[15] Data reported by R.L. Andreano reinforces this point:

If the largest 200 companies of 1968 had made no mergers between 1947 and 1968 their share of total manufacturing sector assets would have risen from 42.4% in 1947 to 45.3% in 1968. The actual change in proportion of total manufacturing assets held by the largest 200 firms of 1968 between that date and 1947 was 60.9% from 42.4%. Thus mergers alone accounted for 15.6 of the 18.5 percentage point increase.[16]

If we accept a "natural" tendency for population – and hence markets – to expand, there should be a "natural" tendency towards diffusion of power because of the creation of more economic units to serve the expanding market. During the advanced stage of capitalism, however, the overall process is the reverse. The largest economic units themselves tend to expand more rapidly than the market, so that we observe the phenomenon of the two hundred largest manufacturers in the United States accounting for 30 per cent of value added in 1947 and 43 per cent in 1970 – in spite of population expansion of some 40 per cent. According to data of the U.S. Federal Trade Commission, Bureau of Economics, the *one hundred* largest manufacturing corporations in 1972 held 48 per cent of all manufacturing assets. Increasing concentration is reflected in the fact that the top *two hundred* corporations in 1950 also held 48 per cent (while the top one hundred then held 40 per cent).[17] Thus fewer corporations account for a greater proportion of an even greater market. This process is reflected in Table 14.

The pattern of growth among the very largest corporations is again evident in Table 15, which is confined to manufacturing corporations with assets greater than $1 billion. It is evident that any analysis that confined itself to manufacturing corporations in the United States with assets over $1 billion would have to take only 124 corporations into account, and these corporations control over half of all the assets and profits of all manufacturing in the United States.

Although the economy of the United States is concentrated, it is not nearly as concentrated as Canada's; it is generally much more diffuse. Its scale is about eleven times larger than that of Canada, but its scale in population alone does not contribute as greatly to its diffuseness as

TABLE 14

Share of Assets Held by the Largest U.S. Manufacturing Corporations, 1950 to 1972 *(percentages)*

	1950	1955	1960	1965	1970	1972
100 largest	39.7	44.3	46.4	46.5	48.5	47.6
200 largest	47.7	53.1	56.3	56.7	60.4	60.0

(SOURCE: United States, *Statistical Abstract of the United States, 1974*:487, Table 799.)

TABLE 15

U.S. Manufacturing Corporations with Assets over
$1 Billion, 1960 to 1973

	1960	1970	1973
Number	28	102	124
Per cent of assets of all mfg. corps.	27.6	48.8	52.9
Per cent of profits of all mfg. corps.	37.1	51.9	52.6

(SOURCE: United States, *Statistical Abstract of the United States, 1974*:488, Table 801.)

might be expected.* Moreover, and retaining the spatial metaphor, scope in the U.S. economy is furthered by wide-ranging markets and outlets outside the country, which permit a good deal more manoeuvrability within the United States.

While it is correct to note that the extent of concentration in Canada is higher than in the United States (the hundred largest manufacturers accounted for 46 per cent of the value added in Canada but only 33 per cent in the United States for 1965),[18] it is also important to point out that at least part of Canada's concentration in manufacturing and resource extraction is the result of the presence of U.S. companies. That is, since only the largest U.S. firms tend to enter Canada, they usually congregate at the top of Canada's economy and are much larger than

TABLE 16

Average Major Characteristics of Corporations in Canada
by Source of Control, 1973 (non-financial)

	Foreign ($'000)	Canadian ($'000)	Proportion Foreign/Canadian
Assets	10,417	2,325	4.48
Equity	5,035	820	6.14
Sales	11,683	2,261	5.17
Profits	1,071	160	6.69

(SOURCE: Calculated from Canada, CALURA *Report for 1973*:1, Statement 1A.)

---

* "Canadian manufacturing industries are much more highly concentrated than corresponding United States industries. Thirty-four per cent of Canadian manufacturing shipments in 1964 came from industries in which eight or fewer firms accounted for eighty per cent of the total value of industry shipments. Only 13.7 per cent of United States manufacturing shipments came from industries concentrated to that extent" (Canada, *Foreign Direct Investment in Canada*, p. 217). This finding is in agreement with an earlier study by Gideon Rosenbluth, who found that in 1947-48 "in 50 of the 56 industries for which a comparison of firm concentration can be made, concentration is higher in Canada than in the United States" ("Industrial Concentration in Canada and the United States," *CJEPS* 22 (1954):336).

Canadian firms in general. In the sphere of production the higher degree of Canadian concentration is therefore in large part a product of U.S. direct investment and is a further distortion of the Canadian economy because of uneven development. This fact is evident in Table 16 (and it will be shown later that these data probably understate the size of U.S. companies operating in Canada).

The only sector that does not follow this pattern, reported by the Corporation and Labour Union Returns Act Division of Statistics Canada (CALURA), is public utilities, where foreign companies averaged $34.4 million in assets and Canadian companies $60.7 million in 1972. Of course, the banks and insurance companies not reported by CALURA would also reverse the trend, but outside these areas, the pattern is clear. Foreign-controlled non-financial firms operating in Canada are on average four and a half times as large by assets as Canadian-controlled firms, over six times as large by equity, five times as large by sales, and almost seven times as large by profits. Since the United States accounts for 80 per cent of foreign direct investment in Canada, the only conclusion must be that U.S. branches add to concentration within Canadian industry.

It is now necessary to analyse the implications of conglomerates, continuity, and concentration for the continental economy.

II. Dominant U.S. Corporations and Their Canadian Relations

Previous chapters have analysed the U.S.–Canadian relationship primarily in terms of aggregate financial statistics. We will now examine more specifically the current structure of this relationship by identifying the 194 dominant U.S. corporations and studying their Canadian operations. This will be done within the context of the nature of concentration and centralization in U.S. corporations. By contrasting the continental and multinational operations of these dominant corporations, it will be possible to come to a better understanding of Canada's particular place within the U.S. sphere of influence.

Although the 113 dominant Canadian companies will also be analysed here,* the focus will be on U.S. dominants because they, primarily, determine the nature of the continental economy. A summary of the methodology used to select dominant corporations appears in Appendix V, while a detailed listing of dominant U.S. corporations by sector is in Appendix VI. Table 17 gives a summary of the Canadian operations of U.S. dominant corporations by sector, and its findings will be discussed in each of the following sections.†

* A more thorough analysis of Canadian dominants is provided in W. Clement, *The Canadian Corporate Elite*, Chapter 4.

† Information and data contained in the following sections on corporate sectors that are not footnoted were derived from personal correspondence or interviews with corporate executives of the companies concerned.

TABLE 17

Number and Proportion of 194 Dominant U.S. Corporations with Dominant and Other Subsidiaries in Canada, 1975

	Number of Dominant U.S. Cos.	Number with Can. Subsid.	Number of Can. Subsid.	Dominant Canadian Subsid.*	Per Cent with Canadian Subsid.
TOTAL FINANCE	35	19	30	2	54
Banks	20	8	11	0	40
Life insurance	9	6	11	2	67
Other finance	6	5	8	0	83
TOTAL TRADE	10	6	8	5	60
TOTAL TRANSPORTATION	17	2	3	0	12
Railways	8	1	1	0	13
Airlines	7	0	0	0	0
Other	2	1	2	0	50
TOTAL UTILITIES	16	6	9	2	38
TOTAL RESOURCES	13	13	37	10	100
Metal mining	2	2	12	0	100
Oil & gas extraction	11	11	25	10	100
TOTAL MANUFACTURING	103	100	304	12	97
Food	9	9	47	0	100
Beverages	2	2	3	0	100
Tobacco	3	2	7	0	66
Textiles	1	1	6	0	100
Apparel	1	0	0	0	0
Paper & wood	7	7	14	2	100
Chemicals	9	9	31	0	100
Petroleum refining	9	9	40	2	100
Rubber	5	5	6	0	100
Pharmaceuticals	4	4	19	0	100
Soap & cosmetics	2	2	3	0	100
Glass, cement, & concrete	2	2	6	0	100
Metal mfg.	14	13	34	0	93
Metal products	3	3	6	0	100
Appliances	5	5	17	2	100
Measuring, scientific	2	2	8	0	100
Motor vehicles & parts	5	5	13	4	100
Aircrafts & parts	7	7	10	1	100
Farm & indus. machinery	4	4	7	0	100
Office machinery	5	5	13	1	100
Other machinery	4	4	14	0	100
TOTAL OF ALL	194	146	391	31	75

*Number with subsidiaries or majority-held affiliates among 113 dominant Canadian corporations (see Clement, *Canadian Corporate Elite*, pp. 400-33).

Financial Corporations

Of the thirty-five dominant financial institutions in the United States, the twenty banks stand out as most important, and among them, the big three (Bank of America, Citicorp, and Chase Manhattan) tower even among the giants. These twenty banks control 42 per cent of the assets and 41 per cent of the deposits of all banks in the United States; the next thirty largest banks add only another 13 per cent to the total assets and 12 per cent to the deposits.* The twenty dominant banks are followed by a myriad of smaller ones. By way of contrast, in Canada there are only ten banks, and the five dominants account for over 90 per cent of all Canadian banking activity. In the U.S. economy, the dominant banks have greater average assets ($17.651 billion) than companies in any other sector.†

The historical trend of concentration within the U.S. banking system has been proceeding rapidly. Between 1960 and 1973, banks with over $100 million in assets have acquired 525 other banks. Of these, 223 had under $10 million in assets, 182 had between $10 million and $25 million, 65 had between $25 million and $50 million, 25 had between $50 million and $100 million, and 30 had over $100 million.[19]

Listing dominant banks, however, does not reveal the community of interest among the banks themselves. The Patman Committee (a subcommittee of the Congressional Committee on Banking and Currency) revealed that U.S. banks can and do hold stock in other banks. For example, in 1966, each of the six largest banks held the following proportions of stock in the other five: Chase Manhattan, 12.4 per cent; First National City Bank, 15.9 per cent; Manufacturers Hanover, 12.4 per cent; Chemical New York, 16.3 per cent; J.P. Morgan and Company, 15 per cent; Bankers Trust New York, 21 per cent.[20] Clearly, this practice cuts across the relative autonomy of each bank and produces a community of interest among the largest bankers.° In addition, there are many areas where joint ownership and investment prevail. This is illustrated in Table 18, showing credits held in estate investment trusts by nine of the dominant banks. The interconnecting ownership and investments of the dominant U.S. banks often make it difficult to distinguish them from each other and, as will be illustrated shortly, from industrial corporations.

Following banks in importance in the financial sector are the nine dominant life insurance companies. They are the second-largest dominant corporations (with average assets of $15.186 billion) compared

---

* Data on concentrations for this and the following sections can be found in Appendix VI, which also lists the dominant corporations and their respective statistics.

† A comparison of the average sizes of dominant corporations for each sector is provided in Appendix VII.

° Life insurance companies in Canada have extensive holdings in Canadian banks ranging between 4 and 11 per cent of the stock, with the largest individual holdings ranging between 1 and 4 per cent (*Financial Post* 15 Nov. 1975:17).

TABLE 18

Real Estate Investment Trust Credits Held by Nine U.S. Banks *($ millions)*

	Chase Manhattan Mortgage & Realty Trust (41 banks)	Continental Mortgage Investors (83 banks)	First Mortgage Investors (100 banks)	Citizens Southern Realty Investors (33 banks)
Chase Manhattan	150.0	18.9	14.5	12.1
Bankers Trust New York	33.9	52.7	27.5	32.6
First Chicago Corp.	38.3	22.1	33.5	6.0
Citicorp	42.7	—	28.5	24.1
Continental Illinois	43.9	28.3	33.5	18.1
Chemical New York	27.7	42.7	34.8	12.1
Manufacturers Hanover	28.9	39.9	6.0	18.1
Bank of America	27.7	10.5	8.0	18.1
J.P. Morgan and Co.	27.7	16.8	5.0	24.1
Total nine banks	420.8	231.9	191.3	165.3
% nine banks	60.1	43.6	47.8	50.2

(SOURCE: *Fortune* 91 (March 1975):168.)

with all other sectors. Although there are not as many dominant corporations in life insurance as in banking, the sector is somewhat more concentrated, with the nine dominants accounting for 54 per cent of the assets and 47 per cent of the value of insurance in force of all insurance companies in the United States. The next forty-one life insurance companies, completing the top fifty, add only another 27 per cent to the total assets and 25 per cent to all the insurance in force. Thus, while the top fifty banks control 55 per cent of the assets and 53 per cent of the deposits of all U.S. banks, the top fifty life insurance companies control 81 per cent of assets and 72 per cent of the insurance in force.

Still, the U.S. sector is not as concentrated as its Canadian counterpart, where thirteen dominants control 86 per cent of the assets and 81 per cent of the income of all life insurance companies in Canada. Two of these Canadian companies are subsidiaries of a dominant holding company, Power Corporation, and two are operations of the two largest dominant U.S. insurance companies, Metropolitan Life and Prudential Insurance, ranking sixth and eighth respectively in Canada.

Like the banks, the dominant U.S. life insurance companies also enter consortia. One of these, the Municipal Bond Insurance Association, was formed in 1973 with the following companies sharing liabilities: Connecticut General Insurance (15 per cent), Aetna Life and Casualty (40 per cent), St. Paul Companies (30 per cent), and Crum and Forester Insurance (15 per cent).[21]

Finally, there are six "other finance" companies, mainly engaged in consumer finance, with sufficient size to be considered dominant. On the average, with assets of $4.672 billion and operating revenues of $1.754 billion, they are about a third the size of the dominants in banking and life insurance but still tend to be larger than the dominants in most other sectors.

Within the U.S. financial sector, five companies stand above all the others: the three giant banks already mentioned and Prudential and Metropolitan Life, each with well over $30 billion in assets. The only other corporation in their league is American Telephone and Telegraph (AT&T). Because of their tremendous assets, and the assets they hold for other corporations in trust, the dominant banks are the most powerful among the financial corporations. Their importance is heightened by their alliance with industrial corporations and the interest groups they form. The prominent role of banks in the remainder of the economy will be examined in connection with other sectors, but some of the relations between finance and industry can be summarized here.

About 1900, banks led the push from the financial sector toward corporate capitalism, and interest groups were formed around giant wholesale banks and key families. For example, "the Mellons formed their Mellon National Bank to control their aluminum monopoly, Alcoa, and their Gulf Oil; J.P. Morgan formed J.P. Morgan & Co. to control his U.S. Steel and General Electric; and Rockefeller had the Chase National Bank for his Standard Oil."[22] Many of these early interest groups persist today. A parallel thrust came from industrial corporations, but as corporate capitalism throve and concerns were linked, the relationship between banks and industrial corporations began to be complementary.

Today, many of the largest banks hold large portfolios of industrial stocks, provide loans for expansion, and perform other financial services. Detailed investigations by the Patman Committee illustrate the intimacy of the relationship and question the extent of separation between ownership and control. The Patman investigators found that "the number of industrial companies in the *Fortune* 500 largest industrial list having 5 per cent or more of their common stock held by one or more of the 49 banks in the Subcommittee survey is 147.... In addition, there are 17 merchandising companies and 17 transportation companies out of the 50 largest in each category."[23] When they applied their findings to a list of corporations previously classified as managerial-run, they found that the top banks held substantial portions of the stock of a quarter of these "managerial" corporations.

In addition to their own holdings of $577 billion in corporate securities in 1971, U.S. banks held another $336 billion in trust, constituting 22 per cent of all the outstanding voting shares of all public corporations in the United States in that year.[24] A further tactic that brings the top banks into the industrial sphere, apart from interlocking directorates (see pp. 162-172), is the formation of the one-bank holding companies. As Robert Fitch and Mary Oppenheimer have shown, "the new structure enables banks to engage in a number of activities previously forbidden to them: control of insurance companies and mutual funds, operation of leasing companies in trucks and computers."[25] Major banks have also kept pace with the recent conglomerate movements, assisting companies like ITT and Gulf and Western; they "financed acquisitions, furnished key financial personnel to conglomerates, and were even willing to clean out stock from their trust departments to aid in takeover bids."[26]

Banks have also been expanding their foreign operations, both independently and to provide for the needs of other U.S. multinationals. "Between 1965 and 1972, U.S. banks more than tripled their foreign locations from 303 to 1,009."[27] Although only Citicorp has a direct affiliate bank in Canada (the Mercantile Bank, which ranks ninth in Canada and is not dominant), U.S. banks are important in the Canadian capital market. U.S. and other international financiers consistently direct their operations in Canada to resource and hydro activities, particularly those with high state involvement. Two outstanding examples of this are Brinco Limited and James Bay. Beginning with hydro, where their major involvement is with the state and bonded debt, they gain access to provincially controlled resources. Robert Davis and his colleagues give some indication of this:

> For lined up behind the James Bay project – which includes not only electricity but also the possibilities for tapping the mineral deposits of the Quebec north and the hard-earned cash of the Quebec taxpayer – is an awesome array of economic power which includes the largest financial houses in the world, such as the Morgan Group, the Humphrey-Hanna Group, the Rockefellers, the Rothschilds and the near-infinite web of their corporate connections.[28]

A similar pattern exists at Brinco, controlled by Rio-Tinto Zinc, part of the House of Rothschild and also associated with the House of Morgan. Top U.S. financiers perform various services for many other Canadian and U.S. companies. For example, Morgan Stanley and Company, the New York investment banker that represented the International Nickel Company of Canada in 1974 in its battle for control of ESB Incorporated (the world's largest battery maker), also raises capital through stock and bond issues. Among its clients are six of the top ten U.S. industrials and eleven of the top twenty, including AT&T, Exxon Corporation, General Motors, Texaco, Mobil Oil, General Electric, International Business Machines, and United States Steel.[29]

Canadian bankers have been active in encouraging U.S. capitalists to enter Canada, as the following report of a New York investors' conference in March 1971 illustrates:

> Eight top Canadian bankers appealed to U.S. financiers yesterday to step up investment in Canada. The bankers indicated they will fight

Canadian government moves to restrict foreign capital.... The panel answering questions from 300 influential U.S. money managers includes G. Arnold Hart, chairman of the Bank of Montreal; W. Earle McLaughlin, chairman and president of the Royal Bank; Allen Lambert, chairman and president of the Toronto-Dominion Bank... J.P.R. Wadsworth, deputy chairman of the [Canadian] Imperial Bank of Commerce; Thomas Boyles, deputy chairman of the Bank of Nova Scotia.[30]

Not only have Canadian financial capitalists promoted U.S. investment but they have also fought to keep barriers to that capital to a minimum (except, of course, on their own turf).

Although only two dominant U.S. insurance companies have Canadian operations large enough to be considered dominant, nineteen of the thirty-five dominant U.S. financial companies have Canadian subsidiaries (see Table 17, p. 142). Only 54 per cent of the dominant U.S. financial companies have any Canadian subsidiaries, a lower proportion than among resource or manufacturing companies. The direct operations of the dominant U.S. banks in Canada are primarily in leasing. Six of the top ten have Canadian leasing operations, but only two of the next ten engage in this activity. In addition to its holding in the Mercantile Bank, Citicorp directly controls Citicorp Leasing International; First Chicago Corporation has First Chicago Leasing of Canada; Continental Illinois has 50 per cent of Builders Financial Company; Chemical New York has Chemco Leasing; Chase Manhattan has Gorwin Properties; Bankers Trust New York has both Killifreth Limited and Ontamont Company. One of the most interesting alliances is that between Bank of America, with a 49 per cent interest in North Continental Capital, a commercial and industrial leasing company, and Laurentide Financial, a subsidiary of the Canadian dominant Power Corporation, which has a 51 per cent interest. Bank of America also has a substantial holding in Montreal Trust, another Power Corporation subsidiary.[31] Power operates with ease in the continental economy. More will be said about the role of financial institutions, but first we will review the other sectors and dominant corporations.

Trade Corporations

The ten dominant U.S. companies in the trade sector have average assets of $2.42 billion and sales of $5.353 billion – less wealthy than the financial companies but about the same as companies in other sectors. Towering above the other nine is Sears, Roebuck and Company with assets of over $10 billion and sales of over $12 billion. Beyond the retail trade, Sears, Roebuck has entered into a joint venture with Aetna Life and MAFCO (a division of Marshall Field) to build a $250-million land development.[32] While the retail trade sector is traditionally one of the most competitive, there is evidence that the competitive spirit does not loom large among the dominants. For example, that "rival" dominants attempt to meet the prices of the others rather than compete is illustrated in an inquiry into Safeway Stores and Great Atlantic and Pacific by the Joint Economic Committee of the Senate and House. Prices on three-quarters of the items were identical, and W.S. Mitchell, president of Safeway, admitted that they check on one another's prices.[33]

In addition to their primary activity, retail trade companies too have been engaged in the process of centralization for some time. For example, since the early 1950s, Sears, Roebuck has held "stock interest in a number of firms (forty-six companies with 109 factories in 1954) selling large portions of their output to Sears...including Whirlpool (8.5 per cent), whose sales to Sears (two-thirds of Whirlpool's output) gave them the largest single share of the home-laundry equipment market, George Roper Corp. (59 per cent), Armstrong Rubber (8.8 per cent), Globe-Union (12 per cent), and Kellwood Company (18.3 per cent)."[34] Just as multinational corporations have deflated the meaning given to the word "trade" because of their intracompany transfers across borders, so the interlocking-ownership pattern between retail and manufacturing companies has reduced the effect of the "marketplace." Small suppliers become dependent upon dominant retailers without whom they could not survive.

As seen earlier, only half of the ten dominant trade companies are multinationals and only six have continental ties. One of the multinationals, Marcor Incorporated (parent of Montgomery Ward), does not appear to have any Canadian subsidiaries, but each of the other four (Sears, Roebuck, Safeway, S.S. Kresge Company, and F.W. Woolworth Company) has a subsidiary in Canada large enough to be dominant. (Actually, Simpsons-Sears, the Canadian operation of Sears, Roebuck, is a joint venture with Simpsons, a dominant Canadian company.) W.T. Grant Company also has a dominant Canadian subsidiary (Zeller's).* Great A&P operates in Canada, but it is not dominant. Five of the six Canadian subsidiaries of U.S. trade companies are among Canada's eleven dominant retail trade companies (one being a joint venture).

One of the U.S. dominants, Safeway, which operates 1,971 stores in the United States, 271 in Canada, and 97 elsewhere, in 1967 transferred its holdings in its Australian, United Kingdom, and West German subsidiaries to Canada Safeway. This turns the Canadian operation into a go-between of the type discussed in Chapter 5 as common among resource and manufacturing companies.

Transportation and Utilities Corporations

There are seventeen dominant transportation companies in the United States – eight railways, seven airlines, and two "other" companies,

---

* Since this list of dominant companies was drawn up, W.T. Grant, the smallest of the dominant retailers, has gone bankrupt (see *Fortune* 93 (April 1976), "W. T. Grant's Last Days"). Also since this time Mobil Oil, dominant in resources, has absorbed Marcor Inc.

Greyhound and Seaboard Coast Line Industries. On the average, the railways have the highest assets ($2.866 billion compared to $1.591 billion for airlines and $1.875 billion for "other") but the lowest average operating revenue ($1.262 billion compared to $1.383 billion for airlines and $2.320 billion for "other"), reflecting the difficult times railways have been experiencing because of increasing shifts to road and air transportation.*

The transportation sector has the lowest degree of multinational operations, with only Greyhound† meeting the definition established earlier. Only two dominant transportation companies have subsidiaries in Canada – Greyhound and Burlington Northern, which owns Burlington Northern (Manitoba) and 125 miles of lines in Canada and leases another 82 miles – neither of which is dominant. Again we see the general tendency for transportation companies to remain national and the fact that transportation is one of the strengths of Canadian capitalism.

The sixteen dominant utilities companies tend to be somewhat larger on the average than the dominants in transportation, averaging $7.864 billion in assets and $2.631 billion in operating revenue. This average is boosted by AT&T, the largest corporation in the United States, with assets of $67 billion and operating revenue of $23.5 billion.

Utilities companies are intimate with the dominant banks, primarily because of their size and the long-term security arising from their monopoly position. For example, six of Consolidated Edison's ten largest stockholders are banks, and "Chase Manhattan is among the top ten holders of 42 utilities, Morgan Guaranty Trust is among the top ten of 41 utilities, Manufacturers Hanover Trust is among the top ten of 31 utilities."[35] Because of the high costs, much of the expansion capital of utilities must be borrowed; over the last five years, "internally generated funds have provided only about 36 per cent of the industry's construction needs."[36] In spite of others' concern about the recent utilities crisis, there appears to be little worry on the part of the big banks. Thomas O'Brien, the specialist in utility lending for Citicorp, which has over $1 billion out in utilities loans, said in 1975, "Basically, we feel our utility portfolio is 'money-good.' Sure, on some loans we're probably not going to get paid in six months. It may take a year. But I really don't think we have to stay awake worrying about it too much."[37] The utilities companies can also expect support from dominant industrials, as a speech in 1975 by Robert Kirby, chairman of Westinghouse Electric, illustrates: "The fact remains that the biggest user of electric en-

---

* The country's largest railway has felt the most dramatic impact, documented in detail by J.R. Daughen and P. Binzen in *The Wreck of the Penn Central* (also see *New York Times* 5 Jan. 1975:40).

† There is some difficulty in classifying Greyhound, one of the two "other" transportation companies, because of its extensive operations in meat-packing since its acquisition in 1970 of Armour & Co., which turned Greyhound into something of a conglomerate. Nevertheless, the principal operation of the company in bus lines allows it to be classified under transportation.

ergy is industry, which must have an adequate supply if it is to create and sustain jobs for its employees" – not to mention corporate profits.[38]

Utilities are second only to transportation in the United States in their tendency to remain domestic. Only two of the sixteen are multinationals, Tenneco Incorporated and El Paso Natural Gas, both oriented to resources. A few venture into Canada, with 38 per cent or six companies having Canadian subsidiaries; these are overwhelmingly concerned with natural gas. One of them, Pacific Gas and Electric, holds a 50 per cent interest in Alberta Natural Gas, a dominant Canadian company. The others are El Paso Natural Gas, with two Canadian subsidiaries, Texas Eastern Transmission and Columbia Gas System, each with one subsidiary, and Tenneco, which has three subsidiaries. They are generally in search of natural resources rather than markets.

This is not to say that there is no close association between U.S. and Canadian utilities except for connections of dominant U.S. gas utilities. Rather the relationships are of a different type. An important illustration is the integration of Bell Canada, and particularly its major manufacturing subsidiary, Northern Telecom (formerly Northern Electric), into the continental and world capitalist order. Northern has extensive multinational activities, and 10 per cent of its sales are in the United States. "Northern, Western [AT&T's manufacturing subsidiary] and ITT operate as a cartel, with ITT (in its telephone operations although not of course in its diverse interests) agreeing to stay out of North America, with Western confined to the AT&T market in the United States [since 1956, following an anti-trust consent decree], and Northern operating in Canada and having a free rein in the American independent market."[39]

Behind this situation is the fact that AT&T has two manufacturing subsidiaries, General Telephone and Electronics and Western Electric (the latter selling only to AT&T), both of which are large enough to be considered dominant in the appliance and electronics sector and are 100 per cent owned by AT&T. General Telephone and Electronics, in turn, holds 100 per cent of Anglo-Canadian Telephone, which shares the Canadian telephone market with Bell Canada, owning over half of British Columbia Telephone (a dominant Canadian company) and Quebec Telephone. In addition, "in 1957, Western sold a 34 per cent interest in Northern Electric to Bell Canada, bringing Bell Canada's share of Northern to 90 per cent and reducing Western's share to 10 per cent; this last chunk was gradually transferred to Bell Canada until it was sole owner."[40] That Bell Canada has extensive relations with AT&T reflects a reciprocity between two utilities giants facing similar problems, using similar technology, and sharing common concerns. That Bell Canada continues in this relationship reflects the benefits that those in control see accruing from the relationship, not that the Canadian company is "dependent" on the other. If the arrangement were not mutually beneficial, Bell Canada could certainly withdraw and, if faced with difficulties, could call on the Canadian state for support. The entire continental telephone system emerged from common origins, and there continues to be a continental division of activity. But aside from this, Canadian ownership dominates other utilities areas, particularly in hydro.

Resource Corporations

Resource companies can be divided into two types, metal mining (with two dominants, Kennecott Copper and AMAX, Incorporated, formerly American Metal Climax) and oil and gas extraction (with eleven dominants). These thirteen companies are not the only dominants involved in resource extraction, for many of the manufacturing companies have resource activities as part of their manufacturing operations through vertical integration. The most obvious ones are the nine dominant manufacturing companies in petroleum refining. But there are also companies, to be discussed shortly, that in Canada are resource companies but whose main activities in the United States are in manufacturing (particularly the steel industry and its iron ore operations in Canada).

The oil and gas extraction companies, on average, are much larger than those in metal mining, with assets of $6.972 billion against $1.845 billion and sales of $6.842 billion against $1.366 billion, and they even tend to be very large compared to other non-financial dominants. As in many other sectors, one company stands well above the others; in this category it is Exxon, with both assets and sales of over $25 billion.

The name of Kennecott Copper suggests its major activity, while AMAX has diverse interests in coal (the fourth largest in the United States), molybdenum, iron ore, nickel, and alumina. In 1975, Standard Oil of California, a dominant petroleum refiner, purchased 19 per cent of AMAX, paying with $333.4 million in cash and stock in Chevron, its subsidiary. Plans were immediately made to add another 700,000 shares to the 5.9 million now held.[41] This development is consistent with the general observation of James Ridgeway:

> By 1970 it was made plain that the oil and gas and coal companies had reorganized themselves into what was called an "energy industry," and were off on a new tack. Not only had the coal industry become more concentrated with ten firms controlling more than two-thirds of all production, but also nearly two-thirds of the top fifty companies were owned by companies in other industries.
>
> Seven of the leading 15 coal producers were oil companies, including 5 of the largest. In the previous five years oil companies had increased their share of the national coal production from 7 to 28 per cent.[42]

There is clearly a movement on the part of the dominant resource companies to diversify beyond a particular resource into a broad range, with the result of centralizing even further the resource industry and squeezing smaller independent resource companies out of the market. Resources are not the only area into which oil companies have diversified. In April 1976 Mobil Oil absorbed Marcor, the parent company of Montgomery Ward and Container Corporation of America.

More than any other sector, the resource companies have spread throughout the world. As mentioned earlier (p. 106), 100 per cent of the dominants in this sector are multinational, and no one will be surprised that all have Canadian subsidiaries. Among them, these thirteen dominant U.S. resource companies control 10 of the 113 dominant Canadian corporations and operate a total of thirty-seven major subsidiaries in Canada. Neither Kennecott nor AMAX has a dominant Canadian subsidiary, but this is attributable more to the way they organize their Canadian operations than to their size. Kennecott has five Canadian subsidiaries and AMAX seven, but neither consolidates its Canadian operations under one company in Canada; rather, all are directly owned by the parent corporation in the United States.

Companies in the oil and gas extraction sector in addition to their dominant holdings in Canadian resources have extensive other holdings, particularly in pipelines, which tend to belong to consortia of U.S. dominants from this sector. Figure 2 illustrates six instances of joint ownership of pipelines. There are other examples of this type of holding – Sun Oil's 55 per cent in Sun-Canadian Pipeline or the joint control by Amerada Hess Corporation, Union Oil Company of California, Gulf Oil, and others of the Peace River Oil Pipeline – and there are also joint holdings in activities other than pipelines. The most important example of this is probably Syncrude Canada.*

Larry Pratt's *The Tar Sands*, a detailed analysis of Syncrude and important aspects of the oil industry in Canada, provides important insights into the nature of control in a consortium:

> Syncrude's decisions are made collectively, with the joint executive and management committees, made up of Syncrude's staff plus executives of the participants, reporting to the owning interests. Power resides in the participating owners and relatively little decision making authority or legal power is delegated to Syncrude's operations staff. All the owners take an interest in Syncrude's affairs, but within the consortium the senior partner is clearly Exxon's Canadian affiliate, Imperial Oil.[43]

Companies in resources more than firms in any other industry tend to form consortia. For example, the Canadian Arctic Gas Study Limited includes among its partners fifteen dominant Canadian and U.S. companies. Discussing the popularity of consortia of this nature, Edgar Dosman said: "Competition has been eliminated in the name of

---

* An in-depth analysis of the relationship between U.S. dominants and Canadian petroleum is beyond the scope of this discussion. A detailed analysis of Canada's relationship with the U.S. in terms of petroleum, gas, electricity, uranium, and water is available in James Ridgeway's *The Last Play*, pp. 86-108.

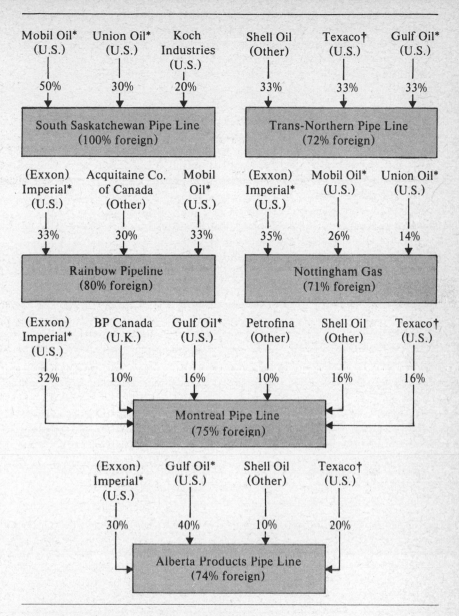

* Dominant U.S. oil and gas company.
†Dominant U.S. petroleum refining company.

NOTE: Percentage of foreign ownership includes partial Canadian holdings in subsidiaries. "Other" refers to companies controlled outside Canada, U.S., or U.K.

Fig. 2.   Holdings of dominant U.S. oil and gas companies in the joint ownership of six pipelines in Canada, 1972.

efficiency. Canadian Arctic Gas, for example, nurtured by Ottawa, solved the problem of competition by including all potential rivals. Both senior officials and corporate executives aimed for industrial stability in a partnership."[44] Centralization can be achieved without concentration; instead of leaving the giants to fight it out, consortia foster a stable and lucrative "partnership."

A Note on INCO Limited (formerly the International Nickel Company of Canada, Limited)

One further company connecting Canada and the United States in the field of resources warrants more detailed discussion. This is the complex multinational, International Nickel Company of Canada (INCO). With sales of $1.685 billion and assets of $2.797 billion, INCO is larger than either Kennecott or AMAX, the two dominant U.S. metal-mining companies. According to the CALURA report filed June 30, 1971, 69 per cent of INCO's shares were held outside of Canada (51,551,128 of 74,473,563 outstanding). And according to the *Financial Post*, over 50 per cent of the shareholders in 1972 lived in the United States.[45] The INCO annual report for 1974, however, said that by the end of that year "Canadian residents of record held 50 per cent of the shares outstanding, United States residents of record 35 per cent, and residents of record in other countries 15 per cent."[46] Moreover, the CALURA *Report for 1972* has reclassified INCO as Canadian-controlled.[47]

It is clear that INCO has historically been controlled from the United States by the Morgan interests (see p. 64), although without a U.S. corporation acting as its parent. As recently as 1972, twelve of its twenty-four directors were U.S. residents, along with eight Canadian residents, three from Britain, and one other. Considered by birth, fifteen were born in the United States, four in Canada, four in the United Kingdom, and one elsewhere. The changes between 1972 and 1975 have led to a board made up of thirteen Canadian residents, eleven U.S. residents, and one other; the pattern by birth changed to eleven born in the United States, nine in Canada, and five elsewhere. As regards shareholdings, the largest insider (executive or director of the company) is George Taylor Richardson, with 31,500 shares. He is a Canadian and is president of the dominant securities company, James Richardson and Sons, a vice-president and director of the Canadian Imperial Bank of Commerce, governor of the Hudson's Bay Company, and a director of Hudson's Bay Gas and Oil. The second largest insider, with 20,095 shares, is Henry Smith Wingate, who resides in New York City and is a director of U.S. Steel, American Standard, J.P. Morgan and Company, and also, in Canada, Canadian Pacific. Of the six largest individual shareholders, two live in Canada and four in the United States, but these individual shareholdings, while important in terms of wealth, are only a fraction of the outstanding shares.

A thorough study of the institutions holding shares does not reveal a clear centre of control, although it does reveal a number of controlling interests. The largest institutional stockholder is a French trust company, Sicovam, which holds between 3 and 4 per cent of the shares; but these investments are in trust, and there is no way of determining from public records who owns them. It is known that when all shareholdings of over 100,000 shares are added together, they total 50.5 per cent of INCO's outstanding stock. Moreover, 65 to 70 per cent of all voting stock is voted at the annual meetings. One reason why such a high proportion is voted is the practice of nominee voting. The breakdown of nominee voting for Canada is banks, 5.4 per cent, trust companies, 10.8 per cent, life insurance companies, 1.5 per cent, pension funds, 1.1 per cent, brokers and others, 1.3 per cent, for a total of 20.1 per cent; for the United States it is banks, 14.5 per cent, brokers and others, 0.8 per cent, life insurance companies, 1.8 per cent, for a total of 17.1 per cent; for nominees from other countries the total is 13.1 per cent. Thus nominees vote 50.3 per cent of INCO's outstanding shares. Nevertheless, no clear centre of control by country emerges from all of this data. The historical tie with Morgan Stanley remains important as a means of obtaining capital and for financial support (see p. 146), but there is no available evidence to prove that Morgan retains a controlling interest. Regarding operations, the U.S. head office is still used for finance and marketing (with the main market in the United States), and the Canadian head office, which is the formal head, looks after management and production.

In a sense, INCO has "dual citizenship," using both the Canadian and the U.S. state apparatus with equal ease. For example, it found the Canadian mechanism helpful in its recent dealings with China and the U.S. apparatus useful for dealings with Indonesia. INCO seems to defy classification by country; its directors and stockholders represent a leading edge of Canadian, U.S., and possibly world capitalists. It appears to be multinational in ownership, markets, production, and (to a lesser extent) executives, who are mainly U.S. and Canadian. It is the embodiment, in one company, of continental capitalism, although there is no suggestion that it represents the way most other continental corporations operate.

Manufacturing Corporations

There are 103 dominant U.S. manufacturing companies in twenty-one subsectors. When unconsolidated subsidiaries and the resource companies are added, there is a total of 119 dominant industrials that can be used to determine levels of concentration and control in this field. The companies have a total of $442.88 billion in sales and $387.035 billion in assets. They account for 66 per cent of all the sales and 70 per cent of the assets of the *Fortune* top 500 industrials. Among the top 1,000 industrials, they account for 60 per cent and 64 per cent, respectively, of sales and assets. Over half the assets and profits of all U.S. manufacturing belong to them. Among them, these corporations have over ten million employees. Concentrated in these dominant manufacturing corporations is enormous economic power.

Of the twenty-one subsectors, metal manufacturing has the most dominants (fourteen), followed by food, chemicals, and petroleum refining (nine each), and paper and wood, appliances/electronics, and aircraft and parts (seven each). Judged by average size, the five dominants in motor vehicles and parts are the largest, with average assets of $8.432 billion and sales of $14.906 billion, led by General Motors with assets of over $20 billion and sales of over $35 billion.

Overall, 97 per cent of the dominant U.S. manufacturing corporations have Canadian subsidiaries, totalling 304 separate major operations. In other words, only 3 of 103 do not have at least one Canadian subsidiary, although many have more than one. Fourteen of the Canadian subsidiaries controlled by these manufacturing corporations are dominant. Like dominants in the resource sector, virtually all U.S. dominants in manufacturing operate on a continental basis. Although one hundred of these companies are continental in their operations, "only" eighty-eight are multinational. For example, all seven dominants in pulp and wood are continental, but only four are multinational; thirteen of the fourteen dominants in metal manufacturing are continental, but only seven are multinational; and all seven dominants in aircraft and parts are continental, but only four are multinational.

Some of the manufacturing companies are difficult to classify. For example, Esmark, Incorporated (formerly Swift) has become a holding company. "Of the company's $68.1 million in profits (on revenues of $4.6 billion), more than half came from nonfood business" in 1974.[48] Nevertheless, it is grouped with foods because this is the single most important activity of the company. Classification problems arise from other factors as well. Many of the U.S. dominants have not consolidated their Canadian operations *within* Canada, making it virtually impossible to determine the exact size of their whole Canadian operation. If it were possible to provide this consolidation, some groups of subsidiaries might well reach a size comparable with Canadian dominants in their sector. An extreme example is Beatrice Foods, with twenty-six separate Canadian operations, all reporting directly to the U.S. parent. The complexity of Beatrice makes it difficult to diagram, but another U.S. dominant with nine Canadian operations, Consolidated Foods, is presented in Figure 3 as an illustration of this problem.

As can be seen, lack of consolidation makes it hard to sort out continental operations and determine in a precise way the entire U.S. impact on Canada by company. Although aggregate data can take the impact into account, there is an overcounting of the actual number of controlling companies involved. That is, statistics for Beatrice's twenty-six Canadian operations would be calculated separately in concentration and size data but should in reality be counted only once, since they are controlled from a single source.

In the paper and wood subsector, all seven U.S. dominants (of which

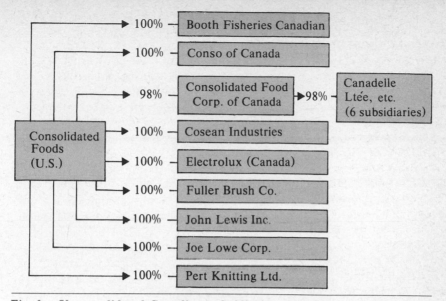

Fig. 3.   Unconsolidated Canadian subsidiaries of the U.S. dominant Consolidated Foods in 1972.

only four are multinational) have Canadian subsidiaries (an average of two each) and two have dominant Canadian subsidiaries. Crown Zellerbach, the smallest of the dominants in both Canada and the United States, has one Canadian dominant in the pulp and paper area, and Champion International, through Weldwood of Canada, has the other in the wood area. Five other dominants are Canadian controlled, including Price Company, controlled in Britain until 1975 when it was bought out by Abitibi Paper.* U.S. holdings tend to be in the middle and smaller ranges of corporations in this subsector in Canada. Neither Canadian nor U.S. dominants are averse to joint ventures in paper and wood, as in the instance of Canadian Overseas Paper: Abitibi Paper, Canadian International Paper, Consolidated-Bathurst, Domtar, and Price each owns 16.5 per cent of the company, with the remaining 16.5 per cent owned by Crown Zellerbach (Canada), a subsidiary of the U.S. dominant.

While none of the nine dominant U.S. companies in chemicals has a dominant Canadian subsidiary, all are multinational and have at least one subsidiary in Canada (the whole group totalling thirty-one). W.R. Grace and Company leads the pack with thirteen subsidiaries. Again, in petroleum refining all nine dominants are multinational, and all have Canadian subsidiaries (forty in all). Both of Texaco's Canadian subsidiaries are dominant, Texaco Explorations Canada in mineral fuels and Texaco (Canada) in petroleum refining. In the United States, Texaco is

* A detailed study of this affair, published as *Takeover: The 22 Days of Risk and Decision That Created the World's Largest Newsprint Empire, Abitibi-Price*, was made by Philip Mathias.

the largest corporation in this subsector with assets of $13.6 billion and sales of $11.4 billion, which would place it only behind Exxon in the oil and gas extraction subsector of resources. The U.S. oil and gas extraction subsector controls ten dominant Canadian subsidiaries, but only Texaco in this subsector has dominant Canadian subsidiaries. Dominant companies in the refining subsector, like those in the resource subsector of oil, are likely to form consortia for pipe lines, although not to the same extent. For example, Cities Service, Atlantic Richfield,* and Marathon Oil, all dominant in refining, hold among them 70 per cent of Key Pipe Line, a Canadian company.

In the rubber subsector, where there are five dominants, pharmaceuticals (four dominants), soaps and cosmetics (two dominants), and glass, cement, and concrete (also with two), all of the dominant corporations are multinational and all have Canadian subsidiaries, although none of the subsidiaries is dominant.

The metal-manufacturing subsector has the largest number of dominant corporations in manufacturing – fourteen – and only half of them are multinational. Thirteen have Canadian operations (totalling thirty-four subsidiaries). As mentioned earlier, manufacturing and resources are simply two parts of a single production process, also illustrated by the operations of companies in this subsector. For example, three U.S. dominants (Armco Steel, National Steel, and Lykes-Youngstown) own among them 72 per cent of Iron Ore Transport in Canada, and these same three companies also own jointly 100 per cent of Carryore, another Canadian company. The complex diagram in Figure 4, involving four of the U.S. and two of the Canadian dominants in this subsector, illustrates both the propinquity to consortia and the interest in Canadian resources of metal-manufacturing dominants from the United States.

Movement across the border by metal-manufacturing companies is not unique to U.S. dominants. According to the Zarb Report on foreign investment in U.S. energy, three of the four dominant Canadian companies in metal manufacturing (Stelco, Dofasco, and Algoma) are "reported to produce nearly 10 million tons of coal from American mines in which they have a total or partial investment."[49]

All ten of the dominants in metal products, appliances and electronics, and measuring, scientific, and photographic equipment are multinational and have at least one Canadian subsidiary, with the ten having thirty-one all together. Only General Electric (discussed in Chapter 3) has a dominant Canadian subsidiary, but here again many of the companies do not consolidate their Canadian holdings within Canada. For example, ITT and Eastman Kodak each holds directly six Canadian subsidiaries.

---

* In 1976, Atlantic Richfield bought a 27 per cent interest in Anaconda Company, a dominant U.S. metal manufacturer, for $162 million in "a big step toward transforming itself from the eighth-largest oil company into a diversified extractor of natural resources" (*Fortune* 93 (May 1976):70).

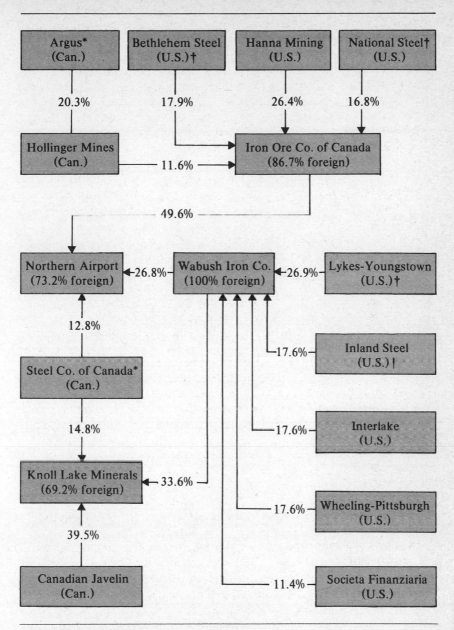

*Canadian dominants
†U.S. dominants in metal manufacturing

NOTE: Percentage of foreign ownership includes partial Canadian holdings in subsidaries.

Fig. 4.   Joint ventures of U.S. and Canadian dominant companies in the metal-manufacturing and resources sectors in 1972.

We have already seen (p. 67) the high degree of concentration within the motor vehicle sector, with the Big Three automakers being much larger than the two dominants in parts and specialties (Bendix Corporation and Signal Companies). General Motors, with assets of over $20 billion and sales of over $35 billion, is about three times the size of Chrysler Corporation, the smallest of the Big Three. All five dominants are multinational and all have subsidiaries in Canada; Bendix has only one and Signal Companies four, but none of these five is dominant in Canada. All the Big Three automakers have dominant Canadian subsidiaries, spreading their virtual monopoly from the United States into Canada. General Motors controls and holds directly 100 per cent of the shares in two dominant Canadian subsidiaries, General Motors of Canada, the largest company in its manufacturing sector, and General Motors Acceptance, the third-largest company in sales finance and consumer loans. The position of the Big Three automakers was formally made secure in 1965 when the Auto Pact guaranteed integration with the United States in a continental market. In the initial years of the pact, although Canadian operations lost any possible autonomy, there was an increase in the amount of production taking place in Canada.[50] More recently, however, there has been a shift away from Canadian production; Canada experienced a $356-million deficit between imports and exports in 1973, $1.2 billion in 1974, and $1.9 billion in 1975, the fifth consecutive year where imports were greater.[51]

Of the remaining twenty dominant manufacturing companies, all but four have extensive foreign holdings. Three of the four are in the aircraft industry (McDonnell Douglas Corporation, Boeing Company, and United Aircraft), and the fourth, Teledyne, Incorporated, is in aircraft parts and machinery. All twenty of these dominants, including the four that are not multinational, have at least one subsidiary in Canada, and the four non-multinationals have ten among them.

A Note on Alcan Aluminium Limited

Another U.S. dominant in the metal-manufacturing sector, Aluminum Company of America (Alcoa),* is important in Canada as the progenitor of Alcan Aluminium Limited. Alcoa formed Alcan in 1928 (see p. 61) and transferred most of its foreign holdings to the Canadian operation (at the same time making it a go-between), but since then its original stock in Alcan has been dispersed. "In 1950, nine individuals (members of the Mellon and Davis families) held 46.3 per cent of the stock in Alcoa and 44.65 per cent of the stock in Aluminium Limited [Alcan]. That year, the [U.S.] courts required the shareholders of Alcoa to dispose of their stock holdings in either Aluminium Limited [Alcan] or Alcoa. Thus, the 1950 ruling completely severed the two companies from one another."[52]

---

* Alcoa continues to operate in Canada only through its subsidiary, Cedar Rapids Transmission Co., which operates an electrical transmission line for its plant in Massena, N.Y.

Alcan's situation is in many ways similar to that of INCO (see p. 154). In fact, when CALURA reclassified INCO as a Canadian-controlled company, it also reclassified Alcan the same way.[53] Like INCO, Alcan has sales ($2.338 billion) and assets ($2.958 billion) that would place it well up among the U.S. dominants in metal manufacturing. Determining the centre of control of Alcan is as difficult as for INCO. The current chairman, Nathanael V. Davis, who was president from 1947 to 1971 and has been chairman since then, is the son of Edward Kirk Davis, who was president of Aluminium Limited (Alcan) from its organization in 1928.* Nathanael V. Davis was born in Pittsburgh, Pennsylvania, and remains a U.S. citizen but lives in Montreal. He owns 38,981 shares of Alcan, certainly a valuable holding and the largest block of shares held by an insider, but not itself a controlling interest.

The largest holding is about two million shares (or about 3 per cent of the outstanding shares), held by a European nominee, and the second largest or just over one million is held by the Kingdom of Norway. There are twelve more nominees with over 1 per cent each of the shares, but there appears to be no clear central control, even though together these major holdings could certainly assume control. The distribution of shares has been shifting back and forth recently, as Table 19 illustrates. The citizenship and residence of the directors would suggest a large Canadian leadership role: ten reside in Canada, two each in the United States and United Kingdom, and one in Norway; nine are Canadian citizens, three American, two British, and one Norwegian. In terms of its operations, Alcan is clearly multinational, with 27 per cent of sales in the United States, 17 per cent in Britain, 15 per cent in Canada, 13 per cent in the European Economic Community outside Brit-

TABLE 19

National Distribution of Common Shares of Alcan,
1965-1974 *(percentages)*

	1965	1972	1974
Residents of Canada	31.1	55.0	45.4
Residents of United States	65.0	32.5	44.1
Residents of other countries	3.9	12.5	10.5
	100	100	100

*Another kinship tie links a current Alcan executive, David Michael Culver, to the earlier executive. Culver's father was an investment dealer who had attended private school and the University of Manitoba and was vice-president of Royal Securities and a director of Atlantic Pacific Grain, Canadian Indemnity, and International Power. The younger Culver went to three of Canada's top private schools (Selwyn House School, Lower Canada College, and Trinity College School) before graduating from McGill and eventually obtaining a Harvard M.B.A. Culver is now an executive vice-president of Alcan and president of Alcan International. His U.S.-born father-in-law, Ray Edwin Powell, was also a member of the economic elite as president of Aluminium Ltd., the predecessor company of Alcan, and a director of Bell Canada and Saguenay Power.

ain and 28 per cent elsewhere. It also uses both Canadian and U.S. capital markets as its source; "new borrowings in excess of $280 million were arranged in 1974, and $53 million in debt was repaid. The largest single issue was a 20-year $75 million long-term publicly-subscribed Canadian issue...other borrowings included a $45 million long-term private placement in the U.S...a U.S. short-term bank loan of $36 million and a U.S. $30 million medium-term loan."[54] Even with these data, we have still not established the country that controls Alcan, and, like INCO, it is best left in a special category of multinationals.

One hundred of the 103 dominant U.S. companies in manufacturing have among them 304 direct Canadian subsidiaries (that is, not consolidated in Canada but owned directly by the U.S. parent). Of the 194 dominants in all sectors, 146 or 75 per cent have subsidiary operations in Canada, totalling 391 direct subsidiaries.

This discussion has shown that there is considerable diversity among companies in the different sectors in their operating practices in Canada. Most Canadian subsidiaries fall into two types of ownership structure, and there is also a system of direct holdings, illustrated by INCO and Alcan. In one of the two main patterns, the parent has a direct holding of between 50 and 100 per cent of a Canadian subsidiary, which in turn holds shares in other subsidiaries. This type can be easily compared with Canadian corporations. The second pattern, in which the parent holds all or many of the Canadian subsidiaries directly (for example, W.R. Grace's thirteen direct subsidiaries or Beatrice Foods' twenty-six) poses a problem in classification. Since these holdings are not organized together (consolidated) within Canada, they cannot be compared with Canadian companies that are consolidated. It is likely that this second method of holding leads to understatement of the degree of concentration within Canada, and government data on corporate concentration must therefore be regarded as conservative. We have also noted a number of instances where joint ownership by U.S. dominants of Canadian operations helps to centralize the continental economy. Now we will turn to another type of relationship between dominant corporations that serves to undercut their "separateness."

III. Interlocking among Dominant U.S. and Canadian Corporations

Interlocking directorships do not constitute the only tie that binds the dominant corporations within Canada and within the United States, or between Canada and the United States, but they are an important component of the general community of interest at the top of the corporate world. Patterns of interlocking are indicative of the centrality of particular corporations, of certain economic sectors, and of a powerful stratum of the economic elite.

Corporate interlocking occurs when one person sits on the boards of directors of two or more companies. We will examine only interlocks between and among the dominant companies. The typical interlocking consists of a senior executive of one company who is an outside director of a second company (that is, he is on the board of directors but not an officer of the second company).

Corporate Interlocks among Dominant Corporations

The following data are based on the 194 dominant U.S. corporations identified earlier and a corresponding set of 113 dominant Canadian corporations.* Once the dominant U.S. corporations were determined, identification of the board members was accomplished by checking several sources. All companies were checked in *Moody's Manuals* and *Standard and Poor's Register*, and many were again cross-checked in the companies' annual reports. All the directors and senior executives of the 194 dominant corporations were selected to represent the U.S. economic elite, and the Canadian economic elite was selected in the same way. Because of some slight discrepancies between *Poor's* (1975), *Moody's* (1975), and the company reports for 1974 (which list officers for 1975), *all* directors and senior executives listed in any one of the three sources were included unless there was a specific reference to their being deceased, retired, or no longer with the company. In Canada the source used to select the elite was the *Financial Post Directory of Directors*, 1972, and in a few instances, when information was not available there, from reports filed with the Department of Consumer and Corporate Affairs.

Table 20 compares and summarizes these findings:†

TABLE 20

Interlocking among Dominant U.S. Corporations and among Dominant Canadian Corporations

Interlocks	U.S.		All Canadian		Canadian-Controlled Only	
	Number	Per Cent	Number	Per Cent	Number	Per Cent
25 or more	20	10.3	28	24.8	24	41.4
10 to 24	84	43.3	35	31.0	17	29.3
Under 10	90	46.4	50	44.2	17	29.3
Total	194	100	113	100	58	100
Average	12.4		16.3		23.4	

*For a review of trends in corporate interlocking in the United States, see Appendix VIII.

†More detail on the results of this analysis of interlocking U.S. corporations can be found in Appendix IX. A more detailed listing of interlocks is in Appendix X. For Canadian corporations, see Clement, *Canadian Corporate Elite*, App. XI.

Since only interlocking among dominant corporations is being measured here, it might be expected that the larger number of U.S. dominants (194) would present more possibilities for interlocking than among the smaller number of Canadian dominants (113). Nevertheless, the Canadian dominants exhibit a much greater tendency to be interlocked. The average Canadian dominant has 16.3 interlocks with other dominants in Canada while the average U.S. dominant has 12.4 domestic interlocks. When Canadian-controlled dominants only are considered, the average increases to 23.4 per dominant.* Only one U.S. dominant has over fifty interlocks (Citicorp, with fifty-three), but five of the Canadian-controlled companies have this many.

The U.S. dominants are clearly not as densely interlocked as the Canadian dominants, but there is still a high degree of interlocking among these largest corporations. Only eight of the 194 dominant U.S. corporations (or 4.1 per cent) are not interlocked with any other dominants. In Canada, three of the 113 (2.6 per cent) are not interlocked. The largest corporations in the United States tend to have the largest number of interlocks, and, as we have seen, they are usually banks. For example, six of the top ten interlocked companies are banks. The thirteen dominants that have thirty or more interlocks are Citicorp, J.P. Morgan and Company, Metropolitan Life, Manufacturers Hanover, Chemical New York, First Chicago Corporation, AT&T, New York Life, General Motors, Continental Illinois, IBM, Chase Manhattan, and U.S. Steel. These stand as the pillars of the U.S. economic elite, among them interlocking over five hundred times within the 194 dominant corporations. In Canada, the top interlocking companies are the banks and the life insurance and transportation/utilities companies, the core of Canadian capitalism.

The average size of boards of directors is similar in the dominant corporations of each nation, although Canadian boards are somewhat smaller (15.5 members) than those in the United States (16.9 members). As Table 21 shows, the U.S. boards are larger in each sector except utilities/transportation, strikingly so in the trade and manufacturing sectors. Canadian bank boards, on the other hand, are almost twice as large on the average as those of the dominant U.S. banks.

Government regulation may be one explanation for the lower degree of interlocking among U.S. corporations. The Clayton Antitrust Act prohibits interlocking directorships between competing corporations and depresses the numbers somewhat. Another possible explanation is based on structural differences between the U.S. and Canadian economies. The Canadian dominants tend to be more interlocked because financial corporations play a more central role in the Canadian economy, and financial corporations, whether in the United States or Canada, have a greater tendency to be interlocked than any other type. An

---

*In contrast, the average dominant U.S. subsidiary in Canada has 7.0 interlocks, the U.K. subsidiary 9.6, and others 16.3.

investigation of the density of interlocks by corporate sector will show this to be the case.*

TABLE 21

Average Size of Board of Canadian and U.S. Corporations by Sector

Sector	Number of Directors U.S. Boards	Number of Directors Canadian Boards
Finance	23.1	19.8
Transportation/Utilities	13.8	14.2
Resources	14.8	13.3
Manufacturing	15.7	12.6
Trade	17.3	11.6
Average	16.9	15.5
Banks	24.4	46.2
Insurance	25.9	14.5

Density of Interlocks

One method of analysing patterns of interlocks is to examine relationships that occur within and among the five sectors. The density established in this way provides a measure of the integration of the elite level between any two sectors. Figures 5 and 6 allow a comparison of patterns within the United States and within Canada; they contrast density of interlocks in each sector and are indicative of the degree of centrality of the sectors within each nation. Finance is the clear centre in Canada, having a very strong relationship with all other sectors. A second minor centre in Canada is the transportation/utilities sector with a particularly strong link to finance. There is a greater diffuseness in relationships between sectors in the United States, mainly accounted for by the equal importance of manufacturing and finance. The pre-

---

*Some interlocking in the United States takes place outside the board room, but as the practice is even more prevalent in Canada, it cannot explain the difference. For example, in the United States an additional forty-six members of the elite sit on the *advisory* boards of dominant banks, another sixteen are on the boards of subsidiaries, and three are honorary directors. These sixty-five persons are not included in the interlocking count. In Canada, however, there are sixty-six members of the economic elite sitting on the advisory boards of dominant corporations who are not included in interlocking. The practice is most actively carried out by trust companies in Canada (accounting for fifty-six directors on advisory boards), and in the United States the most important practitioners are three banks: Chemical New York, Crocker National, and J.P. Morgan and Co. Another aspect of intercompany connection, though it does not explain the different ratios between Canada and the United States, is that an executive of one dominant company may sit on the board of another without being a member of his own board. There are thirty-one instances of this in the United States and fourteen in Canada, about the same proportion of each elite, since the U.S. elite outnumbers Canada's by more than two to one.

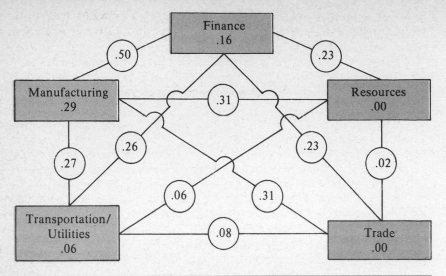

NOTE: Density of interlocks is calculated by dividing the potential number of interlocks by the actual number of interlocks per sector. The figures in the sector boxes represent the density of interlocking *within* each sector. If the density were 1.00, all potential interlocks between sectors would be active; if it were .00, there would be no interlocks. The potential number is determined by the actual number of elite positions within each sector.

Fig. 5.   Density of interlocks among the five sectors (194 dominant U.S. companies) in 1975.

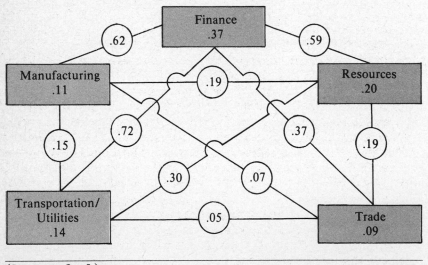

(See note, fig. 5.)

Fig. 6.   Density of interlocks among the five sectors (113 dominant Canadian companies) in 1972.

sence of manufacturing as a second major centre in the United States tends to spread the density of interlocks more evenly among all sectors. This is particularly evident in manufacturing's relationship to resources (.31), trade (.31), and transportation/utilities (.27); by contrast, the relationships in Canada are .19, .07, and .15, respectively. In the United States, transportation/utilities is less important in terms of density of interlocks with other sectors than it is in Canada, and the resource sector is more prominent in its relationship to manufacturing. The trade sector tends to have the lowest density in each country, having its only impressive tie in Canada to finance but with fairly strong ties to both manufacturing and finance in the United States.

The figure in each sector's box is the density of the relationship within sectors. The patterns within are similar to those between sectors, with a much higher relationship within finance in Canada (.37) compared to the density within U.S. finance (.16). This is in spite of Canadian legislation prohibiting banks or insurance companies from interlocking with themselves, although not prohibiting their interlocking with each other. In manufacturing, however, the density is much higher in the United States (.29) than in Canada (.11). Thus it is apparent that dominant manufacturing corporations in the United States have a much more prominent place in their relationships to dominant corporations in their own sector and other sectors than they do in Canada.

The extreme importance of the finance sector in Canada compared with its status in the United States is a reflection of the *relative* importance this sector has in the economic power structure of each nation. Canada's finance sector is dominant opposite a weaker, largely foreign-controlled manufacturing sector, but in the United States both sectors are indigenously controlled and have evolved as relatively equal centres of power. Financial capitalists have had an important place in the U.S. corporate system, but the relationship between financial and industrial capitalists has been more balanced than in Canada.

Chapter 3 offered an explanation of these findings in terms of earlier U.S. industrialization resulting from an earlier breaking of the imperial ties with the United Kingdom. There was also the fact that U.S. manufacturing and resource companies themselves expanded into Canada, where they were promoted as a surrogate for indigenous development by Canadian financial capitalists, and the openings for indigenous Canadian industrialists were thereby reduced. In Canada, elite members in the sphere of circulation are thoroughly integrated with each other but have tenuous connections with the sphere of production, which is foreign controlled. They have consolidated their position only in circulation, while members of the U.S. economic elite have effectively maintained control of all economic activities in their society.

Figures 5 and 6 showed how the dominant corporations were interlocked but did not indicate what the primary affiliations of the directors were. Tables 22 and 23 show the distribution of dominant directorships in various sectors according to the main affiliations of the persons holding these positions.

TABLE 22

**Dominant Directorships (per Sector) Held by Members of
the U.S. Economic Elite by Main Current Affiliation
*(n = 2,007)***

% with dominant directorships* in	Main Current Affiliation (percent)					
	Trans./Util.	Finance	Resources	Manuf.	Trade	ALL
Trans./Utilities	(73)	23	6	11	14	21
Finance	32	(57)	21	24	25	42
Resources	1	8	(78)	4	3	10
Manufacturing	23	42	23	(82)	24	57
Trade	4	6	1	2	(68)	6

*Percentages do not total 100 because multiple directorship holders may appear in more than one sector.

NOTE: These percentages indicate the proportion of 2,007 members of the U.S. economic elite whose main affiliation is in any of the sectors listed along the top who have at least one dominant directorship in any of the sectors along the side. Main current affiliation need not be in a dominant corporation. The percentages in brackets indicate the proportion of persons whose dominant directorships and main current affiliation are in the same sector. For example, of the elite members whose main affiliation is in finance, 57 per cent have at least one dominant directorship in a dominant financial company.

TABLE 23

**Dominant Directorships (per Sector) Held by Members of
the Canadian Economic Elite by Main Current Affiliation
*(n = 798)***

% with dominant directorships* in	Main Current Affiliation (percent)					
	Trans./Util.	Finance	Resources	Manuf.	Trade	ALL
Trans./Utilities	(64)	55	2	19	2	18
Finance	11	(90)	7	22	8	66
Resources	24	45	(70)	12	4	13
Manufacturing	10	52	10	(70)	4	30
Trade	15	38	6	7	(77)	12

*See note, Table 22.

The fact that only 57 per cent of those whose main affiliation is in finance in the United States also have a dominant directorship in finance suggests that many financial executives in smaller corporations are interlocking with dominant companies in other sectors. In fact, additional analysis indicates that 46 per cent whose main affiliation is finance have other than a dominant company as their main affiliation. That is, 54 per cent of those whose main affiliation is finance belong to the elite because of dominant directorships in another company. Therefore, the degree of interconnection between finance as a sector (and not simply dominant companies in finance) and other corporations is greater than the interlocks between only dominant companies suggests. This is especially true for the manufacturing and transportation/utilities sectors, since many of those with main affiliations in smaller than dominant companies interlock extensively with dominants in other sectors.

Table 22 indicates that members of the elite whose main affiliation is in resources or trade are equally likely to hold a dominant directorship in either finance or manufacturing while those in transportation/utilities are more likely to hold a dominant directorship in finance than in manufacturing. Of those whose main affiliation is in finance, 42 per cent have a dominant manufacturing directorship; of those in manufacturing, only 24 per cent have a dominant directorship in finance. Again, the table suggests a greater degree of interlocking by executives of non-financial corporations than indicated only by the interlocks among dominant corporations.

Comparison of Tables 22 and 23 shows that in the United States 57 per cent of those whose main affiliation is finance also have a dominant directorship in finance, but in Canada the proportion is 90 per cent. The implication is a much higher degree of association with dominant companies among Canadian financial capitalists, again reflecting the more diffuse character of U.S. finance because of the larger number of banks. In Canada, financial executives are consistently high in their directorships in other sectors, once again demonstrating their central position. This pattern illustrates that in Canada it is primarily persons with directorships and main affiliations in financial institutions who interlock with other sectors; in the United States the pattern shows persons whose main affiliations are in other sectors holding directorships in dominant financial institutions. Thus, when we see the direction in the interlocking patterns analysed earlier (that is, from main affiliations to outside directorships), it reinforces the argument made throughout this study of the dominance of circulation in Canada and the weaker role of indigenous production.

However the data are examined, the relationship between financial and manufacturing corporations appears to be more balanced in the United States than it is in Canada. Nevertheless, financial institutions remain central in the current stage of U.S. corporate capitalism. Internally generated funds (retained earnings) may be sufficient for normal expansion by industrial corporations, but a need for large external funding remains when huge projects are undertaken or broad new markets tapped; and it is the reserves of financial capital that are able to bridge the gap.

The giant banks are the main source of these capital pools and merit a closer examination. Table 24 gives some indication of the relations of Canadian and U.S. banks with other sectors. U.S. banks have a lower volume of interlocks than their Canadian counterparts and have different patterns of interlocks, again reflecting the basic differences in the two economies. The lower average of interlocks of the twenty dominant U.S. banks with 194 dominant corporations compared to the five dominant Canadian banks with the 113 dominant corporations is significant, as is the larger proportion of interlocks by dominant banks in Canada with other financial institutions (mainly life insurance). As we might expect, interlocks of Canadian banks to the manufacturing sector are less than half the proportion of similar institutions in the United States. Canadian banks are also more likely to be interlocked with resource companies, reflecting Canada's orientation to resources as a major source of revenue.

TABLE 24

Interlocks of Dominant Canadian and U.S. Banks

	Finance	Trade	Trans./ Util.	Resources	Manuf.	Total	Average per Bank
20 U.S. Banks							
Number	66	32	80	35	276	489	24.5
Per cent	13.5	6.5	16.4	7.2	56.4	100	
5 Canadian Banks							
Number	92	28	47	84	54	305	61.0
Per cent	30.2	9.2	15.4	27.5	17.7	100	

Dominant banks and life insurance companies are more completely integrated in Canada than in the United States (and the life insurance companies constitute the second most important capital pool). In the United States, 20 per cent of the elite who hold a dominant insurance directorship also have a dominant bank directorship, and 9 per cent of those with a dominant bank directorship also have a dominant insurance directorship. In Canada, dominant insurance directors hold 28 per cent of dominant bank directorships and dominant bank directors hold 41 per cent of dominant insurance directorships. Here is another indication that financial institutions are much more diffuse in the United States than in Canada. This is not to say that dominant financial institutions are not central in the United States, only that they have a counterbalance there. They are obviously well integrated with other dominant corporations when 61 per cent of those who hold a dominant bank directorship also have at least one other dominant directorship and 48 per cent of those holding a dominant insurance directorship also have at least one other dominant directorship.

Holders of Multiple Directorships

Table 25 summarizes the number of persons holding multiple directorships in the United States and Canada. It shows that only 22 per cent of the U.S. economic elite control 41 per cent of the elite positions, that is, 1,348 elite positions are in the hands of 535 individuals. As would be expected, given the earlier findings on the intensity of interlocks, the Canadian economic elite is even more likely to have multiple dominant directorships: 29 per cent hold 54 per cent of the elite positions. In other words, 274 individuals hold 782 elite positions. Therefore, a greater proportion of the elite have more than one dominant directorship in Canada than in the United States, and they hold a greater portion of the dominant directorships. Reducing these to a common base for comparison, each U.S. multiple directorship holder averages 2.52 dominant directorships while each one in Canada averages 2.85.

TABLE 25

Holders of Multiple Directorships in the United States and Canada

	Number Dominant Directorships	Number Persons*	Number Directorships	CUMULATIVE			
				Number Persons	Per Cent Persons	Number Directorships	Per Cent Directorships
U.S.							
	3 or more	191	660	191	8	660	20
	2	344	688	535	22	1,348	41
	1	1,915	1,915	2,450	100	3,263	100
Canada							
	3 or more	119	472	119	13	472	33
	2	155	310	274	29	782	54
	1	672	672	946	100	1,454	100

*This table includes all members of the Canadian and U.S. economic elites, whether sufficient information was available for analysis of other biographical characteristics or not.

In spite of the facts that the U.S. economic elite outnumbers the Canadian more than two to one and that there are 194 dominant U.S. corporations to Canada's 113, only two members of the elite in the United States have six or more dominant directorships compared to thirteen in Canada. The proportion of persons with three or more dominant directorships (who hold a third of all the dominant positions) is significantly higher in Canada than it is in the United States (where they hold one-fifth). From all the indicators relating to dominant interlocks, the evidence is that there are lower levels of interlocks, that interlocks are spread more evenly among the economic sectors, and that the tendency for members of the elite to hold multiple directorships is less marked in the United States.

The trend in Canada is to increase the extent and expanse of multiple directorship holders. In 1951, 22 per cent of the elite held 46 per cent of the dominant directorships [55] (much like the current U.S. pattern); by 1972, 29 per cent had 54 per cent of the directorships. The Canadian economic elite has become increasingly consolidated, just as the corporate world itself has become more concentrated, centralized, and cornered. While the Canadian pattern is an increase in both the number and density of interlocks, in the United States the trend from 1935 to 1970 is relatively stable with a slight decline in the density of interlocks.*

IV. Continental Connections: Interlocking between Dominant U.S. and Canadian Corporations

We know that international capitalism is not a new phenomenon, and later chapters will illustrate that the tendency of people to follow capital flows is also old. What is relatively new, however, is the multinational corporation with its branch-plant structure, and even more recent is the gravitation of segments of the national capitalist class into direct participation in foreign-based corporations. Nowhere else have these developments been on the scale that has existed in the period since World War II in relations between Canada and the United States. The focus of this section will be on the relations between leading elements of the Canadian and U.S. capitalist classes as they interlock between dominant corporations in both Canada and the United States. This continental pattern is indicative of the relative strengths of various sectors and the way they serve as a base for a continental economic elite.

The two major theoretical issues to be addressed are whether or not there is an international segment of the economic elites of each nation and whether or not all fractions of the dominant class of "dependent" nations are subservient to foreign powers. The empirical issue is

* For a review of the these patterns and for trends in corporate interlocking in the United States between 1899 and 1970, see Appendix VIII.

whether the economic elites of each nation interpenetrate or whether the relationship is exclusively one-sided. While a study of interlocking cannot by itself resolve these complex questions, it can be one useful indicator. Thus it will be important to look outside the structure of parent companies and branch plants to see whether interlocks occur in areas other than those under direct external control.

U.S. Interlocks with Canada

Interlocking in Canada between U.S. and Canadian corporations has to be divided between the relationships of parent companies and branch plants and the direct connection from a U.S. dominant to a Canadian dominant, independent of foreign control. The other aspect to note is the sector to which the U.S. company and the Canadian company in question belong. The same procedures will be followed in examining interlocking in the United States between Canadian and U.S. corporations.

Of the 194 dominant U.S. corporations, fifty-four are interlocked with Canadian dominant companies through directors who are members of the U.S. parent–branch plant structure, and forty-four interlock with Canadian dominants that are not subsidiaries. The fifty-four U.S. companies are interlocked with thirty-two of Canada's 113 dominant corporations, of which six are U.S. subsidiaries interlocking only with their parents, nine are other U.S. subsidiaries, five are U.S. affiliates (over 10 per cent but less than 50 per cent U.S.-owned), one is a joint U.S.-Canadian venture, and eleven are Canadian-controlled companies.

Given a historical pattern in which U.S. direct investment in Canada is centred in the manufacturing, resources, and (in specific instances) trade sectors, it is to be expected that the subsidiary interlocks will conform to this pattern and that there will be lower participation in the predominantly Canadian-controlled finance and transportation/utilities sectors. The conformity does exist among the thirteen dominant U.S. parent companies, which have a total of thirty one interlocks with fourteen of their dominant Canadian subsidiaries. Most of the subsidiaries are in the resource sector (five) followed by trade and manufacturing (four each). There is only one in finance and none in transportation/utilities. Over half of the U.S. parents (eight) have two interlocks with their Canadian subsidiaries, three have only one, one has three, and another (S.S. Kresge Company) has ten. Kresge is an anomaly in the general pattern of two U.S. resident members of the parent board sitting on the Canadian subsidiary's board.

The fact that subsidiary companies share directors in common with parent companies is no surprise, but it is interesting that a relatively low number of interlocks is shared in this way. The remainder of the board positions in Canadian subsidiaries are held by Canadian-resident members of the comprador elite, members of the indigenous Canadian elite, or other outsiders.

TABLE 26

Interlocks between U.S. and Canadian Dominant
Corporations by Sector of Origin in the United States

Sector in the United States	Number of Dominant U.S. Companies	Number of Interlocks in Canada		
		Subsid./Affil.	Direct*	Total
Manufacturing	26	7	36	43
Trans./Utilities	6	0	9	9
Resources	8	6	10	16
Finance	9	2	16	18
Trade	5	17	1	18
Total	54 (of 194)	32	72	104

*"Direct" interlocks occur outside the parent-subsidiary or parent-affiliate relationship through direct connection between a U.S. dominant and a company not dependent on foreign control.

It is evident from Table 26 that the most important source of interlocks with Canadian dominant companies initiated from the United States is the manufacturing sector; half of all the interlocking U.S. companies are from this sector. Moreover, thirty-six of the forty-three interlocks originating in this sector are outside the parent-subsidiary or parent-affiliate company relationship. The finance sector, though second to manufacturing, is much closer to the other sectors as a source of interlocks. Even here most of the interlocks, like those from transportation/utilities, are direct. Few are based on subsidiary or affiliate relations. Trade interlocks are almost entirely with subsidiaries. The resource sector has almost as many subsidiary interlocks as manufacturing and an additional ten direct interlocks.

Where do the interlocks directed mainly from the U.S. manufacturing sector make connection in Canada?* Table 27 shows that the two main target sectors are finance and resources. A larger number of the interlocks to resource companies follow subsidiary or affiliate lines than those to financial corporations, where almost all are direct. Here the dominant banks and the largest life insurance companies stand out, usually having two or three interlocks with dominant U.S. companies by way of U.S.-resident members of the elite. The foreign contacts afford these companies important opportunities to keep in touch with outlets for their capital in the United States. Very few of the lines of connection from the U.S. dominants go to the manufacturing sector, and even fewer to transportation/utilities. Most of the interlocks in trade are accounted for by subsidiaries. Sixteen of the seventy-two direct interlocks are instances of a member of the U.S. economic elite simultaneously holding directorships on the board of another subsidiary or affiliate in Canada and on the board of the U.S. parent.

*There are some restrictions on the numbers of foreign directors on the boards of Canadian banks and trust and loan companies, where three-quarters must be Canadian citizens, and insurance companies, where a majority must be Canadian citizens.

TABLE 27

Interlocks between U.S. and Canadian Dominant
Corporations by Sector of Destination in Canada

Sector in Canada	Number of Dominant Canadian Companies	Number of Interlocks from U.S.		
		Subsid./Affil.	Direct	Total
Manufacturing	5	5	11	16
Trans./Utilities	1	0	3	3
Resources	11	9	20	29
Finance	10	2	26	28
Trade	5	16	12	28
Total	32 (of 113)	32	72	104

Canadian Interlocks with the United States

The most striking difference between interlocks originating in Canada and interlocks initiated from the United States is the complete absence of interlocks from Canadian dominants to subsidiaries in the United States. All of the interlocks are either direct or from a Canadian subsidiary to a U.S. parent. While 54 of 194 U.S. dominant corporations (or 28 per cent) interlocked with dominant Canadian corporations, 48 of 113 (or 43 per cent) of their Canadian counterparts are interlocked through Canadian-resident members of the elite. Most of these interlocks come from Canadian-controlled dominant corporations in Canada: thirty-one Canadian-controlled dominants have a total of eighty-four interlocks, twelve U.S. subsidiaries have twenty-three interlocks, and five controlled elsewhere have eleven interlocks.

TABLE 28

Interlocks between Canadian and U.S. Dominant
Companies by Sector of Origin in Canada

Sector in Canada	Number of Dominant Companies	Number of Interlocks to the U.S.
Manufacturing	10	18
Transportation/Utilities	5	20
Resources	9	20
Finance	22	58
Trade	2	2
Total	48 (of 113)	118

As Table 28 makes evident, the financial sector in Canada is the main source of origin for interlocks with U.S. dominants, accounting alone for almost half of all these interlocks. All five dominant banks and seven of the eleven dominant insurance companies are in the group. Of the ten companies in the manufacturing sector, four are U.S. controlled, two are controlled elsewhere, and four are Canadian controlled (Stelco and Dofasco, which have one interlock each, and Hiram Walker and Massey-Ferguson, with two each). The Canadian companies particularly active in interlocking to U.S. dominants are the Royal Bank (linked to nine), the Canadian Imperial Bank of Commerce and Trans-Canada PipeLines (to seven each), Canadian Pacific and Power Corporation (to five each), and the Toronto-Dominion Bank, Canada Life, and Bell Canada (to four each). Indigenous companies with three each are Calgary Power, MacMillan Bloedel, Sun Life, and Brascan. As it did in the interlocks within Canada, the financial sector occupies the most prominent place in interlocking indigenous Canadian operations with U.S. dominants.

A total of twenty-seven U.S. dominant corporations are linked to forty-eight Canadian dominants through 118 directorships held by members of the Canadian economic elite. Only seven of these interlocks go from subsidiaries in Canada to U.S. parents. What is most striking is that almost half of the sources in Canada come from the financial sector, and exactly half of the recipients in the United States are in the manufacturing sector.* The financial sector in the United States ranks second in this respect, well behind manufacturing and closely followed by the resource sector. Neither the transportation/utilities sector nor the trade sector is an important recipient.

TABLE 29

Interlocks between Canadian and U.S. Dominant Corporations by Sector of Destination in the United States

Sector in the United States	Number of Dominant Companies	Number of Interlocks from Canada
Manufacturing	13	59
Transportation/Utilities	2	8
Resources	5	20
Finance	5	29
Trade	2	2
Total	27 (of 194)	118

*Some sectors cannot have directors living outside the United States. For example, "Communications companies, such as A.T.T. and I.T.T., are forbidden by federal law to have foreigners on their boards" (*Fortune* 85 (Jan. 1972):36).

There is already enough evidence available on the U.S. part of the continental interpenetration so that it is unnecessary to cite examples of U.S. directors on Canadian boards. But because it is a fairly recent phenomenon for members of the Canadian elite to hold dominant U.S. posts directly, it is worthwhile to reinforce the point and illustrate the type of person acting in this capacity from a Canadian viewpoint with some examples. The following are a baker's dozen Canadian directors of U.S. dominant companies.

John Black Aird, a graduate of Upper Canada College and Osgoode Hall Law School, is the son of Hugh Reston Aird, an investment dealer, and the grandson of Sir John Aird, one-time president of the Canadian Bank of Commerce (his other grandfather, John Homer Black, was an executive of Grenville Crushed Stone and a director of Canadian General Electric). He is the son-in-law of Jack H. Housser, stockbroker, who was president of H.B. Housser and vice-president of the Toronto Stock Exchange. Aird typifies Canada's internationalized elite. Although his main affiliation is with the law firm of Aird, Zimmerman and Berlis in Toronto, he has found time for other kinds of pursuits traditional to the upper class: he has been a Liberal senator (from 1964 until recently), vice-chairman of Reed Shaw Osler, a commercial insurance company, chairman of Algoma Central Railway, and a director of such prestigious Canadian firms as Molson Companies, Dominion Glass, and Rolland Paper and such dominants as Consolidated-Bathurst and the Bank of Nova Scotia. It should be evident why AMAX finds him a useful member of its board. To cement his business relations socially, he belongs to the Toronto and York clubs as well as the Canadian Club of New York City.

Alistair Matheson Campbell, chairman of Sun Life, a director and member of the executive committees of Canadian Pacific Investments, Stelco, and Royal Trust and a director of Canadian Industries (a total of four dominant Canadian companies), is also on the board of Textron Incorporated, a dominant in the U.S. aircraft industry.

Frank Elliot Case, chairman of Montreal Trust (and until 1967 domestic general manager of the Royal Bank), is a director of Price Company and Kennecott Copper, itself no stranger to the multinational scene (see p. 152). He also is a member of the Canadian Club in New York City along with the Toronto, St. James's, and Mount Royal clubs in Canada.

Of particular interest is John Hewson Coleman, who was deputy chairman of the Royal Bank until 1973 and is now a director there as well as of three other Canadian dominants, TransCanada PipeLines, Calgary Power, and Chrysler Canada. Added to these he has three U.S. dominant directorships with Colgate-Palmolive, Beatrice Foods, and Chrysler Corporation (Detroit), none of them unfamiliar in Canada.

Falconbridge Nickel's president, Marsh Alexander Cooper, is no stranger to Canadian board rooms as a director of Abitibi Paper, Crown Life, and Canadian Imperial Bank of Commerce. He is also a director of

Texas Eastern Transmission, a dominant U.S. utilities company.

This privilege is not completely confined to English Canadians. Paul Desruisseaux, a Liberal senator since 1966, chairman of Melchers Distilleries, and a director of Canadian General Electric and the Royal Bank, is also a director of PPG Industries. Socially, he does quite well. Besides his membership in the St. James's and Mount Royal clubs in Montreal, he belongs to the Canadian Club in New York City and the ultra-exclusive Duquesne of Pittsburgh.

George Arnold Reeve Hart, chairman and chief executive officer of the Bank of Montreal, a director and member of the executive committees of INCO, Sun Life, and Consolidated-Bathurst and a director of Canadian Pacific, finds time for the board of Uniroyal Incorporated. His memberships in the St. James's, Mount Royal, and Toronto clubs are rounded out by the Metropolitan Club of New York City.

Albert Bruce Matthews, a graduate of Upper Canada College, attended the University of Geneva and spent his early career in the investment business in New York. His father was a lieutenant-governor of Ontario, a director of Toronto General Trust and Excelsior Life, and had his own securities business, R.C. Matthews and Company. Bruce Matthews returned to the family firm and became chairman of Excelsior Life and continues as a director. He is also a director of Domtar, Massey-Ferguson, and Dominion Stores, executive vice-president of Argus, and chairman of Canada Permanent Trust as well as a director of the U.S. dominant Aetna Life. He belongs to five of the six top Canadian clubs as well as the Brook in New York City.

Beverley Matthews, a senior partner with McCarthy and McCarthy, a director of Canada Life, Brascan, Gulf Oil Canada, TransCanada PipeLines, Westinghouse Canada, and 3M Canada and a director and vice-president of the Toronto-Dominion Bank, is also a director of the parent company of Gulf Oil. He belongs to the Toronto, York, and Mount Royal clubs and the Rolling Rock and Duquesne in the United States.

Neil J. McKinnon,* former chairman of the Canadian Imperial Bank of Commerce and a director of Canada Life, TransCanada PipeLines, Ford Motor Canada, Falconbridge, MacMillan Bloedel, and Brascan, managed to hold directorships on the U.S. boards of Campbell Soup, Honeywell Incorporated, and Continental Oil. He also belonged to four of the six exclusive national clubs for men in Canada and was a member of the Links in New York.

William Earle McLaughlin, chairman and president of the Royal Bank, is a director of Power Corporation, Canadian Pacific, Genstar, and Algoma Steel. In the United States he is on the boards of Metropolitan Life, General Motors, and Ralston Purina. He is a first cousin, once removed, of Col. Sam McLaughlin, who sat for years on the parent board of General Motors. In addition to belonging to five of the six top Canadian clubs, he is a member of the Canadian Club in New York.

---

*N.J. McKinnon died in August 1975.

Louis Rasminsky, governor of the Bank of Canada from 1961 to 1973, and currently a director of five dominant Canadian companies (Bell Canada, Shell Canada, Alcan, Canada Trust, and Huron and Erie Mortgage), also finds time for Boise Cascade (dominant in paper and wood products) and American Express in the United States.

Another former member of the state elite, John Robarts, Premier of Ontario from 1961 to 1971 and now a director of Abitibi Paper, Bell Canada, Canadian Imperial Bank of Commerce, and Power Corporation, is also a board member of U.S. Metropolitan Life. This does not exhaust the examples but it does give some indication of the people behind the interlocking statistics.

Overall, 63 of the 113 dominant corporations in Canada (or 56 per cent) are interlocked with U.S. dominants; 73 of the 194 dominant corporations in the United States (or 38 per cent) have interlocks with Canadian dominants. These figures include directorships in U.S. companies held by Canadians and directorships in Canadian companies held by U.S. residents; some companies are interlocked in both ways. Clearly, subsidiary interlocking from U.S. parents to their branch plants and from Canadian branch plants to their U.S. parents is a sign of Canadian dependence. Direct interlocks are signs of strength, both those from U.S. dominants to independent Canadian dominants, which reflect the ability of the Canadian elite to attract important members of the U.S. elite, and those from independent Canadian dominants to U.S. dominants, which reflect a desire by members of the U.S. elite to attract members of the indigenous Canadian elite. They are more characteristic of relations between two elites in alliance than of dependent relations. Both patterns serve to strengthen the continental connection.

The conclusion may be drawn that the economic elites of both Canada and the United States have continental segments and that they operate above and beyond subsidiary relations. A continental elite connecting the sectors of greatest strengths can be said to exist, although it would be wrong to suggest that the entire elite is a continental one. The exchanges, because of the particular historical development of each nation, occur in such a way that they are mainly from Canadian finance to U.S. manufacturing and from U.S. manufacturing to Canadian finance – from strength to strength. It has been demonstrated that there is a reciprocal relationship between powerful sectors, a dependent relationship in other sectors, and relative autonomy in a third group.

An outstanding feature of these continental ties is the effect of economic sectors. They suggest that the financial-industrial axis is continental for Canada but national within the United States. Once again evidence is added regarding the integration of U.S. production and circulation and the unevenness of development within Canada. The ties also reflect a pattern in which a segment of Canada's elite has been drawn into the inner circle of the U.S. elite. While a segment of Canada's elite has gained continental power, Canadian society has been drawn into a relationship of dependence on the United States.

Interlocking between the Indigenous Elite and Branch Plants in Canada

Thus far the relations within Canada between U.S. subsidiaries and the indigenous Canadian elite have not been explored. Drawing the distinction between the dominant indigenous and comprador fractions of the elite must be done with care, because the indigenous and comprador groups overlap. The crucial difference lies in their respective bases of power. The individuals who are comprador have as their main base of power a position, usually in the senior management, in a branch plant of a foreign-controlled firm; the indigenous fraction has independent Canadian-controlled bases of power.* A distinction, therefore, must be made between the comprador roles through the structure and through the individual. "Structural compradorization" represents a set of uppermost positions in the foreign-controlled branch plants, while "individual compradorization" represents a set of persons occupying these positions whose main affiliation is with a branch plant. Some indigenous members also hold comprador positions, but these are secondary to their main Canadian-controlled positions. In this study the distinction between the two forms is made on the basis of a self-reported statement† of the "main occupation" of these persons, and if it was other than corporate, such as a law firm, the country of control of most of their corporate affiliations was used.

It is important to note that persons who are recruited to the highest positions are selected by those in control at that time. There is very little legislation now operating that would dictate the nature of these appointments. As Mitchell Sharp made clear when he was minister of external affairs, the federal government "was aware that a firm required to alter the composition of its board by law might seek out passive directors. And it was aware that key decisions are often taken, not by the board of a subsidiary, but by the board of the parent company itself."[56]

Although 40 per cent of the dominant positions in the Canadian economy are foreign controlled or occupied, the figure represents only the *structural* dimension of compradorization and ignores the other, *individual* compradorization.[57] When the criteria for individual compradorization are applied to the Canadian-born members of the elite hold-

---

* If there are ten elite positions in a branch plant, all ten *positions* are foreign controlled. When some of these positions are occupied by persons with other primary activities that are Canadian controlled, say as insurance company or bank presidents, these persons are *individual* members of the Canadian indigenous elite but hold comprador *positions* in the branch plant along with their main indigenous positions, hence the difference between individual and structural compradorization.

† The statement appears in the *Financial Post Directory of Directors*, which asks each person listed to indicate his "principal occupation."

ing dominant positions, it is found that 74 per cent are indigenous, 17 per cent U.S. comprador, 5 per cent U.K. comprador, and 4 per cent other comprador. In other words, while only 60 per cent of the dominant positions are controlled and held by Canadian residents, 74 per cent of the Canadian-born members of the elite are indigenous and have an independent Canadian base of power. Therefore, some members of the indigenous fraction of the Canadian elite must occupy comprador positions in addition to their primary Canadian activity.* A few examples will illustrate the type:

William Flavelle McLean, who succeeded his father, James Stanley McLean, as president of Canada Packers, is also a vice-president and a director of the Canadian Imperial Bank of Commerce (his father before him was a director of the Commerce); he is besides a director of the U.S.-controlled Canadian General Electric. Jean P.W. Ostiguy, who succeeded his father, Paul E. Ostiguy, in Morgan, Ostiguy and Hudon, investment dealers, members of the Montreal, Toronto, and Philadelphia stock exchanges, is on the board of the Canadian Imperial Bank of Commerce and the U.S.-controlled Ford Motor Company of Canada. William H. Young, fourth generation of his family in what is now called the Hamilton Group, is a director of both the Steel Company of Canada and the National Trust; he became a director of the U.S.-controlled Gulf Oil of Canada in 1973. Charles N. Woodward, who inherited his family's dominant retail firm, Woodward Stores, is a director of both the Royal Bank and the U.S.-controlled Westcoast Transmission Company. Donald G. Willmot, president of Molson Companies, director of the Bank of Nova Scotia and Crown Life, is also a director of Texaco Canada. John P. Gordon, president of the Steel Company of Canada and a director of the Bank of Montreal, is also a director of Gulf Oil of Canada. Robert J. Butler, the first non-Eaton to hold the presidency of the T. Eaton Company, is a director of National Trust and Gulf Oil of Canada. (Fredrik S. and John Craig Eaton are still president and chairman, respectively, of Eaton's of Canada, the fifth generation of the family to have held these posts.)

These and other examples illustrate the way in which members of the indigenous elite are frequently recruited to fill comprador positions in branch plants although in their main economic activities they themselves are not comprador. This practice again suggests an alliance rather than a conflict between the indigenous and the comprador dominant fractions, although there is obviously an unequal entente.

It can be anticipated that as the operations of U.S. branch plants in Canada mature and become established, more of the executives will be recruited from and trained in the Canadian plants, and more members of the indigenous elite will be drafted into their board rooms. This has already been occurring in the oil industry, where a "Canadian execu-

---

* For a more systematic analysis of this phenomenon by fraction of the Canadian elite, see Chapter 9, Table 59.

tive now heads each of the Canadian subsidiary operations of the major U.S. oil companies."[58] This does not mean that control has passed to Canada; as long as 50 per cent or more of the shares are held in the United States, these companies are still under the hand of the U.S. parent. It does mean, however, that the U.S. and Canadian economic elites are becoming increasingly integrated with one another upon a mutually reinforcing power base.

While it is valuable to focus on the activities of elites, it is also necessary to distinguish the effects that U.S. investment patterns in Canada have on the nation as a whole from their effects on the elite. The economy of Canada is very much integrated through resource extraction, power production, transportation, manufacturing, and marketing with the economy of the United States. Moreover, the United States, either directly or through its branch plants, serves as an important outlet for Canadian financial investments. The net impact of this situation is paradoxical; it has produced both economic growth and underdevelopment. As a whole, Canada is dependent on the U.S. economy and the decisions of its economic elite. But many members of Canada's economic elite, who have fostered this arrangement and benefited from it, have integrated themselves as active participants in this system of dominance.

The Economic Elite in Canada and the United States: I. Careers, Class, and Kinship

The corporate world analysed in Chapter 6 operates as a closed social network, an association of like-minded people that limits access to its inner circles, makes investment decisions, and determines who will manage corporations and what skills, products, and life-styles will be valued. It is a world of the rich and powerful. Often, but not always, wealthy before they enter this world, individuals are certainly so when they become established parts of it.* The economic elite is a self-selecting group of persons who provide their own criteria for acceptability. These characteristics are the basis for an elite that is a socially interacting group with the power to direct corporations.

The powers of exclusion of economic elites vary, as argued earlier (pp. 26-32), and conditions created by the nature of the U.S. and Canadian economies and their relationships as we have studied them will be important in analysing and comparing the two elites. This chapter focuses on the types of career avenues that lead to elite positions, the class origins of the elite, and inheritance and kinship ties within it. In the next chapter, corporate and social characteristics of the elite will be analysed. Finally, in Chapter 9, the focus will be on relations between Canadian and U.S. members of the elite.

This study of members of the two economic elites is based on comparable sets of data gathered for both groups.† There have been many earlier studies of the U.S. economic elite and managers, but comparisons cannot be drawn between them and the one undertaken here.° They do, however, add depth to the findings for the United States reported here, particularly in terms of the class origins of top businessmen. Few studies of any kind have been made of the Canadian economic elite or managers.

The major conclusion of these chapters is that entrance to the economic elite is easier for persons from outside the upper class in the United States than it is in Canada. There is indeed a central core of members drawn from the upper class; they inherit their positions and have their main careers in family firms. But outside of this core the U.S. elite is more open, recruiting from a much broader class base than is the case in Canada. This finding is consistent with the other points of comparison made earlier – the lower degree of concentration, the lower

---

* See Appendix XIII for a discussion of ownership and control.
† See Appendix XII for the extent of coverage and sources of the material used here.
° See Appendix XI for a discussion of earlier U.S. studies.

density of interlocks, and the expanding U.S. economy (both at home and abroad). Moreover, the Canadian elite is so closely knit and drawn from such a narrow segment of Canadian society directly because of the penetration of Canada by the United States (see Chapters 4 and 6). The Canadian elite has this character expressly because it has been confined to the sphere of circulation while the sphere of production has been in the hands of outsiders. Confined to this narrow turf, the Canadian upper class has been forced to hold tightly to its position. With the sphere of circulation dominated by the Canadian upper class and the sphere of production controlled by external elements, little room has been left for entrepreneurial indigenous Canadian capitalists outside the sphere of circulation to have an effective role in the elite.

I. Career Patterns of the Economic Elite

The career patterns of most members of the economic elite can be categorized according to the avenues the members have used to gain access to that elite. In this study, each elite member has been classified by the *main* pattern best characterizing his career. Since these patterns are not mutually exclusive, some individuals have secondary patterns, which will be discussed under each career. Table 30 shows a comparison of members of the U.S. and Canadian economic elites according to the main patterns. From this table, it is evident that in the U.S. elite there is little difference between native-born members and the entire elite, while in Canada there is a considerable difference.

TABLE 30

Main Career Patterns of Members of the U.S. and Canadian Economic Elites *(percentages)*

Main Career Pattern	Native Canadian (683)	Canadian, All (798)	Native U.S. (1,894)	U.S., All (2,007)
Engineering and science	10.8	12.8	15.2	14.2
Banking and financial executives	15.4	16.0	12.2	11.9
Law	17.6	15.8	12.0	11.2
Company finance department	6.7	7.8	11.4	11.2
Training in commerce	4.8	5.2	7.1	7.0
Other elite	7.8	7.1	5.8	5.9
Other sector (not elite)	2.5	2.5	3.5	3.7
Family firm	26.8	24.4	19.3	18.6
On own account	1.5	1.8	1.4	1.4
Unclassified	6.1	7.0	12.2	12.6
	100	100	100	100

In the following discussion, the comparisons between Canada and the United States will be made between two mutually exclusive sets of data because the U.S. elite is made up of all persons holding elite positions in the 194 dominant corporations, whether they are resident in the United States or not, while the Canadian elite includes only Canadian residents with positions in the 113 dominant corporations.* (The two comparable sets, dealing with persons native-born and resident in Canada [683] or in the United States [1,894], will be the focus of analysis unless specified otherwise. In both cases, "natives" were actually born in the particular country except for a few persons born to parents who were normally residents there but were temporarily out of the country at the time of the elite member's birth.)

Training in Engineering and Science

Table 30 shows that a higher percentage of the U.S. elite have careers arising from the technical training and skills of engineering and science than their Canadian counterparts,† as might be expected with greater emphasis on research and development in the home country of the parents of most multinational corporations. An additional 4.5 per cent of the U.S. elite whose main careers were in other categories have had a secondary career based on engineering and science. In Canada, engineering and science were the basis for a secondary career of 5.4 per cent. Persons whose careers are in engineering and science tend to operate in particular sectors. The patterns are very similar in both countries: in resources, 43 per cent in the United States and 47 per cent in Canada; in manufacturing, 20 per cent in both countries; in transportation/utilities, 26 per cent in both countries. In trade, there are no persons of this type in Canada and only 7 per cent in the United States. Each country has 1 per cent in finance. It is clear that members of the elite with technical skills have had much better career possibilities in the resource sector than in any other. In Canada, however, the proportion of native-born elite in this sector is depressed because U.S. companies own most of Canada's resources and supply many of the elite having this career pattern. Jerry McAfee is an interesting example of an elite member with this kind of career in the resource sector. Early in 1976 he left the presidency of Gulf Oil Canada to become chairman of U.S. Gulf Oil after the shake-up of executives in connection with illegal political contributions in the parent company. Texas-born, "like his father before him, McAfee is a chemical engineer and a career-man with Gulf."[1]

---

* Foreign-resident members of the Canadian and U.S. elites are discussed on pp. 251-55.

† A higher proportion of the foreign-born elite members in Canada entered through engineering and science than the native-born in either Canada or the United States, with 24.3 per cent. Here again is evidence not only of the historical underdevelopment of technology in Canada but also of high foreign ownership in the sphere of production, the sphere where most technology is applied.

Most of the group in engineering and science do not have upper-class backgrounds.* In fact, of persons in all career types, they are the least likely to come from upper-class origins. In the United States, only 10 per cent of them have upper-class origins and in Canada, "only" 32 per cent (which is extremely low by Canadian standards). On the other hand, among persons whose secondary career is in engineering and science, 58 per cent are of upper-class origin in the United States and 75 per cent in Canada. Nevertheless, this training is the main avenue by which individuals born outside the upper class can become members of the elite. The fact that there are fewer persons of this type in Canada's elite has a considerable effect on the class origin of that elite.

In the United States, these technical types are most often found in "insider" positions in dominant corporations, accounting for 26 per cent of all insiders in dominant corporations and 19 per cent of the "executives" but only 7 per cent of the "outsiders."† The pattern in Canada is similar with persons of this type accounting for only 7 per cent of outsiders but 14 per cent of insiders and 16 per cent of executives. The Canadian elite is composed of more outsiders than the U.S. elite (see p. 219), so that the number of technically trained members in the elite (and therefore the proportion from non-upper-class origins) is smaller.

An illustration of their origin outside the upper class and the value of their skills among the elite is the long "grooming" the science and engineering types receive in the corporation, often followed by a course of more general training. In the United States 10 per cent of the persons in this category also have a secondary career in commerce, while only 4 per cent in Canada have this additional pattern. Many of them go to the Advanced Management Program at the Harvard Business School (see pp. 237-38), where Robert Urey Haslanger (vice-president of Pennzoil Company), Ellison Lockwood Hazard (former chairman of Continental Can and now a director of that board and of Goodyear Tire and Rubber and Southern Pacific Company), John Edward Meyer (president of Cities Service), John Leslie Ross (vice-president of Standard Oil Company (Ohio)), Raymond Camille Tower (vice-president of FMC Corporation and a director of Marathon Oil), and George Raymond Vila (chairman of Uniroyal Incorporated and a director of Bendix Corporation and Chemical New York Bank) were all sent late in their careers after initial training in technical skills. Because they are usually older when they come into the elite than persons in many of the other career types and because they seldom hold on to their elite positions for as long as the others, the engineer and science members are the most "middle-aged" of all types.

---

* For a definition of upper class, see pp. 207-08.

† "Insiders" are vice-presidents and other officials of a company who do not hold "executive" positions. "Executives" are presidents, chairmen, and vice-chairmen of boards of directors. "Outsiders" are members of a company's board of directors who are not officials of the company.

Banking and Financial Executives

The relative importance of the financial sectors in Canada and the United States is reflected in the proportions of persons who enter the elite as financiers and financial executives in the two countries (see Table 30). Canadians lead in this category. Moreover, persons taking this route to the elite usually remain in the finance sector, accounting for 59 per cent whose main affiliation is in the finance sector in the United States and 50 per cent in Canada. There is a secondary pattern in the careers of many of these persons resulting from their education: in Canada, 10 per cent have training in commerce and 12 per cent training in law, in the United States, 21 per cent in commerce and 10 per cent in law. Some members of the elite with main career avenues that led elsewhere also have secondary patterns as financiers or financial executives; these include persons who entered the elite "on their own account," some whose careers are in family firms, and some who changed to the economic elite or had a first career in another sector. One such example is Kenneth Robert MacGregor, now chairman of Mutual Life Assurance and a director of Huron and Erie Mortgage, who had his main career with the Federal Department of Insurance. He joined the department in 1930 and was Superintendent of Insurance with the rank of deputy minister from 1953 to 1964, at which time he left to become Mutual's president.

Except for persons with careers in family firms, more bankers and financial executives are of upper-class origin than any other career type in the United States (32 per cent). In Canada (with 51 per cent upper class), they are only behind careers in family firms and lawyers. In addition, many members who have a secondary pattern in finance have upper-class origins (63 per cent in the United States and 86 per cent in Canada). In the United States, many sons of the upper class who do not continue in family firms or whose families were "well connected" but did not own the companies that projected them into the elite go the financial route. For example: Norborne Berkeley, Jr., whose father was a vice-president of Bethlehem Steel, is now president of Chemical New York Bank and a director of Uniroyal. Joseph William Chinn, whose father was president of Northern Neck State Bank, was chairman of Wilmington Trust Company and is now a director of W.T. Grant Company and Uniroyal. Richard Pierce Cooley's father was chairman of South-West Bell and a director of the First National Bank; the son is now president of Wells Fargo and Company and a director of UAL Incorporated, Westinghouse Electric, and Pacific Gas and Electric. James Henry Higgins's father was president of Pittsburgh Plate Glass, and the younger Higgins is now president of Mellon National Bank and a director of Gulf Oil. Richard Devereux Hill's father was a lawyer and a director of several companies, and the son is now chairman of First National Boston and a director of John Hancock Mutual Life. The son of Arthur W. Page, former vice-president of American Telephone and Telegraph and a director of Chase National Bank, Continental Oil, Westinghouse Electric, Kennecott Copper, and Prudential Insurance, is Walter Hines Page II, now president of J.P. Morgan and Company and a director of Kennecott. Richard Sturgis Perkins's father was president of City Bank Farmers Trust and a director of Union Pacific Corporation, National City Bank of New York, American Tobacco, Consolidated Edison, Anaconda Copper, and others; the son was chairman of the First National Bank of New York and now is a director of Allied Chemical, New York Life, International Telephone and Telegraph, Southern Pacific, and Consolidated Edison. John Bassett Moore Place is the son of Herman G. Place, former vice-president of Chase National Bank and founder of General Precision. J.B.M. Place was president of Chase Manhattan, where he had spent his entire working life until 1971, when he left to become chairman of Anaconda Company (of which he had been a board member since 1969). Besides holding this post, he is a director of Chemical New York, Celanese Corporation, Union Pacific, and Metropolitan Life. The father of James Dixon Robinson III was president of the Trust Company of Georgia and chairman of the First National Bank of Atlanta, and the son is now president of American Express (having attained the position at thirty-nine) and a director of Union Pacific. Walter Bigelow Wriston's father was president of Lawrence College, Canton, New York, and later public governor of the New York Stock Exchange; the son is chairman of First National City Bank and a director of General Electric and J.C. Penney Company. Willsie Winston Wood's father was superintendent of the California state banks; the younger Wood is now chairman of the finance committee of Transamerica Corporation. More than any other career pattern, with the obvious exception of family firms, the top financial executives and financiers come from some of America's "finest" families.

In Canada, financiers follow a very similar pattern while financial executives, especially in banks, have traditionally been "long crawlers" (working over twenty years in the same company before becoming an officer). The pattern in banking has been changing, with more use of university-trained executives than of persons groomed in the organization.[2] The result has been more upper-class recruitment; for example, W. Earle McLaughlin, head of the Royal Bank, has an upper-class background, as does Richard Murray Thomson, head of the Toronto-Dominion Bank, whose father was vice-chairman of the Canadian Imperial Bank of Commerce.

Financiers and financial executives come principally from upper-class families in both countries, and the Canadian economic elite is weighted particularly toward the upper class because the financial sector is high in numbers and importance. From what we have seen of elite members drawn from engineering and science training on the one hand and entering through banking and financial institutions on the other, it is clear that career patterns have some bearing on the unequal rates of upper-class recruitment in Canada and the United States.

Lawyers

Training in law leads to very different career patterns in the economic elites of the two countries. As Table 30 shows, the proportion of lawyers is much greater in the Canadian than in the U.S. elite. Moreover, many of the U.S. lawyers whose main careers are in law have experience outside business and law, primarily in the state or as financial executives, and some have had secondary training in commerce. In Canada, this is less pronounced, although some lawyers are financiers or financial executives or have careers outside business and law. The numbers are more impressive, however, when law is a secondary career, as it is among 47 per cent of those with careers in other sectors, 40 per cent who switched from other elite positions, 16 per cent serving in family firms, and 12 per cent of financial executives with training in law. The trend in the United States, though similar, is much less pronounced: 16 per cent with primary careers in other sectors, 23 per cent who switched from other elite positions, 10 per cent who entered the elite "on their own account," 10 per cent who are financial executives, and about 7 per cent with careers in family firms.

TABLE 31

Primary Affiliation of Those Entering the Economic Elite through Law (percentages)

	Main Current Affiliation			
	Partnership	Executive	Insider	Outsider
United States	46	31	12	11
Canada	68	12	15	5

Types of primary career vary markedly among lawyers in the two elites, as Table 31 illustrates. In Canada, the primary affiliation of over two-thirds is a partnership. In the United States, less than half have a partnership as their primary post. Type of association with law firms also exemplifies this difference. About 12 per cent of the entire U.S. economic elite have been at some time associated with a law firm, but in 1975 only 80 continued this association while 166 have left their law firms, gravitating mainly to the manufacturing sector. In Canada, 18 per cent of the entire economic elite have been associated with law firms, but 115 continue this connection and only 28 have left, while an additional 42 are corporate lawyers only, without association with law firms. Lawyers who leave the firm in Canada generally move either to manufacturing or to finance. It appears that in the United States the law firm is a step on the road to an executive position in a corporation; in Canada lawyers tend to operate in the economic elite mainly as outsiders, keeping the firm as their main base of operation.

Although the "house" lawyer is becoming increasingly important in Canada, only 720 or 3.4 per cent of all Canada's lawyers fall into this category and only twelve Canadian companies have ten or more house lawyers. A different situation prevails in the United States. General Motors, for example, has 120 internal lawyers in the United States but only two in the Canadian branch plant. One reason for this is that General Motors of Canada is a private company, but the parent General Motors is publicly traded and consequently experiences more legal pressure.

Only 26 per cent of the persons in the U.S. elite whose main career is in law have an upper-class background, but the proportion in Canada is more than double this figure (57 per cent), behind only careers in family firms in this respect. Among persons with a secondary career in law, 40 per cent are of upper-class origin in the United States and 75 per cent in Canada. Regarding persons who enter and then leave law firms, in the United States they are 32 per cent of upper-class origin compared to the 40 per cent of those who continue in law; in Canada, this difference does not exist. In both countries, house lawyers are less likely than other lawyers to be drawn from the upper class. The lack of positions as house lawyers in Canada lessens the number of paths into the elite and emphasizes upper-class recruitment.

There are several examples of U.S. lawyers being recruited from fairly low class origins. The most outstanding is Irving Saul Shapiro, the son of poor immigrants from Lithuania, whose father owned a small dry-cleaning shop in Minneapolis. Shapiro spent the first third of his career as an attorney in the Department of Justice in Washington, and then moved to du Pont, where "his reputation within the company rests in his management, in the final stages, of the extraordinarily complex divestiture of Du Pont's stock in General Motors in the early Sixties."[3] According to this report, through Shapiro's work in "one of the most successful corporate lobbying efforts in history, Du Pont got a bill through Congress in 1962 that saved the individual stockholders an estimated $1 billion by permitting them to account for the G.M. stock they received as a return of capital, taxable at capital-gains rates. Shapiro directed the company's campaign in Congress and designed the divestiture plan."[4] Such impressive talents do not go unrewarded. In 1973, he was made chairman and chief executive officer of E.I. du Pont de Nemours with a salary of $250,000 a year, and he is being drawn into upper-class social circles; "Shapiro has been proposed for membership in the Wilmington Club, the downtown bastion of the local establishment, and may not have to wait the usual eight years to get in."[5]

A detailed study of key U.S. law firms, the "spokesmen for big business," was made by Erwin Smigel in 1964. Smigel shows that the senior lawyers in these firms received training mainly (72 per cent) in the law schools of Harvard, Yale, and Columbia, are an integrated part of the upper class (30 per cent are listed in the *Social Register*), and have obtained their positions in the firms through influence in many instances

(29 per cent).[6] The data in the current analysis confirm many of Smigel's findings and indicate that other firms outside New York are also important – Ropes and Gray in Boston, for instance, with such partners as Francis Hardon Burr, a director of American Airlines and Equitable Life, and Edward Benno Hanify, a director of John Hancock Mutual Life and AT&T.

Twenty-three key law firms in Canada have more than one member holding an economic elite position, totalling sixty partners with 106 dominant directorships. To a much greater extent than in the United States law firms in Canada serve to integrate the economic elite further by providing many additional connections between dominant corporations. This situation is to be expected, given the greater use of house lawyers in the United States and the restriction of recruitment of Canada's outside lawyers to only a few of the country's most prestigious firms.

There are nevertheless many lawyers associated with top U.S. law firms who come from well-connected families. Charles Gillespie Blaine's father was president of Marine Midland Banks, a director of Remington Rand, Studebaker, and other companies, and active, as head of the European Advisory Commission mission to Belgium and treasurer-director to the U.S. services to China, in state-associated enterprises. The son is a partner in Phillips, Lytle, Hitchcock, Blaine and Huber and a director of Marine Midland Banks. Grayson Mallet-Prevost Murphy's father was a director of New York Trust, Guaranty Trust, Bethlehem Steel, and Goodyear and was also associated with the state. The younger Murphy is a partner with Shearman and Sterling and a director of Georgia-Pacific Corporation and Celanese. William Piel, Sr., was president of Piel Brothers; William Piel, Jr., is a partner with Sullivan and Cromwell and a director of Phillips Petroleum. Fred Moore Vinson, Jr., son of a chief justice of the U.S. Supreme Court, is a partner with Reasoner, Davis and Vinson and a director of Lockheed Aircraft.

The more typical pattern in the United States, however, is one in which a current member of the elite formerly associated with a law firm has left that firm to take on an executive position with a dominant company. For example, William Graham Claytor IV is the son of an executive with American Gas and Electric; the son was with Covington and Burling for thirty years before becoming president of Southern Railway and a director of J.P. Morgan and Company. R. Heath Larry's father was an executive with Pittsburgh Limestone. After practising law briefly, the son went to United States Steel, where he is a vice-chairman, as well as a director of Textron Incorporated. Then there is George William Miller, who moved to Textron from the prestigious Wall Street firm of Cravath, Swain and Moore "after Royal Little [Textron's chairman] was impressed with his work in a raucous proxy fight with American Woolen."[7] Miller became president of Textron at thirty-five and is now its chairman and a director of Allied Chemical.

Somewhat different is the case of William Prior Patterson, who was in private practice in Dayton, Ohio, and is now chairman of the Third National Bank and Trust Company and also a director of NCR Corporation (formerly National Cash Register); he is the grandnephew of the founder of National Cash Register. George Alfred Ranney, Jr., is particularly well connected. His father, who was once with the Bank of Montreal in Chicago, was chairman of Commonwealth Edison and a director of International Harvester, First National Bank, and other companies. His brother-in-law is a director of Borg-Warner Corporation and First Chicago Corporation. The younger Ranney was with Sidley, Austin, Burgess and Smith of Chicago for over thirty years and is now vice-chairman of Inland Steel.

As was true of the engineering/science and banking/finance routes to the elite, the patterns in law on both sides of the border explain in part differences in class recruitment to the two elites. In Canada lawyers make up a greater proportion of the elite and tend to follow different paths on their way.

The Company Finance Department

The finance department of one's firm is a more popular route to the economic elite than law in the United States. A main career there as a chartered accountant, treasurer, or comptroller brings the member in close contact with the financial workings of the corporation and provides experience in its fiscal operations. As Table 30 shows, in Canada the proportion using this avenue is much lower. U.S. executives whose main careers are in the finance department have frequently added a secondary career and training. The additional training is most often in commerce with a smaller group trained in law and a few rising to the status of financial executives. In Canada, smaller numbers in this category have training in commerce or are financial executives. Unlike those in the United States with their main careers in engineering and science who tend to be sent to Advanced Management Program at Harvard after they have been with the corporation for some time, many elite members who enter via finance departments have taken Master of Business Administration degrees immediately after finishing undergraduate work and then moved directly into the corporation, specializing in the finance department.

Like the engineering and science entrants, persons coming through the finance department are typically career men and are also likely to come from a less than upper-class background in both countries. Only 14 per cent are from upper-class origins in the United States and 35 per cent in Canada. Rawleigh Warner, Jr., is an atypical example: his father was chairman of the Pure Oil Company and a director of various corporations, and the younger Warner worked first in the finance departments of various Mobil Oil subsidiaries, then becoming chairman and a director of Caterpillar Tractor, AT&T, American Express, and Chemical New York. More typical would be Frederic Garrett Donner, whose father was an accountant. The son began as an accountant with General Motors in 1926, became a vice-president in 1941 and chairman in 1958, and retired to become chairman of the Alfred P. Sloan Foundation in 1968, continuing as a GM director. He was important in establishing credit arrangements for wartime expansion under Alfred P. Sloan and Charles E. Wilson. Richard Charles Gerstenberg has a similar story. His father was a factory inspector in the Remington Typewriter Company. Gerstenberg had a career at GM much like Donner's, eventually becoming chairman. Daniel Jeremiah Haughton came out of the Alabama backwoods and rose through the finance departments of aircraft companies to the chairmanship of Lockheed and a directorship in Southern California Edison.

Again the Canadian economic elite has fewer members coming from a career type that is not recruited from the upper class. The company finance department route, like engineering and science, permits upward mobility for persons from outside the upper class, and here again the foreign-born are more prevalent (13.9 per cent) than the native-born (6.7 per cent).

Training in Commerce

The last mode of entry involving a particular training or corporate career experience is taken by graduates in commerce. This route is rapidly becoming important among the economic elite, especially in the United States but also in Canada. Its newness appears in the age profiles for both elites, in which the oldest are least likely to have a career based on training in commerce, followed by the middle age group, but the youngest are using this route in greater numbers (with 7 per cent in Canada and 10 per cent in the United States). Overall, the U.S. elite claims a larger proportion of members of this type (7.1 per cent) than the Canadian (4.8 per cent). Moreover, commerce training leads to more secondary careers in the United States – 11 per cent of all other types, particularly finance departments, finance executives, from other sectors, from family firms, and engineering and science. In Canada, only 6 per cent have commerce as a secondary pattern with finance departments most common, followed by finance executives, from other areas or other elites, and family firms.

Members of the elite trained in business administration vary between Canada and the United States in class of origin. Like lawyers, in the United States few of them come from the upper class (16 per cent). Members with a secondary pattern in commerce are somewhat more likely to be upper class in origin (32 per cent). In Canada, however, 49 per cent of those in commerce as a main career pattern are upper class in origin while 65 per cent of the secondary types are drawn from the upper class. Thus access to this career has been much more open in the United States than in Canada.

The M.B.A. programs at the University of Michigan and Stanford, Dartmouth, and Northwestern universities are outstanding in business administration training, as is the Advanced Management Program at Harvard, but the most noteworthy evidence of education among the current elite is clearly an M.B.A. degree from the Harvard Business School.* The oldest Harvard M.B.A. among the elite is Donald Kirk David, who took his degree in 1919 and remained at Harvard to teach for some years, later returning as a dean. He held executive positions among various dominant corporations, and while now retired, he is still a director of Pan American Airways and Great Atlantic and Pacific in the United States as well as Alcan Aluminium in Canada. Altogether, 174 members of the U.S. economic elite have received Harvard M.B.A.s and sixty are graduates of the Advanced Management Program, many having attended together during the nineteen forties and fifties. Obviously, the Harvard commerce program has provided a common socialization ground for many members of the current U.S. economic elite, where early friendships were forged and a common set of assumptions absorbed.

Recruits from Other Elites and from Careers in Other Sectors

In both Canada and the United States, a fair number of members of the current economic elite have had their main careers in another elite (particularly the state, but also the military and educational) and have then moved into the economic world. A somewhat greater proportion have done so in Canada than in the United States (see Table 30). Another group of elite members have switched to their current positions from other sectors where they did not hold elite positions. The U.S. elite tends to have a slightly higher proportion of members recruited from non-elite positions in the state, military, or university worlds. A major reason for this difference at the lower levels of sector switching is the relationship between universities and the economic elite in the United States in contrast to Canada. Many of the elite and non-elite switchers move from senior university posts, mainly presidents or chancellors, into the economic elite, or they retain these positions and sit as outsiders on the boards of dominant corporations. A further difference is in the relationship with the military, which tends to supply many high-level personnel to the corporate world in the United States but not in Canada. The Canadian economic elite has more recruits from state elite positions.†

Many who switch from another elite in the United States have second-

---

*For a further discussion of the importance of the Harvard Business School for the economic elite, see pp. 237-38.

†These issues will be explored in more detail in a later section on relations between elites, pp. 245-50.

ary careers in law (23 per cent) and science and engineering (16 per cent) and, to a lesser extent, as financial executives (7 per cent). The only secondary pattern prevalent among non-elites switching from another sector is lawyers (11 per cent). In Canada, those coming from other elites have very high secondary patterns in law (40 per cent) with less in other types, while the non-elite are just as high in law. In both countries the two types switching from other sectors most often hold outside directorships in the economic world, with relatively few as insiders or executives. Thus, switchers are valued more for the contacts and experience they can bring to boards than for administrative or executive talents. Both groups tend to come from an upper-class background in Canada (46 per cent) and are somewhat less likely to do so in the United States (29 per cent).

The names of a few members of this group will indicate their status and the importance of their main careers; "making it" in the state elite is a strong recommendation for being drawn into the economic elite. George Wildman Ball, former undersecretary of state in the Johnson administration and now a senior partner with Lehman Brothers, is a director of Burlington Industries and AMAX Incorporated. A former secretary of the treasury, Joseph Walker Barr, is now chairman of American Security Trust and a director of both Minnesota Mining and Manufacturing and Burlington Industries (where he meets his old colleague, George Ball). John Thomas Connor, a former colleague of George Ball and Joseph Barr as secretary of commerce, is now chairman of Allied Chemical and a director of General Foods, General Motors, and Chase Manhattan. Nicholas de Belleville Katzenbach, another former colleague of John Connor, George Ball, and Joseph Barr as attorney general and undersecretary of state, is now vice-president and general counsel of International Business Machines (IBM). When he "prepared to leave the government and transfer to the chancellery at Armonk, another treble damage suit hit IBM, thus assuring Mr. Katzenbach, the new general counsel, that there would be plenty of work for him."[8] Charles Franklin Luce, another colleague of the four mentioned above, was undersecretary of the interior in the Johnson administration and is now chairman of Consolidated Edison and a director of United Air Lines and Metropolitan Life. Peter G. Peterson, who became secretary of commerce under Richard Nixon, is now working with George Ball as chairman of Lehman Brothers and is also a director of Federated Department Stores, General Foods, and 3M. William Marvin Watson, in the Johnson cabinet as postmaster general, is now vice-president of Occidental Petroleum.

Elite recruitment of this kind is even more pronounced in Canada. Among the economic elite of 1972 there were eight former federal cabinet ministers, five former provincial premiers, a former prime minister, and three other members of provincial political elites. The bureaucratic elite also contributed twenty members.[9]

Careers in the Family Firm

In spite of prophecies of the death of family capitalism, there are more persons with careers in family firms than with any of the other types of careers so far examined for both the Canadian and the U.S. economic elites. Members of the Canadian elite lead their opposite numbers in the United States in the proportion having their main career in the family business,* but even in the United States, it is still easiest to make it into the economic elite by being born into it (see Table 30).

The main career in the family firm often overlaps with the other career types already outlined. Nevertheless, the primary reason why these persons are in the elite is that they have an affiliation with a company in which their fathers and often grandfathers or occasionally uncles had some dominant position. Not all persons who have inherited positions are included here nor are all persons born in the upper class, although all those with careers in family firms are upper class in origin, and they make up the solid core of the upper class. They are most likely to have other careers or other training as financiers or financial executives, in law or commerce.

Persons with careers in family firms in both elites average highest of all types in both the oldest and the youngest age groups, which indicates that they enter the elite at an earlier age and remain in it for a longer period than any other type. The continuity in the elite, both their own careers and those of other generations, gives these people the opportunity to have a greater impact than any others on the "character" of the economic elite. They set the tone and standards, and they decide who among the rest of the population may join the elite. This set of people is also the heart of the propertied class because, unlike the executives who are rewarded with stock options that can make them wealthy, they are wealthy before entering the elite and enter the elite because of the wealth and property accumulated by previous generations.†

In dominant U.S. corporations, the group under discussion is more important in outside directorships (holding 26 per cent), having only 10 per cent of the insider positions but 15 per cent of the executive posts in dominant corporations. In Canada their proportion is highest among outside directors (33 per cent), but they also hold many more

---

* In *The Canadian Corporate Elite* I reported that 18.8 per cent of the Canadian-born elite had their careers in family firms. Additional research on the members included in that work and expansion of the coverage of the elite for this study has produced evidence that in fact 26.8 per cent had careers in family firms. This eight-point increase has been the largest difference to appear between the initial gathering of data and the follow-up. Biographical sources do not always reveal whether someone has had a career in a family firm. And since the methodology is "conservative" in this respect, it is likely that the proportion with careers in family firms in the United States would be increased with additional research.

† See Appendix XIII for a discussion of family control of wealth and positions.

executive and insider posts in dominant corporations (20 per cent each). These patterns reveal the existence of two basic types among those with careers in family firms. The first type are persons whose careers are in large family corporations that are not dominant but that provide them with a stepping-stone to outsider positions on the boards of dominant corporations. While their primary inheritance is in a non-dominant corporation, they often follow their fathers in the same dominant outside directorships, although this is, of course, not their primary affiliation. The second type are individuals whose main careers are in the dominant family-controlled companies among the 113 Canadian and 194 U.S. dominant corporations identified earlier. There are numerous examples of these two types, 365 among the current U.S. economic elite and 183 in Canada.

Examples of dominant Canadian family firms would have to include Simpsons department stores and the Burton family. Charles Luther Burton became president of Simpsons Limited in 1929 and was succeeded by his eldest son, Edgar. E.G. Burton was appointed president in 1976; his uncle, G. Allan Burton, is chairman of the company. Five generations of Molsons have controlled what is now called the Molson Companies, and five Eatons have been president of Eaton's of Canada. Two members of the current generation still oversee the department store firm. The Woodward family continues to dominate the Woodward Stores retail empire. The Westons dominate George Weston Limited, the food manufacturing and retail multinational. The Bronfman family remains in control of Distillers Corporation–Seagrams. One branch of the family recently acquired Trizec Corporation, a dominant company dealing primarily in real estate, and holds a 20 per cent interest in IAC Limited, a dominant financial company. The Richardson family controls Richardson Securities, the Billes family Canadian Tire Corporation, the Burns family Crown Life Insurance; the Loebs control M. Loeb Limited, the Scotts control Wood Gundy, the Steinbergs control Steinbergs Limited, the Jeffery family London Life Insurance, the Wolfes the Oshawa Group, and so on.* All of these are dominant Canadian companies. But the decline of family capitalism has never been very loudly proclaimed in Canada; it is in the United States that family continuity and nepotism is supposedly dead.

A few examples provide some indication that continuity of membership in the U.S. elite survives. Among the first sub-group are the following:

Kenneth Karl Bechtel, a son of Warren A. Bechtel who established W.A. Bechtel in 1895, was associated with the company from 1921 to 1970 and now holds a directorship on the Wells Fargo and Company board. His brother, Stephen Davison Bechtel, was president of the family company and a director of Morgan Trust, stepping down in 1961 so that his son, Stephen Bechtel, Jr., could take his place at the age of

* For additional examples, see Clement, *Canadian Corporate Elite*, pp. 183-87.

thirty-five. Now the third generation in command at Bechtel, the grandson of the founder also has directorships in GM, Crocker National, and Southern Pacific.

William S. Beinecke, whose family owns 55 per cent of Sperry and Hutchinson, is a son of Frederick William Beinecke, a former executive of the company; the son is now chairman of Sperry and Hutchinson and a director of Consolidated Edison and Manufacturers Hanover.

Judson Bemis's father was chairman of Bemis Brothers. This position is now held by the son, who is also a director of Northwestern Bancorporation and Northwestern Mutual Life.

William Wade Boeschenstein's father was president of Owens-Corning Fiberglas, a position now held by his son, who sits on the boards of Kroger Company and American Electrical Power.

Otis Chandler's father and grandfather were executives of Times Mirror Company. The youngest Chandler became the publisher at thirty-two and now has directorships in TRW Incorporated and Pan American.

Lester Crown is the son of the former chief executive of Material Service Corporation and a director of General Dynamics. He is now president of Material Service and a director of General Dynamics, Esmark, Incorporated, Continental Illinois, and Trans World Airlines.

Brothers Bruce Bliss Dayton and Donald Chadwick Dayton have both been executives of the family firm, Dayton-Hudson Corporation. Bruce is a director of Honeywell Incorporated and Donald of Northwestern Bancorp and Burlington Northern.

Albert Blake Dick III, grandson of the founder of A.B. Dick Company, is now chairman of the company and a director of Commonwealth Edison. He has another directorship in Marshall Field and Company as his father had before him.

The grandfather of Robert Stanley Dollar, Jr., founded Robert Dollar Company. The son and grandson of the founder have been president of the company with a directorship in Security Pacific.

Gaylord Donnelley's grandfather established R.R. Donnelley and Sons, and his father was chairman of the company as well as a director in International Harvester. The son continues as chairman of the family firm and is a director in Borg-Warner and First Chicago.

John Thompson Dorrance, Sr., was president of Campbell Soup and a director of the Pennsylvania Railway, Prudential Insurance, and Guaranty Trust of New York. John T. Dorrance, Jr., continues as chairman of Campbell Soup and is also a director of J.P. Morgan and Company.

Marshall Field V became a director of Field Enterprises at twenty-four and its publisher at thirty-two, following in the steps of family members right back to his great-great-grandfather. The latest edition is also a director of First Chicago.

Aiken Wood Fisher has had his career in Fisher Scientific, founded by his father in 1902, and is now a director of Mellon National and Equitable Life.

Two members of the fourth generation of the Levi Strauss family, great-grandnephews of Levi, the founder, have had their careers in the family firm. Walter A. Haas, Jr., is also a director of Bank of America, and Peter Edgar Haas is a director of Crocker National, while their father, Walter A. Haas, is a director of Pacific Gas.

Prentis Cobb Hale, Jr., whose father was president of Hale Brothers Stores and vice-president of the Bank of Italy (now Bank of America) and Transamerica Corporation, is now chairman of the family firm and a director of Union Oil Company of California, Santa Fe Industries, and Bank of America.

Henry John Heinz II is now chairman of H.J. Heinz Company and a director of Mellon National. His father, Howard Heinz, was also chairman of the family firm, inheriting it from his father who established it in 1869, and a director of Pennsylvania Railway and Mellon National. "At his grandfather's knee fifty-five years ago, when he was eight, H.J. Heinz II learned that he would one day be expected to run the family business."[10]

Henry Lea Hillman is president of Hillman Company, as was his father. The younger Hillman is also a director of National Steel, Chemical New York, and General Electric.

Amory Houghton, Jr., inherited the chairmanship of Corning Glass Works from his father and grandfather and is also a director of IBM and Citicorp.

Joseph Lowthian Hudson, Jr., inherited the chairmanship of J.L. Hudson Company from his father and is a director of Detroit Edison and National Detroit.

George Magoffin Humphrey was chairman of M.A. Hanna, chairman of the executive committee of National Steel, and president of Iron Ore Company of Canada; his son, Gilbert Watts Humphrey, is chairman of Hanna Mining, chairman of the executive committee of National Steel, and a director of General Electric and Texaco as well as the dominant Canadian companies Massey-Ferguson and Sun Life.

Robert Watt Miller was president of Pacific Lighting Corporation, as was his father before him, and a director of American Airlines, Standard Oil of California, American Trust, and Caterpillar Tractor. His two sons, Richard Kendall Miller and Paul Albert Miller, are now executives of Pacific Lighting. The former is a director of Southern Pacific, and the latter is a director of Wells Fargo.

Roger Milliken, a director of Westinghouse Electric, W.R. Grace and Company, and Citicorp, and Minot K. Milliken, a director of Union Pacific, are both executives of Deering, Milliken Incorporated, following in the footsteps of Seth Mellen Milliken, who was also a director of National City Bank, New York Life, Mercantile Stores, and Monarch Mills.

Henry Thomas Mudd's grandfather, Seeley Wintersmith Mudd, was president of Cyprus Mines. So was his father, Harvey Seeley Mudd, who was also a director of Southern Pacific and Texas Gulf Sulphur.

The representative of the third generation is chairman of Cyprus Mines and a director of Southern Pacific, Western Bancorporation, Union Oil, and Rockwell International.

Daniel Safford Parker's grandfather founded Parker Pens. His father was chairman of the company and a director of Northwestern Mutual Life. Daniel Safford is now chairman of Parker and also a director of Northwestern.

John Sargent Pillsbury, Jr., is the grandson of the founder of Pillsbury Mills. His father was chairman of the company and a director of Northwestern Bancorp. J.S. Pillsbury, Jr., began his career with the family firm, later becoming chairman of Northwestern National Life while retaining a directorship in Pillsbury and is now also a director of Northwestern Bancorp and Boise Cascade Corporation.

John Mortimer Schiff's grandfather was a partner of Kuhn, Loeb and Company as well as a director of Equitable Life, Western Union, and Wells Fargo; his father, Mortimer Leo Schiff, was also a partner with Kuhn, Loeb and a director of Western Union, Pacific Oil, and Chemical Bank. The son continues the partnership at Kuhn, Loeb and is a director of Westinghouse, Uniroyal, Great A&P, Getty Oil, and Kennecott Copper and sits on the advisory board of Chemical New York.

Until 1914, Byron Laflin Smith was president of Northern Trust, followed by his son, Solomon Albert Smith, who added directorships on Commonwealth Edison, U.S. Gypsum, and Montgomery Ward. The current chairman of Northern Trust, grandson of the founder, is Edward Byron Smith, also a director of Commonwealth Edison and Equitable Life.

Lloyd Bruce Smith, grandson of the founder of A.O. Smith Corporation, is now chairman of the company and a director of Goodyear, Continental Can, and Deere and Company.

Robert Douglas Stuart, Jr., is president of Quaker Oats and also a director of First Chicago Corporation, CNA Financial Corporation, and UAL. His father was president of Quaker Oats until 1953, when he became U.S. ambassador to Canada, and also held directorships in the First National Bank of Chicago, Continental Casualty, Canadian Consolidated Grain, and Bell Telephone.

It would be possible to name many more men who have had careers in family firms that are not dominant but who hold directorships in dominant corporations. Among the other sub-groups, those who have their main careers in dominant U.S. corporations controlled by their families, are the following:

Inland Steel was founded in 1893 by Joseph D. Block, who served as board chairman until 1940. His two sons, Leopold E. Block (who was a director of Buffalo Steel, Commonwealth Edison, and First National Bank) and Philip Dee Block (a vice-president of Chicago, Illinois and Indiana Railway and a director of First National Bank of Chicago), followed their father as executives of Inland Steel. Today, three grandsons of the founder wear the mantle. Joseph Leopold Block and Leigh

Bloom Block, both sons of Leopold E. and former executives, are now directors of Inland Steel, while Philip Dee Block, Jr., is chairman of the executive committee.

Ralph Budd, "a protégé of James J. Hill and a legendary president of both the Great Northern and the Burlington" railways,[11] was a director of First National Bank of Chicago, International Harvester, and Equitable Life. His son, John Marshall Budd, is former chairman and now a director of Burlington Northern besides being a director of New York Life and, like his father, International Harvester.

An interesting instance is Hugh Brown Cannon, who was president of Windsor Farm Dairy Importers when the company was merged with Beatrice Foods, of which he then became a director. Brown Woodburn Cannon, his son, is now a vice-president and a director of Beatrice.

Carlyle Robert Carlson, Jr., started a Deere and Company factory in Welland, Ontario, in 1930 and was also a director of Deere in the United States. His son, Robert John Carlson, is now a vice-president and a director of Deere. William Alexander Hewitt married the daughter of Charles Deere, and he is now chairman of Deere as well as a director of AT&T, Continental Oil, and Continental Illinois and sits on the international advisory board of Chase Manhattan Bank.

Lammot du Pont Copeland is the great-great-grandson of Eleuthère Irenée du Pont, founder of the du Pont firm in 1802, and nephew of three successive presidents of the company; he is now a director of du Pont after being its chairman and is also a director of Chemical New York. Norman A. Copeland is a vice-president and director of du Pont. Irenée du Pont, Jr., is also a vice-president and director. His brother-in-law, Crawford Hallock Greenewalt, a former president and chairman of du Pont, is now a director there as well as in Boeing Company; "on Greenewalt's wedding day in 1926, his father-in-law Irenée du Pont gave him 1,000 shares of Christina Corporation, the holding company that owns gobs of du Pont stock. By 1959 Greenewalt owned 4,096 shares of du Pont common (at $250 a share) and 687 shares of Christina common (at $17,000), for total holdings worth about $13 million."[12] Charles Brelsford McCoy, former chairman of du Pont and now a director, is also a director of TRW, Citicorp, and Bethlehem Steel; "McCoy had begun his du Pont career in 1932 as an operator of a cellophane machine, and the fact that his father was a du Pont director [and vice-president] appears to have had nothing to do with his steady progress."[13] Currently, nine family members are on du Pont's board.

In 1848, Ferdinand Cullman established the family tobacco business in the United States. Now two of his great-grandsons are executives: Hugh Cullman is executive vice-president of Philip Morris while Joseph Frederick Cullman II is chairman of Philip Morris, a director of Ford Motor Company, Bankers Trust New York, and IBM World Trade, and chairman of Benson and Hedges (Canada).

William H. Danforth founded Ralston Purina; two of his grandsons, Donald Danforth, Jr., and William H. Danforth II, are now directors.

Charles Crocker DeLimur resigned in 1975 "as senior vice-president of the Crocker National Bank after a 29-year career in banking. His resignation...was said to be based on a desire to give closer attention to his family interests. The last descendant of the Crocker family, which founded the bank, actively involved in the institution, Mr. DeLimur will continue as a director of the bank as well as its parent, the Crocker National Corporation."[14]

Herbert H. Dow established Dow Chemical, and his son, William Henry Dow, assumed the presidency upon the father's death. The last direct descendant in the company is Herbert Henry Doan (whose mother was a sister of Willard Dow, a former president), himself a former president and now a director of the company. Carl Allan Gerstacker, a nephew of James T. Pardee, Herbert Henry Dow's major backer, is now chairman of Dow Chemical and a director of Eaton Corporation.

James C. Donnell was president of Ohio Oil, as was his son Otto Dewey Donnell; now a grandson, James C. Donnell II, is chairman of Marathon Oil (formerly Ohio Oil) and a director of Armco Steel and New York Life.

Benjamin Firestone's father was reputed to be the richest man in Columbiano County, Ohio, and left his son a great deal of land. But Benjamin's son, Harvey Samuel, who founded Firestone Tire and Rubber, certainly left his sons and grandsons a great deal more. Raymond Christy Firestone, son of the founder, is now chairman of Firestone while his brother, Leonard Kimball Firestone, a former president and now a director of the company, is also a director of Wells Fargo. Leonard Kimball's son, Kimball Curtis Firestone, is a vice-president and a director. Martha Firestone, daughter of Harvey Samuel Firestone, Jr., married William Clay Ford, whose grandfather had been Harvey Samuel Firestone's first tire customer in 1905. William Clay Ford is now a vice-president of Ford Motor Company, and his brothers are both chief executives of Ford. All are sons of Edsel Bryant Ford, son of Henry Ford.

Charles Thomas Fisher, Jr., was president of the Bank of Detroit and a director of Detroit Edison, American Airlines, and National Steel. His son, Charles Thomas Fisher III, is not only president of National Detroit and a director of American Airlines, Detroit Edison, and GM, but also a director of Hiram Walker–Gooderham and Worts, a dominant Canadian company.

William Russell Grace founded W.R. Grace and Company, later run by Joseph Peter Grace, his son. Now Joseph Peter Grace, Jr., is chairman of the company, a director of Kennecott and Citicorp, and a director of Brascan, a dominant Canadian company.

Henry J. Kaiser organized Kaiser Steel and sixty years ago founded Kaiser Resources in Vancouver, British Columbia. His son, Edgar Fosburgh Kaiser, is now chairman of Kaiser Aluminum and Chemical and a director of Bank of America; his grandson, Edgar F. Kaiser, Jr., at thirty-two, heads the Kaiser Resources Company in Vancouver. The family continues to own 42 per cent of all stock in Kaiser Industries.

The fourth generation of the Lazarus family continues the family tradition at Federated Department Stores, with Charles Y. as a vice-president and director, Maurice as chairman of the finance committee, and Ralph as chairman and a director of General Electric and Chase Manhattan Bank.

William C. Liedtke, Jr., is president of Pennzoil and John Hugh Liedtke is chairman. At Lykes-Youngstown, in the same pattern, Joseph T. Lykes is chairman, J.M. Lykes is a vice-president and a director, and C.P. Lykes is a director.

Brooks McCormick personifies the entire history of harvester companies in the United States. He is a great-grandson of William Deering, founder of one harvester company, and of William S. McCormick, who founded another. Besides being president of International Harvester, he is a director of Esmark, Commonwealth Edison, and First Chicago.

James Smith McDonnell, John Finney McDonnell, William Archie McDonnell, and Stanford Noyes McDonnell are all members of the executive or directors of McDonnell Douglas Corporation.

Appropriately, the youngest member of the economic elite, born in 1942, is Seward Prosser Mellon, who is on the board of Mellon National, having become president of Richard K. Mellon and Sons at twenty-eight. His great-grandfather was Judge Thomas Mellon, who established T. Mellon and Sons; his grandfather, Richard Beatty Mellon, was president of Mellon National Bank; and his father, Richard King Mellon, was chairman of Mellon Bank and a director of Alcan, General Motors, Gulf Oil, Pennsylvania Railway, Pittsburgh Plate Glass, and Westinghouse. The "Prosser" in his name is from his mother, daughter of New York banker Seward Prosser. He is not much younger than Richard Mellon Scaife, also on the board of Mellon National, born in 1932 to Sarah Mellon and Allan Magee Scaife, chairman of Scaife Steel and a director of Mellon National, Gulf Oil, Bell Telephone, and other companies suitable for an heir to the Mellon fortune.

Three sons of William Francis O'Neil, founder of General Tire and Rubber, now hold the three top posts: John James O'Neil is chairman of the finance committee, Michael Gerald O'Neil is president, and Thomas Francis O'Neil is chairman.

Three Pews, John Glenn Pew, Robert Anderson Pew, and Walter C. Pew, are still on the board of Sun Oil. Four Reynolds brothers, all sons of Richard Samuel Reynolds, the founder of Reynolds Industries, are in the family firm. Julian Louis, William G., and David Parham Reynolds are vice-presidents and directors; Richard S. Reynolds, Jr., is chairman and president as well as a director of Manufacturers Hanover.

David Rockefeller continues a long family tradition with his chairmanship of Chase Manhattan while James Stillman Rockefeller, although retired as chairman of National City Bank, continues as a director of Pan American and NCR.

William Frederick Rockwell, Jr., follows his father as chairman of Rockwell International, adding directorships on El Paso Natural Gas and Mellon National.

Since 1914, the Watson family, beginning with Thomas John, has dominated International Business Machines. "In raising his sons, Thomas J. Watson, Sr., an old fashioned authoritarian with a formidable personality, imposed standards of achievement & decorum similar to those with which he ran IBM, where employees were required to conform to a strict set of rules ranging from white shirts to teetotalism."[15] Until his death in 1974, Arthur Kittredge Watson remained a director, having been president, then chairman from 1954 to 1970, then U.S. ambassador to France. Thomas J. Watson, Jr., continues as chairman of the executive committee and a director of Bankers Trust New York and Pan American.

The final two of many possible examples are both associated with dominant corporations in the wood industry. With a father prominent in the lumber industry and married to the daughter of a well-known lumberman, Frederick Edward Weyerhaeuser was president of Weyerhaeuser Company from 1934 to 1945, and his son, Charles Davis Weyerhaeuser, continues as a director of the company and chairman of Comerco, a wood stains company. George Hunt Weyerhaeuser, son of John Philip Weyerhaeuser, Jr., president of Weyerhaeuser after 1947, became president in 1966 and is also a director of Boeing. Anthony Zellerbach established a small paper company in 1870, carried on by Isador Zellerbach, his son, who became chairman of Crown Zellerbach. Isador's son, Harold Lionel Zellerbach, continues as a consultant and director emeritus after a long career with the company, while the fourth generation is represented by his son, William Joseph Zellerbach, who is president of Zellerbach Paper and an officer and a director of Crown Zellerbach.

These examples actually represent only a quarter of the whole list of persons with careers in family corporations among the U.S. elite. It is clear that family capitalism is not dead there. Instead, its vitality has persisted in the era of corporate capitalism; the form has changed but not the substance. When we examine the class origins of the U.S. economic elite, we will see how some of these transformations of form have taken place. But, before this is done, one final career type that directly contrasts with main career in a family firm will be examined.

"On His Own Account"

To say that someone has "made it on his own" into the economic elite does not necessarily mean that he has risen from the dregs of society. Rather, it means that the person has been able to establish, within the course of his lifetime, a corporation that is either dominant in itself or of sufficient consequence to project the founder into the elite circle through an outside directorship in a dominant corporation or absorption of his company by a dominant corporation. For every single member of the U.S. economic elite that entered "on his own account" there are fourteen who have had careers in family firms. In Canada the ratio is one to eighteen. In fact, the 1.4 per cent of the U.S. elite in this category is about the same as the 1.5 per cent in the Canadian elite. No one in any other category has made it into the U.S. elite "on his own account."

The relatively high class of origin of these persons undoubtedly influenced their careers, since 23 per cent are from the upper class in the United States and 40 per cent in Canada. Nevertheless, the fact that most of them are in the oldest age group and very few in the youngest group in both countries is an indication of the declining importance of this mode of entry and of the advanced age at which members of this type actually achieve elite status.

There are obviously not as many instances of entry to the elite in this category as there were through the family firm (in fact, there are only ten Canadian-born elite members of this type), but some are prominent persons.* Henry Crown, born in 1896 to a Lithuanian immigrant family of suspender makers, began his business life as a partner with his brother Sol in 1916. Eventually, Crown was able to become the owner of 18 per cent of General Dynamics through his Material Service Corporation, which became a division of General Dynamics, and continues as chairman of the executive committee. The climb, of course, was not so difficult for his son Lester, who is now president of Material Service and a director of General Dynamics, TWA, Continental Illinois, and Esmark. Richard Winn Courts is a member of the elite because of his directorship in Delta Air Lines, but his career was made in Courts and Company, which he founded in 1925. Probably the most entrepreneurial of all is Armand Hammer, who salvaged his father's failing pharmaceutical company and later built Occidental Petroleum from scratch, continuing now as its chairman.

William Redington Hewlett and David Packard founded Hewlett-Packard Company in 1939. Each continues as a chief executive of the company, although Packard took time out between 1969 and 1971 to be deputy secretary of defense. Although the company itself is not dominant, it is a sufficient base of power to place Packard on the boards of Standard Oil of California, TWA, and Caterpillar Tractor, and Hewlett on Chase Manhattan, FMC, and Chrysler. The former classmates at Stanford have done well in the field of electronics research.

Earl Robert Kinney was founder of North Atlantic Packers, and his company became a subsidiary of General Mills in 1968. He assumed the presidency of the parent in 1973, also holding a directorship in W.T. Grant. Herman Warden Lay followed a similar pattern; he was founder of H.W. Lay, later known as Frito-Lay, which merged with PepsiCo,

* For Canadian examples of "on his own account," see Clement, *Canadian Corporate Elite*, pp. 187-89.

Incorporated, in 1965, yielding Lay 500,000 shares in the dominant company and making him the largest individual stockholder and chairman of the executive committee of PepsiCo.

James Smith McDonnell, Jr., was, with his brother William Archie McDonnell, a founder of McDonnell Douglas in 1939 and continues as chairman. A second generation of sons of the founding brothers have now taken on executive positions. Leonard Parker Pool was a founder of Air Products and Chemicals and has been its chairman since 1940. He also has a directorship in American Standard. Carleton Putnam was a founder of Chicago and Southern Airlines, briefly becoming chairman of Delta Air Lines in 1953-54 and continuing since as a director. Simon Ramo, another son of Lithuanian immigrants who operated a small clothing store, was a co-founder of The Ramo-Woodridge Corporation, now known as TRW Incorporated, and continues as its vice-chairman. Meshulam Riklis, whose parents were "well-to-do" immigrants from Turkey, created Rapid-American Corporation. Ross David Siragusa, Sr., founder of Admiral Corporation, is now a director of Rockwell International, since Admiral's absorption by Rockwell, as is his son Ross David Siragusa, Jr., who is also a vice-president. Charles Bates Thornton, whose father had made and lost fortunes before him, was involved in the formation of Litton Industries in 1953 and is now its chairman and a director of TWA and Western Bancorp. Theodore Albert von der Ahe founded Von's Grocery Company with his father in 1932; he is still chairman and also a director of Bank of America. Finally, Sam Doak Young was one of the original organizers of the El Paso National Bank in 1925, has been its chairman since 1952, and is also on the board of El Paso Natural Gas.

These examples illustrate that there is still a certain openness to at least some activities within the U.S. elite. This was particularly true at one time of the chemical and airline industries, but the trend is clearly away from this type of entrepreneurship and toward solidifying already established firms into dominant corporations and maintaining family continuity after the founding generations. Earlier elite studies give some sense of patterns of continuity among the elite through class origins,* and now the subject will be examined comparatively for the contemporary period.

II. Class Origins of the Economic Elite

The class of origin of members of the economic elite is a strong indicator of the extent to which privilege is reproduced over generations; in other words, it can be used to judge the relative proportions of persons belonging to a class of reproduction (that is, who gain their position because of kinship) and to a class of nomination (that is, selected by

---

* Appendix XI summarizes these studies.

those in power). In this study, biographical data are used because they are much more precise for determining upper-class origins than surveys conducted by questionnaires, such as those used for the study reported in Chapter 9 on the migration of managers or in many of the studies discussed in Appendix XI.* On the other hand, the questionnaire can be more precise for establishing middle-class or working-class origins. Therefore, the strength of this study is that it is able to establish the crucial dividing line between the upper class and those below it. Certainly, if the major focus is on corporate power, this class division is more important than any of the others.

When the focus is mainly on mobility, as most studies of business leaders have been, more precise definitions of the middle and working classes gain importance. These business leader studies do provide such insights into the mobility patterns of U.S. business. For example, they all conclude that only about 10 per cent of the population has supplied about 70 per cent of the business leaders, suggesting a low rate of mobility into top corporate positions in the United States. Conversely, about 60 per cent of the population of working-class origins employed in wage or office work has supplied only about 10 per cent of the business leaders. The remaining 20 per cent of business leaders are drawn from approximately 30 per cent of the population who are professionals, white-collar workers, or farmers.

Returning to the study of power, as it is defined here only about 2 per cent of the population of either Canada or the United States falls into the very specific category of "upper class." It encompasses only the very highest layer of society. The "missing data"† act as a conservative factor because if it cannot be proved that a person is from the upper class, he must be placed outside it.

It must be stressed that the class of *origin* of the economic elite is

---

* One further advantage of biographical over questionnaire methods for elite studies is that the researcher does not have to depend on the subjects for the response rate. Mailed-out questionnaires normally yield a return of about 50 per cent. Personal interviewing is most difficult for studying members of the national elite because they are dispersed and often inaccessible. Biographical methods are able to get coverage of from 80 to 85 per cent.

† "Missing data" result in a coverage of 82 per cent for the U.S. elite and 84 per cent for the Canadian elite. Nevertheless, there is no distortion of comparisons. The effect of missing data can be seen in the change between the original analysis of the Canadian economic elite (based on 82 per cent coverage) and that reported here (based on 84 per cent coverage). *Increased information and coverage* simply raised the proportion of upper-class origin in the Canadian elite from 59.4 per cent to 60.9 per cent, a difference of 1.5 percentage points. Moreover, the findings of Bendix and Howton, using biographical sources to determine class of origin for businessmen in the United States, suggest that there is no systematic difference between those for whom data was available and those for whom it was not. From criteria including first job and other enabling circumstances, they concluded: "We found only small and random differences between the two groups...it is apparent that a large proportion of those whose father's occupation was *unknown* came from relatively well-to-do families" ("Social Mobility and the American Business Elite," in *Social Mobility in Industrial Society*, ed. R. Bendix and S.M. Lipset, pp. 125-26).

being analysed here, not current class positions. Class of origin indicates where in the class structure the person started life, the upper class offerring advantages before the person enters the labour force. Upper-class origins in Canada and the United States can be easily compared because the criteria are very specific: was the father in the economic elite or another elite of the previous generation? Was the wife from an elite family that provided her husband with an upper-class start? Or was the father in a "substantial" business that while not smaller than middle-range was still not large enough to be considered dominant? These standards exclude many whose fathers may have been with smaller companies or in the occupational classification of businessmen or managers. The designation "upper-middle" class, which is simply grouped with the upper class for broader comparisons, is given to those who attended one of the top private tuitional schools,* if the person fails to meet any of the above criteria or if other information is not available. The private school was used earlier for the Canadian elite and also for the U.S. elite.[16] This indicator is readily used in terms of ascriptive characteristics because the parents send the child to the school and pay the high admission fees. Its effectiveness as an indicator is further reinforced by the fact that most of the current elite members who went to private schools attended during the depression of the thirties when few families had the funds for this luxury. The role of private schools in the elite will be returned to (see pp. 239-41).

In a comparative study of elites using biographical sources, it is often difficult to determine precisely whether a person has middle- or working-class origins. In an earlier study of Canada, two indicators of middle-class origins were used,[17] but for comparison between Canada and the United States use of one of these indicators is problematic. When information on the occupation of the father is available, using the professionals, managers, businessmen, state or federal politicians (besides elites), and large-scale farmers as middle-class occupations, there is no difficulty of classification. The second indicator, education, is less certain. In Canada it is fairly safe to assume that anyone who graduated from university during the late thirties and early forties, the time when the average elite member was of university age, was from a relatively privileged background. Only about 8 per cent of the whole male population even attended university at that time.[18] But the same assumption cannot be made about the United States. At the present time, 19.2 per cent of the population over eighteen years old in the United States has attended university; in Canada, only 9.4 per cent of the same population group has attended university. In fact, while about

---

*The top private schools in the United States used are those listed in E. Digby Baltzell, *Philadelphia Gentlemen* and G. William Domhoff, *Who Rules America?* In Canada, schools of the Headmasters' Association and the most exclusive classical colleges in Quebec were used.

half the U.S. population over eighteen has graduated from high school, only about a quarter of the same group in Canada has completed this level of education. Obviously, the national differences in post-secondary education make it a questionable indicator for comparison. As a result of these difficulties, no attempt has been made to analyse the middle and working classes as sources for the economic elites, aside from the studies in Appendix XI, and the entire focus of this study will rest on the upper class, where comparisons between the United States and Canada can be clearly made.

Applying feasible criteria to the economic elites of Canada and the United States then, we find that there is much more recruitment to the elite from outside the upper class in the United States than there is in Canada. In the United States, 555 members (29.3 per cent) of the economic elite are solidly upper class in origin because of their kinship ties with earlier upper-class generations. The second group of 119 members who attended an exclusive private school (aside from the above 555) brings the total percentage of persons with upper-class background to 35.6 per cent for the U.S. economic elite. In the Canadian elite, 338 members (49.5 per cent) have kin in earlier upper-class generations. Another seventy-eight attended exclusive private schools (aside from the 338), so that 60.9 per cent of this elite is of upper-class origin. Although there is a marked difference between the two elites in the proportion with upper-class origin when Canada has 61 per cent and the United States 36 per cent, they are both well above the rest of the population with respect to upper-class origin (about 2 per cent in both countries).

We have already seen, in discussing family firms, that in both countries there is a solid core of families in the economic elite that transmits elite positions to its children – that is, each country has a class of reproduction. The real difference between the elites lies in the origin of recruits, in the class of nomination. In Canada, the class of nomination is still drawn from a very limited privileged class, but in the United States, it comes from a broader set of people.

In the United States, 13 per cent of the current elite are the sons or, in a few cases, nephews of earlier members of the economic elite. In Canada, 29 per cent have fathers who were in the earlier economic elite. A *greater* proportion of the U.S. elite have had careers in family firms (19 per cent) than have fathers in the economic elite (13 per cent), while in Canada, a *smaller* number have had careers in family firms (27 per cent) than have fathers in the economic elite (29 per cent). As the other upper-class criteria are applied, the differences between Canada and the United States widen and ultimately the U.S. economic elite is 36 per cent upper class in origin and the Canadian 61 per cent. Moreover, an earlier analysis demonstrated that the current trend in Canada is toward greater upper-class recruitment in the elite than twenty years ago, with 50 per cent from the upper class in 1951 and 59.4 per cent in 1972.[19]*

Part of the explanation for these differences between the countries lies in the career types already examined. Members with engineering and science careers are least likely to have upper-class origins in both Canada and the United States, and there are more of them in the United States. Careers in the corporation finance departments account for more elite members in the United States than in Canada and also tend to be characterized by members of less than upper-class origin. Finance executives and financiers, on the other hand, are frequently of upper-class origin in both countries, but they form a much higher proportion of the elite in Canada. Similarly, the lawyers in the elite are often of upper-class origin, and law is a more frequent avenue to the elite in Canada than in the United States. It has already been shown that the Canadian elite has a larger share of members following the career types favoured by the upper class and that the U.S. elite has a greater proportion of members among the career types accessible to non-upper-class persons. Careers in law and financial institutions account for the greatest part of the difference, along with careers in family firms.

A more detailed analysis of additional characteristics and patterns will clarify other factors that explain these differences in class recruitment. It must be stressed that a core made up of over a third of the U.S. economic elite is of upper-class origin. There must be, therefore, a self-reproducing upper class that continues to set the tone for the economic elite. That there continues to be an upper class in the United States is not in doubt; as E. Digby Baltzell has stated, "there exists one metropolitan upper class with a common cultural tradition, consciousness of kind, and 'we' feeling of solidarity which tends to be national in scope."[20] The continuity of this class in the current U.S. economic elite is also evident. For example, 82 per cent of members whose fathers were in the economic elite inherited some position, 80 per cent have had their main career in a family firm, and 28 per cent hold more than one dominant U.S. directorship. A member of the current economic elite whose father was in a previous economic elite in the United States has a 99 per cent chance of not having to make the long crawl of twenty years in a corporation before attaining an executive position (only 2 of 244 in this category had to).

*A study by Craig McKie of business leaders in Ontario's manufacturing companies confirms the general findings for Canada. McKie says: "One immediate conclusion to be drawn therefore is that the characteristics which Porter described as being typical of the Canadian economic elite [for 1951], also characterize those who occupy the next level down in at least the Ontario manufacturing industry" ("An Ontario Industrial Elite," pp. 307-8).

III. Inheritance and Current Kinship Ties in the Economic Elite

The transmission of privilege through inheritance is an important part of the perpetuation of an upper class. Although it is impossible to make a systematic analysis of the inheritance of property here, the inheritance of corporate positions can be traced. The persistence of a core class of reproduction is illustrated by the fact that exactly 20 per cent, or one in every five, of the current members of the U.S. economic elite has inherited some position. This includes 18 per cent who have inherited their main current affiliation and, overlapping with this set, 9 per cent who have inherited a position in a dominant corporation. In Canada, 26 per cent of the entire economic elite, including 29 per cent of the Canadian-born and 10 per cent of the foreign-born, have inherited some position. Twenty-four per cent have inherited their main current affiliation and, overlapping with this set, 13 per cent have inherited a position in a dominant corporation. In the U.S. economic elite there are 183 members who have inherited their main affiliation but not a dominant position, 158 who have inherited a dominant position but not their main affiliation, and 23 who have inherited corporation positions that are neither main nor dominant.

Inheritors in both countries tend to be overrepresented in bank directorships compared to those not inheriting, especially in Canada. Of the U.S. inheritors, 27 per cent have a dominant bank directorship compared to 21 per cent of the non-inheritors while in Canada, 36 per cent of the inheritors have a dominant bank directorship compared to 21 per cent of the others. Inheritance is like the other indicators of privilege: it allows the privileged person to enter the elite at an earlier age and remain longer than the others, and it is possible to observe this phenomenon in both the U.S. and the Canadian elites. In this way the elite preserves continuity.

The continuity of intergenerational transfers of position is reinforced by current kinship ties within the elite. In the United States, there are currently thirty-six father-son combinations, forty-nine brothers, and seventy-two other kinship ties, such as fathers-in-law or uncles, that could be traced through biographical sources. In Canada, there are forty-three father-son combinations, forty-nine brothers, and sixty-three other kinship ties. Because of the difference in size of the two elites, however, current kinship ties apply to 7.3 per cent of the U.S. elite but to 16.8 per cent of the Canadian elite. These persons, along with the inheritors, form the core of the class of reproduction. The continuity of this subset is reflected in the finding that 94 per cent of those with current kin in the U.S. elite are of upper-class origin, as are 91 per cent in Canada.

We have already seen many examples of inheritance and current kinship among persons with careers in family firms, but there are other types of kinship ties that help bind the elite together. The following are some examples from the U.S. elite: George Heguley Lanier, Jr., is now chairman of his father's Mount Vernon Mills and a director of General Public Utilities. He married the daughter of William Jerome Vereen, who was president of Moultrie Cotton Mills. Vereen's son (also Lanier's brother-in-law) is now president of Moultrie Mills and a director of Southern Company. Edward Lasker, a director of Philip Morris, is a brother-in-law of Sidney F. Brody, president of Brody Investments and a director of Security Pacific, and they are both brothers-in-law of Leigh Bloom Block of Inland Steel.

Charles Sherwood Munson, honorary chairman of Airco Incorporated, a director of Greyhound, and a member of the advisory council of Morgan Guaranty Trust, is the father of Charles Sherwood Munson, Jr., chairman of Eaton Corporation's audit committee and president of American European Securities, but there is no apparent corporate connection between them, although both belong to four clubs in common, including the Links and Union. This means they are represented among the current kinship ties but not the inheritors.

Courtland Davis Perkins, who was the chairman of space systems command at NASA and is now a director of American Airlines, is a brother of James Alfred Perkins, former president of Cornell University and now a director of Chase Manhattan; neither appears to have followed their banker father's footsteps.

Gaylord Donnelley of R.R. Donnelley and Sons, a director of Borg-Warner and First Chicago, married the sister of George Alfred Ranney, Jr., the vice-chairman of Inland Steel.

Warren McKinney Shapleigh, the president of Ralston Purina and a director of J.P. Morgan and Company, married the sister of Tom K. Smith, Jr., a vice-president and director of Monsanto Company.

Edson White Spencer, president of Honeywell and a director of Northwestern Bancorporation, married the daughter of Robert Douglas Stuart, already mentioned as father of Robert Douglas Stuart, Jr., the president of Quaker Oats and a director of UAL, CNA Financial, and First Chicago. The elder Stuart, as mentioned earlier, was U.S. ambassador to Canada and president of Quaker Oats as well as a director of several dominant corporations.

Brothers George Latimer Wilcox, vice-chairman of Westinghouse, and Thomas Robert Wilcox, chairman of Crocker National and a director of Boeing and Colgate-Palmolive, have had separate careers.

A final example of kinship ties in the United States is a case where children of current members of the economic elite have married. The daughter of Kendrick Roscoe Wilson, Jr., the vice-chairman of Avco Corporation and a director of Atlantic Richfield, married E. Newton Cutler III, son of E. Newton Cutler, Jr., a director of Consumers Power and American Standard.

To unravel the kinship ties among the Canadian economic elite requires a genealogist with tremendous patience. A systematic analysis has been presented elsewhere,[21] but a few examples will provide some indication of the complexities. Aubrey Wilton Baillie, who is currently a director of the Canadian Imperial Bank of Commerce and who sold half the stock in Bowes Company in 1972 to the Weston empire for $8.5 million, is the son of Sir Frank Wilton Baillie who was a stockbroker, general manager of the Metropolitan Bank, and president of Canada Steel among many other traditional Canadian upper-class activities. The son married Mary Frances Finlayson, daughter of the Hon. William Finlayson, who was a lawyer, Ontario minister of lands and forests, and president of the Simcoe Railway, to name but a few of his activities. Also married to one of Finlayson's daughters (Phyllis) is Lt.-Col. John Wallace Eaton, currently a vice-president and director of the T. Eaton Company, who is a son of Robert Young Eaton, a former president of the T. Eaton Company, director of the Dominion Bank, and a nephew of Timothy Eaton, the founder. John Wallace Eaton's daughter, Cynthia Carol, married L. Yves Fortier who is currently a partner of Ogilvy, Cope, Porteous, Hansard, Marler, Montgomery and Renault of Montreal and a director of Manufacturers Life Insurance.

Gordon Harold Aikins, son of Sir James Aikins, also part of Canada's ruling class, was a director of such companies as Canada Cement, Imperial Bank, and Great-West Life. He had two daughters, Margaret Anne, who married Group Captain George Henry Sellers, now chairman of Federal Grain and a director of the Bank of Montreal (his father also headed Federal Grain and was a director of the CPR, Maple Leaf Mills, Dominion Glass, Winnipeg Electric, Imperial Bank, and Great-West Life), and Mary Frances Myrtle, who married Conrad Sanford Riley, now president of Dominion Tanners and a director of the Canadian Imperial Bank of Commerce (his father was president of Canadian Indemnity and a director of the Hudson's Bay Company, Royal Bank, and Great-West Life). To add to the web of kinship ties, Gordon Peter Osler, vice-chairman of British Steel and director of TransCanada Pipe-Lines, North American Life, and the Toronto-Dominion Bank and a member of the longstanding Osler family (his father was president of Osler, Hammon and Nanton, as was his grandfather, and a director of Great-West Life), married Nancy Adina Riley, daughter of Conrad Stephenson Riley, the father of Conrad Sanford Riley mentioned above. Meanwhile, Jean Elizabeth Riley, another daughter of Conrad Stephenson Riley, married George Montegu Black, Jr., vice-president of Argus Corporation and a director of the Canadian Imperial Bank of Commerce and Dominion Stores (his father was also a member of the economic elite as a financier and president of Western Breweries and director of the Union Bank of Canada, among other activities).

Finally, Gordon Thomas Southam, son of Harry Stevenson Southam, the publisher of the Ottawa *Citizen* and vice-president of Southam Newspapers (and grandson, through his mother, of the Hon. Thomas Ahearn, president of Ahearn and Soper and director of Canada Westinghouse, Bell Telephone, Bank of Montreal, and Royal Trust), is president of Pioneer Envelopes (a family firm) and director of Southam

Press and the dominant MacMillan Bloedel pulp and paper company. Gordon Thomas Southam is the son-in-law of Harvey Reginald Mac-Millan, who died early in 1975, the founder of H.R. MacMillan Export Company, former president of B.C. Packers, and partner to the merger forming MacMillan Bloedel. These kinship ties, in addition to those found in family firms, help to thread an important social web among the elite and are one of the many bonds that form it into an upper class. Further ties that bind will be explored in the following chapter.

This chapter has concentrated on comparisons of the Canadian and U.S. economic elites. It has demonstrated that the U.S. elite has more members with careers in engineering and science, finance departments, and work requiring training in commerce. It is through these career avenues in both countries that most persons from outside the upper class gain access to the elite. The Canadian elite, on the other hand, has a greater representation from banking and financial institutions, law, other elites, and family firms. These are the career avenues used most often by the upper class in both countries for securing their elite positions. This difference in entrance patterns is reflected to some extent in the degree of upper-class recruitment in the two elites, accounting for 36 per cent of the U.S. elite and 61 per cent of the Canadian.

In spite of this great difference, there is still a core within the U.S. elite that inherits its positions (one-fifth of the elite) as there is in Canada (one-quarter). The persistence of this core is also reflected in current kinship ties within each elite and the fact that careers in family firms are the most common patterns in both elites. These findings are consistent with earlier reports that the United States is less concentrated than Canada, less densely interlocked, and because it commands the leading position in the world system, it has a great deal of room for expansion. In contrast, Canadian capitalists have found themselves boxed into a narrow economic space. Most of the areas of innovation in the sphere of production have been taken over by outsiders, particularly U.S. capitalists in command of multinational manufacturing and resource corporations. Nevertheless, within its territory the Canadian elite has been successful in reproducing itself and resisting outside intrusion.

CHAPTER EIGHT

The Economic Elite in Canada and the United States:
II. Corporate, Ascriptive, and Social Characteristics

The corporate characteristics of the economic elite include the economic sectors in which current members have had their careers, the elite positions they hold in the business world (executives, insiders, and outsiders), and their multiple dominant directorships, if any. In this chapter each of these corporate characteristics is to be analysed in terms of upper-class recruitment into the elite. Following this is an analysis of ascriptive characteristics (aside from those based on class and inheritance, discussed in the last chapter), such as region of birth, race and ethnicity, and sex, for both elites. Analysis of these characteristics makes possible an evaluation of factors affecting exclusion from the elite on other than class grounds. The two elites are then examined as social groups by focusing on common university training, private schools, and men's private clubs. The evidence will indicate the extent to which the elite in each country is either simply an elite of position or an interacting set of people. Finally, movement between the economic elite and other elites – the state, the military, and the academic world – is briefly examined.

I. Corporate Characteristics of the Elite

Career Avenues and Class Origins of the Elite

One approach to an understanding of differences in upper-class recruitment between the United States and Canada is to analyse career avenues, both economic and non-economic, to see whether there is any systematic difference in their openness to persons of non-upper-class origin. Table 32 shows that there is actually more variation between the economic sectors in the United States than there is in Canada. The Canadian corporate sectors have a difference of twenty-three percentage points between the high in trade and the low in resources, but in the United States there is a difference of thirty points between the high in finance and the low in transportation/utilities. Upper-class origin in all career avenues is consistently higher in Canada than in the United States. The greatest difference between the two is in trade (with a 49 percentage-point difference) followed by transportation/utilities (with a 42 percentage-point difference). After these two sectors is the non-corporate career avenue of law, with a 25 percentage-point difference.

215

From this it can be concluded that there are no wide-open avenues to the elite for individuals from outside the upper class in Canada, except for the few whose main career is in the academic world or, to a limited extent, the resource sector. The relative openness in Canada's resource sector has to do with the high degree of foreign ownership in this sector (see Chapter 9). By comparison, all avenues in the United States are more open to persons from outside the upper class, although the finance and manufacturing sectors, the two key centres for interlocks, have the highest recruitment from the upper class.

TABLE 32

Upper-Class Origins and Career Avenues
to the Economic Elite

	Per Cent Upper Class		Number of Cases	
	Canada	U.S.	Canada	U.S.
Economic Sectors:				
Transportation/Utilities	58	16	43	130
Finance	65	46	178	333
Resources	47	32	45	117
Manufacturing	61	38	133	811
Trade	70	21	60	88
Law	61	36	144	158
Academic	31	22	16	77
State or Military	57	26	54	110

Law as a career avenue was shown in Chapter 7 to take different routes in the two countries (pp. 189-192), and a similar variation can be seen when law as a career avenue is compared with the main current affiliation by sector. In the United States, only 36 per cent of persons with careers in law still have law as their main current affiliation compared with 90 per cent in Canada. A similar, but less marked, pattern is also evident in the academic world; 55 per cent who entered the elite here in the United States are still in education (primarily as university presidents and heads of commerce schools), compared to 75 per cent in Canada. In contrast, only 5 per cent in the United States and 17 per cent in Canada of those with career avenues in the state or military continue their main current affiliations there. In the United States, elite members from the state or military tend to move to finance (23 per cent), manufacturing (21 per cent), law (13 per cent), education (12 per cent), and transportation/utilities (10 per cent). In Canada, they are likely to enter law (30 per cent) and finance (19 per cent), few moving to manufacturing (9 per cent) or transportation/utilities and resources (6 per cent each).

Unlike persons with non-corporate careers, those with career avenues in economic sectors tend to continue a main affiliation in the same sectors. The continuity varies in the United States from a low of 88 per cent in trade and finance to a high of 94 per cent in manufacturing, and in Canada from 92 per cent in manufacturing to 98 per cent in transportation/utilities.

Some slight difference exists between the two countries as to whether members of their elites have had their careers in dominant or smaller corporations. Of the entire U.S. elite, half have had their main careers in their current dominant corporations, and an additional 7 per cent have had a career in some other dominant corporation. In Canada, only 43 per cent have had their main career in their current dominant corporation, and an additional 8 per cent have had their career in another dominant corporation. There is a considerable difference in Canada between native-born and foreign-born elite members in this respect. While only 48 per cent of the Canadian-born have had their entire careers in dominant corporations, 67 per cent of the foreign-born living in Canada have had this experience. These figures are a reflection of the long crawl described earlier (p. 188). Only 17 per cent of the Canadian-born have had to make the long crawl to the top, but 30 per cent of the foreign-born are long-crawlers. The foreign-born also tend to continue their affiliation with dominant corporations; 62 per cent are currently affiliated with dominant corporations compared to 46 per cent of the Canadian-born. Indeed, only 10 per cent of the foreign-born (as opposed to 26 per cent of the Canadian-born) now have non-corporate affiliations. This difference is attributable to the fact that law firms are the main non-corporate current affiliation of the elite, and very few foreign-born persons are lawyers (17 per cent of the Canadian-born compared to only 1 per cent of the foreign-born).

Similarly, 8 per cent of the Canadian-born but only 4 per cent of the foreign-born used the state or military as a career avenue. This pattern is reversed in the sectors of resources and manufacturing, where so much of the Canadian economy is foreign controlled. Of the foreign-born, 30 per cent have had their main careers in manufacturing and 23 per cent in resources, while the respective percentages of Canadian-born are only 19 and 7. Reflecting the patterns of the Canadian-born outlined in Chapter 6, 92 per cent with careers in finance, 89 per cent with careers in trade, and 84 per cent with careers in transportation/utilities are in Canadian-controlled companies. The manufacturing and resource sectors, however, reflect foreign control. Of the Canadian-born with careers in manufacturing, 58 per cent have been in Canadian-controlled companies and 30 per cent have been in U.S. branches. Where careers have been in resources, only 31 per cent have been in Canadian-controlled resource companies and 62 per cent have been in U.S. branches. It is interesting to see the differences in career patterns in relation to control. Almost two-thirds of all persons with careers in Canadian-controlled corporations have been in family firms (41 per cent) or have served as financiers or financial executives (23 per cent). On the other hand, half of those whose careers have been

in U.S.-controlled branches in Canada have had career patterns in engineering or science (34 per cent) or in the corporate finance department (16 per cent). Again, these facts agree with patterns stressed
throughout the preceding chapters.

Positions within the Economic Elite

The positions in dominant (and smaller) companies held by members of the economic elite represent various degrees of involvement
with the company and can be studied to show further corporate characteristics. *Executives* are officers who hold a corporate post as chairman,
vice-chairman, president, or chief executive officer, or sometimes
more than one post simultaneously. *Insiders* are usually vice-presidents
but sometimes treasurers, house lawyers, or comptrollers who also sit
on the company's board. *Outsiders* sit on a corporation's board of directors but are not executives or insiders of that company, although they
are often executives of other companies. In this way members are recruited to the elite and companies are interlocked. For example, the
group of four hundred top U.S. corporations (250 industrials and 150
non-industrials) consists of the 194 dominants and 206 non-domi-
nants, yet 61 per cent of all the presidents and 69 per cent of all the
chairmen of these four hundred are members of the economic elite –
that is, the chairman *or* the president of 71 per cent of these four hundred largest companies is an elite member. Therefore, it is clear that a
member of the elite who is an executive of a non-dominant company
often achieves elite status through being an outsider of a dominant
company. At the same time, the two companies are interlocked. This
practice is also characteristic of the Canadian economic elite.[1]

Corporate positions can be analysed from two perspectives, a narrow
one – insider, outsider, or executive in a dominant corporation – and a
broader one – insider, outsider, or executive in any corporation, dominant or not. The difference, of course, is that the narrower perspective
uses only dominant corporations as its universe while the broader one
uses any corporation with which an elite member is affiliated. For example, Charles I. Rathgeb, Jr., like his father before him, is chairman
and owner of Comstock International, Canada's largest construction
company but not among the 113 dominants. He is also an outside director of three dominant companies – Algoma Steel, IAC Limited, and the
Royal Bank. From the narrower perspective of dominant corporations
he is only an outsider, but from the broader perspective he is an executive.

Looked at from these two perspectives, the insiders of *dominant* U.S.
corporations also have the greatest likelihood of being insiders of *any*
corporation (82 per cent) and almost all the rest are executives (17 per
cent). In Canada, the results are almost identical (80 and 18 per cent,
respectively). On the other hand, outsiders of dominant U.S. corpora-

tions usually tend to be executives of other non-dominant companies (68 per cent), although some are partners (13 per cent) and 16 per cent are only outsiders in all companies (mainly attached to non-corporate institutions such as universities). The Canadian pattern with respect to outsiders is quite different: only 51 per cent of the outsiders of dominant companies are executives of non-dominant companies, 33 per cent are partners (mainly in law firms), and 11 per cent are only outsiders. Once again, the different role of law firms in the two elites affects the pattern.

The difference between the two perspectives is evident in comparisons of positions by whether or not members of the elite have had their main careers in dominant corporations. The perspective of career in a dominant corporation shows that in both elites 90 per cent of outsiders have not had their main careers in dominant corporations, but over 90 per cent of the insiders and executives have had careers in dominant corporations. In terms of the top posts held in any corporation, about half the executives and outsiders in both elites have had careers in dominant corporations. Virtually none of the partners in both elites have had careers in dominant corporations.

The difference between the two perspectives on corporate positions and differences between the positions themselves are evident in the class origins set out in Table 33. Within dominant corporations, more outsiders are of upper-class origin in both countries than executives or insiders. In any corporation, the pattern shifts and executives are more likely to be from the upper class. Here is further evidence that the executives of non-dominant companies sit on the boards of dominant companies as outsiders. It can be concluded that in both countries a career in a family firm that is itself not dominant provides a stepping stone to the boards of dominant corporations. The pattern also suggests that many outsiders in dominant corporations hold controlling blocks of shares that allow transfer of the outsider position from one generation to another (see the discussion on pp. 196-200) even though their main bases of operation are in smaller companies. It is a common practice for outsiders to hold controlling blocks of shares but to hire execu-

TABLE 33

Upper-Class Origins of the Elite by Corporate Position
(percentages)

	DOMINANT CORPORATION		ANY CORPORATION	
	Canada	United States	Canada	United States
Insider	49	21	49	19
Executive	57	31	69	40
Outsider	67	46	39	35
Partner	—	—	62	44

tives to manage dominant companies (as illustrated in Appendix XIII). The fact that the proportion of persons of upper-class origin who are only outsiders drops significantly between dominant corporations and any corporation suggests that those who are exclusively outsiders, with no corporate executive or insider post or partnership, are the least likely to be upper class. It is in this group that most token outside directors are located.

If this table is looked at in another way, insider positions are the channel through which people outside the upper class are most likely to make it into the elite. Upper-class members are likely to use the offices of chairman of the executive committee or outsider in a dominant corporation as a means of entrance while they are simultaneously chairmen of other corporations.

The same patterns are also evident in terms of inherited positions, where outsiders of dominant corporations have the highest rate in both Canada (37 per cent) and the United States (28 per cent), executives have rates of 20 per cent and 16 per cent respectively, and insiders 20 per cent and 11 per cent. It is clear that outsider positions offer non-upper-class persons more opportunity to enter the elite in the United States than they do in Canada. In Canada, more of the insiders are children of the upper class "learning the ropes" before entering executive positions and moving into the charmed circle of outside directors.

In contrast to the inheritors are the long-crawlers who work in one company for twenty or more years before becoming corporate officials. In terms of career types, long-crawlers are common among persons trained in engineering and science (a third of them in both elites) or, especially in Canada, working in the finance department (46 per cent compared to 17 per cent in the United States). A career outside the corporate world, in a family firm, or law virtually guarantees that there will be no long crawl. Only 7 per cent of the long-crawlers in the United States are from upper-class backgrounds compared to 42 per cent of those not having to take this route. In Canada, 34 per cent of the long-crawlers have upper-class backgrounds while 66 per cent of others have had this wait.

There is a noticeable difference between Canadian-born and foreign-born persons in Canada in the type of positions held within dominant corporations. The Canadian-born tend to be outsiders in dominant corporations (53 per cent compared to 33 per cent of the foreign-born) while the foreign-born are more likely to hold insider positions (26 per cent compared to 21 per cent of the Canadian-born) and especially executive positions (41 per cent compared to 27 per cent of the Canadian-born). These aspects of the Canadian elite, like many others, reflect foreign dominance in manufacturing and resources.

Looking at class origins by type of position helps to account for some of the overall differences in class origins in the Canadian and U.S. elites. The branch-plant structure of most of the resource industry and much of manufacturing in Canada means that fewer insider positions, particularly those associated with engineering and science, are available in Canada. Since this is the main area of mobility for persons outside the upper class, particularly coming up through the long crawl, the branch-plant structure means that chances for mobility are lower in Canada generally than they are in the parent organization (see Chapter 9, pp. 253-255).

Holders of Multiple Dominant Directorships

We saw earlier (pp. 171-172) that 29 per cent of the economic elite in Canada are holders of multiple directorships, among them holding 54 per cent of all dominant positions, and in the United States, 22 per cent of the elite hold 41 per cent of all such dominant positions. The pattern of interlocking is not as "dense" in the United States as in Canada. With regard to class of origin, 55 per cent of holders of single and 73 per cent of holders of multiple directorships are from the upper class in Canada. While the trend is similar in the United States, there is not such a wide gap between the holders of multiple dominant positions (37 per cent) and the holders of single dominant directorships (35 per cent). It is clear that the realm of multiple directorship holders is not so much the preserve of the upper class in the United States as in Canada.

Class of origin has an important effect on disposition of dominant bank directorships in the United States, since 41 per cent of those with one are of upper-class origin compared to 34 per cent of those without. But the spread is even wider in Canada, where 74 per cent of bank directors are drawn from the upper class compared to 56 per cent for those without a dominant bank directorship. The relative class differences in dominant life insurance directorships are the same in both countries. In the United States dominant bank directorships are more likely to be held by inheritors than those not inheriting (24 to 19 per cent), but the rate is even higher in Canada (41 to 25 per cent).

The pattern found earlier (p. 167) for interlocking between sectors in the United States is repeated among holders of multiple directorships. As Table 34 illustrates, the most likely location for at least one of their

TABLE 34

Holders of Multiple Dominant Directorships by Sector

Per cent of multiple directorship holders with a dominant directorship in:	United States	Canada
Manufacturing	79	54
Finance	66	91
Transportation/Utilities	33	30
Resources	16	24
Trade	11	20

dominant directorships is in manufacturing, followed closely by finance, and the others are much lower. As would be expected, in Canada holders of multiple directorships are mainly in the finance sector, well ahead of manufacturing, with the others following. Here is additional confirmation of the more central place of finance in the Canadian economic elite, when 91 per cent of all multiple directorship holders have at least one of their dominant directorships in that sector.

Banks are the most actively used for interlocking of all corporations in both countries. Only 16 per cent of multiple directorship holders in the United States do not have a dominant bank directorship, and 61 per cent of holders of dominant bank directorships have one or more other dominant directorships as well. In Canada, only 21 per cent of holders of two or more dominant directorships lack a top bank directorship, while 71 per cent of the bank directors are multiple directorship holders. Similarly with directorships in dominant life insurance companies: in the United States, 47 per cent of these directors are also multiple directors compared to 24 per cent of multiple holders without an insurance directorship. In Canada, the proportions in the same categories are 62 per cent and 27 per cent.

Holders of single and multiple dominant directorships differ considerably in their positions within corporations, as Table 35 illustrates. From the perspective of both dominant corporations and all corporations, executives in both countries are the most likely of the categories to hold more than one dominant directorship and insiders are the least likely. In all the categories considered (except for outsider directors in any corporation) there are more likely to be more Canadian members of the elite holding multiple directorships than U.S. members, even when they hold the same type of position. The exception concerns the few Blacks and women in the United States who are used as token directors by several dominant companies (see pp. 229 and 232), resulting in a higher proportion of multiple directors among those who are only outsiders. The position in Canada in which there is the second largest holding of multiple directorships is the partnership. This fact again reflects the active role of law firms in binding dominant Canadian corporations together. Table 35 further reinforces the argument made earlier that the outsiders of a dominant corporation are usually executives from other corporations.

TABLE 35

Holders of Multiple Dominant Directorships by Position
(percentages)

	DOMINANT CORPORATION		ANY CORPORATION	
	Canada	United States	Canada	United States
Insider	15	8	15	6
Executive	53	42	43	32
Outsider	31	23	25	29
Partner	—	—	31	25

II. Ascriptive Characteristics of the Elite

Ascriptive characteristics are the features an individual has been endowed with at birth, over which he has no control. By examining the
ascriptive characteristics of members of the economic elite, it is possible to determine to what extent they are used for selection of recruits,
consciously or not, by persons in control of dominant corporations. The
three ascriptive characteristics to be examined here (class of origin and
inheritance have already been analysed in Chapter 7) are region of
birth, race and/or ethnicity, and sex.

Regions of Birth and Residence

Does one's place of birth, in the United States and Canada, affect
one's chances for becoming a member of the economic elite? The
answer is that place of birth is important, but not so important in the
United States as current place of residence. Table 36 shows the birthplaces and residences of the economic elite in the United States compared with the population distribution in 1920 (the mean year of birth
for the current elite) and 1973 (the most recent census data).

TABLE 36

Regions of Birth and Residence of the U.S.
Economic Elite

Region	Birthplace (%)		Percentage Points Difference	Residence (%)		Percentage Points Difference
	Elite	Total Pop. (1920)		Elite	Total Pop. (1973)	
Northeast	35.7	30.0	5.7	45.2	26.3	18.9
North Central	35.9	32.0	3.9	28.3	27.3	1.0
South	17.5	29.3	(11.8)	12.4	28.9	(16.5)
Mountain	3.2	3.2	0.0	1.3	4.4	(3.1)
Pacific	7.7	5.4	2.3	12.6	13.1	(0.5)
	100	100		100	100	

NOTE: The regional divisions are based on census divisions except that two
sub-regions of the West – Mountain and Pacific – have been used because of
their different patterns.

The Pacific, Northeastern, and North Central regions had more elite
births in proportion to the general population (overrepresented)
than the Mountain region (equally represented) and the South (the
most underrepresented region). When viewed by residence, the South
is even more underrepresented than by birth, the Mountain region is
somewhat less underrepresented, and the Pacific region slightly underrepresented. The Northeastern region is more overrepresented than it
was in elite births and the North Central region is only slightly overrepresented. To understand some of the reasons why region of birth and

region of residence affect access to the U.S. economic elite, it is necessary to analyse, in more detail, some of the other characteristics of elite members from those regions.

One of the means of explaining the representation by region is a class profile of each region, showing the differences between births and residence of the elite. Table 37 gives the proportions of elite persons of upper-class origin born and resident in each region. As places of residence, the regions have fairly even proportions, but the range by birth is a good deal wider. What is most interesting is that the region that is the least upper class by birth is the most upper class by residence. This is not because upper-class members have migrated to the Mountain region but because so many working- and middle-class persons have migrated from this region. With the career avenues to the elite in mind, of members born in the Mountain region, only 5 per cent have careers in family firms, but 8 per cent are members on their own account. Conversely, of those now resident there, 24 per cent have a career in a family firm and there are no "own accounts."

TABLE 37

Regions of Birth and of Residence of the U.S. Economic Elite by Upper-Class Origins

Region	Birthplace		Residence	
	Per cent Upper Class	Total Number	Per cent Upper Class*	Total Number
Northeast	42	672	37	856
North Central	30	676	33	540
South	33	329	37	235
Mountain	18	61	40	25
Pacific	43	144	35	238
All	36	1,882	36	1,894

*These percentages are confined to U.S.-"born" members of the elite to see the effect of internal migration on class recruitment by region.

New England is the main recipient of elite members born outside the upper class. A part of the region with the most upper-class elite births (the Northeast), New England itself has an elite with 48 per cent upper-class birth, and the Middle Atlantic sub-region has an elite with 41 per cent upper-class birth. Generally, then, although region of birth affects a person's chances for access to the U.S. elite, class advantage is also a part of the regional influence. There is a clear pattern in the relative movement of persons toward certain regions. The strongest flow is into the northeastern region, and only 16 per cent of these migrants are of upper-class origin.

The Pacific region has also gained migrants, but again, they are less

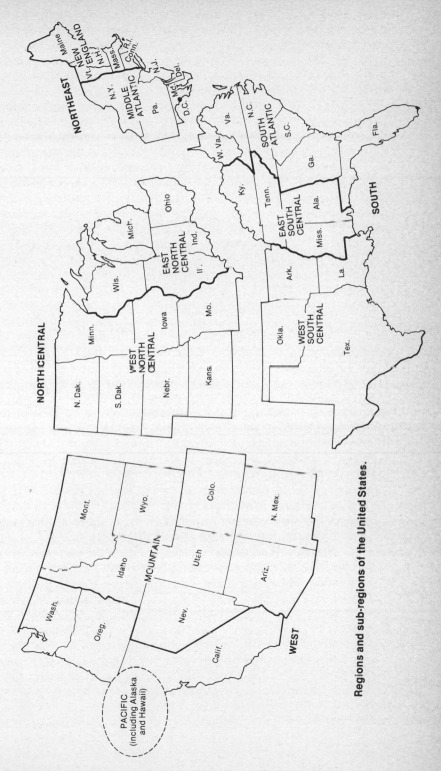

Regions and sub-regions of the United States.

likely than the "native" elite to be upper class. The two regions that lose most members of the elite through migration are the North Central region and the South. These regions tend to lose fewer upper-class members than ones of middle- or lower-class origin. Only 23 per cent of the migrants from the South were born in the upper class and only 17 per cent from the North Central region.

These findings suggest that persons of upper-class origin are likely to remain in their region of birth and that many of those from less privileged classes have to move elsewhere to pursue corporate careers in the elite. This conclusion is reflected in the general distribution of inherited position by region of birth, with the exception of the Mountain region. In that region, only 5 per cent of the elite inherited some position and, as we have seen, they tend to stay in their birthplace while persons of lower class move elsewhere. In the Pacific region, 33 per cent of the elite inherited a position; in all other regions the proportion is about 20 per cent except in the west North Central sub-region, where the proportion is 13 per cent. Patterns of inherited position by current residence are similar except in the east South Central sub-region, where 31 per cent inherited.

Chances for entering the elite because of birthplace are also affected by the distribution of various economic activities. New England and the Middle Atlantic and Pacific regions are most overrepresented by native sons with careers in finance and the east South Central region has the fewest. Among persons with careers in the resource sector the west South Central region is most overrepresented by birth and the east North Central and South Atlantic the least. Similarly, in manufacturing, the east North Central and South Atlantic regions are most overrepresented by birth, with New England and the Pacific the least. In trade, the Mountain region is overrepresented by birth.

Regional differences are also evident in the degree to which elite members of a region are linked with other regions through interlocking directorships. Elite residents of the east South Central, west South Central, and Mountain sub-regions are "isolates," of whom only from 5 to 8 per cent have multiple directorships, while in all the other regions 20 to 30 per cent have multiple directorships.

It is clear from the historical survey of U.S. development why the South is particularly underrepresented in the elite: its early reliance on the plantation economy and late industrialization. Similarly, the Northeast has always been the centre of industrial and financial activity and is also the home of many upper-class institutions such as private schools and men's private clubs.

Regional differences have also had an important effect on the character of the Canadian economic elite. In Table 38, comparisons are made using 1921 as the mean year of birth for the current elite and 1971 as the most recent census year. The most striking feature of this table is that every region in Canada except Ontario is underrepresented in the economic elite by residence of members. By place of birth, Ontario and Manitoba are overrepresented, and British Columbia is about even. The region most underrepresented by birth of elite members is Quebec, followed by Saskatchewan. By residence of the elite, the Atlantic provinces are most underrepresented.

TABLE 38

**Regions of Birth and Residence of the Canadian
Economic Elite**

| Region | Birthplace (%) | | Percentage Points Difference | Residence (%) | | Percentage Points Difference |
	Elite	Total Pop. (1921)		Elite	Total Pop. (1971)	
Atlantic	8.6	11.4	(2.8)	4.0	9.4	(5.5)
Quebec	20.2	26.9	(6.7)	25.2	27.9	(2.7)
Ontario	47.6	33.4	14.2	52.4	35.7	16.7
Manitoba	7.9	6.9	1.0	3.5	4.6	(1.1)
Saskatchewan	4.0	8.6	(4.6)	1.0	4.3	(3.3)
Alberta	5.7	6.7	(1.0)	6.3	7.5	(1.2)
British Columbia	5.9	6.0	(0.1)	7.5	10.1	(2.6)
	100	100		100	100	

The best way to evaluate regional opportunities to enter elite positions is to note how many make it into the elite in the province where they were born. As would be expected, the rate is highest is Ontario (85 per cent of its native-born elite remain there); next is Quebec, retaining 80 per cent of its native elite, followed by British Columbia retaining 78 per cent. Alberta keeps only 54 per cent of future members of the elite, and the other provinces lose more than half their prospective elite members. Saskatchewan keeps the fewest (22 per cent) and somewhat more stay in Manitoba (35 per cent) and the Atlantic region (49 per cent). Ontario receives most of the future elite members from each of the regions. It is now the place of residence of 43 per cent of the elite who were born in Manitoba, 37 per cent born in Saskatchewan, and 31 per cent born in the Atlantic provinces. Ironically, more members born in Manitoba and Saskatchewan now live in Ontario than remain in these provinces. Ontario has also received the lion's share of elite members born outside Canada, 50 per cent of those born in the United States and 58 per cent of those born in Britain. It is clear that Ontario is the centre of the Canadian economic elite, both producing the most and receiving the most members from outside.

Ontario's high proportion of members of the economic elite both by birth and by current residence is related to the fact that so much of Canada's production is located in Ontario. This, in turn, is related to foreign dominance in the sphere of production. This problem will be discussed further in Chapter 10, but it is necessary at this point to see why so much of Canada's manufacturing capacity is Ontario-centred. The importance of industry is evident from the following figures: Ontario receives 43.2 per cent of all taxable income from Canadian-controlled manufacturing. In 1972, it received 72 per cent of its taxes in the manufacturing sector from foreign-controlled companies and in the same year received 62.2 per cent of all taxable income paid by U.S.-owned manufacturing in Canada. Though its tax revenue from Canadian-owned manufacturing centred in Ontario is not insignificant, it is less weighty than the tax received from U.S.-controlled manufacturing.*

Besides being the centre of manufacturing, both foreign- and Canadian-owned, Ontario is also the centre of the financial sector and the upper-class institutions of Canada. It exhibits the paradox of housing over half of the members of the U.S. comprador elite in Canada (53 per cent) as well as a very high proportion of the indigenous Canadian elite (55 per cent). Because it is the centre for both foreign-controlled manufacturing and Canadian-controlled finance, Ontario acts as a magnet, drawing potential elite members into its borders and retaining its native-born. This is reflected in Table 39 on upper-class origin by region. Ontario has a lower percentage of upper-class recruitment than the Canadian total because it is the residence of such a large share of the U.S. comprador elite (see Chapter 9). Be this as it may, the Canadian elite west of Manitoba is clearly less upper-class in origin both by

TABLE 39

Regions of Birth and Residence of the Canadian Economic Elite by Upper-Class Origins

Region	Birthplace		Residence	
	Per cent Upper Class	Total Number	Per cent Upper Class*	Total Number
Atlantic	61	59	75	32
Quebec	78	138	73	201
Ontario	58	326	57	419
Manitoba	70	54	67	28
Saskatchewan	19	27	38	8
Alberta	49	39	41	50
British Columbia	53	40	51	60
All	61	683	61	798

*See note, Table 37.

*For a more detailed analysis of this data, see my "A Political Economy of Regionalism" in *Conflict and Consensus: Multiple Loyalties in the Canadian State*, ed. D. Glenday, A. Turowetz, and H. Guindon (Toronto: Macmillan, 1977).

birth and by residence than is the East. The reason for this is partly that Alberta and British Columbia have the largest comprador elite in relation to population, but this does not account for Saskatchewan's very low percentage. The West's lower rate of upper-class recruitment must be attributed in part to a late start and an immigrant society, so that it has not yet solidified its upper-class institutions.

Various factors account for the difference between the number of upper-class members of the elite born in an area and the number who reside there. In the Atlantic region, the increase in upper-class origins results from the out-migration of lower-class future elite members (as in the U.S. Mountain region). In Quebec and Ontario, on the other hand, although the proportion of upper-class members is greater for birth than for residence, the actual numbers of members of upper-class origin has risen, suggesting some immigration of people born in the upper class but a greater immigration of persons of non-upper-class origin. Manitoba, Saskatchewan, and Alberta have all lost members of upper-class origin numerically, but Saskatchewan has lost a greater proportion of future elite members born outside the upper class. British Columbia has gained a few residents but has dropped slightly in proportion of elite of upper-class origin, suggesting that a slightly greater proportion of the interprovincial migrants are not of upper-class origin.

It may be concluded that region of birth has indeed had an effect on opportunity to enter elite positions in both the United States and Canada. In the United States, the South is clearly the least favourable area in which to be born or reside while the Northeast offers the best chances to natives and residents to enter the elite. In both Canada and the United States, persons who are not of upper-class origin must more often emigrate from their place of birth in order to enter the elite than those of upper-class origin. In Canada, U.S. investment has exaggerated the problem of regionalism and added to Canada's pattern of uneven development (see Chapter 10).

Race and Ethnicity

Of all ascriptive characteristics, being Black in the United States is the one most likely to prevent admission to the economic elite. Although about a fifth of the U.S. population is Black, only ten members, or 0.5 per cent, of the entire economic elite are Black.* Ironically, these few Blacks appear to have been selected for the elite *because* they are Black, since all are outside directors in dominant corporations and appear to be token representatives. It is difficult to make a meaningful analysis of Blacks in the elite because their numbers are so small, but of the ten, five have had their main careers in another elite or another sector and three are involved as lawyers. None belongs to any of the top forty-five exclusive clubs.

---

* Race was determined through biographical sources and the checking of annual reports.

Two Blacks in the elite are of particular interest. The career of one was summarized in a *Fortune* article in 1971:

> The election of Leon H. Sullivan, 48, a black Philadelphia minister, to General Motors Corp.'s board of directors is a landmark event in American business. Pastor of the Zion Baptist Church, Sullivan has been involved in small but socially significant financial ventures since the early Sixties.... High on his priority roster is a plan to increase the number of black G.M. automobile dealers (12 out of 13,600) and black workers...about 15 per cent of 800,000.[2]

It is ironic that the proportion of Blacks in the economic elite is actually greater (0.5 per cent) than that among General Motors auto dealers (0.08 per cent). Blacks are excluded from important positions not simply at the level of the elite but throughout the U.S. class structure.

Jerome Heartwell Holland is important for two reasons: first, he is Black, which makes him rare among the elite, and second, he holds more dominant directorships than any other member of the U.S. economic elite. He sits on the boards of Manufacturers Hanover, Chrysler Corporation, Continental Corporation, Federated Department Stores, American Telephone and Telegraph, General Foods, and Union Carbide. Thus, Holland appears in the annual reports and at the annual meetings of seven dominant U.S. corporations. He has never had a corporate career in a dominant corporation; instead, he has been a college president and is a former U.S. ambassador to Sweden.

Analysis of the U.S. economic elite by ethnic origin or religious affiliation is made difficult because ethnic background is played down in the United States and only 40 per cent of the whole elite report any religious affiliation. The quality of data in these areas does not allow solid comparisons of representation, but some comparisons of types by religious affiliation are possible.

Of elite members born and resident in the United States, forty report their affiliation as Jewish (2.1 per cent). Twelve of these (30 per cent) have had some association with the state and ten belong to one of the top forty-five exclusive clubs. Only 29 per cent of all the Jews in the U.S. economic elite have had their main careers in dominant corporations, the lowest of any racial, ethnic, or religious group except the Blacks, and 36 per cent have had their main careers in family firms, the highest of any group. Jews also have the highest proportion that have made it on their own account – 9 per cent compared to 1 per cent of the others. These same patterns are replicated for Jews in Canada.[3] Depending on how the data are interpreted, Jews represent 2.1 per cent of the entire U.S. elite or 5.2 per cent of those reporting a religious affiliation. Since Jews are more likely to report affiliation than any other group, the lower figure is probably more accurate than the higher one.

Of the religious affiliations reported, the most common is Episcopalian (the equivalent of Anglican in Canada) at 32 per cent, followed by Presbyterian (29 per cent), Methodist (9 per cent), Catholic (8 per cent), Congregationalist (7 per cent), and other affiliations (11 per cent). In the entire U.S. economic elite, only eight Jews, or 18 per cent, have a dominant bank directorship, a lower proportion than Catholics (30 per cent), Episcopalians (25 per cent), or Congregationalists (28 per cent) and the same as Presbyterians and Methodists. Only 7 per cent of the Jews (three) have a dominant insurance directorship, lower than all other religious affiliations. The available evidence clearly indicates that Jews are not in a dominant position in U.S. financial corporations, the same pattern as in Canada. Again as in Canada, a quarter of the Jews in the U.S. elite have kin currently in the elite (compared to 7 per cent among the whole elite), suggesting that the family firm is a major means of access to the elite for them. A high percentage of Jews inherit positions (31 per cent) compared to the total elite, but so do Catholics (28 per cent), Episcopalians (28 per cent), Presbyterians (27 per cent), and Congregationalists (26 per cent). Methodists have the lowest proportion, as with all class indicators. Membership in the top ten clubs shows clear differences by religious affiliation. Between 31 and 35 per cent of Catholics, Episcopalians, and Presbyterians belong to these clubs, but only 7 per cent of Jews are members, and the latter also have the fewest members in the top forty-five clubs.

Specifically, in terms of social class, persons who report a religious affiliation tend to be of higher class of origin than those who do not. While only 30 per cent of those not reporting a religious affiliation are upper class, approximately half of the Catholics, Episcopalians, Presbyterians, Jews, and Congregationalists are upper class in origin. Only Methodists are below a quarter in upper-class origin.

In Canada, origins in the British Isles characterize the dominant ethnic group in the economic elite. "Anglo" origin is reported by only 44.7 per cent of the total population but by 86.6 per cent of the economic elite. French Canadians, on the other hand, make up 28.6 per cent of the population but only 7.9 per cent of the elite. Other studies have supported this finding:

> Despite at least five years of serious social pressure, Quebec's growing economic nationalism has not yet had much impact on the boardrooms of the large companies that do a substantial amount of business in the province.
>
> According to various Quebec Government-sponsored studies, there are very few Quebec enterprises in any sector, except the pulp and paper industry and the banks, that have more than one French-Canadian director.
>
> Of the 93 corporations that employ more than 800 people in Quebec – not including obviously francophone companies such as Caisse Populaire, Desjardins and Sidbec-Dosco Ltd. – 16 had no Francophones on the board and 25 had only one.[4]

Among other ethnic groups, only Jewish Canadians have significant representation among the elite. While 1.4 per cent of Canada's population is Jewish, 4.3 per cent of the elite is of this origin. Jewish Canadians in the elite tend to come from a very few prominent families (twenty-five of the thirty-four come from six families) whose corporations have become dominant in the last few generations. Outside their own firms, they have very little access to the elite. Of the remaining other ethnics (25.3 per cent of the population), only 1.3 per cent are members of the elite.*

While it is clear that in the United States Blacks are systematically excluded from the economic elite and that Jews do not in any way dominate it, it is not possible to analyse the effect of ethnicity systematically in the United States as it is in Canada. First, U.S. census categories do not facilitate aggregate comparisons, and second, U.S. elite members tend not to belong to distinctively ethnic associations or to report their parentage as the Canadian elite does. Baltzell observed that "at the lowest levels of American society, a person is a member of an ethnic group; at the middle levels he is a member of a religious group and at the highest level, he is first a member of his social class,"[5] perhaps an accurate reflection of the effect of religion, ethnicity, and class in the United States. Comparisons with Canada are difficult, to say the least. Blacks are not a large part of the Canadian population and do not have the same type of social and political organizations as Canada's major minority, the French Canadians. Ethnic identification has been promoted in Canada by the bicultural and multicultural policies of the state. Thus, to attempt a systematic comparison is virtually impossible. It is possible, however, to study the ascriptive characteristic of having been born a woman – the second-least advantageous attribute for admittance to the U.S. economic elite after being Black. The only difference in Canada is that being a woman is the *most* disadvantageous attribute.†

Women in the Economic Elite

The place of women in the U.S. economic elite was best summarized by Patricia R. Harris, the only person in it who has three attributes most likely to prevent admission to the elite. Both a woman and Black, she is a partner in a Washington law firm and a director of Chase Manhattan and International Business Machines. She says, "I was probably asked because I am a black and a woman. I come from two groups that have been excluded from all aspects of American life."[6] To round out her

---

* The increased coverage of the Canadian elite discussed earlier has changed some of the data for the ethnic composition of the elite. "Anglo" origin rises from 86.2 to 86.6 per cent, French falls from 8.4 to 7.9 per cent, and Jewish rises from 4.1 to 4.3 per cent, while "other" ethnics remain the same, 1.3 per cent.

† It is interesting that members of the U.S. economic elite who are either Canadian-born U.S. residents or residents of Canada exist in greater numbers than women or Black members of the elite. There are only twenty women (1.0 per cent) and ten Blacks (0.5 per cent) in the entire U.S. economic elite; there are thirty-eight Canadian-born members (1.9 per cent) and twenty-five Canadian residents (1.2 per cent).

disadvantages, her father was a railway dining-car waiter and "among her ancestors were Negro slaves, Delaware and Cherokee Indians."[7] It is interesting that like Jerome Holland, Patricia Harris was also a U.S. ambassador, this time to Luxembourg. But of course one cannot generalize from her case because she is one of the ten Blacks and one of the twenty women in the U.S. economic elite. Proportionately, women have about the same place in the U.S. elite (20 of 2,007, or 1 per cent) and the Canadian economic elite (8 of 798, or 1 per cent).

Again it is difficult to generalize from so few individuals, but recognizing the limitation, some patterns and examples can be discussed. Of the women in the elite, 40 per cent have had their main careers in non-corporate sectors (three in the state elite), 25 per cent in family firms, 10 per cent in law (two), one woman is a financial executive, and four could not be classified. Among them they hold four bank directorships and five insurance directorships; seven have more than one dominant directorship. Only one has had a career in a dominant corporation. The most common avenue to the elite, taken by seven women, was through a career in the academic world; five had careers in publishing. Six are currently affiliated with publishing, three are in education, three have careers in finance, and two in the state. Women in the elite tend to be similar to the men in terms of class of origin, although 25 per cent, compared to 20 per cent of the men, have inherited positions. They are either highly educated or did not reach university: 55 per cent have had postgraduate training, 15 per cent are university graduates, and 30 per cent did not graduate from university.

The woman with the most dominant directorships is Catherine Blanchard Cleary, one of the few who have actually had a corporate career. She became president of First Wisconsin Trust after being trained in law and working her way through the corporation. She now has directorships in AT&T, GM, Kraftco Corporation, and Northwestern Mutual Life, a company of which her father had been president from 1932 on.

Another career woman is Helen K. Copley, whose husband, James S. Copley, died in 1973. She had been his secretary for thirteen years, and they were married in 1965. She is now head of Copley Press, one of the largest privately owned newspaper chains in the United States, and a director of Wells Fargo and Company.

Katharine Graham, who heads the *Washington Post*, of which her father was once chairman, also having held a directorship in Allied Chemical, is now also a director of Allied Chemical. Her family owns large amounts of stock in this dominant company. She is also a director of Bowaters Mersey Paper, a Canadian company in which the *Washington Post* has a 49 per cent interest.

Another woman associated with newspapers is Marian Heiskell, a director of Consolidated Edison who has been with the *New York Times* for some time. Her father was formerly a publisher and president of the *Times*, and her first husband was also a publisher of the *Times*. Her current husband is the chairman of Time, Inc.

Oveta Culp Hobby is head of the Houston *Post* and a director of General Foods. Her father was a Texas legislator and lawyer, but her husband, who died in 1964, was the president of the Houston *Post* and also was acting governor of Texas at one time.

Claire Giannini Hoffman, whose father, Amadeo Peter Giannini, founded the Bank of Italy in 1904 (now the Bank of America), has been a director of this dominant company since 1949.

The woman with the most dominant directorships after Catherine Cleary is Marina Von Neumann Whitman, who has three: Manufacturers Hanover, Westinghouse Electric, and Marcor Incorporated. Both her father and her husband have had distinguished academic careers, and she had one also as a professor of economics at the University of Pittsburgh. More recently she has worked for the Office of the President of the United States.

The final example is Kathryn Ann Dineen Wriston, a lawyer and trustee of Fordham University, who became the first woman director of W.R. Grace and Company in 1975. Her husband is Walter Bigelow Wriston, chairman of Citicorp and a director of General Electric and J.C. Penney Company (also serving as chairman of the Mercantile Bank of Canada).

The histories of the Canadian women in the economic elite (all eight of them) also defy classification. The most recent entrant, who is also the woman with the most dominant directorships, is, however, of some interest. In 1975, Betty Kennedy, public affairs editor of CFRB Limited, was appointed to the boards of the Bank of Montreal and Simpsons, Limited, the dominant retail company controlled by the Burton family. It was announced in August, 1976, that she would marry G. Allan Burton, chairman of Simpsons and a director of Bell Canada, Simpsons-Sears, the Royal Bank, and CFRB Limited, on October 15, 1976.[8]

While in the aggregate little can be said about women in the economic elite, there are certainly some instances of women holding powerful positions. The role of women within the upper class has generally been to "reproduce" that class socially through socialization and philanthropic activities, rather than to hold dominant positions. In an analysis of the upper class *per se* rather than of the elite, a more detailed study of women members would have to be made.[9]

After examining various career types, class origins, career avenues, family connections, inheritance, corporate positions, holding of multiple directorships, and ascriptive characteristics such as region of birth, race, ethnicity, and sex, it is apparent that the U.S. economic elite, like its Canadian opposite number, is not accessible equally to all social types. A substantial proportion of the members of the U.S. elite have their careers in family firms, as is the case in Canada, but the upper-class recruitment to the elite is lower there than it is in Canada. These facts suggest that a core of the elite in both countries acts as a class of reproduction and that the distinguishing features of the two elites come from the types of attributes found in the class of nomination. The findings leave little doubt that on most counts the Canadian elite is more rigid and the U.S. more open. As was suggested, they are indicators of one elite "in retreat" and the other "aggressive."

More evidence appeared in that there were larger numbers in the United States following career types that have proven to be avenues of access for persons born outside the upper class, such as work in engineering and science or in the finance departments of corporations. Furthermore, insiders tend to have easier access to the elite in the United States than in Canada, even though typically they have to wait over twenty years in the corporation before entering the elite and do not have the same continuity as upper-class members. Region of birth, race, and ethnicity proved to be barriers to the elite in both countries, but the most significant barrier in both countries was sex discrimination. Evidence regarding holding of multiple directorships and the class of origin of these types in each country suggests that the Canadian elite is somewhat tighter than the U.S. elite in its interconnections.

III. The Elite As a Social Group

Several factors that make the economic elite a socially interacting set of people were discussed earlier – interlocking directorships, careers in family firms, kinship ties, and class of origin. In this section some institutions that serve to draw the elite into common social circles, such as top universities, private schools, and private clubs will be analysed.

University Training

Several studies of the United States have suggested that the handful of top universities in the United States, particularly the Ivy League schools, helped to forge a national upper class rather than several local ones.[10] Widespread post-secondary education has existed longer in the United States than in Canada, as the statistics presented earlier illustrate (see p. 208). At the level of the economic elite, however, educational differences between the two countries are significantly reduced, as Table 40 shows.

The differences in education at the elite level are minimal, since 86 per cent of the Canadian elite and 89 per cent of the U.S. elite have university degrees.* In both countries the foreign-born are more frequently not educated at the university level and fewer of them have postgraduate education, but the latter phenomenon in Canada can be attributed to inclusion of law students in postgraduate statistics, and more native Canadians are trained in law than foreign-born Canadians.

---

*These figures are almost the same as the results of the surveys made by Heidrick and Struggles of Canadian and U.S. corporate presidents, which showed only 4 per cent of the U.S. presidents and 13 per cent of the Canadian presidents without post-secondary education (*Profile of a President*, p. 7, and *Profile of a Canadian President*, p. 8).

TABLE 40

Educational Levels of the Economic Elite

Educational Level	Canada (percentages)			United States (percentages)		
	Native-Born (683)	Foreign-Born (105)	All (798)	Native-Born (1,888)	Foreign-Born (119)	All (2,007)
Less than university education*	14	17	14	11	15	11
University graduate	46	54	47	41	42	42
Postgraduate†	41	29	39	48	43	48
	100	100	100	100	100	100

*This category includes persons who attended private school only or attended but did not graduate from university.

†Postgraduates include persons trained in law.

TABLE 41

University Attendance of the Elite by Upper-Class Origins and Career in Family Firm

Undergraduate University, United States	Per cent Upper Class	Per cent Career in Family Firm	Undergraduate University, Canada	Per cent Upper Class	Per cent Career in Family Firm
Yale	83	49	Univ. of Toronto	70	28
Princeton	68	34	McGill	72	30
Harvard	60	21	Univ. of Montreal	91	30
MIT	47	30	Univ. of Manitoba	73	30
Dartmouth	44	15	Queen's	50	23
Stanford	35	30	Univ. of B.C.	47	21
Columbia	25	11	One of the Four†	48	20
One of the Nine*	35	24	Other University	55	30
Other University	21	10	Did Not Attend	47	21
Did Not Attend	36	19			

*The nine are Amherst, Cornell, University of California at Berkeley, University of Chicago, Duke University, University of Michigan, University of Pennsylvania, University of Virginia, and Williams. The selection of these universities was based mainly on Baltzell, *Philadelphia Gentlemen*, p. 320.

†The four are Royal Military College, University of Alberta, Dalhousie University, and University of Western Ontario.

Is there a relationship between class of origin and particular universities? Table 41 lists several top Canadian and U.S. universities and reports on the persons of upper-class origin and those with careers in family firms who attended. Both lists are limited to natives of each country. It is clear from these profiles that some universities attract a greater proportion of the elite from upper-class families than do others. The U.S. Big Three, Yale, Princeton, and Harvard, are particularly prominent socializing agents of the upper class. Over four hundred members of the current elite received degrees from these three universities as undergraduates. In Canada, the Big Two are the University of Toronto and McGill, from which 266 members of the Canadian-born elite received degrees as undergraduates.

There is a much greater range among elite members of upper-class origin regarding university attendance in the United States than in Canada, from the highest percentage at Yale to the lowest at "other" universities. With respect to careers in family firms the range is only between 20 and 30 per cent in Canada and from 10 to 49 per cent in the United States. The fact that Yale alone had 172 members of the current U.S. elite as undergraduates of whom 83 per cent were of upper-class origin and half went on to careers in family firms strongly suggests its role in forming the elite into a socially active upper class. In Canada, 178 members of the current elite attended the University of Toronto of whom 70 per cent were upper class and 28 per cent went on to family firms.

Graduate education is concentrated in fewer schools than is undergraduate training. Standing well above all others is Harvard, attended by 341, or a third of all the U.S. elite that pursued postgraduate studies, followed by Columbia with fifty-five, Yale with forty-five, Massachusetts Institute of Technology with thirty-eight, and Stanford with thirty-one. These five institutions account for half of all members of the U.S. elite going to graduate school. For the Canadian elite, three universities account for half of those attending graduate school, the University of Toronto with eighty-three (26 per cent) and McGill with thirty-four (11 per cent), and Harvard, at the top of the U.S. list, with forty (12 per cent).

The Harvard Master of Business Administration program (see pp. 193-194) is attended by large numbers of the elite, many of them at the same time. Of the current members of the U.S. elite, 174 members have gone to Harvard for an M.B.A., and an additional sixty have gone there for the Advanced Management Program. In an article entitled "The Class the Dollars Fell On," Marilyn Wellemeyer reported on a survey of 621 members of the Harvard Business School class of 1949, about 60 per cent of whom replied to the questionnaire. The average income of this group of graduates was $53,561, net worth averaged $251,000, and there were fifty-seven millionaires. Has Harvard been an avenue of mobility for the working class? Not for many; only 6 per cent of the M.B.A. class of 1949 were sons of salesmen and 4 per cent sons of foremen or skilled craftsmen. Of the total of sixty students from outside the United States, twenty-one were from Canada; Harvard served to draw many of Canada's future elite into the continental circles at an early age. Among the current Canadian economic elite, some thirty-four Harvard M.B.A.s can be found; 77 per cent of the holders are of upper-class origin.

As would be anticipated, the trend in the U.S. elite, as in the Canadian, is toward more postgraduate training. While 40 per cent of the oldest group have attended graduate school, 46 per cent of the middle and 59 per cent of the youngest group have postgraduate training. In Canada, 39 per cent of both the oldest and the middle group and 44 per cent of the youngest attended graduate school. One effect of higher education is to remove the burden of having to make the long crawl up the corporate ladder. In the United States 28 per cent of those with less than university education are long-crawlers, 44 per cent of the parallel group in Canada, but only 10 per cent in the United States and 4 per cent in Canada of elite members with postgraduate training have remained in the same corporation for over twenty years before becoming corporate officers. Early socialization in the universities has become a substitute for later socialization in the corporate world.

Table 42 illustrates the curvilinear relationship between education and upper-class origin in the elites of both Canada and the United States. In both countries, members who are simply university graduates are more likely to be of upper-class origin than those who have lower and higher educational levels. From the point of view of inherited position the pattern is much the same. In the United States, only 13 per cent of those who attended graduate school were heirs in contrast to 25 per cent of both the lower levels of education. In Canada, 23 per cent of the least educated, 38 per cent of the university graduates, and only 21 per cent of the postgraduates are inheritors. The privileged who do decide to go on to postgraduate work tend to concentrate on commerce and law rather than science or arts.

TABLE 42

Upper-Class Origin and Educational Level

Educational Level*	(per cent of upper-class origin)	
	Canada	United States
Less than university graduation	47	37
University graduate	66	42
Postgraduate	59	30

*See Table 40, p. 236.

Very few members of the U.S. elite have attended Canadian universities, reflecting the fact that they regard the United States as the intellectual as well as the economic centre. But one member of the U.S. elite who has attended a Canadian university is Cyrus Eaton. In Hamilton, Ontario, on May 31, 1975, he toasted his alma mater, McMaster University, where he graduated in 1905. He said that it was the enthusiasm of "my uncle, the late U.S. Congressman Charles Eaton...as a member of McMaster's Board of Governors, I must mention, that convinced me that this was the college for me."

Private Schools and Private People

Private or "independent" schools are important in the making of a national upper class because they create solidarity within this class by providing common experiences and forging lasting friendships. They exclude outsiders with their admission policies and fees and create in the young of the upper class a consciousness of kind, transmitting traditions over several generations. According to C. Wright Mills, "if one had to choose one clue to the national unity of the upper social classes in America today, it would best be the really exclusive boarding school for girls and the prep school for boys."[11] Their elegant origins placed these schools among the most exclusive institutions in the United States right from the beginning. E. Digby Baltzell tells of the origins of some of them:

> The Taft School in Watertown, Connecticut, was founded by Horace Dutton Taft, a brother of President Taft, in 1890; the Hotchkiss School, Lakeville, Connecticut, was founded and endowed by Maria Hotchkiss, widow of the inventor of the famous machine-gun in 1892; St. George's School, Newport, Rhode Island, which has a million-dollar Gothic chapel built by John Nicholas Brown, was founded in 1896; in the same year, Choate School, whose benefactors and friends include such prominent businessmen as Andrew Mellon and Owen D. Young, was founded by Judge William G. Choate, at Wallingford, Connecticut; while the elder Morgan was forming his steel company in New York and Pittsburgh in 1901, seven Proper Bostonians, including Francis Lowell, W. Cameron Forbes, and Henry Lee Higginson, were founding Middlesex School, near Concord, Massachusetts.[12]

Baltzell found it difficult to make a systematic analysis of persons who attended private schools because many biographies failed to mention prep schools. The result is probably an undercounting of the extent of private school attendance among the elite.[13] Nevertheless, it is clear that many members of the U.S. economic elite have attended these schools, schools attended by only 0.5 per cent of U.S. students.[14] Although a total of 539 schools report to the National Association of Independent Schools, there are really only about twenty that are top-drawer: Andover, Exeter, St. Paul's, St. Mark's, Groton, St. George's, Kent, Taft, Hotchkiss, Choate, Loomis, Middlesex, Deerfield, Portsmouth Priory, Canterbury, Lawrenceville, Hill, Episcopal, and Woodbury Forest being the most important. Many of these schools are wealthy in their own right; for example, Exeter Academy has an endowment of $70 million. Parents of boys attending boarding school can expect to pay about four thousand dollars a year. Boarders' fees for Canada's top private school, Upper Canada College, are equally prohibitive at $4,610 a year.

Among the current U.S. economic elite about four hundred members (or 20 per cent) report attending one of the top private schools (as identified by Baltzell and Domhoff). Andover leads them all with sixty-one, followed by Hill, Hotchkiss, St. Paul's, and Groton. In contrast, 284 members of the Canadian economic elite – 41 per cent – have attended private schools. Of these, forty-one went to Upper Canada College in Toronto, Canada's most prestigious private school. In both countries, however, these percentages probably underestimate actual attendance.

Regional differences in private school attendance in the United States vary from 29 per cent among members born in the Mid-Atlantic region to 31 per cent of those born in New England to a single individual born in the Mountain region (1.6 per cent). The other regions are grouped more uniformly, the South with 17 per cent, the North Central with 14 per cent, and the Pacific with 13 per cent. By religion, Episcopalians are most likely to have attended a top private school (36 per cent).

In Canada, regional differences are again marked. Quebec has the highest attendance with 63 per cent, and 30 per cent attended the top classical colleges such as Jean de Brébeuf in Montreal. Next, in order, are Manitoba (48 per cent), the Atlantic provinces (42 per cent), and Ontario (37 per cent), while the three western provinces bring up the rear with 28 per cent in Alberta, 22 per cent in British Columbia, and only 7 per cent in Saskatchewan. Anglicans in Canada are also the most inclined to attend private schools, accounting for 38 per cent of the whole group and 47 per cent if French Canadians and classical colleges are excluded.

Although region of birth and religion affect private school attendance in both countries, they do not have as much influence as solid upper-class origin. Elite members whose fathers were in the economic elite attended private schools in proportions of 58 per cent in the United States and 68 per cent in Canada. From another point of view, of those in the economic elite who went to private school, 38 per cent in the United States and 32 per cent in Canada had fathers that were elite. Among the few born at or near the top (that is, those whose backgrounds are upper class without considering private schools), 60 per cent in Canada and 45 per cent in the United States attended private schools. In each country, 48 per cent of persons who went to private schools inherited positions, in contrast to 13 per cent in the United States and 18 per cent in Canada who did not attend private schools. There are also more private-school Old Boys among persons who have careers in family firms or kin currently in the elite.

The class profiles of those who attended specific top universities turn up again in the relationship between top private schools and top universities. Baltzell has observed linkages between certain schools and universities, noting that "three-fourths of the Exeter boys have gone to Harvard for generations, just as their rivals at Andover have gone to Yale (in spite of this tradition, the class of 1929 at Princeton included fifty-seven Exeter and Andover alumni). Quite naturally, a vast majority of the Groton and St. Paul's boys go on to Harvard, Yale or Princeton each year. In 1934...over 95 per cent of the 106 graduates of St. Paul's went to one of the 'big three.'"[15] Baltzell's findings carry over into the current economic elite. Fifteen per cent of the Andover and Exeter graduates went to Harvard, 41 per cent to Yale, and 16 per cent to Princeton, a total of 72 per cent going to the Big Three. Hill sent 42 per cent of its elite graduates to Princeton, 8 per cent to Harvard, and 13 per cent to Yale (63 per cent). From Hotchkiss, 59 per cent went to Yale, 26 per cent to Princeton, and 7 per cent to Harvard (92 per cent); from St. Paul's, 25 per cent went to Harvard, 50 per cent to Yale, and 5 per cent to Princeton (80 per cent); and Groton sent 33 per cent to Harvard, 47 per cent to Yale, and 20 per cent to Princeton – 100 per cent of its graduates going to the Big Three. Overall, three-quarters of elite members who attended private schools went to one of the name universities discussed earlier compared to only half of those who did not attend private schools.

The initial advantage conferred by private school attendance expands in later elite interaction. Thirty per cent of those who went to private schools in the United States have more than one dominant position in the elite compared to the 25 per cent who did not attend. In Canada, 40 per cent of private school students and only 28 per cent of those who attended public schools became holders of multiple directorships in the elite.

It can be seen that private school attendance correlates strongly with all of the major class variables – class of origin, inheritance, careers in family firms, and current kin among the elite. It also correlates with other characteristics related to class, such as region of birth and religious affiliation. But private school friendships and ties do not sustain themselves forever if they are not nourished. The major upper-class institutions that maintain these early ties are the exclusive national clubs for men. More explicitly than any other class institutions, the private clubs are sustained by the class of nomination and rooted in the class of reproduction. While providing continuity to the upper class, they simultaneously absorb "properly" socialized members of the economic elite from outside the upper class.

Private National Clubs for Men

In Canada the club circle of the economic elite is extremely small. Three-fifths of the economic elite belong to one or more of seven exclusive clubs (the National, York, or Toronto clubs in Toronto, the Mount Royal or St. James's clubs in Montreal, the Vancouver Club in Vancouver, and the Rideau Club in Ottawa). Among them, these "clubmen" average almost two top club memberships each in the seven. The larger U.S. society, with eleven times the population, would not be expected to have the same degree of closeness characteristic of the Canadian club circuit. But, even beyond these differences, the same degree of emphasis on club life is not evident. For example, a Heidrick and Struggles survey of corporate presidents in Canada and the United States in 1972 found that U.S. companies are less likely than Canadian firms to provide club memberships at company expense. In Canada, 91 per cent of the presidents were given "town club" memberships at company expense compared to 65 per cent in the United States.[16] Nevertheless, clubs remain an important part of elite interaction and upper class continuity within the United States.

The most detailed analysis of club life in the United States was undertaken by E. Digby Baltzell. His description of the admission processes to clubs clearly conforms to the distinction between class of reproduction and class of nomination introduced earlier. The following is his commentary on one of the top U.S. clubs:

> There are, by and large, two ways to enter the Philadelphia Club. First, every year a small group of younger men in their twenties and thirties, invariably relatives of the present members, are taken into the club. This group of younger men forms the nucleus of ascribed members in their generation. Second, certain capable men who have achieved a high and respected position in the business and cultural life of the city are taken into the club each year.... They are rarely proposed for membership, however, until they have proved themselves occupationally...as each generation of ascribed members of the Philadelphia Club take their places in the business and cultural life of the city, they bring into the club those of their contemporaries whom they (and their fathers) consider "worth-while" and, above all, congenial. These "new men," in turn, have sons who will become ascribed members of the club at a young age. The self-made man finds that club membership is one of the best entrees into the upper class, and one of the best ways of passing on his achieved position to his family.[17]

Although certain top American clubs are more exclusive than others, it is not possible, as it is in Canada, to narrow them down to the top seven. Nevertheless, from the research of Baltzell and G. William Domhoff[18] and additional sources on the upper class it is possible to identify the top forty-five clubs, which, in turn, can be subdivided. The top ten U.S. exclusive national clubs are the Brook of New York, the

Chicago, the Detroit, the Duquesne of Pittsburgh, the Links of New York, the Pacific Union of San Francisco, the Philadelphia, the Somerset and the Union of Boston, and the Union of New York. The next fifteen are the Augusta National of Georgia, the Buffalo Club, the California of Los Angeles, the Cincinnati, the Knickerbocker of New York, the Maryland of Baltimore, the Metropolitan of New York, the Metropolitan of Washington, the Piedmont Driving of Atlanta, the Pinnacle of New York, the Pittsburgh, the Queen City of Cincinnati, the Rittenhouse of Philadelphia, the Rolling Rock of Pittsburgh, and the Union of Cleveland. In addition to these is a series of twenty other clubs with a more regional than national flavour, but they help to blend the local with the national upper class. These twenty top regional clubs are the Arlington of Portland, the Bohemian of San Francisco, the Boston of New Orleans, the Burlingame Country of San Francisco, the Century of New York, the Charleston, the Commonwealth of Chicago, the Cosmos of Washington, the Denver, the Everglades of Palm Beach, the Hartford, the Milwaukee, the Minneapolis, the Piping Rock of New York, the Ranier of Seattle, the River of New York, the Saturn of Buffalo, the St. Louis Country, the Sky of New York, and the Woodhill Country of Minneapolis.

Among the U.S. economic elite, 45 per cent claim a membership in at least one of these clubs. At least 26 per cent belong to one of the top ten, 22 per cent to at least one of the next fifteen, and 18 per cent to one of the twenty regional clubs. The problem for the student is that these figures are necessarily conservative because many members of the elite fail to declare their club memberships in the biographical sources examined. Nevertheless, some characteristics of those who do report membership can be examined.

Of those who do *not* belong to one of the top ten U.S. clubs, 33 per cent are upper class in origin compared to 40 per cent of those who belong to one and 46 per cent of those who belong to two or more. Among elite members whose fathers were also in the economic elite, 34 per cent are members of one of the top ten clubs compared to 24 per cent without this advantage. In terms of the entire forty-five clubs, 39 per cent of the "clubmen" are upper class in origin compared to 33 per cent not reporting these memberships. Thirty-six per cent of those who attended private school belong to one of the top ten compared to 24 per cent of public school graduates. Considering the whole group of clubs, 56 per cent of the private school graduates belong to one or more compared to 42 per cent from public schools.

In Canada, the club circuit is much more intimate and even more exclusive than in the United States. Of those without a membership in one of the top seven Canadian clubs, 54 per cent are upper class; of those who have one membership, 63 per cent are upper class, and with two or more, 68 per cent are of upper-class origin. Of those who attended a private school, 71 per cent have at least one membership in one of the top seven clubs. In terms of position in a dominant corporation, 50 per cent of the insiders, 55 per cent of the outsiders, and 79 per cent of the executives belong to one or more of the top seven clubs.

In the dominant U.S. corporation, executives and outsiders are also most likely to be clubmen. More club members tend to be drawn from particular career types, particularly law and banking and finance. Holders of multiple directorships are much more likely to be clubmen than holders of single directorships and long-crawlers. Of those who have a dominant bank directorship, 64 per cent belong to at least one of these forty-five U.S. clubs compared to 39 per cent of the others.

Most of the national exclusive clubs are "town" clubs, meeting places where clubmen can lunch and out-of-town businessmen can stay, but there are also important country clubs where members of the elite come together for recreation. When *Fortune* drew up a list of the "42 best golfers in American business" in 1973, thirty-one of them were members of the U.S. economic elite.[19] Blind Brook, at Port Chester, New York, is the home club of the following: Howard Long-streth Clark, chairman of American Express (and a director of Chrysler and Xerox Corporation); Robert S. Hatfield, chairman of Continental Can (and a director of First National City Bank, Kennecott Copper, and GM); James D. Robinson III, executive vice-president of American Express (and a director of Union Pacific Corporation); Lewis A. Lapham, vice-chairman of Bankers Trust New York (and a director of Mobil Oil); John S. Lawson, chairman of Marine Midland Banks; Clifton C. Garvin, Jr., president of Exxon (and a director of Citicorp); William H. Morton, president of American Express (and a director of Boise Cascade Corporation and the Singer Company); and Jack S. Parker, vice-chairman of General Electric. All these social and recreational ties help to bring the economic elite into an interacting upper class.

Some of the club ties extend from Canada to the United States. At least ninety-six members, or about 12 per cent, of the Canadian economic elite have a club membership in the United States but there may be more that are not listed in biographies. Forty of these are in one of the top ten. There are at least seven in each of the Links (New York) and Rolling Rock (Pittsburgh). The Canadian-born members of the U.S. economic elite are also well integrated in the U.S. club world. Of the thirty-eight in this group, thirteen, or 34 per cent, belong to one or more of the top ten U.S. clubs compared to 26 per cent of all the U.S.-born members. Thus the Canadian economic elite and the Canadian-born segment of the U.S. elite are linked to the social network of the U.S. upper class.

The ties run in the other direction too. Some members of the U.S. economic elite belong to Canada's exclusive clubs, the Mount Royal in Montreal (which has 185 Canadian resident elite members, representing 40 per cent of the club's total membership) apparently being the favourite. Some U.S. members of the Mount Royal are Stephen Davison Bechtel, Jr., chairman of Bechtel Group and a director of GM, Crocker National, and Southern Pacific Company (Bechtel also belongs to the York Club in Toronto); Gilbert Watts Humphrey, chairman of Hanna Mining Company and a director of General Electric, Texaco, and National Steel in the United States and Massey-Ferguson and Sun Life in Canada; Walter Adelbert Marting of Hanna Mining, a director of Bankers Trust New York, Eaton Corporation, and National Steel in the United States and chairman of the Iron Ore Company of Canada; Joseph Paul Monge, chairman of the finance committee of International Paper, chairman of Canadian International Paper, a director of the Royal Bank, and member of the advisory board of Chemical New York (Monge also belongs to the St. James's Club); Ellmore Clark Patterson, chairman of J.P. Morgan and Company, a director of GM and Santa Fe Industries in the United States and Canada Life and the International Nickel Company in Canada (Patterson also belongs to the Toronto Club); Thomas Wright Russell, Jr., president of International Executives and a director of Connecticut General Insurance; James A. Stewart (who was born in Winnipeg and now lives in the United States), executive vice-president of Continental Can and a director of the Toronto-Dominion Bank and Continental Can of Canada; Henry Smith Wingate, member of the executive committee and a director of United States Steel, American Standard, and J.P. Morgan and Company, chairman of the advisory committee and a director of INCO, and a director of Canadian Pacific.

These men's clubs in both Canada and the United States serve as an important meeting ground for the resident elite where they can discuss their common problems and arrange common business. They are also a meeting ground where members of both economic elites come together socially and exchange views and news about the economic and political world. While among the Canadian elite club life is more highly developed and confined to fewer exclusive clubs, there is still an impressive club network in the United States. Canada's elite, being smaller, finds it easier to come together in the club circuit. Together with the private schools and top universities, as well as class and kinship ties, the private clubs help to bind the economic elite into a socially interacting set of people. More than merely elites of position, the economic elites of Canada and the United States are a closely knit group, familiar with each other and each other's business. They take one another into account and frequently enter into joint business ventures (like the consortia discussed earlier), in addition to exchanging goods, capital, and information with one another.

IV. Relations between Elites

Two kinds of connections between the economic and state elites in Canada and the United States will be briefly examined here. The first are the policy-making forums that unify the economic elite on political questions outside the state system and are themselves pressure groups acting for the business viewpoint on state policy making. The second kind is personal ties between members of the economic elite and the state.

In both Canada and the United States, policy-making forums frequented by members of the economic elite have proliferated. Besides the Pacific Basin Economic Council and Canadian Association for Latin America (see Chapter 5), forums important to the Canadian elite are the Canadian Executive Service Overseas, the Canadian-American Committee, the Conference Board in Canada, various advisory boards to the Ministry of Industry, Trade and Commerce, and some others.[20] Many similar associations also exist in the United States. The most important is probably the Council on Foreign Relations, which, according to Domhoff, "limits itself to 700 New York area residents and 700 non-New York residents (no women or foreigners are allowed to join). As of the mid-sixties, 46 per cent of the resident members and 49 per cent of the non-resident members, most of whom are big businessmen and lawyers, were listed in the Social Register."[21] Although not all members of the Council on Foreign Relations list their memberships, biographical sources reveal that 104 current members of the U.S. economic elite belong to it.

Following the Council on Foreign Relations in importance is the Committee for Economic Development, whose purpose is to create and sustain stable economic conditions within the United States by creating policy on questions such as production, employment, and business cycles. Among the current U.S. economic elite, seventy-seven members report belonging to this organization. The next most important elite forum is the Business Council, an organization to which at least sixty-five current members of the elite belong. Other associations that unify the economic elite on political questions include the World Affairs Council and the Foreign Policy Association.

In the current U.S. economic elite, 13 per cent of the members report belonging to one or more of these five associations. While this list cannot be said to be complete, it makes it apparent that some members of the elite are more likely to join one of these groups than are others. For example, 24 per cent of bank directors belong to an important forum compared to only 10 per cent of elite members without bank directorships. The proportions are 20 per cent for insurance directors to 12 per cent of other elite members. Considering career types, members who have had their main careers in non-corporate sectors are most likely to belong: 29 per cent of those whose main career was in another elite and 19 per cent of those whose main career was in another sector but not holding an elite position report at least one membership in the five associations. It is also those who are most active in the elite who tend to belong; while only 8 per cent of the holders of single dominant directorships belong to at least one, 26 per cent of the multiple directorship holders belong to one of the five key associations.

A broader range of policy-making associations have been analysed by G. William Domhoff. He finds that the owners and managers of large banks and corporations, with a little bit of help from their hired academics, lawyers, and public relations people, dominate everything in this country that is worth dominating – foreign policy through such organizations as the Council on Foreign Relations, Council of the Americas, and Trilateral Commission; economic policy through the likes of the Conference Board, Committee for Economic Development and Brookings Institution; population policy through such groups as the Population Council, Population Reference Bureau, and Planned Parenthood; environmental policy through Resources for the Future, Conservation Foundation, and American Conservation Association; legal policies through the American Law Institute and committees of the American Bar Association; and educational policy through such entities as the Ford Foundation, three Carnegie foundations, and the Carnegie Council for Policy Studies in Higher Education. Every one of these organizations is financed and directed by the same few thousand men who run the major banks and corporations.[22]

These policy-making forums do not, in themselves, dominate the state, but they do ensure that the economic elite is the most articulate segment of society and has its views taken into account when state policy is formulated. The economic elite also keeps in touch with the state through personal ties created either by taking on important government positions or by recruiting for the corporate world persons who have valuable inside knowledge of the state.

Although some contend that as societies become more complex (and hence differentiated) individuals become rigidly specialized in their tasks, this kind of restriction does not appear to reign in the upper levels of corporate power in either Canada or the United States. In both, there is extensive shifting of careers from top corporate posts to ones in the military, the cabinet, education, and regulatory agencies, and vice versa. It is worthwhile to give some examples of the type of people involved in this elite switching that brings the various elites together.

In Canada, the distinctions between careers in the economic and political elites are easy to see. There is a tendency to move from the top of the federal bureaucracy or from cabinet posts (which require election in Canada but are appointive in the United States) to the economic elite or, occasionally, from the top of the corporate world to political office. In the United States, on the other hand, the holding of elite positions in the state is often interspersed throughout an individual's career, sometimes for brief periods of two or three years. Part of the reason for this is the patronage element in the upper reaches of the U.S. civil service and appointive cabinet posts.

Although the state is the major locus for careers of this kind outside the dominant corporations, the academic world is drawn somewhat into the corporate world in the United States and to a lesser extent in Canada. Among members of the U.S. economic elite, 231 have been in government (11.5 per cent), twenty-three had high-ranking military positions outside of wartime (1.1 per cent), and 149 have been academics (7.4 per cent). Among the Canadian-born, only one individual has had a senior military post, but 124 have had some career in the state (18 per cent) and thirty-eight have been academics (5 per cent).

Besides the persons who have worked directly in the state system, 114 members of the U.S. elite have sat on one or more presidential commissions and 90 on other high-level government commissions (10 per cent of the entire U.S. elite). In Canada, twenty-six members have been on royal commissions and eighty-four on other commissions or boards while forty-five sit on the boards of crown corporations – about 15 per cent of Canada's elite.

In both Canada and the United States, members of the economic elite tend to shy away from elected office but are readily recruited to appointive positions. For example, only twenty-nine members of the U.S. elite have held elected positions as governors or state or federal legislators, but twenty-seven have been appointed to the federal cabinet, twenty-two have been appointed ambassadors, and one hundred have held high federal bureaucratic positions during peacetime and another eighty-five served in similar offices during the Second World War or the Korean War. The line between public and private power tends to be diminished when the same people operate on both sides.

Some examples of persons who moved from the state elite to the economic elite were given in Chapter 6. The following are a few instances of members of the economic elite who moved into top state positions. *Fortune* noted in 1971: "For the second time in less than a decade, Bell & Howell has lost a chief executive to government service. Charles H. Percy, who has been in the Senate since 1966, gave up the post when he entered politics in 1963. Now Peter Peterson, 44, who took over from Percy, is moving to Washington to be the first Assistant to the President for International Affairs. In addition, Peterson will be executive director of the newly created Cabinet-level Council on International Economic Policy."[23] One reason why individuals seldom move from the economic to the state elite is the great difference in salaries. For example, at Bell and Howell, Peterson was making over $125,000 a year but in his new job made only $42,500. This is sufficient disincentive to keep the general flow away from the state towards the economic elite. This disincentive is somewhat reduced by the short duration of the stays in the state sector, and after returning to the economic world, the ex-civil servants are even more valuable than when they went in for their brief foray. Since 1973, Peterson has found himself back in the economic elite, now chairman of Lehman Brothers and a director of Federated Stores, General Foods, and Minnesota Mining and Manufacturing. Some of the relations can be particularly incestuous; for example, "Secretary of Agriculture Earl L. Butz and his predecessor, Clifford M. Hardin, virtually switched jobs at the Ralston Purina Company and the Agriculture Department."[24]

Not all examples of moves between elites in the United States involve a complete break in career. Some consist of only a few years' sojourn outside the corporate world. The following histories give a further sense of the types that move between top state positions and the U.S. economic elite:

Robert B. Anderson, former secretary of the navy, deputy secretary of defense and secretary of the treasury, is now chairman of Robert B. Anderson and Company and a director of Goodyear Tire and Rubber and Pan American World Airways.

A former chairman of the International Bank for Reconstruction and Development and administrator of the World Bank is Eugene Robert Black, who is now a consultant to American Express and a director of International Telephone and Telegraph and Boise Cascade.

Former governor of Texas and secretary of the U.S. treasury John Bowden Connally, Jr., is now a law partner and a director of both Pan American and Falconbridge Nickel, a dominant Canadian corporation.

Donald Clarence Cook, former chairman of the Securities Exchange Commission and holder of other senior posts, declined an offer from President Johnson to become secretary of the treasury to retain his posts of chairman of American Electric Power and director of Lincoln National.

Gesualdo A. Costanzo, whose brother is an adviser to the Internatinal Monetary Fund and special assistant to the secretary of the U.S. treasury, was deputy director for the Western hemisphere of the International Monetary Fund, among his other senior posts, before becoming vice-chairman of First National City Bank and a director of Beatrice Foods, NCR Corporation, and Owens-Illinois (besides being chairman of the Mercantile Bank of Canada).

Arthur Hobson Dean was an ambassador to Korea and chairman of several U.S. delegations to Geneva and is now a senior partner with Sullivan and Cromwell and a director of AMAX, Incorporated and El Paso Natural Gas.

Robert Fred Ellsworth is former U.S. ambassador to Nato and now general partner of Lazard Frères and Company as well as a director of Allied Chemical and General Dynamics.

Thomas Sovereign Gates, Jr., is following in his father's footsteps as a director at J.P. Morgan and Company but only after having been undersecretary of the navy and secretary of defense; he is also now a director of Bethlehem Steel, INA Corporation, Cities Service, and General Electric.

James Maurice Gavin became a lieutenant-general and later ambassador to France and is now a director of John Hancock Mutual Life and American Electrical Power.

Najeeb Elias Halaby is former head of the Federal Aviation Administration, which he left to become chairman of Pan American, and is now a director of Chrysler and Bank of America.

William McChesney Martin, Jr., was chairman of the Federal Reserve Board from 1951 to 1970, later becoming the first full-time president of the New York Stock Exchange, and is now a director of American Express, General Foods, U.S. Steel, Caterpillar Tractor, and IBM. His case is interesting because Martin was "literally reared in the tradition of the Federal Reserve System,"[25] since his father was a former governor and president of the Federal Reserve Bank.

Donald William Nyrop, former chairman of the Civil Aeronautics Board, is president of Northwest Airlines and a director of First Bank System and Honeywell Incorporated.

Samuel Riley Pierce, Jr., former head of the legal division of the treasury, is a director of Prudential Insurance, International Paper, and Public Service Electric and Gas.

William Warren Scranton, former governor of Pennsylvania, is chairman of the Northeastern Bank of Pennsylvania and a director of Pan American, IBM, and Sun Oil.

Horace Armor Shepard, former chief of staff of the U.S. Air Force, is chairman of TRW Incorporated and a director of Procter and Gamble and Standard Oil Company (Ohio).

George Pratt Shultz, former secretary of the treasury, is now with Bechtel and is a director of J.P. Morgan and Company.

Hobart Taylor, Jr., is a former director of the Export-Import Bank and now a director of Westinghouse Electric, Standard Oil Company (Ohio), Aetna Life and Casualty, and Great Atlantic and Pacific.

Cyrus Roberts Vance, former deputy secretary of defense, is a director of Aetna Life, Pan American, and IBM.

Similar examples of persons who moved from the state to the economic elite in Canada were given in an earlier study.[26] Since that time a few switches have occurred that are worth examining. Before being recruited to head the government's Anti-Inflation Board and after being defeated at the polls when he was minister of industry, trade and commerce, Jean-Luc Pépin was welcomed into the board rooms of Bombardier, Canada Steamship Lines, Celanese Canada, Westinghouse Canada, and Power Corporation. John Turner, former minister of finance and a cabinet minister from 1965 to 1975, was at once recruited to the boards of Crown Life Insurance, Crédit Foncier, and Canadian Pacific after he resigned. Finally, Simon Reisman, Canada's top civil servant as deputy minister of finance, joined George Weston Limited immediately after he resigned and became a director of Burns Foods, also establishing a consulting firm in Ottawa with James Grandy who had also recently resigned as deputy minister of industry, trade and commerce.

Neither in Canada nor in the United States has the state been free of the influence of the economic elite. In both, the state has frequently been used to further private accumulation of capital and the ends of private power. A profile of each economic elite discloses that there have been many close relations between these two systems of power. The focus in this study is on economic, not state, power, but it is clear that the two are in many ways related.

CHAPTER NINE

Relations between the U.S. and Canadian Elites and Managers

Throughout this study the focus has been on economic power relations between Canada and the United States. It is now time to turn to a specific analysis of the relationship between the two economic elites and the implications of the continental economy for elite members. This chapter examines the multinational and continental activities of the U.S. elite and the place of foreign resident members (especially Canadians) in the U.S. elite. To complement this analysis, a survey was made of managers living in the United States who are Canadian born in order to identify in more detail some aspects of these activities. This is followed by an examination of some common associations in which both the Canadian and the U.S. elites participate. Attention is then turned to the multinational and continental activities of the Canadian elite as a result of foreign dominance.

I. Multinational Activities of the U.S. Economic Elite and Foreign-Born in the Elite

We have already seen that "multinational" activity among dominant U.S. corporations is in part based on the economic sector in which they operate. The same distinction holds good for the members of the economic elite, as Table 43 illustrates. The sector in which members of the U.S. economic elite are least likely to be "multinational" (operate in multinational business) is transportation/utilities, where over half of the members have no multinational affiliation, only 20 per cent are multinational because of their main affiliation, and another 25 per cent are multinational because of additional affiliations. For example, Burlington Northern is not a multinational, therefore its chairman, Louis Wilson Menk, is not associated with a multinational because of his main affiliation. Because of his outside directorship in International Harvester, however, he has a secondary multinational affiliation. On the other hand, Robert W. Downing, vice-chairman of Burlington Northern, has no multinational affiliation (although he is an outside director of Northwestern Bancorporation), and so he is not classified as multinational.

TABLE 43

Multinational Status of the U.S. Economic Elite
by Sector *(percentages)*

Dominant Directorship in:*	Main Corporate Affiliation Multinational	Other Dominant Corporate Affiliation Multinational	No Multinational Affiliation
Transport./Utilities (414)	20	25	54
Finance (657)	43	39	18
Resources (202)	72	28	1
Manufacturing (1,147)	57	34	9
Trade (127)	42	32	27
All U.S. born and resident (1,894)	46	30	24

*Columns do not total because some members have directorships in more than one sector.

The most multinational sector, as with dominant corporations, is re-sources, where only 1 per cent of members are not multinational and most are multinational because of their main affiliation. Members in the manufacturing sector and, to a lesser extent, in finance follow the same trend as those in resources. Trade tends not to be extensively multinational compared to the other sectors, but almost equal propor-tions of the elite with directorships in trade and in finance are multina-tional because of their main affiliation.

The same general pattern tends to hold when the U.S. elite members are examined by career avenues and main current affiliations. There are some differences among members whose careers are in some other sec-tor than the economic. For example, only 46 per cent of elite members in publishing are multinational, 4 per cent because of their main af-filiations, and half because of secondary dominant affiliations. On the other hand, those with their careers in the law, the universities, or the state/military are about as likely as the entire elite to be multinational but obviously because of secondary rather than main affiliations.

There are forty-nine foreign-born members of the economic elite now living in the United States, only one of whom is not associated with a multinational corporation and 67 per cent of whom have their main affiliations with a multinational, compared to only 46 per cent of all the elite who have this kind of affiliation. With the internationaliza-tion of capital, a select few from outside have been drawn into the U.S.-resident economic elite, but not in such numbers that the U.S. eco-nomic elite itself can be said to have taken on an international flavour. Only 6 per cent of the entire U.S. elite is foreign born. Among the U.S. elite living outside Canada and the United States (three of whom are U.S. born), seven live in the United Kingdom, three in Belgium and three in Italy, two in Switzerland, and one in each of France, Sweden, Denmark, the Netherlands, and Puerto Rico. Each of these twenty foreign-resident members of the elite (excluding Canada) holds one dominant U.S. directorship. Clearly, the continental ties between members of the Canadian and U.S. economic elites are much stronger than those established by the United States with any other country. The U.S. economic elite remains a national elite with multinational operations, rather than a multinational elite.

Nor could it be said that the U.S. economic elite has become really continental in its composition, although it is clearly continental in its consequences. Among the U.S.-born and resident members of the U.S. economic elite for whom data are available, twenty-five members sit on the boards of Canadian dominant corporations that are not U.S.-affiliated companies. While this represents only a small part of the U.S. economic elite, it is of consequence in Canada because of the smaller Canadian elite. An additional thirty-two members of the U.S. economic elite are on the boards of dominant Canadian subsidiaries of U.S. companies. Fifty-seven of the 1,894 U.S.-born and resident elite members, then, have at least one dominant Canadian post. Another eleven are directors of Canadian-controlled companies that are not dominant, and seventy sit on the boards of non-dominant U.S. subsidiaries in Canada. By their main current affiliation, 6 per cent of the elite in finance, 7 per cent in transportation/utilities, 8 per cent in manufacturing, 12 per cent in trade, and 19 per cent in resources hold Canadian posts.

All together, 7.3 per cent of the U.S. economic elite hold at least one Canadian post. Canadian posts are held by 11 per cent of the presidents of the 194 dominant U.S. companies, 13 per cent of the chairmen, and 17 per cent of the vice-chairmen. To some extent, these personal continental ties bring members of the U.S. economic elite into contact with the members of the Canadian economic elite who are serving as outside directors in the same U.S. subsidiaries or dominant Canadian-controlled corporations.

The Canadian-Born in the U.S. Economic Elite

Adequate biographical data are available for 2,007 (82 per cent) of the 2,450 persons who can be considered members of the U.S. economic elite. Seventeen Canadian-born U.S. residents were found among them, with adequate biographical data for fifteen (88 per cent).* In addition, there are twenty-one members of the U.S. elite who are Canadian born and live in Canada, and four others who live in Canada but were born outside Canada (three in the United States and one in the United Kingdom). Only one of the Canadian residents is not simultaneously part of the Canadian economic elite (John Henry Graflund, born in Illinois and resident in Hamilton, Ontario, who is president of

---

* A few of those for whom data were not available may be Canadian born, but only those for whom data are available will be considered.

John Deere Limited, Hamilton, and a vice-president and director of Deere and Company, the U.S. parent). Overall, forty-three individuals who were born or now live in Canada for whom data could be found are members of the U.S. economic elite. Only 2 per cent of the U.S. economic elite are tied to Canada by either birth or current residence. In terms of all persons who were born outside the United States and currently have a position in a dominant U.S. corporation, Canada is far ahead of any other country. Thirty-eight current members of the U.S. elite were born in Canada, twenty-four in Britain (one of whom migrated to Canada in his early twenties), ten in Germany, and only thirty-five in all other countries combined. Canada is the residence of over half (twenty-six) of all the current U.S. elite living outside the United States. Ten others live in the United Kingdom (three of these U.S.-born) and only thirteen elsewhere.

With regard to the Canadian-resident elite, just over 3 per cent have dominant directorships in the United States, among them holding thirty-two dominant directorships in the United States and eighty-seven in Canada. They hold 6 per cent of all the dominant positions in Canada. The seventeen Canadian-born members of the elite living in the United States have twenty-three dominant U.S. directorships. Among them, the Canadian-born or resident members of the U.S. elite hold only 3 per cent of all the dominant positions in the United States.

Some members of the Canadian economic elite are also connected with the U.S. elite through advisory boards. For example, Ian David Sinclair, chairman of Canadian Pacific and a director of the Royal Bank, Sun Life, TransCanada PipeLines, and MacMillan Bloedel in Canada and of Union Carbide in the United States, is also on the advisory board of Chase Manhattan. An interesting role was recently played by Beverley Matthews, who sits on the boards of seven dominant Canadian companies and Gulf Oil in the United States. Following political scandals among Gulf's executive, it was necessary to find a replacement, and eventually Jerry McAfee, head of Gulf's Canadian subsidiary, was recruited (see p. 185). "Two directors, Beverley Matthews, a Canadian lawyer and a friend of McAfee, and Nathan W. Pearson, who represents the Mellon family's interest in the company, asked if he would accept the job."[1]*

Because the number is so small, it is difficult to make an analysis of the Canadian-born, U.S.-resident component of the U.S. elite. Of the fifteen for whom adequate data are available, two moved to the United States with their parents; five left Canada to attend university in the United States; six migrated on their own; and two were transferred. In only two instances, those of Frederick George Fusee (who left Canada as assistant general manager of Avon Products of Canada in 1956 to become, eventually, chairman of Avon Products and a director of Manu-

---

* Further examples of Canadian-resident members of the U.S. economic elite are found in Chapter 6, pp. 177-179.

facturers Hanover and B.F. Goodrich Company) and John Kenneth Jamieson (who left Canada as vice-president of Imperial Oil in 1959 to become chairman of Exxon Corporation and a director of Chase Manhattan, Equitable Life, and the International Nickel Company of Canada), have Canadians been transferred from branch plants in Canada to elite positions in dominant U.S. corporations. These are impressive instances, to be sure, but that is what they remain – instances.

Among the other thirteen, there are several other impressive histories, although none are transfers from branch plants. For example, the president of Procter and Gamble is Canadian born, as is the president of CNA Financial Corporation, but both left Canada as children; there is a Canadian-born chairman at Xerox Corporation (he is also a director of Citicorp), a vice-president at Inland Steel and another at Bendix Corporation, and directors at Occidental Petroleum, Shell Oil, and Kaiser Aluminum and Chemical, all of whom left Canada for education in the United States; and finally, the president of Connecticut General Insurance (also a director of General Foods), the chairman of Union Oil Company of California (also a director of Rockwell International), the chairman of the executive committee at Consolidated Foods (a member of the executive committee of General Dynamics), as well as directors of Chessie System, the Travelers Corporation, and National Detroit all simply migrated from Canada to the United States. Clearly, these are all prominent and powerful positions, but among them the Canadian-born members of the U.S. elite living in the United States hold only three-quarters as many dominant U.S. positions as the members of the Canadian-resident elite. Because of Canada's smaller scale, the outflow of managerial talent has a considerable impact on Canada but upon entering the vastness of the United States, it becomes minuscule.

Several interesting aspects of Canada's relationship with the United States were revealed in personal exchanges with the Canadian-born U.S.-resident elite. To a man, the Canadian-born members stressed that their Canadian birth was neither a handicap nor an advantage to their careers in the United States. Some comments are worth reproducing to give a sense of the experiences these men had in the two countries. One consistent theme was their international inclination and dislike of nationalism, evident in the following statement:

> I was affiliated with a very large international...company and recognized that if you were offered an opportunity to expand beyond the local affiliate, it was a very challenging opportunity.... I have no strong nationalistic feelings as I firmly believe that the strong nationalistic tendencies that are so evident in the world today are completely out of pace with the economic facts of the world.

A summary of the primary reasons for the pull to the United States was well articulated by an elite member who said:

> One of the major factors affecting my decision to move to the United States was the fact that Canada had relatively few industries that were fully integrated from research and development through manufacturing and marketing. This was an important criterion for me in my career. Another factor was the question of size and, therefore, opportunity. American businesses tend to be much larger than Canadian firms, and on the whole, I felt this offered better opportunities. The third factor is related to risk and innovation. I felt that American businessmen generally were less conservative than Canadian and were willing to take greater risks with the hope, of course, of far greater profits.

These quotations come from two men who attended university in both Canada and the United States and continue to do business in both countries. Thus they have some basis for their comments. But each statement also conveys something of an ideology that permeates the elite. The first reflects an ideology of internationalism (or, in different terms, approval of an open climate for the operations of multinational corporations), the second an ideology of corporate capitalism, of large, highly integrated operations. In each statement there is also reference to greater opportunities in the United States, but the writers have overlooked the fact that the structure of corporate capitalism expressed in multinational operations ensures that opportunities will be greater in the United States than in Canada.

In a way, one member of the U.S. elite whose training as an actuary led him eventually to migrate to the United States reflected the effect of branch-plant structures: "I made a comprehensive search for employment in my field and received very discouraging replies from possible employers. The position in my own company was an unhappy one because of absentee ownership in England. It seemed to me that the only way out of an unhappy situation was to seek employment elsewhere." He then moved to the United States where branch plants are not a problem.

A further set of influences often mentioned were class barriers and ethnic tensions. Both of the next statements include elements of each.

> Obviously, there is much more opportunity in the United States because the school tie is of little, if any, importance. Your opportunity for success depends upon your ability (and, of course, the breaks of life – being in the right place at the right time). I would say that there were more social barriers to succeeding in Canada at the time I left. I think this has diminished in Canada, except perhaps in Quebec.

Whether it is true that the "school tie" is of "little importance" in the United States or not, this person obviously believed it to be the case. This same feeling is again expressed here:

> It appeared to me that the United States had a more fluid society,

with greater opportunity for upward mobility – social and economic – than Canada offered at that time. Canadians were then attached to British class rigidities and emphasis upon birth and racial origin – prejudice from which American society was freer, and which I believed would be frustrating handicaps to an ambitious young man. I concluded that my progress in Canada would be slowed by the fact that I was not of British birth, origin or name.

It is indeed important to grasp what these people are saying, but it is also necessary to understand their place in society and the perspective from which they look back over their careers. The one thing they all have in common is a position at the top of the U.S. class structure and, because of their positions among some of the most powerful multinationals in the world, at the top of the international class structure. What they fail to see is the relationship between opportunities in the United States and the absence of development of the same advantages elsewhere. They fail to see that, as one put it, U.S. dominants are "fully integrated, from research and development through manufacturing and marketing" for the same reason that Canada appears "conservative" in "risk and innovation." It is mainly because U.S. companies are so much larger than Canadian firms and because they have penetrated the Canadian economy with their largesse that it is, in fact, more "risky" for Canadians to innovate. Finally, all of these members of the elite fail to acknowledge that racism and class inequality do exist in the United States when they make their comparative statements. The analysis in Chapter 8 demonstrated that class origins, sex, race, region of birth, and other ascribed characteristics continue to be important factors for entry into the U.S. economic elite, and that while these barriers persist, there remains a powerful self-selecting upper class in control. Nevertheless, their perceptions of the greater accessibility of the U.S. elite to persons born outside the upper class were confirmed in the comparative study of the two elites.

II. Managerial Migration between Canada and the United States

The 1961 Census of Canada illustrates the great change in origin of persons in the classification of "manager" between pre-war and post-war immigrants. The native-born had 8.1 per cent in this category, all pre-war immigrants had 12.7 per cent, and post-war immigrants had 6.1 per cent. The U.S. immigrant population in Canada goes directly counter to this trend: of the pre-war immigrants, 12.5 per cent were in the managerial class compared to 20.8 per cent of the post-war immigrants.[2] Warren E. Kalbach says:

The proportion of post-war immigrants in managerial occupations was slightly more than one and a half times larger than the proportion of pre-war immigrants born in the United States rather than just half the size, as was the case for all origins. It may also be noted that those in managerial occupations constituted 20.8 per cent of all post-war immigrants born in the United States compared to only 6.1 per cent for all origins combined.[3]

This suggests that U.S. immigrants have felt a continental pull in the mobility available to managerial types that was not in the reach of the overall immigrant population. Forces different from those that operate on other immigrants are obviously affecting U.S. managerial mobility.

Why do managers move, and of what relevance are "push-pull" factors? In the simplest terms, the theories surveyed suggest that the prime reasons are either the need to move or the attractiveness of the destination, although the second of these factors may be qualified to include selective immigration policies in the country of destination.* The first consideration seems to be of limited importance in accounting for post-war movement of managers, although the Ugandan refugees who came to Canada in 1972 are a notable exception. Of the 2,053 Ugandans who entered the labour force, 437 or 21.3 per cent were classified as managerial. Push factors obviously should not be ignored as a prime cause of managerial migration, but they do not appear to be the sole explanation in most cases. This does not mean that push factors are not important in combination with pull factors; indeed, they are extremely important. The pull factor of attractiveness, however, seems to warrant greatest attention. Selective immigration policies would seem to be of minor importance for managers because of their high occupational ranking. If anything, the designation "manager" is an asset where immigration policy is selective.

Theories regarding the general mobility of the population as opposed to its sedentary qualities seem to apply to most managers,† but some qualifications must be made here. Managers who are attached to small companies, particularly family firms with mainly local business, would probably be limited in ability to change residence, especially from one country to another. Other managers, however, would be in a position of high mobility, but whether international mobility is included depends on other factors.

It can be argued that earlier periods of managerial migration, particularly when there was open competition in the entrepreneurial stage of capitalism, were characterized by "free" migration. *Free migration*, as used here, means that the individual moves independent of an organization, taking along managerial skills and frequently capital. As entrepreneurial capitalism gives way to corporate capitalism, managerial

---

* See the discussion of P. George's theory in Appendix XIV, pp. 350-52.
† The argument is developed by Anthony Richmond in "Sociology of Migration in Industrial and Post-Industrial Societies," in *Migration*, ed. J.A. Jackson, p. 245. See also W. Petersen, "A General Typology of Migration," in *Readings in the Sociology of Migration*, ed. C.J. Jensen, p. 53.

migration usually has a connotation of intracompany transfer that may take a person across an international boundary.* *Attached migration*, as used here, means an intra-organizational transfer; the individual concerned is simply following a career path that leads across a boundary but within one organization. More recent types of free migration would include the important group that stays abroad in the country where they have gone for their education.[4] Also possible is active international recruitment by organizations, as occurs with university professors, but this is of minor importance for managers.

The transition from predominantly free to attached migration can be related to changing corporate structures, to differences between portfolio and direct investment, and to training practices (as in the case of university students studying abroad).† For example, the dramatic shift from portfolio to direct investment as the major type of capital flow between nations has had enormous effects on migration patterns. Portfolio investment is interest-bearing capital that is lent by capitalists in one country to capitalists in another (see pp. 15 and 18). This means that the capital transferred will be used by indigenous capitalists and does not bring foreign capitalists with it. Direct investment, on the other hand, involves an entire package of capital, technology, and management and promotes international movement of managers. Multinational corporations, of course, are the major agents for carrying direct investment. Thus managers may be migrants because of organizational ties, particularly in the age of multinational corporations. Louis Parai says:

> Often, the movement of some of these people is from one branch plant to another, and such movements are at times a necessary part of the training and organization of the particular firms. In so far as this is true, the movements of such personnel are essentially a matter of company planning and policy, rather than one of migration motivated by economic factors.[5]

Parai's remark about company policy prompts the question, Does the multinational company recruit its managers within the parent organiza-

---

* "Free" migration is, of course, subject to the limitations imposed by immigration laws, as stressed earlier. In this regard, recent changes in the U.S. Immigration and Nationality Act are of interest. Carl Cuneo has noted that in 1970 a subparagraph "L" was added to the act: "The 'L' Classification is for an alien who immediately prior to entry has been employed abroad for at least 1 year by a corporation or other legal entity, in an executive, managerial, or specialized knowledge capacity and who is seeking to enter the United States to continue such service with the same employer or an affiliate" (U.S. Department of Justice, *Report of the Commissioner of Immigration and Naturalization*, Washington, D.C. (1970):8). Cuneo believes that "this amendment is extremely significant because it indicates that intra-company transfers were no longer considered 'normal' immigration. The political border recedes into the background as mobility within the multinational corporation...becomes much more important" ("The Controlled Entry of Canadian Managers to the United States," *International Journal of Comparative Sociology*, forthcoming).

†See Brinley Thomas's remarks on the changing nature of international capital, Appendix XIV, pp. 350-51.

tion or from the society where the branch plant is located? Aside from
its implications for indigenous social mobility, the answer will determine the nature of international managerial migration. If, for example,
the company chooses managers from employees in the parent, movement will be from the parent to the branch plant, or primarily from the
United States to Canada. But if the company recruits its managers from
the branch-plant society, there will be low migration of managers, unless the parent also recruits managers for the parent operation from the
branch plants. This could mean that Canadian managers, after being
recruited in Canada, may be transferred to the United States as part of a
stream of managers moving from Canada to the United States, either
remaining there or eventually returning to Canada later in their career.
Company policy in this respect explains developments in terms of the
migration of managers – whether it will occur and, if so, what direction
it will take. Also, if social mobility is closed to some groups but not to
others, patterns of migration will be affected.*

Parai's observations lead to an examination of the social structure
and the structured international ties that lead to and promote migration. Managerial migration into Canada must be seen within the context of avenues of social mobility open to indigenous Canadians. If
there is a large influx of managers into Canada through multinational
corporations, indigenous Canadians will not be recruited to these positions and a potential avenue of mobility will disappear. Should this be
regarded as advantageous to Canadians? This is a problem not easily
resolved. Some would argue that it is necessary and beneficial to overall
economic development to bring managerial talent from outside because the required skills are not available in Canada. Others would
argue that the necessary manpower is present in Canada or that part of
it could readily be developed through the educational system, thus providing mobility for indigenous Canadians. Before we address ourselves
to this dilemma, a brief overview of recent managerial migration between Canada and the United States will be useful.

Table 44 shows the actual flow of managers between the two countries. In the period between 1961 and 1971 there was an important shift
in the two-way flow. Before 1965 Canada had an overall net loss of
managers to the United States; since then it has had an overall gain –
the net flow pattern has been reversed. Although there is a net loss of
1,738 managers over the whole period, Canada is gaining toward the
end. For example, in 1960 twice as many managers moved from Canada to the United States as came to Canada from the United States; by
1971 only half as many left as came. The final column places the Canadian flow of managers to the United States within the context of the
overall inflow of managers to Canada. Prior to 1965, more Canadian
managers moved to the United States than the overall inflow of managers from all countries to Canada. By 1971, the Canadian outflow to
the United States was only 20 per cent of the entire intake of managers.

---

*See Appendix XIV, pp. 348-350.

TABLE 44

Managerial Migration between Canada and the United States at Year Ends, 1960 to 1971

	From Canada to United States	From United States to Canada	Difference (Can.-U.S.)	Canada to United States as % of *all* Managers to Canada
	(1)	(2)	(2 – 1)	(3)
1960	1,138	550	–588	137.9
1961	1,122	622	–500	125.2
1962	1,107	626	–481	98.7
1963	1,264	608	–656	109.1
1964	1,340	655	–685	110.6
1965	1,282	887	–395	74.2
1966	812	973	+161	35.4
1967	1,028	962	–66	34.0
1968	938	796	–142	39.3
1969	658	956	+298	25.6
1970	675	1,194	+519	21.8
1971	690	1,487	+797	19.9
	12,054	10,316	–1,738	50.8

(SOURCES: U.S. Department of Justice, Immigration and Naturalization Services, "Immigrant Aliens Admitted to the U.S. Whose Last Residence Was Canada by Occupation for Years Ending June 30, 1960-1972"; Canada, *Canadian Statistical Review, History Summary 1970*; Canada, Department of Manpower and Immigration, "Quarterly Immigration Bulletin," December 1972; Department of Manpower and Immigration, *Immigration Statistics*, various years 1960 to 1971.)

These findings can be interpreted in two ways, depending on the perspective used. One interpretation is that with the reversal of flow since the mid-1960s there will be more managers in Canada and an overall upgrading in the occupational composition of the Canadian labour force. In other words, Canada benefits because there are now more managers in Canada than when there was an overall loss of managerial talent. The alternative interpretation is that the increasing inflow of managers from outside and the reduction in the outflow means that indigenous talents will be blocked from attaining managerial occupations. When there is low intake and high outflow, conditions are ripe for upward mobility among Canadians. When the intake is high and outflow low, however, indigenous Canadians are locked into a low mobility situation. An expansion of the proportion of managerial occupations within Canada would counteract the second conclusion because with expansion there would be greater opportunities. But there has been only a 0.8 percentage point increase in the proportion of the Canadian labour force classified as managerial between 1961 and 1971.

Before immigration data can be used to answer important questions about movement of managers, a better quality of information is needed. Distinctions must be made between types and levels of management, definitions must be refined as well as standardized, and more detailed data must be collected before it is possible to make comparisons between Canada and the United States and determine how long managers stay once they have migrated.* The survey of Canadian-born managers living in the United States avoids many drawbacks of immigration data.

Canadian-Born Managers Resident in the United States

The following survey, made necessary by the problems inherent in immigration statistics, is based on a set of Canadian-born, U.S.-resident managers.† All but two of the 302 persons for whom data are available can be readily categorized as four basic types. These four types provide distinct analytical categories reflecting different patterns of migration, and each is sufficiently large to provide the number of cases needed for more refined analysis. The first are those who migrated as children with their parents (41 per cent); the main analysis of this type focuses on their parents and the reasons for their migration. Second are those who decided to go to the United States for a university education (14 per cent) and have taken up residence there. Third are migrants who simply moved to the United States on their own after they entered the labour force (24 per cent). The final type is the product of continental corporations and branch-plant economies, persons who have been transferred to the United States within an organization operating in both Canada and the United States (21 per cent). Probably about half of this sample would have turned up in immigration statistics as managerial migrants from Canada to the United States. The transfers are most likely to have been detected, but not all the independent migrants would have been, and it is unlikely that many of those who remained in the United States after university would be classified by immigration statistics as managerial migrants. Certainly those who moved with their parents would not be, although some of their fathers would have been.

Some general sense of the types of people in each of these four categories is necessary before going on. The main question regarding those who moved with their parents is, why did the parents move? Thirty-eight per cent of the respondents indicated that their parents were either unemployed or lacked opportunities in Canada, the single most frequent answer given. An additional 18 per cent of the parents were returning to the United States, 11 per cent were transferred to the United States, and another 4 per cent either intended to set up a busi-

---

* For an elaboration of problems involved in using immigration statistics, see Appendix XIV.

† For the methods and sources used in this survey, see Appendix XV.

ness in the United States or went for health reasons. It is interesting that 51 per cent of those who moved with their parents from Ontario said that their parents moved because of lack of opportunity or unemployment, while the parents of another 27 per cent were either transferred or returned home to the United States. In one case, the father was a business executive who was transferred when the son was five; later the son returned to McGill University for a Bachelor of Commerce degree and went back to the United States after university because he felt that it had a "more open and competitive business climate" with "greater opportunity." This story is unusual only because the son returned to Canada after leaving as a youth. It is not unusual in the sense that a substantial number of sons of U.S. businessmen, whose fathers were operating U.S. companies in Canada when they were born, later went to the United States, often even without their parents and especially to attend university. The attitude frequently expressed is: "U.S. citizen by parentage – only Canadian by birth." It suggests that many remained a part of U.S. society even though they were born in Canada.

The following is an interesting illustration of migration to the United States with parents:

> My father wanted to be an engineer and specifically wanted to help design and build printing presses. Advances were beginning to be made in two color printing and he felt the opportunity in Canada in his particular field did not exist. He therefore secured a position with a printing press company in the United States.
>
> While in the States, doing work he loved – designing printing presses – he was asked by his father, who was sick, to come back to Montreal to help with the family business. He did go back and while there, I was born in Montreal. When grandpa got well and the business was doing well he left Canada, again, to come to the United States to resume his work.

Later the respondent founded his own textile business and continues to live in the United States.

Most men who went to the United States for education and remained there joined U.S. companies after university, but not all. For example, one respondent, whose father was a manufacturer, went to Queen's University and then to the Harvard Business School. He was hired by a Canadian financial company to work in the United States and stayed with it for thirteen years; then he moved to a U.S. financial company. He liked the climate and geography of New England, the "open opportunities" and "no prejudices." With a Harvard Master of Business Administration degree he was equally at home in either country. As was suggested earlier, not all who came to the United States for education and stayed on were without prior contacts in the United States. For example, one person born in Montreal to U.S. parents (his father headed a U.S. branch plant) attended Lower Canada College and, when it was time to go to university, went to Princeton. He returned briefly to Canada but then went back to the United States (with a Canadian-born wife but not his parents) to found his own manufacturing company. He says he was "castigated" by schoolmates in Montreal because of "American parents." He continues to have social, family, and business contacts in Canada and knows some Canadian businessmen socially in the United States.

The men who simply moved to the United States are typical migrants: persons who pick up and leave to find a job. In some cases, however, there is a slight overlap with other categories. One respondent says, "At the time I came to New York, and it is now 20 years ago, I planned to do graduate work in Security Analysis while doing investment work. To my knowledge, there were then no comparable training facilities in Canada nor was the practice of investment analysis on an adequate level." Although he is classified as a migrant, it is clear that his intention in going to the United States was to further his education as well as to work. More typical would be the many actuaries who were trained in Canada in the early 1950s, found the market glutted at a time when U.S. demand was high in the insurance business, and therefore moved to the United States in search of a job.

Of those who were transferred, only 16 per cent are working for Canadian-controlled companies. One additional person is associated with a joint Canadian-U.S. venture and one of each of the other types (family move, independent migrant, and university student) is associated with a Canadian-controlled company. Of the ten Canadian-born men who have transferred to the United States in Canadian-controlled companies, three are in manufacturing, four in finance, and three in resources; 70 per cent were born in Ontario or British Columbia. Of those transferred in U.S.-controlled companies, 92 per cent were born in Quebec, Ontario, Saskatchewan, or Manitoba. By ethnicity, 90 per cent of persons transferred in Canadian-controlled companies are "Anglo" and only one is French, while in the U.S.-controlled companies, 88 per cent are "Anglo" and 11 per cent are "third ethnic" or of mixed background. The one French Canadian who was transferred in a Canadian company went to the United States to a branch operation of his father's company. While he was there the firm was sold, and he has stayed on under the new owners as an executive. He never actually held a job in Canada and remained in the United States after leaving university. Another respondent went to university in Canada and on to Harvard for a Master's degree in business administration, returning to Canada to work for a Canadian bank. He was then transferred to the United States. Recently he resigned rather than be transferred back to Canada, mainly because of lower costs and climate. He says he is "better off financially on a $30,000 salary here than on $50,000 in Toronto at the present time." The most involved story of a transfer is that of a man of middle-class origin (his father was a minister) who received a commerce degree in Canada, was transferred to the United States by a Canadian company, changed to a U.S. company three years later, was moved back to Canada for six more years, and finally returned to the United States to establish a company in the finance field, of which he is the president and major stockholder. The most common pattern among the transfer group was concisely stated by one of the respondents, who said, "If one works for an American company subsidiary in Canada, it is often necessary to move to the U.S. to have continuing advancement."

Where were these migrants from Canada born? Table 45 compares birthplaces for each type of migrant with the population distribution of 1926, the mean year of birth of the entire group. British Columbia and Alberta lost a greater proportion in these groups, especially among those leaving for university (compared to the population distribution). Half the men who left Alberta to go to university did so in the 1930s. Ontario and Saskatchewan/Manitoba are both overrepresented, but both are underrepresented in those who left for university. Quebec is the most underrepresented in all of the four types. Two-thirds of those who migrated independently from Quebec left after 1950. The pattern in this province is complicated by the ethnic factor. Since only two of the fifteen transferred from Quebec are of French origin, the proportion of non-French transfers is very high, resembling closely the Ontario pattern of transfers. The Atlantic provinces are underrepresented in all types except those leaving with their parents. The few transfers from the Atlantic provinces reflect the lower levels of economic activity there. Of the men who left as children, 30 per cent left Ontario and Alberta after 1930 compared to a 12 per cent average in the other provinces. Only 6 per cent of those transferred left before 1941, all born in Ontario. Among the managers moved by their companies, half came from Ontario in the 1950s, but Ontario and Quebec each contributed 30 per cent in the 1960s.

TABLE 45

Region of Birth of Canadian-Born, U.S.-Resident Managers *(percentages)*

Region (N)	With Parents (125)	To University (42)	Inde- pendent Migrant (71)	Transfer (62)	All (302)	Popu- lation 1926	Birth- place of Canadian Elite*
Atlantic (28)	14	12	7	2	9	31	9
Quebec (50)	12	17	17	24	17	27	20
Ontario (112)	33	29	48	39	37	33	48
Sask./Man. (52)	18	14	16	21	17	15	12
Alberta (29)	13	14	4	7	10	6	6
B.C. (31)	11	14	9	8	10	6	6
	100	100	100	100	100	100	100

* See Table 38, p. 227.

In a comparison of their birthplaces, many more managerial migrants are western born (37 per cent) than the elite (24 per cent), and they are much less Ontario centred than the elite. The analysis of regionalism and the elite revealed that the Ontario-born elite were likely to remain in their province of birth.

Where do members of each of these types settle when they move to the United States? Table 46 places them in the four major regions of the United States by residence and compares them to the U.S. population in 1973. It is evident that these migrants compare with the U.S. elite in choosing the Northeast region and are even less likely to live in the South. Although the North Central region as a choice of residence is closest to the population distribution, it receives more than its share of transferred managers, especially the youngest, 41 per cent of whom live there. The West is overrepresented in those moving with their parents and those migrating for university, especially for the group born in 1926 or later, of whom 43 per cent live in the West. This reflects the fact that these two groups are the highest represented in the West by birth.

TABLE 46

Region of Residence in the United States of Canadian-Born Managers *(percentages)*

U.S. Residence (N)	With Parents (125)	To University (42)	Inde- pendent Migrant (71)	Transfer (62)	All (302)	Popu- lation 1973	Residence of U.S. Elite
Northeast (127)	41	38	44	48	42	26	45
North Central (82)	26	26	24	32	27	28	28
South (24)	6	7	14	3	8	29	12
West (69)	28	29	18	16	23	18	14
	100	100	100	100	100	100	100

When the residence in the United States is related to the province of birth, strong north-south ties are evident. For example, when parents moved, 71 per cent of those from the Atlantic provinces went to the Northeast and 18 per cent to the North Central region; 80 per cent from Quebec went to the Northeast; 76 per cent from Ontario went to the Northeast or North Central; 56 per cent from Alberta and 57 per cent from B.C. went to the West. The most dispersed group came from Saskatchewan and Manitoba, of whom 27 per cent went to the Northeast, 36 per cent to the North Central, and 32 per cent to the West. North-south ties are also evident among those who migrated independently, with 100 per cent from the Atlantic region and 58 per cent from Quebec going to the Northeast, 71 per cent from Ontario to the Northeast or

North Central regions, 55 per cent from Saskatchewan and Manitoba to the North Central, and 50 per cent from British Columbia to the West. Of those transferred from Ontario, 92 per cent settled in the Northeast or North Central regions. As a general rule, managers born in central and eastern Canada tend to go to the Northeast and North Central regions, adjacent to the province of birth, the western-born tend to go to the western region, and the South is consistently avoided by all types. Only independent migrants reach even half the proportion of the U.S. population living in the South, and then only because some of them have retired in Florida and run businesses on the side. The fact that only 3 per cent of the transfers reside in the South reflects the low level of industrialization there and is consistent with the findings on the U.S. economic elite seen earlier, except that managers avoid the South even more strongly.

As in virtually all top economic positions, women are conspicuous by their absence. In this sample of 302 Canadian-born U.S. residents there are only two women (0.7 per cent, but this is almost the same as the proportion of women in either the Canadian or the U.S. economic elite). One moved with her parents and one went to the United States for education. The country of origin of the wives of these managers follows a pattern similar to their career patterns. Of those who moved with their parents, 78 per cent have wives from the United States and only 6 per cent wives from Canada (the remainder have wives from elsewhere or are unmarried). Among those who went to the United States for university, 52 per cent have wives from the United States and 33 per cent from Canada. The proportion is reversed among the independent migrants, 59 per cent of whom have wives from Canada and 38 per cent from the United States. Of the transferred managers, 74 per cent have wives from Canada and 16 per cent from the United States, a reflection of the age at which they left. A similar pattern is evident in citizenship: 65 per cent of those who were transferred remain Canadian citizens, compared to 34 per cent of the independent migrants, 14 per cent of those who left for university, and only 2 per cent of those who left with their parents (many of whom may never have been Canadian citizens, although Canadian-born).

It is interesting that of those who were transferred, 10 per cent had lived temporarily in the United States earlier for schooling, and another 20 per cent were temporary residents there for other reasons. Thus about 30 per cent of the transfers had some preliminary taste of the United States before moving there. Similarly, 14 per cent of the independent migrants reported having lived there temporarily earlier.

What reasons do these people give for migrating? Not one said that being Canadian born was a drawback in the United States; in fact, 20 per cent of those who moved with their parents, went to the United States for university, or were transferred thought it was an asset. Among those who moved on their own, 37 per cent felt Canadian birth was an asset in the United States, particularly the youngest group, of

which 56 per cent thought it an asset. Clearly, one factor in their migration is that they find few, if any, barriers in the United States because of
their Canadian birth. But this is not a reason for moving. The respondents were asked to supply general and specific reasons why Canadians
migrate to the United States, without any possible reasons being suggested to them. Since the reason of those who moved with their parents
is obvious enough, and since they usually cannot speak in comparative
terms, they are left off Table 47.

TABLE 47

**Reasons Given by Canadian-Born Managers
for Migrating to the United States**

	(Percentage mentioning specific reasons)		
	To University	Independent Migrant	Transfer
Greater opportunity	90	77	73
More money	56	52	44
Life-style	41	25	29
Negative reasons in Canada	31	25	10
U.S. more meritocratic	23	15	17
Skill outlet	26	23	5
Larger market	13	17	10
Job offer	10	12	14

A typical response offered by these managers was, "I didn't leave
Canada because I felt there were any barriers to success but simply
because I felt opportunities at the time were much greater in the United
States." Generally, this was the tone of most of the responses, although about a third of those leaving Canada to attend university in the
United States suggested negative reasons in Canada, as did a quarter of
those who migrated themselves, compared to only 10 per cent of those
transferred. But overall, the answers simply reflect a feeling of more,
bigger, better opportunities. Of course, this is to be expected from
people who have moved to the United States and remained there.

Table 48 summarizes their answers to questions asking whether
there were any "barriers" to their succeeding in Canada and if they
thought they had a better chance in the United States than in Canada of
attaining their present positions. As in the "negative reasons" shown
in Table 47, those who went to the United States for university and did
not return to Canada were likely to identify barriers in Canada, independent migrants were less likely to do so, and less than a third of the
transfers found barriers. The same pattern is evident among those saying they felt they had a better chance in the United States, but the fairly
large difference in the proportions of responses to the two questions

suggests that attraction to the United States still has an important place. The responses of the transfer group are consistent with their position in the structure of multinational corporations: relatively few identify barriers in Canada simply because they had to make it in Canada before being transferred. On the other hand, given the movement from branch plants to parent corporations, they had a better chance to go further in the United States than in Canada.

TABLE 48

Barriers in Canada and Better Chance in the U.S. as
Reasons for Migrating

	(per cent yes)		
	To University	Independent Migrant	Transfer
Barriers in Canada	63	45	30
Better chance in the United States	93	88	80

When the answers to the question of barriers in Canada are broken down by region of birth, some interesting differences emerge (Table 49). Immediately apparent are some major differences by region of birth. In the Atlantic provinces and Quebec consistently higher proportions list barriers, particularly among the groups that transferred from the Atlantic provinces and that left Quebec to go to university in the United States. The barriers in Quebec tend to be ethnic and those in Atlantic provinces economic. Those who left the three Prairie provinces to attend university perceive barriers, but few of this type

TABLE 49

Barriers in Canada as Reasons for Migrating,
by Region of Birth

	(per cent yes)		
	To University	Independent Migrant	Transfer
Atlantic	60	40	100
Quebec	86	58	42
Ontario	30	44	29
Saskatchewan/Manitoba	83	36	27
Alberta	75	33	25
British Columbia	63	45	30
All	63	45	30

from Ontario suggest obstacles. The implication is that those who left from Ontario to attend university in the United States were drawn mainly by the "pull" of university education while students in other provinces may have been "pushed."

A further dimension of barriers is revealed in the reasons for migrating given by different ethnic groups, as Table 50 suggests. The "other ethnic" group (which includes all those not reporting origin in the British Isles) in each of the three types reports greater barriers than those whose ethnic origin is in the British Isles. In terms of whether they thought they had a better chance in the United States, there was no difference by ethnicity among those leaving for university (with 92 per cent of the British Isles and 93 per cent of the others). Among the two other types, however, 90 per cent of independent migrants of British origin thought they stood a better chance in the United States to only 80 per cent of the other ethnic groups; in the transfer group, 79 per cent of "Anglo" origin and 100 per cent of other ethnic origin perceived a better chance in the United States. The bitterness of one respondent was reflected in his statement that "Corporate access was very limited in Canada to minorities. CPR, CNR, Sun Life, etc., etc. were closed Anglo-Saxon clubs."

TABLE 50

Barriers as a Reason for Migrating from Canada, by Ethnic Origin (Self-Reported)

	(per cent yes)		
	To University	Independent Migrants	Transfer
British Isles	57	43	29
Other	73	64	50

Table 51 gives more details of the ethnic categories. There are only eight persons of French descent among the U.S.-resident managers, seven of whom moved from Quebec to the Northeast region of the United States. The other ethnics tend to go to the North Central region and those of British origin to the Northeast. Comparing the ethnic origins of these managers to the Canadian population, it is clear that the British Isles group is overrepresented because although it averaged between 52 and 45 per cent of the Canadian population from 1931 to 1971, it has consistently higher representation among all the four types. Similarly, the French are clearly underrepresented in terms of their 28 to 29 per cent of the population over the same period. In only one area is there anything approaching equitable ethnic representation, and that is the proportion of other ethnics leaving Canada to attend university in the United States, where they surpass their 20 to 27 per cent of the population in Canada between 1931 and 1971. Closer examination shows that 58 per cent of the other ethnics going to the United States for education left in 1951 or later, compared to 29 per cent of the British Isles group, that half were born in 1926 or later, compared to a quarter of the British Isles group, and that 58 per cent of the other ethnics came from the West, with only one from Quebec and none from the Atlantic region. This pattern for other ethnics, as would be expected, is evident in the other types as well; for example, two-thirds of the other ethnics who migrated with their parents came from provinces west of Ontario.

TABLE 51

Ethnic Origins of Canadian-Born, U.S.-Resident Managers *(percentages)*

(N)	With Parents (123)	To University (42)	Independent Migrant (69)	Transfer (60)	All (294)
British Isles (220)	66.7	64.3	84.1	88.3	75.0
French (8)	3.3	4.8	—	3.3	2.7
Other (46)	17.1	28.6	14.5	5.0	15.5
American (6)	4.9	—	—	—	2.0
Mixed (14)	8.1	2.4	1.4	3.3	4.7
	100	100	100	100	100

Six of the respondents identified themselves as "American," and all of them returned to the United States with their parents prior to 1930. Fourteen respondents reported "mixed" ethnic origins, of which five were half British Isles and half French, five were half British Isles and half other, and four were half French and half other. Of the fourteen "mixed" ethnics, ten moved to the United States with their parents.

The transfer group has the highest concentration of British ethnics, 25 per cent of whom were transferred during the fifties and 57 per cent in 1961 or later. This suggests that if a branch-plant system with "attached" migrations becomes dominant, there will be few openings for persons from other ethnic groups. Indeed, the numbers of French and other ethnic transfers are already very small. Nor are there many of other origins among those who are independent migrants, although the other ethnics have fared better than the French in this type. Earlier it was suggested that persons born outside of Ontario may have been "pushed" to the United States for education; these findings suggest that it is primarily members of the other ethnic groups that find it difficult to attend university in Canada and, instead, are migrating to the United States and staying there after graduation.

As would be expected, there are considerable variations in the educational patterns of the four types of migrants. Only two people who went to the United States with their parents came back to Canada for university (both attended McGill University). Of those who went to the United States for university and stayed, 60 per cent went for their first degree; 54 per cent received graduate degrees from Harvard; and 24 per cent specialized in science, 12 per cent in engineering, and 44 per cent in commerce, these three specializations accounting for 80 per cent of the whole group. In addition, 13 per cent of those who were transferred had already received commerce training in the United States.

Among those who migrated independently, only 17 per cent had not attended university in Canada. Fifty-eight per cent of the migrants from Quebec had attended McGill University, while of those leaving from Ontario 50 per cent had attended the University of Toronto, 6 per cent had gone to McGill, and 21 per cent had gone to another "name" university (University of British Columbia, McMaster University, University of Western Ontario, Queen's University, or the University of Manitoba).

Among the independent migrants, 17 per cent were trained in science (three-quarters of them from Ontario) and 15 per cent were engineers (half from Ontario); another 29 per cent were trained in commerce and came from all areas except the Atlantic provinces. Similarly, 10 per cent of those transferred were trained in science, 18 per cent were engineers, and a third had training in commerce. Only 15 per cent of the transfers had not attended university, and 67 per cent of those from Quebec attended McGill (all from Quebec went to university). Education obviously is an important key to entering the continental migration stream. Those who went to the United States for university are obviously oriented to education, but even among the transfers, 85 per cent were university educated, as were 83 per cent of the independent migrants.

There is a marked increase in the level of the current managers' education compared to that of their fathers, although their fathers were also well educated compared to the rest of the population. Table 52

TABLE 52

Education of Fathers of Canadian-Born, U.S.-Resident Managers *(percentages)*

Level of Fathers' Education (N)	With Parents (107)	To University (38)	Independent Migrant (55)	Transfer (52)
Public school	28	24	36	29
High school	39	53	42	33
University	33	24	22	39
	100	100	100	100

illustrates that there are some important differences in the educational levels of the fathers of the four types.

Managers who were transferred and those who moved with their parents tend to have the best-educated fathers, but those who went to the United States for university have the lowest percentage of fathers with only public school education and over half had high school education. This suggests that some of the fathers of men going to the United States for university may have experienced educational barriers in Canada, and their sons were avoiding these barriers by going to the United States. Half of the fathers who migrated when these men were children or who were corporate officials had also attended university, but the fathers of only a third of those who migrated to the United States for education and of 17 per cent of those who migrated independently were corporate officials and had attended university. Thus it appears that the fathers of those who migrated themselves and especially those who went for university found educational barriers in Canada, even if they eventually became corporate officials.

In terms of the managers themselves, 15 per cent of those who attended school in Canada and moved with their parents attended private school in Canada, as did 18 per cent of those who went for university, 14 per cent of those who migrated independently, and 11 per cent of those transferred. These figures are considerably lower than the 41 per cent of the Canadian economic elite with private school education and reflect the differences in social class origins of the elite compared to these managers.

A few observations should be made concerning the quality of the data used to determine class origins. In the study of the elite in earlier chapters, the data were drawn from biographical sources, which are excellent for determining those of upper-class origin but more conjectural for distinguishing between middle-class and working-class origins. This study of managers is based on survey data, which are stronger for distinguishing origins within and between the middle and working classes but less reliable than biographical studies for upper-class origins.*

Compared to the Canadian economic elite, the entire group tends to be nearer working-class rather than upper-class origin (see Table 53). Middle class origin is higher among the independent migrants and transfers than among the economic elite; those who moved with their parents have the same proportion as the elite of middle-class origin, and those who went to the United States for university have only slightly lower proportions than the elite. Compared to the proportion of

---

* There is an interesting difference in the response rates of the four types on the class origin question. Between 7.0 and 7.2 per cent of those who moved with their parents, moved to the United States for education, or migrated independently refused to state their fathers' occupations, but 16.1 per cent of those transferred refused this information. Since all the first three types have been in the United States much longer than the transfers, this suggests that there is more openness in the United States about revealing family backgrounds than among Canadian businessmen.

the whole population in each of these social classes,* even these managers are privileged in their origins. Of the population "at risk" in Canada (that is, males of a similar age) only a little over 2 per cent are upper class, but even among the independent migrants, the lowest by social class origin of the four types, over a third are from the upper class.†

TABLE 53

Social Class Origin of Canadian-Born, U.S.-Resident Managers *(percentages)*

(N)	With Parents (116)	To University (39)	Independent Migrant (68)	Transfer (59)	Canadian Economic Elite (686)
Upper class	39	44	34	37	61*
Middle class	35	31	47	46	33
Working class	27	26	19	17	6
	100	100	100	100	100

*See footnote, p. 207.

Additional analysis indicates that 40 per cent of those who moved with their parents and had fathers who were corporate officials were born in Ontario, 23 per cent were from Alberta, and all other areas were underrepresented. This suggests that the largest numbers of the parental generation of the transfer types lived in Ontario, reflecting the high degree of branch-plant activity there, as demonstrated historically. Half of those who moved independently and had fathers who were corporate officials were also born in Ontario. But of those who were transferred and had fathers who were corporate officials, 67 per cent were born in Quebec.

As would be expected, the perceptions of barriers to success in Canada, as identified earlier, differ by the class origins of the types. This is reflected in Table 54. The different overall pattern from one type of migrant to another has already been discussed. The trend in general is for persons born outside the upper class to perceive barriers in Canada and for persons of upper-class origin to be less likely to perceive barriers. In all classes of origin, the transfer types tend to be the least likely to report barriers, suggesting that after they have made it in Canada,

* The definition of upper class used earlier in studying the elite is somewhat more rigorous than the one used here. The main criteria used in that study were an executive position in a substantial business and descent from an earlier elite generation. In the managerial study it was not possible to follow up on the size of companies where the fathers of managers were officials. With this difference, the managers are even less likely to be upper class in the terms used in the elite study.
† For an alternative method of identifying class of origin, see Appendix XVI.

TABLE 54

Perceived Barriers in Canada by Class Origin of Canadian-Born, U.S.-Resident Managers

	(per cent yes)		
	To University	Independent Migrant	Transfer
Upper class	44	39	30
Middle class	91	38	31
Working class	63	69	22
All	63	44	29

class origins have less impact. Independent migrants from the middle class are least likely to perceive barriers, but seven-tenths of this type from working-class origins saw barriers in Canada. In the group that left for university in the United States, the middle-class member is most likely to perceive barriers. One man of working-class origin whose father was a tradesman was able to become a chartered accountant in Canada but found advancement slow. He went to the United States for the reason that "the caste system was less prevalent [there]." While the terminology may be wrong, the sense is still there.

From a somewhat different viewpoint, among the independent migrants only 4 per cent from the upper class mentioned skill outlets as a reason for migrating, but that reason was mentioned by 23 per cent from the middle class and 46 per cent of those from working-class origins. This suggests that men of working-class origin, even when skilled, found difficulty in securing the kind of employment they wanted in Canada, while those from the upper class did not have this problem and left for other reasons.

The final question related to Canadian-born, U.S.-resident managers concerns the kinds of contacts they had before moving to the United States, the contacts they maintain in Canada, and the contacts they have with other Canadian-born businessmen now also resident in the United States. These data provide some idea of the kind of continental social, family, and business contacts that exist among this mobile stratum of the business world. Table 55 shows that, as would be expected, nearly all of the transfers had some contact in the United States before they moved there and four-fifths had contacts with their own company prior to moving. A considerable number of them also had social, other business, and family contacts. Half of those who moved with their parents had family contacts, reflecting the fact that many of them were children of parents who normally lived in the United States and were only temporarily residents of Canada. The most interesting contacts are those of the independent migrants and those who went to the United States for university. About three-fifths of each type had some form of contact in the United States before moving, with family ties most important, followed by social contacts. Ten per cent of the independent migrants already had contacts in their present company and 21 per cent had other business contacts. Although they were not transfers, at least some of these who went to the United States were already somewhat integrated into U.S. business.

TABLE 55

Contacts in the United States of Canadian-Born Managers before Migrating

	(per cent yes)			
	With Parents	To University	Independent Migrant	Transfer
General contacts	49	61	59	94
Social	2	24	17	36
Family	50	29	27	21
Business (own company)	—	2	10	81
Other business	1	7	21	37

Once they have left, what kinds of contacts do these types maintain in Canada? Table 56 suggests that strong ties remain even after the move. It is to be expected that those who left with their parents have somewhat fewer current Canadian contacts than the others, but still, over four-fifths report some type of contact. These are mainly family contacts, with a considerable number of business contacts. Evidently the continental tie is important even for persons who left Canada as children. Virtually all of the other three types have some Canadian contact. Those who went to the United States for university have mainly family and social ties, but more than a third still report business contacts in Canada. The independent migrants and those who have transferred have numerous current business contacts. The strong social, family, and business ties among these managers suggest an important binding network of a continental scope.

TABLE 56

Current Canadian Contacts of Canadian-Born, U.S.-Resident Managers

	(per cent yes)			
	With Parents	To University	Independent Migrant	Transfer
General contacts	83	98	99	100
Social contacts	38	68	61	79
Business contacts	45	37	61	77
Family contacts	61	73	81	92

Within the United States, strong ties persist among businessmen born in Canada. Over four-fifths of the independent migrants and transfers now know other Canadian-born businessmen in the United States; so do almost three-quarters of those who left for university and over half of those who left with their parents. Aside from those who moved with their parents, where the proportions are about identical, more know other Canadian-born businessmen through business than socially. It may well be that there are many more Canadian-born managers living in the United States and that their common roots in Canada have some effect on their ties within the United States. One respondent, who left Canada in 1948 with his parents (his father was a corporate official) after attending a private school in Ontario, went to the University of California at Los Angeles for a law degree and reports, "I know approximately fifty businessmen who have come to California in the past ten years. Primary reasons appear to be economic opportunity, climate and social activities."

TABLE 57

**Canadian-Born, U.S.-Resident Managers Who Know
Other Canadian-Born Businessmen Now in the
United States**

Know other Canadian-born now in the United States:	(per cent yes)			
	With Parents	To University	Independent Migrant	Transfer
General	56	73	81	81
Social	42	51	52	55
Business	41	56	75	73

We have seen how, historically and currently, many ambitious Canadians have found themselves drawn to the United States. Historically, they were drawn by the prospect of economic opportunities befitting the entrepreneurial stage of capitalism. In the present era of corporate capitalism, a new prospect has drawn Canadians to the United States. It is a step in the process of career mobility in a continental corporation – being taken into the U.S. parent company after moving up the ranks in the Canadian branch plant. Some others are drawn to the United States initially for education and find themselves becoming part of the U.S. business world. What is most striking is that all of the types that leave continue to have social, family, and business ties in Canada, which serve to integrate the two societies on yet another level.

Perceived barriers in Canada (particularly class, ethnic, and regional barriers) and opportunities in the United States appear to be factors in stimulating managerial migration to the United States. The continental economy has created a structure in which some people are transferred within corporations across the national boundary, more often at the managerial level (21 per cent) than at the elite level (13 per cent). Nevertheless, it is clear that managerial migration has not provided opportunities for upward mobility for many Canadians. The managerial level is somewhat more open than the elite level, but this would be expected for at least two reasons. Managers have a lower level of power, and many of these migrants, particularly the transfers, are insiders, who tend to be more mobile even within the elite.

The southward pull is very strong for managers, particularly for those born in western Canada. Members of the Canadian elite born in the West, on the other hand, tend to be oriented toward central Canada (see pp. 226-229). Both groups must migrate from their home region to attain their present positions. Like the U.S. elite, migrating managers are drawn to the industrial Northeast and to some extent to the North Central region and the West but avoid the South.

The notions of barriers to advancement in Canada and great opportunities in the United States were strongest among the type of managers who originally left Canada to go to university in the United States. Independent migrants shared these views to a lesser extent. The managers who were transferred by their companies, however, were unlikely to perceive barriers because their transfers were based on their having been successful in Canada.

The managers studied usually had ties that might be described as continental in character. Many had social, family, or business contacts in the United States before they migrated that would have helped to make their migration easier. Moreover, they kept up family and business ties in Canada and had business and sometimes social contacts with other Canadian businessmen living in the United States. It may be possible to conclude that Canadian-born businessmen are far from uncommon in U.S. business circles and that there is something of a continental community in the upper part of the class structure.

All these findings add further evidence to the argument advanced earlier that Canada is integrated with the United States not just on the economic level as recipient of a large volume of U.S. investment. The relationship also involves a good many Canadian capitalists, whether elite members or managers, who have benefited by this arrangement. They project an ideology of internationalism and, related to it, an ideology of corporate capitalism.

III. Multinational and Continental Activities of the Canadian Elite

Before turning to the implications of continental capitalism for the structure of the Canadian elite, it is important to review more closely some of these continental and multinational elite ties.

International Associations

Associations of the Canadian and U.S. elites at various levels have been discussed throughout this study. One level at which the co-ordination between the two elites is explicit is in international policy-making associations. As the North American economy became even more continental after the Second World War, it was important for businessmen to develop forums where they could discuss and resolve their mutual concerns, particularly how to keep national boundaries from becoming barriers to international capital. One of the most important for the continental economy, the Canadian-American Committee, was formed in 1957 "to study problems arising from growing interdependence between Canada and the United States." In its policy statement, the Canadian-American Committee says,

> The Committee believes that good relations between Canada and the United States are essential for the future prosperity, and perhaps even the survival, of both countries. It is therefore seeking not only to encourage a better understanding of the problems which have arisen and may arise, but also to develop solutions for such problems which are in the common interest of both countries. The Committee is taking a North American approach in its search for constructive programs.[6]

Elite members belonging to this committee include William John Bennett, president of the Iron Ore Company of Canada and a director of Canadian Pacific; Herbert Hayman Lank, director of such dominant companies as Bell Canada, Canadian Pacific, Consolidated-Bathurst, Crédit Foncier, Genstar, Hudson's Bay Gas and Oil, Sun Life, and Toronto-Dominion Bank; Brooks McCormick, president of International Harvester and a director of Commonwealth Edison, Esmark, Incorporated, and First Chicago Corporation; Henry Smith Wingate, a director of the International Nickel Company of Canada and Canadian Pacific in Canada and of United States Steel, American Standard, and J.P. Morgan and Company in the United States.

As a reflection of the world system within which these capitalists and their corporations operate, associations have also been created on a broader level than the continental one. An example is the British-North American Committee, sponsored by the British-North American Research Association in the United Kingdom, the National Planning Association in the United States, and the Private Planning Association of Canada (the same U.S. and Canadian associations that sponsor the Canadian-American Committee). There are ninety-three members in all on this committee, twenty-nine of whom are key members of the U.K. economic elite, including Sir David Barran, managing director of Shell Transport and Trading, and Dr. Ernest Woodroofe, chairman of Unilever. The Canadian members have included Robert M. Fowler, who is chairman of the executive committee as well as president of the C.D. Howe Research Institute, chairman of BP Canada, a director of Celanese Canada, the Quaker Oats Company of Canada, and other corporations; Hon. John Black Aird (see p. 177); Hon. J.V. Clyne, former head and now a director of MacMillan Bloedel and a director of Canada Trust and other firms; the late Dr. John J. Deutsch, a director of the Canadian Imperial Bank of Commerce, Alcan Aluminium, F.P. Publications, and INCO, and chairman of the Economic Council of Canada; Derek F. Mitchell, president of BP Canada and a director of Canadian International Paper; J.G. Prentice, chairman of Canadian Forest Products and a director of the Bank of Montreal; William Ian Mackenzie Turner, Jr., president of Consolidated-Bathurst and a director of Power Corporation, Celanese Canada, Dominion Glass, and other corporations; W.O. Twaits, former chairman of Imperial Oil, now vice-president and a director of the Royal Bank, and a director of Abitibi Paper. From the U.S. economic elite are James H. Binger, chairman of Honeywell Incorporated and a director of Northwest Airlines, Northwestern Bancorporation, Chase Manhattan, and Minnesota Mining and Manufacturing; William Blackie, a director of Caterpillar Tractor and Shell Oil; Harold Bridges, president of Shell Oil and a director of Charter New York; Nicholas Joseph Campbell, Jr., senior vice-president and a director of Exxon; Silas Strawn Cathcart, chairman of Illinois Tool Works and a director of General Electric; - Joseph B. Flavin, president of Xerox and trustee of Northwestern Mutual Life; Henry J. Heinz II, chairman of H.J. Heinz and a director of Mellon National; Tom Killefer, vice-president and a director of Chrysler Corporation; Franklin A. Lindsay, president of Itek Corporation and a director of First National Boston; Ray W. Macdonald, president of Burroughs Corporation and a director of Chrysler; Ian K. MacGregor, chairman of AMAX, Incorporated, and a director of American Cyanamid and the Singer Company; General Lauris Norstad, a director of Owens-Corning Fiberglas and Continental Oil, UAL, Incorporated, and the Canadian dominant, Abitibi Paper; J.E. Wallace Sterling, Canadian-born chancellor of Stanford University and a director of Shell Oil and Kaiser Aluminum; Andrew W. Tarkington, member of the executive committee and a director of Continental Oil, a director of Bankers Trust New York and a director of the Canadian dominant, Hudson's Bay Gas and Oil. This far from exhaustive list gives some idea of the elite members from Canada, the United States and the United Kingdom who have a common meeting ground in the British–North American Committee.

Continental and Multinational Ties of the Canadian Elite

Seven per cent of the Canadian-resident members of the Canadian economic elite hold U.S. corporate posts, twenty-four in dominant companies and thirty in others. At least 106 members of the Canadian elite living in Canada have a U.S. club membership, forty of them in one of the top ten clubs and fifty-six in other top U.S. clubs. There is a close relationship between the two sets of facts because half of those who have a dominant U.S. post also report a U.S. club membership. The Canadian elite is centred in central Canada, and the continental ties run from central Canada to the United States. Of the fifty-four members of the Canadian resident elite with a U.S. post (not necessarily dominant), twenty-three were born and twenty-nine live in Ontario, while ten were born and nineteen live in Quebec. Again, of the 106 belonging to U.S. clubs, fifty-three reside in Ontario (exactly half), and twenty-eight in Quebec, while British Columbia follows with only seven. Therefore, the Canadian connection to the United States comes primarily from central Canada, with other peripheral regions tying into central Canada.

Two examples will suffice to give some indication of these and other continental ties. S. Robert Blair, born in Trinidad and now living in Calgary, Alberta, was educated at Choate School in Wallingford, Connecticut, and has an engineering degree from Queen's University, Kingston, Ontario. Blair worked for Canadian Bechtel, a branch of the giant U.S. engineering and construction company, as an engineer from 1951 to 1958, during which time (and until recently) his father was president of Canadian Bechtel, continuing there as a consultant as well as a director of Alberta Natural Gas. The son moved to Alberta Natural Gas in 1958, becoming a director in 1959, vice-president in 1961, and president of Alberta Gas Trunk Line (a joint Canadian-U.S. venture) in 1966. He continues in this position, adding directorships in the Bank of Montreal and Dominion Foundries and Steel.

Admittedly, Blair is exceptionally well integrated in both the Canadian and the U.S. upper class through his schooling and corporate positions, but he is not alone. Another example, concentrating more on the social level of continental integration, is William Cranfield Harris. He was born in Toronto and was graduated with a Bachelor of Commerce degree from the University of Toronto in 1925. He is the son of William Thomas Harris, who was president of Harris Abbatoir and vice-president of Canada Packers. William Cranfield Harris was chairman of Harris and Partners and is now a vice-president and a director of the Bank of Nova Scotia (having once held directorships in other dominant companies such as Brascan and Canada Packers). He also maintains a residence in Florida and mixes with the U.S. upper class in the Links Club of New York and the Rolling Rock of Ligonier, Pennsylvania, while keeping contact with the Canadian upper class in the Toronto, York, and National clubs. His son, William Bowles Harris, is a graduate of Upper Canada College, the University of Toronto, and Oxford and is a chairman of Dominion Securities Harris, the product of a merger between Dominion Securities and Harris and Partners, and a director of National Trust. He too is solidly integrated in the life of the continental business world with memberships in the Toronto and

Mount Royal clubs as well as the Links of New York.

Certainly not all members of the Canadian economic elite are as well commingled with the U.S. upper class as the Blairs and Harrises, but it is clear that at least part of them do operate in the United States as equals. Others are integrated in the continental system of dominance as unequal partners.

A component of Canada's dominant corporations operates multinationally (see Chapter 5), and it is possible to isolate characteristics of the individuals associated with these companies as it was with U.S. multinationals. These individuals can be identified in two ways: either their main corporate affiliation is multinational or one of the companies where they hold an elite position is multinational. It is quite obvious that the members of the elite who hold the most dominant directorships are, in a sense, the most multinational because they are exposed to the operation of a broader range of companies. Seventy-three per cent of those with multiple dominant directorships are multinational compared to 55 per cent of the single directorship holders. Twenty-eight per cent of those whose main affiliation is in the transportation/ utilities sector are multinational, but 65 per cent of those holding a dominant directorship in this sector have some multinational affiliation (the Canadian elite's proportion in this category is actually higher than the U.S. elite's 46 per cent). In finance, 32 per cent are multinational because of their main company and 87 per cent because they have a dominant financial directorship. Once again this is higher than the 82 per cent in the United States. The resource sector has the most multinationals – 60 per cent whose main affiliation is in this sector and 95 per cent of those with a dominant directorship in this sector; in the United States, 99 per cent in resources are multinational. Of those whose main affiliation is in manufacturing, 46 per cent are multinational as are 83 per cent with a dominant directorship in that sector, compared to 91 per cent in the United States. Trade has only 27 per cent multinational as a result of a main affiliation and 70 per cent from a dominant directorship, compared to 73 per cent in the United States. Canada's proportion is higher than that of the United States in the finance and transportation/utilities sectors, but in the sectors where U.S. capital dominates in Canada, manufacturing and resources, the United States has a greater proportion of multinational elite members. As will be illustrated, however, there is an important relationship between Canadian multinational elite members and their U.S. opposite numbers.

Indigenous and Comprador Elites in Canada

The class origins of members of the elite associated with multinationals reveal interesting differences. Forty-eight per cent of those whose main affiliation is in a multinational are upper class in origin; 57 per cent of those with no multinational affiliation are upper class; and those who are multinational because of a secondary affiliation compose the largest upper-class proportion – 75 per cent. The reason for these differences is that many of the Canadian elite whose main affiliation is multinational are affiliated with a foreign-controlled branch plant. These people (the comprador elite) tend to be less upper class in origin than the indigenous elite. The distinction between indigenous and comprador elites by multinational activity is shown in Table 58.

TABLE 58

Multinational Activity of Members of Canadian Indigenous and Comprador Elites *(percentages)*

Multinational Activity (N)	Indigenous (588)	U.S. Comprador (135)	U.K. Comprador (42)	Other Comprador (33)
Main	23	62	79	73
In other dominant	42	18	21	27
In other corporation	3	1	—	—
None	33	20	—	—
	100	100	100	100

It is evident here that all the U.K. and "other" compradors are multinational, and three-quarters of them are multinational because of their main affiliation. Nearly two-thirds of the U.S. compradors also are multinational because of their main activity, but 20 per cent of the U.S. compradors are not multinational because the U.S. branches they work for are only continental in scope. The indigenous elite is least multinational, particularly in terms of their main affiliation. Nevertheless, two-thirds of the indigenous elite is multinational because of some affiliation. Many of the multinational affiliations of the Canadian indigenous elite members are accounted for by their association with foreign-controlled branches in Canada, although there are, of course, a good number of Canadian multinationals, especially in the financial sector.

Before proceeding with a picture of the indigenous and comprador fractions of the Canadian elite, the role of the comprador should be placed in some context. The comprador elite consists of persons whose main affiliation is with a foreign-controlled branch plant in Canada. They are not the equivalent of the foreign-born in the elite (although many foreign-born members do hold comprador positions in Canada). The rapid U.S. takeover and control of the productive sectors of the Canadian economy over the past twenty-five years has already been documented. In the initial stages of this takeover, U.S. managers were often sent to Canada to run the branch operations. As these operations became established and stabilized, however, Canadians were trained and groomed to assume managerial positions and the parent company exercised control through directives, fiscal measures, and the selection of Canadian management that would carry out its policies. In other words, two processes are occurring simultaneously: in one, foreign control increases, and in the other, Canadian management is increasingly used to administer the Canadian branches. Table 59 illustrates these trends.

TABLE 59

**Birthplaces of the Canadian-Resident Economic Elite,
1951 and 1972** *(percentages)*

Birthplace (N)	Economic Elite		Canadian Population	
	1951* (760)	1972 (798)	1951	1972
Canada	80.4	85.6	85.3	84.7
United States	9.9	6.5	2.0	1.4
United Kingdom	8.7	5.5	6.5	4.3
Other	1.1	2.4	6.2	9.6
	100	100	100	100

*(SOURCE: for 1951 elite, John Porter, *The Vertical Mosaic,* p. 287.)

Over the past two decades, there has been an increase in the proportion of Canadian-born members of the elite, even though there has been a slight decrease in the native-born population during the same period. The table shows that the proportion born in the United States is the largest compared to the general population, illustrating that foreign control continues to bring some foreign executives even in the advanced stages of a branch-plant economy. Most underrepresented in the elite are those born in "other" areas (2 per cent of the elite compared to 10 per cent of the population), a reflection of the general pattern of "other" ethnic exclusion.

Among the entire economic elite living in Canada, 74 per cent can be classified as indigenous, 17 per cent as U.S. comprador, 5 per cent as U.K. comprador, and 4 per cent as "other" comprador. Whether a person is comprador or indigenous is determined in large part by the control of the corporation through which he has the main part of his corporate career. Ninety-seven per cent of those whose careers have been in Canadian-controlled corporations are now indigenous members of the elite. Eighty-one per cent are U.S. comprador and 16 per cent indigenous of those whose main careers are in U.S. corporations, and of persons with careers in U.K. corporations, 89 per cent are U.K. comprador and 11 per cent are indigenous. All persons with their main careers in "other"-controlled companies are currently "other" compradors.

Place of birth is another indicator of the kind of elite fraction to which an individual will eventually belong. Of the U.S.-born in the - Canadian-resident elite, 50 per cent are primarily associated with U.S.-controlled companies and 42 per cent with indigenous firms; of the U.K.-born, only 27 per cent remain with U.K. companies and 57 per cent work in indigenous companies; of the others, 21 per cent work for "other"-controlled companies and 68 per cent for indigenous firms. Clearly, the foreign-born in the Canadian elite follow several different patterns. While half of the U.S.-born residents are "attached" to a "home" branch plant, only a quarter of the U.K.-born and a fifth of the others follow a similar pattern.

We have already studied the sectors in which foreign control or Canadian control is dominant, and the differences are dramatically expressed by the career avenues followed by various fractions of the elite. Only 19 per cent of the Canadian-born indigenous elite used either manufacturing or resource companies as their career avenue, but 37 per cent used transportation/utilities or finance. Among the Canadian-born U.S. comprador elite the proportion is 55 per cent using resources or manufacturing and only 18 per cent using transportation/utilities or finance as career avenues. Of the U.S.-born in the Canadian-resident elite who are affiliated primarily with a U.S. corporation, 83 per cent have used manufacturing or resources. U.S. direct investment concentrates in the sphere of production at the corporate level and the resident members of the elite are gathered in this sphere also.

The positions in Canadian corporations that comprador members tend to hold are different from those held by the indigenous elite, as Table 60 illustrates. In a dominant corporation or any corporation, all the comprador elite are more likely than indigenous members to be insiders. In either a dominant corporation or any corporation, the comprador elite members are also more likely than the indigenous to be

TABLE 60

Corporate Positions of Indigenous and Comprador Members of the Canadian Elite *(percentages)*

	Indigenous	U.S. Comprador	U.K. Comprador	Other Comprador
(N)	(588)	(135)	(42)	(33)
DOMINANT POST				
Insider	19	28	36	20
Outsider	55	37	33	32
Executive	26	35	31	48
	100	100	100	100
ANY POST				
Insider	17	26	26	18
Outsider	11	10	5	15
Executive	55	56	57	55
Partner	18	8	12	12
	100	100	100	100

executives. The indigenous member, on the other hand, is more likely to hold an outsider post in a dominant corporation or a partnership than is the comprador member.

These elite fractions have definite roles when corporate career avenues are considered. Only 17 per cent of the indigenous elite experienced the long crawl through the corporate ranks while 26 per cent of the U.S. comprador elite are long-crawlers. Although 44 per cent of the indigenous elite have their main current affiliation in a dominant corporation and 25 per cent have non-corporate affiliations, among the U.S. comprador elite 56 per cent have their main affiliation with a dominant corporation and only 19 per cent have non-corporate affiliations. In part, these ratios reflect the roles lawyers play within the various elite fractions. Of the lawyers now with a law firm, 79 per cent are indigenous members, but only 68 per cent of those who have left their law firms and 60 per cent of house lawyers are indigenous. Lawyers who have switched from the law firm to become house lawyers often tend to be drawn into the ranks of the comprador elite.

The fact that comprador members tend to be insiders and long-crawlers suggests some differing patterns in class recruitment to the elite fractions. In addition, they tend toward careers in science and engineering (the field of only 7 per cent of the indigenous elite but of 27 per cent of the Canadian-born U.S.-comprador elite and 37 per cent of the foreign-born comprador elite), while members of the indigenous elite are overrepresented in law and a third of them have careers in family firms. All these factors contribute to the greater openness of the comprador elite. There are, however, some interesting differences between the fractions of the comprador elite. The origins of the U.S. comprador elite are only 38 per cent upper class, compared to the 57 per cent of the U.K. comprador elite and the 61 per cent of the "other" comprador elite. The indigenous elite is 66 per cent upper class in origin. The differences between the U.S. and the other comprador elites cannot be explained by corporate positions. The explanation may be that the branch plants of companies with headquarters elsewhere than in the United States have a greater degree of autonomy from their parents, which induces them to recruit "reliable" upper-class Canadians to manage their Canadian affairs. It is easier for the U.S. elite to keep a close watch over their Canadian operations. An alternative possibility is that the U.S. branches follow the practice of their parent corporations and recruit more broadly in the population. Earlier evidence tends to confirm both explanations. Since few of the foreign-born from the United Kingdom or "other" areas remain attached to corporations controlled from home, Canadians tend to be recruited to fill these positions. On the other hand, half the U.S.-born in the Canadian-resident elite remain with U.S. branches and would reflect the recruitment patterns of their parent companies. Whatever the explanation, it is clear that broader class recruitment by U.S. companies in Canada does not extend to ethnicity, because 96 per cent of the U.S. comprador elite are

"Anglo" compared to 85 per cent of the indigenous elite.

What social background characteristics tend to ensure that a member of the Canadian economic elite will be indigenous? The strongest guarantee is to inherit some position, particularly a career in a family firm. Aside from this, having a father in the economic elite ensured that 93 per cent would be indigenous; having a father in a substantial business was insurance for 83 per cent; and having a wife from an elite family ensured 81 per cent. Having a father in the state elite, however, does not ensure an indigenous position. Only 67 per cent of those with fathers in the state elite are indigenous; 19 per cent are U.S. comprador and 11 per cent U.K. comprador. Furthermore, only 67 per cent of those who themselves had been in the bureaucracy during the Second World War and 70 per cent of the bureaucrats from other periods are in the indigenous elite. Having held a political office, however, gives an 84 per cent chance of being indigenous.

Finally, what kinds of relationships exist between these various fractions of the elite? Thus far only the primary affiliations of the elite have been examined, yet many of those who hold indigenous positions simultaneously hold comprador positions. Table 61 provides some insight into these secondary affiliations. It is apparent that a high degree of interconnection exists in Canada between indigenous and comprador fractions of the elite. Among the comprador fractions, the "other" compradors are connected mainly to the Canadian corporations and much less to the other comprador fractions. This is also true to some extent of the U.K. compradors. What is most interesting is the proportion of the indigenous elite simultaneously holding comprador positions in U.S. branches or at least one comprador post. Conversely, well over half the compradors hold at least one position in a Canadian-controlled company. As with upper-class origins, it is the United Kingdom and "other" compradors who have the highest ratios of these connections with Canadian-controlled companies. But the indigenous elite is most tightly connected with U.S. branches, in part reflecting the greater dependence that it has on U.S. business in Canada. Since the Canadian elite has overdeveloped the sphere of circulation and allowed the sphere of production to become U.S. dominated, it has put itself in

TABLE 61

Interconnections between Fractions of the Canadian Elite

| Primary Affiliation | Secondary Relations with (percentages): | | | | | |
	U.S.	U.K.	Other	Canada	None	(N=683)
Indigenous	31	11	7	x	58	(528)
U.S. comprador	x	5	4	51	41	(105)
U.K. comprador	14	x	7	57	36	(28)
Other comprador	5	5	x	64	32	(22)

the position of having to find outlets for its capital and services. This is done in part through joint directorships, and it is clear that a good many of the indigenous members have been successful in forging these relations.

Does it make any difference who sits on the boards of branch plants in Canada? From the perspective of actual control of the company, it makes little difference, because the branch must operate within the policies of the parent. Nevertheless, for purposes of ensuring capital sources in Canada access to such services as transportation and utilities, Canadian markets, and contacts with the Canadian state, these connections are of importance. The Canadian elite has been content to allow foreign dominance of the productive sphere of the economy because the members have been able to benefit by its activity. They have been able to gain an important and lucrative position for themselves within the continental structure of dependence.

CHAPTER TEN

Implications of the Continental Economy for Canadian Society

Is it correct to argue that multinational corporations "transcend the nation-state?" In the sense that capitalism is international and not confined to a particular national territory, it is correct. But this is not all that is implied in this argument. To the extent that it implies that multinationals are without national bases, are without important national ties, and do not need the protection, legitimacy, and resources of the home state, the argument is clearly wrong. At the most basic level, and this is what binds the capitalist class together, nationally or internationally, multinationals must maintain a capitalist society where property rights are ensured. To provide this most basic guarantee, multinationals need nation-states. Yet multinational corporations do not promote an equal sharing among or within nations of the resources they control. On the contrary, they ensure that inequality within and between nations will be maintained and even expanded.

Since Canada is located midway in the world economic system, acting as both a receiver of branch plants from foreign-owned multinationals and a base for Canadian multinationals operating in the rest of the world, its place in this world system of inequality is ambiguous. The two types of multinationals dominate Canadian industry, resources, and trade patterns; the nature of the Canadian labour force and of research and development is shaped by their presence; and they have great leverage in dealing with various branches of the Canadian state. The power contained in these companies is private power, exercised by sets of people in ways they feel to be most beneficial to themselves and their companies, with very limited accountability for their actions to the people directly affected. Those who own and control these enormous operations are not subject to popular elections, nor are they often brought to account publicly for their decisions. They are a self-selecting, self-perpetuating set of people who have wide-ranging control over the lives of Canadians and the shape of Canadian society.

In the world system there are some barriers to capital, or more specifically to capitalists, that limit the activities of multinationals. The most important of these is political, and the half of the world that is not capitalist imposes important limits on the "free" movement of multinationals (e.g. China or Cuba). Aside from this, some nations regulate the type, amount, and areas of multinational intrusion from the outside (e.g. Japan or Sweden). Besides political barriers, a strong obstacle to multinational expansion is local capitalists already engaged in economic activities who are able to fight for their turf. This opposition has varied with the period of entry and the kind of economic activity (e.g. Canada or Europe). But to stress these constraints is to miss the tremendous freedom giant capitalists have in much of the world to extract economic surplus. This is nowhere more evident than in the relationship between the United States and Canada, the subject of this study.

Since the end of the Second World War, the United States has lost some of its hegemony in the world system, although it remains the most powerful of the capitalist nations. While the absolute GNP of the United States continues to rise, its share of the "gross world product" is on the decline (from about half in 1950 to about a third in 1976). Countering the United States in the post-war era have been the USSR, China, Japan, and the European Economic Community. Nevertheless, Canada's reliance on the United States has steadily increased and its other outside relations have declined dramatically (Canada's exports to the United States have increased from about half of all exports in 1961 to over two-thirds in 1971). Canada cannot easily withdraw from the continental economy and shift its trade elsewhere because now, unlike earlier periods, much of its "trade" consists of intracompany transfers to U.S. parents. Canada is, therefore, locked into the continental economy, even if other nations challenge the world hegemony of the United States.

I. The Nature of the Canadian Elite: The Question of Domination

As has been stressed throughout this study, multinationals alone do not explain the amount of U.S. direct investment in Canada's sphere of production. At least part of the answer lies in the nature of dominant Canadian capitalists and their essentially complementary relationship with U.S. control in production. These elements in turn are related to the nature of the Canadian elite. For example, the explanation of why the Canadian economic elite is more exclusive in 1972 than it was in 1951 (from 50 per cent upper-class origin to about 60 per cent) is more complex than simply U.S. penetration, because the U.S. comprador elite in Canada is more open to mobility than the indigenous elite. There is, however, a direct relationship. The Canadian indigenous elite is boxed in by its own past, in which most of the productive areas of the economy – manufacturing and resources – were given up to foreign capitalists, and it has meanwhile stayed safely one remove from industrialization and enriched itself on the avails – interest on capital, provision of services such as transportation and utilities, and the buying or selling of existing companies. The narrowness of its recruitment base has been induced by its specialization.

What happened to the powerful Canadian commercial interests at the turn of the twentieth century that saw Canada as the rising centre of a new imperial design? Internationally, they declined with the British

Empire. Internally, they shared their power in an alliance with U.S. industrial capitalists. They have not faded quietly away. Their legacy remains in an overdeveloped financial and transportation/utilities system in Canada and in the remnants of their commercial activities in the rest of the world, particularly in the West Indies. But just as their earlier prosperity depended on the hegemony of the United Kingdom, so their continued prosperity is now predicated on the ascendancy of the United States.

The power of Canadian capitalists in the circulation sector has shaped Canadian society in many ways. An economy dominated by financial capitalists, particularly ones whose business is mainly in long-term interest-bearing investments (unlike the many equity dealers among U.S. financial capitalists), will not strongly resist state ownership of particular sectors such as transportation or utilities because they can still extract their surplus by investing their capital in those enterprises, regardless of ownership. Moreover, these outlets are much more secure than private outlets, at least private entrepreneurial ventures. The financial capitalists are thus unlikely to fund entrepreneurial capitalists in Canada, but when the state takes charge of wavering capitalist ventures – such as the railways that became the CNR – the owners who are bailed out and the financial capitalists who hold their debts can only be pleased.

Nor are Canadian financial capitalists at a loss for a defence. For example, before a Vancouver Board of Trade gathering in late 1975, Earle McLaughlin, president and chairman of the Royal Bank, proceeded to list the major capital-intensive projects in Canada's future such as the Alberta tar sands, James Bay hydro, and Arctic pipelines, going on to explain that

> consortium financing is becoming an important activity of the major Canadian banks. This is a way in which banks can get together to share the financing and to spread out the risks of these gigantic capital projects.
>
> Can you imagine trying to form a loan syndicate to finance a major gas pipeline with hundreds of little banks? So don't underestimate the advantages of the Canadian system with its very big banks.[1]

Whether the project is owned by a consortium of U.S. and state capital, by state capital alone, or by U.S. capital alone, the banks are equally willing to "share." Their correspondent relationships with one another help secure their dominant place rather than threaten it. McLaughlin's logic is sound, given one assumption, which is that the state needs to go to the "private market" to finance such ventures. In a capitalist society, the logic is certainly sound, since it is the private financial capitalists that control the greatest capital reserves; and they determine to whom they will lend these reserves. But what McLaughlin fails to ask is, what are the disadvantages of a banking system where over 90 per cent of all activity is controlled by only five banks?

One disadvantage is well known to small capitalists, who certainly do not need bank consortia to finance them. Because of their orientation to "bigness" (which means security), Canadian financial capitalists were drawn to the industrial corporations controlled from the United States rather than to small Canadian industrialists. At the turn of the century, as Canada began its process of industrialization and as corporate capitalism was taking hold, a major outlet for capital was opened in the sphere of production, and Canadian financial capitalists did not hesitate to enter into this activity, but did so in their own way. If these Canadian financial capitalists were to retain their traditional pattern of stable, long-term, interest-bearing investments, they had to search for appropriate outlets. They would suffer losses if there were no outlets that could generate surplus, but if there were surplus-generating outlets in production, they could maintain their strong and secure position. The need for productive outlets explains the search for them by Canadian financiers, and it did not matter whether they were Canadian or U.S. controlled. Indeed, since the U.S. industrial system was further advanced in technology, management, and marketing, the U.S. companies were often favoured as more secure investments. Complementing the financial capitalists' search was the willingness of U.S. industrialists to expand as their national market was filled and resources were needed.

In the present age of corporate capitalism, which has witnessed the coalescence of industrial and financial capital, it might have been anticipated that the two would become one, but the Canadian dominant capitalists have found it difficult to abandon their past, a past that they have found profitable and secure even in an industrial age. They have remained with financial and related mediating activities, carried over from their old imperial ties with Britain, and from this stable base of power they have entered into an alliance with U.S. industrial capitalists at home and extended their own base of power abroad under the U.S. sphere of influence. The existence of a developed industrial structure to the south that could be imported to Canada by way of branch plants provided the surrogate for indigenous industrial development. Although they are still active in some industrial fields, particularly in steel, so closely tied to earlier railway expansion, and food and beverages, tied to agriculture, they have abandoned most other manufacturing pursuits and almost all resource-related activities outside the traditional pulp and paper field, historically key staples.

While in class societies the various classes are related to each other by unequal exchanges that form asymmetrical relationships based on surplus extraction, various fractions within the same class need not be so related. That is, various class fractions, such as industrial and financial capitalists, may form symmetrical relationships within a broad economic system, each mutually complementary to the other. If these alliances cross political boundaries, then little matter – capitalism is international. But various fractions within a class may make alliances more readily than others. For example, Canadian financial capitalists at the beginning of this century had to choose an ally in moving Canada into an industrial era. They had the choice of the nascent Canadian industrialists, the counterpart of today's middle-range indigenous capitalists, or their powerful U.S. competitors, the counterpart of today's dominant comprador capitalists. Consistent with their philosophy of stable investments, they chose the latter. In some instances compatible with the movement from entrepreneurial to corporate capitalism, they chose to enter industrial activities themselves, not as entrepreneurs or industrialists but as financiers, by consolidating existing small-scale industries into corporate complexes.

The upshot is that the power of Canadians to make decisions about specific economic activities in Canada has regressed to a state of underdevelopment (although not total underdevelopment of "material" well-being), with control over future development and stability lost because of the lack of an indigenously controlled base in manufacturing and resources. In the overdeveloped finance, transportation, and utilities sectors originally built on U.K. portfolio investment, the dominant indigenous capitalists now in control still remain powerful components of the total class. In other words, the process of compradorization has been sector specific and took place in the presence of traditionally powerful Canadian capitalists rather than displacing them. The effect on weak capitalists in production was, of course, to bring about their downfall.

The resulting fragmentation of the capitalist class in Canada does not mean that the whole class is not still powerful vis-à-vis the working class – indeed, it may have gained power because of its alliance with U.S. capitalists in the continental context. It does mean, however, that the Canadian component must commit itself to the continental context. The existence of a powerful Canadian commercial elite, based in the Canadian upper class, and a predominantly foreign-controlled elite in production means that Canada remains a "low mobility" society. Concentration and centralization in commercial sectors have been the work of indigenous forces while the same processes in the productive sectors have been imposed from outside (with the aid of Canadian capitalists in circulation). The result is a highly structured economy with few avenues through which the lower class can rise. The process of compradorization has offered a few middle-class Canadians mobility into the elite, but many of the uppermost positions created by this process have been filled by the indigenous elites. In fact, very few Canadians have moved from the branch-plant structure into the real power positions within the parent company. This middle-class comprador elite is largely trapped in the backwater of the U.S. subsidiaries.

Unlike the portfolio investment typical of the British Empire, the direct investment of the U.S. empire does not eventually break off as a result of economic forces alone but deepens its hold. Nor is there any reason to suspect that the indigenous capitalists in circulation are contemplating taking over the U.S. enterprises.

Is the size of the U.S. economy a sufficient explanation for the dominant position of U.S. capitalists in Canada, particularly in production? The Canadian society is clearly of a much smaller scale than that of the United States (with about one-eleventh the population). Size has two strong effects on the nature of their respective elites. First, because of scale, whenever the interpenetration of the two societies occurs, the United States overwhelms Canada. Secondly, because Canada is much smaller than the United States and the turf of Canadian capitalists is more limited, the Canadian elite is a much closer-knit community in terms of interaction and recruitment. But the difference between Canada and the United States is not only one of scale but also one of type, in the sense of the relative concentration of economic activities and the differing strengths by type of activity, as has been stressed so frequently. Would relations between Canada and the United States be very different if there were only the factor of a giant market 'eleven times the size of the Canadian to the south rather than this factor in combination with U.S. control of over half the entire manufacturing and resource sectors of the Canadian economy? The clear answer is yes. Ownership by Canadian capitalists would allow them to trade outside the United States to a greater degree than branches of U.S. companies are liable to do, thus reducing market dependency. In addition, surplus generated from Canadian operations would remain in the hands of Canadian capitalists for future growth, whereas under current conditions, much surplus is withdrawn to the United States or reinvested in the branch plants. But this discussion is merely an academic exercise. The reality is that the two countries are of radically different size and type. In combination, they have created the present structure of dominance.

As was argued in detail earlier, any attempt to analyse Canada in terms of a simple dominance/subordination dichotomy (as in many of the Latin American models of dependency) necessarily misses the complexity of its internal class and power relations. While *in general* the United States dominates Canada, and the dominant capitalists in Canada hold sway over those of the middle range, there are still important mediations between each and significant political struggles. It is important to look for points of alliance and of tension, points where each gains and where one gains at the expense of the other. While the type of methodology used here can specify *some* of these complexities, the real work in specifying these political struggles remains to be done through detailed case studies (some of which were reviewed earlier). But without some broader context, cases remain simply cases and do not lend themselves to broader trends and developments (such as those outlined here). For example, use of either the automobile or the steel industry in Canada would lead to radically different conclusions if they were not placed in the broader context of the economy as a whole. While one is clearly a dependent industry, the other has enjoyed much more support from and success with indigenous capitalists. To understand how and why they coexist requires a broad understanding of the historical and contemporary development of the entire economic structure in Canada and its complex relationship with the U.S. structure.

II. Effects of the Continental Economy on Canadian Society

The "common sense" of Canadians (and the dominant ideology) would tell them that foreign direct investment means greater investment in their economy, more jobs and better ones, more affluence, and, however vaguely, "progress." On the contrary, the "uncommon" reality is that after a brief period of growth, foreign direct investment means that more capital flows *out* of than into the economy; that there are fewer jobs in the capital-intensive branch plants than in Canadian-controlled firms; that there are few jobs in branch plants requiring highly trained manpower because much of the research and development is done in the country of the parent; and finally, that the "affluence" and "progress" created by these developments are deceptive, favouring the already privileged. Each of these inequalities has been analysed, but one, regional inequality, merits closer examination.

Canada is a particularly fragmented nation. It is a federation of ten provinces and two territories, each of which has increased its demands for power vis-à-vis the central government since the dismantling of the Ottawa war machine created for the Second World War. But do these political boundaries alone explain regionalism in Canada? Are the real regional splits not based more on economics than on politics? While political fragmentation aggravates regionalism, it is not itself the cause of regionalism. That cause must be found in the uneven development of the country and the branch-plant structure of corporate capitalism, both indigenous and foreign.

"Regionalism" is an unequal sharing of the wealth and benefits a nation has to offer, expressed in geographical terms. But alone this is not a sufficient definition. There is also a relationship involved – a region is a part of something else, and herein lies the key to the *unevenness* of economic development. It is only uneven when more capital and profits are extracted than are put in – otherwise it is *un*developed, not *under*developed. A region can only be underdeveloped if it is tied to an external economy that is doing the underdeveloping. The only way it can be truly developed is if all those on site who participate in the development share equally in the surplus produced. If part of the surplus is shipped outside, underdevelopment is occurring. This principle applies equally to class relations or to regionalism, the latter frequently passing for the former.

Upon examination, the issues of class and regionalism become closely intertwined because, at the most basic level, both are rooted in extractive relationships and both, in Canada, are reproduced through the institution of private property. This is not to say that there are no extractive relationships in societies that are not capitalist or that they too do not have a type of regionalism, but they have these problems for different reasons and under different political regimes.

When Canada is referred to as an industrial society, what is really meant is that *part* of it is industrialized – the rest is more aptly characterized as a resource hinterland. Most of Canada's industrial capacity is located below a line beginning at Windsor, encompassing Toronto, and moving on to Montreal. This is industrial Canada; all other areas rely on key resources for their economies. In British Columbia the resources are wood, pulp and paper, with some hydro-electric power; they are gas, petroleum, and potash, along with wheat, in the Prairies; mining and pulp and paper in northern Ontario and Quebec, along with hydro; in the Atlantic region pulp and paper, fish, and some coal along with hydro in Newfoundland. These outliers feed the Ontario-Quebec industrial heartland and the U.S. markets with their resources and, in turn, consume some of the finished products from these regions. In finance the branch structure is represented in the dominant banks, all with headquarters in Toronto and Montreal and branches spread throughout the country to tap capital for the centre. The varied economies in these regions produce different types of class structures. At the same time, the regional economies are tied to national economies, and national economies to international economies. Thus, the regional class structures (and, contingent upon these, the varieties of life-styles and opportunities) are to some extent dependent upon the way they fit into the national and international economic order. Regions that have capital and profits extracted from them will have limited access to the means of obtaining goods, services, and opportunities while regions that receive the extracted capital and profits have greater advantage. The overdevelopment of one region depends on the underdevelopment of another; the overdevelopment of one class depends on the underdevelopment of subordinate ones.

Concretely, how does this pattern express itself in the economies of the various regions? The effects of different types of economies can be examined by looking at the tax bases they provide to the provincial governments. This method is significant because taxes are an important means for securing the revenues necessary to pay for various social services. It can be readily demonstrated that the levels of industrial development impinge on the resources provincial governments have; moreover, it can be demonstrated that the effect of the continental economy is to aggravate regionalism in Canada.

While Ontario has 36 per cent of the Canadian population, in 1972 it received 46 per cent of all provincial corporate taxes paid by non-financial companies, 51 per cent of the taxes paid by foreign-controlled companies, and 54 per cent of the taxes paid by U.S.-controlled non-financials. In the manufacturing sector 72 per cent of Ontario's taxes are from foreign-controlled companies.*

---

*Calculated from CALURA, *Report for 1972*, pp. 21-22, Statements 4 and 5. Data are available only on a provincial basis and do not lend themselves to intraprovincial regionalism.

Table 62 illustrates two aspects of regionalism. The first is seen in Ontario's overrepresentation in taxes from industrial corporations compared to the other areas of Canada. The second is evident in the effect of U.S. direct investments in compounding this overrepresentation in Ontario. Consistently, in all regions, the distribution of tax income by Canadian-controlled industrials is much more in line with the population distribution than is the distribution of taxes paid by U.S.-controlled companies. In other words, if it were not for U.S. industrials, the problems of regionalism would not be as serious as they now are for the Atlantic provinces, Quebec, and British Columbia. In the Prairies the situation is somewhat different because of oil revenues. This is evident in Table 63, which examines only manufacturing. Here every area except Ontario is underrepresented compared to its population base, although for income from Canadian-controlled manufacturing only, Quebec and British Columbia are actually above their proportions of the population. Mining provided the provinces with $279.7 million in taxable income in 1972, compared to $3,344.5 million from manufacturing, and Alberta alone received half of this income ($138.6 million), with 88 per cent of Alberta's share coming from foreign-controlled companies. In this sector all other provinces were well below their proportion of the population, with Ontario's 22 per cent the closest to its population base. Thus, it can be argued that foreign investment in manufacturing, because it has been so Ontario-centred, and in petroleum, because it has been so Alberta-centred, has added greatly to regional disparity in Canada. An understanding of regionalism in Canada requires a look outside to see the forces initiating the problems.

Aggravation of regional inequalities is not the only effect of foreign investment on Canadian society, although it is a major one. Many others have already been explored, such as the implications for research and development, the social rigidity caused by a limited base of power, and the fact that the resource sector of the economy is overdeveloped to meet the demands of the United States.

TABLE 62

Distribution of Non-financial, Industrial Tax Income by Region and Control of Company, 1972 *(percentages)*

Control of Companies	Atlantic	Quebec	Ontario	Prairies	British Columbia	Total
United States	3.2	18.1	53.5	17.6	7.3	100
Canada	5.2	26.0	41.8	13.4	13.0	100
All	4.5	22.5	45.7	15.9	11.0	100
Population	9.5	28.0	35.7	16.4	10.1	100

(SOURCE: Calculated from CALURA, *Report for 1972*, and *Canada Year Book, 1973*.)

TABLE 63

Distribution of Taxable Income from Manufacturing, by Region and Control of Company, 1972 *(percentages)*

Control of Companies	Atlantic	Quebec	Ontario	Prairies	British Columbia	Total
United States	2.7	18.9	62.2	9.6	6.7	100
Canada	3.6	28.8	43.2	9.8	14.4	100
All	3.1	23.3	53.7	10.2	9.6	100
Population	9.5	28.0	35.7	16.4	10.1	100

(SOURCE: See Table 62.)

Based on the proposition that social relations follow from the economic and political organization of society, it is evident that there must be a relationship between foreign ownership in Canada and the class structure of *both* Canada and the United States. And further, these class relations will be affected by the nature of Canada's economic and political position in the world capitalist order. It is therefore useful to look beyond Canada to the United States to gain some perspective on internal Canadian developments. Moreover, this larger perspective allows us to make an analysis of class alliances and conflicts, both nationally and continentally. To do so is of necessity to understand a political relationship; nowhere is the politics of economics more apparent than in foreign investment, since the amount, type, location, and encouragement of foreign investment permitted in a nation is a political act. The class dynamics of foreign investment can also provide important insights into the relationships between classes, class fractions, and the state and its branches. While an analysis of the class dynamics of Canadian society in a continental context is beyond the scope of this study, even a limited exploration will illustrate some of the political dimensions of the power relations created by the continental economy.

III. The Canadian State in the Continental Economy

It would be absurd to suggest that the political boundary has not made a difference – a great difference – in the nature of the continental economic system. It is a system composed of two distinct nation states, one with a much larger population and a much more significant impact on the other. Nevertheless, there are two national political systems. As has already been demonstrated (pp. 124-131), the fact of a political boundary affects the economic system through tariffs (which encourage particular national bases for economic activities), through state rents on resources, and through taxation policies.

The political boundary between Canada and the United States has not, however, been an impediment to the penetration of the sphere of production in Canada by U.S. foreign investment (although circulation, the turf of Canadian capitalists, has been protected). The fact of such extensive U.S. investment reflects political decisions to allow and encourage such a pattern of development. The system has emerged not in spite of politicians but because they have permitted it. Conversely, since they have allowed these events to occur, the national independence has been decreased and much of the control over Canada's economy has been allowed to shift outside the country to the board rooms of U.S. corporations. But even within a country the state does not control the decisions of corporations, whether national or foreign, although it can certainly influence them.

What does national sovereignty mean? It is the right, reinforced by might, to control and regulate developments within a territory. But at what point is this right abdicated if it is not employed? What level of external control is necessary before the original right becomes *de jure* but not *de facto*? Certainly in the public domain the *de facto* rights of sovereignty are intact. But in liberal democracies, there is a very large area of private control beyond the public domain, and it is in this area that sovereignty has been eroded. It is only because of the public/private split of liberal democracies that foreign dominance can prevail in one domain but only to a lesser extent in the other.

How far can foreign dominance be allowed to go? Is the public domain not influenced by what happens in the private sphere? Most certainly it is, and when levels of foreign ownership become high the result is erosion of the autonomy of the state itself. It is at this point that the various systems of power – state, military, and economic – become contingent upon one another. The political and military decisions of one nation begin to have direct effects on the other because their economies are so tightly intertwined.

For example, as early as 1902, Prime Minister Laurier was moved to say to Lord Dundonald, "You must not take the [Canadian] militia seriously, for though it is useful for suppressing internal disturbances, it will not be required for the defense of the country, as the Monroe Doctrine [of the United States] protects us against enemy aggression."[2] Thus in the world political system Canada was perceived as being under the wing of U.S. military power, except for internal uprisings, and that view continues some seventy years later. John Warnock's contemporary review of Canada's military policy concludes that "there is no doubt that the Cold War has intensified the problem of creating a Canadian nation and organizing a rational development of the economy."[3]

The political constraints of foreign ownership greatly affect internal policies. In his review of the politics of northern development between 1968 and 1975, Edgar Dosman points out that "in most well-established countries, the development of a peripheral region would be largely a domestic issue. In Canada, however, the development of the North was inextricably linked to the issue of the Canadian relationship with a foreign power, the United States." The reason was that "northern development after 1968 affected Canadian trade relations with the United States, particularly oil and gas exports."[4] Under such pressures, internal development policies are made in light of continuing cordial political and military relations with the United States.

The capitalists who are actually formulating and benefiting from the politics of development cannot be expected to be guided by the best interests of the nation because they operate for private, not public, interest. As John Porter has written, "Corporations...are governed by human beings who behave in accordance with a set of institutional norms – those of corporate capitalism. To argue that national sentiments and the 'national interest' would supplant the historical and inexorable norms of capitalist enterprise is to reveal an ignorance of the capitalist economy."[5]

On the other hand, state power (whether political, bureaucratic, or judicial) is a very real power in liberal democracies. Ultimately the state does have the power to make decisions about the very existence of private power. Private property is an institution granted by the state. It is thus territorially bounded and sanctioned. In corporate capitalism, the right of private property is embodied in incorporation laws, which sanction the operation of various corporations. Each charter issued by the state (federal or provincial) legitimizes the operation of foreign branches or Canadian companies. Therefore, each and every incorporated company operates in Canada under the wish of the state and only by its consent. Canada is not a puppet state because it is a liberal democracy, a society which maintains a distinction between public and private power. A socialist state, where this dichotomy does not exist, could not have the extent of foreign control that Canada has without in fact being a puppet. But even in liberal democracies, the public/private distinction is frequently transgressed, and the extent to which this occurs in Canada reduces the sovereignty of the Canadian state.

The state's role in foreign investment in Canada is a complex one. In areas where Canadian capitalists have been strong, particularly in banking, life insurance, trust companies, transportation, utilities, and the mass media, the state has provided strong protection. In these areas, legislation prohibits foreign capitalists from owning sufficient stock to control or take over companies. But legislation to protect other areas such as retail trade, manufacturing, and resources, although recommended by many government inquiries, has only recently been enacted. Moreover, the Foreign Investment Review Act simply reviews or examines proposed takeovers of Canadian companies in these sectors by foreign capitalists, and there are no across-the-board prohibitions or any effect on the many companies that already exist. The agency's track record since its inception is to approve 80 per cent of these takeovers; it is certainly not a major barrier to foreign capital.

If the state is to carry out its various functions in society, it must gain revenues from the economic sphere. In a capitalist society, this means ensuring that the state creates the conditions necessary for the orderly extraction of economic surplus to go into private hands. The Canadian state, at both the central and the sub-central levels, finds itself in a paradoxical situation regarding foreign investment. On the one hand, the Canadian state elite, aware of the state's capacity to extract a part of the economic surplus bound up with foreign capital and foreign markets, has acted to facilitate foreign investment in productive activities and assist in searching out foreign markets. On the other hand, there has been growing opposition to foreign control and fear that sovereignty is being eroded. An enormous part of both the federal (45 per cent) and the provincial (41 per cent) corporate tax revenue comes from foreign-controlled corporations. To continue to increase its revenues to meet the growing pressure on its purse, the state is forced to create a favourable investment climate for foreign capital. The common ground between the state and capitalists in a liberal democracy is that both are interested in growth and stability and both see corporate capitalism as *the* way to attain this goal. But inherent in corporate capitalism is division between public and private power, inequality within societies (where some command great economic power and others are excluded), and, as has been seen, inequality between nations, where some gain at the expense of others.

The basic concern over foreign investment is that power is exercised in the board rooms of multinationals, out of the reach of Canadians. Decisions on trade, employment, research and development, promotion of management, and investment are all beyond the control of Canadians. But is this really a consequence of *foreign* investment or of *private* investment? How much more control do the vast majority of Canadians have over the Royal Bank, Sun Life, Stelco, Eaton's, or MacMillan Bloedel than they have over General Motors of Canada, Imperial Oil, Kresge's, Crown Zellerbach, or Canadian General Electric? Is it justifiable to call for decreasing foreign investment in the name of Canada's people? To some extent, yes, the claim is justifiable because Canadian-based companies are *potentially* more susceptible to state regulation. The Canadian state, however, has been very reluctant to tamper with the rights of corporate property, whether foreign- or Canadian-controlled.

The fundamental structure of corporations, based as they are on the claims of capital, invariably leads to a system of extractive power by which those in "command" positions remove degrees of freedom from persons below and increase their own freedom. Private property, the most basic institution in both Canada and the United States, remains the principle for organizing production and circulation. Besides being the foundation of the corporate form of organization and therefore of multinationals, private property is also transmitted between generations in the form of inheritance and remains important as a means of perpetuating privilege in both Canada and the United States. In terms of recruiting highly skilled people without *highly* privileged backgrounds, however, the U.S. corporate system has proven more open than the Canadian (although the two patterns are related). In a broader sense, private property is the central institution of both societies, as it is of all liberal democracies, for it is private property as an institution that legitimizes and gives shape to the control structure of corporations. The power exercised by the economic elite is power made possible by private property concentrated into giant corporations. As long as the dominant mode of ownership continues to be private, the power of the economic elite will continue to dominate at the expense of the citizenry.

Appendices

APPENDIX I

Foreign Ownership of Industrial Groups in Canada, 1972

Major Industry Group	50% or more Foreign Ownership (percentages)		
	Assets	Sales	Profits
Total Mining	65	69	73
Metal mining	55	55	55
Mineral fuels	79	90	84
Other mining	58	65	94
Total Manufacturing	56	56	65
Food	38	32	52
Beverages	18*	17*	16*
Tobacco products	83*	80*	77*
Rubber products	92	90	93
Leather products	21	20	38
Textile mills	56	53	61
Knitting mills	22	17	33
Clothing industries	13	10	20
Wood industries	42	32	24
Furniture industries	19	16	13
Paper and allied products	48	43	20
Printing, publishing	10	11	11
Primary metals	42†	38†	25†
Metal fabricating	41	43	56
Machinery	74	77	85
Transportation equipment	80	90	94
Electrical products	66	68	73
Non-metallic mineral products	61	49	71
Petroleum and coal products	100	99	99
Chemicals	77	81	85
Misc. manufacturing	46	48	71
Total Utilities	7	9	13
Transportation	11	10	22
Storage	9	11	10
Communication	13	12	12
Public utilities	3	5	7
Wholesale Trade	32	27	30
Retail Trade	22	19	22
Finance	10	9	17
TOTAL OF ALL INDUSTRIES	23	34	39
TOTAL OF ALL NON-FINANCIAL	34	36	45

*For 1967, later data not available.
†For 1971, data not reported in 1972.
  (SOURCE: CALURA, *Report for 1972*, Part 1—Corporations, pp. 134-47.)

APPENDIX II

Control of Industrial Groups in Canada, 1972, by Assets, Sales, and Profits

	Per Cent U.S.			Per Cent Other Foreign			Per Cent Private Canadian			Per Cent Canadian Government		
	Assets	Sales	Profits	Assets	Sales	Profits	Assets	Sales	Profits	Assets	Sales	Profits
*Total Mining**	50	58	44	10	7	9	37	33	50	1	1	1
Total Manuf.	41	47	55	15	10	11	41	40	34	1	—	—
Food	31	26	46	16	10	13	50	62	41	—	—	—
Beverages	16	20	18	14	11	9	68	68	73	—	—	—
Tobacco	12	24	14	73	53	79	15	23	7	°	°	°
Rubber	87	86	91	5	4	1	7	8	7	°	°	°
Leather	19	17	32	4	4	4	74	74	64	°	°	°
Textile	48	45	53	8	8	7	42	44	39	°	°	°
Knitting	20†	15†	29†	2†	1†	—	74	80	62	—	—	—
Clothing	11†	9†	16†	1†	—	—	78	80	78	°	°	°
Wood	23	21	14	7	5	−1	66	68	84	°	°	°
Furniture	18	15	10	1	1	3	73	73	81	—	—	—
Paper	32	31	40	14	12	−11	54	56	70	°	°	°
Printing	9	9	10	2	2	1	80	75	87	°	°	°
Primary metals	34†	28†	20†	9	10	13	53†	57†	76†	5	5	5
Metal fabrication	36	39	54	5	5	55	53	48	40	—	—	—
Machinery	65	70	81	9	7	5	24	21	14	°	°	°
Trans. equip.	73	87	92	7	3	2	19	10	6	°	°	°
Electrical	56	59	65	10	9	8	34	31	29	°	°	°
Non-met. mining	15	21	28	50	32	47	33	43	24	°	°	°

Petro. & coal	74	77	77	26	22	22	0	1	1	—	—
Chemicals	55	50	67	21	21	17	13	15	10	9	3
Misc. manuf.	42	43	65	4	5	6	45	41	27	—	—
Total Utilities	8	9	17	2	2	2	33	47	62	56	18
Transportation	11	10	34	1	2	3	40	51	73	45	-13
Storage	10†	6†	12†	1†	1†	—	88	81	90	—	6
Communications	13†	12†	11†	—	—	1†	66	69	81	20	6
Public utilities	2	4	7	4	1	2	12	22	27	81	64
Wholesale Trade	17	16	25	17	13	8	53	62	57	5	5
Retail Trade	14	13	9	7	9	57	58	33	2	6	41
TOTAL NON-FIN.	25	28	36	10	8	8	43	50	44	17	9

*In 1971, mining was: U.S. assets 59%, other 10%, Canadian 29%
U.S. sales 70%, other 6%, Canadian 23%
U.S. profits 74%, other 6%, Canadian 23% (CALURA, *Report for 1972*, reclassified INCO as Canadian controlled).

†For 1971.
°Not available (figures may not total 100% because of "unclassified," some of which are negative profits).
(SOURCE: CALURA, *Report for 1972*, Part 1—Corporations, pp. 154-67.)

APPENDIX IIIa

Value of Insurance in Force of the Thirteen Dominant Canadian Life Insurance Companies in Canada, the United States, and the United Kingdom, 1970

Company	Total Value of Insurance in Force ($000,000)	Per Cent of All in Force	in Canada ($000,000)	Per Cent	in United States ($000,000)	Per Cent	in United Kingdom ($000,000)	Per Cent	Per Cent of Total in Force: Can., U.S., U.K.
Sun Life	$18,924	17	$11,110	59	$4,928	26	$1,839	10	94
Manufacturers Life	9,119	8	2,957	32	4,423	49	749	8	89
London Life	11,417	10	11,417	100	6	–	–	–	100
Great-West Life	10,603	10	5,991	56	4,613	44	–	–	100
Mutual Life	6,972	6	6,951	100	20	–	–	–	100
Confederation Life	7,640	7	4,793	63	2,044	27	480	6	96
North American Life	5,406	5	3,201	59	1,803	33	3	–	92
Canada Life	8,776	8	6,386	73	1,492	17	758	9	99
Dominion Life	2,065	2	1,202	58	754	36	1	–	94
Excelsior Life	1,905	2	1,898	100	6	–	–	–	100
Crown Life	7,661	7	3,667	48	3,481	45	317	4	97
National Life	1,993	2	1,473	74	434	22	–	–	96
Imperial Life	2,879	3	2,060	72	85	3	610	21	96
All Canadian life insurance	$109,241	100	$76,774	70	$24,225	22	$4,758	4	96

(SOURCE: Calculated from *Report of the Superintendent of Insurance for Canada*, vol. I and vol. III, 1970; *Canada Year Book*, 1972.)

APPENDIX IIIb

Assets of Dominant Canadian Life Insurance Companies
Held Outside Canada, 1970

Company	Total Assets ($000,000)	Assets outside Canada ($000,000)	Percentage outside Canada
Sun Life	3,643	1,940	53
Manufacturers Life	2,039	1,114	55
London Life	1,614	—	—
Great-West Life	1,470	560	38
Mutual Life	1,216	5	.3
Confederation Life	799	262	33
North American Life	701	177	25
Canada Life	1,308	480	37
Dominion Life	354	98	28
Excelsior Life	248	—	—
Crown Life	729	285	39
National Life	232	25	11
Imperial Life	498	109	22
TOTAL DOMINANT	14,851	5,055	34%
Average of 10 multinationals			43%

(SOURCE: Calculated from *Report of the Superintendent of Insurance for Canada*, vol. III, 1970.)

APPENDIX IIIc

Value of Insurance in Force of Dominant Canadian Life Insurance Companies in Countries Other Than Canada, the United States, and the United Kingdom, 1970 (*insurance in force in $ millions*)

	All Canadian life insurance other than in Can., U.S.,&U.K.	Sun Life	Manufacturers Life	Confederation Life	North American Life	Canada Life	Dominion Life	Crown Life	National Life	Imperial Life
South Africa	1,214.985* (35%)†	759.279 (72%)	455.573 (46%)							
Jamaica	733.877 (21%)	17.883 (2%)	133.388 (13%)	85.437 (26%)	260.732 (65%)		71.557 (66%)		43.707 (51%)	56.793 (46%)
Trinidad & Tobago	269.965 (8%)		.085 —	99.351 (31%)		15.763 (11%)		71.238 (31%)		14.529 (12%)
Ireland	209.438 (6%)				133.742 (89%)					
Bahamas	163.420 (5%)	1.547 —	8.407 (1%)		13.178 (3%)		35.716 (33%)	51.983 (27%)	.155 —	51.695 (42%)
Philippines	151.174 (4%)	102.681 (10%)	47.052 (5%)					.385 —		
Israel	151.856 (4%)		151.835 (15%)							
Guyana	121.126 (3%)	5.852 (1%)			110.676 (28%)			4.598 (2%)		

Dominican Republic	105.096 (3%)	7.112 (1%)		98.606 (30%)			.378	—	
Rhodesia	74.417 (2%)	33.365 (3%)	41.052 (4%)						
Neth. Antilles	53.855 (2%)	101	25.955 (3%)	1.860 (1%)			16.607 (8%)	9.332 (11%)	
Bermuda	40.559 (1%)	—	10.468 (1%)	.027	14.844 (<%)	.550 (1%)	6.397 (3%)	6.361 (7%)	.207
Venezuela	20.630 (1%)			20.630 (6%)					—

*Dollar amount (in millions) of company insurance in force outside Canada, the United States, and the United Kingdom.

†Percentage of the company total insurance in force outside Canada, the United States, and the United Kingdom.

(SOURCE: Calculated from *Report of the Superintendent of Insurance for Canada*, vol. I and vol. III; *Canada Year Book, 1972*.)

APPENDIX IVa

Branches of Canadian Chartered Banks Outside Canada, 1972

Bank and Branch Location	Number	Bank and Branch Location	Number
Bank of Montreal.	10	Jamaica	10
England	2	St. Lucia	1
Germany	2	St. Vincent	1
Grand Cayman	1	Trinidad & Tobago	10
United States	5	United States	23
Bank of Nova Scotia	69	*Royal Bank of Canada*	85
Antigua	1	Antigua	1
Bahamas	9	Argentina	3
Barbados	4	Bahamas	11
Belgium	1	Barbados	3
British Honduras	2	British Honduras	4
British Virgin Islands	1	Colombia	6
Dominican Republic	5	Dominica	1
England	5	Dominican Republic	12
Germany	1	England	2
Grand Cayman	1	France	1
Greece	2	Grand Cayman	1
Grenada	1	Grenada	2
Guyana	1	Guadeloupe	1
Haiti	1	Guyana	7
Ireland	1	Haiti	1
Lebanon	1	Lebanon	2
Netherlands	1	Martinique	1
Northern Ireland	1	Montserrat	1
Puerto Rico	4	Puerto Rico	6
St. Lucia	2	St. Kitts	1
St. Martin	1	St. Lucia	2
Scotland	2	St. Vincent	1
Trinidad & Tobago	14	Trinidad & Tobago	13
United States	2	United States	1
U.S. Virgin Islands	5	U.S. Virgin Islands	1
Canadian Imperial Bank of		*Toronto-Dominion Bank*	4
Commerce	57	British Virgin Islands	2
Antigua	1	England	2
Bahamas	4	*Banque Canadienne Nationale* . . .	1
Barbados	3	France	1
England	2		
Grand Cayman	1	TOTAL	226
Grenada	1		

NOTE: This table does not include sub-agencies operating outside Canada, of which there were 45 in 1972.
(SOURCE: *Canada Year Book, 1973*:792.)

APPENDIX IV*b*

Foreign Holdings of Canadian Banks, 1971

Royal Bank of Canada
100% The Royal Bank of Canada International Ltd.
100% The Royal Bank of Canada (France) Ltd.
100% The Royal Bank of Canada (Middle East) S.A.L.
100% The Royal Bank of Jamaica Ltd.
100% The Royal Bank of Trinidad & Tobago Ltd.
100% The Royal Bank of Canada Trust Company: New York
100% The Royal Bank Trust Company (West Indies) Ltd.
     which has the following subsidiaries:
     Royal Bank Trust Company (Jamaica) Ltd.
     Royal Bank Trust Company (Barbados) Ltd.
     Royal Bank Trust Company (Trinidad) Ltd.
     Royal Bank Trust Company (Guyana) Ltd.
     Royal Bank Trust Company (Cayman) Ltd.
Jointly with six other financial institutions, RoyWest Banking Corp.: Bahamas
  50% Banco Real do Canada, SA
  20% Royal Benezolanao, CA
  25% Banque Belge pour l'Industrie, SA
  10% Private Investment Company for Asia, SA
      Union Internationale de Financement et de Participation, SA

Canadian Imperial Bank of Commerce
100% California Canadian Bank
100% The Canadian Bank of Commerce Trust Co.: New York
100% Canadian Imperial Bank of Commerce Trust Co. (Cayman) Ltd.

Bank of Montreal
100% Bank of Montreal (California)
100% Bank of Montreal (Bahamas & Caribbean) Ltd.
100% Hochelaga Holdings, NV
100% Hochelaga Jamaica Ltd.
  10% Banque Transatlantique: France
   9% Joh. Berenberg, Gossler & Co.: Germany
     Banco La Guaira International CA: Venezuela
  20% Australian International Finance Corp. Ltd.
  40% Montfield Trust Co.: Bermuda
  50%+Private Investment Co. for Asia, SA

The Bank of Nova Scotia
100% The Bank of Nova Scotia NV
100% BNS International
100% BNS International (Bahamas) Ltd.
100% BNS International (Sterling Bahamas) Ltd.
100% Scotia Nominees Ireland Ltd.
  60% The Bank of Nova Scotia Trust Co. (Bahamas) Ltd.
     which has the following subsidiaries:
     The Bank of Nova Scotia Trust Co. of Jamaica Ltd.
     The Bank of Nova Scotia Trust Co. of the West Indies Ltd.

The Bank of Nova Scotia Trust Co. (Cayman) Ltd.
The Bank of Nova Scotia Trust Co. (Caribbean) Ltd.
100% The Bank of Nova Scotia Trust Co. (United Kingdom) Ltd.
100% The Bank of Nova Scotia Trust Co. of New York
 70% The Bank of Nova Scotia Jamaica Ltd.
 67% The West Indian Co. of Merchant Bankers Ltd.
 40% Bermuda National Bank Ltd.
 30% Maduro & Curiel's Bank NV: Netherlands Antilles
      United International Bank Ltd. (Unibank) with other banks
      Eurofinance with seventeen other banks

The Toronto-Dominion Bank
100% Toronto-Dominion Bank of California
100% Toronto-Dominion Bank Investments (U.K.) Ltd.
 40% International Consolidated Investments Ltd.: South East Asia
 29% World Banking Corporation: Nassau
 10% United Malayan Banking Corporation BHD: Malaysia and Singapore
 15% Allied Irish Investment Bank Ltd.
 26% Midland and International Banks Ltd.; London Headquarters

(SOURCE: *Financial Post Survey of Industrials*, 1972.)

APPENDIX V

Determining Dominance in U.S. Corporations

Economic concentration has two dimensions. One is bigness or "superconcentration," which groups all industries together to illustrate aggregate concentration. The other is market concentration, which is restricted to specific industries. Since our purpose is to analyse first only the key, or the largest, sectors and industries, and second, only the largest corporations within these sectors, the method used here to determine dominant corporations will include both internal and external comparisons based on broad industrial categories, comparing the largest corporations within particular sectors and comparable ones in other sectors. Plant concentration (the enterprise level) is useful if the focus is on production, as it is for many economists. The five-digit Standard Industrial Classification (SIC) used in this type of analysis, however, understates the degree of intersector concentration. If concentration throughout the economy is to be evaluated (the "superconcentration" mentioned above), the focus must be on ownership and control rather than on production. For purposes of control, it is the parent organization, not the plant, that is important. This analysis calls for a less "refined" SIC classification to minimize the extent of interclassification overlap.*

Occasionally there are disparities between the *Fortune* data and reports filed with the U.S. Securities and Exchange Commission (SEC). In these cases, the SEC data have been used. Typically, only the sales and revenue figures, and not the assets, are affected. Remarks concerning *Fortune* categories (the Top 500, Top 1000) use *Fortune* rather than SEC figures.

The results of these procedures are summarized in Appendix VI, grouping corporations by their SIC categories, and are discussed in Chapter 6. By comparing corporations within their sectors and between sectors and measuring with a combination of assets and revenue (where necessary, deposits, insurance in force, or a similar measure was used in place of revenue, but consistency was maintained within sectors), a composite rank (COMP RANK) for each section has been produced. The list contains 194 parent corporations that were considered to be dominant, including thirty-five corporations in finance, ten in trade, seventeen in transportation, sixteen in utilities, thirteen in resources, and 103 in manufacturing.

---

* For an elaboration of the method used to determine dominant corporations, see Clement, *Canadian Corporate Elite*, pp. 396-99. The same procedures were used to determine Canada's 113 dominant corporations.

APPENDIX VI

Dominant U.S. Corporations (All Sectors)

FINANCE

1–Commercial Banks, 1973 (ranked by assets and deposits)

COMP RANK	Name	Assets ($ billion)	Deposits ($ billion)	Net Income ($ million)
1	Bank of America	49.405	41.454	221.074
2	First National City Bank [Citicorp]	44.019	34.942	252.019
3	Chase Manhattan Corp.	36.791	29.913	163.095
4	J.P. Morgan & Co.	20.375	15.367	143.777
5	Manufacturers Hanover Corp.	19.850	17.210	99.406
6	Chemical New York Corp.	18.592	14.374	66.600
7	Bankers Trust New York Corp.	18.515	14.705	60.637
8	Western Bancorporation	17.903	14.245	76.037
9	Continental Illinois Corp.	16.870	12.598	85.470
10	First Chicago Corp.	15.559	12.042	90.849
11	Security Pacific Corp.	13.479	11.404	59.861
12	Marine Midland Banks	13.044	10.989	45.822
13	Wells Fargo & Co.	11.768	9.017	43.459
14	Charter New York Corp.	9.739	8.232	32.211
15	Crocker National Corp.	9.770	8.015	32.078
16	Mellon National Corp.	9.601	7.282	64.915
17	First National Boston	8.005	6.180	51.624
18	National Detroit Corp.	6.712	5.423	40.140
19	Northwest Bancorporation	6.517	5.193	45.651
20	First Bank System	6.514	4.890	51.572
	Total, dominant banks	353.028	283.475	
	Total, all commercial banks*	842.9	687.6	
	Top 50 banks	459.0	364.7	
	Top 50 as per cent of all	54.5	53.0	
	Dominant as per cent of all	41.9	41.2	

*Based on U.S. Federal Deposit Insurance Corporation, *Assets and Liabilities: Commercial and Mutual Savings Banks*. If aggregate data from the *Federal Reserve Bulletin* is used, the proportions of total assets would be 42.4 per cent for the dominant banks and 54.9 per cent for the Top 50 banks. The ratio in deposits would be 41.5 per cent and 53.4 per cent respectively.

2–Life Insurance Companies, 1973
(ranked by assets and value of insurance in force)

COMP RANK	Name	Assets ($ billion)	Insurance in Force ($ billion)	Net Income ($ million)
1	Prudential Insurance	34.964	197.428	1,815.694
2	Metropolitan Life	31.986	198.185	1,752,018
3	Equitable Life	17.153	97.508	864.278
4	John Hancock Mutual Life	11.447	75.056	581.045
5	Aetna Life & Casualty	8.934	71.507	485.208
6	New York Life	12.472	62.843	667.966
7	The Travelers Corp.	6.001	64.759	297.361
8	Connecticut General Insurance	6.662	41.429	363.283
9	Northwestern Mutual Life	7.096	25.722	397.516
	Total, dominant life insurance companies	136.675	834.437	
	Total, all life insurance companies*	252.4	1,778.3	
	Top 50 life insurance companies	204.849	1,274.7	
	Top 50 as per cent of all	81.1	71.7	
	Dominant as per cent of all	54.2	46.9	

*Aggregate data from Institute of Life Insurance, New York, N.Y., *Life Insurance Fact Book*.

3–Other Finance Companies, 1973 (ranked by assets and revenue)

COMP RANK	Name	Assets ($ billion)	Operating Revenue ($ billion)	Net Income ($ million)
1	American Express	6.619	1.905	150.906
2	Transamerica Corp.	4.630	2.110	89.274
3	CNA Financial Corp.	4.593	1.773	15.798
4	Continental Corp.	4.474	1.652	137.736
5	Lincoln National Corp.	4.100	1.187	95.568
6	INA Corporation	3.617	1.895	131.772
		28.033	10.522	

4–Retail Trade, 1973 (ranked by assets and sales)

COMP RANK	Name	Assets ($ billion)	Sales ($ billion)	Net Income ($ million)
1	Sears, Roebuck & Co.	10.427	12.306	679.902
2	J.C. Penney Company	2.440	6.244	185.769
3	Marcor Inc.	2.848	4.077	96.652
4	Safeway Stores	1.341	6.774	86.271
5	S.S. Kresge Co.	1.653	4.633	138.251
6	F.W. Woolworth Co.	1.974	3.722	98.474
7	Federated Department Stores	1.515	2.966	113.732
8	Great Atlantic & Pacific	1.019	6.748	12.227
9	Kroger Co.	.950	4.205	29.916
10	W.T. Grant Co.	1.253	1.854	8.429
		25.420	53.529	

5–Railways, 1973 (ranked by assets and revenue)

COMP RANK	Name	Assets ($ billion)	Operating Revenue ($ billion)	Net Income ($ million)
1	Penn Central Co.	4.263	1.964	(172.55)
2	Southern Pacific Co.	3.415	1.551	100.537
3	Burlington Northern	3.082	1.332	51.514
4	Union Pacific Corp.	2.828	1.224	127.107
5	Chessie System Inc.	2.611	1.124	66.667
6	Santa Fe Industries	2.483	1.219	102.781
7	Norfolk & Western Railway	2.401	.903	68.328
8	Southern Railway Co.	1.841	.779	67.202
		22.924	10.096	

6–Airlines, 1973 (ranked by assets and revenue)

COMP RANK	Name	Assets ($ billion)	Operating Revenue ($ billion)	Net Income ($ million)
1	UAL, Inc.	2.417	2.060	51.128
2	Trans World Airlines	1.920	1.811	46.476
3	American Airlines	1.687	1.482	(48.046)
4	Pan American World Airways	1.684	1.433	(18.402)
5	Eastern Air Lines	1.433	1.260	(51.269)
6	Delta Air Lines	.908	1.050	65.995
7	Northwest Airlines	1.086	.584	51.850
		11.135	9.680	

7–Other Transportation, 1973 (ranked by assets and revenue)

COMP RANK	Name	Assets ($ billion)	Operating Revenue ($ billion)	Net Income ($ million)
1	Greyhound Corp.	1.309	3.409	76.408
2	Seaboard Coast Line Industries	2.441	1.230	75.794
		3.750	4.639	

UTILITIES

8–Gas & Electric, 1973 (ranked by assets and revenue)

COMP RANK	Name	Assets ($ billion)	Operating Revenue ($ billion)	Net Income ($ million)
1	American Telephone & Telegraph	67.051	23.527	2,993.256
2	Consolidated Edison	5.968	1.736	207.707
3	Tenneco Inc.	5.427	3.911	230.211
4	Pacific Gas & Electric	5.471	1.490	243.607
5	Southern Co.	5.378	1.166	148.198
6	Commonwealth Edison	4.649	1.266	184.437
7	Southern California Edison	3.990	1.079	147.731
8	Public Service Electric & Gas	3.897	1.076	150.023
9	American Electric Power	5.071	.967	182.612
10	Columbia Gas System	2.597	1.049	106.230
11	Philadelphia Electric Co.	3.176	.767	122.867
12	Consumers Power Co.	2.845	.835	80.893
13	Detroit Edison Co.	3.061	.753	100.132
14	Texas Eastern Transmission	2.289	.827	88.551
15	El Paso Natural Gas	1.917	.983	68.169
16	General Public Utilities	3.034	.662	92.757
		125.821	42.094	

9–Metal Mining, 1973 (ranked by assets and sales)

COMP RANK Name	Assets ($ billion)	Sales ($ billion)	Net Income ($ million)
1 Kennecott Copper Corp.	1.977	1.395	159.407
2 AMAX, Inc.	1.712	1.337	105.102
	3.689	2.732	

10–Oil & Gas Extraction, 1973 (ranked by assets and sales)

COMP RANK Name	Assets ($ billion)	Sales ($ billion)	Net Income ($ million)
1 Exxon Corporation	25.080	25.724	2,443.286
2 Mobil Oil Corp.	10.690	11.390	849.312
3 Gulf Oil Corp.	10.074	8.417	800.000
4 Standard Oil Co. (Indiana)	7.081	6.379	511.249
5 Shell Oil Company	5.381	5.701	332.694
6 Continental Oil Co.	3.693	4.472	242.664
7 Phillips Petroleum Co.	3.607	2.990	230.411
8 Occidental Petroleum Corp.	2.871	3.456	79.763
9 Union Oil Co. of California	2.909	2.552	108.170
10 Sun Oil Co.	3.382	2.286	229.731
11 Amerada Hess Corp.	1.922	1.896	245.765
	76.690	75.263	

11–Food, 1973 (ranked by assets and sales)

COMP RANK Name	Assets ($ billion)	Sales ($ billion)	Net Income ($ million)
1 General Foods Corp.	1.729	2.632	110.449
2 Kraftco Corp.	1.391	3.602	103.428
3 Borden, Inc.	1.448	2.554	72.962
4 Esmark, Inc.	1.088	3.951	48.802
5 Beatrice Foods Co.	1.088	2.787	90.391
6 Ralston Purina Co.	1.133	2.434	77.550
7 United Brands Co.	1.238	1.991	25.363
8 CPC International Inc.	1.201	1.874	75.493
9 Consolidated Foods Corp.	1.008	2.043	72.133
	11.324	23.868	

12–Beverages, 1973 (ranked by assets and sales)

COMP RANK	Name	Assets ($ billion)	Sales ($ billion)	Net Income ($ million)
1	Coca-Cola Company	1.394	2.145	214.981
2	PepsiCo, Inc.	1.150	1.727	79.596
		2.544	3.872	

13–Tobacco, 1973 (ranked by assets and sales)

COMP RANK	Name	Assets ($ billion)	Sales ($ billion)	Net Income ($ million)
1	R.J. Reynolds Industries	2.612	3.295	263.569
2	American Brands, Inc.	2.161	3.096	131.298
3	Philip Morris, Inc.	2.108	2.603	148.632
		6.881	8.994	

14–Textiles, 1973 (ranked by assets and sales)

COMP RANK	Name	Assets ($ billion)	Sales ($ billion)	Net Income ($ million)
1	Burlington Industries	1.582	2.100	82.391

15–Apparel Products, 1973 (ranked by assets and sales)

COMP RANK	Name	Assets ($ billion)	Sales ($ billion)	Net Income ($ million)
1	Rapid American Corp.	1.756	2.697	29.529

16–Paper & Wood Products, 1973 (ranked by assets and sales)

COMP RANK	Name	Assets ($ billion)	Sales ($ billion)	Net Income ($ million)
1	Minnesota Mining & Manufacturing	2.281	2.546	295.527
2	Weyerhaeuser Co.	2.327	2.302	348.811
3	International Paper Co.	2.197	2.314	159.800
4	Georgia-Pacific Corp.	2.002	2.229	162.810
5	Champion International Corp.	1.700	2.208	86.757
6	Boise Cascade Corp.	1.585	1.324	141.850
7	Crown Zellerbach Corp.	1.238	1.364	102.597
		13.330	14.287	

17–Chemicals, 1973 (ranked by assets and sales)

COMP RANK	Name	Assets ($ billion)	Sales ($ billion)	Net Income ($ million)
1	E.I. du Pont de Nemours	4.832	5.276	585.600
2	Union Carbide Corp.	4.163	3.939	290.942
3	Dow Chemical Co.	3.896	3.086	275.568
4	Monsanto Company	2.545	2.648	238.300
5	W.R. Grace & Co.	2.004	2.808	84.636
6	Allied Chemical Corp.	1.763	1.665	95.071
7	Celanese Corp.	1.747	1.609	81.000
8	American Cyanamid Co.	1.442	1.472	113.962
9	Borg-Warner Corp.	1.172	1.550	113.601
		23.564	24.035	

18–Petroleum Refining, 1973 (ranked by assets and sales)

COMP RANK	Name	Assets ($ billion)	Sales ($ billion)	Net Income ($ million)
1	Texaco Inc.	13.595	11.407	1,292.403
2	Standard Oil Co. of California	9.082	7.762	843.577
3	Atlantic Richfield Co.	5.109	4.489	270.185
4	Cities Service Co.	2.660	2.035	146.900
5	Getty Oil Co.	2.355	1.741	142.237
6	Ashland Oil, Inc.	1.437	2.361	85.219
7	Standard Oil Co. (Ohio)	1.964	1.482	89.385
8	Marathon Oil Co.	1.572	1.579	143.347
9	Pennzoil Company	2.001	1.059	83.661
		39.775	33.915	

19–Rubber, 1973 (ranked by assets and sales)

COMP RANK	Name	Assets ($ billion)	Sales ($ billion)	Net Income ($ million)
1	Goodyear Tire & Rubber	3.871	4.675	184.756
2	Firestone Tire & Rubber	2.669	3.155	164.861
3	Uniroyal, Inc.	1.581	2.083	47.094
4	B.F. Goodrich Co.	1.475	1.661	56.057
5	General Tire & Rubber Co.	1.234	1.380	76.846
		10.830	12.954	

20–Pharmaceuticals, 1973 (ranked by assets and sales)

COMP RANK	Name	Assets ($ billion)	Sales ($ billion)	Net Income ($ million)
1	Warner-Lambert Company	1.389	1.670	138.638
2	American Home Products	1.126	1.784	199.155
3	Johnson & Johnson	1.189	1.612	148.378
4	Pfizer Inc.	1.408	1.284	120.699
		5.112	6.350	

21–Soaps & Cosmetics, 1973 (ranked by assets and sales)

COMP RANK	Name	Assets ($ billion)	Sales ($ billion)	Net Income ($ million)
1	Procter & Gamble Co.	2.687	3.907	302.103
2	Colgate-Palmolive Co.	1.151	2.195	88.769
		3.838	6.102	

22–Glass, Cement, & Concrete, 1973 (ranked by assets and sales)

COMP RANK	Name	Assets ($ billion)	Sales ($ billion)	Net Income ($ million)
1	Owens-Illinois, Inc.	1.643	1.857	130.931
2	PPG Industries	1.491	1.513	104.448
		3.134	3.370	

23–Metal Manufacturing, 1973 (ranked by assets and sales)

COMP RANK	Name	Assets ($ billion)	Sales ($ billion)	Net Income ($ million)
1	United States Steel Corp.	6.919	6.952	325.758
2	Bethlehem Steel Corp.	3.919	4.138	206.609
3	LTV Corp.	1.829	4.175	49.888
4	Armco Steel Corp.	2.259	2.390	107.454
5	Aluminum Co. of America	2.821	2.157	104.188
6	National Steel Corp.	2.024	2.103	98.072
7	Republic Steel Corp.	1.862	2.069	86.744
8	Reynolds Metals Co.	2.118	1.450	45.139
9	Inland Steel Co.	1.559	1.829	83.129
10	Kaiser Aluminum & Chemical	1.815	1.280	44.538
11	Anaconda Co.	1.690	1.343	88.053
12	Illinois Central Industries	1.737	1.172	58.285
13	Lykes-Youngstown Corp.	1.482	1.092	36.408
14	Eaton Corporation	1.140	1.550	85.601
		33.174	33.700	

24–Metal Products, 1973 (ranked by assets and sales)

COMP RANK Name	Assets ($ billion)	Sales ($ billion)	Net Income ($ million)
1 Continental Can Co.	1.753	2.540	95.169
2 American Can Co.	1.544	2.182	66.423
3 Burroughs Corporation	1.696	1.264	115.890
	4.993	5.986	

25–Appliances, Electronics, 1973 (ranked by assets and sales)

COMP RANK Name	Assets ($ billion)	Sales ($ billion)	Net Income ($ million)
1 General Electric Co.	8.324	11.575	585.100
2 International Telephone and Telegraph	10.133	10.183	527.837
3 Westinghouse Electric	4.408	5.702	161.928
4 RCA Corp.	3.301	4.247	183.700
5 The Singer Company	1.897	2.528	94.500
	28.063	34.235	
Dominant Subsidiaries*			
General Telephone & Electronics	10.749	5.105	352.076
Western Electric Co.	4.828	7.037	315.305
	15.577	12.142	

*Both dominant subsidiaries are 100% owned by American Telephone & Telegraph, dominant in utilities.

26–Measuring, Scientific, & Photographic, 1973 (ranked by assets and sales)

COMP RANK Name	Assets ($ billion)	Sales ($ billion)	Net Income ($ million)
1 Eastman Kodak Co.	4.302	4.036	653.475
2 Xerox Corp.	3.102	2.990	300.484
	7.404	7.026	

27–Motor Vehicles & Parts, 1973 (ranked by assets and sales)

COMP RANK	Name	Assets ($ billion)	Sales ($ billion)	Net Income ($ million)
1	General Motors Corp.	20.297	35.798	2,398.103
2	Ford Motor Co.	12.954	23.015	906.500
3	Chrysler Corp.	6.105	11.774	255.445
4	Bendix Corp.	1.427	2.230	68.700
5	The Signal Companies	1.378	1.711	58.371
		42.161	74.528	

28–Aircraft & Parts, 1973 (ranked by assets and sales)

COMP RANK	Name	Assets ($ billion)	Sales ($ billion)	Net Income ($ million)
1	McDonnell Douglas Corp.	2.503	3.003	129.529
2	Lockheed Aircraft Corp.	1.855	2.757	16.812
3	Boeing Co.	1.683	3.335	51.215
4	TRW Inc.	1.446	2.165	95.068
5	United Aircraft Corp.	1.266	2.289	58.136
6	Textron Inc.	1.310	1.859	100.837
7	General Dynamics Corp.	.994	1.642	41.343
		11.057	17.050	

29–Farm & Industrial Machinery, 1973 (ranked by assets and sales)

COMP RANK	Name	Assets ($ billion)	Sales ($ billion)	Net Income ($ million)
1	International Harvester Co.	2.813	4.193	114.296
2	Caterpillar Tractor Co.	2.233	3.182	246.845
3	Deere & Company	1.761	2.003	168.479
4	FMC Corporation	1.380	1.719	79.190
		8.187	11.097	

30–Office Machinery, 1973 (ranked by assets and sales)

COMP RANK	Name	Assets ($ billion)	Sales ($ billion)	Net Income ($ million)
1	International Business Machines	12.290	10.993	1,575.467
2	Honeywell Inc.	2.583	2.391	103.885
3	Litton Industries, Inc.	2.116	2.468	43.030
4	Sperry Rand Corp.	1.841	2.229	90.057
5	NCR Corp.	1.834	1.816	71.961
		20.664	19.897	

31–Other Machinery, 1973 (ranked by assets and sales)

COMP RANK	Name	Assets ($ billion)	Sales ($ billion)	Net Income ($ million)
1	Rockwell International	2.014	3.179	103.983
2	Gulf & Western Industries	2.364	1.927	89.216
3	American Standard Inc.	1.172	1.529	39.523
4	Teledyne, Inc.	1.230	1.456	65.363
		6.780	8.091	

APPENDIX VII

Average Sizes of Dominant U.S. Corporations by Sector

Sector	Number	Assets	Sales	(or)
		($ billions)		
Finance				
Banks	20	17.651	14.169	(deposits)
Life insurance	9	15.186	92.715	(insurance in force)
Other finance	6	4.627	1.754	(operating revenue)
Trade	10	2.542	5.353	(operating revenue)
Transportation				
Railways	8	2.866	1.262	(operating revenue)
Airlines	7	1.591	1.383	(operating revenue)
Other transportation	2	1.875	2.320	(operating revenue)
Utilities	16	7.864	2.631	(operating revenue)
Resources				
Metal mining	2	1.845	1.366	
Oil & gas extraction	11	6.972	6.842	
Manufacturing				
Food	9	1.258	2.652	
Beverages	2	1.272	1.936	
Tobacco	3	2.294	2.998	
Textiles	1	1.582	2.100	
Apparel	1	1.756	2.697	
Paper & wood	7	1.904	2.041	
Chemicals	9	2.618	2.671	
Petroleum refining	9	4.419	3.768	
Rubber	5	2.166	2.591	
Pharmaceuticals	4	1.278	1.588	
Soaps & cosmetics	2	1.919	3.051	
Glass, cement, & concrete	2	1.567	1.685	
Metal manufacturing	14	2.370	2.407	
Metal products	3	1.664	1.995	
Appliances, electronics	7*	6.234	6.625	
Measuring, scientific	2	3.702	3.513	
Motor vehicles & parts	5	8.432	14.906	
Aircraft & parts	7	1.580	2.456	
Farm & indus. machinery	4	2.047	2.774	
Office machinery	5	4.133	3.979	
Other machinery	4	1.695	2.023	

*Includes two dominant subsidiaries.

APPENDIX VIII

Trends in Corporate Interlocking in the United States, 1899 to 1970

Several studies of interlocking directorates in the United States have been made, and a brief review of them will show how the practice has changed. A study by David Bunting and Jeffery Barbour covers the longest period of time. They examined interlocking among 207 companies for the years 1899, 1905, 1935, and 1964, covering "the 100 largest industrial corporations, fifty largest public utilities, twenty-five largest transport companies, twenty largest banks, and twelve largest investment houses."[1] These companies include some on our list of 194 dominants, but there are some important differences. We have systematically selected dominant corporations by comparing their size on two dimensions of control (assets and revenue, or other appropriate indicators) both within and between sectors, and we have also included the trade sector and life insurance companies. It is likely that Bunting and Barbour incorporated resources with manufacturing under the heading "Industrials." While the two studies cannot be directly compared, it is possible to establish some long-term trends because their own data are comparable over the period they review.

The conclusion of Bunting and Barbour is that there is a long-term trend toward less interlocking within their top 207 corporations; they found "more interlocking in 1905 than in 1935 and more in 1935 than in 1964." This was not the result of a lower number of interlocked corporations over the time period; "while the number of interlocked corporations remained virtually the same, the extent to which they were interconnected declined greatly."[2] In other words, the density of interlocking* declined. These 207 corporations averaged thirteen interlocks in 1899; there were eighteen in 1905, but they then began to decline to an average of ten by 1935 and eight by 1964.[3] Even with this relative decline, the authors report that for the most recent period, 1964, 68 per cent of the non-financial corporations in their sample were interlocked with at least one of twenty banks.[4] As one would expect from their general findings, they also report that the proportion of individuals with multiple directorships (that is, in more than one of the top 207 corporations) had also decreased.[5] Two other studies of U.S. interlocks, however, come to somewhat different conclusions.

Peter Dooley's study of interlocking covers a similar but briefer period (1935 and 1965) and uses a somewhat different set of corporations. For 1935, he uses the National Resources Committee study of the two hundred largest non-financial corporations and fifty largest financial corporations ranked by assets and for 1965, the two hundred largest non-financials (115 industrial, 10 merchandising, 25 transportation, 50 public utilities) and fifty financial (thirty-two banks and eighteen life insurance).[6] His study is not directly comparable to

---

* "Density of interlocking" means the frequency with which interlocks occur, not simply that *an* interlock exists. For example, when one person has a position on two boards of directors, the companies concerned are interlocked, but they are not interlocked as *densely* as when two or more persons have positions on the same two boards. Thus the density declines if the number of persons interlocking two companies is reduced from, say, two to one, but the companies remain interlocked.

either this one or that of Bunting and Barbour but is consistent within the two periods he compares. Dooley's results are different from those reported by Bunting and Barbour; he found that in 1935, 18 per cent of the directors held multiple directorships, accounting among them for 37 per cent of all directorships, while in 1965, 18 per cent again held multiple directorships, this time with 35 per cent of the directorships.[7] Among the corporations themselves, "more of the top 250 corporations were interlocked in the later period."[8] The differences between the two studies may be attributable to differences in sample size and the types of companies covered, since Dooley also included life insurance companies and merchandising as well as twelve more banks in his study.

A third study, conducted by Michael Allen, covered two periods, 1935 and 1970. Like Dooley's, the study of 1935 used as the baseline the National Resource Committee study, and the data for 1970 were gathered by Allen himself. Each period includes the two hundred largest non-financial and fifty largest financial corporations ranked by assets. The composition of the two samples differs somewhat, reflecting relative changes in the size of corporations within various sectors. The Allen sample for 1970 includes 33 banks, 17 life insurance companies, 125 industrials, 17 transportation, 10 retailing, and 48 utilities.[9] Allen's results indicate that the 250 major corporations had the same average number of interlocks, 10.4, for each period. There are, however, some interesting differences in the sectors. The financial corporations in the sample increased their averages from 14.8 to 16.9 and the industrials from 8.3 to 9.6 while the non-industrial and non-financial corporations dropped from 10.3 to 7.4.[10] Allen also finds that "the number of corporations with no interlocks declined from 25 in 1935 to 13 in 1970," which confirms and even extends Dooley's finding in this respect, and he adds that "the number of corporations with more than 25 interlocks declined from 23 in 1935 to 14 in 1970."[11] From this evidence he concludes "that the structure of corporate interlocking is becoming more pervasive and integrated through time in that more corporations maintain interlocks with other corporations. However, this structure of corporate interlocking is also becoming less centralized through time in that fewer corporations maintain a large number of interlocks with other corporations."[12] In other words, the general pattern over time calls for an increasing number of interlocked companies but with a lower density of interlocks. Moreover, there is an increasing role for financial corporations (banks and life insurance) in the interlocking patterns. In Canada the pattern between 1951 and 1972 is toward an increasing frequency *and* density of interlocks.[13]

APPENDIX IX

Interlocking Among 194 Dominant U.S. Corporations

Number of Interlocks	Number of Companies	
53	1	Citicorp
44	1	J.P. Morgan & Co.
43	1	Metropolitan Life
41	1	Manufacturers Hanover
40	1	Chemical New York
39	1	First Chicago Corp.
38	1	American Telephone & Telegraph
37	1	New York Life
36	1	General Motors
35	1	Continental Illinois
34	1	International Business Machines
33	1	Chase Manhattan Corp.
30	1	United States Steel
27	1	Westinghouse Electric
26	2	Equitable Life; General Foods
25	4	American Express; Continental Can; Kraftco; Mellon National
24	6	Bank of America; Caterpillar Tractor; Chrysler; General Electric; National Detroit; Sears, Roebuck
23	2	Bankers Trust New York; Continental Corp.
22	2	International Harvester; Union Carbide
20	2	Consolidated Edison; Southern Pacific
19	5	Commonwealth Edison; Federated Department Stores; Goodyear; Kennecott Copper; Western Bancorp
17	3	Charter New York; Pan American World Airways; Uniroyal
16	10	Borg-Warner; Continental Oil; Exxon; W.R. Grace; S.S. Kresge; Mobil Oil; National Steel; Northwestern Mutual Life; Procter & Gamble; Standard Oil of California
15	7	Aetna Life; Aluminum Co. of America; Atlantic Richfield; Burlington Northern; Trans World Airlines; TRW; Wells Fargo & Co.
14	8	Bendix; Detroit Edison; Eastman Kodak; Esmark; NCR Corp.; Prudential Insurance; Singer; Union Pacific
13	9	Allied Chemical; Bethlehem Steel; Borden; Burroughs; FMC Corp.; Getty Oil; Minnesota Mining & Manufacturing; Pacific Gas & Electric; UAL, Inc.
12	15	American Can; Colgate-Palmolive; Crocker National; Ford; General Dynamics; Great Atlantic & Pacific; Honeywell; INA Corp.; International Paper;

Number of Interlocks	Number of Companies	
		Marcor; Ralston Purina; Republic Steel; Rockwell International; Security Pacific; United Aircraft
11	5	Anaconda; First Bank System; International Telephone & Telegraph; John Hancock Mutual Life; Southern California Edison
10	10	American Standard; Boeing; Celanese; CPC International; du Pont; Illinois Central Industries; Inland Steel; Northwestern Bancorp; Sperry Rand; Standard Oil (Indiana)
9	12	American Home Products; Champion International; B.F. Goodrich; Monsanto; Owens-Illinois; PepsiCo; Public Service Electric and Gas; RCA Corp.; Safeway; Santa Fe Industries; Shell Oil; Union Oil
8	13	AMAX; American Airlines; Armco Steel; Cities Service; Consumers Power; Eaton Corp.; First National Boston; Lockheed Aircraft; Marine Midland Banks; Northwest Airlines; Standard Oil (Ohio); Texaco; Warner-Lambert
7	13	American Electric Power; Beatrice Foods; Burlington Industries; CNA Financial; Crown Zellerbach; Deere; Eastern Air Lines; Litton Industries; J.C. Penney Co.; PPG Industries; R.J. Reynolds Industries; Signal Companies; Southern Railway
6	12	Consolidated Foods; Gulf Oil; Kaiser Aluminum; Lincoln National; Norfolk & Western Railway; Reynolds Metals; Seaboard Coast Line Industries; Textron; Transamerica Corp.; Travelers Corp.; F.W. Woolworth; Xerox
5	9	American Cyanamid; Boise Cascade; El Paso Natural Gas; Georgia-Pacific; W.T. Grant; Greyhound; Lykes-Youngstown; Texas Eastern Transmission; Weyerhaeuser
4	6	Amerada Hess; Coca-Cola; Firestone; Pfizer; Tenneco; United Brands
3	6	Connecticut General Insurance; Marathon Oil; Philip Morris; Phillips Petroleum; Southern Co.; Sun Oil
2	5	Delta Air Lines; Kroger Co.; McDonnell Douglas; Penn Central; Philadelphia Electric
1	6	American Brands; Columbia Gas; Dow Chemical; General Public Utilities; LTV Corp.; Teledyne, Inc.
0	8	Ashland Oil; Chessie System; General Tire; Gulf & Western; Johnson & Johnson; Occidental Petroleum; Pennzoil Co.; Rapid-American

APPENDIX X

Interlocking Among Dominant U.S. and Canadian Corporations

	U.S.			Canada (All)			Canadian-controlled		
	Number of Inter-locks	Per cent	Cumu-lative Per cent	Number of Inter-locks	Per cent	Cumu-lative Per cent	Number of Inter-locks	Per cent	Cumu-lative Per cent
Over 50	1	0.5	0.5	5	4.4	4.4	5	8.6	8.6
40-49	4	2.1	2.6	3	2.7	7.1	3	5.2	13.8
30-39	8	4.1	6.7	12	10.6	17.7	11	19.0	32.8
25-29	7	3.6	10.3	8	7.1	24.8	5	8.6	41.4
20-24	12	6.2	16.5	8	7.1	31.9	4	6.9	48.3
15-19	25	12.9	24.9	15	13.3	45.2	10	17.2	65.5
10-14	47	24.2	53.6	12	10.6	55.8	3	5.2	70.7
5-9	59	30.4	84.0	20	17.7	73.5	9	15.3	85.6
0-4	31	16.0	100.0	30	26.6	100.0	8	13.8	100.0
Total	194	100%		113	100%		58	100%	

APPENDIX XI

Studies of the U.S. Economic Elite and Executives

Over the years a variety of studies have been made of members of the U.S. economic elite and executives that are important sources of information for determining broad trends within the upper reaches of U.S. corporate power. Data are not available to make systematic comparisons between Canada and the United States because little work has been done in this area in Canada.

The early U.S. studies are of three types: studies of "business leaders," using mail questionnaires; studies of wealth and power, using less systematic but more detailed interest-group analysis; and "elite" studies, using biographical data. The first type includes the study of prominent business leaders for 1928 by F.W. Taussig and C.S. Joslyn (replicated for 1952 by Lloyd Warner and James Abegglen), which is based on a 49 per cent return of usable responses to over 15,000 questionnaires sent out.[1] The major weakness of this study, and others like it, is the looseness of the definition of a "business leader," identified as "a person occupying a position of major executive, partner, or sole owner in a business of such size as to be of more than local importance."[2] Nevertheless, their study seriously questions the dominant ideology of easy access to the business class in general. Like many other investigators, Taussig and Joslyn found that various ascriptive characteristics, such as region of birth (particularly the Northeast), had a great part to play in determining who became a business leader in the United States during the 1920s.[3]

The important common characteristic of this set of people was its class of origin, 57 per cent having had businessmen as fathers, including about 30 per cent who were "major executives and large owners." As they report:

> The outstanding fact brought to light by our data on occupational origins is that, contrary to an American tradition of long standing, the typical figure among present-day business leaders in the United States is neither the son of a farmer nor the son of a wage-earner. Not more than 12 per cent of our respondents had fathers who were farmers, and only about 10 per cent had fathers who were manual laborers. If it is permissible to speak of a "typical figure" in this connection at all, the business man's son is certainly far more eligible for the title. The proportion of respondents having fathers who were business men of one kind or other (owners or executives) is no less than 56.7 per cent.[4]

Their major conclusion is that only "10 per cent of the American population produces 70 per cent of its business leaders."[5] But the claim they make for their data is that it supports a "superiority" rather than a "privilege" explanation of inequality. They rely, without convincing evidence, on "innate differences" within the population to explain their findings: "Lack of native ability rather than lack of opportunity is primarily responsible for the failure of the lower occupational classes to be as well represented as the higher classes."[6] The researchers, even in the face of their own data, are unable to transcend the dominant ideology. They are content to leave the responsibility on biology, with the onus on individuals from labouring classes, instead of focusing on the structure of corporate capitalism and, in the process, privilege.

The second type of study tends to be less systematic than the first but addresses the questions of wealth and privilege directly through the technique of journalism. Most prominent here is the work of Ferdinand Lundberg in *America's Sixty Families* (1937), but the studies of muck-raking journalists such as Gustavus Myers, *History of the Great American Fortunes* (1910) and *A History of Canadian Wealth* (1914), should also be included. Lundberg's work is much more difficult to summarize than the other types of studies except to extract his conclusion that "the United States is owned and dominated by a hierarchy of sixty of the richest families, buttressed by no more than ninety families of less wealth. Outside this plutocratic circle there are perhaps three hundred and fifty other families, less defined in development and in wealth."[7] Like Taussig and Joslyn, Lundberg did not use strict definitions, probably because of the nature of the wealth and power he described. His focus is less on "social types" and the exercise of power than on the social networks and behaviour of the rich, particularly in terms of the marriage patterns and friendships making up "American ruling class families."

Finally, there are elite studies based on biographical data. One example is Chester McArthur Destler's study of forty-three entrepreneurs from the end of the Civil War to the turn of the century. Even in this select group, he found that only 69 per cent were "first generation entrepreneurs" and that 38 per cent were of upper-class backgrounds, 11 per cent of middle-class origin, and 51 per cent from the petty bourgeoisie, with none from the working class.[8] The most extensive early studies of this type were published by C. Wright Mills in an article on the American business elite covering seven generations, and by

William Miller in a series of articles on the period around 1900, collected mainly in his *Men in Business.*

Mills selected from the *Dictionary of American Biography* 1,464 prominent businessmen who were born betwen 1570 and 1879 and divided them into age groups, the most recent of which would have been between forty and seventy years old during the First World War.[9] His analysis has the advantage of being somewhat systematic and covering a long time period. He found that "of the men born between 1570 and 1759, 80.6 per cent were from upper-class homes. Of the men born between 1760 and 1849, only 59.4 per cent were from the upper classes; whereas of those born between 1850 and 1879, 70.7 per cent originated in the upper economic levels of the American social structure."[10] The upper class obviously supplied most of the prominent businessmen in all eras, particularly during the height of mercantilism and after the emergence of corporate capitalism but somewhat less during the era of entrepreneurial capitalism. The men having easiest mobility were those born about 1835, who reached maturity just following the Civil War. As for the broad profile for the entire period, he concludes:

> The typical member of the American business elite is of northeastern origin (61.2 per cent). He did not migrate westward to success. He was definitely of the upper classes by birth (63.7 per cent) and was educated well above the level of the general population (46.6 per cent being in the "higher" category). The father of the business elite has typically (40.4 per cent) been a businessman. And 45.7 per cent of the business elite of America have held office in its various political structures.[11]

Mills later complemented this analysis of prominent businessmen with a study of 275 of the wealthiest people in the United States, including ninety from 1900, ninety-five from 1925, and ninety from 1950. A clear trend can be seen in the class origins of the three groups, with "only " 39 per cent of upper-class origin in 1900, 56 per cent in 1925, and 68 per cent in 1950.[12]

William Miller's study of the business elite in the decade 1900 to 1910 differs from Mills's primarily in the method of selection and, of course, covers only one period. Instead of using a biographical source for reputedly powerful businessmen, Miller systematically chose his elite by taking the presidents, chairmen, and in some cases (as in investment houses) partners of the largest corporations in "(1) manufacturing and mining, (2) steam railroads, (3) public utilities, (4) finance (commercial banking, life insurance, investment banking)."[13] Of the 190 members of the elite identified in this way, 179 could be classified by class of origin. Half came from upper-class origins, 45 per cent from the middle class, and 5 per cent from the lower classes.[14] Contrary to the mythology of the era, "poor immigrant boys and poor farm boys together actually make up no more than 3 per cent of the business leaders."[15] As to ethnic origin, the ancestors of 79 per cent were from the United Kingdom, 3 per cent from Southern Ireland, 12 per cent from Germany, and only 6 per cent from other countries.[16] Like Mills, Miller found that 61 per cent of the native-born were from the Northeast (compared to 39 per cent of the population).[17]

Using only companies in textiles, railways, and steel, Gregory and Neu replicated Miller's study for the 1870s with essentially the same results, although the occupations of the fathers were of somewhat lower status during the earlier period. Between 1870-80 and 1900-10 the father's occupation for this subset changed as follows: businessmen, a rise from 51 to 55 per cent; professionals, an increase from 13 to 22 per cent; farmers, a drop from 25 to 14 per cent; public officials, a rise from 3 to 7 per cent; and workers, a drop from 8 to 2 per cent.[18] These results conform to the general pattern reported by Mills in terms of the shift from entrepreneurial to corporate capitalism. A similar although not identical study of Canadian manufacturers for approximately the same period (1880 to 1910) produced much the same conclusions, with the proportion of businessmen fathers rising from 60 to 69 per cent and that of craftsmen dropping from 6 to 1 per cent, and no labourers reported for either period.[19]

All three of these early U.S. studies have their contemporary counterparts. Following procedures similar to William Miller's, Suzanne Keller made a study of American business leaders covering the periods 1870, 1900, and 1950 and used the chairmen and presidents of the largest corporations for each. She found that the "largest proportion of business leaders in each generation had fathers who were businessmen. This is true for about one-half of the business leaders of 1870 and 1900, rising to nearly three-fifths for the business leaders of 1950."[20] Table XI-1 summarizes the transformations over the whole period.

TABLE XI-1

Occupations of Fathers of Three Generations of Business Leaders *(percentages)*

Father's Principal Occupation	1870 (254)	1900 (168)	1950 (348)	Population (1870)	Population (1900)
Businessman	47	50	57	6	8
Professional	16	25	14		
Lawyer	(5)	(5)	(5)		
Engineer	(0)	(2)	(0)		
Clergyman	(3)	(9)	(2)		
Other	(8)	(9)	(7)		
Public Official or Politician	3	5	1		
Farmer	26	16	15	32	25
Wage or Office Worker	8	4	12	57	59
	100	100	99		

(SOURCE: Suzanne Keller, "The Social Origins and Career Lines of Three Generations of American Business Leaders," p. 69, Table 17.)

Further evidence of the continuity found by Keller comes from the occupations of the grandfathers of the 1950 sample: "42 per cent of the [1950] business leaders had grandfathers who were businessmen, 12 per cent professional men, 33 per cent farmers and only 8 per cent of the grandfathers were wage or office workers."[21] The conclusion reached by Keller is somewhat ambiguous: "Our data, therefore, provides no support for the familiar, if generally undocumented, assertions about the increasing exclusiveness of the leading business stratum. This stratum has always been more closed than has generally been assumed and is, if anything, somewhat more open in the latest period studied than it was in the earlier periods."[22] The data would suggest mounting exclusiveness in terms of leaders with businessmen for fathers, because there is a steady increase from 47 to 50 to 57 per cent over the period. The patterns for both professionals and wage or office workers are somewhat erratic. There is little doubt, given the evidence, that businessmen are consistently much overrepresented for their proportion of the population, while farmers and wage or office workers are always underrepresented by very substantial amounts. The last period shows contradictory trends in which the numbers for both businessmen and wage or office workers are increasing, suggesting that although the core of business leaders remains intact through the years, there can still be an increase in the proportions drawn into their circles from working-class origins.

A further study using a similar methodology was made by Mabel Newcomer, who selected presidents and chairmen of the largest non-financial corporations in the United States for periods centred on the years 1900, 1925, and 1950. Her study differs from Keller's mainly (aside from the shorter time frame) in its exclusion of financial corporations and somewhat different size of sample. As would be expected, the results are strikingly similar. Newcomer found a similar rise in the proportion of fathers who were business executives from 51 to 56 per cent between 1900 and 1950 (compared to Keller's 50 to 57 per cent) while professionals were falling from 22 to 18 per cent and farmers from 21 to 13 per cent. If Newcomer's categories of clerical, skilled, semi-skilled, and unskilled are combined to compare with Keller's wage or office workers, they show an increase from 6 to 13 per cent between 1900 and 1950 compared to Keller's increase from 4 to 12 per cent.[23]*

Following procedures to replicate the Taussig and Joslyn study for 1928, Warner and Abegglen sent out 17,546 questionnaires to business leaders in 1952 and got back a usable total of 48 per cent,[24] almost the same as in the earlier study. As a replication, it has the same weakness of a loose definition for "business leader" but does make possible comparison over time. These studies cover a broader range of businessmen than those by Mills, Miller, Keller, and Newcomer, consciously including both large and small companies, and may thus reflect more accurately a general category of "manager." This difference may account for the variation the authors found in class origins between 1928 and 1952 compared to Newcomer's findings between 1925 and 1950. Over the period, Warner and Abegglen found that the proportion of leaders with fathers who were business owners or executives fell from 58 to 52 per cent,[25] while Newcomer found an increase in that category from 52 to 56 per cent.[26] Nevertheless, the broad distributions by occupational backgrounds for the fathers in both studies are similar. Controlling for shifts in the population, Warner and Abegglen found that the group with businessmen for fathers had declined as a ratio of the population but remained the most overrepresented category.[27]

A study has been made for Canada in 1967 that roughly replicates the Warner-Abegglen study. Its author found that 55 per cent of the managers had fathers who were business owners or executives, compared to the 52 per cent

---

* It is worthwhile noting Newcomer's remark: "And it may be said without further comment that no woman and no Negro has been found among the top executives of this study" (*The Big Business Executive*, p. 42).

Warner and Abegglen found for 1952 in the United States. There were also lower proportions in Canada whose fathers were farmers (6 compared to 9 per cent) and labourers (9 compared to 15 per cent).[28] But the fifteen-year time difference and different selection criteria for the two studies do not allow them to be directly comparable.

Finally, a study by Reinhard Bendix and Frank Howton uses methods similar to those of C. Wright Mills but in addition provides a comparison of all the findings of studies of "business leaders" and elite members in the United States to the point of writing. They selected a one-in-nine sample of all businessmen listed in the *National Cyclopedia of American Biography*, recognizing the limitations of this procedure for the specificity of the definition "elite." They supplemented this source with the *Dictionary of American Biography* to obtain more names for the earliest and with *Current Biography* for the latest period.[29] Table XI-2 summarizes their findings for the five periods. It shows a consistent pronounced pattern of upper-class origins tending to rise over the time periods and negligible working-class origins tending to fall further. These authors, however, point to a stability in the pattern over time[30] and conclude: "Our data allow us, therefore to question the validity of the doctrine that the successful businessman had proved himself to be the fittest in the struggle for survival."[31]

TABLE XI-2

Class Origins of the U.S. Business Elite for Five Periods
(percentages)

Birthdate	1771-1800	1801-1830	1831-1860	1861-1890	1890-1921
Median (plus 50)*	1835	1865	1895	1925	1955
	(91)	(56)	(225)	(281)	(106)
Upper	65	63	69	73	74
Middle	23	25	19	19	20
Working	12	13	11	8	7
	100	100	100	100	100

*This gives an indication of the year the median member of the elite would be in the prime of life.
(SOURCE: Bendix and Howton, "Social Mobility":122, Table 4.2; upper class: businessmen, gentry farmers; middle class: master craftsmen, small entrepreneurs, professionals, government officials, white-collar workers; working class: farmers, manual workers.)

When they compare all of the studies, they note that the "similarity in the *trends* shown by all...is impressive."[32] Four of the five studies document consistently high upper-class recruitment, and only one period in Mills's study showed any meaningful discontinuity. It may safely be concluded then, that there has been a very high degree of upper-class reproduction among U.S. economic leaders over time, despite the mythology to the contrary. The upper economic levels in the United States have been particularly inaccessible to the working class, which makes up the majority of the population.

These studies are not directly comparable to the study of the U.S. economic elite presented in the text, mainly because they focus on business leaders in a general way and use only presidents and chairmen or businessmen listed in biographical sources, while the present study makes use not only of the senior executives but also of the entire board of directors. This study is also more systematic than any of the others in selecting the dominant corporations used to determine members of the economic elite. Given the large number of studies that have previously dealt with the class origins of the top businessmen in the United States, it is not necessary to provide further documentation of the historical continuity. The current study is instead designed to be comparable with studies already available for Canada[33] and to focus on the relationships between members of the U.S. and Canadian economic elites. It has the advantage of being precise in the meaning given to the term "economic elite" and of examining the broad question of power, rather than the question of "leadership" that has been the concern of most of these U.S. studies. No comparisons between the class origins of the business leaders of these studies and those of the economic elite of the present study would be valid because the meaning given to "upper class" here is much more rigorous than the occupational classifications used in earlier studies.

Two other types of studies are relevant here. The first is concerned primarily with the nature of the U.S. upper class[34] and has already been discussed in the text. The other type consists of a series of surveys by *Fortune* magazine. In 1952, *Fortune* sent questionnaires to the three highest-paid executives of each of the 250 largest industrials, the 25 largest railroads, and the 25 largest utilities (but not to financial or merchandising companies). From the 65 per cent return to a question on fathers' occupations, *Fortune* found that 63 per cent of the respondents had fathers who were in business, 16 per cent who were in a profession or government, and only 21 per cent who were farmers or labourers.[35] A more selective survey of young executives in 1965 by Walter Guzzardi found equivalent responses of 43 per cent upper class, 35 per cent middle class, and 21 per cent working class.[36] In 1970, *Fortune* surveyed the chief executives of its Top 500 industrials and concluded:

> American lore is filled with tales of the up-from-nowhere achiever, but the reality is that most chief executives grew up in comfortable middle- and upper-middle-class surroundings. Only 16 per cent are the sons of blue-collar workers or farmers. All the rest got a first-hand view of the executive world from fathers with an entrepreneurial frame of mind or who closely served those who did. Forty-five per cent of their fathers stood at the top of the business hierarchy either as founder, chairman of the board, or president of the company, or as a self-employed businessman.[37]

This survey clearly confirms the broad patterns found earlier among the more systematic studies. Corporations in the United States have not provided equal opportunities for all classes. Instead, the top positions in U.S. corporations have been the preserve of the most privileged – the children of the upper class.

Very recently (May 1976) *Fortune* conducted another survey of the "Top 800" chief executive officers of the five hundred largest industrials and the fifty largest banks, life insurance, diversified finance, retail, transportation, and utilities companies. From the eight hundred questionnaires sent out they had a return of 492 (or 61.5 per cent), but the published article is based on a return of only 52 per cent. This time the authors state: "One of the hoariest myths about the top corporate officer is that he comes primarily from a wealthy or at least upper-middle-class background, and thus has a special advantage in getting to the top. There may have been a grain of truth to the idea in years past, but the backgrounds of today's chief executives suggest that the notion is now thoroughly obsolete."[38] This claim notwithstanding, their own data show that the fathers of half the subjects in their returns were business executives, and a quarter were professionals. Thus three-quarters of these chief executives had fathers in business and the professions; only a fifth were the children of clerical, skilled, or semi-skilled workers and one-twentieth of farmers.

APPENDIX XII

Methodological Note on Biographical Data for the Elite

In *The Canadian Corporate Elite*, I was attempting to analyse changes that had taken place in the economic elite between 1951 (the date of John Porter's *The Vertical Mosaic*) and 1972, and it was thus necessary to use comparable categories. Since the present analysis relies on two sets of data I have gathered myself, I have adjusted the categories slightly to afford comparisons between the U.S. and Canadian economic elites. In adjusting the Canadian categories I have taken the opportunity to gather additional amplifying material on the nature of the Canadian economic elite. As a result, although the data for Canada presented here are more accurate, they are not strictly comparable with the 1951 Canadian data. The differences between the original and the revised 1972 data on the elite do, however, reflect the "conservative" nature of data based on biographical information as a source.

Combining the senior executives of the 194 dominant U.S. corporations identified in Appendix VI with the directors of these corporations (see Appendix XI) produces a set of 2,450 members of the economic elite. Biographical information was available for 2,007 of these or 82 per cent of the total. This group of 2,007 elite members holds 86 per cent of the dominant U.S. positions and is almost the same proportion of the whole as the original sample of the Canadian economic elite (82 per cent of the elite and 88 per cent of the positions; see Clement, *The Canadian Corporate Elite*, pp. 172 ff). The revised data for the Canadian elite are somewhat improved, increasing the coverage of elite members to 84 per cent holding 90 per cent of the positions.* Since the statistics shown in this study are based on identical criteria and the coverage is virtually the same, there is no problem of comparability.

---

* Adequate biographical material was lacking for 443 members of the U.S. economic elite, holding 461 positions; only one held three dominant positions, sixteen held two, and the remaining 426 held one. In Canada, biographical data were not available for 148 members of the elite, holding 152 positions; only four held two dominant positions, and the rest had one.

Various biographical sources were consulted for both the Canadian and the U.S. economic elites and their relatives. For a listing of the Canadian sources used, see Clement, *The Canadian Corporate Elite*, p. 221. The following are the U.S. sources, both contemporary and historical: *Appleton's Cyclopedia of American Biography; Biographical Dictionary of the United States Executive Branch; Biographical Encyclopedia of America; The Blue Book; Concise Dictionary of American Biography; Current Biography; Dictionary of American Biography; Encyclopedia of American Biography; Fortune* magazine; *International Businessmen's Who's Who; Notable American Women; The International Who's Who; The New York Times Biographical Edition; The New York Times Obituaries Index; Notable Americans; Poor's Register of Corporations – Directors and Executives; Webster's Biographical Dictionary; Webster's American Biographies; Who's Who in America; Who's Who in American History; Who's Who in American Politics; Who's Who in American Women; Who's Who in Banking; Who's Who in Commerce and Industry; Who's Who in the East; Who's Who in Finance and Industry; Who's Who in Government; Who's Who in the West; Who Was Who in America; Who Was Who in American Politics.*

APPENDIX XIII

The "Ownership/Control" Debate in the United States: The Power of Property

Theoretical issues concerning two aspects of the "ownership/control" debate – the role of managers and the dispersal of stock ownership – especially as they apply to Canada, have already been analysed.[1] But since arguments about the power of managers and the dispersal of ownership, particularly as they relate to the decline of family capitalism and private property, play a much greater part in the dominant mythology of the United States, it is necessary to make a further examination of how the same issues are applicable to the United States and the 194 dominant corporations listed in Appendix VI.

As far as Canada's economic relations with the United States are concerned, it can be demonstrated that the separation of ownership and control is a non-issue. Since most U.S. ownership in Canada is in the form of branch plants, ownership of the stock is highly concentrated in the parent corporation. As reliable Canadian management is found, controls in terms of direct overseeing can be loosened. There is no loosening, however, of the tie of subsidiary to parent or the enforced conformity of the subsidiary to the overall policy of the corporate complex set out by the parent's board. It is the kind of ownership in the parents themselves that must now be examined.

Basically, the "ownership/control" debate revolves around whether continuous capital ownership is the main mechanism for controlling corporations or whether the control has passed into the hands of the management of these bureaucratic apparatuses. Another question is whether or not stock ownership has become so dispersed in advanced capitalist societies that it is no longer a bridle on the power of corporate managers, who are not supposed to be accountable to any of the traditional rights of property. The argument is summarized thus by Nichols: "Managerialists have written of a 'divorce' or 'separation' of ownership and control. In this context we find it more fitting to write of a 'marriage of convenience.'"[2] That is to say, the advent of corporate capitalism created a co-operative relationship between owners and managers, and the synthesis of the two is to be found in the board rooms of dominant corporations. The board of directors is now the focal point of power under corporate capitalism, bringing together major stockholders, these stockholders' representatives, and corporate executives.

These issues have been most thoroughly discussed for the United States by Maurice Zeitlin in a paper published in 1974 that draws together the major arguments and relevant evidence. Zeitlin argues that the fact that a process of bureaucratization has accompanied corporate capitalism is not sufficient grounds for contending that control has passed to the administrators of the bureaucracies. Specifically, "there is nothing in bureaucratic management itself that indicates the bureaucracy's relationship to extrabureaucratic centres of control at the apex or outside of the bureaucracy proper, such as large shareowners or bankers."[3] Just because property interests may not engage directly in management activities does not relieve the managers of control by property interests. Zeitlin's argument is based on the common class of the owners and executives of large corporations; that is, "'owners' and 'managers' of the large corporations, taken as a whole, constitute different strata or segments – when they are not merely agents – of the same more or less unified social class."[4]

The project he sets out "demands research concerning the ensemble of social relations, concrete interests, and overriding commitments of the officers, directors, and principal shareowners of the large corporations in general" to prove the common class basis of these three segments of the capitalist class.[5] The one corporate institution that draws these three segments together is the board of directors, and only the board is endowed with the capacity to formulate and implement policies taking each into account. Furthermore, Zeitlin warns that the relationships must not be reduced to the board rooms of individual corporations; instead, the analyst must attempt "to see the pattern of power relationships of which this corporation is merely one element."[6] To do this involves an analysis of an entire web of social, economic, and familial ties that combine to make the individuals in control a social class.

The dispersal of ownership, it has frequently been said, has meant the demise of family capitalism. While family capitalism is not the only means by which ownership can exercise control, it is the one where it is most difficult to demonstrate the relationship between ownership and control. Nevertheless, some evidence has been adduced that family capitalism still has an important place among the largest corporations in the United States. For example, Robert Sheehan found that 150 of the 1967 *Fortune* 500 list of largest industrials were controlled (defined as holding 10 per cent or more of voting stock, compared to the Patman Committee's 5 per cent criterion) by an individual or a single family. Of these corporations, seventy were controlled by the families of the founders.[7] More recently, a systematic study by Philip Burch gives an analysis of the top three hundred industrials and the top fifty companies in the merchandising, transportation, and banking sectors. He groups these 450 corporations into three categories: probably management-controlled, possibly family-controlled and probably family-controlled.*

TABLE XIII-1

Burch's Classification of 450 U.S. Corporations by Control *(percentages)*

	Probably Management	Possibly Family	Probably Family
Top 300 Industrials	40	15	45
Top 50 Merchandising	30	10	60
Top 50 Transportation	46	14	40
Top 50 Banks	48	20	32

(SOURCE: P.H. Burch, *Managerial Revolution Reassessed*, pp. 70, 98.)

Table XIII-1 summarizes Burch's findings for these corporations. Of the whole group, 42 per cent are probably family-controlled, 41 per cent probably management, and 17 per cent possibly family.[8] Equally important are his findings that among the companies classified as family firms, in 93 per cent of the industrials, 97 per cent of firms in the merchandising sector, 77 per cent in the transportation sector, and 80 per cent in banking, the family "has served in various major executive capacities" and that in the overwhelming majority of cases, this family control has persisted for over a decade.[9] Burch concludes:

> The rather pervasive family control exercised over a substantial number of the total 450 industrial, merchandising, transportation, and commercial banking concerns included in this analysis is, for the most part, of a very direct and enduring nature. That is to say, not only is this control exercised through significant stock ownership and outside representation on the board of directors, but also, in a great many cases, through a considerable amount of family managerial direction of these major corporate enterprises.[10]

What is the effect of applying Burch's classifications to the 194 dominant U.S. corporations identified earlier? Table XIII-2 summarizes the results. Thirty-nine of the 194 did not fit Burch's classification. Of the rest, 45 per cent are probably management-controlled, compared to his total of 41 per cent for the 450 firms, 23 per cent are possibly family, compared to 17 per cent, and 32 per cent are probably family, compared to 42 per cent. While more of the 194 dominant corporations tend to be classified as managerial, there is still a proportion of 55 per cent possibly and probably family-controlled firms even among these largest corporations. Furthermore, it was demonstrated in Chapter 7 that many of the outside directors on boards of dominant corporations belong to the economic elite because they have had careers in family firms,

---

* For a detailed discussion of these three categories, see P.H. Burch, *The Managerial Revolution Reassessed*, pp. 29-35. Burch fails to take into account the possibility of financial control, which is an important mechanism of corporate control, as demonstrated in Chapter 6.

TABLE XIII-2

Control of 194 Dominant U.S. Corporations

	Probably Management*		Possibly Family		Probably Family		Not Available
	Number	%	Number	%	Number	%	Number
Finance	11	61	4	22	3	17	17
Trade	3	33	3	33	3	33	1
Transportation/ Utilities	9	56	5	31	2	13	17
Resources	4	33	5	42	3	25	1
Manufacturing	43	43	19	19	38	38	3
	70	45	36	23	49	32	39

*See footnote below.

although these firms themselves are not dominant. Family capitalism remains an important element at the height of the United States economy.

As was suggested earlier, family capitalism is not the only point at which ownership and control converge. Banks (and some of them are controlled by families) have large blocks of stock in dominant corporations. The Senate Government Operations Committee reported that in 1973 four New York banks held "21.9 per cent of United Airlines, 24.7 per cent of American Airlines, and 13.8 per cent of Western Airlines.... Chase (with two other Rockefeller-Morgan banks) has voting rights to 23.1 per cent of the stock of CBS, to 24.6 per cent of ABC, and to 6.7 per cent of NBC.... In 1967, Chase had a 5.5 per cent interest in Reynolds, and Morgan had 17.5 per cent interest in Kennecott."[11] Little wonder that the Patman Report concluded, "Companies which have previously been characterized as 'management controlled' are probably controlled either by banks or by a combination of minority control through bank trust departments, stockholdings and management control."[12] Foundations are another kind of repository of family capitalism. Many families, such as the Dukes, Fords, Kelloggs, Kresges, Lillys, and Rockefellers, use foundations as a means of consolidating and continuing corporate control[13] For example, the Hartford Foundation owns 33 per cent of Great Atlantic and Pacific, while the Hartford heirs own 25 per cent directly.[14]*

On the surface, it may appear that because of the predatory nature of the giant corporations in buying out smaller family-owned corporations the control exercised by these individuals and families will eventually perish. In fact, in a number of cases the process has been quite the reverse. For example, Horace C. Jones II, who was president of Burlington Industries and is now its chairman and "largest stockholder" (at present directly holding 50,735 shares), "joined

*Burch's classification of Great A&P as only "possibly" family-controlled indicates his conservative view. Burlington Industries was classified as "probably management," as was UAL, whereas there is now clearly identifiable control. These changes were *not* made to Burch's original classifications in Table XIII-2.

Burlington in 1960, when it acquired his family business, Lees Carpets, for 2,166,936 shares."[15] Is this an isolated occurrence? Malcom P. McLean, a director of R.J. Reynolds Industries, would not think so. "Mr. McLean obtained 3.5 million shares or about half of Reynolds' preferred stock, in 1969, when he sold McLean Industries, parent company of Sea-Land Services, the nation's leading containerized freight transportation system to Reynolds."[16] Nor would Edward E. Carlson, who became president of United Air Lines in 1971. He had been a director of UAL since 1970, when Western International Hotels, of which he was chairman, merged with UAL. "The Carlson appointment was engineered by an old friend, Thomas F. Gleed, a Seattle businessman who had been on United's board since 1955.... When Carlson and L.P. Himmelman, president of Western International, came on the board in August following the merger, the time was ripe for a showdown. The two hotelmen are no hired hands; between them they own over 220,000 shares of UAL convertible preferred stock and they lead a group of Western International shareholders who now control 17 per cent of UAL stock, a powerful bloc indeed."[17]

It thus appears that ownership continues to be an important basis of control among dominant corporations.* Daniel Bell's argument that the "singular fact is that in the last seventy-five years the old relation between the two institutions of property and family...has broken down"[18] may be correct for some dominant corporations, but not for most. Some families continue to have sizable controlling interests in dominant corporations. For example, "Gulf Oil was founded by the Mellon family, which still owns some 20 per cent of the company's stock."[19] The Mellon family still has sufficient holdings in Aluminum Company of America to have three members on its board. W.R. Grace and Company and other companies have gone public, but the family continues in control. The Kaiser family interests continue to hold 42 per cent of the common and preferred stock in Kaiser Industries.[20] The du Pont and Heinz families continue with great staying power. Further instances of family capitalism are examined in Chapter 7.

Another element of importance in the ownership/control debate is the role of corporate executives in the exercise of corporate control.† Burch has shown that ruling families continue to supply many of the senior executives in the largest corporations, but in some family firms the executives are not family members. High salaries and stock ownership plans soon bring these executives into the propertied class. Averitt puts the salaries of executives into some perspective when he says that for 1962, "the salaries and bonuses paid the fifty-six

---

* For example, "The new chairman [of United Brands], Max M. Fisher, sixty-seven, made his fortune as an independent oil dealer in Detroit. He took charge of a leaderless company last year to protect his family's holding of 297,800 common shares (about 3 per cent of the total) and 14,400 shares of preferred. His ally in this rescue mission (and vice-chairman) is Seymour Miltstein, fifty-five, a New York real-estate developer who along with his brother Paul and other family members owns 9.3 per cent of the common and 18,700 shares of preferred." The largest block, 20.5 per cent of the shares, is held by Carl H. Lindner (*Fortune* 94 (July 1976):145).

† There is not necessarily a conflict of interest between owners and managers. The owners of business are vitally concerned about strong management, for this is a means of attaining profit. They are equally concerned about control, for it is a means of regulating management and keeping an eye on profit. The more confidence they have in management, the looser the immediate control, but because of the claims of private property, the owners through the directors retain the decision on management selection and fiscal policy.

officers and directors of General Motors exceeded the combined remuneration received by the President of the United States, the Vice-President, 100 U.S. Senators, 435 members of the U.S. House of Representatives, the nine Supreme Court justices, the ten cabinet members, and the governors of the fifty states."[21] In other words, the top fifty-six officers and directors of GM received more than the 606 most powerful political officeholders in the United States combined.

Salaries for executives of dominant corporations are even greater today. For example, in 1974, J. Kenneth Jamieson received compensation of $676,667 as chairman of Exxon Corporation, Maurice Granville $460,761 as chairman of Texaco, Rawleigh Warner, Jr., $596,000 as chairman of Mobil Oil, Bob Rawls Dorsey $544,264 from Gulf Oil, William P. Tavoulareas $489,750 from Mobil Oil, John E. Swearingen $487,891 from Standard Oil Company (Indiana) as chairman, C.C. Garvin, Jr., $485,083 as president of Exxon, and Harold S. Geneen a mere $788,610 as chairman of International Telephone and Telegraph.[22] Bankers tend to be paid on a somewhat lower scale than industrialists but not so little that they would have to put their hands in the till; for example, Walter Wriston, chairman of First National City Bank, received remuneration of only $425,422 in 1974 while A.W. Clausen, chief executive of Bank of America, received $245,000.[23]

A *Fortune* survey of chief executives in 1970 found that "nine out of ten have incomes before taxes ranging from $100,000 to over $1 million."[24] A study by Heidrick and Struggles of executive compensation in Canada (1972) and the United States (1971) showed that 77 per cent of the presidents of industrials in Canada with sales of over $100 million made more than $100,000 a year and that in the United States 87 per cent of presidents of industrials with sales of over $165 million made over $100,000.[25] It is difficult to conceive of executives with these high salaries having interests other than those of the propertied class; even if they are not themselves born in this class, their positions soon project them into it.

The holdings of executives may not represent a controlling interest in the corporation, but they do provide enormous wealth and guarantee of commitment to the property system, which is the foundation of the corporation. R.J. Larner's study of ninety-three chief executives found that forty-one owned over $1 million in stock.[26] As of 1975, David R. Foster, chairman of Colgate-Palmolive, held 52,650 shares in his company; William A. Marquard, Jr., president of American Standard, 57,713; Edward Carlson, chairman of UAL, 89,356 directly and 1,100 indirectly; Charles H. Bell, chairman of the finance committee and a director of General Mills, 70,460.[27] What about the executives with stock option plans but no capital? Companies have been looking after them, with what the *New York Times* termed "Fringe Benefits at the Top," by providing no-interest or low-interest loans to cover the purchases.[28]

A survey of the value of shareholdings in their own companies by presidents of U.S. companies found that 29 per cent had over $1 million and 73 per cent over $100,000 worth of their own company's stock.[29] A *Fortune* survey in 1976 of the "Top 800" chief executive officers of the largest U.S. corporations found that 30 per cent own $1 million or more of their own company's stock; 15 per cent own between $500,000 and $999,000, 29 per cent between $100,000 and $499,999, 16 per cent less than $100,000. Only 10 per cent have no stock in their own company.[30]

There has indeed been a broad trend toward wider dispersion of stock in the United States since the rise of corporate capitalism; but blocks large enough to control ownership continue to exist, and much of the dispersed stock has gone to corporate executives. Outside of these holdings, widespread ownership of stock increases the control power of smaller blocks and allows minority interests to expand the power of their capital. But to the extent that shares are distributed, a greater community of interest among the corporations, as opposed to particularistic interests in individual corporations, is created. The general solidarity of the owning class is thus reinforced, consistent with the cooperation of corporate capitalism rather than the competition of entrepreneurial capitalism.

Among the general U.S. population with high incomes, inheritance also plays a large part. Howard Tuckman reports that "over 66 per cent of the consumer units with incomes of $100,000 or more have some inherited assets, and of these, 57 per cent report that inheritances constitute a substantial portion of their total assets."[31] And even within the population as a whole, ownership of stock remains concentrated among the wealthy. In an article entitled "Stock Ownership Remains with Rich," the *New York Times* said that "the richest two-tenths of 1 per cent of Americans owned 30 per cent of all the stock as of mid-1971. The richest 1 per cent owned just over half of it.... In 1958, the top 1 per cent of dividend recipients received 50.6 per cent of all the dividends paid. Their percentage fell in stages, to 45.9 per cent in 1969 but had risen again to 46.9 per cent by 1971."[32] When only 1 per cent of the income earners receive half the dividends and own half the stock, it is clear that dispersion has not penetrated the society very deeply. Nevertheless, dispersion does serve to increase the capital mobilized by large corporations and, as argued, increases the control value of those with blocks of shares. Private property remains intimately related to control over corporate power.

Wealth is not the same thing as corporate power. For example, the Kennedy family has accumulated great personal wealth (about $400 million), largely through real estate speculation, but Joseph Kennedy "banked" his capital in trust funds and foundations. The money is useful for furthering political careers and has potential for corporate control, but it is essentially *rentier* capital or "passive property" not used to exercise corporate control. Large capital pools accumulated over generations provide continuity among the upper class, but the economic elite puts capital to work to gain control of dominant corporations that are repositories of large amounts of other people's capital. As C. Wright Mills stated, "Power has not been split from property; rather the power of property is more concentrated than is its ownership."[33] Private property remains the basic institution upon which corporations are built, and it confers on those in command of these corporations the power to exercise the rights of property. "Active property" invested in corporations for the purpose of control increases the control value and allows its owners to extend their power much farther than was possible during the days of entrepreneurial capitalism, when capitalists tended to confine their control to the power of their own capital only. Now the corporate form of organization is used to extend the power of property. Within the corporation, the board of directors is the body that exercises the rights of property; it represents the focal point of private ownership and bureaucratic control.

Obviously, the persons in the board room have differing degrees of power.

The president and vice-presidents will be principally concerned with operations, while the chairman's orientation will be toward general policy and external corporate relations. Some outside directors may represent specific financial ties or relations with the state, others may have particular legal skills, and some will be simply token representatives to give the corporation legitimacy. There will be internal hierarchies built around particular offices, committees, and large stock ownership. It is not possible to determine *a priori* which of these are the most powerful. Although some individual members of the economic elite may be particularly powerful, power is generally exercised collectively among the elite, as a collegial activity. Thus, it is not simply individuals *per se* but collectivities of individuals that exercise corporate power. The most powerful collectivities are at home in the board rooms of dominant corporations.

It is also impossible to assign the greatest degree of power to members of the company executive. There are too many instances where boards have thrown out executives who have not performed up to their expectations, some of them from important companies: in October 1975, the directors of the Singer Company forced Donald Kircher, the president, to resign when profits were declining.[34] At Gulf Oil, it was the directors that conducted and implemented an investigation that led to the dismissal of the senior executives as a result of political scandals.[35] In recent years, the chief executives of UAL, Pan American World Airways, and American Airlines have all been removed by the directors.[36] Following the suicide of Eli Black, its chairman, and some political adventures, the board of United Brands took over the executive posts temporarily while searching for new talent to fill the jobs.[37] In an unprecedented move, RCA Corporation's board fired Robert Sarnoff as chairman – unprecedented because his father, General David Sarnoff, had built the company.[38]

These examples do not prove that executives are powerless, only that the collective power of the board is often greater than the individual power of an executive. Studies that do not include directors among the elite miss this important collective aspect of power. Moreover, as the interlocking patterns demonstrated (pp. 162-171), this collective power extends beyond the board rooms of specific dominant corporations into the economic elite in all dominant corporations. The fact that there were over 2,400 interlocked elite positions among the 194 dominant corporations in the United States and 1,848 among the 113 dominant Canadian corporations illustrates the broad collegiality among the entire economic elite.

A survey conducted by Heidrick and Struggles found that U.S. directors agreed solidly (38 per cent) on the most important activity of the board, "setting policy." Other functions agreed upon were "counselling management" (23 per cent) and "auditing management's performance" (19 per cent).[39] It is also important to know that for the most part directors are a self-selecting group. The same study shows that the selection of new directors in 94 per cent of all companies (including 97 per cent of all industrials with sales over $350 million) was mainly in the hands of "present directors."[40]

It should be stressed that the power of position such as that held by corporation executives, based on control through the direct exercise of economic power, and the power of ownership, based on stockholdings, are not unrelated forms of power. The power of position allows its incumbents to demand high salaries plus stock options, each of which is turned into ownership. While aspirants to these positions benefit from upper-class origin, they are just as likely to come from the middle class by way of university training and/or to be long-crawlers in the corporate bureaucracy (especially true of insiders and presidents). On the other hand, the power of ownership can be readily transferred from one generation to another, and it allows those who have it to select the executives, directors, and other holders of top positions – even, if they wish, to place themselves in the chief executive positions. Because the largest blocks of stock in dominant corporations, under the conditions of mature capitalism, tend to be acquired mainly through inheritance, persons of upper-class origin are the most important in terms of the power of property. If someone is able to acquire a position of power and by accumulating significant power of ownership transform it into property, the property can be transferred as an ascribed advantage to the children, who are then able to take advantage of this ownership. The other spin-offs of the power of position should not be underestimated, either, as a way of transferring social status and contacts to children; acquired upper-class positions have other intergenerational rewards besides the power of ownership.

APPENDIX XIV

Immigration Data and Migration Theories

Analysing the flow of managers from country to country by using immigration statistics presents several problems. One is the difficulty of distinguishing between nationality, country of birth, and country of last residence, which are not necessarily the same. Immigration data normally record the last residence, and the lack of adequate information is evident in the consideration of the flows between Canada and the United States. For example, over the relatively short period from 1960 to 1965 "Canadian" emigration to the United States ranges from half Canadian-born to three-quarters Canadian-born.[1]

All discussion of movement between Canada and the United States is complicated by returnees. Neither country records the return of its own citizens because immigration relates only to aliens and emigration records are not kept. It is therefore impossible to distinguish, in the immigration data, between what Anthony Richmond calls "quasi-migrants" and "semi-permanent migrants." When managers are being considered the problem is particularly acute, especially when the foreign posting (a training period at the parent company, for example) is for a relatively short time. L.W. St. John-Jones has described this problem that is exacerbated by the relative ease with which people move between the two countries:

Without some assessment of how long the immigrants remain in the U.S.A. or Canada, all the foregoing figures tell only a part of the story of the U.S.A.–Canada exchange. It is true that each immigrant intended to be more than a merely temporary resident at the time of applying to enter the country – and temporary may mean a few months, or in the case of a worker going to the U.S.A. on a firmly fixed-term assignment, a very few years – but having become an immigrant, he may stay for as little as a year or for as long as a lifetime. Indeed, there is nothing to stop him from leaving at any time after his arrival.[2]

The classification "managerial" is obviously of importance to the study of managerial migration, but the distinction made between "managerial" and other categories in immigration statistics is far from satisfactory.* For example, the proprietor of a corner store and the president of a large corporation are placed in the same category. The classification in use does not distinguish between the positions the managers hold, the types of activities they pursue, and the size of the organizations they are associated with, nor does it show whether the move is "attached" to an organization or is "free." Moreover, the classification is based on "intended occupation," and it is not known what correlation there is between intention and the actual occupation entered. Similarly, there is no follow-up to see whether the migrant "falls" from the occupation recorded or "rises" to a higher one.

Comparability of classifications used by the two nations is also problematical, and the same categories may not exist over the same periods of time. For example, "managerial" has existed as a category for immigration purposes only since 1953 in Canada.

Leaving aside the quality of the data, there are some questions regarding correct interpretation. Between unequal entities, it is difficult to say what is an equal exchange. Is it equal if eleven Canadians migrate to the United States for each one coming to Canada from the United States? The ratio would make about the same impact on each receiving country, but the loss of eleven Canadians would have 121 times as much impact on Canada as the one leaving the United States. What if 100,000 people crossed the border each way; would that be equal? It would represent 1/200 of Canada's population but only 1/2,200 of that of the United States. Either way, it is difficult to say which is equal; any quantity must always be qualified in terms of equality with respect to what. This problem is similar to that encountered earlier in interpreting the flow of capital between Canada and the United States. While it may be true that on a per capita basis more investment moves from Canada to the United States than moves from the United States to Canada, the respective impacts are not at all similar. The size of the U.S. economy allows it to absorb the Canadian capital with ease, while in an economy of Canada's size the same per capita inflow of capital will leave its money dominated by U.S. capital. So it is with migration. An equal exchange of managers (in absolute numbers) would mean that Canada would soon be swamped with U.S. managers.

In order to establish the characteristics of managerial migrants, it is necessary to locate a source of data other than immigration statistics, primarily because there is not enough detail in these statistics and especially because of the looseness of the classification "manager." Theoretically, it can be anticipated from the development of a branch-plant system that a change will occur in the flow and recruitment of management. In the early stages of establishing and integrating branches into parent operations, it is to be expected that a large number of management personnel will be sent from headquarters to oversee these operations. As branches mature, local personnel are trained and become

* It has been pointed out by Richmond that high-level and lower-level managers behave quite differently (*Post-War Immigrants in Canada*, p. 232).

responsible for managing the affairs of the branch. At this point there would be a reduction in the flow of managers from the United States to Canada, and a reverse flow would take place if Canadian resident managers are brought into the promotion system of parent companies. The branches are at different stages in this process, however, and aggregate data would tend to mask possible differences. Some of the evidence already presented suggests that this process is occurring among the largest and most firmly established U.S. continental corporations. At the elite level, the proportion of the Canadian economic elite born in the United States declined from 10 per cent to 6 per cent between 1951 and 1972, in spite of the rapid expansion of U.S. control during the period. It is clear that more recently there has not been the same tendency to send U.S. executives to Canada to run branches of dominant subsidiaries, and there has been a heavier reliance on Canadian-recruited management in these branches.

Economic Theories of Migration

Various theories have been developed to explain the relationships between economic development and the movement of people. P. George contends that "economic migration takes place when demographic pressures in one country are met by a corresponding readiness to receive population in another." He maintains that "numerical proportions are rigidly determined by the development requirements of the new country."[3] Emphasis here is on the selection policy of the receiving country which places limits on the migration that takes place and on the conditions in the country of origin that determine whether or not emigration will be stimulated.

F.D. Scott takes a similar position, maintaining that the "phenomenon of the business cycle in relation to migration indicates also that the causes of migration were located both in the country of origin and in the country of destination. Neither the push nor the pull functioned alone."[4] The most noted proponent of this view is Brinley Thomas. He has, however, adjusted his view in light of developments that occurred in the international economy after 1952. Briefly, his theory is that "viewed as an essential part of the process of economic expansion, migration not only induces but is itself partly determined by changes in the structure of the international community." Built into this theory is the dynamic notion that as the structure of the economy changes, so too changes of migration patterns can be anticipated. His analysis is that nineteenth-century migration followed a flow of capital from Europe to North America but that over time the nature of this relationship changed as initial capital expanded and became established; "ultimately migration dwindles, the direction of capital flow changes and the international economy has to adjust itself to a new set of conditions."[5]

The important development that makes 1952 a benchmark, according to Thomas, is the change of direction of international capital investment from the United States to Europe, which stimulated economic growth in Europe and thereby intracontinental migration in Europe and a different pattern of overseas migration. His revised position is that "international migration no longer plays the role in economic growth that it did in the nineteenth century. Legislative restrictions, the changes in the economic determinants, and the population upsurge in different parts of the world have all tended to reduce the scale of movement."[6] There is an essential difference, according to Thomas, between contemporary capital flows and migration and the patterns of earlier periods. He maintains that when "Britain was the world's largest exporter of capital, there were natural and synchronous flows of private capital, technical skills and unskilled labour from the advanced country to the then developing countries overseas."[7] The result was that the gap between the sending and receiving countries closed with increasing speed, to the mutual benefit of each. Now, however, the question arises "whether, in the new setting, the free international flow of human capital continues to be an economic blessing to the sending as well as the receiving countries, as it was in the nineteenth century."[8]

Thomas now maintains that "the international flow of skills is governed by the rate of growth in the richest sector," not in the developing areas, thus perpetuating and reinforcing the gap rather than closing it.[9] In an earlier phase, people tended to bring their capital with them to developing areas or to bring skills that could be used alongside capital from developed areas. Now capital tends to circulate independent of individual migration, and the flow of skills is out of, rather than into, underdeveloped areas. "With the dice loaded in favour of the industrially advanced, the rate of economic growth in these countries exceeds that of the underdeveloped."[10]

A further element of Thomas's theory, and one stressed by a number of other authors, is the relationship between geographical and social mobility as it is affected by stratification. He suggests that the "actual volume of emigration was governed not only by the driving force of the innovations but also by the degree of internal immobility in the 'old' country,"[11] suggesting that in a rigidly stratified society with low social mobility, there is a stimulus for individuals who aspire to rise to emigrate elsewhere where the structure is less restrictive.

On a related matter, Anthony Richmond's finding that among migrants in Canada the most likely to return home are highly qualified persons from the United States led him to propose the distinction between "quasi-migrants" who stay for short terms and longer-term or "semi-permanent immigrants."[12] He found that only a minority of "repatriates" were actually dissatisfied; "the largest proportions appear to be following an occupational career cycle in which the practical experience gained or the capital saved as migrants is a means of achieving upward social mobility."[13]

As corporations spread across political boundaries, at least for a select group of highly skilled migrants there are fewer intervening factors to impede the search for upward mobility. Migration patterns increasingly become products of the ability of differently skilled individuals to operate in a wider market. That is, the market for highly skilled individuals is much wider than that for the low skilled, and, along with recent immigration policies favouring these types, there is lower resistance to their movement. In addition, Thomas's point that the areas of greatest expansion and production are now able to offer the greatest rewards is suggestive of inducements leading to a selective migration in which movement is by a particular class of people from one area to another.

As transportation and communications have expanded within and between nations in the post-war period, the market for highly qualified manpower can be defined as international in scope. With a wider demand for highly skilled labour, the nation-state, even if it is in a period of economic expansion relative to earlier times, is now often part of a larger market within which opportunities may be greater than they are in the nation-state itself. In other words, with expanded markets comparisons must be made not only with the past, where they may indicate great gains, but also with the present, worldwide, in which the nation may be relatively lacking. Once a nation reaches a certain level of development, it may enter this worldwide market for highly skilled labour and only after reaching this level actually begin to experience a loss of manpower. Prior to that point it may have been isolated from the wider market and therefore able to retain its skilled labour. Canada is an example of a nation with expanding industrialization and increasing numbers of positions for highly qualified manpower that has exported large numbers of such people to the United States, a more advanced industrial centre, while at the same time importing manpower from abroad. Once again, Canada tends to act as a way station or go-between, mediating between the United States and the rest of the world. Taiwan and Japan, two other expanding nations, are also losing manpower to the United States.[14] This suggests that the explanation for loss of highly qualified manpower lies not solely in the development of the nation-state but also in its *relative* position in a worldwide market.

APPENDIX XV

Procedures Used in a Survey of Canadian-Born, U.S.-Resident Managers

A sample of U.S.-resident, Canadian-born managers was located by a search of *Standard & Poor's Register of Directors and Executives* for 1975. Of the 68,000 managers listed there, the names of 558 (or about 0.8 per cent of the total) who had been in Canada but were now resident in the United States were located. The *Register* also lists persons resident in Canada and some born and resident outside the United States. Of these 558, it was possible to find addresses for and send questionnaires to 516 persons. Of the 516, 302 responded, or 59 per cent of the total.

The *Register* provides a minimum amount of data so that it is possible to compare the respondents with those who did not respond on some characteristics. In terms of age, the respondents tend to be somewhat younger than average; the greatest disparity occurred in the group born in 1910 or earlier, where 28 per cent did not respond and 15 per cent responded. The 1911-20 category includes the greatest portion of both those who did not respond (38 per cent) and those who responded (43 per cent). Regarding province of birth the two sets were within 2 percentage points of each other, except in Ontario, where 43 per cent of the non-respondents and 37 per cent of the respondents were born. Region of current residence in the United States was even closer for the two sets, with a maximum of 3 percentage points difference in any of the four regions. Aside from the tendency of the respondents to be younger, which may be because some questionnaires were sent to persons who were dead or retired, the sample and the non-returns are very similar in terms of age and region of residence in the United States.

The two documents that follow are the covering letter and the questionnaire sent to Canadian-born, U.S.-resident managers.

McMASTER UNIVERSITY
Department of Sociology

1280 Main Street West, Hamilton, Ontario, L8S 4M4
Telephone: 525-9140 Local 4481

September 15, 1975

Dear Sir:

In this modern era business has become international. I am
attempting to study the migration of important people from Canada
to the United States and am asking you to help me by answering
a few questions to facilitate this.

I have obtained your name along with those of other Canadian
born businessmen from Standard and Poor's Register of Directors
and Executives, 1975. Although I realize you must be a busy
person, your answering this questionnaire will take only five
minutes of your valuable time. Your cooperation is crucial to
our successful understanding of this modern phenomenon. The
questionnaire is anonymous. If these questions do not apply to
you for some reason, please state why.

I had earlier sent similar questions to other Canadian-born
businessmen in the United States and based on their responses it
was felt it would take you less time to fill out this 'structured'
questionnaire than to have a more 'free flowing response'. Therefore, I hope the formality of the questions is compensated for by
its brevity.

Thank you very much for your cooperation.

Sincerely,

Wallace Clement
Dept. of Sociology
McMaster University

WC/sc

Most of these questions can be answered simply by checking the appropriate box or boxes, or with short answers. This questionnaire is anonymous.

Please return to: Professor Wallace Clement,
                              Department of Sociology,
                              McMaster University,
                              Hamilton, Ontario, Canada.

1. What is your year of birth? 1_____

2. Province of birth?_____

3. Your ethnic origin? British Isles ( ), French ( ), Other ( )_____

4. When did you leave Canada to live 'permanently' in the United States? 19___

5. Were you ever 'temporarily' resident there before?_____

    If so, why?_____

6. Did you simply migrate to the United States ( ) or were you transferred
    within a company ( )?

    If transferred, is that your present company?_____

7. Do you know many other Canadian born businessmen now living in the United
    States?_____

    If so, on what basis: social ( )
                                   business( )
                                   other   ( ), specify_____

8. What kinds of contacts did you have in the United States before moving there?

                                   none   ( )
                                   social   ( )
                                   business (within your company) ( )
                                   other business ( )
                                   family   ( )
                                   other   ( ), specify_____

9. Do you maintain contacts with Canadians now?_____

    If so, on what basis: social ( )
                                   business( )
                                   family ( )
                                   other   ( ), specify_____

10. Did you ever go to school in Canada?_____

    If so, where: private   ( ), specify_____
                                   public or high school ( )
                                   university ( ), specify_____

    If university, type of degree specialty:_____

11. Did you ever go to university in the United States?_____

    If so, where:_____

    For what degree:_____

12. Is your wife from Canada ( ), the United States ( ) or elsewhere ( )?

13. Did you move to the United States with your parents?_____

     If so, why did they move?_____

14. What was your father's occupation?_____
     Was he ever a company official?_____
     What was his highest level of education?_____

15. Are you now a citizen of Canada ( ), the United States ( ) or
     elsewhere ( )?

16. What is the main economic activity of your present company:

                 Manufacturing ( )   Transportation ( )
                 Finance   ( )   Utilities   ( )
                 Resouces   ( )   Trade   ( )
                 Other   ( )_____

     Is that company owned mainly from Canada ( ), the United States ( ) or
     elsewhere ( )?

17. In what area of the company has your main career been? (eg. sales, finance,
     law, etc.)_____

18. Do you think your being Canadian born has been an asset ( ), drawback ( )
     or neutral ( ) in attaining an important position in the United States?

19. Were there any 'barriers' to your succeeding in Canada?_____

     If so, specify_____

20. Do you think you stood a better chance in the United States than in Canada
     of attaining your present position?_____

     Why:

21. What were the (three) major factors affecting your decision to move to and
     remain in the United States?
                    i)

                   ii)

                  iii)

     Generally, why do you think many Canadian businessmen migrate to
     the United States?

THANK YOU VERY MUCH FOR YOUR COOPERATION, WITHOUT IT THIS STUDY WOULD NOT
BE POSSIBLE.

APPENDIX XVI

Two Methods of Determining Class Origins of Managers

Two classifications of class origin were used in studying the Canadian-born, U.S.-resident managers. The first, which permits comparison most easily with the elite studies in Chapter 7, is social class origin determined by combining the answers to the questions on father's occupation and whether he was ever a corporate official. If these questions were not answered, the questions on private school education and university attendance in Canada were substituted. In this classification, working-class origin includes farmers. The second classification of class origin is determined solely by the occupation of the father and whether or not he was a corporate official. When these criteria are used, senior civil servants who have not been corporate officials are classified as new middle class rather than upper class, as they had been in the other categorization. The designation of capitalist class is reserved for those who were corporate officials. Within the middle class, a distinction is drawn between "old" and "new" middle class. The old middle class is composed of independent operators (including farmers), and the new middle class consists of persons employed in a bureaucracy and salaried.

It was possible to use two different categorizations because more detailed occupational data were available for persons born outside the dominant class while more detail for the dominant class is available in the biographical data. Comparing the two categorizations, of managers classified as upper class by the first method, 87 per cent fall into the capitalist class, 8 per cent into the new middle class, and 5 per cent into the old middle class; the different proportions in the two categories are accounted for by senior civil servants and a few attending private schools. Persons in the (social) middle class are divided into 57 per cent in the new middle class and 44 per cent in the old middle class; 40 per cent of those in the (social) working class go into the old middle class and the working class by occupation consists of the other 59 per cent, with the difference accounted for by farmers. The accompanying table summarizes the second categorization in terms of the four types of migrants.

TABLE XVI-1

Class Origin by Occupation of Canadian-Born, U.S.-Resident Managers *(percentages)*

Class (N)	With Parents (116)	To University (39)	Independent Migrant (66)	Transfer (52)
Capitalist	36	33	29	31
New middle	22	23	32	29
Old middle	24	31	27	35
Working	18	13	12	6
	100	100	100	100

In Table 53, nine of the thirty-one managers of working-class origin who migrated with their parents were sons of farmers. In this table, fourteen of the twenty-one of working-class origin who migrated with their parents were sons of skilled labourers. Of all those who have working-class origins when the class by occupation classification is used, twenty were sons of skilled labourers. The conclusion is that even in this group it is largely the upper levels of the working class that supplied sons for managerial positions.

Notes

Preface

1. John Porter, *The Vertical Mosaic*, p. 266.

Chapter One   A Continental Economy and Corporate Power

1. *New York Times* 5 Feb. 1967.
2. *Canadian Forum* July 1929.
3. Herbert Marshall et al., *Canadian-American Industry*, pp. ix, 2.

Chapter Two   A Framework for Analysis of the Continental System

1. Paul Baran, *The Political Economy of Growth*, p. 175.
2. Geoffrey Kay, *Development and Underdevelopment*, p. 90.
3. Ibid., p. 93.
4. Ibid., p. 97.
5. See Fred Block, "Expanding Capitalism: The British and American Cases," *Berkeley Journal of Sociology* 15 (1970): 138-65.
6. Theotonio Dos Santos, "The Structure of Dependence," in *Readings in U.S. Imperialism*, ed. K.T. Fann and D.C. Hodges, pp. 227-28.
7. *Globe and Mail* (Toronto) 7 June 1972: B2.
8. See Robert O. Keohane and Joseph S. Nye, "World Politics and the International Economic System," in *The Future of the International Economic Order*, ed. C. Fred Bergsten.
9. Osvaldo Sunkel, "Transnational Capitalism and National Disintegration in Latin America," *Social and Economic Studies* 22 (1973): 170.
10. Johan Galtung, "A Structural Theory of Imperialism," *Journal of Peace Research* 2 (1972): 104.
11. Ralph Turner, "Modes of Social Ascent through Education: Sponsored and Contest Mobility," in *Class, Status and Power*, ed. R. Bendix and S.M. Lipset, 2nd ed., pp. 450-51.
12. Max Weber, *Economy and Society*, ed. G. Roth and C. Wittich, I: 341-42.
13. Gertrud Neuwirth, "A Weberian Outline of a Theory of Community: Its Implications to the 'Dark Ghetto,'" *British Journal of Sociology* 20 (1969): 148-50.
14. Frank Parkin, "Strategies of Social Closure in Class Formation," in *The Social Analysis of Class Structure*, ed. F. Parkin, pp. 3-4.
15. Ibid., p. 6.
16. C. Wright Mills, *The Power Elite*, p. 11.
17. G. William Domhoff, *The Higher Circles*, pp. 106-7.

18. Ibid., pp. 75-88.

19. E. Digby Baltzell, "'Who's Who in America' and 'The Social Register,'" in *Class, Status and Power*, ed. R. Bendix and S.M. Lipset, p. 267; see also *Philadelphia Gentlemen*, p. 7.

Chapter Three   Setting the Stage for a Continental Economy

1. See William A. Williams, *The Contours of American History*, p. 40.

2. Gustavus Myers, *A History of the Great American Fortunes*, p. 51.

3. Ibid., p. 57.

4. Williams, *Contours*, p. 103.

5. L.M. Hacker, *The Course of American Economic Growth and Development*, p. 29.

6. Wallace Clement, *The Canadian Corporate Elite*, pp. 45-59.

7. D.G. Creighton, *The Empire of the St. Lawrence*, p. 2.

8. R.B. Sheridan, "The British Credit Crisis of 1772 and the American Colonies," in *Views of American Economic Growth*, ed. T.C. Cochran and T.B. Brewer, pp. 51-52.

9. J.B. Brebner, *North Atlantic Triangle*, p. 36.

10. Sheridan, "British Credit Crisis," p. 53.

11. H.A. Innis, *The Cod Fisheries*, pp. 212-13.

12. See E.P. Douglas, *The Coming of Age of American Business*, p. 23, and R.W. Van Alstyne, *Empire and Independence*, pp. 22-24.

13. Brebner, *Triangle*, pp. 31-32.

14. Clement, *Canadian Corporate Elite*, pp. 49-52.

15. Hacker, *American Economic Growth*, p. 43.

16. R.W. Van Alstyne, *The Rising American Empire*, p. 38.

17. C.P. Nettels, "The Economics of the Constitution," in *Views of American Economic Growth*, ed. T.C. Cochran and T.B. Brewer, p. 84.

18. Barrington Moore, Jr., *Social Origins of Dictatorship and Democracy*, p. 112.

19. Fritz Redlich, "First Period: Some Characteristics," in *Views of American Economic Growth*, ed. T.C. Cochran and T.B. Brewer, p. 246.

20. See Cleona Lewis, *America's Stake in International Investments*, p. 12.

21. Charles and Mary Beard, *New Basic History of the United States*, p. 194.

22. T.C. Cochran, "Business Organization and the Development of an Industrial Discipline," in *Views of American Economic Growth*, ed. T.C. Cochran and T.B. Brewer, p. 220.

23. Douglas, *Coming of Age*, p. 92.

24. Cochran, "Business Organization," p. 217.

25. Williams, *Contours*, p. 201.

26. Ibid., p. 186.

27. Lewis, *America's Stake*, p. 17.

28. Van Alstyne, *Rising American Empire*, p. 88.

29. O.J. McDiarmid, *Commercial Policy in the Canadian Economy*, p. 11.

30. Brebner, *Triangle*, p. 81.

31. McDiarmid, *Commercial Policy*, p. 32.

32. Brebner, *Triangle*, p. 70.

33. Jacob Spelt, *Urban Development of South-Central Ontario*, p. 55.

34. H.C. Pentland, "The Role of Capital in Canadian Economic Development before 1875," *CJEPS* 16 (1950): 460-61.

35. See Beard, *Basic History*, pp. 190-91.
36. Ibid., p. 201.
37. Douglas, *Coming of Age*, p. 244.
38. See Myers, *American Fortunes*, pp. 146-90, and Hacker, *American Economic Growth*, p. 77.
39. Douglas, *Coming of Age*, pp. 74-75, 247.
40. Lewis, *America's Stake*, pp. 36-37.
41. Mira Wilkins, *The Emergence of Multinational Enterprise*, p. 35.
42. McDiarmid, *Commercial Policy*, p. 58.
43. See Brebner, *Triangle*, p. 157.
44. R.T. Naylor, *The History of Canadian Business*, I: 67.
45. Moore, *Social Origins*, p. 116.
46. Ibid., pp. 125-26.
47. Hacker, *American Economic Growth*, p. 185.
48. T.C. Cochran, *The American Business System*, pp. 79-80.
49. Douglas, *Coming of Age*, pp. 295-96.
50. Beard, *Basic History*, pp. 293-94.
51. D.C. North, "The United States in the International Economy, 1790-1950," in *American Economic History*, ed. S.E. Harris, p. 199.
52. See Allan Nevins, "The Emergence of Modern America, 1865-1875," in *The Historians' History of the United States*, ed. A.S. Berky and J.P. Shenton, pp. 807-8.
53. Ida M. Tarbell, "The Nationalization of Business, 1879-1898," in *The Historians' History of the United States*, ed. A.S. Berky and J.P. Shenton, p. 923.
54. T.W. Lawson, "Pioneers and Speculators–Westinghouse versus 'The System,'" in *The Robber Barons Revisited*, ed. P. Jones, p. 102.
55. Beard, *Basic History*, pp. 292-93.
56. Nevins, "Emergence of Modern America," pp. 808-10.
57. John Moody, *The Truth about the Trusts*, p. 453.
58. Quoted in R.A. Brady, *Business As a System of Power*, p. 192.
59. A.D. Chandler, Jr., "The Role of Business in the United States," in *The American Corporation*, ed. E. Goldstein et al., p. 43.
60. C. Wright Mills, *The Power Elite*, p. 271.
61. A.D. Chandler, Jr., *Strategy and Structure*, pp. 24-25.
62. A.D. Chandler, Jr., and Stephen Salsbury, "The Railroads: Innovations in Modern Business Administration," in *The Changing Economic Order*, ed. A.D. Chandler, Jr., et al., p. 254.
63. Douglas, *Coming of Age*, pp. 239, 248.
64. Gabriel Kolko, *The Triumph of Conservatism*, p. 59.
65. John Moody, "The Masters of Capital," in *The Historians' History of the United States*, ed. A.S. Berky and J.P. Shenton, p. 453.
66. A.S. Berky and J.P. Shenton, *The Historians' History of the United States*, p. 845.
67. Simon Kuznets, "Production of Capital Formation to National Product," *American Economic Review* 42 (1952): 522-23.
68. E. Digby Baltzell, *Philadelphia Gentlemen*, p. 16.
69. Ibid., p. 21.
70. Kenneth Buckley, *Capital Formation in Canada, 1896-1930*, p. 80.

71. H.G.J. Aitken, "Defensive Expansionism: The State and Economic Growth in Canada," in *Approaches to Canadian Economic History*, ed. W.T. Easterbrook and M.H. Watkins, pp. 183-221.

72. Clement, *Canadian Corporate Elite*, pp. 60-71, 75-86.

73. Brebner, *Triangle*, p. 232.

74. H.V. Nelles, *The Politics of Development*, pp. 233-34.

75. Canada, House of Commons, *Debates*, 1878, p. 854.

76. McDiarmid, *Commercial Policy*, pp. 147-48.

77. Naylor, *Canadian Business*, I: 38.

78. T.W. Acheson, "Changing Social Origins of the Canadian Industrial Elite," *BHR* 47 (1973): 189-217; see also Clement, *Canadian Corporate Elite*, pp. 66-71.

79. McDiarmid, *Commercial Policy*, pp. 248-49.

80. See Herbert Marshall et al., *Canadian-American Industry*, p. 11, and Wilkins, *Emergence of Multinational Enterprise*, p. 461.

81. Marshall et al., *Canadian-American Industry*, pp. 72-73; see also Wilkins, *Emergence of Multinational Enterprise*, pp. 58, 93.

82. Marshall et al., *Canadian-American Industry*, , p. 6.

83. Nelles, *Politics of Development*, p. 149.

84. Wilkins, *Emergence of Multinational Enterprise*, pp. 212-13.

85. Ibid., pp. 72 ff.

86. Lewis, *America's Stake*, p. 173.

87. Kari Levitt, *Silent Surrender*, p. 66, Table 3.

88. See Myers, *American Fortunes*, pp. 674-78.

89. C.M. Destler, "Entrepreneurial Leadership among the 'Robber Barons': A Trial Balance," *Journal of Economic History* 6 (1946): 40.

90. Marshall et al., *Canadian-American Industry*, pp. 16-17.

91. Kolko, *Conservatism*, pp. 26-27.

92. Berky and Shenton, *Historians' History*, p. 1026.

93. Hacker, *American Economic Growth*, p. 252.

94. Chandler, "Role of Business," p. 46.

95. See Cochran, *American Business System*, pp. 83-84.

96. Douglas, *Coming of Age*, pp. 297-98.

97. Williams, *Contours*, pp. 350-51.

98. D.L. Smith, "Sociology and the Rise of Corporate Capitalism," in *The Sociology of Sociology*, ed. L.T. and J. Reynolds, p. 68.

99. Kolko, *Conservatism*, p. 145.

100. A.D. Chandler, Jr., "The Structure of American Industry," *BHR* 43 (1969): 79.

101. Kolko, *Conservatism*, pp. 2-3.

102. Ibid., p. 222.

103. Ibid., pp. 5-6, 58-59.

104. See Myers, *American Fortunes*, pp. 594 ff. and Berky and Shenton, *Historians' History*, pp. 1057 ff.

105. Lewis, *America's Stake*, p. 69.

106. Ibid., pp. 73-77.

107. Stanford Rose, "Why They Call It 'Fat City,'" *Fortune* 91 (1975): 108.

108. See Raymond Vernon, *Sovereignty at Bay*, p. 71.

109. T.C. Cochran and W. Miller, *The Age of Enterprise*, p. 298.

110. Wilkins, *Emergence of Multinational Enterprise*, p. ix.

111. H.G.J. Aitken, "The Changing Structure of the Canadian Economy," in *The American Economic Impact on Canada*, ed. H.G.J. Aitken et al., pp. 4-5.

112. H.G.J. Aitken, *American Capital and Canadian Resources*, p. 108.

113. Wilkins, *Emergence of Multinational Enterprise*, pp. 97-98.

114. See Marshall et al., *Canadian-American Industry*, p. 65.

115. Naylor, *Canadian Business*, II: 191.

116. Wilkins, *Emergence of Multinational Enterprise*, pp. 87-89.

117. Naylor, *Canadian Business*, II: 238.

118. Wilkins, *Emergence of Multinational Enterprise*, p. 146.

119. See Lewis, *America's Stake*, pp. 312-13; Wilkins, *Emergence of Multinational Enterprise*, p. 143; Naylor, *Canadian Business*, II: 155-56.

120. Wilkins, *Emergence of Multinational Enterprise*, pp. 143-44.

121. Glen Williams, "Canadian Industrialization: We Ain't Growin' Nowhere," *This Magazine* 9 (1975): 8-9.

122. McDiarmid, *Commercial Policy*, pp. 242-45.

123. Ibid., p. 244.

124. Naylor, *Canadian Business*, II: 186-87.

125. Ibid., I: 109-10.

126. See Aitken, *American Capital*, pp. 100-1.

127. Nelles, *Politics of Development*, p. 307.

128. See Brebner, *Triangle*, p. 234.

129. Aitken, "Changing Structure," pp. 15 ff.

130. Ibid., p. 16.

131. Ibid., pp. 20-21; see also Nelles, *Politics of Development*, pp. 106-7, 309, 327-28.

132. Wilkins, *Emergence of Multinational Enterprise*, pp. 141-42.

133. Brebner, *Triangle*, pp. 235-36.

134. See Jacob Viner, *Canada's Balance of International Indebtedness, 1900-1913*, pp. 92-93.

135. See Lewis, *America's Stake*, p. 567.

136. See Marshall et al., *Canadian-American Industry*, pp. 178-82; Lewis, *America's Stake*, p. 566.

137. Brady, *Business As a System*, p. 194n.

138. Kolko, *Conservatism*, pp. 286 ff.; W.A. Williams, *Contours*, pp. 85 ff.

139. B.I. Kaufman, "The Organizational Dimension of United States Economic Foreign Policy, 1900-1920," *BHR* 46 (1972): 34-35.

140. W.A. Williams, *Contours*, p. 381.

141. Cochran, *American Business System*, p. 78.

142. Ibid., pp. 94-95; *Federal Reserve Bulletin*, 1968, pp. 3 ff.

143. H.H. Liebhafsky, *American Government and Business*, p. 177.

144. See Cochran, *American Business System*, pp. 40 ff.

145. See Chandler, "Role of Business," pp. 275 ff.

146. Liebhafsky, *Government and Business*, p. 177.

147. Based on Lewis, *America's Stake*, pp. 3 ff.

148. H.B. Lary et al., "The United States As an International Creditor," in *American Economic Development*, ed. W. Greenleaf, pp. 361-62.

149. Mira Wilkins, *The Maturing of Multinational Enterprise*, p. 51.

150. Ibid., p. 92.

151. See A.E. Safarian, *The Canadian Economy in the Great Depression*, pp. 28 ff.
152. Ibid., p. 65.
153. See Wilkins, *Maturing of Multinational Enterprise*, p. 31, Table I.3.
154. Aitken, *American Capital*, p. 42.
155. Buckley, *Capital Formation*, pp. 104-5.
156. Nelles, *Politics of Development*, p. 348.
157. Wilkins, *Maturing of Multinational Enterprise*, pp. 74-75.
158. Ibid., p. 76.
159. Safarian, *Canadian Economy*, p. 43.
160. Ibid., p. 44n.
161. Nelles, *Politics of Development*, pp. 461-62.
162. Wilkins, *Maturing of Multinational Enterprise*, p. 9.
163. Ibid., p. 93.
164. Ibid., p. 55, Table III.1.
165. Nelles, *Politics of Development*, p. 152.
166. Ibid., p. 492.
167. Marshall et al., *Canadian-American Industry*, p. 185.
168. *Monetary Times* 3 May 1918, quoted in Viner, *International Indebtedness*, pp. 89-90.
169. Wilkins, *Maturing of Multinational Enterprise*, pp. 169-70.
170. D. Wecter, "The Age of the Great Depression, 1929-1941," in *The Historians' History of the United States*, ed. A.S. Berky and J.P. Shenton, p. 1253.
171. Ibid., p. 1254.
172. Reported in Brady, *Business As a System*, p. 210.
173. Wecter, "Great Depression," p. 1254.
174. Wilkins, *Maturing of Multinational Enterprise*, p. 171.
175. Marshall et al., *Canadian-American Industry*, p. 19.
176. J.J. Deutsch, "Recent American Influence in Canada," in *The American Economic Impact on Canada*, ed. H.G.J. Aitken et al., p. 39.
177. Wilkins, *Maturing of Multinational Enterprise*, p. 182, Table VIII.2.
178. Marshall et al., *Canadian-American Industry*, pp. 22, 26.
179. Ibid., p. 247.
180. Ibid., pp. 61-62.
181. Ibid., pp. 221-22.
182. Ibid., p. 101.
183. Ibid., pp. 154-58.
184. Lewis, *America's Stake*, p. 197.
185. Marshall et al., *Canadian-American Industry*, p. 175.
186. Ibid., pp. 196-97.
187. Ibid., pp. 77-94.

Chapter Four   Consolidating the Continental Economy

1. George Grant, *Lament for a Nation*, pp. 9-10.
2. G. Rosenbluth, "Concentration and Monopoly in the Canadian Economy," in *Social Purpose for Canada*, ed. M. Oliver, p. 206.
3. C. Wright Mills, *The Power Elite*, pp. 100-1.
4. T.C. Cochran, *The American Business System*, p. 160.

5. Ibid., p. 134.

6. Ibid., p. 160.

7. O.J. Firestone, *Canada's Economic Development, 1867-1953*, p. 214.

8. D.A. Wolfe, "Political Culture, Economic Policy and the Growth of Foreign Investment in Canada," p. 43.

9. Ibid., pp. 91-92.

10. Mira Wilkins, *The Maturing of Multinational Enterprise*, p. 251.

11. Quoted in Wilkins, *Maturing of Multinational Enterprise*, p. 311.

12. H.G.J. Aitken, "The Changing Economic Structure of the Canadian Economy," in *The American Economic Impact on Canada*, ed. H.G.J. Aitken et al., p. 11.

13. Ibid., p. 23.

14. Wilkins, *Maturing of Multinational Enterprise*, p. 305.

15. Ibid., p. 392.

16. Wolfe, "Political Culture," p. 123.

17. Quoted in Wolfe, "Political Culture," p. 120.

18. See Dale Thomson, *Louis St-Laurent*, p. 148.

19. Aitken, "Changing Structure," p. 33.

20. H.G.J. Aitken, *American Capital and Canadian Resources*, pp. 74-75.

21. Canada, *Canada Year Book, 1975*, pp. 728, 829.

22. See *Fortune* 84 (1971): 144-149.

23. U.N., *Monthly Bulletin of Statistics*, June 1971: xii-xvi.

24. *Toronto Star* 24 July 1976: D11.

25. Aitken, *American Capital*, p. 7.

26. Mitchell Sharp, "Canada-U.S. Relations: Options for the Future," *International Perspectives*, Autumn 1972: 1, 4.

27. D. Drache, "Canadian Capitalism: Sticking with Staples," *This Magazine* 9 (1975): 7.

28. Ibid., p. 9.

29. P. Bourgault, *Innovation and the Structure of Canadian Industry*, pp. 82-83.

30. Ibid., p. 69.

31. Canada, *Foreign Direct Investment in Canada*, p. 118.

32. Canada, Royal Commission on Canada's Economic Prospects, *Final Report*, p. 97.

33. Aitken, *American Capital*, p. 199.

34. U.N., Dept. of Economic and Social Affairs, *Multinational Corporations in World Development*, p. 193, Table 36.

35. K. Levitt, *Silent Surrender*, p. 94.

36. Canada, *Canadian Statistical Review: Historical Summary, 1970*, pp. 94, 96.

37. Canada, CALURA *Annual Report for 1972, Part I. Corporations*, pp. 39-40.

38. Canada, Statistics Canada, *Canada's International Investment Position, 1968 to 1970*, p. 81.

39. Ibid., pp. 72-80.

40. Ibid., p. 115, Table 15.

41. Ibid., p. 132, Table 22.

42. Ibid., pp. 116-17, Table 16.

43. Ibid., p. 68.

44. *Infomat* 5 Sept. 1975: 3.

45. Canada, Statistics Canada, *Canada's International Investment Position, 1926 to 1967*, p. 31.

46. Ibid., p. 54.
47. Firestone, *Economic Development*, p. 182.
48. J. Porter, *Canadian Social Structure*, pp. 92-93; Canada, Ministry of Industry, Trade and Commerce, *Perspective Canada*, pp. 124-25, Table 6.6.

Chapter Five   Multinational Corporations Operating from the United States and Canada

1. Canada, *Foreign Direct Investment in Canada*, pp. 52, 56.
2. Ibid., p. 51.
3. J.N. Behrman, *Some Patterns in the Rise of the Multinational Enterprise*, p. 85.
4. Canada, Task Force on the Structure of Canadian Industry, *Foreign Ownership and the Structure of Canadian Industry*, pp. 192-93.
5. L. Pratt, *The Tar Sands*, p. 121.
6. Ibid., p. 122.
7. Alcan Aluminium, *Annual Report, 1974*, p. 8.
8. See C. Tugendhat, *The Multinationals*, pp. 96-103; U.N., Dept. of Economic and Social Affairs, *Multinational Corporations in World Development*, pp. 147-49; Alcan Aluminium, *Annual Report, 1974*.
9. C. Gonick, "Socialism and the Economics of Growthmanship," in *Essays on the Left*, ed. L. La Pierre et al., p. 143.
10. Canada, *Foreign Direct Investment*, p. 56.
11. R. Vernon, *Sovereignty at Bay*, p. 194.
12. Ibid., p. 196.
13. *New York Times* 23 April 1975: 55.
14. *Fortune* 85 (June 1972): 103.
15. U.N., *Multinational Corporations in World Development*, p. 151, Table 5.
16. Ibid., p. 140, Table 1.
17. D. Johnson, "Dependence and the International System," in *Dependence and Underdevelopment in Latin America*, ed. J. Cockcroft et al., p. 93.
18. Mira Wilkins, *The Emergence of Multinational Enterprise*, pp. 201-2.
19. Mira Wilkins, *The Maturing of Multinational Enterprise*, pp. 374-75.
20. See Vernon, *Sovereignty at Bay*, pp. 7-11; J.W. Vaupel and J.P. Curhan, *The World's Multinational Enterprises*, p. 2.
21. H. Magdoff, *The Age of Imperialism*, pp. 74-75; R. Wolff, "The Foreign Expansion of U.S. Banks," *Monthly Review* 23 (1971): 21.
22. Wolff, "Foreign Expansion," p. 21.
23. S. Rose, "The Misguided Furor about Investments from Abroad," *Fortune* 91 (May 1975): 108.
24. Wilkins, *Maturing of Multinational Enterprise*, pp. 392-93.
25. See P. Jalée, *The Third World in World Economy*, p. 124 and Magdoff, *Age of Imperialism*, p. 194.
26. See *Fortune* 90 (Nov. 1974): 175.
27. See *Fortune* 88 (Aug. 1973): 54.
28. D. Gilberg, "United States Imperialism," in *Up Against the American Myth*, ed. I. Christoffel et al., pp. 243-44.
29. Jalée, *Third World*, p. 111.
30. J. Petras, "U.S. Business and Foreign Policy in Latin America," in *Eco-*

nomics: Mainstream Readings and Radical Critiques, ed. D. Mermelstein, p. 433.

31. Lewis Turner, *Invisible Empires,* p. 153.
32. Magdoff, *Age of Imperialism,* p. 198.
33. Petras, "Foreign Policy," p. 432.
34. Jalée, *Third World,* p. 113.
35. A.G. Frank, *Latin America: Underdevelopment or Revolution,* p. 389.
36. G. Kolko, *The Roots of American Foreign Policy,* pp. 68-69.
37. D. Horowitz, *The Free World Colossus,* pp. 222-23.
38. Petras, "Foreign Policy," pp. 435-36.
39. Gilberg, "U.S. Imperialism," p. 247.
40. Magdoff, *Age of Imperialism,* p. 162.
41. Wilkins, *Maturing of Multinational Enterprise,* p. 354.
42. *Survey of Current Business,* Oct. 1970: 23.
43. *Fortune* 84 (Aug. 1971): 118.
44. *Globe and Mail* 4 May 1976: B7.
45. *Fortune* 91 (May 1975): 174.
46. *Financial Post* 15 Feb. 1975: 11.
47. See U.N., *Multinational Corporations,* p. 170, Table 21.
48. *New York Times* 17 April 1975: 52.
49. *Ottawa Journal* 18 Feb. 1975: 9.
50. Rose, "Misguided Furor," p. 172.
51. R.T. Naylor, *The History of Canadian Business,* II: 218-19.
52. Ibid., II: 219-20.
53. R.T. Naylor, "Canada's International Commercial Expansion to 1914," *Our Generation* 10 (1975): 37.
54. Naylor, *Canadian Business,* II: 258.
55. See R. Chodos and B. Drummond, "Ma Bell Joins the Jet Set," in *Let Us Prey,* ed. R. Chodos and R. Murphy, pp. 21-23.
56. Canada, Statistics Canada, *Canada's International Investment Position, 1926 to 1967,* p. 104, Statement 63.
57. Canada, Statistics Canada, *Canada's International Investment Position, 1968 to 1970,* p. 27.
58. Ibid., pp. 10-11.
59. Ibid., p. 9.
60. Ibid., pp. 28, 92.
61. Ibid., p. 10.
62. D. Cubberley and J. Keyes, "The Weston Conglomerate," *Last Post* 5 (1975): 18-29.
63. K. Levitt and A. McIntyre, *Canada-West Indies Economic Relations,* p. 24.
64. Ibid., pp. 24-27.
65. Canada, *Investment Position, 1926 to 1967,* p. 75.
66. *Financial Post* 18 Oct. 1975: D6.
67. *Globe and Mail* 28 May 1976: B1.
68. Canada, *Investment Position, 1926 to 1967,* p. 74.
69. Canada, *Canada Year Book, 1972,* pp. 1101-2.
70. Ibid., p. 1103; "The Brascan File," *Last Post* 3 (1973): 29-33.
71. See *Ottawa Journal* 23 May 1975: 18.
72. *Globe and Mail* 16 Dec. 1975: B1.

73. *Financial Post* 13 Dec. 1975: C5.
74. I.A. Litvak and C.J. Maule, "The Multinational Corporation: Some Perspectives," *Canadian Public Administration* 13 (1970): 129.
75. A.G. Frank, "Economic Dependence, Class Structure and Underdevelopment Policy," in *Dependence and Underdevelopment in Latin America*, ed. J. Cockcroft et al., p. 224.
76. T. Balogh, "The Mechanism of Neo-Imperialism," in *Power in Economics*, ed. K.W. Rothschild, p. 339.
77. H.G.J. Aitken, "Government and Business in Canada," in *The Canadian Economy: Selected Readings*, ed. J.J. Deutsch et al., rev. ed., p. 497.
78. R. Jenkins, *Exploitation: The World Power Structure and the Inequality of Nations*, p. 158.

Chapter Six   Continental Corporate Structures and Interlocking

1. See James O'Connor, *The Fiscal Crisis of the State*, pp. 13-18.
2. J.K. Galbraith, *Economics and the Public Purpose*, pp. 55 ff.
3. W.F. Mueller, "The Measure of Industrial Concentration," in *Superconcentration/Supercorporation*, ed. R.L. Andreano, p. 331; see also H.H. Liebhafsky, *American Government and Business*, p. 178.
4. R.L. Nelson, *Merger Movements in American Industry, 1895-1956*, p. 4.
5. E. Bannock, *Economic Report on Corporate Mergers*, p. 101.
6. J. Didrichsen, "The Development of Diversified and Conglomerate Firms in the United States, 1920-1970," *BHR* 46 (1972): 216-17.
7. *Fortune* 91 (May, 1975): 239.
8. Peter C. Newman, *The Canadian Establishment*, I: 64.
9. *New York Times* 25 Nov. 1974: 47.
10. W. Clement, *The Canadian Corporate Elite*, p. 126.
11. See A.D.H. Kaplan, *Big Enterprise in a Competitive Society*, pp. 136-63; A.D. Chandler, Jr., "The Structure of American Industry in the Twentieth Century: A Historical Overview," *BHR* 43 (1969): 290-97.
12. *Fortune* 91 (May, 1975): 241.
13. Ibid.
14. R.J. Barnet and R.E. Muller, *Global Reach*, p. 230.
15. J.R. Felton, "Conglomerate Mergers, Concentration and Competition," *American Journal of Economics and Sociology* (1971): 233. See also Lee Preston, "Economic Concentration, Size Mobility and Competition Concepts and Hypotheses," brief to U.S. Congress, Senate, Committee on the Judiciary, Subcommittee on Antitrust and Monopoly, 88th Congress, 2nd session, 1964, p. 66.
16. R.L. Andreano, *Superconcentration/Supercorporation*, preface.
17. U.S., Federal Trade Commission, Bureau of Economics, *Statistical Abstract of the United States, 1974*: 487, Table 798.
18. Canada, Ministry of Consumer and Corporate Affairs, *Concentration in the Manufacturing Industries of Canada*, pp. 5-6.
19. U.S., Comptroller of the Currency, "Annual Report," *Statistical Abstract of the United States, 1974*: 451, Table 724.
20. Reported in R. Fitch and M. Oppenheimer, "Who Rules the Corporations?" *Socialist Revolution* 4 (1970): 98.

21. *Moody's Bank and Financial Manual* (1974): 3040.
22. R. Pelton, "Who Really Rules America?" *Progressive Labor* 7 (1970): 18-19.
23. U.S., Congress, House, Committee on Banking and Currency, Subcommittee on Domestic Finance [Patman Committee], *Commercial Banks and Their Trust Activities*, 90th Congress, 2nd session, 1969, p. 18.
24. Barnet and Muller, *Global Reach*, pp. 233-34.
25. Fitch and Oppenheimer, "Who Rules the Corporations?" 104-5.
26. Barnet and Muller, *Global Reach*, pp. 239-40.
27. U.N., Dept. of Economic and Social Affairs, *Multinational Corporations in World Development*, pp. 14-15.
28. R. Davis, M. Zannis, and R. Surette, "Why David Rockefeller Was in Quebec City," in *Let Us Prey*, ed. R. Chodos and R. Murphy, p. 96.
29. See *New York Times* 25 May 1975: III, 1, 10.
30. *Toronto Star* 19 Mar. 1971: 1.
31. *Moody's Bank and Financial Manual* (1974): 420-22.
32. Ibid., p. 3200.
33. *New York Times* 18 Dec. 1974: 67.
34. R.T. Averitt, *The Dual Economy*, pp. 66-67.
35. Barnet and Muller, *Global Reach*, p. 244.
36. C.J. Loomis, "For the Utilities, It's a Fight for Survival," *Fortune* 91 (March 1975): 99.
37. Ibid., p. 186.
38. *New York Times* 1 May 1975: C59-60.
39. R. Chodos and D. Burgess, "Ma Bell Joins the Jet Set," in *Let Us Prey*, ed. R. Chodos and R. Murphy, p. 45.
40. Ibid., p. 44.
41. *Ottawa Journal* 2 June 1975.
42. J. Ridgeway, *The Last Play*, p. 77.
43. L. Pratt, *The Tar Sands*, p. 120.
44. E.J. Dosman, *The National Interest*, pp. 214-15.
45. *Financial Post* 5 Aug. 1972: 9.
46. INCO, *Annual Report, 1974*, p. 17.
47. Canada, CALURA, *Annual Report for 1975*, pp. 47, 95.
48. *Fortune* 91 (April 1975): 38.
49. *Ottawa Journal* 18 Feb. 1975: 9.
50. J. Laxer, "Canadian Manufacturing and U.S. Trade Policy," in *(Canada) Ltd.*, ed. R. Laxer, pp. 138-39.
51. *Infomat* 22 March 1974; 26 March 1976.
52. Mira Wilkins, *The Maturing of Multinational Enterprise*, p. 295.
53. Canada, CALURA, *Annual Report for 1972*, p. 16.
54. Alcan Aluminium, *Annual Report, 1974*, p. 6.
55. John Porter, *The Vertical Mosaic*, p. 589.
56. *Globe and Mail* 18 Jan. 1972.
57. Clement, *Canadian Corporate Elite*, pp. 150-55.
58. *Globe and Mail* 3 Jan. 1976: B1.

Chapter Seven The Economic Elite in Canada and the United States: I. Careers, Class, and Kinship

1. *Toronto Star* 17 Jan. 1976: D8.
2. See W. Clement, *The Canadian Corporate Elite*, pp. 195-96.
3. *Fortune* 89 (Jan. 1974): 79.
4. Ibid., p. 152.
5. Ibid., p. 154.
6. E.O. Smigel, *The Wall Street Lawyer*, pp. 39-40, 57.
7. *Fortune* 84 (Oct. 1971): 33.
8. William Rodgers, *Think: A Biography of the Watsons and IBM*, p. 335; *New York Times* 12 Nov. 1972: 3-4.
9. See Clement, *Canadian Corporate Elite*, pp. 182-83, 344-53.
10. *Fortune* 84 (Oct. 1971): 81.
11. *Fortune* 86 (Aug. 1972): 132.
12. Osborn Elliot, *Men at the Top*, p. 22.
13. *Fortune* 87 (Jan. 1973): 70.
14. *New York Times* 14 Mar. 1975: 55.
15. *Current Biography* (1971): 434.
16. See Clement, *Canadian Corporate Elite*, pp. 244-47; C. Wright Mills, "The American Business Elite," in *Power, Politics and People*, ed. I.L. Horowitz, p. 123.
17. See Clement, *Canadian Corporate Elite*, pp. 189-94.
18. Ibid., pp. 192, 461.
19. Ibid., pp. 189 ff.
20. E. Digby Baltzell, *The Protestant Establishment*, p. 389.
21. See Clement, *Canadian Corporate Elite*, pp. 206-8.

Chapter Eight The Economic Elite in Canada and the United States: II. Corporate, Ascriptive, and Social Characteristics

1. See W. Clement, *The Canadian Corporate Elite*, pp. 208 ff.
2. *Fortune* 83 (Feb. 1971): 37.
3. See Clement, *Canadian Corporate Elite*, pp. 237-39.
4. *Globe and Mail* 6 April 1976: B4.
5. E. Digby Baltzell, *The Protestant Establishment*, pp. 52-53.
6. *Fortune* 85 (May 1972): 159.
7. *Current Biography* (1965): 189.
8. Zena Cherry, *Globe and Mail* 12 Aug. 1976: F3.
9. See G. William Domhoff, *The Higher Circles*, pp. 33 ff.
10. See C. Wright Mills, *The Power Elite*, pp. 106 ff; E. Digby Baltzell, *Philadelphia Gentlemen*, pp. 293 ff; G. William Domhoff, *Who Rules America?* pp. 17 ff.
11. Mills, *Power Elite*, p. 64.
12. Baltzell, *Philadelphia Gentlemen*, p. 302.
13. Ibid., pp. 294-95.
14. See Domhoff, *Higher Circles*, p. 36n.
15. Baltzell, *Philadelphia Gentlemen*, pp. 328-29.
16. Heidrick and Struggles, Inc., *Profile of a President*, p. 5; *Profile of a Canadian President*, p. 6.

17. Baltzell, *Philadelphia Gentlemen*, p. 348.
18. Ibid., p. 338; Domhoff, *Higher Circles*, pp. 23-24.
19. *Fortune* 88 (Dec. 1973): 48.
20. See Clement, *Canadian Corporate Elite*, pp. 256-59.
21. Domhoff, *Higher Circles*, p. 116.
22. G. William Domhoff, "Social Clubs, Policy-Planning Groups, and Corporations: A Network Study of Ruling-Class Cohesiveness," *Insurgent Sociologist* 5 (1975): 46.
23. *Fortune* 83 (Mar. 1971): 32.
24. *New York Times* 12 Nov. 1972, sec. 3: 2.
25. *Current Biography* (1951): 35.
26. See Clement, *Canadian Corporate Elite*, pp. 260-66.

Chapter Nine   Relations between the U.S. and Canadian Elites and Managers

1. *Fortune* 93 (Feb. 1976): 27.
2. W.E. Kalbach, *The Impact of Immigration on Canada's Population*, p. 220.
3. Ibid., p. 238.
4. See W.A. Glazer, "The Migration and Return of Professionals," Columbia University, Bureau of Applied Social Research (Sept. 1973).
5. L. Parai, *Immigration and Emigration of Professionals and Skilled Manpower during the Post-War Period*, p. 93.
6. Canadian-American Committee, *Capital Flows between Canada and the United States*, p. ix.

Chapter Ten   Implications of the Continental Economy for Canadian Society

1. *Financial Post* 13 Dec. 1975: C5.
2. Quoted in J.B. Brebner, *North Atlantic Triangle*, pp. 270-71.
3. J.W. Warnock, *Partner to Behemoth*, p. 17.
4. Edgar Dosman, *The National Interest*, pp. xiv-xv.
5. J. Porter, *The Vertical Mosaic*, p. 269.

Appendix VIII   Trends in Corporate Interlocking in the United States, 1899 to 1970

1. D. Bunting and J. Barbour, "Interlocking Directorates in Large American Corporations, 1896-1964," *BHR* 45 (1971): 320.
2. Ibid., p. 327.
3. Ibid., p. 328, Table 5.
4. Ibid., p. 330n.
5. Ibid., p. 335.
6. P.C. Dooley, "The Interlocking Directorate," *American Economic Review* 59 (1969): 314.
7. Ibid., p. 315, Table 1.
8. Ibid., p. 315.
9. M.P. Allen, "The Structure of Interorganizational Elite Cooptation: Inter-

locking Corporate Directorates," *American Sociological Review* 39 (1974): 397.
10. Ibid., p. 399, Table 3.
11. Ibid., p. 403.
12. Ibid., p. 404.
13. See W. Clement, *The Canadian Corporate Elite*, pp. 155-69.

Appendix XI   Studies of the U.S. Economic Elite and Executives

1. F.W. Taussig and C.S. Joslyn, *American Business Leaders*, pp. 9, 23.
2. Ibid., p. 31.
3. Ibid., pp. 92-93.
4. Ibid., pp. 233-34.
5. Ibid., p. 241.
6. Ibid., p. 264.
7. F. Lundberg, *America's Sixty Families*, p. 3.
8. C.M. Destler, "Entrepreneurial Leadership among the 'Robber Barons': A Trial Balance," *Journal of Economic History* 6 (1946): 36 ff.
9. C. Wright Mills, "The American Business Elite: A Collective Portrait," in *Power, Politics and People*, ed. I.L. Horowitz, p. 110-12.
10. Ibid., p. 123.
11. Ibid., p. 139.
12. C. Wright Mills, *The Power Elite*, pp. 104-5.
13. William Miller, "American Historians and the Business Elite," in *Men in Business*, ed. W. Miller, pp. 312-13; "The Recruitment of the American Business Elite," in *Men in Business*, pp. 386-87.
14. Miller, "Recruitment of the American Business Elite," p. 326, Table 8.
15. Ibid., p. 328.
16. Ibid., p. 333, Table 1.
17. Ibid., p. 334.
18. F.W. Gregory and I.D. Neu, "The American Industrial Elite in the 1870's," in *Men in Business*, ed. W. Miller, p. 202, Table 6.
19. T.W. Acheson, "Changing Social Origins of the Canadian Industrial Elite," *BHR* 47 (1973): 206, Table 12; see also W. Clement, *The Canadian Corporate Elite*, pp. 71-73.
20. Suzanne Keller, "The Social Origins and Career Lines of Three Generations of American Business Leaders," pp. 68-69.
21. Ibid., p. 72.
22. Ibid., p. 170.
23. Based on M. Newcomer, *The Big Business Executive*, pp. 53-54, Table 17.
24. L.W. Warner and J. Abegglen, *Occupational Mobility in American Business and Industry, 1928-1952*, p. 24.
25. Ibid., p. 46.
26. Newcomer, *Business Executive*, pp. 53-54.
27. Warner and Abegglen, *Occupational Mobility*, p. 48.
28. W.G. Daly, "The Mobility of Top Business Executives in Canada," p. 119.
29. R. Bendix and F.W. Howton, "Social Mobility and the American Business Elite," in *Social Mobility in Industrial Society*, ed. S.M. Lipset and R. Bendix, pp. 118-21.

30. Ibid., pp. 122-23.
31. Ibid., p. 127.
32. Ibid., p. 131.
33. See John Porter, *The Vertical Mosaic* and Clement, *Canadian Corporate Elite*.
34. E. Digby Baltzell, *Philadelphia Gentlemen* and *The Protestant Establishment*; G. William Domhoff, *Who Rules America?* and *The Higher Circles*; G. Kolko, *Wealth and Power in America*.
35. *Fortune* [magazine], *The Executive Life*, pp. 25, 27.
36. W. Guzzardi, *The Young Executives*, p. 178.
37. *Fortune* 81 (May 1970): 323.
38. *Fortune* 93 (May 1976): 174.

Appendix XIII   The "Ownership/Control" Debate in the United States

1. See W. Clement, *The Canadian Corporate Elite*, pp. 13-23.
2. T. Nichols, *Ownership, Control and Ideology*, p. 141.
3. M. Zeitlin, "Corporate Ownership and Control: The Large Corporation and the Capitalist Class," *American Journal of Sociology* 79 (1974): 1077-78.
4. Ibid., p. 1078.
5. Ibid., pp. 1079-80.
6. Ibid., p. 1091.
7. R. Sheehan, "Proprietors in the World of Big Business," in *American Society, Inc.*, ed. M. Zeitlin, pp. 79-83.
8. P.H. Burch, *The Managerial Revolution Reassessed*, pp. 102-3.
9. Ibid., p. 101.
10. Ibid.
11. Quoted in R.J. Barnet and R.E. Muller, *Global Reach*, pp. 235-36.
12. Quoted in R. Fitch, "Sweezy and Corporate Fetishism," *Socialist Revolution* 12 (1972): 155.
13. See C.H. Anderson, *The Political Economy of Social Class*, p. 206.
14. *Fortune* 91 (Jan. 1975): 21.
15. *Fortune* 87 (April 1973): 22.
16. *New York Times* 21 Feb. 1975: C43.
17. *Fortune* 83 (Feb. 1971): 31.
18. D. Bell, "The Breakup of Family Capitalism," in *The End of Ideology*, D. Bell, p. 40.
19. *New York Times* 13 Mar. 1975: C75.
20. *Fortune* 89 (Jan. 1974): 54.
21. R.T. Averitt, *The Dual Economy*, p. 178.
22. *New York Times* 4 April 1975: 45.
23. *New York Times* 25 May 1975: F11.
24. *Fortune* 81 (May 1970): 181.
25. Heidrick and Struggles, Inc., *Profile of a President*, p. 5; *Profile of a Canadian President*, p. 6.
26. R.J. Larner, "Ownership and Control in the 200 Largest Non-financial Corporations, 1929-1963," *American Economic Review* 56 (1966): 251-62.

27. *New York Times* 15 May 1975: 67; 17 April 1975: 63; 22 May 1975: 65; 28 Mar. 1975: 41.
28. *New York Times* 13 April 1975, sec. 3.
29. Heidrick and Struggles, Inc., *Profile of a President*, p. 11.
30. *Fortune* 93 (May 1976): 176.
31. H.P. Tuckman, *The Economics of the Rich*, p. 15.
32. *New York Times* 16 Dec. 1974: 57-58.
33. C. Wright Mills, *White Collar*, p. 101.
34. *Fortune* 92 (Dec. 1975); 100 ff.
35. *Globe and Mail* 31 Dec. 1975: 3.
36. R. Loving, Jr., "Outsider in the Throne Room at Kaiser," *Fortune* 91 (Mar. 1975): 93.
37. *Fortune* 91 (June 1975): 19.
38. *Fortune* 92 (Dec. 1975): 17.
39. Heidrick and Struggles, Inc., *Profile of a Board of Directors*, p. 5.
40. Ibid., p. 9.

Appendix XIV   Immigration Data and Migration Theories

1. Canada, *Canada Year Book, 1972*, p. 231.
2. L.W. St. John-Jones, "The Exchange of Population between the United States of America and Canada in the 1960's," *International Migration* 11 (1973): 43.
3. P. George, "Types of Migration of the Population According to the Professional and Social Composition of Migrants," in *Readings in the Sociology of Migration*, ed. C.J. Jansen, p. 40.
4. F.D. Scott, *World Migration in Modern Times*, p. 10.
5. B. Thomas, *Migration and Economic Growth*, pp. 30-31.
6. B. Thomas, "Migration: Economic Aspects," *International Encyclopedia of the Social Sciences*, pp. 297, 299.
7. Ibid., p. 250.
8. Ibid., p. 251.
9. Ibid., p. 269.
10. B. Thomas, ed., *Economics of International Migration*, p. 16.
11. Thomas, *Migration and Economic Growth*, p. 25.
12. A. Richmond, *Post-War Immigrants in Canada*, pp. 124-25, 253-54.
13. Ibid., p. 244.
14. J.M. Van der Kroef, "The U.S. and the World's Brain Drain," *International Journal of Comparative Sociology* 11 (1970): 227-28.

References

Abbreviations Used:

BHR – Business History Review
CJEPS – Canadian Journal of Economics and Political Science

Acheson, T.W. "Changing Social Origins of the Canadian Industrial Elite," *BHR* 47 (1973).

Aitken, Hugh G.J. "The Changing Structure of the Canadian Economy." In *The American Economic Impact on Canada*, ed. H.G.J. Aitken et al. Durham, N.C.: Duke Univ. Press, 1959.

——— "Defensive Expansionism: The State and Economic Growth in Canada." In *The State and Economic Growth*, ed. H.G.J. Aitken. New York: Social Science Research Council, 1959; reprinted in *Approaches to Canadian Economic History*, ed. W.T. Easterbrook and M.H. Watkins. Toronto: McClelland & Stewart, Carleton Library No. 31, 1967.

——— *American Capital and Canadian Resources*. Cambridge, Mass.: Harvard Univ. Press, 1961.

——— "Government and Business in Canada." In *The Canadian Economy: Selected Readings*, ed. J.J. Deutsch et al., rev. ed. Toronto: Macmillan, 1965.

Alexander, Malcolm L. "The Political Economy of Semi-Industrial Capitalism: A Comparative Study of Argentina, Australia and Canada." Ph.D. thesis proposal, Dept. of Sociology, McGill University, Montreal, March, 1975.

Allen, Michael P. "The Structure of Interorganizational Elite Cooptation: Interlocking Corporate Directorates," *American Sociological Review* 39 (1974).

Anderson, Charles H. *The Political Economy of Social Class*. Englewood Cliffs, N.J.: Prentice-Hall, 1974.

Andreano, Ralph L., ed. *Superconcentration/Supercorporation*. Andover, Mass.: Warner Modular Publ., 1973.

Averitt, Robert T. *The Dual Economy: The Dynamics of American Industry Structure*. New York: W.W. Norton, 1968.

Balogh, T. "The Mechanism of Neo-Imperialism." In *Power in Economics*, ed. K.W. Rothschild. Harmondsworth: Penguin, 1971.

Baltzell, E. Digby. *Philadelphia Gentlemen: The Making of a National Upper Class*. Glencoe, Ill.: Free Press, 1958.

——— *The Protestant Establishment: Aristocracy and Caste in America*. New York: Random House, 1964.

——— "'Who's Who in America' and 'The Social Register.'" In *Class, Status and Power: A Reader in Social Stratification*, ed. Reinhard Bendix and S.M. Lipset, 2nd ed. New York: Free Press, 1966.

Bannock, E. *Economic Report on Corporate Mergers.* Washington: Federal Trade Commission, 1971.

Baran, Paul A. *The Political Economy of Growth.* New York: Monthly Review Press, 1957.

Barnet, Richard J. and Muller, Ronald E. *Global Reach, the Power of the Multinational Corporations.* New York: Simon & Schuster, 1974.

Beard, Charles and Beard, Mary R. *New Basic History of the United States*, ed. William Beard, rev. ed. Philadelphia: New Home Library, 1968.

Behrman, J.N. *Some Patterns in the Rise of the Multinational Enterprise.* Chapel Hill, N.C.: Univ. of North Carolina Press, 1969.

Bell, Daniel. "The Breakup of Family Capitalism." In D. Bell, *The End of Ideology.* New York: Free Press, 1960.

Bendix, Reinhard and Howton, Frank W. "Social Mobility and the American Business Elite." In *Social Mobility in Industrial Society*, ed. R. Bendix and S.M. Lipset. Berkeley, Calif.: Univ. of California Press, 1959.

Berky, A.S. and Shenton, J.P., eds. *The Historians' History of the United States.* 2 vols. New York: Putnam, 1966.

Bertram, G.W. "Economic Growth in Canadian Industry, 1870-1915: The Staple Model and the Take-Off Hypothesis," *CJEPS* 29 (1963).

Block, Fred. "Expanding Capitalism: The British and American Cases." *Berkeley Journal of Sociology* 15 (1970).

Bourgault, Pierre. *Innovation and the Structure of Canadian Industry*, Science Council of Canada. Ottawa: Information Canada, 1972.

Brady, Robert A. *Business As a System of Power.* New York: Columbia Univ. Press, 1943.

Braverman, Harry. *Labor and Monopoly Capital: The Degradation of Work in the Twentieth Century.* New York: Monthly Review Press, 1974.

Brebner, John Bartlet. *North Atlantic Triangle: The Interplay of Canada, the United States and Great Britain.* New York: Columbia Univ. Press, 1945. McClelland & Stewart, Carleton Library No. 30, 1966.

Buckley, Kenneth. *Capital Formation in Canada, 1896-1930.* Toronto: Univ. of Toronto Press, 1955. McClelland & Stewart, Carleton Library No. 77, 1974.

Bunting, David and Barbour, Jeffery. "Interlocking Directorates in Large American Corporations, 1896-1964," *BHR* 45 (1971)

Burch, Philip H. *The Managerial Revolution Reassessed: Family Control in America's Largest Corporations.* Lexington, Mass.: D.C. Heath, Lexington Books, 1972.

Canada, Government, *Foreign-Direct Investment in Canada* [the Gray Report]. Ottawa: Information Canada, 1972.

———, House of Commons, *Debates*, 1878.

———, Ministry of Consumer and Corporate Affairs, *Concentration in the Manufacturing Industries of Canada.* Ottawa: Information Canada, 1971.

———, Ministry of Industry, Trade and Commerce, *Perspective Canada.* Ottawa: Information Canada, 1974.

———, Ministry of Industry, Trade and Commerce, Statistics Canada, *Annual Report* under the Corporations and Labour Unions Return Act [CAL-

URA], *Part I. Corporations.* Ottawa: The Ministry, 1972, 1973, 1975.

———, *Canada Year Book 1972.* Ottawa: Information Canada, 1972.

———, *Canada Year Book 1973.* Ottawa: Information Canada, 1973.

———, *Canada Year Book 1975.* Ottawa: Information Canada, 1975.

———, *Canadian Statistical Review: Historical Summary, 1970.* Ottawa: Information Canada, 1972.

———, *Canada's International Investment Position, 1926 to 1967.* Ottawa: Information Canada, 1971.

———, *Canada's International Investment Position, 1968-1970.* Ottawa: Information Canada, 1975.

———, Privy Council Office, Task Force on the Structure of Canadian Industry, *Foreign Ownership and the Structure of Canadian Industry* [the Watkins Report]. Ottawa: Information Canada: 1970.

———, Royal Commission on Canada's Economic Prospects, *Final Report* [the Gordon Report]. Ottawa: Queen's Printer, 1958.

Canadian-American Committee. *Capital Flows between Canada and the United States.* Montreal: Private Planning Assoc., 1965.

Chandler, Alfred D., Jr. "The Beginnings of 'Big Business' in American Industry," *BHR* 33 (1959).

——— *Strategy and Structure.* Cambridge, Mass.: M.I.T. Press, 1962.

——— "The Structure of American Industry in the Twentieth Century: A Historical Overview," *BHR* 43 (1969).

——— "The Role of Business in the United States: A Historical Survey." In *The American Corporation*, ed. E. Goldstein et al. Cambridge, Mass.: M.I.T. Press, 1969.

——— and Salsbury, Stephen. "The Railroads: Innovations in Modern Business Administration." In *The Changing Economic Order: Readings in American Business and Economic History*, ed. A.D. Chandler, Jr., et al. New York: Harcourt, Brace & World, 1968.

Chodos, Robert and Burgess, Drummond. "Ma Bell Joins the Jet Set." In *Let Us Prey*, ed. Robert Chodos and Rae Murphy. Toronto: James Lorimer, 1974.

Clement, Wallace. *The Canadian Corporate Elite: An Analysis of Economic Power.* Toronto: McClelland & Stewart, Carleton Library No. 89, 1975.

——— "A Political Economy of Regionalism in Canada." In *Conflict and Consensus: Multiple Loyalties in the Canadian State*, ed. D. Glenday, A. Turowetz, and H. Guindon. Toronto: Macmillan [in press].

Cochran, Thomas C. *The American Business System: A Historical Perspective, 1900-1955.* Cambridge, Mass.: Harvard Univ. Press, 1957.

——— "Business Organization and the Development of an Industrial Discipline." In *Views of American Economic Growth*, ed. T.C. Cochran and T.B. Brewer. New York: McGraw-Hill, 1966.

——— and Miller, William. *The Age of Enterprise: A Social History of Industrial America*, rev. ed. New York: Harper & Row, Harper Torch Books, 1961.

Creighton, D.G. *The Empire of the St. Lawrence.* Toronto: Macmillan, 1956.

Cubberley, David and Keyes, John. "The Weston Conglomerate," *Last Post* 5 (1975).

Cuneo, Carl. "The Controlled Entry of Canadian Managers to the United States," *International Journal of Comparative Sociology* 17 (1977) [forthcoming].

Daly, William G. "The Mobility of Top Business Executives in Canada." Master's thesis, Department of Commerce and Business Administration, University of British Columbia, 1972.

Daughen, Joseph R. and Binzen, Peter. *The Wreck of the Penn Central.* Boston: Little Brown, 1971; reprinted Signet, Mentor Executive Library, 1971.

Davis, Robert, Zannis, Mark, and Surette, Ralph. "Why David Rockefeller Was in Quebec City." In *Let Us Prey,* ed. Robert Chodos and Rae Murphy. Toronto: James Lorimer, 1974.

Destler, Chester M. "Entrepreneurial Leadership among the 'Robber Barons': A Trial Balance," *Journal of Economic History* 6 (Supplementary Issue) (1946).

Deutsch, John J. "Recent American Influence in Canada." In *The American Economic Impact on Canada,* ed. H.G.J. Aitken et al. Durham, N.C.: Duke Univ. Press, 1959.

Deverell, John. *Falconbridge: Portrait of a Canadian Mining Multinational.* Toronto: James Lorimer, 1975.

Didrichsen, Jon. "The Development of Diversified and Conglomerate Firms in the United States, 1920-1970," *BHR* 46 (1972).

Domhoff, G. William. *Who Rules America?* Englewood Cliffs, N.J.: Prentice-Hall, 1967.

_____ *The Higher Circles.* New York: Vintage Books, 1970.

_____ "Social Clubs, Policy-Planning Groups, and Corporations: A Network Study of Ruling-Class Cohesiveness." In "New Directions in Power Structure Research," ed. G.W. Domhoff, *Insurgent Sociologist* 5 (1975).

Dooley, Peter C. "The Interlocking Directorates," *American Economic Review* 59 (1969).

Dosman, Edgar J. *The National Interest: The Politics of Northern Development, 1968-1975.* Toronto: McClelland & Stewart, 1975.

Dos Santos, Theotonio. "The Structure of Dependence." In *Readings in U.S. Imperialism,* ed. K.T. Fann and D.C. Hodges. Boston: Porter Sargent, 1971.

Douglas, Elisha P. *The Coming of Age of American Business.* Chapel Hill, N.C.: Univ. of North Carolina Press, 1971.

Drache, Daniel. "Canadian Capitalism: Sticking with Staples," *This Magazine* 9 (1975).

Elliot, Osborn. *Men at the Top.* New York: Harper, 1959.

Felton, John R. "Conglomerate Mergers, Concentration and Competition," *American Journal of Economics and Sociology* July, 1971.

Firestone, O.J. *Canada's Economic Development, 1867-1953, with Special Reference to Changes in the Country's National Product and National Wealth.* London: Bowes and Bowes, 1958.

Fitch, Robert. "Sweezy and Corporate Fetishism," *Socialist Revolution* 12 (1972).

_____ and Oppenheimer, Mary. "Who Rules the Corporations?" *Socialist Revolution* 4, 5, 6 (1970).

Fortune [magazine]. *The Executive Life.* Garden City, N.Y.: Doubleday, 1956.

Frank, André G. *Latin America: Underdevelopment or Revolution.* New York: Monthly Review Press, 1969.

_____ "Economic Dependence, Class Structure and Underdevelopment Policy." In *Dependence and Underdevelopment in Latin America*, ed. J.D. Cock-croft et al. New York: Doubleday-Anchor, 1972.

Galbraith, J.K. *Economics and the Public Purpose*. Boston: Houghton Mifflin, 1973.

Galtung, Johan. "A Structural Theory of Imperialism," *Journal of Peace Research* 2 (1972).

George, P. "Types of Migration of the Population According to the Professional and Social Composition of Migrants." In *Readings in the Sociology of Migration*, ed. C.J. Jansen. Oxford: Pergamon Press, 1970.

Gilberg, Dan. "United States Imperialism." In *Up Against the American Myth*, ed. T. Christoffel, D. Finkelhor, and D. Gilberg. New York: Holt, Rinehart and Winston, 1970.

Girvan, Norman. "The Development of Dependency Economics in the Caribbean and Latin America: Review and Comparison," *Social and Economic Studies* 22 (1973).

Glazer, William A. "The Migration and Return of Professionals," Columbia University, Bureau of Applied Social Research, September 1973.

Gonick, C. "Socialism and the Economics of Growthmanship." In *Essays on the Left*, ed. L. La Pierre et al. Toronto: McClelland & Stewart, 1971.

Grant, George. *Lament for a Nation*. Toronto: McClelland & Stewart, 1965.

Gregory, Frances W. and Neu, Irene D. "The American Industrial Elite in the 1870's: Their Social Origins." In *Men in Business: Essays on the Historical Role of the Entrepreneur*, ed. William Miller, rev. ed. New York: Harper & Row, Harper Torch Books, 1952.

Guzzardi, Walter. *The Young Executives*. New York: New American Labor, 1965.

Hacker, Louis M. *The Course of American Economic Growth and Development*. New York: John Wiley, 1970.

Heidrick and Struggles, Inc. *Profile of the Board of Directors*. Chicago: Heidrick and Struggles, 1971.

———— *Profile of a President*. Chicago: Heidrick and Struggles, 1972.

———— *Profile of a Canadian President*. Chicago: Heidrick and Struggles, 1973.

Horowitz, David. *The Free World Colossus*, rev. ed. New York: Hill and Wang, 1971.

Innis, Harold. *The Cod Fisheries: The History of an International Economy*. New Haven: Yale Univ. Press, 1940.

———— *Essays in Canadian Economic History*, ed. Mary Q. Innis. Toronto: Univ. of Toronto Press, 1956.

Jalée, P. *The Third World in World Economy*. New York: Monthly Review Press, 1969.

Jenkins, Robin. *Exploitation: The World Power Structure and the Inequality of Nations*. London: Paladin, 1971.

Johnson, D. "Dependence and the International System." In *Dependence and Underdevelopment in Latin America*, ed. J.D. Cockcroft et al. New York: Doubleday-Anchor, 1972.

Kalbach, Warren E. *The Impact of Immigration on Canada's Population*. Ottawa: Dominion Bureau of Statistics, 1970.

Kaplan, A.D.H. *Big Business Enterprise in a Competitive Society*. Washington: Brookings Institution, 1964.

Kaufman, Burton I. "The Organizational Dimensions of United States Economic Foreign Policy, 1900-1920," *BHR* 46 (1972).

Kay, Geoffrey. *Development and Underdevelopment: A Marxist Analysis.* New York: St. Martin's Press, 1975.

Keller, Suzanne. "The Social Origins and Career Lines of Three Generations of American Business Leaders." Ph.D. thesis, Department of Political Science, Columbia University, 1953.

Keohane, Robert O. and Nye, Joseph S. "World Politics and the International Economic System." In *The Future of the International Economic Order: An Agenda for Research*, ed. C.F. Bergsten. Lexington, Mass.: D.C. Heath, Lexington Books, 1973.

Knickerbocker, Frederick T. *Oligopolistic Reaction and Multinational Enterprise.* Boston: School of Business Administration, Harvard University, 1973.

Kolko, Gabriel. *Wealth and Power in America.* New York: Praeger, 1962.

———, *The Triumph of Conservatism: A Reinterpretation of American History, 1900-1916.* New York: Free Press, 1963.

——— *The Roots of American Foreign Policy.* Boston: Beacon Press, 1969.

Kuznets, Simon. "Proportion of Capital Formation to National Product," *American Economic Review* 42 (1952).

Larner, R.J. "Ownership and Control in the 200 Largest Non-financial Corporations, 1929-1963," *American Economic Review* 56 (1966).

Lary, Hal B., et al. "The United States As an International Creditor." In *American Economic Development Since 1860*, ed. William Greenleaf. New York: Harper & Row, 1968.

Lawson, Thomas W. "Pioneers and Speculators – Westinghouse versus 'The System.'" In *The Robber Barons Revisited*, ed. P. Jones. Lexington, Mass.: D.C. Heath, 1968.

Laxer, Jim. "Canadian Manufacturing and U.S. Trade Policy." In *(Canada) Ltd.*, ed. R. Laxer. Toronto: McClelland & Stewart, 1973.

Levitt, Kari. *Silent Surrender.* Toronto: Macmillan, 1970.

——— and McIntyre, Alister. *Canada-West Indies Economic Relations.* Centre for Developing-Area Studies, McGill University. Montreal: Canada Trade Committee, 1967.

Lewis, Cleona. *America's Stake in International Investments.* Washington: Brookings Institution, 1938.

Liebhafsky, H.H. *American Government and Business.* New York: John Wiley, 1971.

Litvak, I.A. and Maule, C.J. "The Multinational Corporation: Some Perspectives," *Canadian Public Administration* 13 (1970).

Loomis, Carol J. "For the Utilities, It's a Fight for Survival," *Fortune* 91 (March 1975).

Loving, Rush, Jr. "Outsider in the Throne Room at Kaiser," *Fortune* 91 (March 1975).

Lundberg, Ferdinand. *America's Sixty Families.* New York: Vanguard, 1937.

Magdoff, H. *The Age of Imperialism.* New York: Monthly Review Press, 1969.

Marshall, Herbert, Southard, Frank A., and Taylor, Kenneth W. *Canadian-American Industry: A Study of International Investments.* New Haven: Yale Univ. Press, 1936.

Mathias, Philip. *Takeover: The 22 Days of Risk and Decision That Created the*

World's Largest Newsprint Empire, Abitibi-Price. Toronto: Financial Post, 1976.

Martin, Linda G. "The 500: A Report on Two Decades," *Fortune* 91 (May 1975).

McDiarmid, O.J. *Commercial Policy in the Canadian Economy.* Cambridge, Mass.: Harvard Univ. Press, 1946.

McKie, Donald Craig. "An Ontario Industrial Elite: The Senior Executives in Manufacturing Industry." Ph.D. thesis, Department of Sociology, University of Toronto, 1974.

Miller, William. "American Historians and the Business Elite," *Journal of Economic History* 9 (1949). Reprinted in *Men in Business: Essays on the Historical Role of the Entrepreneur*, ed. William Miller, rev. ed. New York: Harper & Row, Harper Torch Books, 1962.

———— "The Recruitment of the American Business Elite." In *Men in Business: Essays on the Historical Role of the Entrepreneur*, ed. William Miller, rev. ed. New York: Harper & Row, Harper Torch Books, 1962.

Mills, C. Wright. "The American Business Elite: A Collective Portrait." In *Power, Politics and People*, ed. I.L. Horowitz. New York: Oxford Univ. Press, 1945.

———— *White Collar.* New York: Oxford Univ. Press, 1951.

———— *The Power Elite.* New York: Oxford Univ. Press, 1956.

Moody, John. *The Truth about the Trusts.* New York: Moody Publ., 1904.

———— "The Masters of Capital." In *The Historians' History of the United States*, ed. A.S. Berky and J.P. Shenton. New York: Putnam, 1966.

Moore, Barrington, Jr. *Social Origins of Dictatorship and Democracy.* Boston: Beacon Press, 1966.

Mueller, Willard F. "The Measure of Industrial Concentration." In *Superconcentration/Supercorporation*, ed. Ralph L. Andreano. Andover, Mass.: Warner Modular Publ., 1973.

Myers, Gustavus. *A History of the Great American Fortunes*, 1919; New York: Modern Library, 1936.

———— *A History of Canadian Wealth*, 1914; Toronto: James Lorimer, 1972.

Naylor, R.T. "Canada's International Commercial Expansion to 1914," *Our Generation* 10 (1975).

———— *The History of Canadian Business, 1867-1914*, 2 vols. Toronto: James Lorimer, 1975.

Nelles, H.V. *The Politics of Development: Forests, Mines and Hydro-Electric Power in Ontario, 1849-1941.* Toronto: Macmillan, 1974.

Nelson, Ralph L. *Merger Movements in American Industry, 1895-1956.* Princeton, N.J.: Princeton Univ. Press, 1959.

Nettels, Curtis P. "The Economics of the Constitution." In *Views of American Economic Growth*, ed. T.C. Cochran and T.B. Brewer. New York: McGraw-Hill, 1966.

Neufeld, E.P. *A Global Corporation: A History of the International Development of Massey-Ferguson Limited.* Toronto: Univ. of Toronto Press, 1969.

Neuwirth, Gertrud. "A Weberian Outline of a Theory of Community: Its Application to the 'Dark Ghetto,' " *British Journal of Sociology* 20 (1969).

Nevins, Allan. "The Emergence of Modern America, 1865-1875," 1927; reprinted in *The Historians' History of the United States*, ed. A.S. Berky and

J.P. Shenton. New York: Putnam, 1966.

Newcomer, Mabel. *The Big Business Executive: The Factors That Made Him, 1900-50.* New York: Columbia Univ. Press, 1955.

Newman, Peter C. *The Canadian Establishment*, vol. I. Toronto: McClelland & Stewart, 1975.

Nichols, Theo. *Ownership, Control and Ideology.* London: Allen and Unwin, 1969.

North, Douglass C. "The United States in the International Economy, 1790-1950." In *American Economic History*, ed. S.E. Harris. New York: McGraw-Hill, 1961.

O'Connor, James. *The Fiscal Crisis of the State.* New York: St. Martin's Press, 1973.

Parai, Louis. *Immigration and the Emigration of Professional and Skilled Manpower during the Post-War Period.* Special Study No. 1, Economic Council of Canada. Ottawa, 1965.

Parkin, Frank. "Strategies of Social Closure in Class Formation." In *The Social Analysis of Class Structure*, ed. F. Parkin. London: Tavestock, 1974.

Pelton, Richard. "Who Really Rules America?" *Progressive Labor* 7 (1970).

Pentland, H.C. "The Role of Capital in Canadian Economic Development before 1875," *CJEPS* 16 (1950).

―――― "The Development of a Capitalist Labour Market in Canada," *CJEPS* 25 (1959).

Perry, Robert L. *Galt, U.S.A.* Toronto: Maclean-Hunter, 1971.

Petras, J. "U.S. Business and Foreign Policy in Latin America." In *Economics: Mainstream Readings and Radical Critiques*, ed. David Mermelstein. New York: Random House, 1970.

―――― "Class Structure and Its Effects on Political Development." In *Radical Sociology*, ed. J.D. Colfax and J.L. Roach. New York: Basic Books, 1971.

Porter, John. *The Vertical Mosaic: An Analysis of Social Class and Power in Canada.* Toronto: Univ. of Toronto Press, 1965.

―――― *Canadian Social Structure: A Statistical Profile.* Toronto: McClelland & Stewart, Carleton Library No. 32, 1967.

Pratt, Larry. *The Tar Sands: Syncrude and the Politics of Oil.* Edmonton: Hurtig, 1976.

Preston, Lee. "Economic Concentration, Size Mobility, and Competition Concepts and Hypotheses." Hearings before the Subcommittee on Antitrust and Monopoly of the Committee on the Judiciary, U.S. Senate, 88th Congress, 2nd Session, Part 1, July 1, 2 and Sept. 9-11, 1964. Reprinted in Warner Modular Publications, No. 574. Andover, Mass.: Warner Modular Publ., 1974.

Redlich, Fritz. "The First Period: Some Characteristics." In *Views of American Economic Growth*, ed. T.C. Cochran and T.B. Brewer. New York: McGraw-Hill, 1966.

Reynolds, Lloyd G. *The Control of Competition in Canada.* Cambridge, Mass.: Harvard Univ. Press, 1940.

Richmond, Anthony H. *Post-War Immigrants in Canada.* Toronto: Univ. of Toronto Press, 1967.

―――― "Sociology of Migration in Industrial and Post-Industrial Societies." In *Migration*, ed. J.A. Jackson. London: Cambridge Univ. Press, 1969.

Ridgeway, James. *The Last Play*. New York: E.P. Dutton, 1973.

Rodgers, William. *Think: A Biography of the Watsons and IBM*. New York: Stein & Day, 1969.

Rose, Stanford. "Why They Call It 'Fat City,'" *Fortune* 91 (March 1975).

———— "The Misguided Furor about Investments from Abroad," *Fortune* 91 (May 1975).

Rosenbluth, Gideon. "Industrial Concentration in Canada and the United States," *CJEPS* 20 (1954).

———— "Concentration and Monopoly in the Canadian Economy." In *Social Purpose for Canada*, ed. M. Oliver. Toronto: Univ. of Toronto Press, 1961.

Ryerson, Stanley B. *The Founding of Canada, Beginnings to 1815*. Toronto: Progress Books, 1960.

Safarian, A.E. *The Canadian Economy in the Great Depression*. Toronto: Univ. of Toronto Press, 1959. Toronto: McClelland & Stewart, Carleton Library No. 54, 1970.

Scheinberg, Stephen. "Invitation to Empire: Tariffs and American Economic Expansion in Canada," *BHR* 47 (1973).

Scott, Franklin D., ed. *World Migration in Modern Times*. Englewood Cliffs, N.J.: Prentice-Hall, 1968.

Sharp, Mitchell. "Canada-U.S. Relations: Options for the Future," *International Perspectives*. Ottawa: Information Canada, Autumn, 1972.

Sheehan, Robert. "Proprietors in the World of Big Business." In *American Society, Inc.*, ed. M. Zeitlin. Chicago: Markham Publ., 1970.

Sheridan, Richard B. "The British Credit Crisis of 1772 and the American Colonies." In *Views of American Economic Growth*, ed. T.C. Cochran and T.B. Brewer. New York: McGraw-Hill, 1966.

Smigel, Erwin O. *The Wall Street Lawyer*. New York: Free Press, 1964.

Smith, Dusky Lee. "Sociology and the Rise of Corporate Capitalism." In *The Sociology of Sociology*, ed. L.T. and J. Reynolds. New York: David McKay, 1970.

Spelt, Jacob. *Urban Development of South-Central Ontario*. Toronto: McClelland & Stewart, Carleton Library No. 57, 1972.

St. John-Jones, L.W. "The Exchange of Population between the United States of America and Canada in the 1960's," *International Migration* 11 1973.

Sunkel, Osvaldo. "Transnational Capitalism and National Disintegration in Latin America," *Social and Economic Studies* 22 (1973).

Tarbell, Ida M. "The Nationalization of Business, 1879-1898." In *The Historians' History of the United States*, ed. A.S. Berky and J.P. Shenton. New York: Putnam, 1966.

Taussig, F.W. and Joslyn, C.S. *American Business Leaders*. New York: Macmillan, 1932.

Thomas, Brinley, ed. *Economics of International Migration*. London: Macmillan, 1958.

———— "Migration: Economic Aspects." *International Encyclopedia of the Social Sciences*, 1966.

———— *Migration and Economic Growth: A Study of Great Britain and the Atlantic Economy*. 2nd ed. Cambridge: Cambridge Univ. Press, 1973.

Thomson, Dale. *Louis St-Laurent: Canada*. Toronto: Macmillan, 1967.

Tuckman, Howard P. *The Economics of the Rich*. New York: Random House, 1973.

Tugendhat, Christopher. *The Multinationals.* New York: Random House, 1972.

Tulchinsky, Gerald. "The Montreal Business Community, 1837-1853." In *Canadian Business History: Selected Studies, 1497-1971*, ed. D.S. Macmillan. Toronto: McClelland & Stewart, 1972.

Turner, Lewis. *Invisible Empires.* New York: Harcourt Brace Jovanovich, 1971.

Turner, Ralph H. "Modes of Social Ascent through Education: Sponsored and Contest Mobility." In *Class, Status and Power: A Reader in Social Stratification*, ed. Reinhard Bendix and S.M. Lipset. 2nd ed. New York: Free Press, 1966.

United Nations, Department of Economic and Social Affairs. *Multinational Corporations in World Development.* New York: Praeger Publ., 1974.

U.S., Congress, House, Committee on Banking and Currency, Sub-committee on Domestic Finance [Patman Committee], *Commercial Banks and Their Trust Activities*, 90th Cong. 2nd Sess., 1968.

————, Department of Commerce, Bureau of the Census, *Statistical Abstract of the United States, 1974.* Washington: U.S. Govt. Printing Office, 1974.

Van Alstyne, R.W. *The Rising American Empire.* New York: Oxford Univ. Press, 1960.

———— *Empire and Independence.* New York: John Wiley, 1965.

Van der Kroef, J.M. "The U.S. and the World's Brain Drain," *International Journal of Comparative Sociology* 11 (1970).

Vaupel, James W. and Curhan, Joan P. *The World's Multinational Enterprises.* Cambridge, Mass.: Harvard Univ. Press, 1973.

Vernon, Raymond. *Sovereignty at Bay, the Multinational Spread of U.S. Enterprises.* New York: Basic Books, 1971.

———— *Manager in the International Economy.* 2nd ed. Englewood Cliffs, N.J.: Prentice-Hall, 1972.

Viner, Jacob. *Canada's Balance of International Indebtedness, 1900-1913.* Cambridge, Mass.: Harvard Univ. Press, 1924.

Wallerstein, Immanuel. *The Modern World System: Capitalist Agriculture and the Origins of the European World Economy in the Sixteenth Century.* New York: Academic Press, 1974.

Warner, Lloyd W. and Abegglen, James. *Occupational Mobility in American Business and Industry, 1928-1952.* Minneapolis: Univ. of Minnesota Press, 1955.

Warnock, John W. *Partner to Behemoth: The Military Policy of a Satellite Canada.* Toronto: New Press, 1970.

———— "Free Trade Fantasies: The Case of the Farm Implements Industry," *This Magazine* 9 (1975).

Weber, Max. *Economy and Society*, ed. G. Roth and C. Wittich. New York: Bedminster Press, 1968.

Wecter, Dixon. "The Age of the Great Depression, 1929-1941." In *The Historians' History of the United States*, ed. A.S. Berky and J.P. Shenton. New York: Putnam, 1966.

Weldon, J.C. "Consolidations in Canadian Industry, 1900-1948." In *Restrictive Trade Practices in Canada*, ed. L.A. Skeoch. Toronto: McClelland & Stewart, 1966.

Wilkins, Mira. *The Emergence of Multinational Enterprise: American Business Abroad from the Colonial Era to 1914.* Cambridge, Mass.: Harvard Univ. Press, 1970.

_____ *The Maturing of Multinational Enterprise: American Business Abroad from 1914 to 1970.* Cambridge, Mass.: Harvard Univ. Press, 1974.

Williams, Glen. "Canadian Industrialization. We Ain't Growin' Nowhere," *This Magazine* 9 (1975).

Williams, William Appleman. *The Contours of American History.* Chicago: Quadrangle Books, 1966.

Wolfe, David A. "Political Culture, Economic Policy and the Growth of Foreign Investment in Canada." M.A. thesis, Department of Political Science, Carleton University, Ottawa, 1973.

Wolff, R. "The Foreign Expansion of U.S. Banks," *Monthly Review* 23 (1971).

Zeitlin, Maurice. "Corporate Ownership and Control: The Large Corporation and the Capitalist Class," *American Journal of Sociology* 79 (1974).

Index

Abegglen, James, 332, 336, 371n
Abitibi Power and Paper (now Abitibi
    Paper),71, 136, 157,157n,177,179
Academics, 216-17, 247, 259
Accountability, 10, 12
Acheson, T.W., 371n
Acquired characteristics, 28-29
Acquisitions. See Mergers
Acquitaine Co. of Canada, 153
Act for International Development
    (AID), 109-10
Actuaries, 264
Administration, 48, 55-57, 56n,
    99-101
Admiral Corp., 206
Advertising, 9, 11
Aetna Explosives, 70
Aetna Life and Casualty, 144, 147,
    178, 250, 316, 330
Africa, 106-07, 116, 123
Agriculture, 41, 43, 50-51, 50n,
    58-59, 69, 72, 74, 75n, 95-96, 292
Aikenhead Hardware, 135n
Aikens, Gordon Harold, 213
Aikens, Margaret Anne, 213
Aikens, Mary Frances Myrtle, 213
Aircraft industry, 70-71, 106, 156,
    206, 325
Aird, Hon. John Black, 177, 280
Aird, Zimmerman and Berlis (To-
    ronto law firm), 177
Airlines, 148-49, 206, 319
Aitken, Hugh G.J., 33n, 54n, 84-86,
    361n-62n, 364n, 367n
Aitken, Max (Lord Beaverbrook),
    62, 62n
Alberta Gas Trunk Line, 280

Alberta Natural Gas, 281
Alberta Products Pipe Line, 153
Alexander, Malcolm L., 23n
Algoma Central Railway, 177
Algoma Steel, 76-77, 158, 178, 218
Allen, Michael P., 327, 370n-71n
Alliance, 6-7, 17-18, 22, 79, 90, 94,
    129, 131, 179-80, 182, 288,
    292-94, 298
Allied Chemical, 188, 191, 195, 233,
    249, 322, 329
Aluminum Co. of America (Alcoa),
    61, 70n, 145, 160, 160n, 323, 330,
    344
Aluminium Co. of Canada (Alcan),
    81-82, 99-100, 100n, 115n, 120,
    120n, 123, 160-62, 161n, 179, 194,
    203, 280, 365n
Amalgamated Copper, 56n
AMAX, Inc., (formerly American
    Metal Climax), 151-52, 154, 177,
    195, 249, 280, 320, 331
Amerada Hess Corp., 152, 320, 331
American Airlines, 191, 199, 202,
    212, 319, 331, 343, 347
American Brands, 321, 331
American Can, 46, 323, 330
American Cyanamid, 280, 322, 331
American Electrical Power, 198, 249,
    319, 331
American Express, 179, 188, 192,
    244, 249-50, 317, 330
American Gas and Electric, 191
American Home Products, 323, 331
American Revolution, 8, 35, 37-40,
    44, 49, 78, 137
American Sales Book Co., 65

American Security Trust, 195
American Standard Inc., 206, 212,
    245, 279, 326, 331, 345
American Sugar Refining Co., 48
American Telephone and Telegraph
    (AT&T), 46, 60, 66, 76, 145-46,
    150, 164, 176n, 187, 191-92, 201,
    230, 233, 319, 324n, 330
American Tobacco, 46, 48, 188
American Trust, 199
American Woolen, 191
Ames, A.E., & Co. Ltd., 76-77
Anaconda Copper Co., 68, 74, 158n,
    188, 323, 331
Anderson, Charles H., 372n
Anderson, Robert B., 249
Andover (School), 240-41
Andreano, Ralph L., 138-39, 367n
"Anglo", 231-32, 232n, 264, 270-71,
    286-87
Anglo-Canadian Telephone, 119
Annexation Manifesto of 1849,
    42-43, 42n
Anti-trust legislation, 48, 61, 135,
    150, 164
Appleton, Nathan, 38
Argentina, 121
Argus Corp., 24n, 120, 135, 159, 178,
    213
Armco Steel Corp., 84, 158, 202, 323,
    331
Armour & Co., 47, 135, 149n
Armstrong Rubber Co., 148
Ascriptive characteristics, 28-29, 208,
    223, 257, 332
Ashland Oil, Inc., 322, 331
Asia, 58, 76, 91, 106-07, 116
Atlantic Refining, 134
Atlantic Richfield, 158, 158n, 212,
    322, 330
Augusta National Club (Georgia),
    345-46
Australia, 25n, 74, 107n, 116-17,
    122n, 124, 148
Auto Pact, 2, 160
Automobiles, 9, 12, 55, 59-60, 59n,
    67-70, 74, 76, 122, 294, 325
Avco Co., 212
Averitt, Robert T., 344, 368n, 372n

AVM Corp., 111
Avon Products, 254

Bahamas, 121
Baillie, Aubrey Wilton, 213
Ball, George Wildman, 195
Balogh, T., 127, 367n
Baltimore and Ohio Railroad, 46
Baltzell, E. Digby, 31, 49, 208n, 210,
    236n, 239-42, 359n-60n,
    369n-70n, 372n
Bank of America (formerly Bank of
    Italy), 43, 144, 147, 199, 202, 206,
    234, 249, 312, 330, 345
Bank of Canada, 179
Bank of Detroit, 202
Bank of Manhattan, 134
Bank of Montreal, 54, 114, 119, 147,
    178, 181, 192, 213, 234, 280-81,
    312-13
Bank of Nova Scotia, 54, 119, 121,
    147, 177, 181, 281, 312-14
Bank of the United States, 39
Bankers Trust New York, 143-44,
    147, 201, 204, 244-45, 280, 316,
    330
Bank directors, 46, 51, 55, 211,
    221-22, 231, 233, 244, 246, 328-29
Banking and financial executives,
    184, 187-88
Banks, 10, 17, 38, 39, 41, 43-44,
    46-47, 50-51, 55-57, 63-64, 66-69,
    72, 76-77, 95, 102, 104-05, 113-14,
    116n, 118-21, 119n, 124, 133,
    143-47, 143n, 164-71, 165n, 174,
    174n, 176, 231, 291-92, 296, 300,
    312-14, 316, 343-45
Bannock, E., 367n
Banque Canadienne Nationale, 312
Baran, Paul, 15-16, 15n, 358n
Barbados, 119
Barbour, Jeffery, 328-29, 388n
Barclay's Bank, 121
Barnet, Richard J., 367n-68n, 372n
Barr, Joseph Walker, 195
Barran, Sir David, 279
Barriers, 268-71, 274-75, 277
Baruch, Bernard, 65
Bata Shoes, 124

Bata, Thomas, 124
B.C. Packers, 214
Beard, Charles and Mary, 359n, 360n
Beatrice Foods, 134n, 135, 156, 162, 177, 201, 249, 320, 331
Beaver Lumber, 135n
Bechtel Group, 244, 250
Bechtel, Kenneth Karl, 197
Bechtel, Stephen Davison, 197
Bechtel, Stephen Jr., 197, 244-45
Bechtel, W.A., Ltd., 197
Behrman, J.N., 98, 365n
Beinecke, William S., 198
Belgium, 103, 191, 252
Bell and Howell, 248
Bell, Charles H., 345
Bell, Daniel, 344, 372n
Bell Telephone of Canada, 60, 76, 111, 120, 150, 161n, 176, 179, 200, 203, 213, 234, 279
Bemis Brothers, 198
Bemis, Judson, 198
Bendix Aviation, 74
Bendix Corp., 160, 186, 255, 325, 330
Bendix, Reinhard, 207n, 335, 371n-72n
Bennett, William John, 279
Benson and Hedges (Canada) Ltd., 201
Berkeley, Norborne, Jr., 187
Berky, A.S., 360n-61n
Bermuda, 311
Bertram, G.W., 54n
Bethlehem Steel Corp., 159, 187, 191, 201, 249, 323, 330
Biggers, John D., 80
Billes family, 197
Binger, James, 280
Binzen, P., 149n
Biographical sources, 207, 207n
Black, Eli, 347
Black, Eugene Robert, 249
Black, George Montegu, Jr., 213
Blackie, William, 280
Blacks, 14, 29, 229-32, 232n, 336n
Blaine, Charles Gillespie, 191
Blair, Robert S., 281
Blind Brook Club (Port Chester, N.Y.), 243-44

Block family, 200-01
Block, Fred, 358n
Block, Joseph Leopold, 200-01
Block, Leigh Bloom, 200-01, 212
Block, Philip Dee, Jr., 201
Board size, 164
Boeing Co., 160, 201, 204, 212, 325, 331
Boeschenstein, William Wade, 198
Boise Cascade Corp., 179, 200, 244, 249, 321, 331
Bombardier Corp., 250
Booth Fisheries of Canada, 157
Borden Co., 67, 320, 330
Borg-Warner Corp., 192, 198, 212, 322, 330
Boundaries, 1-2, 4, 11, 21, 39, 57, 73, 131, 259, 289-90, 292, 298-99
Bourgault, Pierre, 87-88, 120n, 364n
Bowaters Mersey Paper Co., 233
Bowes Co., 213
Boyles, Thomas, 147
BP Canada, 153, 280
Brady, Robert A., 360n, 362n-63n
Branch plants, 3, 18, 20, 22, 26, 52-53, 61, 64, 68, 68n, 70-71, 73-74, 76, 86, 89, 93, 95, 99, 102, 113, 115n, 124, 128, 141, 162, 172, 174, 179-82, 218, 221, 255-56, 259-60, 269, 271, 283, 286-89, 292-93, 295, 96, 340, 349. See also Multinational corporations; Subsidiaries
Brascan (formerly Brazilian Traction, Light, Heat and Power Corp.), 114, 116n, 121-24, 122n, 176, 178, 202, 281
Brazil, 122, 123
Braverman, Harry, 32n
Brebner, John Bartlet, 33n, 36, 40, 50, 64, 359n-62n, 370n
Bridges, Harold, 280
Brinco Ltd., 146
British Columbia Forest Products, 135
British Columbia Telephone, 150
British North America (BNA), 33, 35-36, 37n, 40, 42-45, 48
British-North America Committee, 279-80

British Petroleum, 112
British Steel, 213
Brody Investments, 212
Brody, Sidney F., 212
Bronfman family, 197
Brook Club (N.Y.), 178, 242
Buckley, Kenneth, 49-50, 360n, 363n
Budd, John Marshall, 201
Budd, Ralph, 201
Builders Financial Co., 147
Bunting, David, 328-29, 370n
Burch, Philip, 341-44, 342n-43n,
    372n
Bureaucratic elite, 195, 247-50
Burgess, D., 368n
Burlington Industries, 195, 321, 322,
    343, 343n
Burlington Northern (Manitoba),
    149
Burlington Northern Railway, 198,
    201, 251, 318, 330
Burma Oil, 112
Burns family, 197
Burns Foods, 250
Burr, Francis Hardon, 191
Burroughs Corp., 280, 324, 330
Burton, Betty Kennedy, 234
Burton, Charles Luther, 197
Burton, Edgar E.G., 197
Burton family, 197, 234
Burton, G. Allan, 197, 234
Business Council, 246
Business leaders, 207, 207n
Butler, Robert J., 181
Butz, Earl L., 248-49

Calgary Power, 62n, 176-77
Camaguey Electric and Traction, 62n
Campbell, Alistair Matheson, 177
Campbell, Nicholas Joseph, Jr., 280
Campbell Soup, 178, 198
Canada Car & Foundry Co., 62n
Canada Cement, 62n, 213
Canada Development Corp., 111
Canada Life, 176, 178, 245, 308-10
Canada Packers, 77, 181, 281
Canada Permanent Trust, 178
Canada Power and Paper, 62n, 71
Canada Rand Drill Co., 60

Canada Steamship Lines (CSL),
    135-36, 250
Canada Trust, 179, 280
Canada Wire and Cable, 124
Canadelle Ltée, 157
Canadian-American Committee, 2,
    246, 279, 370n
Canadian Arctic Gas Study Ltd., 152,
    154
Canadian Association for Latin
    America, 124, 246
Canadian Bechtel, 281
Canadian Club (N.Y.C.), 177-78
Canadian Consolidated Grain, 200
Canadian Executive Service Over-
    seas, 246
Canadian Forest Products, 280
Canadian General Electric, 53, 70,
    178, 181, 301
Canadian Grand Trunk, 64
Canadian Imperial Bank of Com-
    merce, 114, 119, 147, 154, 176-79,
    181, 188, 213, 280
Canadian-Ingersoll-Rand Co., 60
Canadian International Paper, 245,
    280
Canadian International Power, 119
Canadian Javelin, 159
Canadian Manufacturers' Associa-
    tion, 20, 124
Canadian National Railways (CNR),
    124, 270
Canadian Northern Railway, 64
Canadian Overseas Paper, 157
Canadian Pacific Investments, 135,
    177
Canadian Pacific Railway (CPR), 54n,
    63-64, 120, 135, 154, 176, 178,
    213, 245, 250, 254, 270, 279, 291
Canadian Pacific Steamships, 136
Canadian Pacific Transport, 136
Canadian Tire Corp., 197
Canals, 15, 41, 48, 50, 72, 103
Cannon, Brown Woodburn, 201
Cannon, Hugh Brown, 201
Canterbury (School), 240
Cape Breton Trust, 62n
Capital, 9, 16, 17, 18, 20, 30, 31, 38,
    40, 129, 133, 289-90

Capital drains, 3, 15, 22, 25, 126, 294
Capital sources, 10, 16, 39, 42, 44-45, 48, 50-53, 56, 62n, 64-66, 68n, 70, 72-73, 79, 84, 88-90, 92-93, 101, 108, 128, 133, 146, 169-70, 288, 295, 350
Career avenues, 29, 215-18, 233, 252
Career patterns, 184-206, 210, 233
Caribbean, 113-14, 120, 123
Carlson, Edward E., 343, 345
Carlson, Robert John, 201
Carnegie, Andrew, 57
Catelli Ltd., 135n
Caterpillar Tractor Co., 192, 199, 205, 250, 280, 325, 330
Cathcart, Silas Strawn, 280
Cayman Islands, 119
Cedar Rapids Transmission, 160n
Celanese Canada, 250, 280
Celanese Corp., 188, 191, 322, 331
Central America, 76, 116, 121
Centralization, 98, 132, 154, 172, 293. See also Concentration; Consolidations
Centre (or Metropolitan) nations, 6-7, 15, 19, 22-23, 36, 98-99, 113
CFRB Ltd., 234
Chains, 133
Champion International, 157, 321, 331
Chandler, Alfred D., Jr., 48, 56, 56n, 350n-62n, 367n
Chandler, Otis, 198
Charter companies, 34
Charter New York, 280, 316, 330
Chase Manhattan Corp., 102, 134, 137, 143-44, 147, 149, 164, 188, 195, 201, 203, 205, 212, 232, 254-55, 280, 316, 330, 343
Chase Manhattan Mortgage & Realty Trust, 144
Chase National Bank, 134, 145, 188
Chavteau Clique, 36
Chemco Leasing, 147
Chemical Corn Exchange, 135
Chemical New York, 135, 137, 143-44, 147, 165n, 186-88, 192-93, 199, 200-01, 245, 316, 330
Chemicals, 55, 59n, 75, 93, 156, 206, 322

Cherry, Zena, 369
Chessie System, 255, 318, 331
Chevron, 151
Chicago and Southern Airlines, 206
Chicago Club, 243
China, 154, 191, 289-90
Chinn, Joseph William, 187
Choate (School), 49, 239-40, 281
Chodos, Robert, 366n, 368n
Christina Corp., 201
Chrysler Canada, 177
Chrysler Corp., 67, 70, 115n, 160, 177, 205, 230, 244, 249, 280, 325, 330
Circulation, sphere of, 6, 15n, 16, 16n, 18, 24, 80, 127, 167, 169, 184, 287, 291, 299
Citicorp. See First National City Bank
Citicorp Leasing International, 147
Cities Service, 158, 186, 249, 322, 331
Citizens Southern Realty Investors, 144
City Bank Farmers Trust, 188
Civil War (American), 8, 33, 41, 44, 78, 334
Clark, Howard Longstreth, 244
Clark, K.H.J., 123-24
Class, 1, 4, 8, 17n, 20-22, 26-32, 32n, 34, 78, 127, 131, 257, 282-87, 292-93, 295-96, 298, 347, 351; barriers, 256-67; mobility, 30, 183, 207; of nomination, 28-29, 206-07, 209, 235, 241; of reproduction, 20, 206, 209-11, 214, 234-35, 241, 337, 347; origins, 2, 27, 29, 186, 206-10, 215-17, 220-21, 224-25, 228-29, 233, 237-41, 272-75, 273n, 282-83, 286, 333-39, 356-57
Clausen, A.W., 345
Clayor, William Graham IV, 191
Cleary, Catherine Blanchard, 233-34
Cleveland Trust Co., 65
Clyne, Hon. J.V., 280
CNA Financial Corp., 200, 212, 255, 317, 331
Coal, 72, 94n, 296
Coca-Cola Co., 321, 331
Cochran, Thomas C., 57n, 58, 359n, 361n-64n

Coleman, John Hewson, 177
Colgate-Palmolive Co., 177, 212, 323, 331, 345
Colonies, 6-7, 15, 18-19, 34-38, 41, 43-44, 54, 102
Columbia Gas System, 150, 319, 331
Columbia University, 190, 236-37
Combinations, 47, 55-56
Cominco, 119, 136
Commerce, 11, 14, 29, 34, 40, 58-59, 63; training in, 184, 186-87, 189, 192-94, 196, 214, 237-38
Commercial capital, 36, 38; class, 15, 19, 43n, 50-51, 50n, 124, 290-91
Committee for Economic Development, 246-47
Commonwealth Edison, 192, 198, 200, 203, 270, 319, 330
Competition, 27, 34, 39, 41, 46, 55, 125, 132-33, 147-49, 152, 154
Comprador, 24n, 181, 228-29, 282-83; individual, 173, 180-81, 180n, 290; structural, 24-26, 94, 180-81, 180n, 293
Comstock International, 218
Concentration, 3, 33, 46, 48, 73-74, 103, 132-34, 138-41, 140n, 143, 162, 183, 293, 315. See also Centralization; Consolidations
Confederation, 49-50
Confederation Life, 121, 308-10
Conference Board in Canada, 246
Conglomerates, 12, 134-36, 134n
Connally, John Bowden, Jr., 249
Connecticut General Insurance, 144, 245, 255, 317, 331
Connor, John Thomas, 195
Consolidated-Bathurst, 120, 135-36, 157, 177-78, 279-80
Consolidated Coal, 134
Consolidated Edison, 149, 188, 195, 198, 233, 319, 330
Consolidated Food Corp. of Canada, 157
Consolidated Foods, 157, 255, 320, 331
Consolidated holdings, 162
Consolidations, 33, 46-47, 52-53, 55-56, 59, 62, 70n, 78-79, 136. See

also Centralization; Concentration; Mergers
Conso of Canada, 157
Consortia, 132, 147, 152-54, 158, 291-92
Consumerism, 11
Consumers Power, 212, 319, 331
Contacts, continental, 2, 275-78
Container Corp. of America, 134
Continental Baking, 135
Continental Can Co., 186, 200, 244-45, 324, 330
Continental Casualty, 200
Continental Corp., 230, 317, 330
Continental elite, 22, 26, 172-80, 253-57
Continental Illinois Bank, 144, 147, 164, 198, 201, 205, 316, 330
Continental Mortgage Investors, 144
Continental Oil, 134, 178, 188, 201, 280, 320, 330
Continental system, 2, 3, 6-9, 12, 20-23, 26n, 53-54, 59, 63-64, 70, 78-79, 82-83, 85-86, 112, 124, 130-31, 141, 150-51, 154, 156, 179-80, 251, 258, 279-82, 290, 298
Continuity, 137-38
Cook, Donald Clarence, 249
Cooley, Richard Pierce, 187
Coopery, Marsh Alexander, 177-78
Copeland, Lammont du Pont, 201
Copeland, Norman A., 201
Copley, Helen K., 233
Copley, James S., 233
Copley Press, 233
Core institutions, 164
Corning Glass Works, 199
Corn Laws of 1846, 18, 42
Corporate capitalism, 8, 19, 33, 41-42, 46, 54-57, 59, 62, 78-79, 81, 133, 179-80, 204, 256, 258, 278, 292, 300
Coscan Industries, 157
Costanzo, Gesualdo A., 249
Costs, 9-10
Cotton, 17n, 34, 41, 44, 52, 63
Council on Foreign Relations, 246-67
Courts and Co., 205
Courts, Richard Winn, 205

Covington and Burling, 191
Cox, Sen. George Albertus, 114
CPC International Inc., 320, 331
Cravath, Swain and Moore (N.Y. law firm), 191
Crezdit Foncier, 250, 279
Credito Italiano, 102
Creighton, Donald G., 35, 37n, 39n, 42n, 359n
Crocker National Bank, 155n, 198-99, 202, 212, 244, 316, 330
Crown corporations, 82, 133, 248
Crown, Henry, 205
Crown, Lester, 198, 205
Crown Life, 121, 177, 181, 197, 250, 308-11
Crown Zellerbach, 157, 204, 321, 331
Crown Zellerbach (Canada), 157, 301
Crum and Forester Insurance, 144
Cuba, 289
Cubberley, D., 366n
Cullman, Hugh, 201
Cullman, Joseph Frederick II, 201
Culver, David Michael, 161n
Cuneo, Carl, 4, 259n
Curhan, J.P., 365n
Cutler, E. Newman, Jr., 212
Cutler, E. Newman III, 212
Cyprus Mines, 199

Dairy industry, 67
Daly, W.G., 371n
Danforth, Donald, Jr., 201
Danforth, William H. II, 201
Dartmouth University, 194, 236
Data coverage, 4, 164, 183n, 185, 196n, 297n, 253, 262, 262n, 273, 273n, 339n, 340-41, 352
Daughen, Joseph R., 149n
David, Donald Kirk, 194
Davis family, 160, 161
Davis, Nathaneal V., 161
Davis, Robert, 146
Dayton, Bruce Bliss, 198
Dayton, Donald Chadwick, 198
Dayton-Hudson Corp., 198
Dean, Arthur Hobson, 249
Declaration of Independence, 33

Deere & Co., 200-09, 254, 325, 331
Deere, John, 119
Deere, John, Ltd., 254
Deerfield (School), 240
Deering, Milliken Inc., 199
Deering, William, 203
Defensive expansionism, 3, 50
DeLimur, Charles Crocker, 202
Delta Air Lines, 205-06, 319, 331
Demerara Electric Co., 62n
Denmark, 253
Density of interlocks, 165-67, 166n, 184, 328-29, 328n
Dependency, 6-8, 18, 21-24, 21n, 88-89, 125-27, 172, 179-80, 182, 288, 294
Depression, Great, 67, 73-74, 81
Desmarais, Paul, 136
Desruisseaux, Paul, 178
Destler, Chester McArthur, 333, 361n, 371n
Detroit Club, 243
Detroit Edison, 199, 202, 319, 330
Deutsch, Dr. John J., 280, 363n
Deverell, John, 101n, 120n
Diamond Match Co., 47, 74
Dick, A.B., Co., 198
Dick, Albert Blake III, 198
Didrichsen, Jon, 135, 367n
Direct interlocks, 174, 174n, 179
Direct investment, 2, 15, 18, 25, 42, 54, 67-68, 68n, 74, 78, 80n, 88, 90, 93-94, 103-04, 107, 114-15, 121-22, 126-27, 259, 290, 293, 295, 297
Distillers Corporation-Seagrams, 77, 111, 119, 121, 197
Doan, Herbert Henry, 202
Dodge Co., 67
Dollar, Robert, Co., 198
Dollar, Robert Stanley, Jr., 198
Dome Mines, 68
Domhoff, G. William, 30-31, 208n, 240, 242, 246-47, 358n, 359n, 369n-70n, 372n
Dominant corporations, 3, 4, 9, 24, 24n, 26, 32, 59, 132-33, 141-64, 141n, 167-78, 172-73, 179, 197, 217-19, 315, 347

Domination, 3, 7, 22, 121, 182, 290-95

Dominican Republic, 121, 311

Dominion Bridge, 119

Dominion Foundry and Steel Co. (Dofasco), 158, 176, 281

Dominion Glass, 177, 213, 280

Dominion Life, 308-11

Dominion Securities, 77, 114

Dominion Steel and Coal, 76

Dominion Stores, 76, 135, 178, 213

Dominion Tanners, 213

Domtar, 157, 178

Donnelley, Gaylord, 198, 212

Donnelley, R.R., & Sons, 198, 212

Donnell, James C. II, 202

Donner, Frederick Garrett, 193

Dooley, Peter, 328-29, 370n

Dorrance, John Thompson, Jr., 198

Dorrance, John Thompson, Sr., 198

Dorsey, Bob Rawls, 342

Dosman, Edgar, 152, 154, 299-300, 368n-70n

Dos Santos, Theotonio, 19, 358n

Douglas Aircraft, 134

Douglas, Elisha P., 45, 359n-61n

Dow Chemical, 202, 322, 331

Dow, Herbert H., 202

Downing, Robert W., 251

Dow, William Henry, 202

Drache, Daniel, 4, 87, 364n

Drummond, B., 366n

Duke family, 343

Dundonald, Lord, 299

du Pont family, 57, 201, 344

du Pont, E.I., de Nemours & Co., 201, 322, 331

du Pont, Irenée, Jr., 201

Duquesne Club (Pittsburgh), 178, 243

Eastern Air Lines, 319, 331

Eastman Kodak Co., 46, 57, 158, 324, 330

Eaton Corp., 202, 212, 245, 323, 331

Eaton, Cynthia Carol, 213

Eaton, Cyrus, 239

Eaton family, 181, 197, 213

Eaton, John Wallace, 213

Eaton, T., Co., 181, 197, 213, 301

Economic Council of Canada, 280

Edison Electric Light Co., 47

Edison, Thomas A., 47

Education, 29, 65, 208-09, 233, 235-41, 272-73

Electrical Development Co., 51

Electrical industry, 47, 59n, 75

Electrolux (Canada), 157

Elite, 1-2, 4, 20, 26-32, 101-02, 293-94; economic, 4, 6, 9-10, 12-13, 24, 26, 28-30, 32, 98, 130-31, 133, 162, 167, 171, 173, 179, 183, 206-10, 214, 245, 273, 290-95, 302, 332-39, 347, 349; forums, 65-66, 245-47; switchers, 194-95

Elliott, Osborn, 369n

Ellsworth, Robert Fred, 249

El Paso National Bank, 206

El Paso Natural Gas, 106, 150, 204, 206, 249, 319, 331

Embargo Act of 1807, 40

Engineering and science, 11, 29-30, 65, 184-86, 195, 210, 214, 286

Entrepreneurial capitalism, 16, 33, 46, 48, 57, 78-79, 128, 184, 206, 258, 291

Episcopal (School), 240

Equitable Life, 191, 198, 200-01, 255, 317, 330

Erie Canal, 39

ESB Inc., 111, 146

Esmark Inc. (formerly Swift Co.), 156, 198, 203, 205, 279, 320, 330

Ethnicity, 29, 229-32, 232n, 255-56, 264, 270-71, 287-88, 334

Europe, 18, 44, 58, 61, 63, 71, 76, 82-83, 86, 91, 100, 107, 112, 117, 126, 290, 350

European Economic Community (EEC), 100, 107, 116, 161-62, 290

Excelsior Life, 178, 308-09

Exclusion, 27-28, 215

Executives, 24, 163, 165n, 169, 186, 186n, 189, 196-97, 218-23, 253, 285-86, 345

Exeter Academy, 240-41

Export Development Corporation

(EDC), 123
Exxon Corp., 95, 101, 146, 151-53, 244, 255, 280, 320, 330, 344

Falconbridge Nickel Mines, 101n, 109, 119n, 177-78, 249
Family capitalism, 28, 31, 196-97, 204
Family Compact, 36
Family firms, 57, 183-84, 187, 189, 193, 196-204, 196n, 209, 211, 214, 224, 230-31, 236-37, 286, 341-44
Farm machinery, 93-94, 325
Farrell, James, 66
Federal Grain, 213
Federal Reserve Bank Act of 1913 (U.S.), 56
Federal Reserve Board (U.S.), 57n
Federal Trade Commission (U.S.), 135, 139
Federated Department Stores, 195, 203, 230, 248, 318, 330
Felton, John R., 138, 367n
Field, Marshall, & Co., 147, 198
Field, Marshall V, 198
Finance (sector), 3, 6, 8, 10, 24, 45, 76, 94, 96, 106, 122, 137, 142-48, 155, 164-71, 173-76, 185, 189, 214-17, 221-22, 228, 252-53, 282
Finance departments, 184, 192-93, 210, 214
Financial capitalists, 6, 8, 10, 15, 17, 17n, 19, 24n, 33, 45-48, 51-53, 56, 59, 62, 64, 66-67, 79, 167, 292-93
Financial corporations, 3, 6, 8, 10, 24, 45, 76, 95, 106, 122. See also Banks; Insurance
Finlayson, Hon. William, 213
Finlayson, Mary Francis, 213
Finlayson, Phyllis, 213
Firestone, Kimball Curtis, 202
Firestone, Leonard Kimball, 202
Firestone, Martha, 202
Firestone, O.J., 50n, 95, 364n-65n
Firestone, Raymond Christy, 202
Firestone Tire and Rubber, 70, 202, 322, 331
First Bank System, 250, 316, 331
First Chicago Corp., 144, 147, 164, 192, 198, 200, 203, 212, 279, 316, 330

First Chicago Leasing of Canada, 147
First Mortgage Investors, 144
First National Bank, 45, 187, 192
First National Bank of Atlanta, 188
First National Bank of Chicago, 200-01
First National Boston, 187, 280, 316, 331
First National City Bank (Citicorp), 45, 58, 106, 137, 143-44, 147, 149, 164, 188, 199, 201, 234, 244, 249, 255, 316, 330, 345
First Wisconsin Trust, 233
First World War, 33, 65-66, 68-70
Fish, 15, 17n, 37n, 43, 87, 296
Fisher, Aiken Wood, 198
Fisher, Charles Thomas III, 202
Fisher, Max M., 344
Fisher Scientific, 198
Fitch, Robert, 146, 367n-68n, 372n
Flavin, Joseph B., 280
FMC Corp., 186, 205, 325, 330
Food and beverages, 25n, 41, 58-59, 62, 70n, 77-78, 94, 112, 156, 292, 320-21
Ford family, 202, 343
Ford, Henry, 60
Ford Motor Co., 25n, 59n, 60-61, 66, 70, 70n, 115n, 201-02, 325, 330
Ford Motor Co. of Canada, 120, 178, 181
Ford, William Clay, 202
Foreign born elite, 185n, 217, 227, 235, 246, 252, 283
Foreign control, 1-2, 4, 14, 66, 68, 78, 80, 91-92, 99, 227-28, 295-98, 305-06
Foreign investment, 2, 8, 14, 16, 23-24, 42, 53-54, 58, 67-68, 68n, 73-74, 82-83, 87, 90, 97. See also Direct investment; Portfolio investment
Foreign Investment Review Act, 300
Foreign Policy Association, 246
Foreign resident directors, 173-80, 174n, 252-53
Forget, Louis, 62
Fortier, L. Yves, 213
Fortune magazine, 338-39, 345

Foster, David R., 345
Foundations, 343
Fowler, Robert W., 279-80
F.P. Publications, 280
Fractions, capitalist class, 14, 17-18,
    17n, 20, 22-27, 78, 90, 93-95, 98,
    131, 180-81, 181n, 283-87, 292-93
France, 61, 73, 103, 111, 253
Franchises. See Chains
Frank, André Gunder, 21n, 126,
    366n-67n
Fraser Companies, 77
Frechette, W.D.H., 124
French Canadians, 8, 14, 231-32,
    232n, 264-65, 270-71
Frito-Lay, 205
Fuller Brush Co., 157
Fur, 15, 17n, 36, 37n, 39-40, 87
Fusee, Frederick George, 254-55

Galbraith, J.K., 133
Galtung, Johan, 21n, 23, 358n
Gardiner, W.D.H., 124
Garfield, Harry A., 65
Garvin, Clifton C., 246, 344
Garvin, James Maurice, 251
Gates, Thomas Sovereign, Jr., 251
Geneen, Harold S., 344
General Dynamics Corp., 198, 205,
    249, 255, 325, 330
General Electric Co., 45-47, 53, 57,
    74, 76, 80, 115n, 145-46, 158, 188,
    199, 203, 234, 244-45, 249, 280,
    324, 330
General Foods, 70n, 195, 230, 233,
    248, 250, 255, 320, 330
General Mills, 205, 345
General Motors Acceptance, 160
General Motors Corp., 59n, 60, 66,
    80-81, 115n, 146, 160, 164, 178,
    190, 193, 195, 198, 202-03, 230,
    233, 244-45, 325, 330, 344
General Motors of Canada, 60, 160,
    301
General Precision, 188
General Public Utilities, 212, 319,
    331
General Telephone & Electronics,
    150, 324

General Tire and Rubber, 203, 322,
    331
Genstar, 178, 279
George, P., 258n, 349-50, 373n
Georgia-Pacific Corp., 191, 321, 331
Gerard, Robert, 112
Germany, 100, 102-03, 111, 148, 254
Gerstacker, Carol Allan, 202
Gerstenberg, Richard Charles, 193
Getty Oil, 134, 200, 322, 330
Giannini, Amadeo Peter, 234
Gilbert, Dan, 365n-66n
Girvan, Norman, 21n
Glassco, Grant, 124
Glazer, William A., 370n
Gleed, Thomas F., 343
Globe-Union (Co.), 148
Go-between investment, 24-25, 25n,
    61, 70n, 97, 103n, 115-17, 148
Go-between nations, 1, 23, 50n, 114,
    125, 129, 351
Gonick, C., 365n
Goodrich, B.F., and Co., 70, 255,
    322, 331
Goodyear Tire and Rubber, 70, 186,
    191, 200, 249, 322, 330
Gordon, John P., 181
Gorwin Properties, 147
Gould family, 57
Grace, Joseph Peter, Jr., 202
Grace, William Russel, 202
Grace, W.R., and Co., 157, 162, 199,
    202, 234, 322, 330, 344
Grady, James, 250
Graflund, John Henry, 253-54
Grant, George, 80, 361n
Grant, W.T., Co., 148, 148n, 187,
    205, 318, 331
Granville, Maurice, 344
Great Atlantic and Pacific Tea Co.
    (A&P), 76, 148, 194, 200, 250, 318,
    330, 343, 343n
Great Lakes Paper, 136
Great Northern Electric, 80
Great West Life Assurance, 120, 135,
    213, 308-09
Greenewalt, Crawford Hallock, 201
Green, H.L., Co., 76
Gregory, F.W., 371n

Greyhound Corp., 106, 135, 149, 149n, 212, 319, 331
Groton (School), 49, 240-41
Guaranty Trust, 135, 191, 198
Guggenheim family, 57
Guinea, 100
Gulf and Western Industries, 135, 146, 326, 331
Gulf Oil, 115n, 145, 152-53, 178, 185, 187, 203, 254, 320, 331, 344, 347
Gulf Oil Canada, 178, 181, 185
Guyana, 100, 119-21, 311
Guzzardi, Walter, 338, 372n

Haas, Peter Edgar, 199
Haas, Walter A., Jr., 199
Hacker, Louis M., 41n, 45, 359n-61n
Halaby, Najeeb Elias, 249
Hale Brothers Stores, 199
Hale, Prentis Cobb, Jr., 199
Hamilton Group, 181
Hammar, Armand, 205
Hancock, John, Mutual Life, 187, 191, 249, 317, 331
Hanify, Edward Benno, 191
Hanna, M.A., Co., 199
Hanna [Ore] Mining, 84, 159, 245
Hanover Bank, 134
Hardin, Clifford M., 248
Harris Abbatoir, 281
Harris, Patricia R., 232-33
Harris, William Bowles, 281-82
Harris, William Cranfield, 281
Harris, William Thomas, 281
Hart, A.H., 124
Hartford Foundation, 343
Hart, George Arnold, 147, 178
Harvard University, 161n, 186, 190, 192, 194, 194n, 236-38, 241, 263, 272
Haslanger, Robert Urey, 186
Hatfield, Robert S., 244
Haughton, Daniel Jeremiah, 193
Hawley-Smoot Tariff (1930), 73
Hazard, Ellison Lockwood, 186
Headmasters' Association Schools, 208n
Heidrick and Struggles, 345, 347, 369n, 372n-73n

Heinz family, 344
Heinz, Henry John II, 199, 280
Heinz, H.J., Co., 60, 280
Heinz, Howard, 199
Heiskell, Marian, 233
Hewitt, William Alexander, 201
Hewlett-Packard Co., 205
Hewlett, William Redington, 205
Higgins, James Henry, 187
Hill (School), 240-41
Hill, James T., 54, 201
Hill, Richard Devereux, 187
Hillman Co., 199
Hillman, Henry Lea, 199
Himmelman, L.P., 343
Hiram Walker-Gooderham & Worts, 77, 119, 176, 202
Hobby, Oveta Culp, 234
Hoffman, Claire Giannini, 234
Holding companies, 56n, 70n, 119-20, 145-46
Holland, Jerome Hartwell, 230, 233
Hollinger Mines, 84, 120, 135, 158
Holt, Herbert, 114
Honeywell Inc., 178, 198, 212, 250, 280, 322, 330
Hoover, Herbert, 65
Horowitz, David, 366n
Hotchkiss (School), 49, 239-40
Houghton, Amory, Jr., 199
Houston Post, 234
Howe, C.D., 82, 83n, 85
Howe, C.D., Research Institute, 280
Howton, Frank, 207n, 335, 371n-72n
Hudson, J.L., Co., 199
Hudson, Joseph Lowthian, Jr., 199
Hudson's Bay Co., 35, 54, 154, 213
Hudson's Bay Gas and Oil, 154, 279-80
Humphrey, George Magoffin, 199
Humphrey, Gilbert Watts, 199, 245
Humphrey-Hanna Group, 146
Hurley, Edward, 66
Huron & Erie Mortgage, 179, 187
Hydro, 51, 58, 72, 72n, 296

IAC Ltd., 197, 218
IBM World Trade, 201
Identity, 7

Ideology, 27, 55-56, 102, 255, 278, 295, 332
Illinois Central Industries, 323, 331
Illinois Tool Works, 280
Immigration, 4, 39-40, 45, 50-51, 59, 254-78, 259n, 348-51
Imperial Bank, 213
Imperialism, 8, 34-38, 42, 55, 66, 131
Imperial Life Assurance, 120, 121, 135, 308-11
Imperial Oil, 70, 72, 76, 84, 95, 115n, 152-53, 255, 280, 303
Imperial preference (Ottawa Agreements), 60, 74
Imperial Wire and Cable, 60
INA Corp., 249, 317, 330
INCO Ltd. (formerly International Nickel Co. of Canada), 63-64, 68, 72n, 76, 100n, 111, 115n, 120, 120n, 123, 146, 154-55, 161, 178, 245, 255, 279-80, 307n
India, 61
Indigenous capitalists, 8, 17n, 21, 25, 25n, 79, 94, 125, 129, 167, 173, 179-82, 282-87, 290, 293-95
Indigenous power bases, 6, 51, 115, 122, 125, 180-81, 293
Indonesia, 154
Industrial capitalists, 15-18, 24-26, 33, 45-47, 62, 66-67, 79, 292-93
Industrialization, 6, 15, 15n, 18-19, 34, 37, 40-43, 46n, 52-53, 54n, 59, 63, 79-80, 83, 95-96, 128-29, 292-93, 296
Ingersoll Rock Drill Co., 60
Inheritance, 29, 183, 196-97, 209, 210-14, 219-21, 226, 238, 241, 301, 345, 347
Inland Steel Co., 159, 192, 200-01, 212, 255, 323, 331
Innis, Harold, 36, 359n
Insider positions, 186, 186n, 196-97, 218-23, 243-44, 285-86
Insurance companies, 10, 17, 45, 77, 96, 104-06, 113-14, 116n, 118, 118n, 121, 143-45, 143n, 164-70, 174, 300, 308-11, 317
Insurance directors, 51, 221-22, 232, 246, 328-29

Inter-American Development Bank, 124
Interlake Steel, 159
Interlocking directors, 2, 3, 26, 51, 162-71, 163n, 165n, 172n, 214, 218, 226, 328, 332, 347. See also Density of interlocks
International Business Machines (IBM), 68, 115n, 146, 164, 195, 199, 204, 232, 250, 326, 330
International Harvester Co., 45, 65, 75n, 119n, 192, 198, 201, 203, 251, 279, 325, 330
Internationalism, 255-56, 275
Internationalization, 22, 26, 252
International Paper and Power (now International Paper), 71, 245, 250, 321, 330
International Telephone and Telegraph (ITT), 68, 135, 146, 150, 158, 176n, 188, 249, 324, 331, 344
Interprovincial Pipe Line, 84
Investors Group, 135
Ireland, 308
Iron and steel, 25n, 34, 46, 50, 52, 58-59, 62-63, 72, 74, 76-78, 84, 94, 158, 292, 294, 323
Iron Ore Co. of Canada, 84, 159, 199, 245, 279
Iron Ore Transport, 158
Israel, 310
Italy, 102-03, 253
Itek Corp., 280

Jalee, P., 365n-66n
Jamaica, 100, 118-21, 310
James Bay project, 146
Jamieson, John Kenneth, 255, 344
Japan, 102-03, 111, 124, 289-90, 351
Jean de Brezbeuf College, 240
Jefferson, Thomas, 39
Jeffers, William, 81-82
Jeffery family, 197
Jenkins, R., 367n
Jewish ethnicity, 230-32, 232n
Johnson and Johnson, 323, 331
Johnson, D., 103
Joint ownership. See Consortia
Jones and Laughlin, 135

Jones, Horace C. II, 343
Joslyn, C.S., 332-33, 371n

Kaiser Aluminum and Chemical, 202, 255, 280, 323, 331
Kaiser, Edgar Fosburgh, 202
Kaiser, Edgar F., Jr., 202
Kaiser family, 344
Kaiser Industries, 344
Kaiser Resources, 202-03
Kalbach, Warren E., 257-58, 370n
Kaplan, A.D.H., 81, 367n
Kaufman, Burton I., 66, 362n
Kay, Geoffrey, 16n, 17-18, 358n
Keck, Howard B., 120n
Keller, Suzanne, 335-36, 371n
Kellogg family, 343
Kellwood Co., 148
Kelly Oil, S., 134
Kennecott Copper, 84, 123, 151-52, 154, 177, 188, 200, 244, 320, 330, 343
Kennedy family, 346
Kent (School), 240
Keyes, J., 366n
Key Pipe Line, 158
Killefer, Tom, 280
Kinder, Peabody, 45
Kinney, Earl Robert, 205
Kinship ties, 161, 161n, 209, 211-14, 231
Kirby, Robert, 149
Kircher, Donald, 346-47
Knickerbocker, Frederick T., 83n
Knoll Lake Minerals, 159
Knudsen, William S., 80
Koch Industries, 153
Koehane, Robert O., 356n
Kolko, Gabriel, 48, 56-67, 360n-61n, 366
Korea, 82, 84, 248
Kraftco Corp., 233, 320, 330
Kresge family, 343
Kresge, S.S., Co., 76, 148, 173, 303, 318, 330
Kroger Co., 198, 318, 331
Kuhn, Loeb & Co., 45, 200
Kuznets, Simon, 360n

Labatt, John, Ltd., 122n, 135n
Labour, 3, 4, 9-12, 17n, 18, 26, 37,
44, 48, 65, 68, 82, 95-96, 133, 289, 350. See also Working class
Lambert, Allen, 147
Land, 34, 37, 39, 59n
Lanier, George Heguley, Jr., 212
Lank, Herbert Hyman, 279
Lapham, Lewis A., 244
Larner, R.J., 345, 372n
Larry, R. Heath, 191
Lary, H.B., 362n
Lasker, Edward, 212
Latin America, 19, 21, 58, 82-85, 89, 91, 104, 106-10, 112-14, 123-25, 127-29, 294
Laura Secord, 135n
Laurentide Financial Corp., 120, 135, 147
Laurier, Sir Wilfrid, 299
Law partnerships, 180, 189-91, 218-20, 222, 286. See also Lawyers
Lawrenceville (School), 240
Lawson, John S., 244
Lawson, Thomas W., 47, 360n
Lawyers, 11, 29-30, 47, 65, 184, 186, 189-92, 195-96, 214, 215-17, 219, 222, 229, 252, 286. See also Law partnerships
Laxer, James, 368n
Lay, Herman Warren, 205-06
Lazard Frères, 42, 249
Lazarus, Charles Y., 203
Lazarus family, 203
Lazarus, Maurice, 203
Lazarus, Ralph, 203
Leasing, 147
Lee Carpets, 343
Lehman Bros., 195, 248
Leman, Paul, 123
Levitt, Kari, 68n, 89, 121, 361n, 366n
Lewis, Cleona, 33n, 53, 57, 59n, 67n, 359n, 360n
Lewis, John, Inc., 157
Libbey-Owens-Ford, 80
Liebhafsky, H.H., 362
Liedtke, John Hugh, 203
Liedtke, William C., Jr., 203
Liggett Co., 76
Lilly family, 343

Lincoln National, 249, 317, 331
Linder, Carl H., 344n
Lindsay, Frank A., 280
Links Club (N.Y.C.), 178, 212,
    243-44, 281-82
Little, Royal, 191
Litton Industries, Inc., 206, 326, 331
Litvak, I.A., 125, 367n
Lockheed Aircraft Corp., 191, 193,
    325, 331
Loeb family, 197
Loeb, M., Ltd., 197
London Life, 197, 308-09
Long crawl, 29, 188, 210, 217,
    220-21, 238, 244, 286, 347
Loomis (School), 240
Loomis, C.J., 368n
Loving, R., Jr., 373n
Loyalists, 36
Lowe, Joe, Corp., 157
Lower Canada College, 161n, 263
LTV Corp., 135, 323, 331
Luce, Charles Franklin, 195
Lundberg, Ferdinand, 333, 371n
Lykes, C.P., 203
Lykes, J.M., 203
Lykes, Joseph T., 203
Lykes-Youngstown Corp., 158-59,
    203, 323, 331

Macdonald, Sir John A., 51
MacDonald, Ray W., 280
MacGregor, Ian K., 280
MacGregor, Kenneth Robert, 187
Machinery, 55, 75, 326
MacMillan Bloedel, 111, 121, 176,
    178, 214, 254, 280, 303
MacMillan, Harvey Reginald, 214
Magdoff, Harry, 108, 365n-66n
Malaysia, 25n
Managers, 4, 101, 133, 136-37, 183,
    257-78, 341, 344n, 348-50, 348n,
    356-57
Manufacturers Hanover, 198,
    254-55, 316, 330
Manufacturers Hanover Trust, 135,
    143-44, 149, 164, 203, 232, 236
Manufacturers Life, 118, 213, 206-09
Manufacturers Trust, 134

Manufacturing (sector), 3, 8, 14,
    19-20, 22, 24, 34, 38-41, 43, 43n,
    46-47, 46n, 50-52, 50n, 52n,
    55-56, 58, 60n, 61, 65, 67-69, 71,
    73-74, 80, 89, 91-92, 92n, 94, 101,
    103-08, 106n, 115-16, 127, 134,
    139, 140, 140n, 142, 150-62,
    164-69, 173-76, 185, 189, 215-17,
    221-22, 226-28, 252-53, 256, 282,
    290, 297, 320-26
Maple Leaf Mills, 213
Marathon Oil Co. (formerly Ohio
    Oil), 158, 186, 202, 322, 331
Marathon Realty, 136
Marcor Inc., 148, 148n, 152, 234,
    318, 331
Marine Midland Banks, 191, 244,
    316, 331
Maritime Oligarchy, 36
Markets, 3, 6, 9-10, 16, 20, 38,
    44-45, 47-48, 50, 53-54, 59, 63,
    75-76, 78, 83-84, 87, 107, 113,
    131, 292, 294
Market strategy, 68-69, 68n
"Market system," 133
Marquard, William A., Jr., 345
Marquez, V.O., 20
Marriage, 29, 31, 211-13, 333
Marshall, Herbert, et al., 12, 33n, 77,
    358n, 361n, 363n
Martin, William McChesney, Jr., 249
Marting, Walter Adelbert, 245
Massachusetts Institute of Technol-
    ogy, 236-37
Massey-Ferguson, 102, 111, 119-21,
    119n, 135, 176, 178, 199, 245
Massey-Harris Harvester, 52n, 64,
    75, 75n, 77
Material Service, 198, 205
Mathias, Philip, 157n
Matthews, Albert Bruce, 178
Matthews, Beverley, 178, 254
Matthews, R.C., & Co., 178
Maule, C.J., 125, 367n
Mayne, A.F., 123
McAfee, Jerry, 185, 254
McCarthy & McCarthy (Toronto law
    firm), 178
McCormick, Brooks, 203, 279

McCormick, Vance, 65
McCormick, William S., 203
McCoy, Charles Brelsford, 201
McDiarmid, O.J., 33n, 51-52, 52n, 359n-62n
McDonnell Aviation, 134
McDonnell Douglas Corp., 160, 203, 206, 325, 331
McDonnell family, 202, 206
McDonnell, James Smith, Jr., 203, 206
McDonnell, William Archie, 203, 206
McGill University, 161n, 236-37, 272
McGregor, Gordon M., 60
McIntyre, Alister, 121, 366n
McIntyre Mines, 120
McKie, Donald Craig, 210n
McKinnon, Neil J., 178, 178n
McLaughlin Carriage Co., 60
McLaughlin family, 60
McLaughlin, G.W., 60
McLaughlin Motor Car Co., 60
McLaughlin, Robert, 60
McLaughlin, R.S., 60, 178
McLaughlin, W. Earle, 124, 147, 178, 188, 291
McLean, Malcolm P., 343
McLean, William Flavelle, 181
McMaster University, 239, 272
Meat packing, 47, 77
Media, 3, 8, 300
Melchers Distilleries, 178
Mellon family, 57, 145, 160, 203, 254, 344
Mellon National Bank, 145, 187, 198-99, 203-04, 280, 316, 330
Mellon, Stewart Prosser, 203
Mellon, T., & Sons, 203
Menk, Louis Wilson, 251
Mercantile Bank of Canada, 104, 146-47, 234, 249
Mercantile Stores, 76, 199
Mercantilism, 2, 15-19, 15n, 34-41, 49, 75, 334
Mergers, 46, 54-56, 60, 62, 66-67, 70n, 71, 79, 81n, 132-39, 134n. See also Consolidations; Takeovers
Metals, 55, 69, 75, 106, 156, 158

Metropolitan Club (N.Y.C.), 178
Metropolitan Life, 144-45, 164, 178-79, 188, 195, 317, 330
Mexico, 76, 114, 121
Meyer, John Edward, 186
Middle class, 29, 31, 49, 65, 207, 224, 273-75, 293, 337, 356-57
Middle range capitalists, 24-26, 94, 94n, 208, 293-94
Middlesex (School), 239-40
Migration, "attached," 259, 271, 348-49; "free," 258-59, 259n, 348-49; managerial, 4, 257-78
Military, 12, 29, 83-84, 114, 123, 126, 131, 194, 216, 247-48, 252, 299
Miller, George William, 191
Miller, Paul Albert, 199
Miller, Richard Kendall, 199
Miller, Robert Watt, 199
Miller, William, 58, 332-33, 337, 371n
Milliken, Robert, 199
Milliken, Seth Mellon, 199
Mills, C. Wright, 30, 81, 239, 331-33, 335, 344, 358n, 360n, 363n, 369n, 371n-72n
Miltstein, Seymour, 344n
Mining, 46, 50n, 51, 55, 58, 63, 67-68, 71-72, 75, 80, 84-85, 87, 91-93, 106, 115-16, 122, 128, 134, 151-55, 297, 320
Minnesota Mining and Manufacturing, 195, 248, 280, 321, 330
Mitchell, Derek S., 280
Mitchell, W.S., 148
Mitsubishi Bank, 102
Mobility, contest, 27, social, 4, 27, 30, 257, 260-61, 293; sponsored, 27n, 29-30
Mobil Oil, 146, 148, 152-53, 192, 244, 320, 330, 344
Molson Companies, 135n, 177, 181, 197
Molson family, 197
Monarch Mills, 199
Monge, Joseph Paul, 245
Monsanto, 212, 322, 331
Montgomery Ward, 134, 148, 152, 200

Montreal Pipe Line, 153
Montreal Trust, 120, 135, 147
Moody, John, 360n
Moore, Barrington, Jr., 38, 44,
    359n-60n
Moore Corp., 64, 77, 111, 119
Moore, J.H., 122n
Moore, S.J., 64
Moore, W.H., 47
Morgan Guaranty Bank, 112, 135,
    149
Morgan, House of, 42
Morgan interests, 146, 164, 343
Morgan, J.P., 45-47, 57, 64, 145
Morgan, J.P., and Co., 135, 143-45,
    154, 164, 165n, 188, 191, 198, 212,
    245, 249-50, 279, 316, 330
Morgan, J.S., and Co., 38, 45
Morgan Stanley and Co., 146, 155
Morgan Trust, 197
Morris Co., 47
Morton, William H., 244
Moultrie Cotton Mills, 212
Mount Royal Club (Montreal),
    177-78, 242, 244-45, 282
Mount Vernon Mills, 212
Mudd, Harvey Seeley, 199
Mudd, Henry Thomas, 199-200
Mueller, Willard F., 134
Muller, Ronald E., 367n-68n, 372n
Multinational corporations, 2-4, 6, 8,
    15, 19, 22, 25, 58, 64, 68n, 77-78,
    83, 88-89, 97-110, 104n, 119-27,
    130, 150, 152, 155-56, 161-62,
    259, 289. See also Branch plants;
    Subsidiaries
Multinational elites, 26n, 251-53,
    280-83
Multiple directorship holders, 168n,
    171-76, 210, 221-22, 241, 244,
    246, 282, 328-29
Municipal Bond Insurance Assoc.,
    144
Munson, Charles Sherwood, 212
Murphy, Grayson Mallet-Prevost,
    191
Mutual Life, 186, 191, 308-09
Myers, Gustavus, 34, 331, 359n,
    360n-61n

National Assoc. of Manufacturers
    (NAM), 47
National Biscuit Co., 47, 70n
National City Bank of New York,
    188, 203
National Club, 242, 281
National Dairy Products, 67
National Detroit, 199, 202, 255, 316,
    330
National Foreign Trade Council
    (NFTC), 66
Nationalism, 110, 255-56
National Lead, 46
National Life, 308-11
National Planning Association, 279
National policy, 51-52, 83
National Steel Corp., 84, 158-59, 199,
    202, 245, 323, 330
National Trust, 181, 281
National Westminster Bank, 102
Natural Gas, 150-52
Naylor, R.T., 33n, 43, 50n, 52, 60,
    62-63, 62n, 113-15, 360n-62n,
    366n
NCR Corp. (formerly National Cash
    Register), 192, 203, 249, 326, 330
Nelles, H.V., 51, 71-72, 72n,
    361n-63n
Nelson, Donald, 80
Nelson, Ralph L., 55n, 134, 367n
Netherlands, 91, 103, 111, 115n, 253
Netherlands Antilles, 121, 311
Nettels, C.P., 359n
Neu, I.D., 371n
Neufeld, E.P., 119n
Neuwirth, Gertrud, 28, 358n
Nevins, Allan, 360n
Newcomer, Mabel, 336-37, 336n,
    371n
New France, 35
Newman, Peter C., 367n
New York Central Railroad, 46
New York Life, 164, 188, 199, 201,
    202, 317, 330
New York Stock Exchange, 188
New York Times, 233
New York Trust, 135, 191
New Zealand, 25n, 124
Niagara Frontier (Ontario), 76

Nicholls, Sen. Frederick, 53
Nichols, Theo., 331, 372n
Nickel, 63-64, 72, 72n, 85
Nonintercourse Act of 1809, 40
Noranda Mines, 111, 119-20
Norfolk and Western Railway, 318, 331
Norstad, General Lauris, 280
North (U.S.), 33, 35, 44, 77
North American Life Insurance, 121, 213, 308-11
North Atlantic Packers, 205
North Continental Capital, 147
North, D.C., 360n
Northern Airport, 159
Northern Neck State Bank, 187
Northern Telecom (formerly Northern Electric), 20, 60, 119-20, 150
Northern Trust, 200
Northwest Airlines, 250, 280, 319, 331
Northwestern Bancorporation, 198, 200, 212, 251, 280, 316, 331
Northwestern Mutual Life, 198, 200, 233, 280, 317, 330
Northwestern National Life, 200
Northwestern University, 194
Norway, 100
Nova Scotia Power Corp. (NSPC), 95
Nye, Joseph S., 358n
Nyrop, Donald William, 250

O'Brien, Thomas, 149
Occidental Petroleum, 195, 205, 255, 320, 331
O'Connor, James, 367n
Ogilvy, Cope, Porteous, Hansard, Marler, Montgomery and Renault (Montreal law firm), 213
Oil (petroleum), 12, 47, 53, 55, 63, 67n, 68-69, 71-72, 75-76, 78, 84-85, 87, 91-93, 94n, 99, 112, 115-16, 122, 128-29, 151-52, 156, 181-82, 296-97, 300, 320, 322
O'Neil family, 203
Ontamont Co., 147
Oppenheimer, Mary, 146, 367n-68n
Opportunities, 256-67, 263
Organization of Petroleum Exporting

Countries (OPEC), 112
Orion Bank, 102
Osgoode Hall Law School, 177
Oshawa Group, 197
Osler family, 213
Osler, Gordon Peter, 213
Ostiguy, Jean Paul, 181
Other, elite, 184, 187, 194-95, 246; sectors, 184, 194-95
Outsider positions, 186, 186n, 189, 196-97, 218-23, 229, 243-44, 285-86, 346
Overdeveloped nations, 126-27, 296
Owens-Corning Fiberglas, 198, 280
Owens-Illinois, Inc., 249, 323, 331
Own account, 184, 204-06, 187, 189, 224, 230
Ownership and control, 6, 10, 20-21, 31-32, 92-93, 145-46, 182n, 340-47

Pacific Basin Economic Council (PBEC), 123-24, 246
Pacific Gas and Electric, 187, 199, 319, 330
Pacific Lighting Corp., 199
Pacific Oil, 200
Pacific Petroleums, 120
Pacific Union Club (San Francisco), 243
Packard, David, 205
Page, Arthur W., 187
Page, Walter Hines II, 188
Paley Report (Resources for Freedom), 84
Pan American World Airways, 194, 198, 203-04, 249-50, 319, 330, 347
Pan Canadian Petroleum, 136
Parai, Louis, 259-60, 370n
Parasitic relations, 126
Pardee, James T., 202
Parker, Daniel Safford, 200
Parker, Jack S., 244
Parker Pens, 200
Parkin, Frank, 28, 358n
Patents, 59n, 61, 74, 88-89
Patino Mines, 120
Patman Committee Report, 143, 145, 341, 343
Patterson, Ellmore Clark, 245

Patterson, William Prior, 192
Peabody, George, 38
Peace River Oil Pipeline, 152
Pearson, Lester B., 7
Pearson, Nathan W., 254
Pelton, Richard, 368n
Penn Central, 149n, 318, 331
Penney, J.C., Co., 61, 88, 234, 318, 331
Pennsylvania Railway, 198-99, 203
Pennzoil Co., 186, 203, 322, 331
Pentland, H.C., 18n, 40, 41n, 359n
Pezpin, Jean-Luc, 250
PepsiCo Inc., 135, 205-07, 321, 331
Percy, Charles H., 248
Peripheral (or marginal) nations, 7, 15-16, 22-23, 98, 113
Perkins, Courtland Davis, 212
Perkins, James Alfred, 212
Perkins, Richard Sturgis, 188
Perry, Robert, 99n
Pert Knitting, 157
Peru, 61, 72
Petersen, W., 260n
Peterson, Peter G., 195, 248
Petras, J., 365n-66n
Petrofina, 112, 153
Petroleum. See Oil
Pew family, 203
Pfizer Inc., 323, 331
Philadelphia Club, 242-43
Philadelphia Electric Co., 319, 331
Philip Morris, Inc., 135, 201, 212, 321, 331
Philippines, 311
Phillips, Lytle, Hitchcock, Blaine and Huber (law firm), 191
Phillips Petroleum, 191, 318, 331
Piel, William, Jr., 191
Pierce, Samuel Riley, Jr., 250
Pillsbury, John Sargent, Jr., 200
Pillsbury Mills, 200
Pipelines, 150-54
Pittsburgh Limestone, 191
Place, Herman G., 188
Place, John Bassett, 188
Placer Development, 120
"Planning system", 133
Plantations, 35-37, 41

Political economy, 2, 7, 55, 298
Political elite, 29-30, 51, 130, 194-95, 247-50
Pool, Leonard Parker, 206
Porter, John, 1-2, 5, 210n, 339, 358n, 365n, 368n, 370n, 372n
Portfolio investment, 2, 15, 41, 54, 57-58, 62, 68n, 93, 102-03, 113, 115, 128-29, 259, 293
Portsmouth Priory (School), 240
Power, 4, 9-13, 28-29, 139, 289-90, 300, 302, 338, 347
Power Corp., 24n, 120, 135-36, 144, 147, 176, 178-79, 250, 280
Power elite, 30-31
PPG Industries (formerly Pittsburgh Plate Glass), 46, 178, 187, 203, 323, 331
Pratt, Larry, 99, 152, 365n, 368n
Prentice, J.C., 280
Preston, Lee, 367n
Price Company, 136, 157, 157n, 177
Prices, 9-10, 148
Princeton University, 236-37, 241, 264
Private clubs, 2, 27, 30-31, 49, 226, 229-31, 242-45, 281
Private Planning Association of Canada, 279
Private schools, 29, 31, 49, 208-09, 208n, 226, 239-43, 256-57, 273
Proclamation Line (1763), 37
Procter and Gamble Co., 70, 250, 255, 323, 330
Production, sphere of, 6, 10, 15-17, 15n, 16n, 17n, 24, 52, 80, 167, 169, 184, 287, 290, 298
Profits, 10-12, 51-52, 68, 88-89, 98, 108-09, 126, 133, 140, 256, 296, 344n
Progressives, 48-49, 56
Property, 10, 28-29, 31-32, 196, 211, 295-96, 300-02, 339-47
Prosser, Stewart, 203
Proximity, 18, 68, 130, 294
Prudential Life Insurance, 144-45, 188, 198, 250, 317, 330
Public Service Electric and Gas, 250, 319, 331

Puerto Rico, 253
Puerto Rico Co., 62n
Pulp and paper (newsprint), 25n, 34, 43, 58-59, 63, 69, 71-72, 75-78, 84-85, 88, 91, 94, 106, 122, 129, 156-67, 231, 292, 296, 321
Pure Oil Co., 192
Putnam, Carleton, 206
Pyramiding, 136, 136n

Quaker Oats Co., 60, 200, 212
Quaker Oats Co. of Canada, 280
Quebec Act, 37
Queen's University, 236, 263, 272, 281

Race, 27-29
Railways, 15, 41, 43-48, 50-51, 54-55, 58, 63-65, 68-69, 72, 75, 77, 91-93, 95, 103, 113-14, 148-49, 292, 318
Rainbow Pipe Line, 153
Ralston Purina, 178, 201, 212, 248, 320, 331
Ramo, Simon, 206
Ranney, George Alfred, Jr., 192, 212
Rapid American Corp., 206, 321, 331
Rasminsky, Louis, 179
Rathgeb, Charles I., Jr., 218
RCA Corp., 324, 331, 347
Reasoner, Davis and Vinson (law firm), 191
Reciprocity Trade Agreements (1935), 74
Reciprocity Treaty (1854), 43, 74
Redfield, William C., 65
Redlich, Fritz, 359n
Reed Shaw Osler, 177
Regionalism, 14, 21n, 22, 27, 37, 44, 62, 76, 223-29, 240, 265-67, 269-70, 281, 295-300, 332
Reisman, Simon, 250
Relations between elites, 1, 65-66, 81-82, 245-50
Religious affiliation, 27, 230-31, 240
Remington Rand, 191
Remington Typewriter, 193
Rentiers, 31, 94
Republic Steel Corp., 84, 323, 331

Research and development, 10, 185, 256-67, 289, 295. *See also* Technology
Residence, 27, 154, 252-53
Resources, natural (sector), 3, 6, 8-9, 11, 14, 17-18, 23-24, 50n, 63, 68, 74, 78, 81, 83-84, 87, 89-90, 94n, 104-07, 106n, 113, 128-29, 131, 142, 150-55, 164-70, 173-76, 185, 215-17, 221-22, 226, 252-53, 282, 290, 292, 296, 320
Resources, power, 9, 28, 132
Reynolds family, 203
Reynolds Industries, 203, 312, 343
Reynolds, Lloyd G., 70n
Reynolds Metals Co., 323, 331
Reynolds, Richard S., Jr., 203
Reynolds, R.J., Industries, 321, 331, 343
Rhodesia, 311
Richardson family, 197
Richardson, George Taylor, 154
Richardson, James, and Sons, 154
Richardson Securities, 197
Richfield Oil, 134
Richmond, Anthony II., 258n, 348, 348n, 351, 373n
Rideau Club (Ottawa), 242
Ridgeway, James, 151, 152n, 368n
Riklis, Meshulam, 206
Riley, Conrad Sanford, 213
Riley, Jean Elizabeth, 213
Riley, Nancy Adina, 213
Rio Algom Mines, 120
Rio-Tinto Zinc, 146
Robarts, John, 180
Robb Engineering Co., 62n
Robinson, James Dixon II, 188, 244
Rockefeller, David, 102, 203
Rockefeller family, 57, 145-56, 343
Rockefeller, James Stillman, 203
Rockefeller, John D., 47, 53
Rockwell International, 204, 206, 255, 326, 331
Rockwell, William Frederick, Jr., 204
Rodgers, William, 369n
Rolland Paper, 177
Rolling Rock Club (Ligonier, Pennsylvania), 178, 243-44, 281

Roosevelt, Theodore, 57
Roper, George, Corp., 148
Ropes and Gray (Boston law firm), 191
Rosenbluth, Gideon, 140n, 363n
Rose, Stanford, 112, 361n, 365n-66n
Ross, John Leslie, 186
Rothschild, House of, 146
Royal Bank of Canada, 102, 114, 119-21, 124, 188, 213, 218, 234, 245, 254, 280, 291, 301, 312-13
Royal Bank Trust Co. (West Indies) Ltd., 119
Royal Trust, 177, 213
Rubber, 55, 70, 75, 93, 158, 322
Russell, Thomas Wright, Jr., 245
Ryerson, Stanley B., 41n

Safarian, A.E., 59n, 363n
Safeway Stores, 106, 135n, 148, 318, 331
St. George's (school), 239-40
St. James Club (Montreal), 177-78, 242, 245
St. John-Jones, L.W., 348, 373n
St. Paul Companies, 144
St. Paul's (school), 240-41
St-Laurent, Louis, 85
St. Lawrence River, 37, 40, 43, 50
St. Mark's (school), 240
Salaries, 10, 133, 190, 264, 344-45, 347
Sample. See Data coverage
Santa Fe Industries, 199, 245, 318, 331
Sarnoff, Robert, 347
Scaife, Richard Mellon, 203
Scaife Steel, 203
Scheinberg, Stephen, 54n
Schiff, John Mortimer, 200
Schiff, Mortimer Leo, 200
Scott family, 197
Scott, F.D., 350, 373n
Scranton, William Warren, 250
Seaboard Coast Line Industries, 149, 319, 331
Seagram and Sons, Joseph E., 111
Sears, Roebuck & Co., 77, 80, 106, 147-48, 318, 330

Second World War, 18-19, 69, 78, 80, 82, 91, 125, 248, 295
Sectors, economic, 8, 24-26, 92-95, 104-06, 165-71, 252, 293, 305-06, 327. See also Finance; Manufacturing; Resources; Trade; Transportation; Utilities
Security Pacific, 198, 212, 316, 331
Seiberling, 70
Sellers, George Henry, 213
Selwyn House (school), 161n
Service, 19, 95-96, 107
Sex, 29
Shanghai, 61
Shapiro, Irving Saul, 190
Shapleigh, Warren McKinney, 212
Sharp, Mitchell, 87, 180, 364n
Shearman and Sterling (law firm), 191
Sheehan, Robert, 341, 372n
Shell Canada, 179
Shell Oil, 67n, 111-12, 115n, 153, 255, 280, 320, 331
Shell Transport and Trading, 279
Shenton, J.P., 360n-61n
Shepard, Horace Armor, 250
Sheridan, R.B., 359n
Sherman Antitrust Act (1890) (U.S.), 48, 61
Sherritt Gordon Mines, 120
Sherwin Williams Paints, 60-61
Shultz, George Pratt, 250
Sicovam, 155
Sidley, Auston, Burgess and Smith (Chicago law firm), 192
Signal Companies, 160, 325, 331
Simpsons Ltd., 197, 234
Simpsons-Sears, 148, 234
Sinclair, Ian David, 254
Sinclair Oil, 134
Singapore, 25n
Singer Co., 244, 280, 324, 330, 346
Siragusa, Ross David, Jr., 206
Siragusa, Ross David, Sr., 206
Sloan, Alfred P., 193
Small businessmen, 12, 16, 39, 43, 59, 62, 133, 136-37, 258, 291-92
Smigel, Erwin O., 190-91
Smith, A.O., Corp., 200

Smith, Byron Laflin, 200
Smith, Donald Alexander, 54
Smith, Dusky Lee, 55-56, 361n
Smith, Edward Byron, 200
Smith, Lloyd Bruce, 200
Smith, Solomon Albert, 200
Smith, Tom K., Jr., 212
Social closure, 27-29
Societa Finaziaria, 159
Solidarism, 27-28
Somerset Club (Boston), 243
South (U.S.), 17n, 33, 35-36, 38, 41,
    44, 78, 226
South Africa, 25n, 61, 107n, 118, 310
South America, 76, 113, 117, 121
Southam family, 213
Southam, George Thomas, 213
Southam, Gordon Thomas, 214
Southam Newspapers, 213
Southam Press, 213-14
Southern California Edison, 193,
    319, 331
Southern Co., 212, 319, 331
Southern Pacific Co., 186, 188,
    198-200, 244, 318, 330
Southern Railway Co., 191, 318, 331
South Saskatchewan Pipe Line, 153
South-West Bell, 187
Sovereignty, 289-90, 299
Spelt, Jacob, 41n, 359n
Spencer, Edson White, 212
Sperry and Hutchison, 198
Sperry Rand Corp., 326, 331
Stamp Act (1765), 37
Standard Brands (U.S.), 70n
Standard Broadcasting, 135
Standard Ideal Co., 62n
Standard Oil Co. (Indiana), 320, 331, 344
Standard Oil of California, 151, 199,
    205, 322, 330
Standard Oil of New Jersey, 46-48,
    53, 61, 70, 72, 74, 76, 145
Standard Oil (Ohio), 47, 111, 186,
    250, 322, 331
Stanford University, 194, 205,
    236-37, 282
Staples, 15-16, 17n, 34, 36, 37n, 39,
    41, 43-44, 50, 63-64, 71, 87, 129,
    292, 296

State, 1, 10, 12, 14, 18, 20, 34, 37,
    43-44, 48-49, 50-51, 56-57, 61,
    65-66, 69, 71, 72-73, 72n, 78-79,
    81, 85, 92, 99, 101, 101n, 123-24,
    127-28, 150, 154, 165, 216, 245-50,
    289-90, 295, 298, 301-02; elite,
    1, 7, 12, 29, 65-66, 194-95, 344;
    power, 12, 29, 44, 49, 72, 98n,
    102, 126, 250, 289-90, 299, 300;
    sector, 1, 10, 12, 14, 18, 20, 34, 37,
    43-44, 48-51, 54, 56-57, 61, 65-66,
    69, 71-73, 72n, 78-79, 81, 85, 92,
    99, 101, 101n, 122-24, 127-28,
    133, 150, 154, 165, 166, 245-50,
    252, 258, 259n, 291
Steel. See Iron and Steel
Steel Co. of Canada (Stelco), 62n, 72,
    76-77, 119, 158-59, 176-77, 181,
    301
Steinberg family, 197
Steinbergs Ltd., 197
Stephen, George, 54
Sterling, J.E. Wallace, 280
Stettinius, Edward R., 80
Stevens, J.H., 124
Stockbrokers, 48, 69-70, 73, 76-77,
    95n
Stock ownership, 10, 30, 66, 73, 137,
    145-46, 154-55, 160-61, 189, 201,
    219-20, 340-47
Strauss, Levi, family, 199
Stuart, Robert Douglas, Jr., 200, 212
Studebaker, 191
Subsidiaries, 23, 26, 59n, 60, 68, 89,
    98-99, 101, 127, 156-58, 162, 173,
    174. See also Branch plants; Multi-
    national corporations
Sugar refineries, 52, 63
Sullivan and Cromwell (law firm),
    191, 249
Sullivan, Leon H., 230
Sun-Canada Pipeline, 152
Sunkel, Osvaldo, 21n, 22, 358n
Sun Life, 118, 176-78, 199, 245, 254,
    270, 279, 301, 308-11
Sun Oil Co., 152, 203, 250, 320, 331
Superior Oil, 120n
"Supply strategy," 68-69, 68n
Swearingen, John E., 344

Sweden, 103, 230, 253, 289
Swift-Armour, 121
Swift Co., 47. *See also* Esmark Inc.
Switzerland, 103, 111, 253
Symbiotic relations, 126
Syncrude Canada, 152, 152n

Taft (school), 49, 239-40
Taiwan, 351
Takeovers, 88, 134-36. *See also*
   Mergers
Tarbell, Ian M., 360n
Tariffs, 38, 43-44, 47, 51-52, 60-61,
   68, 73, 75n, 83, 85, 110, 123, 298
Tarkington, Andrew W., 280
Taussig, F.W., 332-33, 371n
Taxes, 296-98, 301
Taylor, Hobart, Jr., 250
Tavoulareas, William P., 344
Tea Act (1773), 37
Technology, 10, 16, 18-20, 23, 53,
   55, 59, 63, 71, 79, 87-88, 99, 99n,
   101, 119n, 129, 150, 185n, 292. *See*
   also Research and development
Teledyne, Inc., 160, 326, 331
Tenneco Inc., 106, 150, 319, 331
Texaco (Canada), 157, 181
Texaco Explorations Canada, 157
Texaco Inc., 115n, 146, 153, 157-58,
   199, 247, 322, 331, 344
Texas Eastern Transmission, 150,
   178, 319, 331
Texasgulf Inc., 111
Texas Gulf Sulphur, 199
Textiles, 17n, 38, 41, 62, 76
Textron Inc., 135, 191, 325, 331
"Third" ethnics, 264, 270-71, 284
Third National Bank and Trust Co.,
   192
"Third" World, 1, 7, 14, 20-23,
   108-09
Thomas, Brinley, 259n, 350-51, 373n
Thompson, Richard Murry, 188
Thornton, Charles Bates, 206
3M Canada, 178
Tidewater Oil, 134
Timber, 15, 40
Timiskaming and Northern Ontario
Railway, 63
Times Mirror Co., 198
Tobacco, 34
Tobago, 118, 121
Toronto Club, 49, 177-78, 242, 245,
   281
Toronto-Dominion Bank, 118-19,
   119n, 147, 176, 178, 188, 213, 245,
   279, 312-13
Tower, Raymond Camille, 186
Townshend Duties (1767), 37
Trade (exports and imports), 2, 17n,
   34, 37, 40, 43, 50, 50n, 71, 73-74,
   75n, 84-86, 109, 113, 290, 294
Trade (sector) (wholesale and retail)
   (merchandising), 41, 69, 74-75,
   77, 92, 96, 104-05, 107, 116, 122,
   133, 142, 147-48, 160, 164-70,
   173-76, 185, 215-17, 221-22,
   252-53, 282, 318, 328-29
Trade Commissioner Service, 123
Transamerica Corp., 135, 188, 199,
   317, 331
TransCanada PipeLines, 176-78, 213,
   254
Transfers, 254-55, 260, 262-64
Trans-Northern Pipe Line, 153
Transportation (sector), 3, 6, 8, 17n,
   24, 38-39, 41-44, 48, 55, 79, 91,
   94, 99, 104-06, 112, 115-16, 122,
   127-28, 142, 148-51, 164-70, 173-
   76, 185, 215-17, 221-22, 252-53,
   282, 290, 300, 318-19, 328-29
Trans World Airlines (TWA), 198,
   205-06, 319, 330
Travelers Corp., 255, 317, 331
Trinidad, 118-19, 121, 281, 310
Trinity College School, 161n
Trizec Corp., 197
Trust Co. of Georgia, 188
Trusts, 47-48
TRW Inc. (formerly The Ramo-
   Woodridge Co.), 198, 201, 206,
   250, 325, 330
Tuckman, Howard, 345, 373n
Tugenhat, C., 365n
Tulchinsky, Gerald, 41n
Turner, John, 250
Turner, Lewis, 366n

Turner, Ralph, 27, 348n
Turner, William Ian Mackenzie, Jr., 280
Twaits, W.O., 280

UAL Inc. (formerly United Airlines), 187, 195, 200, 212, 280, 319, 330, 343, 343n, 345, 347
Uganda, 258
Underdeveloped nations, 7, 15n, 16, 18, 89, 107, 126-28, 295-96
Underhill, Frank, 8
Underdeveloped nations, 126-27, 295, 350
Uneven development, 7-8, 14, 19, 80, 95, 127-28, 141, 229, 257, 295, 350
Unilever, 279
Union Bank of Halifax, 62n
Union Carbide, 70n, 230, 254, 322, 330
Union Club (Boston), 243
Union Club (N.Y.), 212, 243
Union of the Canadas, 42
Union Oil Co. of California (Union Oil), 152-53, 199-200, 255, 320, 331
Union Pacific Corp., 46, 82, 188, 199, 244, 318, 330
Unions, 10
Uniroyal, Inc., 178, 186-87, 200, 322, 330
United Aircraft Corp., 81, 160, 325, 331
United Brands, 320, 331, 344n, 347
United Fruit Co., 57
United Kingdom (Great Britain), 2, 6, 8, 16, 18-19, 25, 33-34, 36, 38, 39n, 42, 44, 51, 54, 57-58, 60, 62, 65, 73-74, 76, 80, 83, 91, 100, 102-03, 110-11, 113-14, 115n, 117-18, 119n, 120, 126-27, 131, 148, 154, 167, 252-54, 256, 279-80, 290-92, 350
United Shoe Machinery, 46
United States Rubber, 46, 70
United States Steel Corp., 45, 56n, 57, 64, 66, 74, 76, 80, 84, 145-46, 154, 164, 191, 245, 250, 279, 323, 330

Universities, 49, 194, 235-39
University of British Columbia, 236, 272
University of Manitoba, 236, 272
University of Michigan, 194
University of Montreal, 236
University of Toronto, 236-37, 272, 281
University of Western Ontario, 272
Upper Canada College, 49, 177-78, 240, 281
Upper class, 29-31, 36, 49, 183-84, 186-88, 190, 192-93, 195, 196, 205, 207-11, 207n, 214-17, 220-21, 224-25, 228-29, 236-41, 243, 273-75, 274n, 281-83, 286, 290, 293, 333-34, 347, 356-57
U.S. Gypsum, 200
U.S.S.R., 290
Utilities (sector), 3, 6, 8, 24, 51, 68-69, 72, 75-76, 79, 91-95, 103, 106, 114-16, 122, 141, 142, 148-51, 164-70, 173-76, 185, 215-17, 221-22, 252-53, 282, 290, 300, 319, 328-29

Values, 11, 31
Van Alstyne, Richard, 37-38, 359n
Van der Kroef, J.M., 373n
Vance, Cyrus Robert, 250
Vancouver Club, 242
Vaupel, J.W., 365n
Venezuela, 121, 311
Vereen, William Jerome, 212
Vernon, Raymond, 83, 361n, 365n
Vila, George Raymond, 186
Viner, Jacob, 362n-63n
Vinson, Fred Moore, Jr., 191
Von der Ahe, Albert, 206
Von's Grocery Co., 206

Wabash Iron Co., 159
Wadsworth, J.P.R., 147
Wages, 10
Wallerstein, Immanuel, 23n
War, 44, 69, 73, 81-82, 83n
Warner-Lambert Co., 323, 331
Warner, Lloyd, 332, 336, 371n
Warner, Rawleigh, Jr., 192-93, 344

Warnock, John W., 75n, 299, 370n
War of 1812, 39
Washington *Post*, 233
Watkins Report, 98-99
Watson, Arthur Kittredge, 204
Watson family, 204
Watson, Thomas J., Jr., 204
Watson, William Marvin, 195
Wealth, 31-32, 49, 183, 334, 345-46
Weber, Max, 27-28, 358n
Wecter, Dixon, 363n
Weldon, J.C., 70n
Weldwood of Canada, 157
Wellemeyer, Marilyn, 237
Wells Fargo & Co., 187, 197,
    199-200, 202, 233, 316, 330
Westcoast Petroleum, 120
Westcoast Transmission, 181
Westdeutsche Landesbank, 102
Western Airlines, 343
Western Bancorp, 200, 206, 316, 330
Western Canada Power, 62n
Western Electric, 61, 150, 324
Western Union, 200
West Indies, 39-40, 76, 118-19, 121, 291
Westinghouse Canada, 178, 213
Westinghouse Electric, 47, 74, 149,
    187-89, 199, 200, 207, 212, 234,
    250, 324, 330
Westinghouse, George, 47
Weston family, 197, 213
Weston, George, Ltd., 77, 119, 197, 250
Weyerhaeuser, Charles Davis, 204
Weyerhaeuser Co., 204, 321, 331
Weyerhaeuser, Frederick, 57
Weyerhaeuser, George Hunt, 204
Wheat, 17n, 34, 39-40, 43, 50, 58-59,
    87, 296
Wheeling-Pittsburgh, 159
Whirlpool, 148
Whitman, Mariana Von Neumann, 234
Wilcox, George Latimer, 212
Wilcox, Thomas Robert, 212
Wilkins, Mira, 33n, 42, 53, 58, 59n,
    60-61, 68, 68n, 70n, 72n, 104,
    104n, 110, 360n-68n
Williams, Glen, 59n, 362n
Williams, William Appleman, 38n,
    39, 55, 66, 359n, 361n

Willmot, Donald G., 181
Wilmington Club, 190
Wilmington Trust Co., 187
Wilson, Charles, 80
Wilson, Charles E., 80, 193
Wilson, Kendrick Roscoe, Jr., 212
Wilson, Woodrow, 57, 66
Wingate, Henry Smith, 154, 245, 279
Winters, Robert, 124
Wolfe, David A., 81, 83n, 364n
Wolfe family, 197
Wolff, R., 365n
Women, 29, 232-34, 232n, 246, 267,
    336n
Woodbury Forest School, 240
Wood, Edward Rogers, 62, 114
Wood Gundy & Co., 77, 197
Wood, Willsie Winston, 188
Woodroofe, Dr. Ernest, 279
Woodward, Charles N., 181
Woodward family, 197
Woodward Stores, 181, 197
Woolworth, F.W., Co., 106, 148,
    318, 331
Working class, 29, 31-32, 207, 224,
    273-75, 293, 337, 356-57. *See also*
    Labour
World Affairs Council, 246
World system, 1, 7-8, 14, 17, 20-23,
    23n, 65, 74, 79, 97, 122, 125-26
Wriston, Kathryn Ann Dineen, 234
Wriston, Walter Bigelow, 188, 234, 345

Xerox Corp., 244, 255, 280, 324, 331

Yale University, 190, 236-37, 241
York Club (Toronto), 177, 242, 245,
    281
Young, Sam Doak, 206
Youngstown Sheet and Tube, 84
Young, William H., 181

Zarb Report, 112, 158
Zatzenbach, Nicholas de Belleville,
    195
Zeitlin, Maurice, 341, 372n
Zellerbach family, 204
Zellerbach Paper, 204
Zellerbach, William Joseph, 204